Stevens and Borrie's
Elements of Mercantile Law

Edited by T. M. Stevens, M.A., B.C.L.

First edition 1890
Second edition 1897

Edited by Herbert Jacobs, B.A.

Third edition 1900
Fourth edition 1903
Fifth edition 1911
Sixth edition 1920
Seventh edition 1925
Eighth edition 1930
Ninth edition 1934
Tenth edition 1938

Edited by John Montgomerie, B.A.

Eleventh edition . . . . . June 1950
First reprint . . . . . . September 1953
Twelfth edition . . . . . . February 1955
First reprint . . . . . . August 1958
Thirteenth edition . . . . . . February 1960
First reprint . . . . . . October 1963

Edited by Gordon J. Borrie, LL.M.

Fourteenth edition . . . . . May 1965
Fifteenth edition . . . . . April 1969
First reprint . . . . . . January 1971
Sixteenth edition . . . . . March 1973

Stevens and Borrie's Elements of Mercantile Law

SIXTEENTH EDITION

by

GORDON J. BORRIE, LL.M.,

of the Middle Temple, Barrister,
Professor of English Law at the
University of Birmingham

LONDON
BUTTERWORTHS
1973

ENGLAND:	BUTTERWORTH & CO. (PUBLISHERS) LTD. LONDON: 88 Kingsway, WC2B 6AB
AUSTRALIA:	BUTTERWORTHS PTY. LTD. SYDNEY: 586 Pacific Highway, Chatswood, N.S.W. 2067 MELBOURNE: 343 Little Collins Street, 3000 BRISBANE: 240 Queen Street, 4000
CANADA:	BUTTERWORTH & CO. (CANADA) LTD. TORONTO: 14 Curity Avenue, 374
NEW ZEALAND:	BUTTERWORTHS OF NEW ZEALAND LTD. WELLINGTON: 26–28 Waring Taylor Street, I
SOUTH AFRICA:	BUTTERWORTH & CO. (SOUTH AFRICA) (PTY.) LTD. DURBAN: 152–154 Gale Street

ISBN Casebound: 0 406 66084 0
Limp: 0 406 66085 9

Reproduced and printed by photolithography and bound in
Great Britain at The Pitman Press, Bath

Preface

The purpose of this work has always been to provide a wide-ranging survey of the whole subject of Mercantile Law in one volume. The need to keep a proper balance between the many different topics considered and to keep the book to a reasonable length have continued to be borne in mind in this edition. The object of providing a general study of the whole field is thought to be worthwhile because while the lawyer who wishes to investigate a detailed point on, say, Sale of Goods or Partnership, may turn to *Chalmers* or *Lindley*, there is a real need for people in industry and commerce to have a guide to Mercantile Law generally in a single volume. Mr. T. M. Stevens in the Preface to the First Edition of this work, published in 1890, wrote that while "few mercantile men are unwise enough to deal with any legal matter of serious importance without the aid of their solicitors, yet in the affairs of everyday life it will frequently happen that a knowledge of Mercantile Law is almost a necessity. . . . " There is no doubt that this is even more true today than it was some 80 years ago.

Students too, whether they are studying to be lawyers or concerning themselves with Mercantile Law (or Commercial or Business Law, as the subject is often called) as part of the professional courses of the various accountancy, secretarial and insurance bodies, have a need for a book on the subject as a whole.

Changes in the law since the last edition was published in 1969, both case-law and statute law, have been taken into account. The law in this field is never standing still and many important statutes have been passed, such as the Merchant Shipping Act 1970, the Carriage of Goods by Sea Act 1971, the Industrial Relations Act 1971, and the Contracts of Employment Act 1972. The European Communities Act 1972 comes into effect today, bringing with it a host of regulations affecting particularly trade between member-States of the E.E.C. By the time the next edition is published, its impact in areas like restrictive practices and its indirect effect in bringing about greater harmonisation between the differing mercantile laws of England and the other States, will be more clearly seen. A Note follows the Preface on the Supply of Goods (Implied Terms) Bill and the Fair Trading Bill, both Government Bills, and expected to become law in 1973.

The law is given as it stands on January 1, 1973.

GORDON J. BORRIE

University of Birmingham,
January 1, 1973.

NOTE

Supply of Goods (Implied Terms) Bill; Fair Trading Bill

I. SUPPLY OF GOODS (IMPLIED TERMS) BILL

This Bill, which received its second reading in the House of Lords in November 1972, is intended to give effect to the First Report of the Law Commissions on Exemption Clauses in Contracts[1]. It also makes amendments to the law implying certain terms in hire-purchase agreements and on a redemption of trading stamps.

1. Amendments to the Sale of Goods Act 1893

(a) *Implied conditions and warranties as to title* (*post*, p. 196). A new section is substituted for s. 12 of the Sale of Goods Act[2]. The implied *condition* as to title remains and there are reworded implied *warranties* as to the goods being free from undeclared encumbrances and for quiet possession. However, the contract may show an intention that the seller should transfer only such title as he has, in which case there are only implied *warranties* as to the goods being free from undeclared encumbrances and for quiet possession. By clause 4 of the Bill, any contractual term purporting to exclude or restrict the operation of the new s. 12 of the Sale of Goods Act is void.

(b) *Implied condition as to description.*—Section 13 of the Sale of Goods Act (*post*, p. 196) is amended so as to make clear that a sale is not prevented from being a sale by description by reason only that, being exposed for sale, the goods are selected by the buyer as in a self-service store[3].

(c) *Implied condition of merchantable quality.*—Section 14(2) of the Sale of Goods Act (*post*, p. 197) is replaced as follows[4]:

> "Where the seller sells goods in the course of a business, there is an implied condition that the goods supplied under the contract are of merchantable quality, except that there is no such condition—
>> (a) as regards defects specifically drawn to the buyer's attention before the contract is made; or
>> (b) if the buyer examines the goods before the contract is made, as regards defects which that examination ought to reveal"

---

1. Law Com. No. 24 (1969).
2. Clause 1 of the Bill.
3. Clause 2 of the Bill.
4. Clause 3 of the Bill.

By a definition clause[5]:

> "Goods of any kind are of merchantable quality . . . if they are as fit for the purpose or purposes for which goods of that kind are commonly bought as it is reasonable to expect having regard to any description applied to them, the price (if relevant) and all the other circumstances. . . ."

(*d*) *Implied condition of fitness for purpose.*—Section 14(1) of the Sale of Goods Act (*post*, p. 198) is renumbered as s. 14(3) and will now read as follows[6]:

> "Where the seller sells goods in the course of a business and the buyer, expressly or by implication, makes known to the seller any particular purpose for which the goods are being bought, there is an implied condition that the goods supplied under the contract are reasonably fit for that purpose, whether or not that is a purpose for which such goods are commonly supplied, except where the circumstances show that the buyer does not rely, or that it is unreasonable for him to rely, on the seller's skill or judgment."

(*e*) *Exemption Clauses.*—Section 55 of the Sale of Goods Act (*post*, p. 195) is renumbered s. 55(1) and other subsections are added[7]. In a "consumer sale", any term of the contract purporting to exclude or restrict the operation of all or any of the provisions in ss. 13–15 of the Sale of Goods Act, or the exercise of a right conferred by such provision, or any liability of the seller for breach of a term implied by such provision, is void. A "consumer sale" means a sale, other than by auction or by competitive tender, by a seller in the course of a business where the goods are of a type ordinarily bought for private use or consumption, and are sold to a person who does not buy or hold himself out as buying them in the course of a business.

In the case of a sale other than a "consumer sale", any exemption clause is not enforceable "to the extent that it is shown that it would not be fair and reasonable to allow reliance on that term". In considering this question, a court should have regard to all the circumstances and in particular to (i) whether the buyer knew or ought reasonably to have known of the extent of the term, and (ii) whether the buyer was able to choose whether to buy the goods (from the seller or someone else) under a contract without such term.

The prohibitions and restrictions on exemption clauses do not apply to contracts for international sales of goods[8].

---

5. Clause 7(2) of the Bill.
6. Clause 3 of the Bill.
7. Clause 4(2) of the Bill.
8. Clause 6 of the Bill.

2. Hire-purchase agreements

Substantially the same terms are implied in the case of all hire-purchase agreements and they can be excluded only in substantially the same circumstances[9]. This means that both the Common Law obligations of the owner (*post*, pp. 219–21) and the provisions of the Hire Purchase Act 1965, ss. 17–20 (*post*, pp. 228–9) cease to have effect. Moreover, the criterion for control over exemption clauses in hire-purchase agreements is to be whether or not the agreement is a "consumer agreement" (defined on similar lines to "consumer sale", *ante*) and not the amount of the hire-purchase price.

3. Trading stamps

The terms implied where goods are obtained on a redemption of trading stamps by the Trading Stamps Act 1964, s. 4 (*post*, p. 201) are amended by and are set out in clause 16 of the Bill. These terms cannot now be excluded.

II. FAIR TRADING BILL

This Bill, which received its second reading in the House of Commons in December 1972, creates a new office, that of the Director General of Fair Trading, (hereafter called the Director), supported by a Consumer Protection Advisory Committee. This new official is to have the task of keeping under review trade practices which may adversely affect the interests of consumers as well as keeping under review commercial activities which involve monopoly or restrictive practices.

1. Orders against unfair trade practices

Unlike the Trade Descriptions Act 1968 (*post*, pp. 552–5) the Fair Trading Bill does not create any new offences itself but it does provide the machinery whereby new offences may be created by order of the Secretary of State for Trade and Industry. There are several stages in the process. First, the Director may make a reference to the Advisory Committee if he considers that a trade practice has the effect or is likely to have the effect (a) of misleading or confusing consumers with regard to the nature, quality or quantity of goods or services; (b) of misleading consumers as to their rights and obligations; (c) of subjecting consumers to undue pressure; or (d) of causing the terms of consumer transactions to be so adverse to consumers as to be inequitable. (Professional services and the nationalised industries are excluded.) If he thinks fit, the Director may include in his reference proposals for recommending an order forbidding or regulating the practice. Normally the Advisory Committee

---

9. Clauses 8–12 of the Bill.

will have only 3 months in which to make a report and if it agrees with the Director's proposals, perhaps with modifications, the Secretary of State may make an appropriate order. Such order may, for example, prohibit the trade practice, prohibit exemption clauses in specified consumer transactions, or require that contracts relating to specified consumer transaction should include certain terms. Like the Trade Descriptions Act 1968 (*post.* pp. 552–5), responsibility for enforcing any new offences created by order will rest with the weights and measures authorities (or trading standards authorities) of the local authorities. The Bill allows the same defences as the Trade Descriptions Act.

2. Persistent breaches of criminal or civil law

Part III of the Bill gives the Director power to seek orders from the Restrictive Practices Court against traders who persistently maintain a course of conduct detrimental to the interests of consumers by breaking the criminal law, *e.g.*, the Trade Descriptions Act, or by breaking their civil obligations, such as under the Sale of Goods Act, and who refuse to give written assurances that they will desist. Breach of any order of the Restrictive Practices Court would be punishable as a contempt of court.

3. Monopolies and restrictive trade practices

Under the Fair Trading Bill, the Director is empowered to make references to the Monopolies Commission (renamed the Monopolies and Mergers Commission) subject to the Secretary of State's veto. The proportion of the market by reference to which monopolies are defined (see *post*, p. 519) is reduced from one-third to one-quarter.

The Director takes over the functions of the Registrar of Restrictive Trading Agreements (*post*, p. 523) and the Bill extends the application of the Restrictive Trade Practices Act 1956 to agreements between suppliers of *services*, other than services of a professional nature.

Table of Contents

Part IV

BANKRUPTCY

Part V

ARBITRATIONS

Part VI

PROTECTION OF COMMERCE

INDEX

Table of Statutes

In the following Tables references are given to Halsbury's Statutes of England (Third Edition) showing the volume and page number at which the annotated Act is printed.

Table of Cases Cited

A.

PART I

General View of the Law of Contracts

CHAPTER I

The Different Types of Contract and their Form

MEANING OF CONTRACT

In modern law, the word "contract" generally means an agreement intended by the parties to it to have legal consequences and to be legally enforceable[1]. Thus, there is a contract when one person agrees to sell something to another, when a bank agrees to lend money to a company, and when a builder agrees to repair a damaged chimney. These are common examples of contracts in everyday life, but they are sometimes referred to as *simple contracts* to distinguish them from *specialty contracts* or contracts by deed, and *contracts of record* which are obligations recorded by a court of law in its official records, *e.g.*, judgments and recognisances.

Contracts of record need no further reference and contracts by deed need only a brief further description[2]. The significance of both these types of contract is overshadowed today by the importance of *simple contracts*.

Simple contracts

A simple contract has been defined above as an *agreement* intended to have legal consequences and to be legally enforceable. Its main essential is mutual agreement and this connotes that (1) *at least two parties* have expressed themselves (2) *with sufficient certainty* (3) *in terms which correspond* upon the subject.

For an agreement there must be at least two parties. A man cannot contract with himself. If a person agrees with himself and one or more other persons, the agreement will be construed and enforced as if it had been entered into with the other person or persons alone[3].

Certainty.—The details of the bargain must be certain or ascertainable.

In *Scammell (G.) and Nephew. Ltd.* v. *Ouston*[4],

A agreed to buy a van from B "on hire-purchase terms": *Held:*

---

1. *Rose and Frank Co.* v. *J. R. Crompton & Bros., Ltd.* [1923] 2 K. B. 261, *per* BANKES, L.J., at p. 282; affirmed [1925] A. C. 445.
2. See p. 5, *post.*
3. Law of Property Act 1925, s. 82.
4. [1941] 1 All E. R. 14; [1941] A. C. 251.

no precise meaning could be attributed to these words because there was a wide variety of hire-purchase terms and therefore there was no contract. The parties had never got beyond negotiations. Similarly, there is no contract if a vital term, such as the price to be paid for goods sold, has not been agreed and remains to be settled by further negotiation[5].

On the other hand in *Foley* v. *Classique Coaches, Ltd.*[6]

A agreed to buy petrol from B at a price to be agreed and there was a provision for the submission of any dispute to arbitration. The parties never did agree a price. *Held:* since the price was ascertainable otherwise than by the parties themselves, *i.e.* by arbitration, the parties had made a concluded contract.

And in an agreement otherwise sufficiently precise a meaningless clause may be ignored. In *Nicolene, Ltd.* v. *Simmonds*[7],

A offered to buy some steel bars from B. B agreed to do so, adding: "I assume that we are in agreement that the usual conditions of acceptance apply." B failed to deliver the goods and A sued B for breach of contract. *Held:* since there were apparently no "usual conditions of acceptance", this meaningless phrase could be ignored. There was a clear concluded contract and B was liable for breach of it.

The terms must correspond.—The parties must be *ad idem*. This is usually expressed in the form that an offer by one party must be accepted in corresponding terms by the other. If the outward expressions of the parties correspond, there will be a contract[8], even if inwardly the intentions of one or both the parties are different; but in certain cases mistake or misrepresentation vitiates the contract[9].

Intention to create legal relations.—An agreement will not amount to a contract if the parties expressly agree that it is not to be enforceable in the courts—by saying, for example, that it is only "binding in honour"[10]. The rules of football pools usually contain a rule to this effect[11].

The circumstances may also be such that the court will infer that the parties did not intend it to have legal consequences and this is

5. *May and Butcher, Ltd.* v. *R.* [1934] 2 K. B. 17.
6. [1934] 2 K. B. 1.
7. [1953] 1 All E. R. 822; [1953] 1 Q. B. 543.
8. *Frederick E. Rose (London), Ltd.* v. *William H. Pim, Jnr. & Co., Ltd.* [1953] 2 All E. R. 739; [1953] 2 Q. B. 450.
9. See Ch. III.
10. *Rose and Frank Co.* v. *J. R. Crompton & Bros., Ltd.* [1923] 2 K. B. 261.
11. *Appleson* v. *H. Littlewood, Ltd.* [1939] 1 All E. R. 464.

particularly likely in family or domestic arrangements. Thus in *Balfour* v. *Balfour*[12],

> A husband verbally promised to make his wife an allowance of £30 a month while he was abroad in consideration of her agreeing to support herself without calling upon him for any further maintenance. *Held:* this was a domestic arrangement not intended to create a binding contract.

On the other hand, in *Merritt* v. *Merritt*[13],

> A husband left his wife and made her a written promise to pay her £40 a month and transfer the matrimonial home to her sole ownership in consideration of her making the mortgage repayments still due on the home. *Held:* this was a binding contract. Lord DENNING, M.R. said that where parties are living in amity their domestic arrangements are ordinarily not intended to create legal relations but it is different when the parties are separated or about to separate.

However, it is always a matter of interpretation for the court to determine, when the agreement is not explicit as to whether the parties intended it to be a legally binding contract. In *Parker* v. *Clark*[14],

> C wrote to P offering to share his house with P and Mrs. P on terms as to sharing expenses, also offering that he and his wife would on their death leave the house to Mrs. P and suggesting that P and Mrs. P should sell their cottage. P accepted the offer and the two couples lived together until P and Mrs. P were asked to leave. *Held:* both parties did intend to create a legally binding contract, and Mr. and Mrs. P were entitled to damages for breach.

In commercial agreements, an intention to create legal relations is normally presumed and although a collective agreement between a trade union and an employer was held not to be legally binding because of lack of contractual intention[15], by s. 34(1) of the Industrial Relations Act 1971 every collective agreement made in writing after the commencement of the Act is conclusively presumed to be legally enforceable unless it contains a provision to the contrary.

By the Law Reform (Miscellaneous Provisions) Act 1970, an engagement to marry is no longer enforceable as a legal contract.

---

12. [1919] 2 K. B. 571 followed in *Spellman* v. *Spellman* [1961] 2 All E. R. 498; [1961] 1 W. L. R. 921 and *Jones* v. *Padavatton*, [1969] 2 All E. R. 616; [1969] 1 W. L. R. 328 (Mother and daughter).
13. [1970] 2 All E. R. 760; [1970] 1 W. L. R. 1121, C. A.
14. [1960] 1 All E. R. 93; [1960] 1 W. L. R. 286.
15. *Ford Motor Co.* v. *Amalgamated Union of Engineering and Foundry Workers*, [1969] 2 All E. R. 481; [1969] 2 Q. B. 303.

FORM OF CONTRACT

A *simple contract* may be
1. Drawn up in writing;
2. Partly written and partly oral;
3. Entirely oral; or
4. Inferred from, and created by the mere conduct of the parties.

The contract may be completely performed at once or it may consist of or include promises to perform or not to perform some act in the future. Thus the purchase of a packet of cigarettes over the counter is a contract which is completed at once, while an order for a suit of clothes to be made involves mutual promises on the part of the tailor to make the suit properly and on the part of the customer to pay for it. The distinction is sometimes expressed by dividing contracts into "executed" and "executory" contracts, but even when a contract appears to be completed at once, the effects of it may continue, as when a man buys a bun for a penny and subsequently breaks his teeth on a stone in it[16].

Specialty contracts

Specialty contracts, also called *deeds*, are contracts under seal. It is necessary that a deed should be written, sealed, and delivered, and the person who executes it must also sign it or place his mark on it[17]. The writing may be by hand or in print, and on paper or parchment. In modern times the seal has become a wafer or a mere piece of wax which has been previously attached to the document. In *Stromdale and Ball, Ltd.* v. *Burden*[18], DANCKWERTS, J., said:

> "Meticulous persons when executing a deed may still place their finger on the wax seal or wafer on the document but it appears to me that, at the present day, if a party signs a document bearing wax or wafer or other indications of a seal, with the intention of executing the document as a deed, that is sufficient adoption or recognition of the seal to amount to due execution as a deed."

Delivery of a deed may be
(i) Actual—*i.e.* handing over the instrument; or
(ii) Constructive—*i.e.* speaking words importing an intention to deliver[19], *e.g.* "I deliver this as my act and deed".

---

16. *Chapronière* v. *Mason* (1905), 21 T. L. R. 633.
17. Law of Property Act 1925, s. 73. A deed is executed by a company when its seal is affixed in the presence of and attested by its secretary and a director: s. 74.
18. [1952] 1 All E. R. 59; [1952] Ch. 223.
19. *Doe* d. *Garnons* v. *Knight* (1862), 5 B. & C. 671.

Specialty contracts differ from simple (or parol) contracts in the following respects:

(i) No consideration is required[20].

(ii) Right of action arising out of a contract under seal is normally barred by non-exercise for twelve years; right of action on a simple contract is normally barred in six[21].

CONTRACTS REQUIRING A SPECIAL FORM

In general the parties to a contract may make it in any form they choose. Apart from special circumstances, a contract will be equally binding whether it is made under seal, in writing or by word of mouth alone though naturally the terms of a contract will generally be easier to prove if the contract is under seal or otherwise in writing.

Sometimes, however, some special form is necessary; if so, this will be either writing under seal or writing under hand; and sometimes, though a verbal contract may be valid, it may be unenforceable by action unless evidenced by writing.

Contracts which must be entered into by deed

Among these may be mentioned:

1. Gratuitous promises[1];
2. Leases for upwards of three years[2].

Contracts which must be in writing

These include:

1. Bills of exchange and promissory notes; this is required by the Bills of Exchange Act 1882, and was formerly so by the common law[3];
2. Contracts of marine insurance[4];
3. Hire-purchase contracts governed by the Hire-Purchase Act 1965[5].

In addition there are certain transactions, closely connected with or involving contracts, where writing is necessary; for instance, an acknowledgment of a debt so as to start time running again under the

---

20. See *post*, p. 20.
21. See *post*, pp. 99–103.
1. See *post*, pp. 20–21.
2. Law of Property Act 1925, ss. 52 and 54.
3. S. 3 (1), (2).
4. See *post*, p. 295.
5. See *post*, p. 224.

Limitation Act must be in writing[6]; transfers of shares in companies are required to be in writing[7].

Contracts which are unenforceable by action unless evidenced by writing

By s. 4 of the Statute of Frauds 1677 it was provided that no action could be brought upon any of a number of contracts unless they were evidenced by some *note or memorandum* in writing, signed by the party to be charged, or by his authorised agent. From an early date, however, it was found that the Act was more frequently used as an instrument of frauds than to prevent frauds and the requirements of the Act were repealed in relation to most of the transactions mentioned in it by the Law Reform (Enforcement of Contracts) Act 1954.

There remain only the two following cases where a memorandum is required:

1. A promise to answer for the debt, default, or miscarriage of another person, *i.e.* a contract of guarantee[8];
2. A contract for the sale or other disposition of land or any interest in land[9].

The requirement of a memorandum does not affect the validity of the contract; it merely renders the contract unenforceable by action, unless it is evidenced by writing which fulfils the conditions of the statute. Accordingly, as the contract exists independently of the writing, the writing may be made at any time preceding the commencement of the action. Where it is made afterwards it will support the action[10] only if the proceedings are completely reconstituted or a new writ is issued after discontinuing the old proceedings[11]. Any document signed by the party to be charged, or his agent, and containing the terms of the contract, is sufficient to satisfy the statute; *e.g.*, a will or an affidavit[12]. A contract for the disposition of land not evidenced by a note or memorandum is only unenforceable *by action* so that if the purchaser repudiates such a contract the vendor is entitled to retain any deposit paid by the purchaser.

---

6. See *post*, p. 102.
7. Companies Act 1948, s. 75.
8. Statute of Frauds 1677, s. 4. See Ch. 22.
9. Law of Property Act 1925, s. 40. The section is not confined to contracts for the *sale* of an interest in land (*McManus* v. *Cooke* (1887), 35 Ch. D. 681, *per* KAY, J., at p. 687).
10. *Lucas* v. *Dixon* (1889), 22 Q. B. D. 357.
11. *Farr Smith & Co.* v. *Messers Ltd.* [1928] 1 K. B. 397.
12. *Re Hoyle* [1893] 1 Ch. 84.

The memorandum must contain details of the contract, including the names of the parties[13], the subject-matter, the consideration[14] and any other special terms in reasonable detail[15].

Note or memorandum

The note or memorandum need not be on one piece of paper; it may extend over several, provided that these are so connected and consistent that they can be read together[16]. If the signed paper does not itself contain all the contractual terms, there must be a sufficient reference, express or implied, in that document to some other document or documents, so that when all are read together they comprise a complete note or memorandum, *e.g.*,

> the term "our arrangement" was used in a letter, and this was allowed to be connected with an arrangement set out in a previous note, the whole being then taken as the true contract[17].

This case may usefully be contrasted with *Timmins v. Moreland Street Property Co., Ltd.*[18]:

> The buyers of houses sent the seller a cheque for £3,900 payable to the seller's solicitors. The seller gave the buyers a receipt for £3,900 which he (the seller) signed and the receipt contained the terms of the sale. Later the buyers countermanded the cheque and repudiated the contract. *Held:* the document signed by the party to be charged, *i.e.* the cheque, did not contain all the contractual terms and did not expressly or by implication refer to any other document. In consequence the two documents could not be read together so as to comprise a complete memorandum. Judgment was given for the buyers. (It may well have been different had the cheque been made out in favour of the seller personally as the seller had signed the receipt.)

---

13. So long as two parties are named who are contractually bound, it does not matter that one is really acting as an agent for someone else. Thus, where an estate agent signed in his own name without qualification a receipt for a deposit which described the property being sold, and contained the names of the estate agent (who was acting for the vendor) and of the purchaser, but not the name of the vendor, it was held to be a sufficient memorandum to bind the vendor: *Davies v. Sweet*, [1962] 1 All E. R. 92; [1962] 2 Q. B. 300.
14. The consideration for a guarantee need not be stated: Mercantile Law Amendment Act 1856, s. 3.
15. *Pocock v. A. D. A. C., Ltd.*, [1952] 1 All E. R. 294.
16. *Boydell v. Drummond* (1809), 11 East, 142.
17. *Cave v. Hastings* (1881), 7 Q. B. D. 125. It does not matter that the other document contains the words "subject to contract": *Griffiths v. Young* [1970] 3 All E. R. 601; [1970] Ch. 675.
18. [1957] 3 All E. R. 265; [1958] Ch. 110; earlier cases are summarised in the judgments.

A letter, which would be a sufficient compliance with the statute if it contained the name of the person to whom it is addressed, may be made complete by means of the envelope in which it was sent[19]. And where a signed letter sets out the terms of a contract for the purpose of repudiating it, if the ground of repudiation is not good in law, it will not prevent the letter from being a sufficient memorandum within the statute[20].

The name of the party charged must be on the paper, but, in addition, the name of the other party, or a sufficient description (with which he may be connected by parol evidence), must be included[1]. Thus, a description of a party as "the proprietor"[2] or "personal representative"[3] has been held sufficient; on the other hand, "vendor" has been considered an insufficient description[4].

Only the signature of the party sought to be charged is requisite, though in most cases both parties would sign[5]. The signature may be in ink or pencil, printed or stamped[6]; an identifying mark or mere initials will suffice[7]. The signature must be so placed as to show that it was intended to relate and refer to every part of the instrument[8]. If it governs the whole document it need not be at the end—*e.g.* if a man begins "I, A.B., agree, etc," and does not sign the paper at the foot, the statute is satisfied[9]. The signature may be that of the party to be charged, or of his duly authorised agent.

Agents

Whether a person is agent for the purpose of binding his principal by his signature is in each case a question of fact which must be determined according to the circumstances, and with the assistance of the general principles of agency law. It is not necessary that the principal should have authorised the agent to sign the document as a record of the transaction[10]:

---

19. *Pearce* v. *Gardner*, [1897] 1 Q.B. 688.
20. *Dewar* v. *Mintoft*, [1912] 2 K. B. 373.
1. *Champion* v. *Plummer* (1805), 1 B. & P. N. R. 252; *Williams* v. *Lake* (1860), 2 E. & E. 349; 29 L. J. Q. B. 1.
2. *Sale* v. *Lambert* (1874), 18 Eq. 1.
3. Even though it is not stated of whom he is the representative: *Fay* v. *Miller, Wilkins & Co.*, [1941] K. B. 360; [1941] 2 All E. R. 18.
4. *Potter* v. *Duffield* (1874), 18 Eq. 4.
5. *Reuss* v. *Picksley* (1866), L. R. 1 Ex. 342.
6. *Schneider* v. *Norris* (1814), 2 M. & S. 286; *Leeman* v. *Stocks*, [1951] 1 All E. R. 1043; [1951] Ch. 941.
7. *Baker* v. *Dening* (1838), 8 A. & E. 94.
8. *Caton* v. *Caton* (1867), L. R. 2 H. L. 127, *per* LORD WESTBURY.
9. *Evans* v. *Hoare*, [1892] 1 Q. B. 593.
10. *John Griffiths Cyle Corporation* v. *Humber & Co., Ltd.*, [1899] 2 Q. B. 414.

the signature of counsel to a pleading may constitute a sufficient memorandum of a contract by his client, although the pleading was signed without the slightest intention of bringing about that result[11].

A person may be agent for both parties, but if he is himself one of the parties, he cannot be agent to sign for the other. An auctioneer is agent to sign for the vendor, and for the buyer also after the lot has been knocked down to the buyer; his signature will then bind both parties unless indeed he is himself the vendor[12]. This authority to sign cannot be revoked after the fall of the hammer[13]; nor does it continue for an indefinite period after the sale.

A signature made a week after the auction was held to be too late[14]; but the auctioneer need not sign in the auction room if his signature can be fairly said to be part of the transaction of sale[15].

Part performance

It is possible to obtain a court order of specific performance of an agreement relating to land, of which there is no written evidence, provided that there has been part performance of the agreement by the plaintiff with the defendant's consent. Thus, in *Rawlinson* v. *Ames*[16]:

> The plaintiff agreed orally to let his flat to the defendant for twenty-one years and to make certain alterations whose execution the defendant supervised. Later, the defendant refused to take the flat. *Held:* the plaintiff was entitled to an order of specific performance because, although there was no written evidence of the contract, the plaintiff had partly performed the contract with the defendant's consent by doing acts which were explicable only on the basis of some such contract as the plaintiff alleged had been made.

Equivocal acts, like the mere payment of money, which are explicable on other grounds than the existence of a contract such as that alleged by the plaintiff, are not treated as acts of part performance. However, it is not necessary for the plaintiff to show that his acts establish the exact terms of the contract he alleged. Thus, in *Kingswood Estate Co., Ltd.* v. *Anderson*[17]:

---

11. *Grindell* v. *Bass*, [1920] 2 Ch. 487; *Farr Smith & Co.* v. *Messers*, [1928] 1 K. B. 397.
12. *Farebrother* v. *Simmons* (1822), 5 B. & Ald. 333.
13. *Van Praagh* v. *Everidge*, [1902] 2 Ch. 266; reversed on another point [1903] 1 Ch. 434.
14. *Bell* v. *Balls*, [1897] 1 Ch. 663.
15. *Chaney* v. *Maclow*, [1929] 1 Ch. 461.
16. [1925] Ch. 96.
17. [1962] 3 All E. R. 593; [1963] 2 Q. B. 169 C. A.; followed in *Wareham* v. *Mackenzie*, [1968] 2 All E. R. 783.

The elderly tenant of a house, living with her invalid son, enjoyed security of tenure under the Rent Acts. She agreed to give up possession to the landlords in return for an oral tenancy of a flat in which they could live for the rest of their lives. After they moved to the flat, the landlords served a four weeks' notice to quit. *Held:* although the contract relating to the flat was oral, the tenant's acts in leaving the controlled premises and entering into possession of the flat were sufficient acts of performance to defeat the landlord's claim for possession.

Variation of contract

The terms of a valid contract required by the Statute of Frauds to be evidenced in writing cannot be varied orally or by a document which does not comply with the statute. However, a subsequent parol contract may operate as an express or implied dissolution of the previous written contract, if it discloses an intention not merely to vary the original contract, but to set it aside[18]. A subsequent parol contract which purports not only to discharge the earlier written contract, but also to substitute for it a new one, has the effect of dissolving the earlier contract, but if the new one also comes within the provisions of the Statute of Frauds, it will be unenforceable because of the lack of written evidence.

At common law a contract under seal could not be dissolved or varied by a parol agreement, but such agreement now affords a defence to any action brought to enforce the contract on its original terms[19].

---

18. *Morris* v. *Baron & Co.*, [1918] A. C. 1; *British and Benington's, Ltd.* v. *N. W. Cachar Tea Co.*, [1923] A. C. 48.
19. *Berry* v. *Berry*, [1929] All E. R. Rep. 281; [1929] 2 K. B. 316.

CHAPTER 2

Essentials of a Contract

Every contract can be analysed into an offer and a corresponding acceptance[1]. The offer and the acceptance may be express or implied from conduct. In addition to these essentials, all contracts not under seal (and contracts in restraint of trade, though under seal) require consideration to support them.

1 OFFER AND ACCEPTANCE

In either of the following cases these is a clear contract—a definite offer and acceptance; in the latter case to pay the fair reward for the work done.

A may offer to sell B a ring at a certain price and B may say, "I'll take it." Or A may request B to erect a shed for him without any mention of the remuneration and B may agree to do so.

The offer need not be made, in the first instance, to any particular offeree but may be made to anyone in a given category of persons or to the general public, if that is the reasonable inference from the terms of the offer. In *Carlill* v. *Carbolic Smoke Ball Co.*[2], the facts were these:

Defendants issued an advertisement in which they offered to pay £100 to any person who should contract a certain disease after using a certain remedy in a specified manner and for a specified period; the plaintiff duly used the remedy, and contracted the disease, whereupon the Court of Appeal *held* her entitled to the £100.

Here was a definite offer to anybody who would perform the conditions, and it was accepted by one of the persons to whom it was made. Another example of this kind is advertising a reward for services to be rendered[3].

It is not always the party who makes the first overture who makes the offer. For instance,

A shopkeeper displays priced articles in his window or on shelves in his shop: he is not making an offer for a contract of sale, but

1. See p. 4, *ante*.
2. [1893] 1 Q. B. 256.
3. *Williams* v. *Carwardine* (1833), 4 B. & Ad. 621.

13

he is holding himself ready to consider offers made to him. He is said to be merely issuing an "invitation to treat", *i.e.* an invitation to make offers. So too if someone puts an advertisement in a newspaper that he has goods for sale[4].

Similarly in *Pharmaceutical Society of Great Britain* v. *Boots Cash Chemists (Southern), Ltd.*[5]:

> The defendants had a self-service system in their shop. The goods were exposed on the shelf with the prices marked. The customer helped himself and took the goods to the cash desk where he paid for them. *Held:* a sale was not completed till the customer's offer to buy had been accepted by the defendants' acceptance of the purchase money.

So when a company issues its prospectus, and asks for applications for shares, it is very seldom that the company so words the prospectus as to make it an offer to the public—it is usually only an advertisement that the company is ready to consider offers—an invitation to treat. The application for shares is then the offer and the allotment is the acceptance. It is a question of construction in each case, and must depend for its solution on the circumstances of each case. If someone, *e.g.* a local authority, advertises for tenders for the supply of "such coal as we may require" during the next year, this would only be an invitation to treat, but any trader who says he is willing to supply such coal as the local authority orders next year at £x per ton is making a tender or offer. The offer is accepted whenever a specific quantity of coal is ordered in accordance with that tender[6].

Further, the offer must be accepted absolutely, and on the same terms as offered. If there is an offer to go to London for £50, which is accepted subject to a call being made at Guildford on the way, there is no contract; but if the first party assents to this, there is an agreement based not upon the original offer, but on the acceptance of the counter-offer[7].

An acceptance "subject to contract" is not an absolute acceptance. The matter remains in negotiation until a formal contract is executed, and, if it is recorded in two parts, until the formal contracts are exchanged[8]. An extreme example is *Eccles* v. *Bryant and Pollock*[9]:

> The plaintiff bought a house "subject to contract." The terms of the formal contract were agreed and each party signed his part.

4. *Partridge* v. *Crittenden*, [1968] 2 All E. R. 421, [1968] 1 W. L. R. 1204.
5. [1953] 1 All E. R. 482; [1953] 1 Q. B. 401.
6. *Great Northern Rail. Co.* v. *Witham* (1874), L. R. 9 C. P. 16.
7. *Hyde* v. *Wrench* (1840), 3 Beav. 334.
8. *Chillingworth* v. *Esche*, [1924] 1 Ch. 97.
9. [1947] 2 All E. R. 865; [1948] Ch. 93.

The plaintiff posted his part but the vendor before posting his part changed his mind. *Held:* there was no binding contract.

The same result will follow whenever it is clear that the parties intended a formal contract to be executed before the obligations became operative. But the parties may reach a binding contract and then decide to record it. In such a case the agreement is binding even if no formal contract is executed[10]. Moreover, a provisional or temporary agreement may be made to take effect at once and constitute a binding contract until a more formal contract is executed[11].

Communication of acceptance

An unaccepted offer will not affect the rights of the parties, nor will a mere mental acceptance, uncommunicated to the offeror[12]; but the offeror may waive notification by specifying a particular act which he will agree to take as effective acceptance—*e.g.* if the person making the offer expressly or impliedly intimates in his offer that it will suffice to act on the offer, so acting will be a sufficient acceptance[13]. This is so where a reward is offered for the return of lost goods. Anyone who acts on the offer by returning the goods is deemed to have accepted the offer.

Where the terms on which an offer is made are contained in or referred to in a document handed to the offeree, his acceptance of the document amounts to tacit acceptance of the terms, provided that a reasonable person would expect the document to contain or refer to terms. Where a person buys a railway ticket containing words that the passenger agrees to take it subject to conditions on the back or in time-tables and posters, the acceptance of the ticket will be deemed to be a tacit acceptance of the conditions as part of the contract[14]. Contrast the following case of *Chapelton v. Barry Urban District Council*[15]:

The plaintiff hired a deck chair on a beach. He paid 2*d.* and received a ticket. On the back was a condition, which he did not read, excluding liability. The deck chair collapsed injuring the plaintiff. *Held:* the plaintiff in the circumstances could not be expected to look at the back of the ticket which was a mere

---

10. *Bolton Partners v. Lambert* (1889), 41 Ch. D. 295.
11. *Branca v. Cobarro*, [1947] 2 All E. R. 101; [1947] K. B. 854.
12. *Felthouse v. Bindley* (1862), 11 C. B. (N.S.) 869.
13. *Carlill v. Carbolic Smoke Ball Co.*, [1893] 1 Q. B., at p. 270.
14. *Parker v. South Eastern Rail. Co.* (1877), 2 C. P. D. 416; *Richardson v. Rowntree*, [1894] A C. 217; *Thompson v. London, Midland and Scottish Rail. Co.*, [1930] 1 K. B. 41. It is different if the words "see back" are obliterated: *Sugar v. London, Midland and Scottish Rail. Co.*, [1941] 1 All E. R. 172.
15. [1940] 1 All E. R. 356; [1940] 1 K. B. 532.

receipt. He could not therefore be said to have accepted the condition and was entitled to recover damages.

Moreover, if the term sought to be relied on is unusual (*e.g.* a car parking ticket excluding any liability for personal injury) a court may rule that it cannot be relied on unless it is drawn explicitly to the customer's notice[16]. And if a written term is contradicted by an oral undertaking, the latter may be held to prevail[17].

But normally in commercial transactions (apart from misrepresentation) if a document is handed by one party to another and accepted by the latter as the contractual document (by signature or otherwise), there is no obligation to call the attention of the recipient to its conditions, and he will generally be bound by them, whether he reads it or not[18], unless the conditions are ambiguous[19], or unless he is misled by representations as to the contents of the document[20]. If parties have frequently contracted on the basis of particular written terms and subsequently a similar transaction is entered into without any written terms being used, the previous transactions may amount to a *course of dealing* and the written terms previously used will be treated as incorporated into the later contract[1].

Exemption clauses.—In a number of recent cases it has been held that if a contractual term purports to exempt a party from some liability he would otherwise be under, such exemption clause is normally construed by the courts as not being intended to apply if that party has failed to carry out the basic essential terms of the contract, *i.e.*, he has committed a *fundamental breach* of contract. In *Karsales (Harrow), Ltd.* v. *Wallis*[2],

> The defendant inspected a second-hand Buick car which was in excellent condition and he agreed to take it on hire-purchase. The contract contained a clause to the effect that (contrary to the normal conditions implied by law in such case) there was no condition that the vehicle was roadworthy or as to its fitness for

---

16. *Thornton* v. *Shoe Lane Parking, Ltd.*, [1971] 1 All E. R. 686; [1971] 2 Q. B. 163, C. A.
17. *Mendelssohn* v. *Normand*, [1969] 2 All E. R. 1215; [1970] 1. Q. B. 177, C. A.
18. *L'Estrange* v. *F. Graucob, Ltd.*, [1934] 2 K. B. 394.
19. *White* v. *John Warwick & Co., Ltd.*, [1953] 2 All E.R. 1021; [1953] 1 W. L. R. 1285.
20. *Curtis* v. *Chemical Cleaning and Dyeing Co.*, [1951] 1 K. B. 805; [1951] 1 All E. R. 631 ; followed in *Jaques* v. *Lloyd D. George & Partners, Ltd.*, [1968] 2 All E. R. 187; [1968] 1 W. L. R. 625 and *Mendelssohn* v. *Normand*, [1969] 2 All E. R. 1215; [1970] 1 Q. B. 177, C. A.
1. *Cf. Hollier* v. *Rambler Motors* (AMC), *Ltd.*, [1972] 1 All E. R. 399; C. A. [1971] 2 W. L. R. 401.
2. [1956] 2 All E. R. 866; [1956] 1 W. L. R. 936; followed in *Yeoman Credit, Ltd.* v. *Apps*, [1961] 2 All E. R. 281; [1962] 2 Q. B. 508.

any purpose. When the car was delivered, it was found to be in a deplorable condition, having been substantially altered since it was inspected. *Held:* the exemption clause was not effective as there had been a fundamental breach of contract.

Contrast the case of *Smeaton, Hanscomb & Co., Ltd.* v. *Sassoon I. Setty, Son & Co.*[3]:

The plaintiffs contracted to buy from the defendants mahogany logs of a certain size and quality. The contract contained a clause to the effect that the defendants were under no liability as to defects unless complaint was made within fourteen days of delivery. Five weeks after delivery, the plaintiffs complained of defects in quality and size. *Held:* the alleged breach was not fundamental and, therefore, the defendants were protected by the time clause. The position would have been different if the logs delivered had been pine logs instead of mahogany logs.

The House of Lords indicated in 1966 that there is no rule of law that a party is unable to rely on an exemption clause if he has committed a fundamental breach of contract—it depends on the construction of the contract[4]. However, in *Harbutt's Plasticine, Ltd.* v. *Wayne Tank and Pump Co., Ltd.*[5], the Court of Appeal took the view that, if as a result of a fundamental breach of contract, the contract was automatically brought to an end or the innocent party properly disaffirmed the contract, the exemption clause ceases to have any effect. On the other hand, if after a fundamental breach of contract the innocent party is able and chooses to affirm the contract, it is a matter of construction whether the exemption clause applies to such breach though there is a presumption against it.

B agreed to install certain equipment in A's factory and because B used unsuitable material the factory was destroyed by fire. A clause in the contract limited B's liability to the contract price for the work. *Held:* B had committed a fundamental breach of the contract which because of the factory's destruction automatically brought the contract to an end and the limitation clause (really one kind of exemption clause) could not be relied on so B was fully liable in damages.

---

3. [1953] 2 All E. R. 1471; [1953] 1 W. L. R. 1468.
4. *Suisse Atlantique Société d'Armement Maritime S.A.* v. *Rotterdamsche Kolen Centrale,* [1966] 2 All E. R. 61; [1967] 1 A. C. 361.
5. [1970] 1 All E. R. 225; [1970] 1 Q. B. 447; see also *Farnworth Finance, Ltd.* v. *Attryde,* [1970] 2 All E. R. 774. [1970] 1 W. L. R. 1053, C. A. and *Kenyon, Son and Craven* v. *Baxter Hoare & Co., Ltd.,* [1971] 2 All E. R. 708; [1971] 1 W. L. R. 519.

Mode of acceptance.—An offer which insists on a specified mode of acceptance is not properly accepted unless it is accepted in the prescribed manner—*e.g.*,

> If the offeror says you must reply by wire in twenty-four hours, he cannot be bound by any acceptance not conforming to this direction. It would be different if the offeror merely suggested a particular mode of acceptance.

Where the *offeree* specifies a mode of acceptance such mode can be waived by the offeree[6].

Revocation of offer.—An offer may be withdrawn at any time before acceptance; thus, a bid at an auction is not binding till accepted by the fall of the hammer[7]; but for such withdrawal to be effectual the revocation must be communicated to the other party or his agent[8]. The revocation need not, however, be communicated *by* the offeror—it suffices if the offeree learns of the offeror's intention to revoke from any reliable source[9]. If, when the offer is made, the offeror says that he will keep the offer open for a certain time, he may nevertheless revoke his offer before the expiration of the time, if he has received no consideration for the promise to keep his offer open[10], and if he communicates his revocation before the other party accepts[11].

Acceptance by post

When the offer is made by post, and whenever the circumstances are such that, according to the ordinary ways of mankind, the post might be used as a means of communicating the acceptance of an offer, the acceptance is complete as soon as it is posted, and the offer cannot be revoked after that time[12]. A revocation cannot take place after the acceptance has been duly posted[13], although the acceptance may not have arrived[14], or may never arrive[15]; and to be of any avail the revocation of

6. *Manchester Diocesan Council for Education* v. *Commercial and General Investments, Ltd.*, [1969] 3 All E. R. 1593; [1970] 1 W. L. R. 241.
7. *Payne* v. *Cave* (1789), 3 T. R. 148.
8. *Byrne* v. *Van Tienhoven* (1880), 5 C. P. D. 344; *Stevenson* v. *McLean* (1880), 5 Q. B. D. 346; *Financings, Ltd.* v. *Stimson*, [1962] 3 All E. R. 386; [1962] 1 W. L. R. 1184.
9. *Dickinson* v. *Dodds* (1876), 2 Ch. D. 463.
10. *Routledge* v. *Grant* (1828), 4 Bing. 653; *Dickinson* v. *Dodds* (1876), 2 Ch. D. 463. The right to revoke an application for shares is restricted by statute; Companies Act 1948, s. 50 (5).
11. *Byrne* v. *Van Tienhoven, supra.*
12. *Henthorn* v. *Fraser*, [1892] Ch. 27. Probably a posted acceptence cannot be cancelled by a later communication, *e.g.* a telegram, even though this reaches the offeror before the posted acceptance: Treitel, *The Law of Contract*, (3rd ed., 1970, p. 28).
13. *Byrne* v. *Van Tienhoven, infra.*
14. *Dunlop* v. *Higgins* (1866), 1 H. L. Cas 381; *Harris' Case* (1872), L. R. 7 Ch. 587; *Byrne* v. *Van Tienhoven, infra; Stevenson* v. *McLean, supra.*
15. *Household Fire Insurance Co.* v. *Grant* (1879), 4 Ex. D. 216.

an offer (whether made by post or otherwise) must reach the offeree before he posts or telegraphs his acceptance[16].

The offeree, by posting the letter, has put it out of his control, and done an extraneous act which clinches the matter, and shows beyond all doubt that each side is bound[17]. In this connection the following cases are in point.

In *Adams* v. *Lindsell*[18]:

A wrote on September 2nd, offering to sell wool at a price, and asking for an answer in course of post; the letter being misdirected, reached B only on the 5th; the answer, an acceptance, was sent at once, and arrived on the 9th, but the wool had been sold to third parties on the 8th. It was *held* that B could recover damages for non-delivery of the wool.

In *Byrne* v. *Van Tienhoven*[19]:

Defendants posted an offer to sell goods to the plaintiff on October 1st; on the 11th the offer arrived and the plaintiff at once accepted by telegram. On the 8th the defendants had posted a letter withdrawing the offer, and this was received on the 20th. The withdrawal was *held* to be too late.

LINDLEY, J., said:

"It has been urged that a state of mind not notified cannot be regarded in dealings between man and man, and that an uncommunicated revocation is, for all practical purposes, and in point of law, no revocation at all."

This view the learned judge adopted.

Telephone and teleprinter

The rules applicable to negotiations by post do not apply to communications by telephone or teleprinter. Where the communication is instantaneous, or nearly so, acceptance is effective only when it reaches the offeror. In *Entores, Ltd.* v. *Miles Far East Corporation*[20], DENNING, L.J., said—

"Suppose, for instance, that I make an offer to a man by telephone and, in the middle of his reply, the line goes 'dead' so that I do not hear his words of acceptance. There is no contract at that moment."

---

16. *Byrne* v. *Van Tienhoven* (1880), 5 C. P. D. 344.
17. Lord BLACKBURN in *Brogden* v. *Metroplitan Rail. Co.* (1877), 2 App. Cas. 666, 691.
18. (1818), 1 B. & Ald. 681.
19. (1880), 5 C. P. D. 344.
20. [1955] 2 All E. R. 493 at p. 495; [1955] 2 Q. D. 327 at p. 332.

The offeree in such cases will normally be able to tell if his message has not been received and if the offeror does not ask to have a message repeated which he has not properly heard, he may be estopped from saying he did not receive it[21].

The offer may lapse otherwise than by revocation—*e.g.*:

(i) By rejection or counter offer, so that if the offer is to sell goods at £10 and the offeree makes a counter offer to buy them at £9 the offer has lapsed and the offeree cannot now accept the original offer[22]. A counter offer must, however, be distinguished from an offeree's request for information, *e.g.* "may I pay next month?";

(ii) By lapse of the time specified in the offer as being the time within which it might be accepted;

(iii) If no such time is specified, the lapse of a reasonable time, *i.e.* the lapse of such time that in all the circumstances the offeree may fairly be regarded as having rejected the offer[23].

(iv) By death of the offeree before he has accepted the offer, but the death of the offeror before acceptance will cause the offer to lapse only where it involves personal performance by the offeror as in the case of an offer to write a book[24].

II CONSIDERATION

This has been defined as

"some right, interest, profit, or benefit accruing to the one party, or some forbearance, detriment, loss, or responsibility given, suffered, or undertaken by the other"[25].

Consideration must be distinguished from motive. If a promise is made in the hope that it will induce a course of conduct, but the promisee gives no undertaking, there is no consideration.

In *Guiness (Bob), Ltd.* v. *Salomonsen*[1]:

A promised to pay a betting debt by instalments in the hope that he would not be reported to the National Turf Protection Society. The bookmaker gave no promise but in fact did not report him. *Held:* there was no consideration for the promise to pay.

Had the bookmaker given a promise not to report A so long as the

---

21. *Per* DENNING, L.J., [1955] 2 All E. R. at p. 495; [1955] 2 Q. B. at p. 333.
22. *Hyde* v. *Wrench* (1840), 3 Beav. 334.
23. *Manchester Diocesan Council for Education* v. *Commercial and General Investments, Ltd.*, [1969] 3 All E. R. 1593; [1970] 1 W. L. R. 241.
24. *Bradbury* v. *Morgan* (1862), 1 H. & C. 249.
25. *Currie* v. *Misa* (1875), L. R. 10 Ex., at p. 162.
1. [1948] 2 K. B. 42; but see *Crears* v. *Hunter* (1887), 19 Q. B. D. 341.

instalments were paid, there would have been consideration although the contract would then have been void under the Gaming Act 1845[2].

Sir William Anson laid down the following general rules as to consideration:

1. It is necessary to the validity of every contract not under seal.
2. It need not be adequate to the promise, but must be of some value in the eye of the law.
3. It must be legal.
4. It must not be past.

1. *It is necessary to the validity of every contract not under seal.*—It is a principle of our law that there must be some consideration to support even a written contract, unless the contract is under seal: for *Ex nudo pacto non oritur actio.* This was clearly expressed in the case of *Rann* v. *Hughes*[3], where SKYNNER, L.C.B., delivering the opinion of the judges, said:

> ". . . the law of this country . . . affords no remedy to compel the performance of an agreement made without sufficient consideration."

2. *It need not be adequate to the promise, but must be of some value in the eye of the law.*—Once consideration is proved, adequacy is not important: a promise to sell a car may be in consideration of £10 or £100, or of 10p. The contract may be enforced, if the promise is

> "Either for the benefit of the defendant, or to the trouble or prejudice of the plaintiff"[4].

BLACKBURN, J., has said:

> "The adequacy of the consideration is for the parties to consider at the time of making the agreement, not for the court when it is sought to be enforced"[5].

Thus, in *Thomas* v. *Thomas*[6]:

> The executors of T agreed to allow his widow to remain in the matrimonial home in consideration of T's wishes, her paying £1 a year and her keeping the house in repair. *Held:* consideration for the executors' promise consisted in the widow's promises of payment and doing the repairs and the agreement was enforceable.

---

2. *Hill* v. *William Hill (Park Lane), Ltd.,* [1949] 2 All E. R. 452; [1949] A. C. 530; and see *post,* p. 50.
3. (1778), 7 T. R. 350.
4. Com. Dig, Action on the case in Assumpsit, B. 1
5. *Bolton* v. *Madden* (1873), L. R. 9 Q. B., at p. 57. Inadequacy may be evidence of fraud.
6. [1842] 2 Q. B. 851.

In *Chappell & Co., Ltd.* v. *Nestlé Co., Ltd.*[7],

A promise to supply gramophone records for 1s. 6d. plus three chocolate wrappers was held enforceable—the delivery of the wrappers was considered to form part of the consideration.

The following are sufficient to support a contract:

(i) Payment of money.

(ii) Compromise of an action.

(iii) Giving up a claim which has been honestly made, though in fact the claim is one which would not have been successful.

The following are examples of agreements which do not constitute binding contracts because of the non-existence of consideration:

(i) A promise founded on moral obligation alone[8];

(ii) A promise to do what the promisee can legally demand already. Thus, in *Stilk* v. *Myrick*[9]:

> After two seamen had deserted a ship, the remaining seamen agreed to work the ship home in return for a promise of extra wages. *Held:* since the seamen were bound already by their existing contracts to work the ship home, their promise could not constitute consideration for the promise of extra wages and their claim, therefore, failed.

In *Foakes* v. *Beer*[10]:

> A debtor agreed to pay a judgment debt by a part payment down, the remainder by instalments, the creditor meanwhile agreeing not to proceed with his legal remedies. The House of Lords *held* that the debtor gave no consideration, as he could have been made to do what he did independently of his later promise.

On the other hand, if A promises to carry out his existing contractual obligations with B in return for a promise by C, A's performance of those obligations is good consideration for C's promise. Thus, in *Shadwell* v. *Shadwell*[11]:

> An uncle offered an annuity to his nephew if he would carry out a previously arranged engagement to marry and fulfilment of the latter promise was held enough to support the uncle's promise.

---

7. [1959] 2 All E. R. 701; [1960] A. C. 87.
8. *Eastwood* v. *Kenyon* (1840), 11 A. & E. 446.
9. (1809), 2 Camp. 317.
10. (1884), 9 App. Cas. 605.
11. (1850), 9 C. B. (N. S.) 159. Yet the benefit to the uncle was "a purely sentimental one" and SALMON, L.J., has recently doubted if there was any contractual intention (*Jones* v. *Padavatton*, [1969] 2 All E. R. 616, at p. 621).

(iii) A promise to do what the promisor is already bound to do as a matter of public duty. Thus in *Collins* v. *Godefroy*[12], it was held that a promise to attend court proceedings, given by someone who was bound to attend because a subpoena had been served upon him, could not constitute consideration for a promise of six guineas for his trouble. But, in *Ward* v. *Byham*[13]:

> A man offered £1 a week to a woman with whom he had been living in return for the woman agreeing to look after their illegitimate child properly and in return for permitting the child to decide whether she wished to live with the woman. *Held:* although the mother of an illegitimate child is under a statutory duty to maintain the child, her promise to allow the child a choice as to her home was consideration for the man's promise of payment.

(iv) Payment of a smaller amount cannot alone be consideration for discharge from an agreement to pay a larger amount[14].

Similarly, variations in the mode of paying a debt made at the debtor's request for his sole benefit are not consideration which would support a promise.

In *Vanbergen* v. *St. Edmunds Properties, Ltd.*[15]:

> A owed B £208. B at A's request agreed not to serve a bankruptcy notice if A would pay the £208 into a bank in the country on the next day. A paid the £208 but B not knowing it had been paid served the notice. *Held:* by the Court of Appeal, A was not entitled to damages as there was no consideration for B's promise. The choice of the country bank was made entirely for A's convenience.

On the other hand, if at the *creditor's* request, a smaller sum is paid at an earlier date than the date when the full sum became due, or at a different place from that where payment is due, there is good consideration for the creditor's promise to take it in full settlement.

Equitable Estoppel.—Though breach of a promise not to enforce a legal right cannot give rise to an action for damages unless the agreement is supported by consideration, such a promise, if it is intended to have legal consequences and to be acted on and if it is in fact acted

---

12. (1831), 1 B. & Ad. 950.
13. [1956] 2 All E. R. 318; [1956] 1 W. L. R. 496.
14. *Cumber* v. *Wane* (1721), 1 Sm. L. C. (13th ed.) 373. A composition with creditors imports mutual promises by the creditors to reduce their claims: *Good* v. *Cheesman* (1831), 2 B. & Ad. 328.
15. [1933] 2 K. B. 223.

upon, may afford a defence to an action to enforce that right even without consideration. Thus in *Central London Property Trust, Ltd.* v. *High Trees House, Ltd.*[16]:

> The plaintiffs by a lease under seal let a block of flats at £2,500 a year. Subsequently when many flats were vacant owing to the war the plaintiffs by letter agreed to accept a reduced rent of £1,250. *Held:* by DENNING, J., although there was no consideration for the plaintiffs' agreement not to enforce their strict legal right to the full rent, the plaintiffs should not be allowed to go back on that agreement and claim arrears of rent strictly due.

Thus a gratuitous promise by one party to suspend his rights under a contract will prevent him from proceeding to enforce them until he has given reasonable notice of his intention to resume them. This is known as "equitable estoppel"[17]. The principle does not apply if it would be inequitable to apply it. In *D. and C. Builders, Ltd.* v. *Rees*[18].

> D owed P £482 and when P, in urgent need of money, sought payment. D insisted that his payment by cheque of £300 must be accepted by P "in completion of the contract". *Held:* there was no consideration for P's agreement to take less than was due to him, nor was P estopped in the circumstances from claiming the balance of £182.

3. *It must be legal.*—The legality of the consideration is dealt with in Chapter 4.

4. *It must not be past.*—The consideration must not be past. Thus, if A delivers goods to B or does some service for B and subsequently B promises A that in consideration of what A has done for him, he (B) will pay A a sum of money, there is no consideration to support B's promise and B's promise cannot be sued on[19].

The following appear to be exceptions to the general rule:

(i) It is said that a past consideration will be enough, if it has been given at the request of the person making the subsequent promise—*e.g.*,

---

16. [1947] K. B. 130; for the limitations of the doctrine, see *Combe* v. *Combe*, [1951] 1 All E. R. 767; [1951] 2 K. B. 215. In *Woodhouse A. C. Israel Cocoa, Ltd., S. A.* v. *Nigerian Produce Marketing Co., Ltd.*, [1972] 2 All E. R. 271 at p. 282. Lord HAILSHAM, L.C., said the time may soon come when the sequence of cases based on promissory estoppel beginning with the *High Trees House Case* may need to be reviewed and reduced to a coherent body of doctrine by the courts.

17. DENNING, J.'s statement of the principle was *obiter*, but it was accepted by the House of Lords in *Tool Metal Manufacturing Co.* v. *Tungsten Electric Co., Ltd.*, [1955] 2 All E. R. 675; [1955] 1 W. L. R. 761. The result of these recent cases is to throw doubt on the earlier House of Lords decision in *Foakes* v. *Beer* (1884), 9 App. Cas. 605.

18. [1965] 3 All E. R. 837; [1966] 2 Q. B. 617.

19. The law is otherwise with bills of exchange. See *post*, p. 253.

If A requests B to do certain work for him, and some time afterwards says, "You shall have £10 for that,"

the consideration, though past, is good[20];

(ii) If a man makes a written acknowledgement of a past "debt or other liquidated pecuniary claim" which cannot be enforced against him it is statute-barred by lapse of time since the claim accrued, he is liable on that acknowledgement although the consideration for it is past[1].

Consideration, it is said, must "move from the promisee."—This means that a party seeking to enforce a promise must show that he has furnished the consideration. Thus, if A in return for services to be performed by B agrees with B to pay money to C, C cannot enforce the promise even if he is made a party to the agreement, but B can do so, for B furnished the consideration. A, however, can insist on performing his contract by paying C and B has no right to demand payment to himself[2].

It is clear, however, that the consideration need not move from the promisee to the promisor. Thus, if A takes a car on hire-purchase from X Co. Ltd. and B promises X Co. Ltd. that he will pay the instalments if A fails to do so, X Co. Ltd. may enforce B's guarantee promise—consideration for B's promise has moved from the promisee, X Co. Ltd., though X Co. Ltd. has given that consideration, namely the car, to A, not to B.

---

20. Possibly this is no exception to the general rule; a promise to pay may be implied from A's request and the £10 may be evidence of what would be the proper sum (*Stewart v. Casey*, [1892] 1 Ch. 115).
1. Limitation Act 1939, s. 23 (4). See *post*, p. 101.
2. *Re Schebsman, Ex parte Official Receiver*, [1943] 2 All E. R. 768; [1944] Ch. 83; and see *post*, p. 67.

CHAPTER 3

Mistake, Misrepresentation and Undue Influence

INTRODUCTORY

As has been stated[1], where one party has made an offer and the other party has accepted it in corresponding terms, a contract is concluded, even if one or both of the parties did not intend what he said. And the same is generally true if the parties entered into the contract under some misapprehension as to the circumstances. Thus—

A agrees to buy "horsebeans" from B. Both A and B wrongly believe that "horsebeans" are the same thing as "feveroles" which a customer has ordered from A. There is a binding contract between A and B[2].

But in certain circumstances mistake may be a ground for relief. Moreover, if a misapprehension has been induced by a misrepresentation made by the other party or if one party has been induced to enter into the agreement by some unfair pressure brought to bear upon him by the other party, then the innocent party may again have some remedy.

MISTAKE

The Common Law

The *general rule* of the Common Law was stated by BLACKBURN, J., in *Smith* v. *Hughes*[3]:

"If, whatever a man's real intention may be, he so conducts himself that a reasonable man would believe that he was assenting to the terms proposed by the other party, and that other party upon that belief enters into the contract with him, the man thus conducting himself would be equally bound as if he had intended to agree to the other party's terms."

Thus, if a man buys a horse mistakenly believing it is sound or a dwelling-house mistakenly believing it is habitable, the contract would

---

1. See p. 4, *ante.*
2. *Frederick E. Rose (London), Ltd.* v. *William H. Pim Jnr. & Co., Ltd.,* [1953] 2 All E. R. 739; [1953] 2 Q. B. 450.
3. (1871) L. R. 6 Q. B., 597, 607.

be valid[4]. Similarly, if a man sells 100 chests of tea for a given price, mistakenly believing that the chests contain a lower quality of tea than in fact they do, the contract is valid[5]. Provided that the terms of the contract are clear and it seems, objectively speaking, that a definite contract has been concluded, the parties will be held bound by the contract though one or other of them, or even both of them (as in the "horsebeans" case referred to) are mistaken as to what is involved. In *Tamplin* v. *James*[6]:

> J made a bid at an auction sale for a public house believing that a certain field was included in the lot. This was a misapprehension on his part. The lot was knocked down to him. There was no ambiguity in the particulars as to what was included in the lot and J was *held* bound to the contract.

A most important case on this matter is *Bell* v. *Lever Brothers, Ltd.*[7]:

> B and S were employed by Lever Bros. on five-year service contracts and Lever Bros. wished to dispense with their services before the expiry of this period. Lever Bros. made compensation agreements with B and S under which they received £50,000 for loss of office. Lever Bros. later discovered that B and S had committed certain breaches of duty which, had Lever Bros. known of these breaches earlier, would have entitled them to dismiss B and S without compensation. The House of Lords accepted that these breaches were not in the minds of B and S at the time of the compensation agreements. The House *held* that despite the mistake of both parties, *i.e.* the assumption that the services of B and S could only be dispensed with by compensation agreements, these agreements were valid contracts. The parties were mistaken only as to the quality of the service contracts (which were the subject-matter of the compensation agreements), *i.e.* their mistake was only as to whether the service contracts were voidable.

As a result of this decision, it has been thought that no mistake as to quality can ever have the effect of invalidating a contract and Lord ATKIN did say that if A buys a picture from B which both believe to be the work of an old master and a high price is paid, but it turns out to be a modern copy, the contract is valid—A has no remedy in the absence of a representation or warranty. However, one author has doubted this illustration and suggested that if some particular quality is so important in the minds of the parties that they use it to identify

---

4. *Per* Lord ATKIN in *Bell* v. *Lever Brothers, Ltd.*, [1932] A. C. 161, 224.
5. *Scott* v. *Littledale* (1858), 8 E. & B. 815.
6. (1879), 15 Ch. D. 215.
7. [1931] All E. R. Rep. 1; [1932] A. C. 161.

the thing, and the thing lacks that quality, the contract is void[8].

There are a number of well recognised circumstances where, exceptionally, a mistake does render a contract void at common law and any money paid or property handed over under such contract is recoverable:

1. *Where it is not clear what the terms are because of ambiguity.*—Thus, in *Raffles* v. *Wichelhaus*[9]:

> A agreed to buy cotton from B to arrive "ex *Peerless* from Bombay". There were two ships of that name coming from Bombay—A had one in mind, B the other. The terms of the contract could apply to either and it was *held* that the contract was void.

In *Scriven Brothers & Co.* v. *Hindley*[10]:

> A bid for a lot at an auction sale which consisted of tow but A thought he was bidding for hemp. The lot was knocked down to him. Both tow and hemp were being sold at the auction, but the bales were not properly described in the auctioneer's catalogue and the samples were confusingly marked. *Held:* contract void.

2. *Where the thing bargained for does not exist.*—If both parties are mistaken as to the existence of the subject-matter of the contract, this mistake nullifies consent and renders the contract void. Thus, in *Galloway* v. *Galloway*[11], a separation deed had been entered into on the basis that A was married to B—their marriage was the subject-matter of the contract. It was held void when it was established that they were not in fact married. Similarly, if A sells B a portrait which, unknown to both, has just been destroyed in a fire, the contract is void for mistake[12]. Again, should A sell B something which, unknown to both, already belongs to B, the sale is void for mistake.

3. *In certain cases of unilateral mistake, i.e.* mistake by one party to the contract only, such mistake being known to the other party. *Mistake as to the identity of the other party* can thus make a contract void if the mistake is material and known to the other party.

A leading case is *Cundy* v. *Lindsay*[13]:

> One Blenkarn ordered goods from L, fraudulently using the name

---

8. G. H. Treitel, *The Law of Contract* (3rd ed., 1970, pp. 215-218). In *Leaf* v. *International Galleries*, [1950] 1 All E. R. 693; [1950] 2 K. B. 86, the sale of a picture believed to be painted by Constable, was held not to be void, but the question of mistake was not argued.
9. (1864), 33 L. J. Ex. 160.
10. [1913] 3 K. B. 564.
11. (1914), 30 T. L. R. 531.
12. The rule is now embodied in the Sale of Goods Act 1893, s. 6, see *post*, p. 184. Of course, if the seller warranted that the portrait existed, he would be liable to the buyer should the portrait not be in existence: see *McRae* v. *Commonwealth Disposals Commission* (1950), 84 C. L. R. 337.
13. (1878), 3 App. Cas. 459.

of Blenkiron & Co. L despatched the goods and Blenkarn sold them to C. L sued C to recover the goods. *Held:* the contract between L and Blenkarn was void for mistaken identity—L intended to deal with Blenkiron & Co., Blenkarn knew of L's mistake, and it was a material mistake. Hence, neither Blenkarn nor C had any title to the goods and C was liable to L.

The position is different if the other party merely used an alias, not the name of another real person. In *King's Norton Metal Co., Ltd.* v. *Edridge, Merrett & Co., Ltd.*[14]:

> The plaintiffs agreed to sell goods on credit to one Wallis who had ordered goods in the name of "Hallam and Co." This was merely an alias used by Wallis. The goods were despatched to Wallis and he sold them to the defendant. *Held:* the contract between the plaintiffs and Wallis was valid. The plaintiffs could not establish they intended to contract with someone other than Wallis, and their mistake was one as to the creditworthiness rather than as to the identity of the other party.

In both these cases, the parties dealt with one another by correspondence. Where parties deal with one another face to face, it may be more difficult for one to establish that he made a material mistake as to the identity of the other party. Thus in *Lewis* v. *Avaray*[15]:

> L advertised his car for sale in a newspaper. A man came to see L about the car, saying he was "Richard Green" and purporting to be a well known actor of that name. L agreed to sell his car to this man in return for a cheque for £450. The man was allowed to drive away the car and he promptly sold it to A. The cheque was dishonoured. *Held:* where the transaction is between parties face to face there is a presumption in law that there is a contract even though a fraudulent impersonation has been made. L therefore had no right to recover the car from A.

Another type of case where unilateral mistake makes a contract void is a *mistake* by A *as to the terms of the contract* and B knows A is mistaken as to the terms. As has already been said, if the terms of a contract are clear and unambiguous and A makes a mistake as to what is involved (*Tamplin* v. *James*[16]), the contract is binding. But if A's mistake is as to what are the terms or as to the meaning of the terms, *and* B is aware of that mistake, the contract is void. Thus if in buying oats, A mistakenly thinks not merely that they are old oats but that

---

14. (1897), 14 T. L. R. 98.
15. [1971] 3 All E. R. 907; [1972] 1 Q. B. 198, C. A., following *Phillips* v. *Brooks*, [1919] 2 K. B. 243, *cf. Ingram* v. *Little*, [1960] 3 All E. R. 332; [1961] 1 Q. B. 31.
16. (1879), 15 Ch. D. 215.

they are being offered to him as old oats (*i.e.* warranted as old oats), and B knows of A's mistake, the contract is void[17].

Remedies at Common Law

At common law the effect of mistake, if it operates at all to invalidate the contract, is simply to make the contract void.

If a mistake sufficient to annul the contract is established to the satisfaction of the court, the contract may be set aside, although completed. Thus, in *Scott* v. *Coulson*[18]:

> A contract for the sale of a life policy was entered into in the belief that the assured was alive. The contract was completed by assignment. *Held:* the contract could properly be set aside for mistake.

Money paid under a mistake of fact may generally be recovered back, because the receiver not being entitled to the money nor intended to have it, its retention is against conscience[19]. The mistake must be as to a fundamental fact but it does not appear to be necessary to establish that there would have been a legal liability to pay had the facts been as thought. Thus, in *Larner* v. *London County Council*[20]:

> When L was called up into the R.A.F., the L.C.C. gratuitously agreed to make up his service pay to his civil pay. After the war, the L.C.C. discovered that they had overpaid L because he had failed to notify them of changes in his service pay. *Held:* the L.C.C. were entitled to recover these overpayments although they had not been under any *legal* liability to pay even if the facts had been as they thought since their undertaking was made without consideration.

Equity

Where the plaintiff seeks an equitable remedy, *e.g.* specific performance of the contract, and it is argued that mistake affects the validity of the contract, the court will normally determine the case according to the principles of the common law already examined. If, therefore, at common law, mistake does not affect the validity of the contract as in *Tamplin* v. *James*[1] the court will be prepared to grant specific performance of it. If, on the other hand, on common law principles, the contract is void for mistake, specific performance will normally be refused.

17. *Smith* v. *Hughes* (1871), L. R. 6 Q. B. 597.
18. [1903] 2 Ch. 249.
19. *Kelly* v. *Solari* (1841), 9 M. & W. 54; *R. E. Jones* v. *Waring & Gillow*, [1926] A. C. 670.
20. [1949] 1 All E. R. 964; [1949] 2 K. B. 683.
1. (1879), 15 Ch. D. 215.

Thus, in *Webster* v. *Cecil*[2]:

> C had refused to sell land to W at £2,000 but C then wrote offering to sell the land to W at £1,200. C had mistakenly written £1,200 instead of £2,200. W realised C had made this error but immediately purported to accept C's offer to sell at £1,200. *Held:* there was no binding contract of sale at £1,200 as C had made a unilateral mistake in writing down the terms and W knew this. Specific performance was refused.

But equity is more flexible than the common law. A court may, for example, by applying equitable principles, set aside a contract, *i.e.* rescind it, for mistake although the common law would not regard the mistake as operative to render the contract void. The court may exercise this equitable jurisdiction where the justice of the case seems to require it, but the extent of this jurisdiction is uncertain. In *Solle* v. *Butcher*[3]:

> The parties agreed to the lease of a flat in the common belief that owing to alterations it was no longer subject to the Rent Acts restricting the amount of rent chargeable and that a rent of £250 was permissible. The flat was still subject to the Rent Acts and the legal rent was £140. *Held:* the lease was not void at common law—the mistake was only as to the quality of the flat—but it would be set aside on equitable principles on terms that were just to both parties.

Where on common law principles a contract is void, the court may, in order to do justice, impose equitable terms on the parties in setting the contract aside, as in *Cooper* v. *Phibbs*[4].

> A took a lease of a fishery from B, both parties mistakenly believing B owned it. Actually the fishery belonged to A, but B had incurred expense in improvements. *Held:* the lease would be set aside on terms that A would reimburse B's expenses.

It is doubtful whether equity would grant relief where the mistake is as to the general law but it may do so where, as in *Cooper* v. *Phibbs,* the mistake is as to private rights under the law.

Rectification.—Where parties have reached an agreement (which need not be a concluded binding contract) and this is then embodied in a

---

2. (1861), 30 Beav. 62.
3. [1949] 2 All E. R. 1107; [1950] 1 K. B. 671. Followed in *Grist* v. *Bailey,* [1966] 2 All E. R. 875; [1967] Ch. 532. Lord DENNING, M.R., also purported to follow *Solle* v. *Butcher* in *Magee* v. *Pennine Insurance Co.,* [1969] 2 All E. R. 891, [1969] 2 Q. B. 507 but it is not clear whether the other majority judge, FENTON ATKINSON, L.J., supported Lord DENNING's reasoning.
4. (1867), L. R. 2 H. L. 149.

document but this document fails to record the agreement accurately, though they both mistakenly think it does, either party may ask the court to rectify the written document in order to bring into line with their prior agreement[5]. However, although a contract will normally be rectified only if *both* parties have made a mistake as to its contents, a party may be granted the remedy of rectification on proof that he believed a certain term was included and the other party concluded the contract with the omission of that term in the knowledge that the other party believed the term was included[6].

Mistake in signing a written document

If anyone signs a written document which is radically different in effect from the document he thinks he is signing and this mistake has been induced by a misrepresentation, he may plead *non est factum* (it is not my deed) and he is not bound by it[7].

In *Foster* v. *Mackinnon*[8]:

> M, "a gentleman far advanced in years and of poor sight", was induced by C to sign a piece of paper described by C as "a guarantee". In fact, the document was a bill of exchange and M's signature appeared to be that of an endorser and, therefore, to make him liable to a later holder for value. *Held:* M was not bound by his signature as he had signed the paper under a mistake as to its nature.

However, it is difficult for an adult literate person to succeed in the defence of *non est factum* and the defence is not available if the signer is negligent. The signer must at least take reasonable care to find out the general effect of the document before signing. The House of Lords has recently clarified the law in *Saunders* v. *Anglia Building Society*[9]:

> An elderly lady had mislaid her spectacles and did not read the document she was asked to sign by her nephew which she mistakenly thought was a deed of gift of her house to him so that he could raise money on it. In fact the document was an assignment of the house to her nephew's business associate, and the latter mortgaged it to the defendants but defaulted in his repayments. The elderly lady sought a declaration that she was not bound by

---

5. *Joscelyne* v. *Nissen*, [1970] 1 All E. R. 1213, [1970] 2 Q. B. 86, C. A.
6. *A. Roberts & Co.* v. *Leicestershire County Council*, [1961] 2 All E. R. 545; [1961] Ch. 555.
7. *Mercantile Credit Co., Ltd.* v. *Hamblin*, [1964] 3 All E. R. 592; [1964] 3 W. L. R. 798, C. A.
8. (1869), L. R. 4 C. P. 704.
9. [1970] 3 All E. R. 961; [1971] A. C. 1004. The distinction formerly drawn between the character and the contents of the document was regarded by the House of Lords as unsatisfactory.

her signature. *Held:* The effect of the document was not so fundamentally different from the document she thought she was signing and her action failed.

MISREPRESENTATION

A contractual term or a representation?

A statement of fact made by one party to the other before a contract between them is completed may be a term of the contract or a mere representation. There are two kinds of contractual terms: a condition[10] is a term of the contract which the parties consider of such importance that breach justifies the other party in repudiating the contract entirely as well as in suing for damages, whereas a warranty is a less important term for breach of which damages alone are obtainable[11]. For misrepresentation, there is the remedy of rescission of the contract but this remedy is lost if, for example, there is undue delay in pursuing it and, until the Misrepresentation Act 1967, no damages were obtainable unless the misrepresentation was fraudulent. Now, by s. 2 (1) of this Act,

"... if the person making the representation would be liable to damages in respect thereof had the misrepresentation been made fraudulently, that person shall be so liable notwithstanding that the misrepresentation was not made fraudulently, unless he proves that he had reasonable ground to believe and did believe up to the time the contract was made that the facts represented were true."

But even now, as no damages are obtainable unless the misrepresentation has been made fraudulently or negligently, it is still of some importance to know whether a statement is a contractual term or only a representation.

The distinction is a difficult one to determine and is said to depend on the intention of the parties, as inferred from all the facts. It appears from the decided cases that a statement is more likely to be interpreted by the courts as a contractual term if it was made by someone with

---

10. See p. 84, *post.* A "condition" as a term of the contract should be distinguished from a "condition precedent". A contract is subject to a "condition precedent" of the obligations of the contract are only binding if a certain event occurs, such as a third party approving the terms of the contract: *United Dominions Trust (Commercial), Ltd.* v. *Eagle Aircraft Services, Ltd.,* [1968] 1 All E. R. 104; [1968] 1 W. L. R. 74, C. A. (repurchase contract binding only if notice to repurchase given in reasonable time). A contract is subject to a "condition subsequent" if the obligations of the contract are to cease on the happening of a certain event: *Head* v. *Tattersall* (1871), L. R. 7 Ex. C. H. 7.
11. See p. 84, *post.*

particular knowledge of the facts and was made close to the time when the contract was completed. In *Oscar Chess, Ltd.* v. *Williams*[12]:

> W, a private individual, offered to sell a car to the plaintiff car dealers. He described the car as a 1948 model, which was the year given in the car's registration book, and the sale was completed. Eight months after the sale, it was discovered that the car was a 1939 model and that the registration book had been fraudulently altered by a previous owner. *Held:* since W did not have any personal knowledge of the car's age, nor any expert knowledge of cars in general, it was not reasonable to interpret his statement as a contractual promise but only as a misrepresentation. Owing to the delay since the sale, rescission for misrepresentation would not be granted, and there being no fraud, damages were not available either.

Contrast *Bannerman* v. *White*[13]:

> When B offered hops for sale, W asked if any sulphur had been used in their cultivation, adding that he would not even ask the price if sulphur had been used. B assured W that no sulphur had been used and the sale was completed. It was later learned that sulphur had been used in the treatment of some of the hops and W refused to accept them. *Held:* B's statement was clearly intended by both parties to be a term of the contract, in fact a condition, and W was entitled to repudiate the contract. Even if W had delayed before seeking a remedy, he would still have been entitled to damages for breach of a contractual term.

If a tradesman praises his wares in general terms that will usually be regarded as a mere puff and not a representation, far less a promise amounting to a term of the contract. Thus, a seller's description of a second-rate house as "a desirable house for a family of distinction" is no more than a sales puff[14].

Meaning of Misrepresentation

A misrepresentation is a false statement of fact made by one party to a contract (A) to the other (B) which is a factor inducing that other (B) to enter into the contract. Its effect is to render the contract voidable at the option of B. If the misrepresentation is fraudulent, *i.e.* made without an honest belief in its truth, B has the additional remedy of damages, and since the Misrepresentation Act 1967 B may also claim damages for negligent misrepresentation. The remedies will be examined in detail after the meaning of misrepresentation has been analysed more closely.

---

12. [1957] 1 All E. R. 325; [1957] 1 W. L. R. 370.
13. (1861), 10 C. B. (N.S.) 844.
14. *Magennis* v. *Fallon* (1828), 2 Mol. 561, at p. 588.

False statement.—It is possible for the representation to be made by conduct so that if A induces B to give him credit by dressing up as a military officer, the contract is voidable for misrepresentation. Normally, however, the representation is a statement made orally, or in writing. Silence cannot amount to a misrepresentation, but the assertion of a half-truth may be a misrepresentation. Lord CAIRNS in *Peek* v. *Gurney*[15] said:

> "There must, in my opinion, be some active misstatement of fact, or, at all events, such a partial and fragmentary statement of fact, as that the withholding of that which is not stated makes that which is stated absolutely false".

In *Dimmock* v. *Hallett*[16] the vendor of farms induced the sale by the statement that they were let to tenants. This was true so far as it went, but the statement amounted to a misrepresentation because the tenants had given notice to quit. Further, where a representation is made during negotiations which, though true at the time it is made, becomes untrue before the contract is made, it amounts to a misrepresentation— if, therefore the person who made the statement fails to disclose the change, the contract is voidable[17]. In some contracts there is a positive obligation on a party to disclose all material facts within his knowledge. These contracts, known as contracts *uberrimae fidei*, of which insurance contracts are the most important are referred to below[18].

Of fact.—This excludes false statements of law so that if A induced B to buy goods from him by falsely stating that the law no longer permitted goods to be taken on hire-purchase, the contract is not voidable. But a false statement of a person's private rights under the law is equivalent to a false statement of fact[19]. A statement of intention is usually not a statement of fact, but if it can be proved that the stated intention was not in fact held, there is a misrepresentation. As BOWEN, L.J., said in *Edgington* v. *Fitzmaurice*[20]:

> "The state of a man's mind is as much a fact as the state of his digestion".

Similarly, a mere statement of opinion is not a statement of fact, but where the facts are not equally known to both parties and an opinion stated by the party who knows the facts best is not in fact held, or there are no reasonable grounds for such opinion, the opinion amounts to a misrepresentation of fact[1]. Thus where the vendor of a hotel described

---

15. (1873), L. R. 6 H. L. 377, 403.
16. (1866), 2 Ch. App. 21.
17. *With* v. *O'Flanagan*, [1936] 1 All E. R. 727; [1936] Ch. 575.
18. *Post*, p. 41.
19. See *ante*, p. 31.
20. (1885) 29 Ch. D. 459, 483.
1. *Brown* v. *Raphael*, [1958] 2 All E.R. 79; [1958] Ch. 636.

it as let to "Mr. Flack, a most desirable tenant" and as BOWEN, L.J.,
put it, Mr. Flack paid his rents only "in driblets under pressure",
the vendor's statement of opinion was held to amount to a misrepresentation of fact[2].

Inducement.—The statement by A must have been intended by A
to be acted upon and it must actually have been relied on by B as at
any rate one of the factors that induced B to make a contract with A.
If B is not deceived by or does not rely on the representation, the
contract will not be set aside[3].

Thus,

> a purchaser did not examine his purchase, a gun; it contained a
> flaw, which rendered it worthless and this flaw had been actively
> concealed. *Held:* as no inspection had been made and the conceal-
> ment therefore never affected the mind of the purchaser, he had
> no remedy[4].

So too if A tells B that the horse which A is proposing to sell to B
has two eyes and B knows the horse does not have two eyes, there is no
operative misrepresentation. But if B was not aware of the falsity
of A's statement, it is no ground for refusing B a remedy that B had
every opportunity of discovering the truth. Thus in *Redgrave* v. *Hurd*[5]:

> a solicitor (A) made false statements of fact about the finances
> of his firm and an intending partner (B) relied on these statements
> when entering into partnership. *Held:* B was entitled to have the
> partnership contract rescinded on the ground of misrepresentation
> although A had given B the opportunity of examining certain
> papers from which B could have discovered the true position.

Fraudulent Misrepresentation and Remedies therefor

A fraudulent misrepresentation is a statement of fact made by A
knowing it is false, or without belief in its truth, or recklessly, without
caring whether it is true or false. At one time, some judges considered
that false statements carelessly made without reasonable ground of
belief in their truth, apart from actual dishonesty, constituted a species
of "legal fraud". This doctrine was exploded by the important case
of *Derry* v. *Peek*[6]:

> A company issued a prospectus, stating that the company had a
> right to use steam power for its tramway cars; as a fact, the consent
> of the Board of Trade was required before steam could be used,

---

2. *Smith* v. *Land and House Property Corporation* (1884), 28 Ch. D. 7.
3. *Smith* v. *Chadwick* (1884), 9 App. Cas. 187.
4. *Horsfall* v. *Thomas* (1862), 1 H. & C. 90.
5. (1881), 20 Ch. D. 1.
6. (1889), 14 App. Cas. 337.

and when, afterwards, consent was applied for, it was refused. The directors believed the truth of their statements, and pleaded that they had reasonable ground for believing them to be true.

In the House of Lords it was definitely settled that, in order to maintain an action for deceit, a false statement must be

(i) false to the knowledge of the person making it; or
(ii) untrue in fact and not believed to be true by the person making it; or
(iii) untrue in fact and made recklessly—*e.g.* without any knowledge on the subject, and without caring whether it is true or false.

But a false statement honestly made without any reasonable grounds for belief in its truth is not sufficient; in other words, in an action for deceit the plaintiff must prove actual dishonesty, not mere negligence or blundering.

If the representation is made innocently by an agent but the principal knew of facts which rendered it untrue, that will only amount to fraud if the principal authorised it or deliberately concealed the facts from the agent in the hope that the latter would make the representation in question.

In *Armstrong* v. *Strain*[7]:

An estate agent made a representation to the plaintiff about a house, which was untrue. The owner knew the facts but did not know of the agent's statements or authorise them. *Held:* there was no fraud for there is no way of combining an innocent principal and an innocent agent so as to produce dishonesty.

If the representation in fact is fraudulent within the definition above given, honesty of motive in making it will not be an answer to an action of deceit[8].

Remedies

A defrauded person has several remedies open to him. He may:

1. Rescind the contract, *e.g.* by communication with the fraudulent party or by conduct which manifests unequivocally his intention no longer to be bound by the contract or by obtaining a court order of rescission. At one time it was thought that communication with the fraudulent party was essential unless a court order was obtained but in *Car and Universal Finance Co., Ltd.* v. *Caldwell*[9], the Court of Appeal held that where a car owner was induced by fraud to sell it to a

7. [1952] 1 All E. R. 139; [1952] 1 K. B. 232.
8. *Polhill* v. *Walter* (1835), 3 B. & Ad. 114; *Foster* v. *Charles* (1830), 7 Bing. 105.
9. [1964] 1 All E. R. 290; [1965] 1 Q. B. 525.

rogue who disappeared, the owner had rescinded the sale when he informed the police to try and recover the car.
2. Resist any action to enforce the contract.
3. Sue for damages in which case he must prove that he has suffered actual damage. This right is normally open to the defrauded person irrespective of whether he is rescinding the contract or affirming it[10]. The measure of damages is not the same as for breach of a term of the contract since damages are not meant to put the innocent party in the same position as he would have been in had the contract not been broken: all damage flowing directly from the fraud is recoverable[11].

The limits that exist on the right of a defrauded party to rescind the contract, *e.g.* lapse of time and affirmation of the contract, are discussed under the head of **Innocent Misrepresentation** below. Certainly if B is induced to buy land or goods by A's fraud and B disposes of the property to C, C has no remedy against A because the representation was not addressed to C[12].

Fraud as to credit.—It remains to add that by s. 6 of the Statute of Frauds Amendment Act 1828:

> "no action will lie on a representation, though false and fraudulent, as to the character, conduct, credit, ability, trade, or dealings of any person, made to the intent or purpose of enabling such person to get credit, money, or goods, unless the representation be made in writing signed by the party to be charged therewith."

The section was passed to prevent evasion of the requirement of s. 4 of the Statute of Frauds[13], that guarantees must be evidenced in writing, by alleging that an oral representation was made fraudulently and suing for damages in an action for deceit; and the Amendment Act applies to *fraudulent* misrepresentations only and not to cases where the claim is based upon any contractual or other breach of duty[14]. The signature of an agent is not sufficient to charge his principal so that before a bank or other limited company can be sued for fraud the dishonest reference must have been impressed with the embossed "common seal" of the company[15].

---

10. Anyone induced to subscribe for shares in a company may only claim damages if he also rescinds the contract: *Holdsworth* v. *City of Glasgow Bank* (1880), 5 App. Cas. 317.
11. *Doyle* v. *Olby (Iron mongers), Ltd.*, [1969] 2 All E. R. 119, [1969] 2 Q. B. 158. (fraudulent inducement to buy a business—damages included reasonable expenses of running it).
12. *Gross* v. *Lewis Hillman, Ltd.*, [1969] 3 All E. R. 1476, [1970] Ch. 445.
13. *Ante*, p. 8.
14. *Banbury* v. *Bank of Montreal*, [1918] A. C. 626, *Rhodes (Liverpool), Ltd.* v. *W. B. Anderson & Sons, Ltd.*, [1967] 2 All E. R. 850.
15. *Hirst* v. *West Riding Union Banking Co., Ltd.*, [1901] 2 K. B. 560.

Innocent misrepresentation and remedies therefor

Any misrepresentation which is made without an honest belief in its truth is a fraudulent misrepresentation. It has been customary to refer to any other misrepresentation as an innocent misrepresentation. Neither the common law nor equity gave a remedy in damages for innocent misrepresentation but in equity rescission of the contract was permitted. As we have seen, the Misrepresentation Act 1967 now allows damages to be claimed for negligent misrepresentation and it may be convenient in future to talk of *three* types of misrepresentation: fraudulent, negligent, and innocent. For the present, however, the traditional categories are adopted and *innocent misrepresentation* taken to mean any non-fraudulent misrepresentation.

Remedies

1. *Rescind the contract, e.g.* by B communicating with the party who made the misrepresentation (A), or by conduct which manifests unequivocally B's intention not to be bound by the contract, or by B obtaining a court order of rescission. In some cases, *e.g.* where the seller of a second-hand car innocently misrepresents the mileage done in the car since its engine was last overhauled, rescission of the contract may be an unduly drastic remedy, and the court now has the power to award damages instead. By s. 2 (2) of the Misrepresentation Act 1967,

> "Where a person has entered into a contract after a mis-representation has been made to him otherwise than fraudulently, and he would be entitled, by reason of the misrepresentation, to rescind the contract, then, if it is claimed, in any proceedings arising out of the contract, that the contract ought to be or has been rescinded, the court or arbitrator may declare the contract subsisting and award damages in lieu of rescission, if of opinion that it would be equitable to do so, having regard to the nature of the misrepresentation and the loss that would be caused by it if the contract were upheld, as well as to the loss that rescission would cause to the other party."

In any case, there are a number of circumstances in which the right to rescind a contract for misrepresentation is lost:

    (*a*) *By affirmation*—the person to whom the misrepresentation has been made (B) loses his right to rescind the contract if he has affirmed it expressly or by conduct after he has knowledge of the falsity of the representation. Unreasonable delay by B after he has knowledge of the falsity is evidence of affirmation[16].

    (*b*) *Third party rights*—the right to rescind is lost if a third party has acquired rights in the subject-matter of the contract

---

16. *Cf. Allen* v. *Robles*, [1969] 3 All E. R. 154; [1969] 1 W. L. R. 1193, C. A.

for value before B has manifested his intention to rescind the contract[17].

(c) *Restitution impossible*—where the parties cannot be restored to their original position, rescission is not permissible. It may still be permitted where someone is induced by misrepresentation to purchase property and the property deteriorates in the hands of the purchaser as a result of inherent defects in the subject-matter, but in *Lagunas Nitrate Co.* v. *Lagunas Syndicate*[18], rescission was refused where a change in the parties' position had resulted from the plaintiffs working certain nitrate deposits purchased from the defendants after misrepresentation by the defendants.

(d) *Lapse of time*—this is no bar to rescission in the case of fraudulent misrepresentation, but where the misrepresentation is innocent, the lapse of such time as would enable a reasonable person to discover the truth does mean that the right to rescind is lost. In *Leaf* v. *International Galleries*[19]:

> the seller of a picture misrepresented it as being one painted by Constable. The purchaser claimed rescission to recover the purchase price five years after the sale. *Held:* although there was no evidence of affirmation as the purchaser had only just discovered the falsity, it was too late for him to rescind.

Until the Misrepresentation Act 1967, the mere execution or performance of a contract had been held in some cases[20] to bar the right to rescind for innocent misrepresentation but these cases have been abrogated by s. 1 of this Act[1].

2. *Resist any action to enforce the contract.*

3. If the misrepresentation has been made negligently, *damages* may be claimed under s. 2 (1) of the Misrepresentation Act 1967[2].

---

17. See *Car and Universal Finance Co., Ltd.* v. *Caldwell*, [1964] 1 All E. R. 290; [1965] 1 Q. B. 525 and *Lewis* v. *Averay* [1971] 3 All E. R. 907; [1972] 1 Q. B. 198, C. A., *ante* p. 29.
18. [1899] 2 Ch. 392.
19. [1950] 1 All E. R. 693; [1950] 2 K. B. 86.
20. *Seddon* v. *N.E. Salt Co.*, [1905] 1 Ch. 326; *Angel* v. *Jay*, [1911] 1 K. B. 666.
1. The Act also provides in s. 1 that the right to rescind is not lost because the representation has become a term of the contract.
2. See *ante*, p. 33 and *Gosling* v. *Anderson* (1972), Times, February 8, C. A. Where no damages can be claimed because the defendant is able to prove he had reasonable ground to believe and did believe the representation to be true, the only possible monetary claim is for an indemnity. Such claim, however, does not cover all the natural consequences of the misrepresentation but only the expense of carrying out the actual obligations of the contract: *Whittington* v. *Seale-Hayne* (1900), 82 L. T. 49. A claim for indemnity may only be made if the plaintiff is entitled to rescind.

Avoidance of Exemption Clauses

Generally speaking, no contractual clause exempting a party from liability for misrepresentation is effective. By s. 3 of the Misrepresentation Act:

> "If any agreement ... contains a provision which would exclude or restrict:
>
> (a) any liability to which a party to a contract may be subject by reason of any misrepresentation made by him before the contract was made, or
>
> (b) any remedy available to another party to the contract by reason of such a misrepresentation;
>
> that provision shall be of no effect except to the extent (if any) that, in any proceedings arising out of the contract, the court or arbitrator may allow reliance on it as being fair and reasonable in the circumstances of the case."

Contracts uberrimæ fidei

There is a certain group of contracts which are voidable by a party misled who enters into them unless each party had disclosed to the other every material fact within his own knowledge, or that of his agent, at the time when the contract is made. These are styled contracts *uberrimæ fidei*. They include

1. All contracts of insurance[3], and are not limited to contracts of marine, fire and life[4] insurance;
2. Family arrangements[5];
3. *Directors' liability in respect of statements in a prospectus.*

Section 43 of the Companies Act 1948 applies to statements made in a prospectus inviting persons to subscribe for shares in or debentures of a company, and entitles persons so subscribing on the faith of untrue or misleading statements to proceed for damages against any of the following:

1. Directors at the time of issuing the prospectus;
2. Persons who have authorised their names to be placed on a prospectus as being directors or as having agreed (at once or after an interval) to become directors;
3. Promoters—*i.e.* persons being parties to the preparation of the prospectus, and not being engaged in such preparation merely in a professional capacity;
4. Any person who authorised the issue of the prospectus.

---

3. *Seaton* v. *Heath*, [1899] 1 Q. B. 782; 4 Com. Cas. 193, reversed on the facts *sub nom. Seaton* v. *Burnand*, [1900] A. C. 135; 5 Com. Cas. 198.
4. *London Assurance* v. *Mansel* (1879), 11 Ch. D. 363.
5. *Gordon* v. *Gordon* (1817), 3 Swan 400.

Liability may be avoided if the party attacked shows that:

1. He has reasonable ground to believe and did believe in the truth of the statements contained in the prospectus; or
2. That he withdrew his consent to be a director before the issue of the prospectus and it was issued without his authority or consent; or
3. That the prospectus being issued without his knowledge or consent, he at once, on becoming aware of the issue, gave reasonable public notice that it was so issued; or
4. That after the issue of the prospectus and before allotment under it he became aware of any untrue statement therein and gave reasonable public notice of the withdrawal of his consent thereto and of his reason for so doing.

Moreover, the directors and other persons referred to above, may successfully defend themselves if they can show that the false statement was a correct and fair copy of or extract from a public official document, or was a fair representation of the statements or report of an expert published with his consent; though if any person had not reasonable grounds for believing in the competency of the expert who makes the statement or report, this last ground of defence is not available to him.

The expert himself may be liable in respect of statements in his report unless:

1. He was competent and believed on reasonable grounds that the statement was true; or
2. He withdrew his consent before delivery of the prospectus for registration; or
3. He withdrew his consent between delivery of the prospectus and allotment and gave reasonable public notice.

Estoppel

In some cases a person who makes a statement, even though innocently, is not allowed subsequently to deny its truth: for as Lord DENHAM said in *Pickard* v. *Sears*[6]:

> "Where one by his words, or conduct, wilfully causes another to believe the existence of a certain state of things, and induces him to act on that belief, so as to alter his own previous position, the former is concluded from averring against the latter a different state of things as existing at the same time."

Thus, suppose that in error a company makes out a share certificate to the effect that X is a shareholder, thus enabling X fraudulently to sell the shares to Y. Since the company will be estopped from denying Y's right to be put on the register of shareholders, Y will be entitled to damages in respect of the company's refusal to place him on the register.

---

6. (1837), 6 A. & El. at p. 474.

UNDUE INFLUENCE AND DURESS

Undue influence is the improper use of any power possessed over the mind of a contracting party, and it may in all cases be proved as a fact[7]. Moreover, according to the doctrine expounded in *Huguenin v. Baseley*[8], undue influence is presumed (in the absence of rebutting evidence) in all cases where the relative position of the parties is such as to render it probable that such influence exists and has been exerted; *e.g.*,

1. Between solicitor and client;
2. Trustee and *cestui que trust*;
3. Guardian and ward, etc.

But the presumption is not limited to such relationships and in *Re Craig*[9] undue influence was presumed where an elderly man had made substantial gifts to a woman secretary of strong personality. The presumption will be rebutted if it can be shown that the transaction was entered into voluntarily after full, free, and informed thought about it and most effectively if there has been independent legal advice. The relation of husband and wife is not one of those to which the doctrine applies[10], and there is not necessarily a presumption of undue influence where the relationship is that of fiancé and fiancée[11].

Duress is actual or threatened violence to the person, or imprisonment. Whether the coercion amounts to duress depends upon the facts of each particular case. Thus, in *Scott v. Sebright* it was said,

"whenever from natural weakness of intellect or from fear—whether reasonably entertained or not—either party is in a state of mental incompetence to resist pressure improperly brought to bear, there is no more consent than in the case of a person of stronger intellect and more robust courage yielding to a more serious danger"[12].

In cases of undue influence and duress the law considers that consent is not freely given, and it allows the contract to be avoided at the will of the party coerced; the contract can subsequently be made good if ratified when that party is absolutely free from the influence or power. The right to rescind a contract for undue influence is barred by affirmation after the influence has ceased, by undue delay after such time and if a third party has acquired rights in the subject-matter for value in good faith.

---

7. *Smith* v. *Kay* (1859), 7 H. L. Cas., at pp. 778, 779; *Mutual Finance, Ltd.* v. *Wetton & Sons, Ltd.*, [1937] 2 All E. R. 657; [1937] 2 K. B. 389 (threat of prosecution).
8. (1807), 14 Ves. 273.
9. [1970] 2 All E. R. 390; [1971] Ch. 95.
10. *Howes* v. *Bishop*, [1909] 2 K. B. 390.
11. *Zamet* v. *Hyman*, [1961] 3 All E. R. 933; [1961] 1 W. L. R. 1442.
12. (1887), 12 P. D., at p. 24.

CHAPTER 4

Contracts which the Law will not Enforce

INTRODUCTORY

Some agreements are *unenforceable* because of their failure to comply with statutory requirements[1]; some are merely *voidable* or subject to repudiation at the option of one of the parties. Such are contracts induced by misrepresentation which may in certain cases be set aside by the party induced[2]. Other contracts are absolutely *void, i.e.* they are altogether destitute of any legal effect. The latter class includes *illegal* contracts, *i.e.*, contracts which have all the proper characteristics of a contract but a court will not enforce them because they offend against public policy.

Clearly, any agreement to commit a crime will be an *illegal* contract but also classed as illegal are contracts which do not involve the commission of any crime or tort but are not enforced by the courts simply because they are considered to be injurious to the public good. When a contract is illegal, a court will of its own motion refuse to enforce it, even though the illegality has not been pleaded by the defendant[3].

The presumption is in favour of validity, and it is doubtful whether any contract will be declared void unless it falls within one or more of the classes mentioned below; if there is any serious doubt, the court inclines rather towards supporting than towards upsetting an agreement.

CONTRACTS CONTRARY TO PUBLIC POLICY

At one time the tendency was to avoid many agreements on this ground, but the modern tendency is the reverse.

The limits of the doctrine of public policy were settled by the House of Lords in the case of *Janson* v. *Driefontein Consolidated Mines, Limited*[4]. A judge is not at liberty to declare a contract to be contrary to public policy merely because in his view it is inexpedient.

---

1. See *ante*, p. 7.
2. See *ante*, pp. 36–40.
3. *Snell* v. *Unity Finance, Ltd.*, [1963] 3 All E. R. 50; [1964] 2 Q. B. 203.
4. [1902] A. C. 484.

"This is always an unsafe and treacherous ground of legal decision"[5].

In *Printing and Numerical Co. v. Sampson*[6], JESSEL, M.R., said:

"You have this paramount policy to consider—that you are not lightly to interfere with the freedom of contract."

Amongst contracts recognised by the common law to be illegal are:

1. Contracts tainted with immorality. The common law rule is, *Ex turpi causa non oritur actio*. A contract for an object in itself innocent may be void if an illegal or immoral purpose is intended.

Thus in *Pearce* v. *Brooks*[7]:

Where a brougham was hired out to a prostitute, and the evidence showed that the payment to be made was not to depend upon amounts earned, yet that the owner knew of the immoral object for which the carriage was hired, the court declared the contract illegal and *held* that the owner could not recover the hire charges.

On the same ground a promise of marriage made by a person who is already married to the knowledge of the promisee cannot be enforced after the death of the promisor's spouse[8]; but if the promise is made during the interval between a decree nisi and a decree absolute, it is enforceable after the decree has been made absolute[9].

2. Agreements to commit a crime or a civil wrong; the doctrine extends to contracts which have for their object the commission of an offence in a foreign and friendly country[10].

In *Regazzoni* v. *K. C. Sethia (1944) Ltd.*[11]:

A agreed to buy jute bags from B. They were to be shipped from India to a European port. But it was intended that they should be resold to a South African customer. Export to South Africa was prohibited by the Indian government. *Held:* the contract was not enforceable in the English Courts.

3. Contracts for the sale of public offices;

4. Contracts to procure a title to be conferred on another, even in consideration of a gift to charity[12];

5. *Per* Lord DAVEY, *ibid.*, at p. 500.
6. (1875), L. R. 19 Eq. 462.
7. (1866), L. R. 1 Ex. 213.
8. *Wilson* v. *Carnley*, [1908] 1 K. B. 729.
9. *Fender* v. *Mildmay*, [1938] A. C. 1.
10. *Foster* v. *Driscoll*, [1929] All E. R. Rep. 130; [1929] 1 K. B. 470.
11. [1957] 3 All E. R. 286; [1958] A. C. 301.
12. *Parkinson* v. *College of Ambulance*, [1925] 2 K. B. 1.

5. Contracts whereby a person undertakes for reward to use his position and influence to obtain a benefit from the Government[13];

6. Trading with an enemy, including anyone voluntarily residing in enemy territory in time of war[14];

7. Contracts impeding justice [*e.g.* taking money to stifle a prosecution unless it is a prosecution for an offence of a private nature, like assault, where there is an alternative remedy in damages[15]]; and

8. Contracts in fraud of the Revenue.

9. Marriage brokage contracts are illegal, whether the object is to bring about a marriage with a particular person, or to introduce a number of persons with a view to marriage with one of them[16].

10. An agreement with newspaper proprietors to suppress comment is illegal, if it is not consistent with the proper conduct of the newspaper in the public interest[17].

Two classes of contract require fuller treatment under this head, *viz.* contracts in restraint of trade and contracts involving maintenance or champerty.

Contracts in restraint of trade

A contract in restraint of trade is one which restricts a person from freely exercising his trade, skill, or profession.

A contract in general restraint is one which prohibits the exercise of a trade throughout the kingdom, and such a contract was formerly regarded as *ipso facto* void. This rule cannot now be considered as universally applicable. The changed conditions of modern commerce have involved corresponding changes in the views of judges as to what is, and what is not, contrary to the public interest, and accordingly in a very special case a restraint unlimited in area or unrestricted as to time will be upheld[18]. A partial restraint is one that prohibits the exercise of a trade or skill for a limited term, or within a certain area, or with particular persons. Partial restraints have long been upheld provided they are reasonable.

Test of validity.—The true test is whether, in view of all the facts, the restraint imposed (whether general or partial) is reasonable and

---

13. *Montefiore* v. *Motor Components Co.*, [1918] 2 K. B. 241.
14. *Potts* v. *Bell* (1800), 8 T. R. 548. This is now regulated by the Trading with the Enemy Act 1939.
15. *Williams* v. *Bayley* (1866), L. R. 1 H. L. 200.
16. *Hermann* v. *Charlesworth*, [1905] 2 K. B. 123.
17. *Neville* v. *Dominion of Canada News Co.*, [1915] 3 K. B. 556.
18. *Nordenfelt* v. *Maxim Nordenfelt Co.*, [1894] A. C. 535; *Mason* v. *Provident Clothing and Supply Co., Ltd.*, [1913] A. C. 724; *Morris (Herbert), Ltd.* v. *Saxelby*, [1916] 1 A. C. 688.

necessary for the protection of the party intended to be benefited, and then, if not otherwise injurious to the public interest, it will be valid[19]. The nature of the contract must be regarded, for a much wider restraint will generally be justified to protect the goodwill of a business for which a full consideration has been paid, or to guard against the divulging of trade secrets, than would be lawful in the ordinary case of master and servant[19].

An example of the operation of this test will be found in *Mason v. Provident Clothing and Supply Co., Ltd*[19]:

> The defendant was employed as canvasser by a clothing and supply company and agreed that he would not within three years after the termination of his employment engage or assist in a similar business within twenty-five miles of London. *Held:* the restriction was wider than was reasonably necessary for the plaintiffs' protection. "Had they been content with asking him to bind himself not to canvass within the area where he had actually assisted in building up the goodwill of the business, or in an area restricted to places where the knowledge which he had acquired in his employment could obviously have been used to their prejudice, they might have secured a right to restrain him within these limits." (*Per* Lord HALDANE, L.C.)

However although a restriction when read literally may be wider than reasonably necessary for an employer's protection, if it was clearly in the parties' contemplation that the restriction should have a more limited scope, the restriction may be upheld[20].

Since the decision in *Mason's Case*[1], restrictive covenants contained in contracts of service have been treated as invalid where the employer endeavours merely to protect himself from the competition of his former servant. The employer is entitled to protect his trade secrets and trade connection with both present and former customers, but not to prevent the servant from using skill or knowledge acquired in the course of his employment, such as general details of organisation and management[2]. Covenants contained in contracts made *between employers* imposing restraints on their employees have similarly been held void. In *Kores Manufacturing Co., Ltd. v. Kolok Manufacturing Co., Ltd.*[3]:

---

19. [1913] A. C. 724. *Cf. G. W. Plowman & Son, Ltd. v. Ash,* [1964] 2 All E. R. 10; [1964] 1 W. L. R. 568, C. A.
20. *Home Counties Dairies, Ltd. v. Skilton,* [1970] 1 All E. R. 1227; [1970] 1 W. L. R. 526, C. A., followed in *Marion White, Ltd. v. Francis,* [1972] 3 All E. R. 857, C. A.
1. *Mason v. Provident Clothing and Supply Co., ante,* p. 47; *Morris (Herbert), Ltd. v. Saxelby, ante,* p. 44; *Attwood v. Lamont,* [1920] 3 K. B. 571.
2. *Morris (Herbert), Ltd. v. Saxelby, ante,* p. 44.
3. [1958] 2 All E. R. 65; [1959] Ch. 108, followed in *Eastham v. Newcastle United Football Club, Ltd.,* [1963] 3 All E. R. 139; [1964] Ch. 413.

Two companies, both manufacturers of carbon paper, agreed that neither would employ anyone who had been in the employment of the other company during the previous five years. *Held:* since the agreement was so expressed as to cover the most junior employee who had been in the employment of the other company for only one day, it was much wider than necessary to protect the companies' legitimate interests and was void.

Questions of restraint of trade usually arise in connection with contracts between—

1. Master or servant; or
2. The vendor and purchaser of a business. A promise by the vendor not to compete with the purchaser in the same line of business as that which he has sold for a reasonable period and over the same area as the business sold covers will be upheld as reasonable. A bare promise by one trader not to compete with another would be void—for a restraint to be valid there must be an interest, *e.g.* a purchaser's interest in the goodwill of the business bought, that deserves protection.

But any other type of contract may offend against this head of public policy. Thus, in *Esso Petroleum Co., Ltd.* v. *Harper's Garage (Stourport), Ltd.*[4]:

Esso had solus agreements with the Garage whereby the Garage agreed to buy all the petrol for their filling stations from Esso. With regard to one filling station, the agreement was to last four and a half years, and with regard to the other filling station for twenty-one years. On the latter Esso had a mortgage to secure £7,000 lent to the Garage which could not be redeemed till the twenty-one years was up. *Held:* the agreements were in restraint of trade and had to be justified by the test of reasonableness. The crucial consideration was the length of period each agreement was to last and in the circumstances the agreement in regard to the first filling station was valid but that relating to the second was invalid and the Garage was entitled to redeem the mortgage on it and buy petrol for it elsewhere.

If an owner in possession ties himself for more than five years to take all his supplies from one company, that is likely to be considered an unreasonable restraint of trade. But if a man, out of possession, is let into possession by the oil company on the terms that he is to tie himself to that company for so long a period, such tie is valid[5].

---

4. [1967] 1 All E. R. 699; [1968] A. C. 269, H. L., followed in *Texaco Ltd.* v. *Mulberry Filling Station, Ltd.*, [1972] 1 All E. R. 513; [1972] 1 W. L. R. 814.
5. *Cleveland Petroleum Co., Ltd.* v. *Dartstone, Ltd.*, [1969] 1 All E. R. 201; [1969] 1 W. L. R. 116, C. A.

A proposed rule of a professional body was declared to be an unreasonable restraint of trade in *Pharmaceutical Society of Great Britain* v. *Dickson*[6]. The proposed rule sought to limit the range of non-pharmaceutical goods sold in chemists' shops.

Even the person for whose benefit a restraint is imposed may object that it renders a contract invalid[7].

All contracts in restraint of trade, even though under seal, require consideration to support them[8].

If a covenant in restraint of trade is unreasonable as drawn, and the covenant contains several separate clauses, some valid and some void, the court may be prepared to sever the valid clauses from the void and enforce the valid clauses. Thus, in *Goldsoll* v. *Goldman*[9]:

> When X sold an imitation jewellery business to Y, Y agreed that he would not for two years deal in real or imitation jewellery in any part of the U.K., France, U.S.A., etc. *Held:* the covenant as drafted was void, but it could be severed by removing from it the reference to "real" jewellery and the reference to countries other than the U.K. The remaining part of the covenant was enforceable.

However, a court will not order severance if this would affect the meaning of the rest of the contract, nor if it involves altering or adding words. Moreover, the courts are reluctant to sever unreasonably wide covenants contained in contracts of employment[10].

A contract in restraint of trade is part of the goodwill of a business, and for this reason is treated as assignable in the absence of any special provision to the contrary; it accordingly passes with the goodwill so as to enable the purchaser to enforce the contract in his own name[11]. If a contract of service is repudiated on the part of the master by the wrongful dismissal of the servant, the latter is no longer bound by a clause restrictive of his right to trade[12].

Contracts involving maintenance or champerty

Maintenance is committed

> "whenever a third party aids the prosecution or defence of an action in the absence of circumstances sufficing in law to justify

---

6. [1968] 2 All E. R. 686.
7. *Evans & Co.* v. *Heathcote*, [1918] 1 K. B. 418.
8. See *Mitchel* v. *Reynolds* (1711), 1 Sm. L. C. (13th ed.) at p. 465.
9. [1915] 1 Ch. 292.
10. *Attwood* v. *Lamont*, [1920] 3 K. B. 571. This is because of the lack of bargaining equality between the parties. But see *T. Lucas & Co., Ltd.* v. *Mitchell*, [1972] 3 All E. R. 689, C. A.
11. *Jacoby* v. *Whitmore* (1883), 49 L. T. 335.
12. *General Billposting Co.* v. *Atkinson*, [1908] 1 Ch. 537; [1909] A. C. 118. The Compulsory winding-up of a company is equivalent to a wrongful dismissal (*Measures Bros., Ltd.* v. *Measures*, [1910] 2 Ch. 248).

the giving of such aid, whatever the motive or purpose of the person giving such aid may have been"[13].

A definition of champerty is

". . . a bargain by some person, with a plaintiff or defendant, to divide the land or other matter sued for between them, if they succeed at law; whereupon that person, who is called the *champertee*, agrees to carry on the party's suit at his own expense"[14].

Taking a transfer of an interest in litigation as security is not champerty.

Moreover, maintenance is lawful where the persons maintaining have a legal (not a mere sentimental) interest in the subject-matter of the action[15]. And a supply of funds fairly and openly, and with an intention partly charitable, is not necessarily against the policy of the law[16]. So an association formed to protect the interests of a class of individuals against large commercial corporations may give financial assistance to its members towards the cost of litigation[17].

He who wrongfully maintains another in litigation is no longer since 1968 liable to an action for damages at the suit of the person injured[18] but agreements for maintenance and champertous (including "contingency fee" agreements between solicitor and client) continue to be contrary to public policy and unlawful.

STATUTORY PROVISIONS

Contracts forbidden by statutes cannot be enforced, whether they are forbidden expressly or impliedly. Thus it is a criminal offence to sell a flick knife[19] and a contract to sell a flick knife is void. Where a contract is not expressly forbidden by statute, it is a matter of construction of the statute whether it is aimed at the contract so as to make it impliedly forbidden[20].

A contract is not illegal merely because a statute is contravened

---

13. *Per* JENKINS, L.J., in *Martell* v. *Consett Iron Co.*, [1954] 3 All E. R. 339; [1955] Ch. 363 at p. 399.
14. Chitty, *Contracts* (22nd. ed.), para. 808.
15. See *Guy* v. *Churchill* (1889), 40 Ch. D. 481; *British Cash and Parcel Conveyors* v. *Lamson Store Service Co.*, [1908] 1 K. B. 1006.
16. *Harris* v. *Brisco* (1886), 17 Q. B. D. 504; *Alabaster* v. *Harness*, [1895] 1 Q. B. 339.
17. *Martell* v. *Consett Iron Co., Ltd.*, [1955] 1 All E. R. 481; [1955] Ch. 363; followed in *Hill* v. *Archbold*, [1967] 3 All E. R. 110.
18. Criminal Law Act 1967, s. 14. Maintenance and champerty have also ceased to be crimes: *ibid.*, s. 10.
19. Restriction of Offensive Weapons Acts 1959 and 1961.
20. *St. John Shipping Corporation* v. *Joseph Rank, Ltd.*, [1956] 3 All E. R. 683; [1957] 1 Q. B. 267.

in the execution of the contract. In *Archbolds (Freightage), Ltd.* v. *S. Spanglett, Ltd.*[1]:

> X engaged Y to carry whisky for X from Leeds to London. Unknown to X, Y used a van which had no A licence and Y was thus in contravention of the Road Traffic Act. The whisky was stolen owing to negligence on the part of Y's driver. *Held:* the contract was not illegal and Y was liable to X for the loss. HOLROYD PEARCE, L.J., said: "To hold the contract illegal would injure the innocent, benefit the guilty and put a premium on deceit."

Similarly in *Shaw* v. *Groom*[2]:

> L let an unfurnished room to T and, in contravention of the Landlord and Tenant Act 1962, L failed to provide T with a rent book in the prescribed form. *Held:* Although L had committed an offence, L was still entitled to sue T for rent due. The Act had not impliedly rendered illegal a tenancy agreement where a prescribed rent book was not provided.

Further, if a statute imposes a penalty for entering into a certain kind of contract, and the purpose of the penalty is merely to obtain revenue (as distinct from protecting the public), the contract is not illegal. Thus, in *Smith* v. *Mawhood*[3]:

> A tobacconist was liable to a statutory penalty for selling tobacco without a licence. *Held:* the contract of sale was not illegal and the tobacconist could recover the price from the purchaser.

If a contract is illegal unless one party to it has obtained a licence, it cannot be enforced in the absence of such a licence; but the other party may be entitled to rely upon a warranty or promise, express or implied, that the first party has or will obtain the necessary licence[4].

The following are cases of contracts made void by statute:

1. *Gaming and wagering contracts.*—By the Gaming Act 1845, s. 18,

> "all contracts or agreements, whether by parole or in writing, by way of gaming or wagering, shall be null and void; and no suit shall be brought or maintained in any court of law or equity for recovering any sum of money or valuable thing alleged to be won upon any wager, or which shall have been deposited in the hands of any person to abide the event on which any wager shall have been made."

Securities deposited with a stockbroker to *secure* payment of "differences" in favour of the broker are not deposited to "abide the event," and may be recovered from the stockbroker[5]; but not money

---

1. [1961] 1 All E. R. 417; [1961] 1 Q. B. 374.
2. [1970] 1 All E. R. 702; [1970] 2 Q. B. 504. C. A.
3. (1845), 14 M. & W. 452.
4. *Strongman (1945), Ltd.* v. *Sincock*, [1955] 3 All E. R. 90; [1955] 2 Q. B. 526.
5. *Universal Stock Exchange* v. *Strachan*, [1896] A. C. 166.

so deposited if it has been appropriated to losses, because that is equivalent to a voluntary payment with knowledge of the facts[6]. Money deposited with a stakeholder to abide the event of a wager may be recovered if its return is demanded before it has been paid over to the winner[7].

It has been held that:

> "The essence of gaming and wagering is that one party is to win and the other to lose upon a future event which at the time of the contract is of an uncertain nature—that is to say, if the event turns out one way A will lose, but if it turns out the other way he will win."[8]

This definition cannot be treated as exhaustive and must be read as subject to the qualification that neither of the parties has any other interest in the contract than the sum or stake he will win or lose[9]. An insurance contract is not a wager because the insured must have an insurable interest in the subject-matter of the insurance. There cannot be more than two parties or two sides to a wager and each side must stand to win or lose. The Horserace Totalisator Board cannot lose on bets placed with it so such bets are not void and the Board is entitled to sue for lost bets[10]. A multipartite agreement to contribute to a sweepstake is not a wager, but may be illegal as a lottery.

The Gaming Act makes void not only the original bet but also any subsequent promise to pay the bet even if supported by a fresh consideration[11].

Gaming and wagering contracts are *void* but not *illegal*[12]; so that a partnership formed for the purpose of carrying on a bookmaker's business is not *per se* illegal[13]. No offence is committed in making a wager, but the courts will not enforce the contract. Thus it will be entirely at the option of the promisor whether or not he pays the debt; he may do so if he likes; if he does, the money cannot be recovered.

It would follow from this, that if an agent is employed to make the bet, the principal cannot set up the statute as a defence to an action by the agent for money paid in respect of a loss; the agent could sue on the implied contract to indemnify him in regard to moneys properly

---

6. *Strachan* v. *Universal Stock Exchange*, [1895] 2 Q. B. 697.
7. *Hampden* v. *Walsh* (1876), 1 Q. B. D. 189.
8. *Thacker* v. *Hardy* (1879), 4 Q. B. D., at p. 695, *per* COTTON, L.J.
9. See *Weddle, Beck & Co.* v. *Hackett*, [1929] 1 K. B. 321, at pp. 329-334.
10. *Tote Investors, Ltd.* v. *Smoker*, [1967] 3 All E. R. 242; [1968] 1 Q. B. 509; *Ellesmere* v. *Wallace*, [1929] 2 Ch. 1, *per* RUSSELL, L.J. In this case the earlier judicial definitions of gaming and wagering were exhaustively discussed.
11. *Hill* v. *Hill (William) (Park Lane), Ltd.*, [1949] A. C. 530.
12. See *Saxby* v. *Fulton*, [1909] 2 K. B., at p. 227, *per* BUCKLEY, L.J.
13. *Jeffrey* v. *Bamford*, [1921] 2 K. B. 351.

expended for his principal, as there is no violation of the law in paying bets at the request of the principal[14]; and until the Gaming Act 1892 such was the law; but by that Act it is provided that

"any promise, express or implied, to pay any person any sum of money paid by him or in respect of any contract or agreement rendered null and void by the [Gaming Act 1845], or to pay any sum of money by way of commission, fee, reward, or otherwise in respect of any such contract, or of any service in relation thereto or in connection therewith, shall be null and void, and no action shall be brought or maintained to recover any such sum of money."

But this statute does not enable an agent who has *received* money for bets made by him on behalf of another to retain it[15].

Negotiable securities such as cheques given in payment of bets on games and horse races, or for the repayment of money knowingly lent for gaming, are deemed to have been given on an *illegal* consideration; as between immediate parties they are unenforceable, but holders in due course may sue upon them[16]. By the Gaming Act 1968, s. 16 (4), a cheque accepted in exchange for cash or tokens to be used by a player in gaming on licensed or registered premises is valid and enforceable even between the parties. Money lent without security in England expressly for the purpose of paying betting debts is irrecoverable, but not if it is merely lent to enable the borrower to pay the debts with no obligation upon him to do so[17]. Probably, money lent without security in England for the purpose of gaming in this country is recoverable if the gaming is legal under the Gaming Act 1968 provided there is no obligation on the borrower to use the loan for wagering[18]. However the Gaming Act 1968, s. 16 (1) provides that where gaming takes place on licensed premises the licensee shall not make any loan to enable someone to take part in gaming or in respect of losses incurred by anyone in gaming.

Although money lent in a foreign country for the purpose of gambling abroad, where the game in question is not illegal, *e.g.* to play roulette

---

14. *Read* v. *Anderson* (1884), 13 Q. B. D. 779.
15. *De Mattos* v. *Benjamin* (1894), 63 L. J. Q. B. 248.
16. See the Gaming Act 1710, as amended by the Gaming Act 1835. Negotiable instruments given in payment of other kinds of bets are not enforceable as between the immediate parties but any subsequent holder for value may sue upon them.
17. *Re O'Shea, Ex parte Lancaster*, [1911] 2 K. B. 981; *Macdonald* v. *Green*, [1950] 2 All E. R. 1240; [1951] 1 K. B. 594; *C.H.T., Ltd.* v. *Ward*, [1963] 3 All E. R. 835; [1965] 2 Q. B. 63 (lender paying winner direct unable to recover loan).
18. *C.H.T., Ltd.* v. *Ward*, [1963] 3 All E. R. 835; [1965] 2 Q. B. 63. *Contra* if the loan is secured by a cheque—then it seems neither the loan nor the cheque may be sued on: *Carlton Hall Club, Ltd.* v. *Laurence*, [1929] 2 K. B. 153.

at Monte Carlo, may be recovered by action in England[19], if a negotiable instrument payable in England be given for the amount advanced, the security will be bad[20].

2. *Leeman's Act* (30 & 31 Vict. c. 29) renders void the sale of shares in a joint stock banking company, unless the contract sets forth in writing the numbers of the shares as stated in the register of the company.

3. *Contracts contravening the Moneylenders Acts* 1900–1927.—See *post*, pp. 389–395.

4. *Registration of Business Names Act* 1916.—See *post*, pp. 157–158.

EFFECT OF ILLEGALITY

As a rule, illegality avoids the whole contract, but this is not so if the illegality can be severed from the rest of the contract. Thus, the presence in a contract of employment of an unreasonably wide covenant in restraint of trade does not render the rest of the contract illegal or unenforceable.

Can money paid under an *illegal* contract be recovered? This will depend upon whether the contract has been executed or is still executory. In *Taylor* v. *Bowers*[1], MELLISH, L.J., said:

"If money is paid, or goods delivered, for an illegal purpose, the person who had so paid the money or delivered the goods may recover them back before the illegal purpose is carried out; but if he waits till the illegal purpose is carried out, or if he seeks to enforce the illegal transaction, in neither case can he maintain the action."

It has been decided that he cannot recover if the illegal contract has been carried out even partly[2]; because "where the illegal purpose has been wholly or partially effected the law allows no *locus pœnitentiæ*"[3]. But where a prohibition has been imposed for the benefit of a particular class of the community, money paid by a member of that class under a prohibited contract may be recovered[4].

---

19. *Saxby* v. *Fulton*, [1909] 2 K. B. 208; *Baumgart's* case (1927), 96 L. J. K. B. 789.
20. *Moulis* v. *Owen*, [1907] 1 K. B. 746.
1. (1876), 1 Q. B. D. 291.
2. *Kearley* v. *Thompson* (1890), 24 Q. B. D. 742; *Bigos* v. *Bousted*, [1951] 1 All E. R. 92. Marriage brokage contracts are an exception (*Hermann* v. *Charlesworth*, [1905] 2 K. B. 123).
3. This statement from Salmond and Winfield's *Law of Contract* was approved by the Court of Appeal, in *Alexander* v. *Rayson*, [1935] All E. R. Rep. at p. 195; [1936] 1 K. B., at p. 190.
4. *Kiriri Cotton Co., Ltd.* v. *Dewani*, [1960] 1 All E. R. 177; [1960] A. C. 192; *Chettiar* v. *Chettiar* (No. 2), [1962] 2 All E. R. 238; [1962] 1 W. L. R. 279.

Generally, where a person must prove his own immoral or illegal act to establish his claim, the court will not lend its aid to enable him to do so. *Ex turpi causa non oritur actio*[5]. Thus if a service agreement provides for a salary and "expenses" when no genuine expenses are incurred, the intention being to mislead the revenue authorities, the employee will not be able to bring successfully proceedings for wrongful dismissal[6]. So in *Alexander* v. *Rayson*[7]:

A leased property to B with certain services. The real rent was £1,200 per annum, but to deceive the rating authority two documents were executed, a lease at £450 per annum without the services, and a further agreement for the services at £750 per annum. *Held:* A could not sue for rent or enforce the covenants of the lease. But B's interest in the land had been validly created and he was entitled to remain in possession for the remainder of the term.

Contrast with the above case *Bowmakers, Ltd.* v. *Barnet Instruments, Ltd.*[8]:

A Co. delivered goods to B Co. on hire-purchase terms. Apparently, the agreement infringed war-time controls. B Co. defaulted on the instalments and sold some of the goods. *Held:* although the contract was illegal, A Co. could recover the tools. It was not necessary for them to set up the illegal contract, they merely claimed the tools as their own property leaving B Co. to prove a valid ground for retaining them which B Co. could not and the agreement by its own terms had come to an end when B Co. broke the agreement.

Where a contract of sale is illegal, once the contract is executed the property in the goods passes to the buyer (irrespective of whether he has taken delivery) so that he may exercise the normal remedies of an owner, *e.g.* sue in trespass or conversion anyone who interferes with his rights[9].

---

5. *Yin* v. *Sam,* [1962] A. C. 304; [1962] 2 W. L. R. 765.
6. *Napier* v. *National Business Agency,* [1951] 2 All E. R. 264.
7. [1935] All E. R. Rep. 185; [1936] 1 K. B. 169. *Cf. Berg* v. *Sadler and Moore,* [1937] 1 All E. R. 647; [1937] 2 K. B. 158; *Edler* v. *Auerbach,* [1950] 1 K.B. 359.
8. [1944] 2 All E. R. 579; [1945] K.B. 65.
9. *Belvoir Finance Co., Ltd.* v. *Stapleton,* [1970] 3 All E. R. 664; [1971] 1 Q. B. 210, C. A.

CHAPTER 5

Capacity to Contract

I PRESUMPTION OF CAPACITY

Every person is presumed to have capacity to contract, but there are certain persons whose status, age, or condition renders them wholly or partly incapable of binding themselves by a contract—*e.g.* minors (alternatively referred to as infants). Incapacity must be proved by the party claiming the benefit of it, and until proved the ordinary presumption remains. The incapacity may be such as to make the attempted contract null and void, or it may be such as to render it voidable; in the latter case the contract remains valid until the option to render it invalid is exercised by the person entitled to avoid it.

II MINORS

A person under eighteen years of age is a minor and a person is deemed to attain the age of eighteen at the commencement of the eighteenth anniversary of his birth. The age of majority was reduced from 21 to 18 by the Family Law Reform Act 1969.

Categories of minors' contracts

(a) Void contracts

Some contracts cannot be validly made by a minor. Section 1 of the Infants' Relief Act 1874 enacts that:

"All contracts, whether by specialty or by simple contract, henceforth entered into by infants for the repayment of money lent or to be lent, or for goods supplied or to be supplied (other than contracts for necessaries), and all accounts stated with infants, shall be absolutely void: Provided always, that this enactment shall not invalidate any contract into which an infant may, by any existing or future statute, or by the rules of common law or equity, enter, except such as now by law are voidable."

This section, it will be observed, applies only to contracts relating to the supply of goods, the loan of money, and accounts stated, *i.e.* admissions of debt[1].

A minor cannot be made liable in respect of a contract which is void under the Infants' Relief Act 1874, in any form of action. Thus,

---

1. See *Duncan* v. *Dixon* (1890), 44 Ch. D. 211. A mortgage of land belonging to a minor to secure advances which the minor has expended in building on the land will be set aside (*Nottingham, etc. Building Society* v. *Thurston*, [1903] A. C. 6).

if a minor induces a person to lend him money by fraudulently representing himself to be of full age, he cannot be sued for money lent, or for money had and received by him for the use of the lender, or for damages for fraud[2]. It seems that if an adult purports to *guarantee* a contract which is void under the Infants' Relief Act, the adult cannot be sued[3], but it is otherwise if the adult's promise is one of indemnity[4]. Despite the statutory words "absolutely void," it seems that the minor may sue on such a contract.

Property which has come into the possession of the minor under a void contract can be recovered from him if it is still in the ownership of the plaintiff. So in *Ballett* v. *Mingay*[5]:

> A lent an amplifier and microphone to B, a minor, in return for a weekly payment. A demanded them back but B had parted with them. *Held:* B was liable in conversion. He could not have been sued for damaging the microphone by using it negligently. Such an act would not be distinct from the contract of hire, but within the four corners of it.

The Betting and Loans (Infants') Act 1892 makes absolutely void an agreement by a person after he comes of age to pay any money which in whole or in part represents, or is agreed to be paid in respect of, any loan advanced to him during his minority; and any instrument, negotiable or not, given in pursuance of such agreement is also absolutely void against all persons whomsoever.

(b) *Voidable contracts*

Certain classes of contracts are binding on the minor unless he expressly repudiates them during his minority or within a reasonable time[6] of reaching his majority; and the minor's ignorance of his right to repudiate will not relieve him from the consequences of undue delay in exercising that right[7]. What amounts to a reasonable time is in each case to be determined on the particular facts[8].

This group of contracts consists of those which are incident to interests in permanent property, and includes:

1. Contracts of tenancy;
2. Partnership;

---

2. *Leslie (R.), Ltd.* v. *Sheill*, [1914] 3 K. B. 607. However, if goods or money obtained by such fraud are still in the infant's possession, he may be required by the court to return them in accordance with the equitable doctrine of restitution.
3. *Coutts & Co.* v. *Browne-Lecky*, [1946] 2 All E. R. 207; [1947] K. B. 104.
4. *Yeoman Credit, Ltd.* v. *Latter*, [1961] 2 All E. R. 294. For the difference between a guarantee and an indemnity, see *post*, p. 377.
5. [1943] 1 K. B. 281; [1943] 1 All E. R. 143.
6. *Re Blakely Ordnance Co.* (1869), L. R. 4 Ch. 31; and *Ebbett's Case* (1870), L. R. 5 Ch. 302.
7. *Carnell* v. *Harrison*, [1916] 1 Ch. 328.
8. *Edwards* v. *Carter*, [1893] A. C. 360, a marriage settlement case.

3. Contracts to take shares; and
4. Marriage settlements.

A minor who remains in partnership after attaining his majority will be held liable as a partner for debts accruing after he comes of age. BEST, J., in a similar case, said:

"If he wished to be understood as no longer continuing a partner, he ought to have notified it to the world"[9].

A minor may hold shares in a company, and if when he becomes of age he does not repudiate them, he will be deemed to have ratified the contract to purchase, and will be liable to be placed on the list of contributories[10]. If he makes a lease and accepts rent after coming of age[11], or if he continues to occupy under a lease[12], in either case he will be considered to have adopted the contract; though, had he wished to do so, he could have avoided the lease[13].

(*c*) *Valid contracts*

There are two contracts of a nature similar to each other, which are valid and binding on a minor if, taken as a whole, the agreement is not so much to the detriment of the minor as to render it unfair that he should be bound by it[14]; such are contracts of:

1. Apprenticeship;
2. Service.

The court, if satisfied that the contract is reasonable and for the benefit of the minor, will enforce its provisions even against him[15], even if the contract is executory[16], and will not allow him to repudiate such a contract. If the contract is not reasonable and for the minor's benefit, the court will not enforce it[17]. If a minor's contract of service contains unreasonable stipulations in restraint of trade and these are severable, the void stipulations may be rejected and the operative part of the contract, if otherwise unobjectionable, enforced[18].

A contract akin to or closely associated with a contract of employ-

---

9. *Goode* v. *Harrison* (1821), 5 B. & Ald. 159, 160; and see *per* Lord HERSCHELL, in *Lovell* v. *Beauchamp*, [1894] A. C., at p. 611.
10. *Re Blakely Ordnance Co., supra.*
11. *Baylis* v. *Dineley* (1815), 3 M. & S. 477, 481.
12. 1 Rolle Abr. 731.
13. *Per* GIBBS, C. J., in *Holmes* v. *Blogg* (1818), 8 Taunt. 508.
14. SMITH, L.J., in *Flower* v. *London and North Western Rail. Co.*, [1894] 2 Q. B., at p.68.
15. *Clements* v. *London and North Western Rail. Co.*, [1894] 2 Q.B. 482; *Green* v. *Thompson*, [1899] 2 Q. B. 1.
16. *Roberts* v. *Gray*, [1913] 1 K. B. 520 (contract to tour as professional billiard player).
17. *De Francesco* v. *Barnum* (1890), 43 Ch. D. 165; 45 Ch. D. 430; *Corn* v. *Matthess*, [1893] 1 Q. B. 310.
18. *Bromley* v. *Smith*, [1909] 2 K. B. 235.

ment is governed by the same principles as a direct contract of service. In *Doyle* v. *White City Stadium*[19],

> the plaintiff minor obtained a licence from the British Boxing Board of Control authorising him to box under its auspices and subject to its rules. Pursuant to this licence the plaintiff agreed to box for a promoter on the terms that he should receive £3,000 win, lose, or draw. Before the fight the promoter paid £3,000 to the Board of Control, one of the rules of which authorised the Board to stop payment of the money to the boxer if he should be disqualified. During the contest the plaintiff was disqualified and the Board refused to pay the money to him. The plaintiff sued the Board for the £3,000 but failed to recover on the ground that the agreement to abide by the rules of the Board was not void but was analogous to a contract of service and being for the minor's benefit would be enforced against him.

An apprentice cannot be sued for damages on his covenant in the deed to serve[20], but a covenant for the payment of a fair and reasonable premium may be enforced against him[1] and so may a reasonable restrictive covenant not to compete in business after the cessation of the apprenticeship[2].

If a minor carries on business, he is not liable on contracts made by him in the course of trade irrespective of whether or not the contract is beneficial to him[3].

Necessaries.—A minor is bound to pay a reasonable price for "necessaries"[4]. They include, says Coke[5]:

> "his necessary meat, drink, apparel, physic, and such other necessaries, and likewise for his good teaching or instruction, whereby he may profit himself afterwards."

Necessaries may include goods supplied to the minor for gifts to his fiancée[6] or sums for the support of his wife[7]. In an old case[8] it was held that tobacco was not a necessary, but the decision might now be different.

---

19. [1934] All E. R. Rep. 252; [1935] 1 K. B. 110; followed in *Chaplin* v. *Leslie Frewin (Publishers), Ltd.,* [1965] 3 All E. R. 764; [1966] Ch. 71.
20. *Gylbert* v. *Fletcher* (1860), Cro. Car. 179. The apprentice can sue his master for breach of contract and claim as damages the diminution of his future prospects as well as for loss of earnings. *Dunk* v. *George Waller & Son, Ltd.,* [1970] 2 All E. R. 630; [1970] 2 Q. B. 163, C. A.
1. *Walter* v. *Everard,* [1891] 2 Q. B. 369.
2. *Gadd* v. *Thompson,* [1911] 1 K. B. 304.
3. *Mercantile Union Guarantee Corporation* v. *Ball,* [1937] 2 K. B. 498.
4. Sale of Goods Act 1893, s. 2.
5. Co. Litt. 172 a.
6. *Elkington & Co., Ltd.* v. *Amery,* [1936] 2 All E. R. 86.
7. *Turner* v. *Trisby* (1719), 1 Stra. 168.
8. *Bryant* v. *Richardson* (1866), L. R. 3 Exchn. 93, n.

Where goods are supplied to a minor they must be suitable to his condition in life and to his actual requirements at the time of the sale and delivery; and it is for the *plaintiff* to prove that the minor was not sufficiently supplied with similar goods at the times in question. For example in *Nash* v. *Inman*[9]:

> A tailor provided an undergraduate with clothing including eleven fancy waistcoats. *Held:* the plaintiff must prove (either by direct evidence or by cross-examining witnesses called by the defendant to prove infancy) not only that they were suitable to the defendant's condition in life but also that he was not adequately provided. If he established these facts he was entitled to a reasonable price which would not necessarily be the agreed price.

But a minor cannot be sued on a bill of exchange or promissory note, even if it is given for necessaries[10]. And though a minor can enter into a contract to pay for necessaries, he cannot be bound by a bond with a penalty, even though the consideration is necessaries supplied[11].

Section 2 of the Infants' Relief Act, 1874

> "No action shall be brought whereby to charge any person upon any promise made after full age to pay any debt contracted during infancy, or upon any ratification made after full age of any promise or contract made during infancy, whether there shall or shall not be any new consideration for such promise or ratification made after full age."

Recovery of money paid by infants

Whether a minor can recover money paid under a contract entered into by him which he either avoids, having a right to do so, or which *per se* is void, depends upon whether there has or has not been a total failure of consideration.

Thus, in *Steinberg* v. *Scala (Leeds)*[12]:

> the plaintiff, while still a minor, was held entitled to repudiate shares in a company and have her name removed from the register so as to escape future liability for calls, but not entitled to recover the money she had paid to the company for her shares, although she had received no dividends and attended no meetings. It

---

9. [1908] 2 K. B. 1. See also *Rayder* v. *Wombwell* (1868), L. R. 4 Exch. 32.
10. *Re Soltykoff*, [1891] 1 Q. B. 413. But if a bill is given to a person who has supplied necessaries his right to sue on the *original contract* is not prejudicially affected. *Ibid.*
11. *Walter* v. *Everard*, [1891] 2 Q. B. 369.
12. [1923] 2 Ch. 452. See also *Holmes* v. *Blogg* (1888), 8 Taunt. 508, where an infant who had occupied premises failed to recover a premium he had paid to the lessor.

was proved that the shares were of substantial value and conferred rights which she could have exercised, so that there was no total failure of consideration; the test as to this being the same in the case of an infant and of a person of full age.

In *Valentini* v. *Canali*[13], the contract was partially within s. 1 of the Infants' Relief Act 1874 and to that extent void:

> The minor had hired a house, and had bought the furniture in it; he paid part of the price for the furniture, and had occupied the house, and used the furniture for several months; the court held that, although the contract in respect of the furniture was void, as the infant had used the furniture, he could not recover the money already paid under the contract.

So, although a minor's contract for the exchange of chattels is void, he cannot recover the chattel transferred by him unless there was a total failure of consideration[14].

Bankruptcy of minor[15].

III MENTALLY DISORDERED AND DRUNKEN PERSONS

A contract made with a person who by reason of mental disorder does not know what he is doing, will, unless the other contracting party was, at the date of the contract, aware of his state hold good[16]; in other cases it is voidable. A mentally disordered person must pay a reasonable price for necessaries[17]. A contract may in any case be ratified when he recovers from his disorder.

Under the Mental Health Act 1959, the High Court has power to make orders for the management of the property and affairs of those who by reason of mental disorder are incapable of managing their own affairs.

The contracts of elderly people, whose powers are failing, are treated on the same principles. Thus in *Manches* v. *Trimborn*[18]:

> The defendant, an elderly woman, drew a cheque in favour of the plaintiff. She was capable of understanding that she was signing a cheque but, to the plaintiff's knowledge, she was incapable of understanding the transaction to which the cheque related. *Held:* she had a good defence to the action on the cheque.

A person who enters into a contract when to the knowledge of the other party he is in a state of complete drunkenness, so that he does not

---

13. (1890), 24 Q. B. D. 166.
14. *Pearce* v. *Brain*, [1929] All E. R. Rep. 627; [1929] 2 K. B. 310.
15. See *post*, p. 443.
16. *Imperial Loan Co.* v. *Stone*, [1892] 1 Q. B. 599.
17. *Re Rhodes* (1890), 44 Ch. D. 94.
18. (1946), 115 L. J. K. B. 305.

know what he is doing, may avoid such contract[19]; but it remains good unless he does so[20]. If the contract is for the supply of necessaries at a fair price, in the absence of unfair dealing, it is good[1].

IV CORPORATIONS AND COMPANIES

A *corporation* is an artificial person created by special authority, and endowed with special capacity. It may consist of one person or of many, and in the former case is then known as a corporation sole[2]. Coke says,

> "A corporation aggregate of many is invisible, immortal, and rests only in intendment and consideration of the law; it has no soul, neither is it subject to the imbecilities of the body".

A corporation may be created by Royal Charter or by Act of Parliament. Various institutions are holders of charters from the Crown. Public utilities and nationalised industries are managed by corporations created under special legislation. Trading companies are usually companies incorporated under the Companies Act 1948 or earlier Acts superseded by that Act.

Contractual capacity.—A statutory corporation or company has its powers defined by the statute under which it is created. But although the powers of a corporation must be ascertained by reference to its constitution, these are sometimes implied. Thus,

> a trading corporation has, in the absence of express restriction, power to borrow money for the purposes of its business[3].

Within the limits imposed by the statute it would seem that a corporation has the same power to contract, subject to the same restrictions as a natural person, and that it can act in any matter of business in the manner in which an individual conducting the same kind of business can act[4].

In the case of companies governed by the Companies Act 1948 a contract made in excess of the powers given to the company is said to be *ultra vires* and invalid[5].

---

19. *Gore* v. *Gibson* (1845), 13 M. & W. 623.
20. *Matthews* v. *Baxter* (1873), L. R. 8 Ex. 132.
1. *Gore* v. *Gibson, supra*, at p. 627.
2. *E.g.*, the vicar of a parish.
3. *General Auction, etc. Co.* v. *Smith*, [1891] 3 Ch. 432.
4. *Breay* v. *Royal British Nurses' Association*, [1897] 2 Ch. 272.
5. *Ashbury Carriage Co.* v. *Riche* (1875), L. R. 7 H. L. 653. See also *Introductions Ltd.* v. *National Provincial Bank*, [1969] 1 All E. R. 887; [1970] Ch. 199.

But by s. 9 of the European Communities Act 1972, in favour of any person dealing with a company in good faith, any contract made by directors is deemed to be one within the capacity of the company.

Corporations created by Royal Charter are not subject to the *ultra vires* rule. As BOWEN, L.J., said in *Wenlock (Baroness)* v. *River Dee Co.*[6],

"At common law a corporation created by the King's Charter has *prima facie* the power to do with its property all such acts as an ordinary person can do, and to bind itself to such contracts as an ordinary person can bind himself to".

However, if such a corporation does exceed the powers set out in the Charter, the Crown may forfeit the Charter.

Abolition of formal requirements.—At common law there was a rule that, in general, a corporation must contract under seal. Contracts not made under seal were void[7]. The rule did not apply to companies registered under the Companies Acts, and there were several other exceptions. The rule was finally abolished by the Corporate Bodies' Contracts Act 1960. In any contract made by a corporation after the commencement of this Act, no more formality is required than if the contract is made by an individual.

V BANKRUPTS

A person who is made bankrupt is not incapacitated from contracting, but if while undischarged he obtains credit to the extent of £10 or upwards, or trades under a different name from that under which he was adjudged bankrupt, without informing his intended creditor that he is an undischarged bankrupt, or without disclosing the name under which he was adjudged bankrupt, he will be liable to imprisonment[8].

If a contract is entered into, and one of the parties is adjudged bankrupt, the rights and liabilities under the contract pass to his trustee[9]; but the trustee may by disclaimer abandon the contract[10].

Personal services.—Contracts requiring the personal services of the

---

6. (1887), 36 Ch. D. 674, at p. 685.
7. *A. R. Wright & Son, Ltd.* v. *Romford Corporation*, [1956] 3 All E. R. 785; [1957] 1 Q. B. 431.
8. Bankruptcy Act 1914, s. 155. See *R.* v. *Doubleday* (1964), 49 Cr. App. Rep. 62.
9. Bankruptcy Act 1914, s. 38; this is subject to the exception that if the contract be one affecting merely the person of the debtor, *e.g.*, to cure, it will not pass to the trustee.
10. *Ibid.*, s. 54. See *post*, p. 478.

bankrupt cannot be enforced by the trustee in bankruptcy against the other party unless the bankrupt is willing to render the services[11]. The rights of the other party are:

1. To prove for loss sustained by non-fulfilment of the contract if the liability of the bankrupt be of a provable nature[12];
2. In the case of a contract to deliver non-specific goods by instalments, to refuse to deliver instalments after the bankruptcy begins until he is paid for them[13]; and
3. He may apply to the court to have the contract terminated, and the court may rescind it on terms that such party do pay damages to the trustee or prove for damages against the estate, or otherwise[14].

VI MISCELLANEOUS CASES

An alien enemy is incapacitated during the continuance of a war from contracting with British subjects, and his power to sue or exercise rights in relation to property in this country is suspended. But an alien enemy may be sued during war, and if sued, he may defend himself[15].

Foreign sovereigns and states may contract, but the contract cannot be enforced against them unless they consent.

Diplomatic representatives of foreign and Commonwealth countries are to some extent privileged from being sued in the English courts but the privilege may be waived with the sanction of the Sovereign or the official superior of the representative[16]. By the Diplomatic Privileges Act 1964, members of a diplomatic mission fall into three classes:

(i) Members of the diplomatic staff have full personal immunity, civil and criminal, with three exceptions—a real action relating to private immovable property in England unless the diplomatic agent held it on behalf of his State for the purposes of the mission, an action relating to succession in which the agent is involved as a private person, and an action relating to any professional or business activity exercised by the agent in England outside his official functions;

---

11. Williams' Bankruptcy (18th ed.), p. 316.
12. Bankruptcy Act 1914, s. 30.
13. Williams' Bankruptcy (18th ed.), p. 313.
14. Bankruptcy Act 1914, s. 54 (5).
15. *The Hoop* (1799), 1 C. Rob. 1906; *Porter* v. *Freudenberg*, [1915] 1 K. B. 857; *Robson* v. *Premier Oil & Pipe Line Co.*, [1915] 2 Ch. 124.
16. *Dickinson* v. *Del Solar*, [1929] All E. R. Rep. 139; [1930] 1 K. B. 376.

(ii) members of the administrative and technical staff, who enjoy immunity for official acts but who are liable civilly (not criminally) for acts performed outside the course of their duties;

(iii) members of the service staff, who enjoy immunity for official acts, but are liable civilly and criminally for acts performed outside the course of their duties.

Where the privileges and immunities granted by a country to the diplomatic missions of the U.K. are less than those conferred by the Diplomatic Privileges Act on the mission of that country, the privileges and immunities granted under the Act may be withdrawn by Order in Council[17].

A barrister cannot sue for his fees; nor can a Fellow of a College of Physicians, the fellows of which are prohibited by byelaw from recovering at law their expenses, charges or fees[18].

---

17. Diplomatic Privileges Act 1964, s, 3.
18. Medical Act 1956, s. 27 (2).

CHAPTER 6

Rights and Duties under the Contract

I POSITION OF THIRD PARTIES

The first point to consider is—Who may enjoy the rights, and who is subject to the obligations arising under a contract? The general rule is clear. As Lord HALDANE said in *Dunlop Pneumatic Tyre Co., Ltd.* v. *Selfridge & Co., Ltd.*[1],

"In the law of England certain principles are fundamental. One is that only a person who is a party to a contract may sue on it".

It is a natural corollary of this to say that no one who is not a party to a contract can be bound by obligations contained in it. Under the principle or doctrine of *privity of contract*, only someone who is privy to the contract may sue or be sued under the contract[2]. Thus,

if A agrees with B to give C £100, C cannot compel payment but A does properly perform his contract with B by paying C, and, of course, B can sue A if A does not pay C the £100. It would seem that the measure of damages resulting from A's failure to pay C is loss to B, which may only be nominal but the court may give B an order of specific performance to compel A to pay C. If an order of specific performance is granted in an action by B against A, the Rules of the Supreme Court permit C to enforce such order against A[3].

In *Scruttons, Ltd.* v. *Midland Silicones*[4].

A drum of chemicals was shipped under a contract which limited the carrier's liability to $500. The drum was damaged by the negligence of stevedores engaged by the carrier and damage in excess of $500 resulted. The owner sued the stevedores. *Held:* The stevedores were not parties to the contract of carriage and,

---

1. [1915] A. C. 847, 853.
2. In *Beswick* v. *Beswick*, [1967] 2 All E. R. 1197; [1968] A. C. 58, the House of Lords referred to this as the commonly accepted view but in the Court of Appeal, Lord DENNING, M.R., not for the first time, had taken the opposite view. Contrary to the majority opinion of the Court of Appeal, the House of Lords ruled that the privity rule had not been altered by the Law of Property Act 1925, s. 56.
3. *Beswick* v. *Beswick*, [1967] 2 All E. R. 1197; [1968] A. C. 58.
4. [1962] 1 All E. R. 1; [1962] A. C. 446.

therefore, were not entitled to the benefit of the contractual clause limiting liability. They were liable for the damage in full.

However, *Snelling v. John G. Snelling, Ltd.*[5] is an interesting case:

X, Y and Z, directors of a company, agreed that if one of them resigned he would forfeit money due to him from the company. X resigned and sued the company for money due to him and the company joined Y and Z as co-defendants. *Held*: although the company was not a party to the agreement between X, Y and Z, X had broke that agreement and with all concerned before the court, further proceedings by X would be stayed under the Supreme Court of Judicature (Consolidation) Act 1925, s. 41, and X's claim dismissed.

It is possible that a contract between A and B to benefit C will be construed as creating a trust in C's favour so that C, as the beneficiary, may in equity enforce it, but this will only be the case where a clear intention to create a trust is shown[6]. The courts are not in practice very willing to employ the trust device as a method of avoiding the rigours of the doctrine of privity, and this is more the position now than at some times in the past. An agreement between A and B to benefit C will not be construed as a trust if either A or B is entitled to alter the terms of their agreement without C's assent.

Thus, in *Re Schebsman*[7], *ex parte Official Receiver*,

In an agreement between S and two companies (both of which employed S), one of the companies agreed in certain circumstances to pay a sum of money to S's widow and daughter. It was *held* that the agreement did not constitute a trust as the parties to the agreement reserved the right to vary the terms.

If A has a fund in his hands over which B has a right of disposal and B directs him to pay it to C, C may sue A if A has acknowledged C's rights[8].

A statutory exception to the rule that a contract is not binding on third parties was created by s. 25 of the Restrictive Trade Practices Act 1956, which (subject to the Resale Prices Act 1964)[9] entitles a supplier of goods who sells them subject to a condition as to the price at which they may be resold to enforce the condition against a third

---

5. [1972] 1 All E. R. 79; [1972]; 2 Q. B. 71.
6. *Les Affréteurs Société Anonyme* v. *Leopold Walford, London, Ltd.*, [1919] A. C. 801.
7. [1943] 2 All E. R. 768; [1944] Ch. 83.
8. *Shamia* v. *Joory*, [1958] 1 All E. R. 111; [1958] 1 Q. B. 448.
9. See p. 533, *post.* S. 25 of the 1956 Act still operates in respect of goods for which exemption has been claimed under s. 6 of the 1964 Act unless and until the Restrictive Practices Court refuses to make an exemption order.

person not a party to the sale who subsequently acquires the goods for resale with notice of the condition.

Another statutory exception to the privity rule arises in the field of motor vehicle insurance. Suppose A insures his car with B Co. and the policy is expressed to cover not only A when he is driving his car but also anyone else when driving A's car with A's consent. If C is driving A's car with A's consent and C incurs liability to someone as a result of his negligent driving, C may claim to be indemnified by B Co. in respect of that liability[10].

A principal may take the benefit of a contract made on his behalf by an agent, but this is because the contract of the agent is regarded in law as being made by the principal; *qui facit per alium facit per se.* Thus:

> If A agrees to carry B on the terms that neither he nor his servants will be liable for negligence, this clause may protect not only A but also A's servants, but only if it can fairly be said that A contracted as agent for his servants as well as on his own account[11].

Agency is further dealt with, *post* pp. 119 *et seq.*

Another possible exception to the privity rule was suggested by Lord DENNING, M.R., in *Morris* v. *C. W. Martin & Sons, Ltd.*[12].

> X sent her mink stole for cleaning to Y, a furrier, who (with X's consent) despatched it for cleaning to Z. In the contract between Y and Z, Z was exempt from liability for loss of goods "belonging to customers". The stole was stolen by a servant of Z to whom Z, had entrusted it and Z was *held* vicariously liable to X for the loss. The exemption clause could not apply as it referred only to goods belonging to customers and X was not a customer of Z. But Lord DENNING, M.R., said that if the clause had been wide enough to cover X's stole, X would have been bound by such clause though not a party to the contract between Y and Z if she could be taken to have impliedly assented to Y despatching the stole to Z on these terms.

II INTERFERENCE BY THIRD PARTY

But though no contractual obligation can be cast upon a person by a contract to which he is a stranger, yet interference with such contract may subject him to liability. In *Lumley* v. *Gye*[13]:

> a singer agreed to sing at a particular theatre, and the defendant, without legal justification or excuse, induced her to break the

---

10. Road Traffic Act 1972, s. 148 (4).
11. see *Adler* v. *Dickson*, [1954] 3 All E. R. 397; [1955] 1 Q. B. 158.
12. [1965] 2 All E. R. 725; [1966] 1 Q. B. 716.
13. (1853), 2 E. & B. 216.

contract. The majority of the court held that an action in tort would lie for interfering with an existing contract.

This principle is not limited to contracts of personal service. In *British Motor Trade Association* v. *Salvadori*[14],

> A sold a car to B and B promised that if he wished to resell it within a year he would offer it first to A. B sold the car to C within the year without first offering it to A and C knew of B's promise. *Held:* C was liable to A for interfering with the contract between A and B.

To excuse interference the justification must exist in fact, and must be founded on a right equal or superior to that of the plaintiff. Thus

> A father may persuade his daughter to break her engagement to marry a scoundrel. The justification arises from a moral duty (per LORD SIMON, L.C.[15]).

To induce a person not to make a contract or to terminate a contract by proper notice is not wrongful in an individual unless he employs unlawful means such as threats of violence, or threatens to commit a tort or breach of contract[16].

Industrial disputes.—By s. 132 (1) of the Industrial Relations Act 1971, an act done by a person in contemplation of furtherance of an industrial dispute is not actionable in tort on the ground that it induces another person to break a contract to which that other person is a party or prevents another person from performing such a contract. However, if such contract is not a contract of employment but is, for example, a commercial contract with an employer who is a party to the industrial dispute, the interference may be an "unfair industrial practice" in respect of which compensation may be awarded by an industrial tribunal or the National Industrial Relations Court[17].

III ASSIGNMENT OF CONTRACTS

How effected.—In many cases a contract may be assigned, and then its rights and duties go with it accordingly. Such assignment or devolution may take place.

1. By operation of law; or
2. By act of parties.

Amongst assignments by operation of law may be mentioned the assignment of a bankrupt's contracts to his trustee, of a deceased's

---

14. [1949] 1 All E. R. 208; [1949] Ch. 556.
15. *Crofter Hand Woven Harris Tweed Co., Ltd.* v. *Veitch*, [1942] A. C. 435, 442; [1942] 1 All E. R. 142.
16. *Crofter Hand Woven Harris Tweed Co., Ltd.* v. *Veitch*, [1942] All E. R. 142; [1942] A. C. 435, at p. 442.
17. Industrial Relations Act 1971, s. 96.

contracts to his personal representative[18]. In dealing with an assignment by act of party the assignment of rights and the assignment of duties must be separately considered.

Assignment of Rights

1. Equitable assignments.—Courts of equity always gave effect to assignments of debts and other choses in action. A *chose in action* is any personal right of property which is enforceable only by action—as opposed to a *chose in possession, i.e.* a thing in actual possession. Thus a debt, a share in a company, and any right arising under a contract are all choses in action. If the right is one which, before the Judicature Acts, could be claimed only in the Common Law Courts—such as a right to recover a contract debt—it is known as a *legal chose in action*; if the right is one which could be claimed only in the Court of Chancery —such as a right to a share in a trust fund—it is known as an *equitable chose in action*.

There can be an effective equitable assignment of a *legal* chose in action by any words (oral or written) which show a clear intention to transfer the benefit of the subject matter. As Lord MACNAGHTEN said:

> "It may be addressed to the debtor. It may be couched in the language of command. It may be a courteous request. It may assume the form of mere permission. The language is immaterial as long as the meaning is plain[1]."

But the assignment of an *equitable* chose in action requires to be in writing[2].

The effect of a valid equitable assignment of a chose in action, is that the assignee may sue to enforce the right, but he has to join the assignor as co-plaintiff (or, if unwilling to co-operate, as co-defendant) unless the assignment is an absolute assignment of an equitable chose in action. An assignment is complete in equity as between the assignor and assignee without the assent of, or notice to, the debtor.

Thus, in *Holt* v. *Heatherfield Trust, Ltd.*[3],

> A had a judgment debt against B. A assigned the debt to C. Before notice of the assignment had been given to B, D, a creditor of A, tried to claim the money from B to satisfy his own judgment: *Held:* the debt had been validly assigned in equity to C who therefore had a better title to it than D.

---

18. There is no assignment by operation of law of contracts relating to purely personal services, rights, and liabilities (*Baxter* v. *Burfield* (1747), 2 Str. 1266).
1. *William Brandt's* v. *Dunlop Rubber Co.*, [1905] A. C., at p. 462. But telling the debtor to pay X is only an assignment to X if intended to be an irrevocable transfer of rights to X.
2. Law of Property Act 1925, s. 53 (1).
3. [1942] 1 All E. R. 404; [1942] 2 K. B. 1.

Notice to the debtor is, however, advisable so as to prevent the debtor paying the assignor. If, without having received notice of the assignment, the debtor pays the assignor, the assignee has no right of action against the debtor. It is otherwise if the debtor pays the assignor after having notice of the assignment. Moreover, notice to the debtor is also advisable to obtain priority over any other assignee because a subsequent assignee without notice of an earlier assignment will have priority if he is first to give notice to the debtor[4].

An assignment which is not a legal assignment because it does not comply with the requirements of s. 136 of the Law of Property Act 1925 (to be discussed below) may be a valid equitable assignment.

2. *Legal assignments.*—At common law choses in action could only be assigned with the assent of the debtor, or in accordance with the law merchant[5]. So, unless the contract were one of a negotiable character (see *post*, p. 236), the rights given by it could not be assigned; to transfer these rights a new contract of a trilateral nature, a *novation* was required, *i.e.* the creditor A agreed to release the debtor B from his liability to A in return for B agreeing to pay the debt to C. C could only enforce B's promise if he gave consideration for it.

The common law rule was altered by the Judicature Act 1873, s. 25 (6), which was repealed and re-enacted by s. 136 of the Law of Property Act 1925. These Acts provided that a debt or other legal chose in action may be assigned so as to entitle the assignee to sue in his own name without joining the assignor as a party if:

(i) the assignment is absolute, and not by way of charge;

(ii) the assignment is in writing;

(iii) notice in writing of the assignment has been given to the debtor[6].

An absolute assignment of a debt is one where the assignor retains no interest in the property. An assignment by way of charge is not an absolute assignment, but an assignment by way of mortgage with a proviso for redemption is within s. 136. Thus, in *Durham Brothers* v. *Robertson*[7],

> A, a builder, had a claim for a contract debt against B, and when borrowing money from C he assigned the debt to C as security for the loan "until the money lent be repaid". This was *held* to be an assignment by way of charge of B's debt.

It would not be appropriate in such a case for C to sue B without

---

4. *Dearle* v. *Hall* (1828), 3 Russ. 1.
5. See remarks of Martin, B., in *Liversidge* v. *Broadbent* (1859), 4 H. & N. 603, 610.
6. The notice must actually reach the debtor; *Holt* v. *Heatherfield Trust, Ltd.*, [1942] 2 K. B. 1; [1942] 1 All E. R. 404.
7. [1898] 1 Q. B. 765.

joining A as a party since the court would need to examine the
state of accounts between A and C in order to determine whom
B should pay. If, on the other hand, A had assigned the debt
to C as security for the loan unconditionally but with a proviso
for reassignment upon repayment of the loan, there would have
been an absolute assignment. Until the debtor B had notice of
the reassignment, both B and any court would be entitled to assume
that B should pay the debt to C.

Clearly, the assignment of a debt is only *absolute* within the terms
of the section if it is an assignment of the assignor's entire interest.
Thus, in *Jones* v. *Humphreys*[8],

> A schoolmaster assigned to X that part of his future salary as
> would be necessary to repay £22 10s. already borrowed from X,
> and any further sums which he might borrow in future. *Held:*
> This was not an absolute assignment.

Even the assignment of a definite part of a debt is not an absolute
assignment[9]. Of course, if an assignment is not absolute and, therefore, cannot be valid as a legal assignment under s. 136 of the Law of
Property Act, it may be valid as an equitable assignment.

3. *Points common to both equitable and legal assignments*

(a) *"Subject to equities."*—Every assignment (whether legal or
equitable) is "subject to equities". This means that when
sued by the assignee, the debtor can raise against him all
defences (including rights of set-off) that he could have
raised against the assignor at the time he received notice of
the assignment. A claim for damages against the assignor
arising out of the contract under which the assigned debt
arises, is an equity which may be set up by way of defence
in an action by the assignee for the debt[10]. But if the assignor
induced the defendant to enter into the contract by fraud
and the latter is not in a position or does not claim to rescind
it, the defendant cannot set off the damages for fraud to
which he is entitled against the assignor as an answer in
whole or in part to the claim of the assignee[11].

(b) *Consideration.*—Although equity would not assist an assignee
to whom a debt or other legal chose in action had been
transferred without valuable consideration, where the

---

8. [1902] 1 K. B. 10.
9. *Williams* v. *Atlantic Assurance Co.*, [1932] All E. R. Rep. 32; [1933] 1 K. B.
   81, C. A., approving *Re Steel Wing Co.*, [1921] 1 Ch. 349.
10. *Newfoundland (Govt.)* v. *Newfoundland Rail. Co.* (1888), 13 A. C. 199.
11. *Stoddart* v. *Union Trust*, [1912] 1 K. B. 181.

provisions of s. 136 have been complied with, a voluntary assignment will confer the legal right to sue[12]. Moreover, it is now generally believed that even in equity a voluntary assignment is valid if it is an absolute assignment and the assignor has done everything which is necessary according to the nature of the property to transfer the title to it to the assignee[13].

(c) *No assignment of some rights.*—Some rights, such as the right to sue for damages in tort and rights under personal contracts like contracts of employment, cannot be assigned at all. COZENS-HARDY, L.J., in *Tolhurst* v. *Associated Portland Cement Manufacturers*, said:

"The section relates to procedure only. It does not enlarge the class of choses in action, the assignability of which was previously recognised either at law or in equity."[14]

Assignment of Duties

A person cannot assign his obligation to perform any contract so as to shift from himself the liability for non-performance, although he may in many cases perform by the act of another. Thus, a buyer of goods need not personally hand over the price to the seller, though where the contract involves personal confidence or ability, it can be performed only by the contracting party himself and not vicariously. Thus an artist cannot pass on to another artist the performance of a contract to paint a portrait.

The person to whom performance is due may consent to a *novation* creating a new contract under which the original contractor gets his release and the liability of another is substituted. Thus, when there is a change in the membership of a partnership, the creditors of the partnership may agree to release the obligations of the retiring partners for existing debts in return for the partnership as newly constituted taking on the liability[15].

Negotiability

A distinction must be drawn between assignability and negotiability. Negotiability implies

---

12. *Re Westerton*, [1919] 2 Ch. 104.
13. *Holt* v. *Heatherfield Trust, Ltd.*, [1942] 1 All E. R. 404; [1942] 2 K. B. 1. For the facts, see *ante*, p. 70. The equitable assignee was held to have a good title to the property assigned although there appeared to be no consideration for the assignment.
14. [1902] 2 K. B., at p. 676.
15. See *post*, p. 162.

(i) that the contract (*e.g.* the liability embodied in a cheque) may
be passed from hand to hand without notice of the transfer
to the party under liability;

(ii) that the *bona fide* transferee for value of a negotiable instrument
holds it free from any defects in title which might have affected
the prior holders, and not subject to equities.

The law on this subject is dealt with in the chapter on "NEGOTIABLE
INSTRUMENTS".

CHAPTER 7

Performance and Breach

I INTRODUCTORY

Performance should be complete, and according to the terms of the agreement—*e.g.*

an agreement to pay a sum of money is not performed by mere readiness to pay, the debtor must go to his creditor and offer to pay[1].

Where no time for performance is fixed, there is an implied undertaking that the performance shall be completed within a reasonable time, having regard to the circumstances of the particular case[2]. Where a time for performance is fixed, the other party is entitled to treat the contract as discharged if performance is not completed within the time fixed only if time is of the *essence of the contract*, *i.e.* a condition of the contract. Time of payment is not generally of the essence of the contract. However, in mercantile contracts, the time of performance of other terms, *e.g.* as to delivery date, is generally of the essence of the contract. Thus, failure by the seller of goods to meet a delivery date entitles the buyer to repudiate the contract. Moreover, even if the buyer waives the seller's breach (as by continuing to press for delivery) the buyer may again make time of the essence of the contract by giving reasonable notice that he will not take delivery after a certain date. The buyer will then be entitled to refuse to take delivery unless delivery is made by that date[3].

Performance may be waived by *accord and satisfaction*. This is

"the purchase of a release from an obligation, whether arising under contract or tort, by means of any valuable consideration, not being the actual performance of the obligation itself".

The consideration on each side may be an executory promise[4].

Thus a new contract, if made and accepted *in discharge* of the old liability, may, even if unperformed, be a good accord and satisfaction,

---

1. Co. Litt. 340; *Cranley* v. *Hillary* (1813), 2 M. & S. 120.
2. *Charnock* v. *Liverpool Corporation*, [1968] 3 All E. R. 473; [1968] 1 W. L. R. 1498.
3. *Charles Rickards, Ltd.* v. *Oppenheim*, [1950] 1 All E. R. 420; [1950] 1 K. B. 616.
4. *British Russian Gazette, etc., Ltd.* v. *Associated Newspapers, Ltd.*, [1933] All E. R. Rep., at p. 327; [1933] 2 K. B., at pp. 643, 644, *per* SCRUTTON, L.J.

the creditor having his remedy for breach of the substituted contract[5].

Set-off.—To an action for non-performance there are various defences, but these, as a rule, arise out of circumstances which are sufficient to discharge the contract and will therefore be examined in the next chapter under "TERMINATION OF THE CONTRACT"—*e.g.* impossibility. But *set-off* is not of such a nature. That is a right on the part of a defendant to avail himself of a debt due to him from the plaintiff in extinction or reduction of the claim in the action, and so to avoid the consequence of non-performance.

The common law courts before 1875 only allowed a set-off in respect of a liquidated claim. Now, a claim for any monetary sum (whether liquidated or not) may be made by way of set-off but the claim and the set-off must exist between the same parties in the same capacity. Claims that cannot be raised by way of set-off, *e.g.* a claim for a sum in excess of the plaintiff's claim, may generally be made the subject of a counter-claim. Such questions belong rather to the law of procedure than of contract.

II PAYMENT

This may be defined as the performance of a contract by delivery of money or of some negotiable instrument. It may be of two kinds—

1. Either absolute; or
2. Conditional.

E.g.

A owes B £20, he may pay this in cash, or by cheque; if B takes the cash or the cheque in full payment, this is full satisfaction. If he takes the cheque subject to its being honoured at maturity, this is a conditional payment and, in the absence of contrary agreement, payment by cheque is usually regarded as conditional payment. No creditor is *bound* to take a cheque or other negotiable instrument in payment of a debt.

A debtor is bound to seek his creditor[6], and is not entitled to wait until demand has been made. This obligation may, of course, be varied by special agreement, and then, in addition to the demand, the debtor is entitled to an allowance of a reasonable time to enable him to fetch the money[7].

Tender

When money is tendered, the whole amount should be offered,

---

5. There must be consideration for the new arrangement; therefore, a promise to pay a smaller sum instead of a larger, is not good satisfaction. See *ante*, p. 23.
6. *Fessard* v. *Mugnier* (1865), 34 L. J. C. P. 126.
7. *Massey* v. *Sladen* (1869), L. R. 4 Ex. 13.

without imposing conditions[8]; but a tender may be made *under protest*, so as to reserve any right of the debtor to dispute the amount[9]. A debtor who is always ready to pay and actually offers to do so in effect performs his contract, so that tender is a defence to an action to recover a debt if the money is brought into court[10].

1. *Payment in cash.*—The amount must be tendered in a manner consistent with the Coinage Act 1971, in accordance with which the following are legal tender:

(i) gold coins, which have been issued by the Mint up to any amount[11];

(ii) silver or cupro-nickel coins of denominations of more than 10p for payment of any amount not exceeding £10;

(iii) Silver or cupro-nickel coins of denominations of not more than 10p for payment of any amount not exceeding £5;

(iv) bronze coins for payment of any amount not exceeding 20p.

Bank of England notes are legal tender for the payment of any amount in England and Wales[12].

Further, the exact amount must be produced, as a creditor cannot be compelled to give change[13]. But in all the above examples the creditor may waive his strict rights, and on slight evidence uncontradicted by other facts the court would probably infer that he had done so—*e.g.*

a debtor offers to pay by cheque; the creditor objects on the ground of insufficiency of amount only; here the creditor has waived his right as to the quality of the tender[14].

Again, though the debtor must actually produce the money, production may be expressly or impliedly waived. If the creditor says—

"Do not produce it; I will not take it if you do,"

the tender will be good[15].

If payment is made in accordance with the direction of the creditor, the debtor will not be liable if the money is lost—*e.g.*

a creditor sometimes directs his debtor to pay into a certain bank; if after the payment the bank fails, the debtor is discharged as

---

8. *Dixon* v. *Clarke* (1847), 5 C. B. 365; *Evans* v. *Judkins* (1815), 4 Camp. 156.
9. *Scott* v. *Uxbridge Rail. Co.* (1866), L. R. 1 C. P. 596; *Greenwood* v. *Sutcliffe*, [1892] 1 Ch. 1.
10. The costs of the action will be borne by the creditor: *Griffiths* v. *School Board of Ystradyfodwg* (1890), 24 Q. B. D. 307.
11. Payments in gold are subject to the Exchange Control Act 1947.
12. Currency and Bank Notes Act 1954, s. 1.
13. *Robinson* v. *Cook* (1816), 6 Taunt. 336.
14. *Polglass* v. *Oliver* (1831), 2 Cr. & J. 15.
15. *Douglas* v. *Patrick* (1789), 3 T. R. 683.

fully as if he had paid the money into the hands of the creditor himself[16].

If a debtor is expressly or impliedly requested or authorised by his creditor to make a payment through the post, then although the money may be lost in course of transit and never reach the creditor, it will amount to payment.   So

> where a company is authorised or directed to send a dividend warrant by post, the stockholder cannot sue for the dividend, if the warrant has been lost in the post[17].

But apart from special directions a request to remit money through the post only authorises the debtor to do so in the manner in which a prudent person would make the remittance in the ordinary course of business, and the sending of a large sum in Treasury notes, which were stolen before they reached the creditor, has been held not to discharge the debt[18].   A request by the creditor to remit through the post will not be inferred from a mere practice between the parties to make payments by cheques in that way[19].   Moreover, the debtor should be careful to carry out strictly the directions given; thus, if asked to send by post, he should not send by commissionaire[20].

Again, where the debtor gives an order on a third person to pay to the creditor, the payment is complete if the creditor, without consulting the debtor, arranges special terms with the third party, and in consequence loses the money[1].   The following are examples of payments which are good, though not made in the usual way:

> (i) money paid by consent of the creditor for his benefit by the debtor[2];
>
> (ii) payment in goods according to agreement[3].

2. *Payment by bill or note.*—Apart from agreement the creditor cannot be compelled to take, nor the debtor to make himself liable on a negotiable instrument in payment.   If a bill or note is taken, then in the absence of stipulation such payment is presumed to be conditional, and if the instrument is not taken up, the original liability revives[4]; while, if the bill is met, the payment relates back to the time

---

16. *Eyles* v. *Ellis* (1827), 4 Bing. 112.
17. *Thairlwall* v. *Great Northern Rail. Co.*, [1910] 2 K. B. 509.
18. *Mitchell-Henry* v. *Norwich Life Insurance Co.*, [1918] 2 K. B. 76, C. A.
19. *Pennington* v. *Crossley & Son* (1897), 77 L. T. 430.   But see *International Sponge Importers, Ltd.* v. *Watt (Andrew) & Sons*, [1911] A. C. 279.
20. *Hawkins* v. *Rutt* (1793), Peake, 186.
1. *Smith* v. *Ferrand* (1827), 7 B. & C. 19, 24.
2. *Waller* v. *Andrews* (1837), 3 M. & W. 312, 318.
3. *Cannan* v. *Wood* (1836), 2 M. & W. 465, 467; but see the Truck Acts 1831–1896 (*post*, pp. 439–440) which, subject to exceptions, forbid the payment of wages in kind to "workmen".
4. If the debtor after giving a bill commits an act of bankruptcy the original debt revives, though the bill has not yet matured (*Re Raatz*, [1897] 2 Q. B. 80).

when it was given[5]. If a buyer offers cash, but the vendor prefers a bill, the payment is absolute, and all right of action upon the original consideration goes and the vendor must sue on the bill[6].

If, owing to the negligence of the creditor, the negotiable instrument becomes valueless, the payment is treated as an absolute payment— *e.g.*,

> if a debtor is the holder of a bill and indorses it to his creditor by way of payment, and when the bill is dishonoured, the creditor fails to give proper notices of dishonour, and thereby releases the drawer and indorsers the creditor has no further claim on the debtor[7].

3. *Time of payment.*—As a general rule, if a time for payment is specified in the contract, failure to comply with that term does not entitle the other party to treat the contract as discharged. This general rule of equity, that time is not deemed to be of the essence of a contract, has been put into statutory form so far as contracts of sale of goods are concerned. By section 10 of the Sale of Goods Act 1893, *unless a different intention appears* from the terms of the contract, stipulations as to time of payment are not deemed to be of the essence of a contract of sale.

4. *Who may pay.*—It is the duty of the debtor to pay, but a third party may do so for him. In this latter case, the debtor should either give his authorisation or ratification[8], though either may be implied from the facts. Until such affirmation by the debtor, the money may be repaid to the payer, and then the original debtor's liability does not cease[9].

5. *To whom payment may be made.*—The payment should be made to the creditor, and if there are several joint creditors then to any one of them. If one of several joint creditors collusively with the debtor forgives the debt, the release may be set aside by the court.

Payments may be made to the creditor's agent, if made:

(i) in and according to the usual course of business[10]: and

(ii) before the principal gives notice that he requires payment to be made to himself[11].

When an agent has a lien on the proceeds of goods sold by him in his own name, *e.g.* as a factor or auctioneer, payment to the principal

5. *Marreco* v. *Richardson,* [1908] 2 K. B., at p. 593, *per* FARWELL, L.J. But see *Re Hone,* [1950] 2 All E. R. 716; [1951] Ch. 85.
6. *Cowas-Jee* v. *Thompson* (1845), 5 Moo. P. C. C. 165.
7. *Bridges* v. *Berry* (1810), 3 Taunt. 130.
8. *Simpson* v. *Eggington* (1855), 10 Ex. 845, 847.
9. *Walter* v. *James* (1871), L. R. 6 Ex. 124.
10. *Saunderson* v. *Bell* (1834), 2 C. & M. 304; *Catterall* v. *Hindle* (1867), L. R. 2 C. P. 186.
11. *Gardiner* v. *Davis* (1825), 2 C. & P. 49.

is no defence to an action by the agent for the price unless the contract of sale permitted payment direct to the principal[12].

An express authority to an agent to sell goods does not necessarily authorise him to receive payment[13].

6. *Appropriation of payments.*—If a debtor owes more than one debt to a creditor, and makes a payment insufficient to satisfy the whole indebtedness, the money is appropriated as follows:

   (i) To whichever debt the debtor desires, provided he exercises his option at the time of payment;

   (ii) If he does not elect, the creditor may do so at any time;

   (iii) If there is a current account between the parties the presumption is that payments have been appropriated to the items in order of date; but the presumption may be rebutted[14].

7. *Debtor's appropriation.*—Lord Campbell has laid it down that:

"There is an established maxim of law that, when money is paid, it is to be applied according to the expressed will of the payer, not of the receiver. If the party to whom the money is offered does not agree to apply it according to the expressed will of the party offering it, he must refuse it, and stand upon the rights which the law gives him"[15].

The appropriation may be by word or by conduct—*e.g.*

if the debtor owes two debts, one of £30 and another of £37 10s., and pays the latter sum, it will be presumed that the latter is the debt intended to be paid[16].

But an undisclosed intention on the part of the debtor to appropriate a payment to a particular debt is ineffective. The debtor's intention must be communicated to the creditor either expressly or by implication arising from circumstances known to both parties[17].

8. *Creditor's appropriation.*—The creditor may appropriate when the debtor has not done so, but the debtor must first have had an opportunity of electing; so if a debtor's money comes to a creditor's hands, the right of the creditor to apply it to a particular debt will arise only after the debtor has had knowledge of the circumstances[18]. The creditor's appropriation is revocable till communicated; so if he enters in his books a payment to a certain debt, he can afterwards alter this,

---

12. *Williams* v. *Millington* (1788), 1 H. Bl. 81; *Robinson* v. *Rutter* (1855), 4 E. & B. 954.
13. *Butwick* v. *Grant*, [1924] 2 K. B. 483.
14. *The Mecca*, [1897] A. C. 286; *Clayton's Case* (1816), 1 Mer. 585, 608.
15. *Croft* v. *Lumley* (1858), 5 E. & B. 648.
16. *Marryatts* v. *White* (1817), 2 Stark. 101.
17. *Leeson* v. *Leeson*, [1936] 2 K. B. 156.
18. *Waller* v. *Lacy* (1840), 1 M. & G. 54.

unless he has disclosed the account[19]. In *City Discount Co.* v. *McLean*, BLACKBURN, J., said:

> "If the debtor does not appropriate it, the creditor has a right to do so to any debt he pleases, and that not only at the instant of payment, but up to the very last moment"[20].

He may even appropriate when being examined as a witness in an action brought by him against the debtor[1].

There is in this respect no difference between a specialty and a simple contract debt, and if both exist the creditor may appropriate to either. If there is a real debt, the creditor may appropriate the payment to it, though the right of action is unenforceabie, *e.g.* because the agreement was not evidenced in writing as required by the Statute of Frauds, or the right of action is gone, for instance a debt barred by the Limitation Act[2]. The creditor must, however, have some legal or equitable claim, though it may not be enforceable by action; he cannot appropriate a payment to a demand arising out of a contract forbidden by law[3], nor does his right to appropriate remain after a judgment which does not give effect to it[4].

9. *Current accounts.*—Where there is an account current between the parties—*e.g.* a banking account or a current account for goods supplied —the general rule is that

> "If there is nothing to show a contrary intention, the items of credit must be appropriated to the items of debt in order of date"[5].

This, however, is but a presumption, and it may be rebutted by evidence showing a contrary intention.

> "A particular mode of dealing, and more especially any stipulation between the parties, may entirely vary the case"[6].

In the case of a current account between banker and customer the rule in *Clayton's Case* may operate to the disadvantage of the banker unless care is taken to prevent it from so doing. Thus,

> where a mortgage is given to a bank to secure a running account and the customer subsequently creates a second mortgage on the property in favour of a third person, the banker cannot, after notice

---

19. *Simson* v. *Ingham* (1823), 2 B. & C. 65.
20. (1874), L. R. 9 C. P. 692, 700; *The Mecca*, [1897] A. C. 286.
1. *Seymour* v. *Pickett*, [1905] 1 K. B. 715.
2. *Mills* v. *Fowkes* (1839), 5 Bing. N. C. 455.
3. *Lamprell* v. *Guardians of Billericay Union* (1849), 3 Exch. 283, 307; *A. Smith & Son (Bognor Regis)* v. *Walker*, [1952] 1 All E. R. 1008.
4. *Smith* v. *Betty*, [1903] 2 K. B. 317.
5. BLACKBURN, J., in *City Discount Co.* v. *McLean* (1874), L. R. 9 C. P. 692, 701.
6. *Henniker* v. *Wigg* (1869), L. R. 4 Q. B. 792; *Re Hallet's Estate* (1880), 13 Ch. D. 696.

of such second mortgage, make *further* advances to the prejudice of the second mortgagee[7].

If the banker continues the account, all further advances will be unsecured and all payments in will be appropriated to the previous advances secured by the mortgage, so that in the end the banker may find that the security has been wholly or in part satisfied, while the debt in substance remains unpaid, for there is no ground of presuming any intention on the part of the bank to apply payments in to the unsecured items in order of date in priority to the secured items[8]. The same result may happen in the case of a continuing guarantee which has been determined by notice. However, if the banker does not wish to enforce immediate payment of the secured balance, he can avoid the operation of the rule in *Clayton's Case* by the simple device of breaking the account and opening a new and distinct account for fresh transactions[9].

Trust moneys.—As against his *cestui que trust* a trustee who has mixed trust money with his own moneys in his banking account may not set up the rule in *Clayton's Case*, and it will be presumed that in drawing from the bank he drew on his own and not on the trust money[10]; but if the trustee exhausts his own money and draws out part of the trust moneys, the charge of the *cestui que trust* upon the credit balance is limited to the lowest sum to which the trust moneys have at any time been reduced, although afterwards further moneys may be paid into the account by the trustee; unless he has expressly appropriated such further moneys to the replacement of the amount improperly withdrawn[11]. Where the contest is between two claimants to a mixed fund consisting of moneys belonging to both, the rule in *Clayton's Case* applies if the money has been paid into an active banking account. Otherwise the claimants share *pari passu*[12]. The position is the same where an innocent party has received trust money without consideration and mixed it with his own[13].

10. *Receipts.*—A receipt is the best evidence of payment, but it is not the only evidence, nor is it, unless under seal, conclusive in favour of the payer—*e.g.* its effect may be rebutted by evidence; it may be

---

7. *Hopkinson* v. *Rolt* (1861), 9 H. L. Cas. 514. But by s. 94, Law of Property Act 1925, notice of the second mortgage would not prevent the bank claiming priority if it was under a contractual obligation to allow the overdraft.
8. *Deeley* v. *Lloyds Bank*, [1912] A. C. 756.
9. Remarks of Lord SELBORNE, *Re Sherry* (1884), 25 Ch. D., at p. 702.
10. *Re Hallett's Estate* (1880), 13 Ch. D. 696.
11. *James Roscoe (Bolton), Ltd.* v. *Winder*, [1915] 1 Ch. 62.
12. *Re Stenning*, [1895] 2 Ch. 433; *Diplock, Re, Diplock* v. *Wintle*, [1948] 2 All E. R. 318; [1948] Ch. 465; *affd. sub nom. Ministry of Health* v. *Simpson*, [1950] 2 All E. R. 1137; [1951] A. C. 251, H. L.
13. *Re Diplock, supra.*

upset by proof of error. Where a cheque, whether indorsed or not, appears to have been paid through the payee's bank account, that is evidence of payment[14]. The stamp duty on a receipt for £2 or more was abolished by the Finance Act 1970.

III INTEREST

Interest is not generally allowed at common law in the absence of agreement, but in certain cases a creditor is entitled to simple interest. Compound interest is never allowed, unless by express or implied contract[15].

Interest is chargeable as of right:

1. Where there is an express or implied agreement to pay it;
2. Where the usage of trade allows it;
3. On money obtained by fraud and retained by fraud[16];
4. On a judgment debt interest runs at $7\frac{1}{2}$ per cent. until the judgment is satisfied[17];
5. On a sum directed to be paid by an arbitration award interest is payable from the date of the award at $7\frac{1}{2}$ per cent, per annum, unless the award otherwise directs, *i.e.* directs that the award will carry no interest at all[18].
6. When by Act of Parliament it is provided that interest shall be payable. The Bills of Exchange Act 1882, for instance, provides that interest from time of maturity, or (in the case of a bill payable on demand) from date of presentment for payment, shall be payable by the party liable on a dishonoured bill[19].

In any proceedings tried in any court of record[20] for the recovery of any debt or damages, the court may, if it thinks fit, order that there shall be included in the sum for which judgment is given interest at such rate as it thinks fit on the whole or any part of the debt or damages for the whole or any part of the period between the date when the cause of action arose and the date of the judgment. The above powers were conferred on the court by s. 3 of the Law Reform (Miscellaneous

---

14. Cheques Act 1957, s. 3.
15. *Fergusson* v. *Fyfe* (1841), 8 C. &. F. 121.
16. *Johnson* v. *R.*, [1904] A. C. 817.
17. Judgments Act 1838, s. 17 amended by the Administration of Justice Act 1970, s. 44 and the Judgment Debts (Rate of Interest) Order 1971 (S. I. 1971 No. 491).
18. Arbitration Act 1950, s. 20 and *Timber Shipping Co. S.A.* v. *London and Overseas Freighters, Ltd.*, [1971] 2 All E. R. 599; [1972] A. C. 1, H. L.
19. Section 57.
20. An arbitrator has the same power (*Chandris* v. *Isbrandtsen-Moller Co. Inc.*, [1950] 2 All E. R. 618; [1951] 1 K. B. 240).

Provisions) Act 1934, but the statute does not authorise the giving of compound interest, or apply to any debt upon which interest is payable as of right.

IV BREACH OF CONTRACT

Upon any breach of contract, there is always a right of action for damages, and even where no actual loss or damage can be proved, nominal damages will be awarded.

If the contract *as a whole* is broken or there is a breach of a *condition* of the contract, *i.e.* one of the more important terms of the contract, the injured party has several remedies including the right to treat the contract as discharged. On the other hand for breach of a warranty, *i.e.* a less important term of the contract, damages alone may be claimed.

Thus in *The Mihalis Angelos*[1]

> Owners of a ship promised the charterers that it would be expected ready to load "about July 1st" at the port of Haiphong. On July 17th it was clear that it would be some time before the ship would reach Haiphong and the charterers cancelled the charterparty. *Held:* the clause that the ship would be ready to load was a condition of the contract and its breach entitled the charterers to repudiate the contract.

However, some terms of contract may not be categorised as either conditions or warranties but are complex terms and the remedy for breach will depend on whether the breach that occurs is so serious as to frustrate the commercial purpose of the contract. Thus, where there was a breach of an owner's undertaking in a charterparty to provide a "seaworthy" ship, the charterers were held not entitled to treat the contract as discharged because the delays consequent on the breach did not frustrate the commercial purpose of the contract[2].

1. *Total Breach.*—If in a contract between A and X, X expressly or impliedly repudiates the contract entirely or is in breach of a condition of the contract, A has the following remedies:

> (i) he may treat the breach as a discharge, refuse to perform his part, and resist successfully any action brought upon the contract[3];

---

1. [1970] 3 All E. R. 125; [1971] 1 Q. B. 164, C. A.
2. *Hong Kong Fir Shipping Co., Ltd.* v. *Kawasaki Kisen Kaisha, Ltd.*, [1961] 2 All E. R. 257, *on appeal*, [1962] 2 Q. B. 26. Moreover, the word "condition" in a contract may be construed to mean simply a term of the contract especially if it would be unreasonable for *any* breach to entitle the other party to treat the contract as at an end: *Wickman Machine Tool Sales, Ltd.* v. *Schuler*, [1972] 2 All E. R. 1173; [1972] 1 W. L. R. 840, C. A.
3. See *General Billposting Co.* v. *Atkinson*, [1908] 1 Ch. 537; affirmed, [1909] A. C. 118, *ante*, p. 49.

(ii) he may bring a claim for damages either by an action of his own, or by way of counterclaim in an action brought against him by the other party;

(iii) he may, if he has performed any part of the agreement, bring an action for an amount equivalent to the work done: this is called suing on a *quantum meruit*, and the claim should be co-extensive with the work done[4];

(iv) in certain cases he may bring an action for specific performance;

(v) where there is a dispute as to whether the contract has been repudiated he may (unless he has refused to accept the repudiation) ask the court for a declaration and his refusal to perform his part of the contract meanwhile will not be treated as repudiation[5].

Although the injured party is always entitled to treat the contract as discharged when the other party has broken the contract as a whole or broken a condition of the contract, he is not bound to do so. It follows that such a breach does not of itself terminate the contract. Thus, if X expressly or impliedly repudiates his contract with A, A may decline to "accept" the repudiation; and if this is possible without X's concurrence, proceed to perform his side of the contract and claim the full consideration agreed for A's work.

In *White and Carter (Councils), Ltd.* v. *McGregor*[6],

A agreed to display advertisements for X's garage for 3 years. Later the same day, X repudiated the agreement but A declined to accept the repudiation, proceeded with the advertisement display, and sued for the contract price. *Held:* A was not obliged to accept the repudiation or sue for damages but was entitled instead to carry out his side of the contract as he had, and claim the full contract price.

However if X, an employer, has wrongfully dismissed A, his employee, this does automatically bring the contract of employment to an end[7].

2. *Anticipatory breach.*—The repudiation of a contract by one party, X, at once entitles the other, A, to treat the contract as discharged and to sue for damages, even though time for performance has not yet arrived.

For an example, see *Hochster* v. *De la Tour*[8],

where plaintiff on April 12th was engaged to act as courier to the defendant, the employment to begin in June. In May the

---

4. *Farnsworth* v. *Garrard* (1807), 1 Camp. 38; *Planché* v. *Colburn* (1831), 8 Bing. 14.

5. See *Howard* v. *Pickford Tool Co., Ltd.*, [1951] 1 K. B. 417.

6. [1961] 3 All E. R. 1178; [1962] A. C. 413.

7. *Denmark Productions, Ltd.* v. *Boscobel Productions Ltd.*, [1968] 3 All E. R. 513; [1969] 1 Q. B. 699, C. A.

8. (1853), 2 E. & B. 678. See also *Frost* v. *Knight* (1872), L. R. 7 Ex. 111.

defendant wrote to inform plaintiff that his services would not be required, and an action was at once commenced, although June had not arrived.

It was held that the action would lie, Lord CAMPBELL saying:

"Where there is a contract to do an act on a future day, there is a relation constituted between the parties in the meantime by the contract, and they impliedly promise that in the meantime neither will do anything to the prejudice of the other inconsistent with that relation".

However, as has been seen, repudiation of the contract by X does not automatically discharge the contract. It is only discharged if A accepts the repudiation. If A does not accept the repudiation, but keeps the contract open, X may change his mind and perform his side of the contract. In this event, X would of course be under no liability for his breach. Moreover, if A does not accept X's repudiation, a supervening event may cause "frustration" of the contract so that both parties are discharged from any liability[9]. In *Avery* v. *Bowden*[10],

X chartered A's ship and agreed to load the ship with cargo at Odessa within 45 days. Before this period elapsed, X repudiated the contract by informing the ship's captain that the cargo was not available. This repudiation was not accepted by A and the outbreak of the Crimean War caused the contract to be discharged by frustration. *Held:* Since the contract had been discharged by frustration, not by X's breach, X was not liable to A in damages.

Repudiation during performance will have a similar effect. In *Cort* v. *Ambergate Rail. Co.*[11],

the plaintiffs agreed to supply the defendants with 3,900 tons of railway chairs at a certain price, the chairs to be delivered in certain quantities on certain dates. These were partially delivered, when the defendants said they would take no more.

It was held that an action could be brought at once, without showing further actual delivery, mere readiness to deliver being sufficient. Lord CAMPBELL said:

"When there is an executory contract for the manufacturing and supply of goods from time to time, to be paid for after delivery, if the purchaser, having accepted and paid for a portion of the goods contracted for, give notice to the vendor not to manufacture any more as he has no occasion for them, and will not accept or pay for them, the vendor having been desirous and able to complete

---

9. See *post*, p. 96.
10. (1856) 6 E. & B., 953.
11. (1851), 17 Q. B. 127.

the contract, he may, without manufacturing and tendering the rest of the goods, maintain an action against the purchaser for breach of contract".

If one party makes the performance of a contract impossible, this also gives an immediate right to treat the contract as at an end and sue for damages. In *Lovelock* v. *Franklyn*[12],

> the defendant agreed to assign his interest in a lease to the plaintiff, but before the date agreed upon for performance arrived, he assigned to another.

It was held that the plaintiff could bring an action without waiting the expiration of the time.

3. *Lump sum contracts.*—If X agrees with A to do an entire work (*e.g.* to build, or to serve as an employee for a fixed time) for a specified sum, and the entire work is not carried out, this amounts to a total breach of contract. As a general rule, X cannot claim the specified sum nor can X sue on a *quantum meruit*. Thus, a builder who abandons an entire contract to erect houses after partly constructing them can recover nothing, even though the owner takes the benefit of his work by completing the building[13]. However, X can recover from A in respect of partial performance where it has been so agreed or where it can be shown that the non-fulfilment was caused by the fault of A or (probably) where the non-fulfilment is due to a frustrating event[14].

The performance of the whole work is in such cases a condition precedent to the right to sue. But under a builder's contract to erect or repair a house, if the *work* has been *substantially completed*, then although part of the work has been omitted or done badly, the builder can recover the contract price subject to a deduction for defective work[15].

4. *Partial breach.*—Where the contract between A and X is not a lump sum contract, then if there is a failure by X to perform part only of the contract or a repudiation by X of part only of the contract, it is a matter of construction whether the court considers such part so vital to the contract that the other party should be entitled to treat the contract as discharged as well as to claim damages. Otherwise, the

---

12. (1846), 8 Q. B. 371.
13. *Sumpter* v. *Hedges*, [1898] 1 Q. B. 673. See also *Forman & Co.* v. *The Ship "Liddesdale"*, [1900] A. C. 190; *Vigers* v. *Cook*, [1910] 2 K. B. 475.
14. See *post*, p. 98.
15. *Dakin (H.) & Co., Ltd.* v. *Lee*, [1916] 1 K. B. 566; *Hoenig* v. *Isaacs*, [1952] 2 All E. R. 176, *cf. Bolton* v. *Mahadeva*, [1972] 2 All E. R. 1322; [1972] 1 W. L. R. 1009, C. A. It has been held by the Divisional Court and SCRUTTON, L.J., that this principle does not apply against a surety who has only guaranteed payment of the contract price on the work being "duly executed": *Eshelby* v. *Federated European Bank, Ltd.*, [1931] All E. R. Rep. 840; [1932] 1 K. B. 254, 433, C. A.

other party is entitled to a remedy in damages for the particular breach, but is not entitled to treat the contract as discharged[16]. Lord BLACKBURN in *Mersey Steel and Iron Co.* v. *Naylor*, said:

> "The rule of law . . . is that, where there is a contract in which there are two parties, each side having to do something . . . If you see that the failure to perform one part of it goes to the root of the contract, goes to the foundation of the whole, it is a good defence to say, 'I am not going to perform my part of it.' . . . But Mr. Cohen contended that whenever there was a breach of a material part of the contract, it necessarily went to the root of the matter. I cannot agree with that at all"[17].

Frequently it happens that the contract is divisible into various stipulations—*e.g.*

> to deliver cargo at certain stated intervals, on March 1st, April 1st, and so on, in which case the question whether the breach of one of them constitutes repudiation of the contract depends mainly on the ratio of the instalment to the whole contract and the probability of repetition of the breach[18].

If, however, the parties expressly agree that breach of a single term shall entitle the other party to treat the contract as abandoned, the general rule is inapplicable[19]. And if a party shows by his acts, or otherwise, an intention not any longer to be bound by his contract, this gives the other a right to refuse further performance, though, so far, one term only has been broken.

In the case of *Freeth* v. *Burr*[20],

> the plaintiff agreed to buy of defendants some iron, to be delivered in two instalments, net cash within a fortnight of delivery; after delivery, and when the first payment was due, plaintiff refused to pay, mistakenly believing he had a right of set-off for late delivery.

After Lord COLERIDGE had said:

> "The real matter for consideration is, whether the acts or conduct of the one do or do not amount to an intimation of an intention to abandon and altogether to refuse performance of the contract,"

it was *held*, that the buyer's acts did not exhibit an intention to break the entire contract, so as to justify the defendant's refusal to continue performance as the buyer had acted *bona fide* under a mistake of law;

---

16. See notes to *Pordage* v. *Cole* (1669), 1 Wm. Saund. 548 (ed. 1871).
17. (1884), 9 App. Cas. 434, 443.
18. *Cf.* p. 206. In some cases each instalment is treated as a separate contract: see *Jackson* v. *Rotax Motor and Cycle Co.*, [1910] 2 K. B. 937, and contrast *Thorpe* v. *Fasey*, [1949] 2 All E. R. 393; [1949] Ch. 649.
19. *Cutter* v. *Powell* (1807), 2 Sm. L. C. (13th ed.) 1.
20. (1874) L. R. 9 C. P. 208.

the defendant's remedy was in damages for breach of contract[1]. The House of Lords approved the principle in *Mersey Steel and Iron Co. v. Naylor*[2].

V DAMAGES

Whenever a contractual term is broken, the injured party is entitled to claim damages. However, damages cannot be claimed in respect of every loss which may result from the breach. The loss must not be too remote:

> "The damages should be such as may fairly and reasonably be considered either arising naturally, *i.e.* according to the usual course of things, from such breach of contract itself, or such as may reasonably be supposed to have been in the contemplation of both parties at the time they made the contract, as the probable result of the breach of it"[3].

In *Victoria Laundry (Windsor), Ltd. v. Newman Industries, Ltd.*[4],

> B agreed to sell to A, a laundry company, a boiler to be delivered on a certain date. B did not deliver the boiler until five months after the agreed delivery date. B was aware of the nature of A's business. A claim (i) for loss of profits that would have been earned through the extension of the business, and (ii) for loss of highly lucrative dyeing contracts. *Held:* A was entitled to damages for loss under head (i) but since B had no knowledge of the particular dyeing contracts made by A, A was entitled under head (ii) only to a normal rate of profit from dyeing contracts and not to the exceptional profit A would have made.

In *The Heron II*[5],

> A chartered a ship from B to carry 3,000 tons of sugar from Constanza to Basrah with the intention of selling the sugar at Basrah. B made deviations in breach of the contract so that the sugar arrived in Basrah 9 days later than expected and the price obtainable for the sugar was some £4,000 less than it would have been had the sugar arrived on time. B did not know of

---

1. *Freeth* v. *Burr* (1874), L. R. 9 C. P. 208, 213; see also *Withers* v. *Reynolds* (1819), 2 B. & Ad. 882; *Simpson* v. *Crippin* (1873), L. R. 8 Q. B. 14; and *cf. Honck* v. *Muller* (1881), 7 Q. B. D. 92.
2. (1884), 9 App. Cas. 434. See also *Thorpe* v. *Fasey*, [1949] 2 All E. R. 393; [1949] Ch. 649; *Peter Dumanil & Co., Ltd.* v. *James Ruddin, Ltd.*, [1953] 2 All E.R. 294.
3. *Hadley* v. *Baxendale* (1854), 9 Ex. Ch. 341.
4. [1949] 1 All E. R. 997; [1949] 2 K. B. 528.
5. [1967] 3 All E. R. 686; The House of Lords said that the rule in tort—that all damage reasonably foreseeable was recoverable (*The Wagon Mound No. 1*, [1961] 1 All E. R. 404; [1961] A. C. 388, P. C.)—was not the same as the rule in contract enunciated in *Hadley* v. *Baxendale* (1854), 9 Exch. 341.

A's intention to sell the sugar in Basrah but the House of Lords *held* that B must have realised it was *not unlikely* that the sugar would be sold on arrival at the then market price and that prices were apt to fluctuate daily. A was entitled to his loss of profit as damages for B's breach of contract.

Assessment of Damages

Assuming that the loss is not too remote from the breach of contract, the amount of damages recoverable is the amount necessary to put the injured party in the same position (so far as money can do it) as if the contract had been performed[6]. Thus, the principle on which damages are assessed is compensatory and exemplary damages cannot be awarded for breach of contract[7]. However, although when a breach of contract has occurred the injured party is entitled to damages sufficient to compensate him for his loss, he is himself under a duty to take any reasonable steps which would mitigate his loss. Thus, in *Brace* v. *Calder*[8],

B agreed to work for a partnership C & Co. for a certain period. Before the period expired, two of the four partners retired. The remaining partners continued the business and were willing to continue to employ B, but B refused. *Held:* The dissolution of the partnership caused by the retirements was a wrongful dismissal of B, but B was entitled to nominal damages only since he had failed to mitigate his loss by accepting the offer of continued employment made by the remaining partners.

An estimate of damages may be based on probabilities, but a court will not award damages of a problematical character upon the assumption that numerous events of a contingent nature would have happened[9]. However, although damages which are incapable of assessment cannot be recovered, the fact that they are difficult to assess with certainty of precision, does not deprive the plaintiff of the right to recover them. The Court must do its best to estimate the loss, and a contingency may be taken into account. In *Chaplin* v. *Hicks*[10],

the defendant advertised that he would employ, as actresses at remunerative salaries, twelve ladies to be selected by him out of fifty whom the readers of various newspapers, in which the candidates' photographs were published, had adjudged to be the most beautiful. The plaintiff won her section and became one of the fifty eligible for selection by the defendant; but the defendant

---

6. *Wertheim* v. *Chicoutimi Pulp Co.*, [1911] A. C. 301.
7. *Addis* v. *Gramophone Co., Ltd.*, [1909] A. C. 488.
8. [1895] 2 Q. B. 253.
9. *Sapwell* v. *Bass*, [1910] 2 K. B. 486.
10. [1911] 2 K. B. 786.

made an unreasonable appointment which the plaintiff could not keep, and proceeded to select twelve out of the forty-nine who were able to keep the appointment. The jury assessed the plaintiff's damages at £100 for the loss of her chance of obtaining a prize and the Court of Appeal refused to disturb the verdict.

Effect on damages of tax liability

Since damages are compensatory, whenever a claim for damages includes a claim for loss of income, the income tax (and surtax) that would have been payable on such income must be taken into account[11]. In *Parsons* v. *B.N.M. Laboratories, Ltd.*[12]

> P claimed damages for wrongful dismissal from his employment, the loss of salary and commission amounting to £1,200. *Held:* That sum must be reduced by £320 being the amount of income tax which would have been payable on the lost salary and commission.

Liquidated damages

If the parties to a contract agree that, in the event of a breach, the party in default shall pay a specified sum to the other party, that sum is claimable on breach if it is a genuine pre-estimate of the probable loss which will be caused by the breach. The sum is then termed "liquidated damages", and even if the actual loss incurred is greater, only that sum may be claimed[13]. If, however, the sum specified as payable on breach is not a genuine pre-estimate of loss but is meant instead to deter a party from breaking the contract, the sum is known as a "penalty" and is not recoverable. In this latter case, the plaintiff will instead recover damages assessed in accordance with the general principles already discussed.

In determining whether the sum fixed is in the nature of damages, or of a penalty, the court looks not to the name by which the parties have called it, but to its actual nature—*e.g.*

> if the parties fix a very large sum, and call it damages for non-payment of a small sum, the court will regard it as a penalty[14];

and the same view will be taken by the court if the sum fixed is extravagant, exorbitant or unconscionable in regard to any possible amount

---

11. *British Transport Commission* v. *Gourley*, [1955] 3 All E. R. 796; [1956] A. C. 185.
12. [1963] 2 All E. R. 658; [1964] 1 Q. B. 95, C. A. See Law Reform Committee, Seventh Report (*Effect of tax liability on damages*), Cmnd. 501. Where the damages for loss of earnings exceeds £5,000, the court will have to take account of the fact that the excess is taxable under the Income and Corporation Taxes Act 1970, ss. 187, 188 (3).
13. See *Cellulose Acetate Silk Co.* v. *Widnes Foundry* (*1925*), *Ltd.*, [1925] A. C. 20.
14. See *Kemble* v. *Farren* (1829), 6 Bing. 141. See also *Alder* v. *Moore*, [1961] 1 All E. R. 1; [1961] 2 Q. B. 57.

of damages or any kind of damage which may be conceived to have been within the contemplation of the parties when they made the contract.

Further, a sum payable on one event only will in general be regarded as liquidated damages[15]; but if payable on the breach of one or more stipulations of different degrees of importance, the presumption is that the parties intended the sum to be penal[16]. But even in the latter case, if the damage is the same in kind for every possible breach, is incapable of being precisely estimated, is a fair pre-estimate of the probable damage and not unconscionable, the sum named will not be treated as a penalty. In *Dunlop Pneumatic Tyre Co. v. New Garage, etc., Co.*[17]:

> Purchasers of tyres agreed not to tamper with the marks on them, not to sell them below listed prices, not to exhibit without consent, and to pay £5 as "liquidated damages" for every breach. *Held:* The £5 sum was claimable as liquidated damages and was not a penalty.

Foreign currency

Where the amount payable for damages for breach of contract requires in the first instance to be assessed in foreign currency, as an English judgment must be expressed in sterling, the proper date for conversion into English money of a loss proved in foreign currency is the date when it was incurred, and not the date when the judgment is pronounced. An alteration in the rate of exchange subsequent to a breach of contract is not an element in the assessment of damages[18].

VI SPECIFIC PERFORMANCE

This is a discretionary remedy granted formerly by courts of equity but now by all courts, where damages of themselves will not be a sufficient compensation. It is used mostly with regard to contracts concerning land, but in certain cases the courts will compel performance of other contracts. Thus, a contract for the sale of a thing of rare beauty, or of one with regard to which there is a fancy value—*e.g.* heirlooms—may be ordered to be specifically performed[19]. But specific performance of an agreement will not be granted:

---

15. *Clydebank, etc. Co. v. Don José Castaneda*, [1905] A. C. 6.
16. *Elphinstone (Lord) v. Monkland, etc. Co.* (1886), 11 App. Cas. 332; *Law v. Redditch Local Board*, [1892] 1 Q. B. 127; *Strickland v. Williams*, [1899] 1 Q. B. 382; *Willson v. Love*, [1896] 1 Q. B. 628; *Pye v. British Automobile Syndicate*, [1906] 1 K. B. 425.
17. [1915] A. C. 79; followed in *Bridge v. Campbell Discount Co., Ltd.*, [1962] 1 All E. R. 385; [1962] A. C. 600, H. L.
18. *S. S. Celia v. S. S. Volturno*, [1921] 2 A. C. 544; *Di Ferdinando v. Simon, Smits & Co.*, [1920] 3 K. B. 409. See also *post*, p. 110.
19. *Dowling v. Betjemann* (1862), 2 J. & H. 544. See also Sale of Goods Act 1893, s. 52, *post*, p. 206.

1. If the contract is for personal services, *e.g.* a contract of employment[20].
2. If the constant supervision of the court would be necessary to secure obedience to the order. Thus, where the lessor of a flat broke a contractual term to provide a resident porter with certain defined duties, the court declined to order specific performance[1].
3. If it would be unenforceable against the person asking for specific performance, *e.g.* where the plaintiff seeking specific performance of an agreement to sell land is a minor[2].

VII INJUNCTION

This too is a discretionary remedy which a court may award where damages would not be an adequate remedy. An injunction is a court order restraining a party to a contract from acting in breach of it. Thus, if a servant is bound by a valid covenant in restraint of trade, his master may obtain an injunction to prevent him from acting in breach of it. Disobedience to the order is punishable as a contempt of court.

It has been noted that a court will not grant an order of specific performance of a personal contract and it follows from this that no court will award an injunction to restrain a servant from breaking his promise to serve as this would indirectly amount to compelling him to perform a personal contract. Even where the servant has entered into a negative stipulation, *i.e.* an express promise not to enter into other employment, no injunction will be ordered if the effect of granting it would be to compel the servant to serve. In *Page One Records, Ltd.* v. *Britton*[3]:

> a group of pop musicians, The Troggs, agreed to let X manage their careers and not to let anyone else act as their manager.

---

20. Similarly, by the Industrial Relations Act 1971, s. 128 (1), no court may compel an employee to work either by way of an order of specific performance or injunction. On a complaint of "unfair dismissal" an industrial tribunal may order a complainant employee to be re-engaged but if this order is disobeyed the tribunal is empowered only to award compensation: s. 106.
1. *Ryan* v. *Mutual Tontine Westminster Chambers Association*, [1893] 1 Ch. 116.
2. *Flight* v. *Bolland* (1828), 4 Russ. 298.
3. [1967] 3 All E. R. 822. *Cf. Lumley* v. *Wagner* (1852), 1 D. M. & G. 604 and *Warner Brothers Pictures Incorporated* v. *Nelson*, [1936] 3 All E. R. 160; [1937] 1 K. B. 209, (injunction preventing film star from working for X would not compel her to work for Y with whom she was already in contract because she could instead pursue another albeit less remunerative occupation). And see *Hill* v. *C. A. Parsons & Co., Ltd.*, [1971] 3 All E. R. 1345; [1972] Ch. 305, C. A. *post*, p. 438.

After a year, The Troggs repudiated their contract with X and X sought an injunction to restrain The Troggs from engaging someone else as their manager. *Held:* an injunction would in effect compel The Troggs to continue to employ X and this would amount to enforcing performance of a contract for personal services. The injunction sought was, therefore, refused.

CHAPTER 8

Termination of Contract and Limitation of Actions

I TERMINATION OF CONTRACT

1. By agreement

The obligations under any contract may be discharged and the contract terminated by mutual agreement, provided that this agreement is by deed or backed by consideration so that it is itself a binding contract.

If neither party has yet performed his obligations under the contract, the mutual release of premises will provide the necessary consideration. Thus, where a contract of sale of goods has been made, a subsequent agreement, whereby the seller is released from his obligation to deliver the goods and the buyer from his obligation to pay for them, effectively terminates the original contract. If, however, A has performed his side of the contract, any promise by A to release B from his obligations will only be a binding contract if it is made under seal or if A obtains some consideration (which may be a promise by B) in return. Where the agreement to discharge a contract is binding because supported by consideration, it is said to comprise an *accord and satisfaction*.

An agreement to discharge a contract which is supported by consideration does not generally have to be in any particular form, so that an oral agreement is effective to discharge a written contract. There are special rules where the original contract is one required by law to be evidenced in writing and the later agreement is intended not merely to terminate it (in which case the agreement of discharge may be oral) but is intended to vary it or substitute a fresh agreement[1].

A contract may be said to be discharged by agreement when it terminates owing to the occurrence of an event, on the happening of which it was previously agreed that all rights and liabilities should cease—*e.g.* A agrees to be bound to B for £500, but if he does a certain act, the bond is to be void. Upon his doing this act, A and B are freed one from the other; the contract is at an end.

2. By performance

See *ante*, pp. 75–84 *et seq.*

---

1. See *ante*, p. 12.

3. By breach

See *ante*, p. 84 *et seq.*

4. Frustration

If, between the time when a contract is made and when it is completed, an event occurs which destroys the basis of the contract, but which is not the fault of either party, the contract is said to be frustrated and, therefore, terminated. The parties are excused from further performance and neither is liable to the other in damages or otherwise[2]. Thus, in *Poussard* v. *Spiers and Pond*[3],

> an actress, engaged to play a leading role in an operetta, was prevented through illness from taking up her role until a week after the season began. *Held:* the contract had terminated and no action lay against her for breach of contract.

In *Taylor* v. *Caldwell*[4],

> an agreement to let a music hall for four days was held to be terminated when the music hall was burnt down before the first day for which it had been let.

If a contract is made on the basis that a certain event will take place, the contract will be discharged by frustration should that event not occur. In *Krell* v. *Henry*[5],

> A hired out the use of a room to B so that B could watch the coronation procession of Edward VII. When the procession was cancelled, it was held that the contract between A and B terminated.

However, the doctrine has no application unless the happening of the event is assumed by both parties to be the sole basis of the contract. So,

> a person, who hired a steamship for the purpose of seeing an intended royal naval review *and* for a day's cruise round the fleet, was held not entitled to refuse payment on ground that the review had been cancelled[6].

Clearly, if further performance of a contract is rendered illegal, for example, because an Act of Parliament has been passed having this effect, the contract is frustrated. Similarly a contract with someone abroad is frustrated if war is declared and performance of the contract would involve trading with the enemy. Even temporary prohibition of a contract by lawful Government action may cause frustration of it. Thus in *Metropolitan Water Board* v. *Dick, Kerr & Co.*[7].

---

2. The doctrine of frustration does not apply to an event for which the parties have expressly and completely provided in their contract.
3. (1876), 1 Q. B. D. 410.
4. (1863), 3 B. & S. 826.
5. [1903] 2 K. B. 740.
6. *Herne Bay Steam Boat Co.* v. *Hutton*, [1903] 2 K. B. 683.
7. [1918] 1 A. C. 119.

the Ministry of Munitions in the exercise of statutory powers conferred by the Defence of the Realm Act required contractors to cease work under a contract for the construction of a reservoir and to place their plant at the disposal of the Ministry of Munitions. By its terms the contract enabled the engineer to grant an extension of time for completion where the contractors had been unduly delayed or impeded; but the House of Lords *held*

    (*a*) that this provision did not apply; and

    (*b*) that the contract had ceased to be operative because the character and duration of the interruption would make it when resumed a really different contract based on changed conditions.

If only a part of the contract becomes impossible of performance, that may not be regarded as going to the length of preventing substantial performance of the contract as a whole[8].

Impossibility arising from a lawful act of Her Majesty's Government will excuse performance, *e.g.*,

if the Government has requisitioned specific goods in the hands of the seller before the property in them has passed to the buyer, the seller will be excused from carrying out his contract[9].

Change not fundamental.—Mere delay, difficulty or loss of profit will not of themselves discharge the parties from their contract. An uncontemplated turn of events making the contract more difficult to perform is not sufficient. In *Davis Contractors, Ltd.* v. *Fareham Urban District Council*[10].

Contractors agreed to build 78 houses for the U.D.C. within 8 months. Owing to a severe labour shortage, completion of the work took 22 months and the work cost exceeded the contract price agreed. The contractors argued that the contract had been frustrated and therefore they were not confined to the contract price, but were entitled to a large sum based on the extra costs incurred. *Held:* The contract had not been frustrated.

In *Tsakiroglou & Co. Ltd.* v. *Noblee and Thorl G.m.b.H.*[11],

A contract made in October, 1956, provided for the sale and delivery of groundnuts from the Sudan to Germany, shipment to be made November/December, 1956. The Suez Canal was closed from November, 1956, to April, 1957, and shipment via the Cape of Good Hope would have involved the sellers in additional expense. The sellers failed to deliver. *Held:* The sellers were

---

8. *Eyre* v. *Johnson*, [1946] 1 All E. R. 719; [1946] K. B. 481.
9. *Re Shipton Anderson & Co. and Harrison Bros. & Co.'s Arbitration*, [1915] 3 K. B. 676.
10. [1956] 2 All E. R. 145; [1956] A. C. 696.
11. [1961] 2 All E. R. 179; [1962] A. C. 93. See also *Ocean Tramp Tankers Corporation* v. *v/o Sovfracht*, [1964] 1 All E. R. 161, C. A.

liable for breach of contract. The contract had not been frustrated by the closing of the Suez Canal because the change of circumstances was not sufficiently fundamental.

Self-induced frustration.—It follows from the definition of frustration, given above, that if one party to a contract deliberately brings about the event which destroys the basis of the contract, the doctrine of frustration has no application. The party in breach is, of course, liable in damages to the other if he fails to perform the contract. Thus, in *Maritime National Fish, Ltd.* v. *Ocean Trawlers, Ltd.*[12],

> the appellants chartered a trawler from the respondents for use in otter fishing. The Canadian Ministry of Fisheries allowed the appellants 3 licences for trawlers which could be used for otter fishing and the appellants applied these licences to 3 trawlers that they owned. *Held:* The charter contract was not frustrated because it was the appellants' own action that prevented them using the chartered trawler for otter fishing. They were still liable for the contract charges.

Leases.—There is considerable uncertainty as to whether the doctrine of frustration has any application to leases. A number of cases do establish that if, during the continuance of a lease, the premises are burnt down by fire or requisitioned by the Government in wartime, the obligations under the lease, for example, the tenant's obligation to pay rent, continue[13]. The reason is that the basis of the contract is the *estate* and whatever happens, that continues to exist. However, two Law Lords *obiter* in *Cricklewood Property and Investment Trust, Ltd.* v. *Leighton's Investment Trust, Ltd.*[14] expressed the view that if after a building lease, for say 99 years, was executed, the land is permanently zoned as open space, the lease would be discharged by frustration.

Effect of frustration.—The effect of frustration at common law was that the contract automatically came to an end and that any obligation that arose before the frustrating event remained enforceable[15]. However, in 1942 the House of Lords ruled that money paid for a consideration that had *wholly* failed was recoverable[15]. But this did not prevent injustices where one party had incurred expense in carrying out part of the contract. Now, the Law Reform (Frustrated Contracts) Act

---

12. [1935] All E. R. Rep. 86; [1935] A. C. 524. It is uncertain whether the negligent as distinct from deliberate action of a party which destroys the basis of the contract also prevents the operation of the doctrine of frustration.
13. *Redmond* v. *Dainton*, [1920] 2 K. B. 256.
14. [1945] 1 All E. R. 252; [1945] A. C. 221.
15. *Chandler* v. *Webster* [1904] 1 K. B. 493; *Fibrosa Spolka Akcyjna* v. *Fairbairn Lawson Combe Barbour, Ltd.*, [1942] 2 All E. R. 122; [1943] A. C. 32.

1943, provides that upon frustration, except in so far as it is expressiy provided for by the contract the following results ensue:

   (i) all sums paid or payable in pursuance of the contract before its discharge are recoverable or cease to be payable;

  (ii) the court may make an allowance in respect of expenses incurred by the other party if it deems it just to do so, but only up to the amounts paid or payable before the frustrating event occurred;

 (iii) where one party has benefited by acts of partial performance done by the other party, the court may order him to pay such a sum as is reasonable in all the circumstances;

The Act has no application to contracts for the carriage of goods by sea, to voyage charter parties, to contracts of insurance, or to contracts for the sale of goods which perish before the risk passes to the buyer[16].

5. Miscellaneous

A contract may be put an end to—

   (i) by merger. Where a judgment is obtained for breach of contract, the original cause of action is merged in the judgment and no further action is possible for breach of the contract, even if fresh damage results[17];

  (ii) by bankruptcy (unless the contract is one which the trustee in bankruptcy can and does adopt), so far as the contract gives rise to a debt provable in bankruptcy;

 (iii) if the contract is in writing, by an unauthorised alteration in a material part made by a party seeking to enforce the contract.

II LIMITATION OF ACTIONS

The Limitation Act 1939 provides that actions founded on simple contract shall not be brought after the expiration of six years from the date on which the cause of action accrued; while an action on a contract under seal must be brought within twelve years of the accrual of the cause of action. A judgment debt is similarly barred after twelve years and interest on the judgment debt cannot be recovered more than six years after it accrued due.

If the damages claimed include damages for personal injuries, the time limit is reduced to three years[18]. To cover the position where the injuries resulting from a tort or breach of contract only become manifest after a considerable time-lag, the Limitation Act 1963 as amended by the Law Reform (Miscellaneous Provisions) Act 1971, allows an action

---

16. See *post*, p. 184.
17. *Conquer* v. *Boot*, [1928] 2 K. B. 336.
18. Law Reform (Limitation of Actions, etc.) Act 1954, s. 2 (1).

to be brought despite the expiry of three years from the accrual of the cause of action in certain circumstances. Where an action includes a claim for personal injuries, and the material facts[19] relating to the cause of action were at all times outside the knowledge of the plaintiff until a date falling outside the three-year period, leave of the court may be obtained for an action to be brought more than three years after the cause of action accrued. It must, however, be brought within three years of the date when the plaintiff learns of the material facts. If the injured party dies, his personal representatives must bring the action either within three years of the death or within three years of their learning the material facts.

Parties under disability.—The running of time may be suspended if the parties are under certain disabilities. If a plaintiff, when the cause of action arises,

(i) is a minor, *i.e.* under eighteen years of age; or
(ii) is of unsound mind;

the period of limitation does not begin to run against him until he ceases to be under such disability or he dies, whichever event first occurs[20]. But where the time has once begun to run, no subsequent disability *i.e.* becoming of unsound mind, will suspend the operation of the statute[1], and if a person has no disability when the right action of accrues, time continues to run although he is succeeded by operation of law by someone who is under a disability[2]. If there are several joint creditors, the disability of some will be no answer by the others for neglect in bringing the action within the time.

Concealed fraud or mistake.—If the action is based on fraud, or the right of action has been concealed by fraud, or is for relief from the consequences of a mistake, the period of limitation does not begin to run until the plaintiff has discovered the fraud or the mistake or could with reasonable diligence have discovered it[3]. "Fraud" in relation to concealment has a somewhat wider meaning than the fraud which would give rise to a separate cause of action. It means conduct on the part of the defendant which hides from the plaintiff his cause of

---

19. In *Central Asbestos Co., Ltd.* v. *Dodd*, [1972] 2 All E. R. 1135; [1972] 3 W. L. R. 333, the House of Lords *held* by a majority that the "material facts" which a man had to prove he did not know in order to bring an action outside the three-year period were matters of fact so that lack of knowledge that there was in law a cause of action did not suffice.
20. Limitation Act 1939, ss. 22, 31 (2). In claims for personal injury, there is no extension of time at all for a minor if he was "in the custody of a parent" at the time the cause of action accrued. The word "custody" denotes a state of fact and it is irrelevant that such custody is inadequately exercised: *Todd* v. *Davison*, [1971] 1 All E. R. 994; [1972] A. C. 392, H. L.
1. *Homfray* v. *Scroope* (1849), 13 Q. B. 509, 512.
2. Limitation Act 1939, s. 22, proviso (*a*).
3. Limitation Act 1939, s. 26.

action so that it would be inequitable for the defendant to rely on the lapse of time as a bar to the claim.

Thus in *Archer* v. *Moss*[4]:

> the defendant developer agreed to build a house for the plaintiff on a concrete raft foundation. Eight years later the plaintiff discovered that the foundation was not as specified in the contract and that the house was unsafe. *Held:* the plaintiff was entitled to sue because his right of action had been concealed by the defendant's fraud in covering up the bad work so that it might not be discovered for a long time.

Where mistake is relied on, it must be an essential ingredient in the action. Thus:

> If A by mistake has overpaid B, A can recover the excess within six years of discovering the mistake in an action for money paid under a mistake of fact. But if B by mistake has claimed too little, he cannot rely on the mistake to extend his time for claiming the balance[5].

Revival of the remedy.—Although the right of action is already barred by lapse of time, it may be revived by acknowledgement of the debt, or by (what is much the same) part payment provided it is clearly referable to the contract.

Section 23 (4) of the Limitation Act 1939 provides:

> "Where any right of action has accrued to recover any debt or other liquidated pecuniary claim . . . and the person liable or accountable therefor acknowledges the claim or makes any payment in respect thereof, the right shall be deemed to have occurred on and not before the date of the acknowledgement or the last payment".

However, neither an acknowledgement nor a part payment is effective to revive a cause of action unless it concerns a "debt or other liquidated pecuniary sum". The debt must be quantified in figures or it must be liquidated in the sense that it is capable of assessment by calculation or by extrinsic evidence without further agreement of the parties. In *Good* v. *Parry*[6],

> a landlord who had received no rent from a tenant of certain premises since 1951, claimed in 1962 for arrears of rent as from 1951. A letter had been sent to the landlord in 1957, signed by

---

4. [1971] 1 All E. R. 747, [1971] 1 Q. B. 406, C. A. See also *Beaman* v. *A.R.T.S. Ltd.*, [1949] 1 All E. R. 465; [1949] 1 K. B. 550; and *King* v. *Victor Parsons & Co.*, [1972] 2 All E. R. 625; [1972] 1 W. L. R. 801.
5. *Phillips-Higgins* v. *Harper*, [1954] 2 All E. R. 51, C. A.
6. [1963] 2 All E. R. 59; [1963] 2 Q. B. 418.

the tenant's agent, saying: "the question of outstanding rent can be settled as a separate agreement as soon as you present your account". *Held:* the letter was merely an admission that there might be some justified claim, but it was not an acknowledgement of a liquidated debt. The landlord's claim for arrears of rent was statute-barred except for arrears due from the last six years.

The acknowledgement must be in writing signed by the debtor or his agent and must be made to the creditor or his agent[7]. It binds the acknowledgor and his assigns but not a joint debtor[8], unless the acknowledgor can be regarded as agent for himself and the joint debtor, as for example if they are partners. A payment made before the period of limitation has expired binds all persons liable for the debt, but a payment made after the expiration of the period binds only the person making the payment and his assigns[9]. An acknowledgement or payment by one of several personal representatives binds the estate[10].

Acknowledgements.—It is an important question in practice whether an acknowledgement is or is not sufficient.

The acknowledgement must be made to the creditor or his agent, but it may be sufficient if it is contained in a balance sheet which a company sends to a creditor who is also a shareholder[11]. And if the balance sheet includes an item "sundry creditors", parol evidence is admissible to show that the debt in question is included in that item[12].

A bare admission of liability is sufficient even if coupled with a refusal or a conditional offer to pay—it need not amount to an implied promise to pay. However, an admission by X that he has signed a promissory note and that no part of the money referred to in it had been paid did not constitute an acknowledgement when the admission formed part of a defence pleading that in effect denied liability[13].

The acknowledgement must be made before action brought[14], and if lost, its contents may be proved by oral evidence[15].

---

7. Limitation Act 1939, s. 24.
8. *Ibid.*, s. 25 (5), (8).
9. *Ibid.*, s. 25 (6), (8).
10. *Ibid.*, s. 25 (7).
11. *Ledingham* v. *Bermejo Estancia Co., Ltd.*, [1947] 1 All E. R. 749. But it depends on the circumstances, *Consolidated Agencies, Ltd.* v. *Bertram, Ltd.*, [1964] 3 All E. R. 282; [1964] 3 W. L. R. 671, P. C. A director cannot make an acknowledgement to himself so as to bind the company: *Coliseum (Barrow) Ltd., Re*, [1930] All E. R. Rep. 221; [1930] 2 Ch. 44. Nor will the auditors' certificate be an acknowledgement to him: *Re Transplanters (Holding Company), Ltd.*, [1958] 2 All E. R. 711.
12. *Jones* v. *Bellegrove Properties, Ltd.*, [1949] 2 K. B. 700; [1949] 2 All E. R. 198.
13. *Re Flynn, (deceased) (no. 2)*, [1969] 2 All E. R. 557; [1969] 2 Ch. 403.
14. *Bateman* v. *Pinder* (1842), 3 Q. B. 574.
15. *Read* v. *Price*, [1909] 2 K. B. 724.

Part payment.—A payment to revive a debt must be clearly referable to the contract. If a debtor owes his creditor several distinct debts, and, in making a payment to the creditor, does not appropriate it to any particular debt, the appropriation by the creditor towards a statute-barred debt does not revive his right of action for the balance of that debt. But, a payment of part of the amount owing on a current account and made "generally on account" starts time running afresh on the whole amount outstanding because the balance is a single debt[16].

The Act of 1939 does not affect actions for which a period of limitation is prescribed by any other enactment[17]. The Crown, public authorities, and the corporations created under nationalization Acts are now in the same position as other persons or bodies[19].

---

16. *Re Footman Bower & Co., Ltd.*, [1961] 2 All E. R. 161; [1961] Ch. 443. The balance is regarded as a single and undirected debt although, under the rule in *Clayton's Case* (*ante*, p. 81) a payment of part of the amount due on a current account has to be appropriated to the earliest outstanding debt.
17. Limitation Act 1939, s. 32. As to moneylenders, see *post*, p. 393.
18. Law Reform (Limitation of Actions, etc.) Act 1954, ss. 1, 5.

CHAPTER 9

Foreign Law

I PROPER LAW OF THE CONTRACT

Conflict of laws

A dispute sometimes arises as to what is to be the law by which a contract or some part of it is to be governed. The uncertainty may be brought about by a variety of causes: for instance, the contract may be entered into in one country with a view to its being wholly or partly performed in another, and the laws of the two countries may materially differ as to the validity or effect of one or more stipulations in the contract.

It is impossible either to exhaust the circumstances which may give rise to the dispute or to lay down hard and fast rules for the determination of any particular case, but all the authorities agree that the point to be ascertained is—

> what was or must be presumed to have been the intention of the parties with respect to the system of law which is to govern the contract?

The most satisfactory evidence of the intention of the parties is, of course, that appearing on the face of the contract, and it is only where this leaves the question in doubt that there is any occasion to resort to other considerations. If the parties to a contract expressly agree that it is to be governed by Ruritanian law, then provided that the intention so expressed is *bona fide* and legal, Ruritanian law is "the proper law of the contract", irrespective of whether the contract or the parties to it have any connection with Ruritania[1].

Further, if instead of a contract expressly providing that it should be governed by the law of Ruritania, it states that the courts of Ruritania are to have jurisdiction in any dispute arising out of the contract or that any disputes are to be settled by arbitration in Ruritania, Ruritanian law may still be "the proper law of the contract". In *Hamlyn Co. v. Talisker Distillery*[2],

> a contract was entered into in England between parties residing

---

1. *Vita Food Products Incorporated* v. *Unus Shipping Co.*, [1939] 1 All E. R. 513; [1939] A. C. 277.
2. [1894] A. C. 202. Followed in *N.V. Kwick Hoo Tong Handel Maatschappij* v. *James Finlay and Co., Ltd.*, [1927] A. C. 604, and *Tzortzis* v. *Monark Line A/B*, [1968] 1 All E. R. 949, C. A.

in England and Scotland respectively, but was mainly to be performed in Scotland, the House of Lords largely based their judgment upon the following clause in the contract:

"Should any dispute arise out of this contract the same to be settled by two members of the London Corn Exchange or their umpire in the usual way".

This was considered to be a clear indication that the parties contemplated that the contract should be interpreted according to the rules of English law. English law was the proper law of the contract.

However, the House of Lords has recently made it clear that any presumption arising from an arbitration clause may be rebutted, *e.g.* by evidence that the contract is more closely connected with some country other than the one where arbitration is to take place[3].

Presumptions.—Where the doubt is not removed by the language of the contract, the broad rule is that the court will apply the system of law with which the contract, on an objective assessment, has its closest and most real connection[4]. *Prima facie*, there is a presumption in favour of the legal system prevailing in the place where the contract is made[5]. This presumption gives way to a presumption in favour of the law of the place where the contract is to be performed (*lex loci solutionis*) if *both* parties have to perform their obligations in a country other than where the contract is made[6]. This is not so, however, where each party has to perform his obligations in different countries. In the case of *Jacobs* v. *Credit Lyonnais*[7],

a contract was made in England by a French company carrying on business in England to sell a quantity of esparto to another company carrying on business in England. The esparto was to be shipped from Algeria but payment was to be made in England. Owing to an insurrection in Algeria and the consequent military operations, the collection and transport of this particular merchandise was prevented, at a time when the contract had not been wholly completed, thereby excusing further performance according to the French law of "force majeure".

It was, however, decided that the proper law of the contract was English, and by English law the obligation to deliver being absolute

---

3. *Compagnie d'Armement Maritime S.A.* v. *Compagnie Tunisienne de Navigation S.A.*, [1970] 3 All E. R. 71; [1971] A. C. 572, H. L.
4. *Bonython* v. *Commonwealth of Australia*, [1951] A. C. 201, P. C.; *James Miller & Partners, Ltd.* v. *Whitworth Street Estates, Ltd.*, [1970] 1 All E. R. 796; [1970] A. C. 583, H. L. (Varying views expressed as to whether the proper law of the Contract was English or Scottish.)
5. *Peninsular and Oriental Steam Navigation Co.* v. *Shand* (1865), 3 Moo. P. C. C. N. S. 272.
6. *Benaim & Co.* v. *Debano*, [1924] All E. R. Rep. 103; [1924] A. C. 514.
7. (1884), 12 Q. B. D. 589.

the subsequent impossibility afforded no defence to an action for damages.   In contracts relating to immovables, *i.e.* interests in land, the general rule is that the *lex situs* is the proper law of the contract.

The foregoing rules for ascertaining the proper law of the contract, *i.e.* the law by which the parties intended it to be governed, may apply to cases where a Sovereign State is a party to the contract, although due weight must be given to that circumstance.   Accordingly where a loan was issued by the British Government in the United States, the rights and obligations under the contract were held to be governed by American law, because the proper inference from the terms of the loan and the relevant surrounding circumstances was that the parties intended that should be so[8].

II ILLEGALITY

If a contract is illegal by the proper law, the English courts will refuse to enforce it[9].   Furthermore, it seems that the English courts will refuse to enforce a contract which is illegal by the law of the country where performance is to take place, even though it is valid by the proper law.   This is certainly so if the proper law of the contract is English.   Thus in *Ralli Brothers* v. *Compania Naviera Sota y Aznar*[10],

> An English firm chartered a Spanish ship to carry jute from India to Spain, freight payable in part in pesetas in Barcelona. After the contract was made, Spanish law prohibited payment of freight at more than a certain fixed sum which was below the freight charges provided for in this contract.   *Held:* The English courts could not allow a claim for any excess over the freight permitted by Spanish law, although the proper law of the contract was English.

Probably, if a contract is legal by the proper law of the contract, it will be upheld though its terms are illegal by the *lex loci contractus*[11].

However, whatever the proper law of a contract, an English court will not enforce it if it contravenes certain fundamental principles of justice and morality as accepted by the common law.   Thus, a contract in unreasonable restraint of trade[12] or a champertous agreement[13] will not be upheld by the English courts although the proper law may regard the contract as valid.   Moreover, an English court will not

---

8. *R.* v. *International Trustee*, [1937] 2 All E. R. 164; [1937] A. C. 500.
9. *Kahler* v. *Midland Bank, Ltd.*, [1949] 2 All E. R. 621; [1950] A. C. 24.
10. [1920] 2 K. B. 287. See also *Regazzoni* v. *K. C. Sethia* (1944), Ltd., [1957] 3 All E. R. 286; [1958] A. C. 301.
11. *Re Missouri Steamship Co.* (1889), 42 Ch. D. 321.
12. *Rousillon* v. *Rousillon* (1880), 14 Ch. D. 351.
13. *Grell* v. *Levy* (1864), 16 C. B. (N. S.) 73.

enforce a contract if it is contrary to an English Act of Parliament if the Act's provisions were intended to have extra-territorial effect[14]. Statutes concerning wagering contracts and the Sale of Goods Act have no effect on contracts where the proper law is not English[15].

III THE LEX FORI

Whatever law governs the interpretation of the contract, anything which relates to the remedy to be enforced must be determined by the *lex fori*, the law of the place where proceedings on the contract are brought. The practice of those courts must be followed, their rules as to the admissibility of evidence will apply, and so will any provision which bars the remedy, such as the Limitation Act 1939[16]. If the remedy is barred by lapse of time according to the law of the country in which enforcement is sought, it does not matter that it is not so barred by the proper law[16]. Where parties accepted Scottish arbitration, Scottish law was the *lex fori* and therefore governed the arbitration so that, for example, the arbiter had no jurisdiction to state a case for the High Court[17].

Conversely, an action on a foreign contract may be maintained here, even though the time has expired for enforcing the contract in the foreign country, provided that the period laid down by the English statute has not been exceeded[18]. It would be otherwise if the foreign statute destroyed the debt as well as the remedy[18]. If an action is brought in England on a contract which by English law has to be evidenced in writing (*e.g.* a contract relating to land), there must be a sufficient note or memorandum of the contract whatever is the proper law of the contract[19].

Foreign law will not be judicially noticed in the English courts. It must be proved, as a fact, by the evidence of a competent witness; until the contrary be proved, the general law of a foreign State is presumed to be the same as the English law[20]. But questions of foreign law must be decided by the judge and not by a jury[1].

---

14. *Boissevain* v. *Weil*, [1950] 1 All E. R. 728; [1950] A. C. 327.
15. *Saxby* v. *Fulton*, [1909] 2 K. B. 208.
16. *Don* v. *Lippmann* (1838), 5 Cl. & F. 1.
17. *James Miller and Partners, Ltd.* v. *Whitworth Street Estates, Ltd.*, [1970] 1 All E. R. 796; [1970] A. C. 583, H. L.
18. *Harris* v. *Quine* (1869), L. R. 4 Q. B. 653.
19. *Leroux* v. *Brown* (1852), 12 C. B. 801.
20. *Dynamit Aktiengesellschaft* v. *Rio Tinto Co.*, [1918] A. C. 260, 292 *et seq.*
1. Judicature Act 1925, s. 102; County Courts Act 1959, s. 97.

IV FOREIGN JUDGMENTS

Registration and enforcement

Judgments given in the superior courts of foreign or Commonwealth countries, which accord substantial reciprocity of treatment to judgments given in the superior courts of the United Kingdom, can be registered as of right and enforced under the provisions of Part I of the Foreign Judgments (Reciprocal Enforcement) Act 1933 in cases where the Act has been extended by Order in Council to the country in which the judgment was obtained[2]. The judgment must be final and conclusive as between the parties and must be for a sum of money, not being a sum payable for taxes or in respect of a fine or other penalty. If the requirements of the Act are satisfied, the High Court must, on the application of the judgment creditor[3] made within six years of the date of the judgment, order it to be registered.

On registration the judgment will for the purposes of execution (or, *e.g.*, as the basis of a bankruptcy petition) be of the same force and effect as if it had been originally given in the registering court and entered on the date of registration; and the sum for which the judgment is registered will carry interest.

The registration of a foreign judgment will be set aside on the application of any party against whom it may be enforced on the following grounds:

(*a*) the judgment is not one to which the Act applies; or

(*b*) the court pronouncing judgment had no jurisdiction over the defendant; or

(*c*) the judgment debtor, being the defendant before the foreign court, did not receive notice of the proceedings in sufficient time to enable him to appear and he did not appear; or

(*d*) the judgment was obtained by a fraud on the court[4]; or

(*e*) the enforcement of the judgment would be contrary to public policy[5]; or

(*f*) the rights under the judgment are not vested in the person who applied for registration.

Registration *may* be set aside if the English court is satisfied that the matter had already been the subject of a final judgment of a competent court.

---

2. Earlier Acts, the Judgments Extension Act 1868, and the Administration of Justice Act 1920, contain limited provisions for the registration of judgments of the Courts of Scotland, Northern Ireland, and the Commonwealth.
3. Or any person in whom the rights under the judgment have become vested (s. 11).
4. See, *e.g.*, *Syal* v. *Heyward*, [1948] 2 All E. R. 576; [1948] 2 K. B. 443.
5. Foreign Judgments (Reciprocal Enforcement) Act 1933, s. 4.

A foreign judgment which can be registered cannot be enforced by action[6].

Enforcement by action

Except in cases where the enforcement of foreign judgments by action is prohibited by the Foreign Judgments (Reciprocal Enforcement) Act 1933 because it is registrable under that Act, any *final* judgment of a foreign, Commonwealth or colonial court, which has *jurisdiction* over the subject-matter and the parties will be acted on here as conclusive of any matter of law or fact thereby decided provided the judgment was for a definite sum. It may also be enforced by action here unless the foreign proceedings are in conflict with English views of natural justice[7], or the judgment was obtained by fraud[8].

In actions *in personam* the courts of this country will treat the defendant as subject to the jurisdiction of a foreign court in the following cases:

1. Where he was present in the foreign country when the action began;
2. Where he has voluntarily submitted to the jurisdiction of the foreign court by appearing as plaintiff, or by entering an appearance, or by agreeing expressly or impliedly to submit to its jurisdiction[9].

But the ownership of property abroad is not sufficient to give the foreign court jurisdiction in a personal action[10]. In actions *in rem*, jurisdiction belongs solely to the courts of the country where the *res* is situated.

The fraud of the plaintiff in obtaining the judgment may be pleaded as a defence to an action brought on the foreign judgment, even though the defendant relied on this in the foreign proceedings and the merits of the foreign judgment are therefore being reopened[11].

An English court will also grant an injunction restraining a person who is subject to its jurisdiction from enforcing a judgment of a foreign court which he has obtained by breach of contract or fraud. In doing so the English court does not set aside the judgment or purport to interfere with the foreign court; such injunction is directed only against the *person* over whom the English court has jurisdiction[12].

---

6. *Ibid.*, s. 6.
7. *Pemberton* v. *Hughes*, [1899] 1 Ch. 781. A mere irregularity in procedure will not affect the validity of the foreign judgment.
8. *Vadala* v. *Lawes* (1890), 25 Q. B. D. 310.
9. *Emanuel* v. *Symon*, [1908] 1 K. B. 302, at p. 309, *per* BUCKLEY, L.J.
10. *Emanuel* v. *Symon*, [1908] 1 K. B. 302.
11. *Godard* v. *Gray* (1871), L. R. 6 Q. B. 139; and see *Syal* v. *Heyward*, [1948] 2 All E. R. 576; [1948] 2 K. B. 443.
12. *Ellerman Lines* v. *Read*, [1928] 2 K. B. 144.

In an action upon a foreign judgment expressed in foreign currency, the English court will award a sum in sterling calculated according to the rate of exchange ruling at the date of the foreign judgment[13]. Where a debt other than a judgment debt is payable abroad in foreign currency it ought, for the purpose of an English judgment, to be converted into English money at the rate of exchange of the day when the debt became due[14].

---

13. *Scott* v. *Bevan* (1831), 2 B. & Ad. 79.
14. *Re United Railways of Havana and Regla Warehouses, Ltd.*, [1960] 2 All E. R. 332; [1961] A. C. 1007.

CHAPTER 10

Construction of Contracts

The construction or interpretation of a written contract is aimed at ascertaining the true meaning of the contract where it is capable of more than one meaning; or where the language is doubtful or obscure, to try if possible to extract some definite meaning.

The construction of a document is a matter of law for the court and in many cases raises questions of great difficulty upon which different minds may come to different conclusions.

Many general rules have been laid down to assist the court in construing contracts. These rules are of varying degrees of importance and in particular cases there may be a conflict as to what rule or rules ought to be applied to enable a court to discover the true meaning of the document under consideration.

The following rules of construction are those usually applied:

1. *A contract must be read as a whole,* that is to say, effect must, if possible, be given to every part of it[1]. Where necessary the resultant of conflicting clauses must be ascertained.

> The lease of a shop occupied by a watchmaker and jeweller contained a covenant by the lessee that he would not make any "alteration" to the demised premises without the consent of the lessor. The lessee fixed a large clock to the exterior wall of the house by means of bolts driven into the wall, and the lessor had refused to consent to this being done. The lessor sued for an injunction ordering the lessee to remove the clock; but the action failed on the ground that there had been no breach of covenant[2].
> In delivering judgment VAUGHAN-WILLIAMS, L.J., said:—
>> "The decision in this case depends on the construction of a short covenant in a lease. We have to take into consideration the whole of the lease and the purposes for which it was granted, and then to see what is the proper construction of the particular covenant. . . . We have to construe the word 'alteration' in this covenant. It would be really impossible to hold that every addition to the premises, whether it does or does not alter the form or structure of the premises, is within the meaning of the word 'alteration' in the covenant. The result would be that this tenant carrying on the business

---

1. *Elderslie S.S. Co.* v. *Borthwick,* [1905] A. C. 93.
2. *Bickmore* v. *Dimmer,* [1903] 1 Ch. 158.

of a watchmaker and jeweller would not be able to put up a fixed blind on the outside of the window of his shop, or put a lamp outside in front of his main door or even to place a knocker upon the door. That would really be an impossible construction."

2. *The parol evidence rule.* If the whole contract is in writing, no oral evidence will be permitted which would add to, vary, or contradict the written terms. The rule is, however, subject to a number of exceptions. Thus, evidence may be given to show that the contract was not meant to operate until a certain condition was satisfied[3]. If a contract is reduced into writing there is a presumption that the writing is intended to include all the contractual terms, but evidence may be admitted that it represents only part of the terms and then evidence is admissible as to the oral terms. Moreover, if X refuses to enter into a written contract with Y until Y gives an oral assurance, the court may rule that Y's assurance and X's promise thereupon to enter into the written contract comprise a separate *collateral contract* and is enforceable as such[4]. In *City & Westminster Properties* (1934), *Ltd.* v. *Mudd*[5],

a tenant declined to sign a lease containing a covenant that he would use the premises for business purposes only until the lessor gave him an oral assurance that he could continue to reside there. *Held:* that the tenant could rely on the oral assurance as a contractual promise.

3. Relevant surrounding circumstances must always be looked at to show the relation of the document to the facts. Such extrinsic evidence is admissible, *not to contradict or vary the contract,* but to apply it to the facts which the parties had in their minds and were negotiating about. Thus, in *Newell* v. *Radford*[6],

a contract read: "Mr. Newell, 32 sacks of culasses at 39s. 280 lbs. to await orders. John Williams." Oral evidence was admissible as to the occupations of Newell and Williams to show which was the seller and which the buyer.

4. The first general rule of construction, sometimes referred to as the *golden rule,* is that the language of the instrument is to be understood in its ordinary and natural meaning unless this leads to absurdity.

"The grammatical and ordinary sense of the words is to be adhered to, unless that would lead to some absurdity, or some repugnance or inconsistency with the rest of the instrument, in which case the grammatical and ordinary sense of the words may

---

3. *Pym* v. *Campbell* (1856), 6 E. & B. 370.
4. *De Lassalle* v. *Guildford*, [1901] 2 K. B. 215.
5. [1958] 2 All E. R. 733; [1959] Ch. 129.
6. (1867) L. R. 3 C. P. 52.

be modified, so as to avoid the inconsistency, but no further"[7].

In *Smith* v. *Cooke*[8],

Two partners assigned the business and property of the firm to trustees for the benefit of creditors. The deed contained no provision in the event of their being a surplus. A surplus was realised and the House of Lords *held* that it belonged to the creditors.

Lord HALSBURY, L.C., said:—

"I cannot get out of the language of this instrument, a resulting trust except by putting in words which are not there. I must say I for one have always protested against endeavouring to construe an instrument contrary to what the words of the instrument itself convey, by some sort of preconceived idea of what the parties would or might or perhaps ought to have intended when they began to frame their instrument".

In *Blore* v. *Giulini*[9],

A lease provided that the lessees should have power to determine it at the end of the first seven years on notice and that on the expiration of the notice *every clause matter and thing contained in the lease should cease and determine and be void*. *Held:* on determination of the lease by the lessees by notice the lessor was entitled to sue them for *existing* breaches of covenants notwithstanding that his right to do so was not expressly reserved.

WRIGHT, J., observed—

"that it was impossible to suppose that it was ever intended by the parties that the liability of the lessees to pay damages for breaches of covenant already committed by them should be put an end to by mere determination of the lease".

5. But the general rule requiring words to be used in their primary and ordinary sense must yield in cases where the circumstances or the context show that the parties must have used the words in a special sense. This often happens where the words are peculiar to a trade or locality or where the parties must be presumed to have contracted with reference to a trade custom or usage. "The meaning of a particular word may be shown, by parol evidence, to be different in some particular place, trade or business, from its proper and ordinary acceptation"[10].

Thus in *Grant* v. *Maddox*[11],

the plaintiff agreed to perform at the defendant's theatre and

---

7. *Grey* v. *Pearson* (1857), 6 H. L. C., at p. 106, *per* Lord WENSLEYDALE.
8. [1891] A. C. 297.
9. [1903] 1 K. B. 356.
10. *Mallan* v. *May* (1844), 13 M. & W., at pp. 517, 518, *per* POLLOCK, C.B.
11. (1846), 15 M. & W. 737.

the defendant agreed to engage her for three *years*, and to pay her a salary of £5, £6 and £7 per week in each of those *years* respectively. *Held:* that according to the uniform usage of the theatrical profession the plaintiff was only entitled to be paid during the theatrical season in each of those years. In this case, therefore, the word "year" was cut down to mean a season which was less than a year.

6. The *ejusdem generis rule*, where it applies, is that general words must be restricted to the same genus as the specific words which precede them[12]. This means that if the things described by the particular words have some common characteristic which constitutes them a genus, the general words which follow must be limited to that genus, and will apply only to things of the same nature.

The *prima facie* rule is that general words are to be considered as having their full and natural meaning. The *ejusdem generis* rule will only be applied if the context requires it. The justification of the rule is that if the general words have an unrestricted meaning, the enumerated items are surplusage. But this argument has little force in construing commercial documents which often contain such surplusage. In *Chandris* v. *Isbrandtsen-Moller Co. Inc.*[13], DEVLIN, J., said:

> "The charter-party in the present case refers, for example, to 'a full and complete cargo of wheat and/or maize and/or other lawful merchandise'. Nobody has ever, I think, suggested that by such a charter-party the merchandise has to be similar to wheat or maize; although the first question which would occur to a lawyer would be to ask himself why the parties bothered to refer to wheat or maize if they meant that the cargo might be anything from chalk to cheese, including turpentine".

7. The introduction into a contract of an *implied* term can only be justified when the implied term is not inconsistent with some express term of the contract, and where there arises from the language of the contract itself, and the circumstances under which it was entered into, an inference that it is *necessary* to introduce the term to effectuate the intention of the parties[14]. This doctrine is often invoked in connection with commercial contracts. A common matter of dispute is whether there is an implied term that a company which has entered into a contract to sell its products over a fixed period will continue to carry on business throughout that period[15].

---

12. *Thames and Mersey Marine Ince. Co.* v. *Hamilton, Fraser & Co.* (1887), 12 A. C., at p. 490, *per* Lord HALSBURY, L.C.
13. [1950] 1 All E. R. 768, at p. 773; [1951] 1 K. B. 240, at p. 246.
14. *Brodie* v. *Cardiff Corporation*, [1919] A. C., at p. 358, *per* Lord ATKINSON.
15. *Hamlyn & Co.* v. *Wood & Co.*, [1891] 2 Q. B. 488. Contrast *General Publicity Services, Ltd.* v. *Best's Brewery Co., Ltd.* (1951), 2 T. L. R. 875.

In *Samuels* v. *Davis*[16], it was held that,

> where a dentist undertakes to make a denture for reward there is an implied term that it will be reasonably fit for the purpose.

SCOTT, L.J., said in delivering judgment:—

> "In my view it is a matter of legal indifference whether the contract was one for the sale of goods or one of service to do work and supply materials. In either case, the contract must necessarily, by reason of the relationship between the parties and the purpose for which the contract was entered into, import a term that, given reasonable co-operation by the patient, the dentist would . . . produce a denture which could be used by the patient for the purpose of eating and talking in the ordinary way".

In *Reigate* v. *Union Manufacturing Co. (Ramsbottom)*[17], SCRUTTON, L.J., said

> "an implied term is not to be added because the court thinks it would have been reasonable to have it inserted in the contract. A term can only be implied if it is necessary in the business sense to give efficacy to the contract; that is, if it is such a term that it can confidently be said that if at the time the contract was being negotiated someone had said to the parties, 'What will happen in such a case', they would both have replied, 'of course, so and so will happen; we did not trouble to say that; it is too clear'."

8. Words may be supplied or struck out to give effect to the manifest intention of the parties.

A bond provided for payment of £100 by equal instalments of £16 13s. 4d. until the sum of "one pounds" was paid. *Held:* "one pounds" must be read as "one hundred pounds"[18].

9. Where a contract is partly written and partly a printed form a conflict may arise between the printed and written words because the latter may have called for consequential alterations in the printed form which the parties have omitted to make. In such cases:

> "the written words must have a greater effect attributed to them than the printed words, inasmuch as the written words are the

---

16. [1943] 1 K. B. 526; [1943] 2 All E. R. 3. See also *Charnock* v. *Liverpool Corporation*, [1968] 3 All E. R. 473, C. A. (term in contract of repairs implied that repairs would be effected with reasonable expedition) followed in *Brown and Davis, Ltd.* v. *Galbraith*, [1972] 3 All E. R. 31; [1972] 1 W. L. R. 997, C. A.

17. [1918] 1 K. B. 592, 605. And see dicta of MACKINNON, L.J., in *Shirlaw* v. *Southern Foundries (1926), Ltd. and Federated Foundries, Ltd.*, [1939] 2 All E. R. 113, 124; [1939] 2 K. B. 206, 227. Both dicta were followed by CROSS, J., in *Gardner* v. *Coutts & Co.*, [1967] 3 All E. R. 1064. *Cf. The Moorcock* (1889), 14 P.D. 64.

18. *Waugh* v. *Bussell* (1814), 5 Taunt. 707.

immediate language and terms selected by the parties themselves for the expression of their meaning, and the printed words are a general formula adapted equally to their case and that of all other contracting parties upon similar occasions and subjects"[19].

10. An *ambiguity* may be *patent* or *latent*. A *patent* ambiguity is one which appears on the face of the instrument itself, such as the existence of the two apparently contradictory clauses in an agreement. It cannot be solved by parol evidence as to the meaning of the parties, but must be solved by the court as a matter of construction[20]. If that cannot be done the agreement will be void for uncertainty.

A *latent* ambiguity is one which is created where the surrounding circumstances show that the language of the instrument may apply to two or more persons or things although the instrument itself is otherwise clear. In such cases parol evidence is admissible to define the subject-matter to which the instrument was intended to apply. Thus in *Robinson* v. *Great Western Rail. Co.*[1]:—

Horses were consigned by rail to Wolverhampton. Evidence was admitted to show which station in Wolverhampton was intended.

The court prefers an interpretation which will make the instrument valid, rather than one which will make it invalid. Between two rival constructions of the same words the court will lean towards that construction which preserves, rather than towards that which destroys. This is a rule of law which is expressed in the maxim—*Ut res magis valeat quam pereat*[2]. So, where a contract requires an act to be done which may according to the circumstances be lawful or unlawful, it will not be presumed that the contract was to do the unlawful act; the contrary is the proper inference[3].

---

19. *Robertson* v. *French* (1803), 4 East, at p. 136, per Lord ELLENBOROUGH, C.J.; see also *Western Assurance Co. of Toronto* v. *Poole*, [1903] 1 K. B. 376.
20. *Committee of London Clearing Bankers* v. *Inland Revenue Commissioners*, [1896] 1 Q. B., at p. 227, *per* WRIGHT, J.; *Saunderson* v. *Piper* (1839), 5 Bing. N. C. 425.
1. (1865), Har. & Ruth, 97.
2. *Langston* v. *Langston* (1834), 2 Cl. & F., at p. 243, *per* Lord BROUGHAM, L.C.
3. *Lewis* v. *Davison* (1839), 4 M. & W. 654.

PART II

Agency and Partnership

CHAPTER II

Agency

I INTRODUCTORY

An agent is "he who is employed to do anything in the place of another"[1], and the person who employs him is called the principal. Most frequently, an agent is employed for the purpose of bringing about a contract between his principal and another person, usually referred to as the third party. In the language of commerce a person who buys goods and resells them is frequently described as an agent, *e.g.* a motor dealer may be described as sole agent for a particular make of car, but that does not necessarily mean that he is acting in *law* as agent for the manufacturer. In practice, such a dealer buys the cars from the manufacturer and sells on his own account to a purchaser so that he is selling not as an agent at all but as his own principal.

An agent may or may not be a servant of the principal, and this distinction may have important results in considering how far the agent is entitled to be given work to enable him to earn his commission and how far he is entitled to notice[2].

Agents may be divided into various types. Some of the most important, together with the chief variations in their legal characteristics, will be described later[3]. A broader division may be made as follows:

1. *Special*, viz., those who have authority to do a specific act, *e.g.* buy a particular thing;

2. *General*, viz., those who may do anything coming within certain limits, *e.g.* agent to manage a business;

3. *Universal*, viz., those who may do anything on behalf of their principal, and whose authority is unlimited.

This classification may be relevant in considering how far the principal may be bound by those acts of his agent which have not been specifically authorised. Thus to make the principal liable for the acts of a special agent the third party will normally have to prove that the agent had *actual* authority to do what he did, but *actual* authority covers not only those things which the agent has *express* authority to do but also

---

1. Comyns' Digest, Attorney A.
2. See *Bauman* v. *Hulton Press*, [1952] 2 All E. R. 1121, *post*, p. 436.
3. *Post*, p. 144 *et seq.*

anything that is necessary for or reasonably incidental to carrying out the authority expressly given. He is said to have *implied* authority to do the latter things. Acts of a general agent will be binding on his principal if they are within the agent's express or implied authority or if they are within his *usual* authority, *i.e.* are of a kind that someone in his trade or profession ordinarily has authority to do. Because it is still necessary to investigate the express, implied, or usual authority of the agent in question, whether he is classified as a specific or general agent, the utility of these terms is now doubted[4].

Capacity.—Those who do not have legal capacity to make contracts[5] cannot get rid of their disabilities by the employment of agents, but if, for example, a minor can lawfully do an act on his own behalf, so as to bind himself *e.g.* in a contract for necessaries, he can instead appoint an agent to do it for him[6]. Moreover, incapacity to contract for himself will not prevent a person from being appointed agent to contract for another. Thus, a minor can make a contract on behalf of a principal for the purchase of non-necessary goods though he could not validly make such a contract for himself.

II APPOINTMENT OF AGENTS

As a rule, no formal mode of appointment is required; in fact, the vast majority of agencies are created verbally, often without any express arrangement at all, and unless these were recognised by law, mercantile business could hardly proceed. The agent does not have to be appointed in writing merely because his task is to bring about a contract which itself has to be evidenced in writing such as a contract for the sale of land[7]. But if the agent is to have authority to contract under seal (*e.g.* to execute a conveyance), the authority must also be under seal, and it is then called a power of attorney, though the want of a deed will be of no avail as a defence to a principal who is present and allows the agent to enter into the contract for him[8].

The principal–agent relationship may arise in the following ways:

1. By *contract* under seal.
2. By *contract* in writing or verbal.
3. By *contract* implied from the conduct or situation of the parties.
4. By *consent* express or implied where there is no contract as the agent is acting gratuitously.

Although the above methods of establishing the principal–agency

---

4. See Fridman, Law of Agency (3rd ed. 1971), pp. 25–27.
5. See *ante*, p. 56.
6. *G(A)* v. *G(T)*, [1970] 3 All E. R. 546, at p. 549 *per* Lord DENNING, M.R.
7. *Heard* v. *Pilley* (1869), 4 Ch. App. 548.
8. *Ball* v. *Dunsterville* (1791), 4 T. R. 313.

relationship depend on the consent of the principal and the agent, it is clear from 3 and 4 above that such consent may be implied. Lord PEARSON in *Garnac Grain Co. v. H. M. Faure and Fairclough and Burge Corporation*[9] said:

"They will be held to have consented if they have agreed to what amounts in law to such a relationship, even if they do not recognise it themselves and even if they profess to disclaim it. . . . Primarily one looks to what they said and did at the date of the alleged creation of the agency. Earlier words and conduct may afford evidence of a course of dealing in existence at that time and may be taken into account more generally as historical background".

5. By *estoppel*, *i.e.* a person may so act as to be precluded from denying that he has given authority to another to act on his behalf. In *Pickering* v. *Busk*[10],

a broker was employed by a merchant to buy hemp; the broker did so, and, at the merchant's request, the hemp was left at the broker's wharf; the broker sold the goods, and the purchaser was held to have obtained a good title to the goods on the ground that the broker was the apparent agent, and that the merchant was estopped by his conduct from denying the agency.

6. By *ratification*. Although an agency may be non-existent when the "agent" enters into a contract with the third party, it may arise and be made restrospective by ratification, *i.e.* adoption of the contract as made by·express words or by conduct. However, ratification is only possible if certain conditions are satisfied:—

(i) the agent in making the contract must purport to act as an agent and name or clearly identify his principal—a contract made by someone in his own name with an undeclared intention to make it on behalf of another, for whom he then had no authority to act, cannot be ratified[11].

(ii) The principal must be in existence and competent to make the contract when the contract is made. Thus—

A principal who was an enemy alien when the contract was made cannot ratify it after he ceases to be an enemy alien[12].

---

9. [1967] 2 All E. R. 353, 358. Lord WILBERFORCE has said that while agency must ultimately derive from consent, the consent need not necessarily be to the relationship of principal and agent itself but may to be a state of facts on which the law imposes the consequences which result from agency: (*Branwhite* v. *Worcester Works Finance, Ltd.*, [1968] 3 All E. R. 104, 122, H. L.).
10. (1812), 15 East, 38.
11. *Keighley, Maxsted & Co.* v. *Durant*, [1901] A. C. 240.
12. *Boston Deep Sea Fishing and Ice Co., Ltd.* v. *Farnham*, [1957] 3 All E. R. 204.

Similarly, a company cannot adopt or ratify a contract entered into on its behalf before the company was incorporated[13]; it may make a new contract to the same effect, unless such contract would be *ultra vires*[14];

(iii) Generally, a principal can only ratify if, at the time of ratification, he could lawfully do the act himself. Thus, in *Grover and Grover, Ltd.* v. *Mathews*[15],

A contract of fire insurance had been taken out by A on P's behalf (without authority) and P purported to ratify this contract *after* a fire had taken place. *Held:* the purported ratification was ineffective.

Apart from this point ratification must be either within any time fixed for ratification or, if none, within a reasonable time.

(iv) Void contracts cannot be ratified. Therefore a company cannot ratify a contract purported to have been made on its behalf if that contract was then *ultra vires* the company. But an issue of shares *intra vires* the company, though voidable because made by the directors for improper motives, is rectifiable by the company[16].

(v) Where ratifying, the principal must either have full knowledge of the facts or be shown to have adopted the agent's acts, whatever they were[17].

Effect of ratification.—If a contract is properly ratified, the ratification is thrown back to the time when the act was done. In consequence, it has been held that where a third party's offer is unconditionally accepted without authority by an agent, the principal may ratify even after the third party has purported to revoke his offer[18]. This is not so, if the agent's acceptance is made expressly or impliedly subject to ratification[19]. There is authority for saying that ratification does not enable the principal to sue for breach occurring before ratification[20].

---

13. *Kelner* v. *Baxter* (1866), L. R. 2 C. P. 174; European Communities Act 1972, s. 9.
14. *Ashbury Carriage Co.* v. *Riche* (1875), L. R. 7 H. L. 653.
15. [1910] 2 K. B. 401.
16. *Bamford* v. *Bamford*, [1969] 1 All E. R. 969; [1970] Ch. 212, C. A.
17. *Marsh* v. *Joseph*, [1897] 1 Ch. 213.
18. *Bolton Partners* v. *Lambert* (1889), 41 Ch. D. 295.
19. *Watson* v. *Davies*, [1931] 1 Ch. 455; *Warehousing and Forwarding Co. of East Africa, Ltd.* v. *Jafferali and Sons, Ltd.*, [1963] 3 All E. R. 571; [1964] A. C. 1.
20. *Kidderminster Corporation* v. *Hardwick* (1873), L. R. 9 Exch. 13. But is this reconcilable with the later decision in *Bolton Partners* v. *Lambert* (1889), 41 Ch. D. 295?

It may be added that where an agent makes a contract in the name of his principal, but with the intention of fraudulently taking the benefit of the contract for himself, the principal may nevertheless ratify and enforce the contract as against the other parties to it[1].

III TERMINATION OF AGENCY

This may occur either by the act of the parties themselves or by operation of law.

1. *By act of the parties.*—Apart from termination by mutual agreement, an agency may as a general rule, be terminated by the unilateral action of either party. Thus, irrespective of any express words in the agency contract, P can revoke A's authority so that any further acts of A, purporting to be done on P's behalf, will render A liable to third parties for pretending to have an authority that has been withdrawn from him, *i.e.* for breach of warranty of authority. But it must be noted that the principal will be liable on contracts entered into on his behalf after the termination of the agency, unless he has caused notice of such termination to reach third parties, who may act on the faith of the previous authority, until such a time has elapsed or such circumstances have happened, as would lead a reasonable man to infer that the agent's authority had been countermanded. This is based on the estoppel principle. Thus,

> a servant who had authority to receive, borrow, and pay money for his master, borrowed 200 guineas in his master's name after he had quitted the service; and the lender recovered against the master on the ground that he had not been aware of the revocation of authority[2].

So, in the case of a partnership (which is in many respects a kind of agency), the partner who leaves the firm but remains ostensibly a member, is liable for debts incurred after his retirement[3].

However, although either party to an agency contract may unilaterally bring it to an end, such action may well be a breach of the agency contract for which damages are payable. Thus, if the agent is engaged for a fixed period, revocation of his authority before the end of that period is a breach[4].

If the agent is a salaried servant of the principal he will have an implied right to reasonable notice in the absence of agreement to the contrary[5]. Even where the agent is not a servant of the principal,

---

1. *Re Tiedemann and Ledermann Frères*, [1899] 2 Q. B. 66.
2. *Monk* v. *Clayton*, Molley, De Jure Maritimo, bk. 2, c. 10, s. 27.
3. Partnership Act 1890, s. 36. See *post*, p. 164.
4. *Turner* v. *Goldsmith*, [1891] 1 Q. B. 544.
5. *Bauman* v. *Hulton Press*, [1952] 2 All E. R. 1121.

a term *may* be implied that he is entitled to notice and therefore unilateral revocation of his authority is a breach of contract. In *Martin-Baker Aircraft Co., Ltd.* v. *Canadian Flight Equipment Ltd*[6],

> The plaintiff appointed M sole selling agent of their products. The agreement imposed various duties on M but contained no provision for determination except in the case of misconduct. *Held*, the agreement was neither terminable summarily nor permanent but could be terminated by reasonable notice which in the particular case meant 12 months' notice. The contract was analogous to a master-servant contract because M was a sole selling agent, had to expend much time and money, and was subject to restrictions as to sale of other persons' goods.

A limit to this power of revocation at any time is found where an

"*interest* has been coupled with an authority";

e.g. when the principal has entered into an agreement to give something to a person, and has appointed the latter an agent to collect and secure it for himself. In such case the authority cannot be revoked. So, although the authority of an agent to sell goods is generally revocable it will become irrevocable if the agent has made advances to his principal in consideration of the latter giving him authority to sell at the market price and retain his advances out of the proceeds[7].

Further, by virtue of the Powers of Attorney Act 1971, s. 5, the donee of a power of attorney who acts in pursuance of the power at a time when it has been revoked shall not, by reason of the revocation, incur any liability (either to the donor or to any other person) if at that time he did not know that the power had been revoked. Where a power of attorney has been revoked and a person without knowledge of the revocation deals with the donee of the power, the transaction between them shall, in favour of that person, be as valid as if the power had then been in existence.

2. *By operation of law.*—Subject to exceptions depending upon the special terms of the appointment and the types of irrevocable agency just referred to (agency coupled with an interest and the provisions of the Powers of Attorney Act 1971)—

> (i) Death: The principal's death generally puts an end to the authority of the agent. A case illustrating this is *Smout* v. *Ilbery*[8] in which

---

6. [1955] 2 All E. R. 722; [1955] 2 Q. B. 556.
7. *Raleigh* v. *Atkinson* (1840), 6 M. & W. 670. See also Powers of Attorney Act 1971, s. 4.
8. (1842), 10 M. & W. 1. In so far as this case decided that the agent would not be liable in such circumstances for damages for breach of warranty of authority, it must be treated as overruled. See *post*, p. 138.

it was decided that a butcher was unable to recover from the husband's estate the price of meat supplied to a woman, at a time when her husband, supposed to be alive, was in reality dead; her authority to buy was gone.

(ii) Bankruptcy: The agent's authority is generally revoked by the bankruptcy of his principal; not necessarily by that of himself.

(iii) Insanity: The insanity of the agent will determine his authority, and the insanity of the principal seems equivalent to a revocation, but if third parties have dealt with the agent on the faith of an authority previously given, and without notice of a determination or revocation, the principal will be precluded from denying the continuance of the authority. Thus, in *Drew v. Nunn*[9];

a man gave his wife authority to buy, then became insane. When he had recovered, he repudiated her contracts, but was held liable in an action for the price because his subsequent insanity did not relieve him from the consequences of the representation he had previously made by giving his wife a general authority to buy, upon the faith of which the plaintiff acted.

(iv) Supervening illegality or frustration: Thus, a contract of agency involving personal services is dissolved if the principal or agent is compelled to join the armed forces because he is no longer available to perform his duties[10].

Similarly, a contract of agency is terminated by destruction of the subject-matter, so that the employment of an estate agent to let a house is determined if the house is burnt down.

(v) expiration of the time agreed upon for its continuance;

(vi) complete performance; *e.g.*

when an agent to procure a buyer has procured one who is accepted.

IV RIGHTS AND DUTIES OF AGENT AS AGAINST PRINCIPAL

Duties of an agent to his principal

1. *To obey his principal's instructions.*—Unless he is acting gratuitously the agent is liable in damages for failure to do what he has agreed to

---

9. (1879), 4 Q. B. 661.
10. *Marshall v. Glanvill*, [1917] 2 K. B. 87; *Morgan v. Manser* [1948] 1 K. B. 184; [1947] 2 All E. R. 666.

do[11]. Provided what the agent has to do is not illegal[12], then whether the agent is acting gratuitously or not, if he proceeds to carry out the agency, he must do so as agreed and comply with his principal's lawful instructions or be liable in damages.

2. *To exercise due care and skill.*—The exact amount of skill and care required varies with the circumstances, but generally a man who undertakes to act for another must not show less diligence than he would have shown if exercising his own affairs. If in addition, he is engaged upon an understanding that he must show special skill, this skill he must show, or he is liable to indemnify his principal, even though he has done his best.

In this respect a difference is to be observed between:

1. a gratuitous agent;
2. a paid agent.

Whilst the gratuitous agent is not bound to proceed to carry out the agency work at all, he is liable if he is negligent in carrying out a matter actually commenced.

Even then, however, the responsibility may not be so great as that of a paid agent, for it seems that whereas the latter is liable for ordinary negligence, the voluntary agent is liable in damages only if he is guilty of gross negligence[13], unless, indeed, his profession is such as to imply skill, in which case, if he enters upon the work at all, he must do so with that skill[14].

The question then arises, what is gross negligence? CROMPTON, J., laid down the law in *Beal* v. *South Devon Rail. Co.*[15]. thus:

"Gross negligence includes the want of that reasonable care, skill, and expedition, which may properly be expected from persons so holding themselves out (*i.e.* as agent for anything), or their servants. . . . The failure to exercise reasonable care, skill, and diligence, is gross negligence. What is reasonable varies in the case of a gratuitous bailee, and that of a bailee for hire. From the former is reasonably expected such care and diligence as persons ordinarily use in their own affairs, and such skill as he has. From the latter is reasonably expected care and diligence such as are exercised in the ordinary and proper course of similar

---

11. *Turpin* v. *Bilton* (1843), 5 Man. & G. 455.
12. *Cohen* v. *Kittell* (1889), 22 Q. B. D. 680.
13. *Beauchamp* v. *Powley* (1831), 1 Moo. & R. 38; *Doorman* v. *Jenkins* (1835), 2 A. & E. 256.
14. Lord LOUGHBOROUGH, in *Shiells* v. *Blackburne* (1789), 1 H. Bl. 158.
15. (1864), 3 H. & C., at pp. 341, 342.

business, and such skill as he ought to have, viz., the skill usual and requisite in the business for which he receives payment"[16].

3. *To act in good faith.*—Whatever the agent does must be done in good faith for the benefit of his principal. An agent must never place himself in such a position as to cause his duty and his interest to conflict. It is for this reason that he must not act for the advancement of his personal interests nor turn himself into a principal without his principal's assent. Therefore, if a broker is employed to buy as an agent, he may not sell his own goods to his principal unless the latter assents[17]. For the same reason an agent cannot accept commission from both parties to a contract without the fullest disclosure to and the consent of each principal[18].

Secret profits.—It follows also that an agent must not make any secret profit out of the agency. He stands in a fiduciary position and anyone who acquires profits by reason of such position and by reason of the opportunity of knowledge resulting from it most account for it to the person to whom he stands in fiduciary relationship[19]. In *Kimber v. Barber*[20]:

> the plaintiff desired to procure shares, and defendant agreed to buy some for him at a price; in fact, defendant had already bought some for less and he sold these to the plaintiff, and the Lord CHANCELLOR held that defendant was an agent and must hand over the difference between the bought and sold price.

It is not necessary that the principal should have suffered any loss or even that the agent should have been acting directly in his principal's business. In *Reading v. Att.-Gen.*[1]:

---

16. "Gross negligence" has, however, been described as the same thing as negligence, with the addition of a vituperative epithet. The point to bear in mind is that what amounts to actionable negligence in a paid agent may not amount to actionable negligence in a gratuitous negligence, but it has been suggested that one of the effects of the House of Lords' decision in *Hedley Byrne, & Co., Ltd. v. Heller and Partners, Ltd.*, [1963] 2 All E. R. 575; [1964] A. C. 465, may be that a gratuitous agent is liable for any lack of reasonable care if he has undertaken to perform the task and in reliance on such promise the principal acts to his detriment (Fridman, Law of Agency, 3rd ed. 1971, p. 126).
17. *Lucifero v. Castel* (1887), 3 T. L. R. 371; *Armstrong v. Jackson*, [1917] 2 K. B. 822.
18. *Fullwood v. Hurley*, [1927] 1 K. B. 498; *Anglo-African Merchants, Ltd. v. Bayley*, [1969] 2 All E. R. 421; [1970] 1 Q. B. 311; *North and South Trust Co. v. Berkeley*, [1971] 1 All E. R. 980; [1971] 1 W. L. R. 471 (practice criticised of Lloyd's insurance brokers, agents of insured, acting also for underwriters).
19. *Regal (Hastings), Ltd. v. Gulliver*, [1942] 1 All E. R. 378; [1967] 2 A. C. 134; *Phipps v. Boardman*, [1966] 3 All E. R. 721; [1967] 2 A. C. 46, H. L.
20. (1873), L. R. 8 Ch. 5.
1. [1951] 1 All E. R. 617; [1951] A. C. 507, H. L.

A soldier wearing uniform rode on civilian lorries carrying illicit spirits. His presence ensured that the lorries were not inspected by the police. He received £20,000 for this service. *Held:* the Crown could claim this sum as the soldier had used his authority as a means of obtaining a profit for himself.

A sub-agent who is aware that he is being employed by an agent of the principal stands in a fiduciary relationship to the principal, and will be accountable to him for any secret commission received, even though no privity of contract has been established between the sub-agent and the principal[2].

An agent who takes a secret commission is a debtor to his principal for the amount thus received; but the principal cannot claim that the agent is trustee for him of the actual money, and so cannot follow the money into and claim the investment in which the agent has placed it; the principal's remedy is to bring an action and get judgment for an amount equivalent to that received by the agent[3]. An agent who receives a secret profit must not only account for it to his principal, but also forfeits his right to commission in respect of the transaction in connection with which the corrupt bargain was made[4]. However, if the agent has acted *bona fide*, then although he will have to give up to his principal any secret profit, he may be permitted to retain his remuneration[5].

Bribes are a particular kind of secret profit. A bribe is a payment to the agent by a third party who knows the agent is acting as such and the payment is kept secret from the principal. An agent who receives a bribe may be dismissed without notice[6] and may be required to pay the bribe over to his principal.

The fact that the principal has recovered from his agent a bribe received, will not of itself prevent him from proceeding for damages against the third party who paid the bribe and the agent for conspiracy to defraud—they are jointly and severally liable[7]. And further, where a contract has been entered into with an agent who has been induced to accept a bribe, the principal may refuse to be bound by the contract, irrespective of any effect the bribe may have had on the agent's mind[8].

The agent or third party, or both, may also be prosecuted under the Prevention of Corruption Acts 1906 and 1916, but proof of corrupt motive is necessary.

---

2. *Powell* v. *Evan Jones & Co.*, [1905] 1 K. B. 11. See also, *post*, p. 130.
3. *Lister* v. *Stubbs* (1890), 45 Ch. D. 1.
4. *Andrews* v. *Ramsay & Co.*, [1903] 2 K. B. 635.
5. *Hippisley* v. *Knee Brothers*, [1905] 1 K. B. 1.
6. *Boston Deep Sea, etc., Co.* v. *Ansell* (1888), 39 Ch. D. 339.
7. *Mayor of Salford* v. *Lever*, [1891] 1 Q. B. 168; *Grant* v. *Gold, etc., Syndicate, Ltd.*, [1900] 1 Q. B. 233.
8. *Shipway* v. *Broadwood*, [1899] 1 Q. B. 369.

Misuse of confidential information.—It is part of the agent's duty of good faith not to misuse confidential information. An agent may not employ, save in his principal's interest, materials and information which the agent has obtained or been supplied with only for his principal and in the course of his agency[9]; he owes a duty to keep secret information given to him and documents entrusted to him for the purpose of his agency. But an agreement not to disclose offences which ought to be divulged to a third party in the interests of justice is contrary to public policy, and disclosure will not expose the original recipient of the information to an action for damages[10].

4. *To act personally.*—A further duty of the agent is to do the work himself, and not to commit it to others for performance, for the old maxim applies—*Delegatus non potest delegare.*

"One who has authority to do an act for another must execute it himself, and cannot transfer it to another"[11].

But this needs some modification, for though it applies where personal trust is put in the agent, or where personal skill is required, yet in many cases it does not, especially under these circumstances:

(*a*) Where custom sanctions delegation;
(*b*) Where delegation is necessary to proper performance;
(*c*) Where there is an agreement, express or implied, to allow it.

The leading case on this part of the subject is *De Bussche* v. *Alt*[12]:

There, a plaintiff (resident in England) consigned a ship to G. & Co., in China, for sale on certain terms, and G. & Co., with the knowledge of the plaintiff, employed the defendant in Japan to sell it.

A point arose in the action whether or not the delegation was good, and THESIGER, L.J., in giving the judgment of the court, said:

The maxim (*delegatus non potest delegare*) "when analysed, merely imports that an agent cannot, without authority from his principal, devolve upon another obligations to the principal which he has himself undertaken to personally fulfil; and that, inasmuch as confidence in the particular person employed is at the root of the contract of agency, such an authority cannot be implied as an ordinary incident in the contract. But the exigencies of business do from time to time render necessary the carrying out of the instructions of a principal by a person other than the agent

---

9. *Lamb* v. *Evans*, [1893] 1 Ch. 219; *Robb* v. *Green*, [1895] 2 Q. B. 315. See also *post*, p. 434.
10. *Howard* v. *Odham's Press*, [1937] 2 All E. R. 509; [1938] 1 K. B. 1.
11. Bacon's Abr. Auth. D.
12. (1878), 8 Ch. D. 286.

originally instructed for the purpose . . . And we are of opinion that an authority to the effect referred to may and should be implied, where from the conduct of the parties to the original contract of agency, the usage of trade, or the nature of the particular business which is the subject of the agency, it may reasonably be presumed that the parties to the contract of agency originally intended that such authority should exist, or where in the course of the employment unforeseen emergencies arise which impose upon the agent the necessity of employing a substitute".

In this case, the agent was authorised to create privity of contract between his principal and the sub-agent in Japan, but the general rule is that the sub-agent is the agent's agent and no privity is created between the principal and the sub-agent.   In consequence, therefore, the sub-agent cannot normally claim remuneration or indemnity from the principal and the principal cannot normally claim direct against the sub-agent if the latter has displayed a lack of due care[13].

5. *To account to the principal.*—The agent must not intermix his affairs with those of the principal, *e.g.* he should not pay money received as agent into his own private account[14] and he must always account to his principal for money received on the latter's behalf[15].

Rights of an agent as against his principal
1. In the first place, the agent has a right to the remuneration agreed upon, or if none has been fixed, then in cases where a contract to pay for his services is to be implied from the circumstances, the agent is entitled to be paid what is usual and customary in the business in which he has been employed, or, in the absence of custom or usage, to a reasonable remuneration.

Where the terms on which commission is to be paid are clearly stated in the contract there is no room for an implied term.   So in *Luxor (Eastbourne), Ltd.* v. *Cooper*[16]:

An agent was employed on terms that he should be paid a commission on completion of a sale.   He produced a person ready able and willing to buy but the owners refused to sell.   *Held:* the agent was not entitled to commission.

---

13. However, since the House of Lords decision in *Hedley Byrne & Co. Ltd.* v. *Heller and Partners, Ltd.*, [1963] 2 All E. R. 575; [1964] A. C. 465, the lack of privity would seem not to prevent an action in the tort of negligence against the sub-agent, at any rate where the agent gives the sub-agent possession of the principal's goods and there is lack of care as to their safety: *Gilchrist Watt and Sanderson Pty., Ltd.* v. *York Products, Pty., Ltd.*, [1970] 3 All E. R. 825; [1970] 1 W. L. R. 1262, P. C.
14. *Gray* v. *Haig* (1854), 20 Beav; 219.
15. *De Mattos* v. *Benjamin* (1894), 63 L. J. Q. B. 248.
16. [1941] A. C. 108; [1941] 1 All E. R. 33.

In that case there was no room for an implied term that the agent should be paid on the basis of a *quantum meruit* or that the owner would accept a reasonable offer. If the agency contract is designed to attract commission on no more being done than the provision of an offer, then that result must be stated in quite clear and precise terms[17].

Thus, if an estate agent is engaged on the basis that commission will be paid to him by the vendor "on introducing a purchaser", that means someone who does purchase and not one who merely makes a definite offer to purchase[18]. Once there is a binding contract of sale, however, the vendor cannot wrongfully withdraw from it except at the risk of having to pay his agent commission, because it is his own fault that the sale has not been completed[19]. If it is not the vendor but the purchaser who withdraws, the case is entirely different and no commission is payable[20].

In *Midgley Estate, Ltd.* v. *Hand*[1], commission was payable to the agents as soon as someone introduced by them "shall have signed a legally binding contract effected within a period of three months from this date". The person introduced signed a legally binding contract within that period but was unable to raise the money to complete the purchase. The Court of Appeal ruled that, on the terms of the agents' contract, they had earned their commission; the terms were clear and unambiguous.

Where an agent is to be paid commission "on securing an offer to purchase", normally at not less than a specified price, commission is payable as soon as such an offer is made. The effect of an agent being appointed "sole agent" is that commission is payable even if the ultimate purchaser is introduced by another agent but not if the vendor himself sells. If the agent is given "the sole right to sell", it seems that he may claim commission even if the owner himself sells.

Generally speaking, when a contract of agency is terminated, no further commission is payable to the agent even though the principal obtains the benefit of making contracts with persons introduced by the agent before such termination[2]. It is, however, a matter of con-

---

17. See *Dennis Reed, Ltd.* v. *Goody*, [1950] 1 All E. R. 919; [1950] 2 K. B. 277: *Christie Owen and Davies, Ltd.* v. *Stockton*, [1953] 2 All E. R. 1149.
18. *Jones* v. *Lowe*, [1945] 1 All E. R. 194; [1945] K. B. 73.
19. *E. P. Nelson & Co.* v. *Rolfe*, [1949] 2 All E. R. 584; [1950] 1 K. B. 139.
20. *Dennis Reed, Ltd.* v. *Goody*, [1950] 1 All E. R. 919; [1950] 2 K. B. 277.
1. [1952] 1 All E. R. 1394; [1952] 2 Q. B. 432. See also *Ackroyd & Sons* v. *Hasan*, [1960] 2 All E. R. 254; [1960] 2 Q. B. 144, C.A.; and *Wilkinson, Ltd.* v. *Brown*, [1966] 1 All E. R. 509; in the latter case, commission was payable when the agent introduced someone "prepared to enter into a contract of purchase". This phrase was held to mean someone ready, willing and able to enter such a contract.
2. *Nayler* v. *Yearsley* (1860), 2 F. & F. 41.

struction and if commission is payable on all business done with persons introduced by the agent "as long as we do business", the obligation is a continuing one[3]. However, the court may decline to order an account to be taken every year till "the crack of doom". Instead it may award compensation to be assessed on the basis that after termination of the agency the agent is entitled to go on receiving commission on repeat orders with a reduction to take account of expenses saved[4].

On termination of an agency, the agent may, depending on the construction of the contract, be required to repay any commission paid to him on account if it has not actually been earned by him before the agency terminated[5].

2. An agent is entitled to be indemnified for losses and liabilities incurred by him in the course of the agency. Thus, in one case,

> where the agent was made liable in damages for seizing goods improperly, and it was shown that he did it *bona fide*, and at the command of his principal, he was adjudged to be entitled to indemnity[6].

So if a principal directs his agent to engage in any enterprise in which by any particular custom or usage of the market, liabilities are incurred, the agent will be entitled to be indemnified against these unless the custom is inconsistent with the contract. WILLES, J., in *Whitehead* v. *Izod*, said:

> "It is familiar law that a principal who employs an agent to purchase goods for him in a particular market is to be taken to be cognizant of and is bound by the rules which regulate dealings therein; and the agent is entitled to be indemnified by his principal for all he does in accordance with those rules"[7].

To this last proposition limits have to be placed.

(i) If the loss is caused by default of the agent himself, his right disappears[8];

(ii) the custom must be one that is well known; so notorious in the market that those dealing there may easily ascertain it, and may well be supposed to have knowledge of it[9];

---

3. *Wilson* v. *Harper*, [1908] 2 Ch. 370; see also *Sellers* v. *London Counties Newspapers*, [1951] 1 All E. R. 544; [1951] 1 K. B. 784.
4. *Roberts* v. *Elwells Engineers, Ltd.*, [1972] 2 All E. R. 890; [1972] 2 Q. B. 586, C. A.
5. *Bronester, Ltd.* v. *Priddle*, [1961] 3 All E. R. 471; [1961] 1 W. L. R. 1294.
6. *Toplis* v. *Crane* (1838), 5 Bing. N. C. 636; *Betts* v. *Gibbins* (1834).
7. (1867), L. R. 2 C. P. 228.
8. *Duncan* v. *Hill* (1873), L. R. 8 Ex. 242; *Ellis* v. *Pond*, [1898] 1 Q. B. 426.
9. *Grissell* v. *Bristowe* (1868), L. R. 3 C. P. 112.

(iii) the custom must be legal and reasonable, or else express knowledge of the custom should be shown to exist[10].

It has been held that when a person at the request of another incurs some liability, which, though not legally enforceable, is paid in consequence of some moral pressure (*e.g.* danger of expulsion from a society), the principal may be legally liable to indemnify his agent. In *Read* v. *Anderson*[11],

> an agent was employed to make a bet; the horse lost, and the agent paid; had he not done so, he would have been posted as a defaulter; it was decided that he could recover from his principal the amount paid[12].

3. An agent has a right to a lien, the particular kind varying with the class of agent. See the chapter on "LIENS"[13].

4. In some cases an agent has a right to stop goods *in transitu*[14] as when, being agent of the consignee, he has made himself liable for the price by having pledged his own credit[15]. This right may not be exercised if the general balance between the principal and agent is in favour of the former.

V AUTHORITY OF AN AGENT

Actual authority—express, implied, and usual authority

In considering the authority of an agent two questions arise, firstly, the extent of the actual authority of the agent and, secondly, the degree to which the principal may become bound to third parties by acts of the agent which are outside that authority. If the agent acts within his actual authority to effect a contract with a third party, then the third party and the principal are bound by it; if the agent exceeds his actual authority, he is guilty of a breach of duty and may be liable both to dismissal and to indemnify his principal. Actual authority includes express, implied, and usual authority. *Express* authority is authority specifically given to the agent and the extent of the agent's express authority is a matter of construction, if the authority is written, or a question of fact if it is verbal. Acts done within the agent's *implied* authority are those that are necessarily required for or

---

10. *Neilson* v. *James* (1882), 9 Q. B. D. 546; *Perry* v. *Barnett* (1885) 14 Q. B. D. 467; 15 Q. B. D. 388; *Seymour* v. *Bridge* (1885), 14 Q. B. D. 460.
11. (1884), 13 Q. B. D. 779.
12. This case was decided before the passing of the Gaming Act 1892; through the principle of the decision is still good law, that Act would, in this particular case, have procured an opposite result.
13. *Post*, pp. 411–413.
14. *Post*, pp. 211–214.
15. *Hawkes* v. *Dunn* (1830), 1 C. & J. 519.

reasonably incidental to the carrying out of the purposes for which the agency was created. An agent has *usual* authority to do these acts that are of the kind that someone in the agent's trade or profession usually has authority to do. Various examples of implied or usual authority may be given. Thus in *Johnston* v. *Kershaw*[16].

> A principal gave an agent abroad authority to purchase 100 bales of cotton and the agent purchased 94 only, this being all that was practicable. *Held:* the agent had authority to use his discretion according to the state of the market.

In *Wallace, Re, Ex parte Wallace*[17]:

> A solicitor was authorised to conduct legal proceedings. *Held:* he was justified in presenting a bankruptcy petition against a debtor of his principal.

So, also, a man put in charge of a shop will have implied authority to order goods for the purposes of the trade carried on; and to receive payments from customers, and give receipts. But an agent to sell does not necessarily have implied authority to receive payment[18] and an agent who is appointed to receive a debt must normally take cash and is not impliedly authorised to take a cheque[19].

An estate agent has implied authority to receive a deposit from a prospective purchaser and the vendor is normally liable for any default of the estate agent whereby the deposit is lost[20].

But where the terms of the authority are clearly defined there is no room for implied terms. Thus in *Catlin* v. *Bell*[1]:

> Goods were delivered to an agent for sale at a certain place, and he was unable to sell them there; it was decided that he had no authority to send them elsewhere in search of a market.

So in *Jonmenjoy Coondoo* v. *Watson*[2]:

> An authority to "sign for me and in my name . . . any and every contract . . . and from time to time to negotiate, make sale, dispose of, assign and transfer," certain property was held to authorise sale but not pledge.

---

16. (1867), L. R. 2 Exch. 82.
17. (1884), 14 Q. B. D. 22. As to counsel's authority, see *Matthews* v. *Munster* (1887), 20 Q. B. D. 141; *Neale* v. *Gordon Lennox*, [1902] A. C. 465.
18. *Butwick* v. *Grant*, [1924] 2 K. B. 483.
19. *Williams* v. *Evans* (1866), L. R. 1 Q. B. 352.
20. *Burt* v. *Claude Cousins & Co., Ltd.*, [1971] 2 All E. R. 611; [1971] 2 Q. B. 426, C. A. However, where an estate agent received the deposit as 'stakeholder' and an unsatisfied judgment was obtained by the purchaser against the estate agent for the return of the deposit, the purchaser was debarred from claiming its return from the vendors: *Barrington* v. *Lee*, [1971] 3 All E. R. 1231; [1972] 1 Q. B. 326, C. A.
1. (1815), 4 Camp. 183.
2. (1884), 9 App. Cas. 561.

If the authority is ambiguous and the agent *bona fide* adopts one interpretation and acts upon it, the principal cannot repudiate the transaction on the ground that he meant the authority to be taken in the other sense[3].

If a third party has actual knowledge of the extent of the agent's express authority, he cannot make the principal liable for acts of the agent outside that authority. But where the agent is acting within his implied or usual authority a secret limitation of the authority is no answer to the claims of those who are not aware of any limitation. Thus, in *Watteau* v. *Fenwick*[4],

> B was manager of A's beerhouse and A forbad him to purchase cigars for the business from third parties. B did order cigars from C on credit such being within the authority usually given to such an agent. C was unaware B was an agent and unaware of the secret limitation on his authority. *Held:* C could claim the price of the cigars from A.

Factors Act 1889.—Agents in possession of goods or documents of title relating to them have by virtue of this Act implied authority to dispose of the title to the goods A "document of title" is defined by s. 1 (4) of the Act to include,

> "any bill of lading, dock warrant, warehouse-keeper's certificate, and warrant or order for the delivery of goods, and any other document used in the ordinary course of business as proof of the possession or control of goods, or authorising or purporting to authorise, either by endorsement or by delivery, the possessor of the document to transfer or receive goods thereby represented".

The Act applies mainly to "mercantile agents", and a mercantile agent means one

> "having in the customary course of his business as such agent authority either to sell goods, or to consign goods for the purpose of sale, or to buy goods, or to raise money on the security of goods"[5].

A mere servant or shopman is not a mercantile agent, but the fact that a person is acting for one principal only and has no general occupation as an agent does not exclude him from filling that character[6].

---

3. *Ireland* v. *Livingston* (1872), L. R. 5 H. L. 395.
4. [1893] 1 Q. B. 346; *cf.* Partnership Act, s. 5, *post.* p. 159. *A fortiori*, if the agent was acting within his actual authority, it is no defence that he was using that authority for his own ends (*Hambro* v. *Burnand*, [1904] 2 K. B. 10).
5. Factors Act 1889, s. 1.
6. *Lowther* v. *Harris*, [1927] 1 K. B. 393.

The following are the chief provisions of the Act:

"Where a mercantile agent is, with the consent of the owner[7], in possession[8] of goods or of the documents of title to goods, any sale, pledge[9], or other disposition of the goods, made by him[10] when acting in the ordinary course of business of a mercantile agent, shall, subject to the provisions of this Act, be as valid as if he were expressly authorised by the owner of the goods to make the same; provided that the person[11] taking under the disposition acts in good faith, and has not at the time of the disposition notice that the person making the disposition has not authority to make the same"[12].

These provisions only apply if the mercantile agent is in possession of goods or of the documents of title to goods in his capacity *as* a mercantile agent, *i.e.* for some purpose connected with a possible sale, such as display. They do not apply if the mercantile agent is in possession for some other purpose, such as repair or safe custody[13].

The sale by a mercantile agent of a car without its registration book is not a sale "in the ordinary course of business"[14]. Hence, if the owner of a car gives possession of it to a dealer with a view to its being displayed for sale, but retains the car's registration book no buyer of the car from the dealer could claim to have a good title under the Factors Act.

Where documents of title to goods were pledged with a bank and re-delivered to the pledgor under a trust receipt for sale on behalf of the bank, an unauthorised pledge of the goods to third parties acting in good faith was held good against the bank; because where rights of ownership are divided between different persons and one of them is given possession with the consent of the other, those persons together

---

7. Such consent is presumed, unless there is evidence to the contrary (Factors Act 1889, s. 2 (4)). The fact that the consent has been obtained by fraud does not exclude the section. See *Pearson* v. *Rose and Young*, [1950] 2 All E. R. 1027; [1951] 1 K. B. 275; *Du Jardin, Ltd.* v. *Beadman Brothers*, [1952] 2 All E. R. 160; [1952] 2 Q. B. 712.
8. *I.e.*, when the goods or documents are in his actual custody, or in the custody of some other person subject to his control, or for him, or on his behalf (*ibid.*, s. 1 (2)).
9. Including lien or giving security on goods or documents (Factors Act 1889, s. 1 (5)).
10. Or his clerk or other person authorised in the ordinary course (s. 6).
11. In the case of joint purchasers, the transaction will not be upheld unless they have all acted in good faith (*Oppenheimer* v. *Fraser*, [1907] 2 K. B. 50).
12. Factors Act 1889, s. 2 (1).
13. *Pearson* v. *Rose and Young, Ltd.*, [1950] 2 All E. R. 1032; [1951] 1 K. B. 275, at p. 288, *per* DENNING, L.J.
14. *Pearson* v. *Rose and Young, Ltd.*, [1950] 2 All E. R. 1027; [1951] 1 K. B. 275; *Stadium Finance, Ltd.* v. *Robbins*, [1962] 2 All E. R. 633; [1962] 2 Q. B. 664.

are the "owner", and the one in possession acting as mercantile agent can sell or pledge the goods so as to bind all interests[15].

The general authority of a mercantile agent to pledge goods cannot be restricted by the custom of any particular trade (not known to the pledgee) which purports to deprive the mercantile agent of such authority[16].

If the owner withdraws his consent, a disposition to any person acting in good faith will nevertheless remain good, provided such person has not at the time of the sale or disposition received notice of such withdrawal[17]. The agent who, by reason of being or having been in possession of goods with the owner's consent, obtains possession of the documents of title to them, is deemed to hold these documents with the owner's consent[18].

Section 3 enacts that:

"A pledge of documents of title to goods shall be deemed to be a pledge of the goods;"

but when a mercantile agent pledges goods as security for a debt or liability due from the pledgor to the pledgee before the time of the pledge, the pledgee can acquire no further right to the goods than could have been enforced by the pledgor at the time of the pledge[19].

Agency by estoppel

If someone has so acted as from his words or conduct to lead another to believe that he has appointed A to act as his agent, he will generally be estopped from denying the agency. A is said to have apparent or ostensible authority. Thus, where P appoints A as his agent to purchase goods and A does purchase goods from T, if subsequently P dismisses A, P will still be liable on later contracts made by A with T (even though A is acting fraudulently for his own benefit) unless P has expressly informed T that A no longer has authority. So, a principal who entrusts title deeds to an agent for the purpose of borrowing a limited sum of money, will, as a condition of recovering the deeds, be liable to repay the whole amount, though the agent exceeds the limit, if the excess was advanced in ignorance of the limitation: and where the principal permits the agent to have possession of the title deeds, the principal will be so liable although the lender (acting in good faith) did not know that the agent had no authority to borrow at all, and made no inquiry[20].

---

15. *Lloyds Bank* v. *Bank of America, etc., Association*, [1938] 2 K. B. 147, C.A.
16. *Oppenheimer* v. *Attenborough & Son*, [1908] 1 K. B. 221.
17. Factors Act 1889, s. 2 (2).
18. *Ibid.*, s. 2 (3).
19. Factors Act 1889, s. 4.
20. *Brocklesby* v. *Temperance Building Society*, [1895] A. C. 173.

Breach of warranty of authority

An agent who represents himself to have an authority from a principal which he really does not possess, or exceeds that which he does possess, is liable to an action at the suit of third parties for breach of warranty of authority, provided the want of authority was not known to such parties[21]. Nor is it different if the agent *bona fide* supposed himself to have authority[22]; even though his original authority has ceased by reason of facts of which he has not knowledge or means of knowledge, *e.g.* by the death or insanity of his principal, or in the case of a company by its dissolution[23].

This doctrine is not limited to cases where the professing agent purports to *contract* on behalf of an alleged principal: any person who suffers damage by acting on the untrue assertion of authority may sue for breach of the implied warranty. Thus, in *Starkey* v. *Bank of England*[24],

a broker, innocently acting under a forged power of attorney for the transfer of Consols, required the Bank of England in performance of their statutory duty to transfer the Consols in their books. Upon discovery of the forgery, the true owner of the Consols compelled the bank to make good the loss, and the bank was held entitled to indemnity from the broker.

It will be observed that the bank made no contract of any kind, but simply performed a duty upon the faith of the alleged agency.

But in cases where a breach of warranty of authority, or an undertaking to indemnify, is sought to be implied the facts must not be such as to negative that implication[25].

VI WHO CAN SUE AND BE SUED

Whether principal, or agent, or both, are liable on a given contract

---

21. *Collen* v. *Wright* (1856), 7 E. & B. 301; 8 E. & B. 647; *Firbank's Executive* v. *Humphreys* (1887), 18 Q. B. D. 54; *Halbot* v. *Lens*, [1901] 1 Ch. 344; *Salvesen* v. *Rederi Aktiebolaget Nordstjernan*, [1905] A. C. 302.
22. *Polhill* v. *Walter* (1832), 3 B. & Ad. 114. As to the measure of damages, see *Meek* v. *Wendt* (1888), 21 Q. B. D. 126; and *Re National Coffee Palace Co.* (1883), 24 Ch. D. 367.
23. *Yonge* v. *Toynbee*, [1910] 1 K. B. 215.
24. [1903] A. C. 114. Apart from agency, a person who presents a forged transfer for registration impliedly undertakes to indemnify the company or corporation against any loss resulting therefrom (*Sheffield Corporation* v. *Barclay*, [1905] A. C. 392). In *Bank of England* v. *Culter* [1908] 2 K. B. 208, a broker who identified as the registered holder of certain stock a person who was fraudulently personating such holder, was held liable to indemnify the bank for the consequent loss on the ground that his conduct amounted to a request to the bank to permit the entry and registration of the forged transfer.
25. *Gowers* v. *Lloyds and National Provincial Foreign Bank, Ltd.*, [1938] 1 All E. R. 766.

is a matter depending upon the intention of the parties and authority of the agent.

Generally, an agent is not liable on the contract, and a principal is; but to this rule many exceptions are found, most of them depending upon the rule that if by his conduct one person causes another to believe that a principal is being dealt with, he cannot put that other in a worse position by any subsequent disclosure of his character as agent; *e.g.*

> A owes B money, and B buys goods to the amount, supposing A to be vendor; A cannot afterwards, by showing himself to be an agent only, prevent B from setting off the debt against the price.

Relations with third persons where principal disclosed

Here, in the absence of evidence to the contrary, the principal, and he alone, has liabilities and rights. But an agent, under certain circumstances, may be liable even in this case, *e.g.*

(i) if he agrees to be so[1];
(ii) where the principal does not exist, or is not in a condition to be bound by the contract[2];
(iii) if the contract is by deed, and the agent executes it in his own name though he describes himself as signing "for and on behalf of" another.
(iv) when the custom of trade makes him liable.

If the contract has been reduced into writing it is a question of construction whether the agent contracted personally, or for a princial, and where a person signs a contract in his own name, without qualification, he is *prima facie* to be deemed to be contracting personally. But where the signature is qualified, *e.g.* by adding the words "on account of" or "as agent", then whether the principal is named or not, the qualified signature must be taken as intended to negative personal liability, although other words and clauses in the body of the document may indicate the contrary[3].

If upon the terms of a written contract the agent appears as principal, he is bound, though as a fact it was known at the time that he was bargaining as agent only, unless he can show that the contract was so

---

1. See, *e.g. International Rail. Co.* v. *Niagara Parks Commission*, [1941] 2 All E. R. 456; [1941] A. C. 328.
2. *Kelner* v. *Baxter* (1866), L. R. 2 C. P. 174.
3. *Gadd* v. *Houghton* (1876), 1 Ex. D. 357; *Ariadne S.S. Co.* v. *James McKelvie & Co.*, [1922] 1 K. B. 18, C. A.; affd. *sub nom. Universal Steam Navigation Co.* v. *James McKelvie & Co.*, [1923] A. C. 492.

drawn up by mistake; and this follows from the general rule, that oral evidence cannot be admitted to vary a written contract[4].

It was at one time thought that where a home agent contracts on behalf of a foreign principal there is a presumption that the agent alone could sue and be sued unless the contrary intention plainly appears from the contract itself or the surrounding circumstances[5]; but the Court of Appeal has now held that no such presumption exists[6]. The nationality of the principal is merely one factor in determing whether T has shown he is willing to treat P as a party to the contract and if so whether A is a party too.

An agent may sue on a contract even if his principal is disclosed, if he has an interest (*e.g.* lien) in the proceeds; for this reason an auctioneer may sue for the price of goods[7].

Settlement with the agent.—If the principal owes money to the third party under the contract, then generally speaking he remains liable although he has paid his agent. In *Irvine & Co.* v. *Watson and Sons*[8],

> the defendants employed C to buy oil; C bought some of plaintiffs', saying it was for principals, but not naming them; the terms were cash on delivery; it was not an invariable custom to pay on delivery; the oil was delivered and defendants, supposing the cash had been paid (which was not the fact), settled with C; when C became insolvent, plaintiffs sued the defendants. *Held:* defendants must pay, though if the plaintiffs had led the defendants to believe that the agent and they had settled matters, the defendants would have been protected.

Relations with third persons where principal undisclosed

In this case the general rule is that the contract may be adopted against or by the principal or the agent at the wish of the parties. In *Sims* v. *Bond*[9] one branch of the rule was thus expressed

> "where a contract not under seal is made by an agent in his own name for an undisclosed principal, either the agent or the principal may sue on it."

In *Thomson* v. *Davenport*[10], the other branch of the rule was stated by TENTERDEN, C.J., as follows:

---

4. *Higgins* v. *Senior* (1841), 8 M. & W. 834. See notes to *Thomson* v. *Davenport* (1829), 2 Sm. L. C. (13th ed.) 336; and see *Wake* v. *Harrop* (1861), 6 H. & N. 768; 1 H. & C. 202, as to mistake.
5. Lord TENTERDEN in *Thomson* v. *Davenport* (1829), 9 B. & C., at p. 87.
6. *Teheran-Europe Co., Ltd.* v. *S. T. Belton (Tractors), Ltd.*, [1968] 2 All E. R. 886, C. A.
7. *Williams* v. *Millington* (1788), 1 H. Bl. 81; *Chelmsford Auctions Ltd.* v. *Poole*, (1972), *Times*, December 19, C. A.
8. (1879) 5 Q. B. D. 102; affirmed (1880), 5 Q. B. D. 414.
9. (1833), 5 B. & Ad., at p. 393.
10. (1829), 9 B. & C. at p. 86.

"If a person sells goods (supposing at the time of the contract that he is dealing with a principal) but afterwards discovers that the person with whom he has been dealing is not the principal in the transaction, but agent for a third person, though he may in the meantime have debited the agent with it, he may afterwards recover the amount from the real principal."

But an agent contracting merely as such for an *unnamed* principal will not incur personal liability, unless by reason of some usage or custom which is not inconsistent with any express term of the contract[11].

If the principal sues upon the contract, he must do so subject to any right of set-off that the third party may have acquired against the agent before he knew him to be acting for a principal[12]. In *Rabone v. Williams*[13],

factors sold to W, and when the undisclosed principal sued, W claimed to set-off a debt due by the factors to him, and the claim was allowed.

This set-off cannot be allowed if the third party was aware that the agent was really such, although he was not aware of the identity of the principal; thus in the case of a sale he should show that the contract was made by a person to whom the principal had entrusted possession of the goods, that that person sold them as his own goods in his own name, and that he (the buyer) believed the agent to be the principal, and that the set-off claimed accrued before he was undeceived[14].

In *Cooke v. Eshelby*[15],

L & Co. sold C cotton in their own names, really on behalf of M. C knew that L & Co. sometimes sold for principals and sometimes on their own account, but did not know, and did not inquire whether or not in this case they had principals. It was decided that money owed by L & Co. could not be set-off against the price of the cotton; Lord WATSON saying, that to entitle a purchaser to set-off a debt due by an agent against one due to the principal, it must be shown "that the circumstances attending the sale were calculated to induce, and did induce, in the mind of the purchaser, a reasonable belief that the agent was selling on his own account, and not for an undisclosed principal."

As the doctrine of constructive notice does not extend to ordinary commercial transactions, a person dealing with an agent in the honest belief that he is the principal is not affected by mere notice of facts

---

11. *Hutchinson v. Tatham* (1873), L. R. 8 C. P. 482.
12. *George v. Clagett* (1797), 2 Sm. L. C. (13th ed.) 131, and for a later example, see *Montagu v. Forwood*, [1893] 2 Q. B. 350.
13. (1785), 7 T. R. 360, n.
14. *Semenza v. Brinsley* (1865), 18 C. B. N. S. 467; *Borries v. Imperial Ottoman Bank* (1874), L. R. 9 C. P. 38.
15. (1887), 12 App. Cas. 271.

which might on inquiry lead to the discovery of the existence of a principal[16].

If in the contract the agent expressly or impliedly contracts that he is the only principal, there is no right of action in the actual principal; the agent alone can sue or be sued. In *Humble* v. *Hunter*[17],

> an agent entered into a charter-party and described himself as "owner" of the ship; it was held that evidence was not admissible to show that another was principal, nor could that other sue on the contract. For if the principal allows the agent to represent himself as principal, the agent alone can sue on the contract made.

Subject to this, the third party (as stated above) may bring his action against either the agent or the undisclosed principal, and oral evidence will be admitted to show that a written contract purporting to be made by a certain person is in reality made by him as agent.

The liability of principal and agent is alternative and not joint, and though the creditor may be entitled to elect against which of them he will enforce his remedies, any unequivocal acts showing an intention to hold one of them liable will discharge the other[18]. If the creditor obtains judgment on the contract against the principal, he cannot afterwards get judgment against the agent, nor, if he gets it against the agent, can he afterwards succeed against the principal[19]. Moreover, the remedy against the undisclosed principal may be lost if the principal has settled with the agent before the third party was aware that there was a principal. Thus, in *Armstrong* v. *Stokes*[20],

> P engaged A to buy goods and A bought from T without disclosing he was acting as an agent. P paid A the price of the goods but A did not pass this on to P. *Held:* P was not liable to T as P had paid the price to A at a time when T did not know of P and was giving credit to A alone.

Rights and duties when the principal is non-existent

Although an agent expressly contracting as such cannot generally

---

16. *Greer* v. *Downs Supply Co.*, [1927] 2 K. B. 28.
17. (1848), 12 Q. B. 310. *Cf. Formby Bros.* v. *Formby* (1910), 102 L. T. 116, C. A.; *Fred. Drughorn, Ltd.* v. *Rederiaktiebolaget Transatlantic*, [1919] A. C. 203; *Epps.* v. *Rothnie*, [1946] 1 All E. R. 146; [1945] K. B. 562.
18. *Scarf* v. *Jardine* (1882), 7 App. Cas. 345. The institution of proceedings against either the principal or the agent does not necessarily amount to a binding election so as to bar proceedings against the other: *Clarkson Booker, Ltd.* v. *Andjel*, [1964] 3 All E. R. 260; [1964] 2 Q. B. 775.
19. *Kendall* v. *Hamilton* (1879), 4 App. Cas., *per* CAIRNS, L.C., at p. 514.
20. (1872), L. R. 7 Q. B. 598. This decision was criticised by the Court of Appeal in *Irvine & Co.* v. *Watson & Sons* (1880), 5 Q. B. D. 414, discussed *ante*, p. 140.

sue in his own name, he may do so if the contract has been partly performed after the other party has had full notice that the supposed agent was the real principal[21], and in a charter-party a person contracting as "agent of the freighter" may declare himself to be the real principal and adopt the character of freighter himself[1]. A contract purporting to be made by a non-existent company will normally take effect as a contract entered into by the person purporting to act for the company[2].

If a professing agent names a principal who is non-existent or incapable of contracting, the agent may himself be sued. In *Kelner* v. *Baxter*[3]:

> the defendants, on behalf of an intended company agreed with the plaintiffs to pay for goods to be supplied to the company; after formation of the company, the goods were supplied and consumed, but the court held that defendants, having contracted as agents for a non-existent company, were personally liable, and that no subsequent ratification or substitution of liability was of any avail to them without the consent of the plaintiffs.

Equitable liability of principal for money borrowed without authority

In some cases where an agent borrows money on behalf of another without any authority or in excess of his authority, although the mere fact of the borrowing may impose no liability on the principal, yet the lender acting in good faith has an equitable right to recover against the principal any part of the money borrowed which has in fact been applied in paying legal debts and obligations of the principal[4]. The lender is subrogated to the position of P's creditor. And even where the agent is known to have no authority to borrow, yet to the extent to which the money borrowed is applied to payment of legal debts of the principal, the lender may assert this equitable right[5].

This equity may also protect an agent who pays his principal's debts without authority. Thus, where a bank contrary to instructions

---

21. *Rayner* v. *Grote* (1846), 15 M. & W. 359.
1. *Schmaltz* v. *Avery* (1851), 16 Q. B. D. 655. The agent could not have enforced the contract himself if he had purported to contract for a named principal whose identity was material.
2. European Communities Act 1972, s. 9, overruling *Newborne* v. *Sensolid (Great Britain), Ltd.*, [1953] 1 All E. R. 708; [1954] 1 Q. B. 45.
3. (1866), L. R. 2 C. P. 174; see also European Communities Act 1972, s. 9.
4. *Blackburn, etc., Building Society* v. *Cunliffe, Brookes & Co.* (1883), 22 Ch. D. 61; affirmed *sub nom. Cunliffe Brooks & Co.* v. *Blackburn, etc., Building Society* (1884), 9 App. Cas. 857; *Bannatyne* v. *MacIver*, [1906] 1 K. B. 103.
5. *Reversion Fund and Insurance Co.* v. *Maison Cosway*, [1913] 1 K. B. 364.

honoured the cheques of a company on the signature of one director only, the cheques having been drawn in favour of and the proceeds received by ordinary trade creditors of the company, so that its liabilities were not thereby increased, the bank on being sued by the company for the amount of the cheques was held entitled to take credit for such payments[6].

VII PARTICULAR TYPES OF AGENTS[7]

1. Factors
A factor is an agent

> "employed to sell goods or merchandise consigned or delivered to him by or for his principal for a compensation"[8].

He is sometimes called a consignee and sometimes a commission agent; but a salaried servant who holds goods for his master is not of necessity a factor, although he may have a special power of sale. A broker and a factor are different sorts of agents, the chief points of difference being that the broker has not possession of the goods, whereas the factor has[9], and whilst the factor *may* sell in his own name, the broker may not[10].

The powers of a factor:

(i) to sell in his own name[11], subject to the ordinary rules relating to sale for undisclosed principals;

(ii) to give a warranty, if it is usual in the course of the business[12];

(iii) to receive payment and give valid receipts[13]; to sell on credit to a reasonable extent[14];

(iv) he has an insurable interest in the goods[15];

(v) he has powers of pledging under the Factors Act.

(vi) he has a general lien, *i.e.* in respect of the general balance of his charges on any goods that have come to him *quâ* factor and

---

6. *Liggett (Liverpool)* v. *Barclays Bank*, [1928] 1 K. B. 48.
7. "Mercantile agent" is a term which covers many of the following: the meaning of the term "mercantile agent", and the position of those who fall within it are referred to *ante*, pp. 135–137.
8. Story, Agency, s. 33.
9. See judgment in *Stevens* v. *Biller* (1884), 25 Ch. D. 31.
10. See *Baring* v. *Corrie* (1818), 2 B. & Ald., at p. 143.
11. See *Baring* v. *Corrie* (1818), 2 B. & Ald., at p. 143.
12. *Brady* v. *Todd* (1861), 9 C. B. N. S. 592; 30 L. J. C. P. 223.
13. *Drinkwater* v. *Goodwin* (1775), 1 Cowp. 251; *Fish* v. *Kempton* (1849) 7 C. B. 687; 18 L. J. C. P. 206.
14. *Houghton* v. *Matthews* (1803), 3 B. & P., at p. 489.
15. *Post*, p. 283.

on the proceeds of such goods[16]. This lien he loses if he delivers possession of the goods to the owner[17], but a right of set-off which the third party may have against his principal will not affect his lien[16].

2. Brokers

A broker is defined by Story[18] to be

"an agent employed to make bargains and contracts in matters of trade, commerce, or navigation between other parties for a compensation commonly called brokerage."

He is an agent of a mercantile character, and one who makes a merely personal contract for another is not strictly a broker; *e.g.* A makes an agreement on behalf of B to sing at a concert; A would not be a broker[19].

Brokers are distinguishable from factors; factors have possession of the goods[20], and brokers have not; factors may buy and sell in their own names; brokers (apart from special custom) cannot[1].

Generally speaking a broker is not liable on the contract, if he is known to be contracting *quâ* broker merely, though the name of the principal be not given in the contract note[2], but he may be made liable by

   (i) custom[3], or

   (ii) contract, or

   (iii) if on the note he appears to contract for himself as principal.

In accordance with general principles of agency, the other party may hold the undisclosed principal liable.

As brokers have not possession of goods they have no lien; but to this there is an exception in the case of an insurance broker, who has a lien on the policy for his general balance, and this extends even against

---

16. *Drinkwater* v. *Goodwin, supra.*
17. *Kruger* v. *Wilcox* (1755), Amb. 252.
18. Story, Agency, s. 28; and see *per* Brett, J., in *Fowler* v. *Hollins* (1872), L. R. 7 Q. B., at p. 623.
19. See *Milford* v. *Hughes* (1847), 16 M. & W. 174.
20. Brokers are mercantile agents, but as they are not, as brokers, entrusted with possession of the goods, they do not come within the Factors Act 1889. See *ante*, p. 135, and see *Cole* v. *North Western Bank* (1874), L. R. 9 C. P. 470; 10 C. P. 354.
1. See *Baring* v. *Corrie* (1818), 2 B. & Ald. 137, 143, 148; *Fairlie* v. *Fenton* (1870), L. R. 5 Ex. 169.
2. *Southwell* v. *Bowditch* (1876), 1 C. P. D. 374.
3. *Fleet* v. *Murton* (1872), L. R. 7 Q. B. 126; in *Pike* v. *Ongley* (1887), 18 Q. B. D. 708, a hop-broker was, in consequence of custom, held liable for non-delivery when a contract note was worded thus: "Sold by [*defendant*] to [*plaintiff*] for and on account of owner."

the principal of an agent who employed him, provided that he had no notice of the agent's character[4].

3. Insurance brokers

An insurance broker is the name given to an agent who is employed to negotiate a policy of insurance. He stands in a peculiar position. In *Power* v. *Butcher*, it was said by BAYLEY, J., that:

> "According to the ordinary course of trade between the assured, the broker, and the underwriter, the assured do not in the first instance pay the premium to the broker, nor does the latter pay it to the underwriter. But as between the assured and the underwriter the premiums are considered as paid. The underwriter, to whom in most instances the assured are unknown, looks to the broker for payment, and he to the assured. The latter pay the premiums to the broker only, and he is a middleman between the assured and the underwriter. But he is not solely agent; he is a principal to receive the money from the assured and to pay it to the underwriters"[5].

Hence the broker is debtor to the underwriter and creditor of the assured for the premiums; he receives the policy from the underwriters, over which he has a lien as against the assured for the premiums and charges[6]; the underwriters cannot sue the assured for the premiums; but in the event of a loss the assured may sue the underwriters direct.

It may be that the underwriter and the broker have cross-claims against one another. Can the underwriter asset such set-off against the claim of the assured? As a rule he cannot, but usage, known to the assured at the date of effecting the policy, will authorise such a set-off; so also may undue delay on the part of the assured prejudicing the position of the underwriter or the state of his accounts with the broker[7]. The insurance broker must prepare for his principal a proper policy duly stamped; and he must exercise diligence in procuring an adjustment in the event of a loss covered by the policy.

4. Shipbrokers

A shipbroker is an agent employed to arrange for the chartering of ships; if a charter-party is signed, he generally becomes entitled to commission from the shipowner.

---

4. *Mann* v. *Forrester* (1816), 4 Camp. 60.
5. (1830), 10 B. & C., at pp. 339, 340; Marine Insurance Act 1906, s. 53 (1); and see *Universo Insurance Co. of Milan* v. *Merchants' Marine Insurance Co.*, [1897] 2 Q. B. 93.
6. Marine Insurance Act 1906, s. 53, (2). This lien extends to any balance on any insurance account due to the broker from the person who employed him to effect the policy, unless when the policy was effected the broker had reason to believe that such person was only an agent (*ibid.*).
7. *Scott* v. *Irving* (1831), 1 B. & Ad. 605, 613.

5. Bankers

The banker is the agent of the customer to pay sums of money as ordered, but the ordinary relationship between banker and customer is that of debtor and creditor; the banker being creditor when the customer's account is overdrawn, the customer being the creditor when the balance is in his favour[8]. However the ordinary rule that a debtor must seek his creditor does not apply; and the obligation to pay does not arise until the customer or banker, as the case may be, has made a demand for payment upon the other. Accordingly, the period of limitation will only commence to run from the date of such demand[9].

The customer is entitled to draw cheques on the banker to the extent of the money standing to his credit[10]; the banker has a general lien on all securities of the customer deposited with him as banker to secure any sum in which the customer may be indebted to the banker unless there be an express contract, or circumstances that show an implied contract inconsistent with lien[11]. With regard to bills of exchange: a banker has authority to pay bills accepted by the customer and made payable at his bank[12], but he is not bound to do so[13].

A banker is under a qualified duty to keep secret the state of his customer's account, his customer's transactions and information relating to the customer acquired through keeping the account, and disclosure (except with the consent of the customer) is only justifiable:

(i) where made under compulsion of law;

(ii) where made in pursuance of a duty to the public;

(iii) where necessary to protect the interests of the banker[14].

The banker's duty of secrecy continues after the closing of the customer's account.

If a bank, with its customer's express or implied assent, answers enquiries regarding the customer's credit, it owes a duty of care to the enquirer and will be liable for loss suffered as a result of careless

---

8. *Foley* v. *Hill* (1848), 2 H. of L. Cas. 28.
9. *Joachimson* v. *Swiss Bank Corporation* [1921] 3 K. B. 110; C. & T., p. 239.
10. *Pott* v. *Clegg* (1847), 16 M. & W. 321. When the cheque has been paid it becomes the property of the drawer, but the banker may keep it so long as it was wanted as a voucher.
11. *Brandao* v. *Barnett* (1846), 12 Cl. & F. 787.
12. *Kymer* v. *Laurie* (1849), 18 L. J. Q. B. 218.
13. Lord MACNAGHTEN in *Bank of England* v. *Vagliano*, [1891] A. C., at p. 157. The position of a banker who pays a forged instrument or a genuine instrument with a forged indorsement is dealt with, *post*, p. 274.
14. *Tournier* v. *National Provincial and Union Bank of England*, [1924] 1 K. B. 461. By statutory authority, the Inland Revenue is empowered in certain circumstances to require a banker to give information about a customer's account.

misstatements unless it has excluded liability, for example, by giving the advice "without responsibility"[15].

6. Auctioneers

An auctioneer is a person employed to sell property by auction. The following points should be noticed:

(i) He is an agent for the seller (with authority to do all such acts as come within an auctioneer's province), and when the goods have been knocked down, for the buyer also, and his signature is then sufficient to satisfy the requirements of s. 40 of the Law of Property Act 1925[16].

(ii) He may not give warranties as to the property unless expressly so authorised.

(iii) The auctioneer may himself sue for or receive the price of goods even where the principal is disclosed[17].

(iv) He must not delegate his authority[18].

(v) He should sell only for cash[19], and at the best price.

(vi) He is responsible to his principal for loss sustained through his delivering the goods without receiving the price[20], and he is answerable for the proper storage of goods whilst they are with him.

(vii) He has possession of the goods, and a lien on them[20].

(viii) He has implied authority to sell goods without reserve, but if a sale is notified as being subject to reserve and the auctioneer knocks down goods to a "buyer" at less than the reserve price the buyer has no right to the goods and cannot sue the auctioneer for breach of warranty of authority.[1]

(ix) An auctioneer who sells on behalf of A goods which really belong to B, and who delivers the goods to the purchaser, is liable in damages for conversion at the suit of B, though he acted without knowledge of B's rights[2]. If the true owner recovers the goods from the person to whom the auctioneer has sold them, the auctioneer may be liable to that purchaser.

---

15. *Hedley Byrne & Co., Ltd.* v. *Heller & Partners, Ltd.*, [1963] 2 All E. R. 575; [1964] A. C. 465.
16. See *ante*, p. 8.
17. *Williams* v. *Millington* (1788), 1 Hy. Bl. 81; *Chelmsford Auctions Ltd.* v. *Poole* (1972), *Times*, December 19, C. A. As to land, he may only receive the deposit: *Sykes* v. *Giles* (1839), 5. M. & W. 645.
18. *Coles* v. *Trecothick* (1804), 9 Ves. 234, 251.
19. Unless it is customary to accept a cheque, and he acts without negligence in taking one (*Farrer* v. *Lacy* (1886), 31 Ch. D. 42).
20. *Williams* v. *Millington* (1788), 1 H. Bl. 81, at p. 84. See *ante*, p. 140.
1. *McManus* v. *Fortescue* [1907] 2 K. B. 1, *cf. Fay* v. *Miller, Wilkins & Co.* [1941] 2 All E. R. 18; [1941] K. B. 360.
2. *Consolidated Co.* v. *Curtis & Son*, [1892] 1 Q. B. 495, 500.

The auctioneer's obligations to the purchaser were listed by SALTER, J., in *Benton* v. *Cambell, Parker & Co.*[3] as follows:

(*a*) he warrants his authority to sell;

(*b*) he warrants he knows of no defect in his principal's title;

(*c*) he undertakes to give possession against the price paid into his hands;

(*d*) he undertakes that such possession will not be disturbed by his principal or himself.

> However, an auctioneer does not warrant his principal's title to sell *specific goods* if he discloses he is acting for a principal even though he does not name his principal. With unascertained goods, an auctioneer warrants his principal's title if the principal is either undisclosed or merely unnamed.

As to illegal biddings at auctions, see *post*, p. 218.

7. Stockbrokers

A person who employs a broker[4] on the Stock Exchange impliedly gives him authority to act in accordance with its rules, though these may not be known to the principal, and the broker is entitled to be indemnified by his client for all that he does in accordance with those rules[5]; but the client is not bound by the rules if they are either illegal or unreasonable *and* not known to him[6]. The printed rules of the Stock Exchange are now taken to be known to the client, but he is not bound by a custom as such without evidence of his being acquainted with it[7].

The fact that the custom is unreasonable or illegal, such as the custom to disregard Leeman's Act[8], is good ground for supposing that the client has not consented to be bound by it[9], but it is not conclusive[10]; nor is the client discharged merely because the custom contradicts the ordinary law of contract; thus:

---

3. [1925] 2 K. B. 410.
4. Owing to the fact that members of Stock Exchange are personally liable to one another, whether they are agents for an outside client or not, and that disputes arise only upon the failure of a member, the form of contract about which there is litigation is usually one made by a broker on behalf of a client with a jobber acting as principal. At any rate it will be convenient in considering the legal effect of the rules to have this kind of contract chiefly in view.
5. *Sutton* v. *Tatham* (1839), 10 A. & E. 27; *Chapman* v. *Shepherd* (1867), L. R. 2 C. P. 228, *per* WILLES, J., at p. 238; *Forget* v. *Baxter*, [1900] A. C. 467, at p. 479. See *ante*, pp. 132–133.
6. *Smith* v. *Reynolds* (1892), 66 L. T. 809, C. A.
7. *Benjamin* v. *Barnett* (1903), 8 Com. Cas. 244; *Robinson* v. *Mollet* (1875), L. R. 7 H. L. 818; *Neilson* v. *James* (1882), 9 Q. B. D. 546.
8. See *ante*, p. 54.
9. *Perry* v. *Barnett* (1885), 15 Q. B. D. 388.
10. *Seymour* v. *Bridge* (1885), 14 Q. B. D. 460.

there is a well-recognised usage that a purchaser of securities is not entitled to refuse acceptance of part only of the securities, though according to ordinary law he could insist on a tender of the whole amount or none; a broker may obtain securities from different sellers and the client must indemnify him for those which he has paid for[11].

The following points should be noticed:

1. The broker, being an agent, must not make a secret profit, and he must act in accordance with the authority given to him by his client[12].

2. If the broker sells before the date upon which he is instructed to sell, the client may repudiate the contract[13].

3. If instead of making a contract for his client with a jobber he acts as principal without the knowledge or consent of his client and sells to him securities of his own, the client may repudiate the transaction altogether[14]. Of course there is nothing to prevent a broker acting as principal if the client consents; and in every case it is a question of fact whether or not a broker is acting as principal, and if he is a principal whether or not the client has consented to deal with him as such. Thus:

> a broker may purchase a block of shares on the market, allocating some to his client and keeping the rest for himself, but this does not make him a principal in respect of the shares he allocates[15].

4. The client is bound as principal to indemnify the broker against the personal liability which the broker incurs under the rules of the Stock Exchange. Thus:

> if A acting as principal instructs a broker to sell the shares of B, A thereby undertakes that B is and will continue to be ready and willing to complete the transfer. If B refuses and the broker has to purchase other shares to fulfil his bargain, A must indemnify the broker[16].

5. Since the client is bound to indemnify the broker against the claims of the jobber it is the duty of the broker, in the event of the client not being able to meet his engagements, to minimise the loss

---

11. *Benjamin* v. *Barnett* (1903), 8 Com. Cas. 244.
12. This is the ordinary law of agency, but it was specially applied to Stock Exchange transactions in *Johnson* v. *Kearley*, [1908] 2 K. B. 514; *Stubbs* v. *Slater*, [1910] 1 Ch. 632, C. A.; *Aston* v. *Kelsey*, [1913] 3 K. B. 314, C. A.   See *ante*, pp. 125–129.
13. *Ellis* v. *Pond*, [1898] 1 Q. B. 426, C. A.
14. *Johnson* v. *Kearley*, [1908] 2 K. B. 514. See *ante*, p. 127.
15. *Scott* v. *Godfrey*, [1901] 2 K. B. 726.
16. *Hichens, Harrison, Woolston & Co.* v. *Jackson & Sons*, [1943] A. C. 266; [1943] 1 All E. R. 128.

as far as possible[17]. If the client declares his inability to complete the purchase of securities the broker may immediately close the account, *i.e.* pay for and take up the securities instead of arranging for a "carry over". A subsequent sale of the securities at the best price obtainable so as only to charge the client with the difference between the purchase price and the price at which they were sold is the ordinary and legitimate method of minimising the client's loss[18].

8. Wives

By virtue of cohabitation, a man's wife (or mistress) is presumed to have authority to pledge the man's credit for necessaries. In determining whether goods supplied are necessaries, regard is had to the man's style of living rather than to his actual means[19].

However, a man is not liable on contracts made by his wife for necessaries if:

(i) the trader has been warned expressly not to supply goods to the wife on credit;
(ii) the wife has been forbidden to pledge her husband's credit;
(iii) the wife was supplied with sufficient means to purchase necessaries without pledging her husband's credit;
(iv) the trader gave credit exclusively to the wife; or
(v) the household already had a sufficient supply of the particular goods bought.

However, where a man has in the past held out his wife to a trader as having his authority to pledge his credit (for necessaries or otherwise), the husband will be liable on any later contract made by his wife unless the trader has been expressly told that the authority has been withdrawn. This is merely another example of agency by estoppel[1].

The former law, that a deserted wife was an agent of necessity with authority to pledge his credit, was abrogated by the Matrimonial Proceedings and Property Act 1970, s. 41.

9. Agents of necessity

In an emergency, A may have power to bind P without prior authority, and even though P refuses to ratify A's actions. Thus, the master of a ship may borrow money on the owner's credit to purchase necessaries required during a voyage where it is impracticable to communicate with the owner. In *Great Northern Rail. Co. v. Swaffield*[2]:

---

17. *Walter* v. *King* (1897), 13 T. L. R. 270.
18. *Macoun* v. *Erskine, Oxenford & Co.*, [1901] 2 K. B. 493, C. A.; *Lacey* v. *Hill (Crowley's Claim)* (1874), L. R. 18 Eq. 182.
19. *Phillipson* v. *Hayter* (1870), L. R. 6 C. P. 38.
1. See *ante*, p. 121.
2. (1874), L. R. 9 Ex. Ch. 132.

the railway company incurred the expense of stabling a horse after it had been carried to its destination and there was no one to receive it. Although the company had no express or implied authority to incur such expense, it was entitled to claim an indemnity from the owner of the horse as an agent of necessity.

No one may claim to be an agent of necessity unless it is impossible or impracticable to communicate with the principal in order to obtain his instructions[3]. In any case, any action taken must be reasonably necessary in the circumstances[4] and taken in good faith in the interests of the principal[5].

10. Del Credere Agents

A *del credere* agent is an agent for sale who undertakes to pay if the buyer becomes insolvent; but such an agent does not guarantee the due performance of the contract in the sense that the seller may sue him in respect of any breach by the buyer other than his failure to pay. Such disputes must be fought out between the principals, the agent only guaranteeing that the buyer will prove solvent and not default in payment[6].

The *del credere* agent will be liable though the arrangement has not been reduced to, or evidenced by, writing, as his guarantee promise is only part of the larger contract of agency and the courts have held that the provisions of the Statutes of Frauds are excluded in such a case[7].

---

3. *Springer* v. *G. W. Rail. Co.*, [1921] 1 K. B. 257.
4. *Prager* v. *Blatspiel, Stamp and Heacock, Ltd.*, [1924] All E. R. Rep. 524; [1924] 1 K. B. 566.
5. *Sachs* v. *Miklos*, [1948] 1 All E. R. 67; [1948] K. B. 23.
6. *Gabriel & Sons* v. *Churchill and Sim*, [1914] 3 K. B. 1272.
7. *Sutton & Co.* v. *Grey*, [1894] 1 Q. B. 285, and *post*, p. 379.

CHAPTER 12

Partnership[1]

I INTRODUCTORY

The law of partnership is concerned partly with the rights and duties of partners between themselves and partly with the legal relations between partners and third persons which flow from or are incident to the formation of a partnership. The Partnership Act 1890 is a statute which declared and amended the law of partnership; and though it does not contain the whole of that law, the main principles of it are authoritatively settled by the statute[2].

II DEFINITION OF A PARTNERSHIP

Section 1 of the Partnership Act 1890 defines partnership as follows:

"Partnership is the relation which subsists between persons carrying on a business in common with a view of profit. But the relation between members of any company or association which is—

"(i) registered as a company under the Companies Act 1862 or any other Act of Parliament for the time being in force and relating to the registration of joint stock companies[3], or

"(ii) formed or incorporated by or in pursuance of any other Act of Parliament or letters patent, or Royal Charter; or

"(iii) a company engaged in working mines within and subject to the jurisdiction of the Stannaries[4];

"is not a partnership within the meaning of this Act."

Distinctions from a company.—Partnerships, then, must be distinguished from trading companies. Companies engaged in trade are almost invariably incorporated under the Companies Acts and such companies are governed by a completely different code of law.

The main practical difference between a company and a partnership is that the formation and existence of a partnership depends upon

---

1. In this chapter the references to sections are to those of the Partnership Act 1890.
2. The principal practitioner's work is Lindley on Partnership (13th ed., 1971).
3. The Act at present in force is the Companies Act 1948.
4. The Stannaries Court has been abolished, and the Act must now be construed as referring to mines which would otherwise have been subject to its jurisdiction. See Stannaries Court Abolition Act 1896, s. 3.

mutual trust and the personal relationship of the members to each other, whereas the formation and existence of a company does not depend to any extent on this; further, whilst in a partnership every member is entitled to take part in the management of the business unless he bargains away his right, in a company the management is left to specified officers[5]. In law, the essential difference is that a company is regarded as being a separate entity from its members[6], while a partnership is not, although, as a matter of procedure, many things can be done in the name of the firm. "The firm" is simply a short name substituted for the names of the members composing the partnership and every partner is liable *personally* to the full extent of his fortune for any debt of the firm. When an action is brought against partners in the firm name, it is still in effect an action against each of the individual partners[7].

Limit on numbers.—By the Companies Act 1948, a banking partnership may not consist of more than ten persons but the Companies Act 1967 allows a banking partnership of not more than twenty persons each of whom is for the time being authorised by the Department of Trade to be a member of such partnership[8].

With regard to other partnerships, the general rule is that the partnership may not consist of more than twenty persons but this restriction does not apply to partnerships of solicitors, or accountants or members of a recognised stock exchange. The Department of Trade has powers by regulations to exempt other types of partnerships from the general rule[9].

How to identify a partnership.—In addition to defining "partnership" in a general way, and then expressly excluding bodies which would otherwise answer the terms of the definition, the Act lays down certain further rules for determining the existence of a partnership. These rules, set out in section 2, define the principles applicable to the consideration of typical cases, and serve very materially to elucidate and explain the meaning of "partnership". They are as follows:

> "(1) Joint tenancy, tenancy in common, joint property, common property, or part ownership does not of itself create a partnership as to anything so held or owned, whether the tenants or owners do or do not share any profits.

5. It may be doubted whether these differences always exist when the company is a "private company". In such cases the fact of incorporation and the wording of the Partnership Act distinguish companies from partnerships.
6. *Salomon* v. *Salomon & Co.*, [1897] A. C. 22.
7. See *per* JAMES, L.J., in *Shand, Re, Ex parte Corbett* (1880), 14 Ch. D. 122.
8. Companies Act 1948, s. 429 as amended by Companies Act 1967, s. 119.
9. Companies Act 1948, s. 434 as amended by Companies Act 1967, s. 120. Various regulations have been made exempting from the general rule partnerships of specified descriptions such as estate agents and actuaries.

"(2) The sharing of gross returns does not of itself create a partnership, whether the persons sharing such returns have or have not a joint or common right or interest in any property from which or from the use of which the returns are derived.

"(3) The receipt by a person of a share of the profits of a business is *prima facie* evidence that he is a partner in the business, but the receipt of such a share, or of a payment contingent on or varying with the profits of a business, does not of itself make him a partner in the business, and in particular—

"(*a*) The receipt by a person of a debt or other liquidated amount by instalments or otherwise out of the accruing profits of a business does not of itself make him a partner in the business or liable as such:

"(*b*) A contract for the remuneration of a servant or agent of a person engaged in a business by a share of the profits of the business does not of itself make [him] a partner in the business or liable as such:

"(*c*) A person being the widow or child of a deceased partner, and receiving by way of annuity a portion of the profits made in the business in which the deceased person was a partner, is not by reason only of such receipt a partner in the business, or liable as such:

"(*d*) The advance of money by way of loan to a person engaged or about to engage in any business on a contract with that person that the lender shall receive a rate of interest varying with the profits, or shall receive a share of the profits arising from carrying on the business, does not of itself make the lender a partner with the person or persons carrying on the business or liable as such. Provided that the contract is in writing, and signed by or on behalf of all the parties thereto[10]:

"(*e*) A person receiving by way of annuity or otherwise a portion of the profits of a business in consideration of the sale by him of the goodwill of the business is not by reason only of such receipt a partner in the business or liable as such."

Whether a given person is or is not a partner depends upon the facts of the case and the intention of the parties. At one time it was considered that receipt of part of the profits was of itself conclusive proof of partnership, but this is not so[11]. In *Cox v. Hickman*[12],

---

10. The absence of a written and signed contract will not automatically make the lender a partner, but the fact that the lender is to share in the profits is then *prima facie* evidence of partnership—the whole agreement will be looked at to ascertain the real intention of the parties.
11. *Mollwo, March & Co. v. Court of Wards* (1872), L. R. 4 P. C. 419.
12. (1860), 8 H. L. Cas. 268.

A trader owed money to many creditors, and these entered into an arrangement with him, whereby he agreed to carry on the business under their superintendence, and gradually to pay off their debts out of a share of the profits. The case was carried up to the House of Lords, where it was *held*—somewhat against what then seemed the current of authority—that such an arrangement did not constitute a partnership *per se*, and it would only be a partnership if the debtor carried on the business for and on behalf of the creditors, so as to constitute the relation of agent and principal between them. On the facts, there was no partnership.

The Act now states the law as declared in *Cox* v. *Hickman*. If the "lender" is to have a voice in the management, or he is to be repaid only out of the business, or he is to take an interest in the capital, the agreement probably will be considered a partnership.

It is clear that partnership is not the same as co-ownership; the former may include the latter, but the converse will not apply. They may be thus distinguished:

1. Co-ownership is not necessarily the result of agreement, partnership is; *e.g.* A gives land to B and C in common; B and C are not partners, but may become so by agreement among themselves. So the co-owners of a ship are not necessarily partners, and it needs an agreement, express or implied, to make them so;
2. Co-ownership does not, of necessity, involve the idea of working for profit, partnership does;
3. A co-owner has a right of free disposition over his property without the consent of his co-owner; a partner who desires to replace himself by another cannot, in the absence of agreement, do so without the consent of his co-partner.

Sharing profits is strong, though not conclusive, evidence of partnership[13]. At the same time the court will look at the whole of the evidence, and draw the fair inference of fact; only when nothing more is known than that profits are shared, does it *necessarily* follow that there must be a partnership[13]. Persons who work together with a view to forming a company are not normally partners within the meaning of section 1 of the Partnership Act. In *Keith Spicer, Ltd.* v. *Mansell*[14],

M and B agreed to form a limited company and, in the 3 weeks prior to its formation, decided to do certain acts so that the company could start business at once on its formation. B ordered goods

---

13. *Badeley* v. *Consolidated Bank* (1888), 38 Ch. D. 238; and see *Davis* v. *Davis*, [1894] 1 Ch. 393, 399, 401; *Hollom* v. *Whichelow* (1895), 64 L. J. Q. B. 170; *King* v. *Whichelow, ibid.*, 801.
14. [1970] 1 All E. R. 462; [1970] 1 W. L. R. 333, C. A.

from KS Ltd intending them to be used by the company and M and B opened a bank account in the name of the proposed company B became insolvent and KS Ltd sued M for the price of the goods on the basis that M and B were partners when they were ordered. *Held:* M and B were not partners and M was therefore not liable for the price of the goods.

It may be difficult to determine whether discussions with a view to partnership or other evidence tending to point towards a partnership necessarily establish that a partnership in fact exists[15].

Postponement of lender's rights in case of insolvency.—The Act further provides[16] that if any person to whom money has been advanced on a contract[17] to pay a rate of interest varying with the profits, or any buyer of a goodwill who has engaged to pay the vendor a portion of the profits in consideration of the sale, shall be adjudged a bankrupt, or enter into an arrangement to pay his creditors less than 100 pence in the pound, or die in insolvent circumstances, the lender of any such loan shall not be entitled to recover anything in respect of his loan, nor shall any such vendor of a goodwill as aforesaid be entitled to recover anything in respect of the share of profits contracted for, until the claims of the other creditors of the borrower or buyer for valuable consideration in money or money's worth have been satisfied.

III THE FIRM NAME

In the case of a firm having a place of business in the United Kingdom, if the firm name does not consist of the true surnames of all partners who are individuals and the corporate names of all partners who are corporations without any addition except the true christian names or initials of the individual partners and in cases where a partner has changed his name (except in the case of a woman who marries) the firm must be registered under the Registration of Business Names Act 1916. The particulars requiring registration include the business name and the general nature and principal place of the business, and in respect of every individual partner must disclose:

1. His present christian name and surname;
2. Any former christian name or surname;
3. His present nationality;
4. His usual residence; and
5. Any other business occupation that he follows;

---

15. *Floydd* v. *Cheney*, [1970] 1 All E. R. 446; [1970] 1 Ch. 603.
16. Partnership Act 1890, s. 3.
17. Whether such contract is in writing or not (*Re Fort*, [1897] 2 Q. B. 495).

and in respect of every corporation which is a partner the corporate name and registered office must be stated.

Particulars of changes in the constitution of the firm must also be registered.

If there is default in registration the firm cannot sue on any contract entered into while it was in default, unless the court grants relief against the disability, but if the firm is sued on such a contract it will not be precluded from asserting rights under the contract by way of counter-claim or set-off[18]. The court may, *e.g.* if satisfied that the default was an accident or that on other grounds it is just and equitable to grant relief, grant relief generally; or it may do so as respects any particular contract in the course of proceedings to enforce it, and if such relief is granted it will operate retrospectively so as to validate the contract *ab initio* and all subsequent proceedings in respect of it[19]. The title to property of which the defaulter has obtained complete possession is not affected[20].

All registered firms must publish particulars of the names and nationality of the partners in their trade catalogues, trade circulars, show cards and business letters[1].

IV FORMATION OF THE CONTRACT

The contract is formed by consent alone, and no particular formality is required. The agreement may therefore be verbal or implied from conduct, but the general practice is to have a written agreement containing the terms on which the partners are to carry on their business, and this document is styled the *Articles of Partnership*, if under seal, or a *Partnership Agreement*, if not under seal. If an informal partnership is entered into the court will not imply into the agreement more terms than are strictly necessary[2].

V WHO MAY BE PARTNERS

1. Alien *enemies* or persons adhering to the enemy may not be partners of an Englishman, and a partnership between such persons and an Englishman is dissolved when war breaks out[3]; but, where for

---

18. Registration of Business Names Act 1916, s. 8.
19. *Re Shaer*, [1927] 1 Ch. 355.
20. *Daniel* v. *Rogers*, [1918] 2 K. B. 228.
1. Registration of Business Names Act 1916, s. 18, as amended by the Companies Act 1947, s. 123, Sched. IX, Part II.
2. *Miles* v. *Clark*, [1953] 1 All E. R. 779.
3. *Hugh Stevenson & Sons* v. *Aktiengesellschaft für Cartonnagen-Industrie*, [1917] 1 K. B. 842, C. A. This case went to the House of Lords, where it was not disputed that the partnership had been dissolved by the outbreak of war. As to the rights of the enemy partner, see *post*, p. 172.

the purpose of winding up the affairs of a dissolved partnership an action is brought to recover a debt due to the firm, an alien enemy partner may be joined as a co-plaintiff[4].

2. Insanity of a partner will not *ipso facto* dissolve an already existing partnership, but it will be a ground on which the court may decree dissolution.

A minor may be a partner, and, unless he repudiates the contract during his minority or within a reasonable time of becoming 18 (as he may), he remains a member of the firm, though he does not thereby render himself personally liable to creditors for partnership debts contracted during his minority[5]. However, an infant partner cannot prevent partnership debts being discharged out of the partnership assets, including any capital which he may have supplied.

New partners may be admitted, provided the legal number is not exceeded[6], but, of course, the consent of all the existing partners must first have been obtained, either in the original articles or agreement or by subsequent agreement.

VI RIGHTS AND DUTIES OF THE PARTNERS IN RELATION TO THIRD PARTIES

Liability on contracts.—Every partner is an agent of the firm and his other partners for the purpose of the business of the partnership; and, in general, every partner who does any act for carrying on in the usual way business of the kind carried on by the firm binds the firm and his partners[7].

But partners are not liable (*a*) on a contract entered into by a partner outside the scope of the business of the firm, unless the partner was, in fact, specially authorised to make the contract[8], or (*b*) on a contract entered into by a partner without authority if the third party either knows the partner has no authority or does not know or believe him to be a partner[9].

The liability on a partnership debt is joint, not several[10]. But the

---

4. *Rodriguez* v. *Speyer Bros.*, [1919] A. C. 59.
5. *Lovell* v. *Beauchamp*, [1894] A. C., at p. 611, *per* HERSCHELL, L.C.
6. *Ante*, p. 154.
7. Partnership Act 1890, s. 5.
8. Partnership Act 1890, s. 7.
9. *Ibid.*, ss. 5, 8. *Cf.* the rule in ordinary agency law that if an agent acts within his usual authority for an undisclosed principal the principal is bound even though the agent has acted contrary to secret restrictions on his authority: *Watteau* v. *Fenwick*, [1893] 1 Q. B. 346; *ante*, p. 135.
10. *Ibid.*, s. 9; and see *Kendall* v. *Hamilton* (1897), 4 App. Cas. 504; *Badeley* v. *Consolidated Bank* (1887), 34 Ch. D. 536; reversed on another point, 38 Ch. D. 238.

estate of a deceased partner is severally liable in due course of administration for the debts and obligations of the firm while he was a partner, subject to the prior payment of his separate debts[11]. This must not be misunderstood. As a general rule every partner is liable for every penny of the firm's debts, and the creditor has the option to sue any or all of them. If he obtains judgment against the firm, he may issue execution against the property of the members, and is not confined to satisfaction out of the joint property. The liability is joint, but all are liable. He may sue each partner separately, but if he obtains *judgment* against any of them he cannot enforce the judgment against any but those against whom it was pronounced, nor can he afterwards get judgment against the others; for the liability, being a joint—*i.e.* a single liability, has become merged in the judgment. Nor are his rights different, where he does not get any payment under the judgment. Thus in *Kendall* v. *Hamilton*[12],

> A and B (partners) borrowed money from C; eventually C sued them on the loan, and obtained a judgment which was not satisfied. Afterwards C discovered that D was a partner with A and B at the date of the loan, but it was *held* that C had lost his remedy against D, as the joint liability had merged in a judgment which was not pronounced against D. Had D been dead, and his estate been in course of administration, D's estate would have been severally liable, *i.e.* liable on a separate contract to the same effect as the joint one, and this would not have been merged by a judgment against the other contractors.

The above doctrine of merger has no application where there are distinct causes of action; so that if a partner gives his own cheque for the price of goods sold to the firm, the creditor may, if the cheque is dishonoured, recover judgment upon it, without prejudicing his rights to sue the firm or any member of it for the price of the goods, if his judgment on the cheque remains unsatisfied[13].

Implied authority of a partner.—It is quite settled that all partners are bound by the acts or admissions of one, if done within the scope of the business. Story says,

> "a partner, indeed, virtually embraces the character both of a principal and of an agent"[14].

---

11. *Ibid.*, s. 9. In *Bagel* v. *Miller*, [1903] 2 K. B. 212 M's estate was held not liable for the price of goods ordered by the firm at a time when M was a partner but the goods were not delivered until after M's death, since the obligation to pay only accrued on delivery.
12. (1879), 4 App. Cas. 504.
13. *Wegg Prosser* v. *Evans*, [1895] 1 Q. B. 108.
14. *Partnership* § 1.

And in *Baird's Case*[15], JAMES, L.J., said,

> "as between the partners and the outside world (whatever may be their private relations between themselves), each partner is the unlimited agent of every other in every matter connected with the partnership business, or which he represents as partnership business, and not being in its nature beyond the scope of the partnership."

But a partner is an agent only so far as he is acting upon, and within the scope of, the firm's ordinary affairs; that the act is useful to the firm is not sufficient, neither is it necessary; the act done must be a furtherance of the ordinary business of the firm. Even then (as has already been pointed out), the firm will not always be bound, for if a partner attempts to make a firm liable, though within his apparent authority, the firm will not be bound, if in fact he has no authority, and if this was known to the other contracting party, or by the exercise of reasonable diligence could have been known; *e.g.*

> a partner gives a partnership security in discharge of a private debt; the recipient must show that he took it without knowledge, and without such negligence as would amount to knowledge.

In *Kendal* v. *Wood*, COCKBURN, C.J., said, that in a case such as this, the recipient would deal with the partner at his peril[16].

Sir Frederick Pollock[17] dealt with certain of the more ordinary transactions, thus:

1. Every partner may bind his firm by any of the following acts:
   (i) He may sell any goods or personal chattels of the firm;
       [Legal estate in land must be conveyed by all the partners, or by one authorised by *deed*.]
   (ii) He may purchase on account of the firm any goods of a kind necessary for or usually employed in the business carried on by it[18];
   (iii) He may receive payment of debts due to the firm[19], and give receipts and releases for them;

---

15. (1870), 5 Ch. App., at p. 733.
16. (1871), L. R. 6 Ex. 243.
17. Pollock on Partnership (15th ed.), pp. 31, 32.
18. A partner has no implied authority to make his co-partners partners with other persons in another business. But where a partner in a firm of produce merchants agreed with X to buy and re-sell potatoes on joint account, MEGARRY, J., *held* the partner had implied authority to bind his co-partners to such joint venture or partnership with X—such partnership was not "another business": *Mann* v. *D'Arcy*, [1968] 2 All E. R. 172; [1968] 1 W. L. R. 893.
19. In the absence of express or implied authority, a private debt due to one partner is not discharged by payment to the firm of which he is a member (*Powell* v. *Brodhurst*, [1901] 2 Ch. 160).

(iv) He may engage servants for the partnership business.

2. If the partnership is in trade, that is, if the business is one which depends on the buying and selling of goods[20], every partner may *also* bind the firm by any of the following acts:

(i) He may make, accept and issue bills and other negotiable instruments in the name of the firm[1];

[A member of a *non-trading* partnership may bind the firm by negotiable instruments, but only in those cases where it is shown to be within the usual course to issue negotiable instruments, the burden of showing this being on the person attempting to make the firm liable.]

(ii) He may borrow money on the credit of the firm;

(iii) He may, for the purpose, pledge any goods or personal chattels belonging to the firm.

3. A partner has no implied authority to bind the firm by a deed[2], or to give a guarantee in the name of the firm[3], or to bind the firm by a submission to arbitration[4].

The authority continues even after a dissolution, so far as is necessary properly to wind up the business and complete pending transactions, save that a bankrupt partner cannot bind the firm by his acts[5]. And where one of two partners dies, the surviving partner may carry on the business for the purpose of finally winding it up, and may mortgage the real or personal property of the late firm for the purpose of securing a partnership debt[6].

Outgoing partners.—When a partner retires, the other partners may agree to hold him free of all liabilities already incurred, and this, *if* assented to by the creditors, will give him a complete release; if the creditors are not parties to this agreement, either expressly or by implication, then so far as they are concerned, he is still a debtor[7]; but he may have rights of indemnity against his late partners.   Agree-

---

20. *Higgins* v. *Beauchamp*, [1914] 3 K. B. 1192, *per* LUSH, J., at p. 1195, in which case it was *held* that the business of cinema proprietors was not a trading business and in consequence a partner had no implied authority to borrow on behalf of the firm.

1. When a partner's individual name coincides with the firms name and he does not carry on a separate business, his acceptance of a bill of exchange is *prima facie* the acceptance of the firm. See *Yorkshire Banking Co.* v. *Beatson* (1880), 5 C. P. D. 109.

2. *Steiglitz* v. *Eggington* (1815), Holt, N. P. 141.

3. *Brettel* v. *Williams* (1849), 4 Exch, 623.

4. *Stead* v. *Salt* (1825), 3 Bing. 101.

5. Partnership Act 1890, s. 38.

6. *Re Bourne*, [1906] 2 Ch. 427.

7. Partnership Act 1890, s. 17 (2), (3).

ment by the creditors to release a retired (or deceased) partner may be implied from a course of dealing with the firm as newly constituted[8].

A and B are bankers. C and D are admitted as partners, and notice of this reaches the customers; soon after, A and B die, but C and D carry on the business under the old name, and depositors, prior to the death of A and B, leave their money with C and D, receiving interest from the bank after the death of the old partners; the bank fails, and the depositors prove against C and D; this conduct as a whole may amount to a tacit acknowledgment of the release of A and B, and of the substitution of C and D as debtors.

Such an agreement, express or implied is said to be a *novation*[9].

If a member of a firm retires on an agreement with his partners that he shall in future be regarded merely as a surety for the firm's existing debts, the creditors who know this must treat the retiring partner as a surety, and may release him if they give time to the other parties[10].

A change in the constitution of a firm will terminate a continuing guarantee given to the firm or to a third party in respect of the transactions of the firm so far as relates to future transactions, unless agreement to the contrary be made[11].

Incoming partners.—A new partner is not liable for debts incurred before he entered the firm[12] save by special agreement; this agreement can be enforced by any of the parties to it, but not by any creditors merely as such. Thus,

if on June 1st A & Co. owe B £500 and on June 2nd C joins A & Co., agreeing to give a premium and to be answerable proportionately to his interest for the £500, B cannot sue C unless he, B, is a party to the contract, and gives consideration; *e.g.* agrees, if C makes himself partly responsible, to give time to the firm or to release an old partner[13].

Persons liable as partners by holding out.—Generally speaking, the partners alone are liable, but there are classes of persons who, although not partners, are treated by law as such; are, in fact, estopped by their conduct from denying themselves to be members of the debtor firm.

---

8. *Rouse* v. *Bradford Banking Co.*, [1894] 2 Ch., at p. 54; and see *Re Head*, [1893] 3 Ch. 426, with which *cf. Bilborough* v. *Holmes* (1877), 5 Ch. D. 255.
9. See *ante*, p. 73.
10. *Rouse* v. *Bradford Banking Co.*, [1894] A. C. 586.
11. Partnership Act 1890, s. 18.
12. *Ibid.*, s. 17 (1).
13. See *Rolfe* v. *Flower* (1866), L. R. 1 P. C. 27 (a case where such an arrangement was implied).

Those who, not being partners, are so treated, have been styled *quasi*-partners, and they become such by virtue of the rule in section 14 (1):

> "Everyone who by words spoken or written or by conduct represents himself, or who knowingly suffers himself to be represented, as a partner in a particular firm, is liable as a partner to anyone who has on the faith of any such representation given credit to the firm, whether the representation has or has not been made or communicated to the person so giving credit by or with the knowledge of the apparent partner making the representation or suffering it to be made."

The contract is made on his credit, and he is answerable if loss is incurred.

An example of this is to be found in the case of *Martyn* v. *Gray*[14],

> where A introduced B to C as the moneyed partner; B was not a partner, but he stood by, and did not deny the statement, and he was *held* answerable for a loss incurred.

It is sometimes rather harsh, but as EYRE, C.J., said in *Waugh* v. *Carver*[15], it is necessary

> "upon the principles of general policy, to prevent frauds to which creditors would be liable."

But representations of this kind cannot be used against a man unless his conduct causes others to alter their position on the faith of them.

Upon the principle of *"holding out"*, where two persons, who though not in fact partners have traded as such, become bankrupt, the assets of the business will be administered as joint estate[16]. The executors of a deceased partner are not bound by the mere use of the old partnership named by the survivors[17].

A retiring member is not as such liable for debts contracted subsequently to his retirement, but he may be so if he continues an apparent member of the firm as regards persons who are not aware that he had ceased to be a partner. In order to escape liability for future transactions of the firm, he should give actual notice to persons who were in the habit of dealing with it, but a notice in the *London Gazette* will be sufficient as regards persons who had no dealings with the firm before the date of the dissolution or change[18], and it is advisable in the case of local firms to give further notice through the local papers.

---

14. (1863), 14 C. B. (N. S.) 824.
15. (1793), 2 H. Bl. 235.
16. *Ex parte Hayman* (1878), 8 Ch. D. 11.
17. Partnership Act 1890, s. 14 (2). See also *Bagel* v. *Miller*, [1903] 2 K. B. 212, *ante*, p. 160.
18. Partnership Act 1890, s. 36 (1), (2).

The estate of a partner who dies or becomes bankrupt is not liable for partnership debts contracted after the date of death or bankruptcy. Moreover, a partner who retires is not liable for debts contracted after his retirement to persons who did not know he was a partner. This is so even where the partner has taken an active part in managing the firm's business but the third party who deals with the firm after his retirement only learns of his membership of the firm after he has retired[19]. In *Tower Cabinet Co., Ltd.* v. *Ingram*[20],

> X and Y carried on a partnership business and both their names were on the firm's notepaper. The partnership was dissolved but no notice was put in the London Gazette. After the dissolution X continued to trade in the firm name and ordered goods from T using the old notepaper without Y's authority. T sought to make Y liable on the contract. *Held:* there was no holding out under s. 14 as Y had not *knowingly* suffered himself to be represented as a partner and, as T did not know Y to be a partner before Y's retirement, s. 36 (3) relieved him from liability as an apparent partner.

Liability for wrongs.—This rests on a somewhat different footing, for only those who are actual members of the firm are held liable for the consequences; and the principle of "holding out" has no application. Even true partners are not answerable for all wrongs of their co-partners, but only if the wrongful act was committed whilst the partner was acting with his co-partner's authority, or in the ordinary course of the firm's business when the firm is liable to the same extent as the partner who has committed the wrong. In *Hamlyn* v. *Houston & Co.*[1],

> It was within the ordinary course of a business firm of grain merchants to obtain information by legitimate means as to contracts made by competing firms. One partner in the business bribed the clerk of a competitor to disclose such information thereby inducing the clerk to break his contract of employment. *Held:* the firm was liable in damages to the competitor.

The firm is also liable if the tort is misapplication of property, and either the money was received by the misapplying partner within the scope of his apparent authority, or was received by the firm, and misapplied by one or more of the partners whilst in its custody[2].

The liability rests upon the fundamental principle, that within a certain limit, dependent upon the nature of partnership business, each

---

19. *Ibid.*, s. 36 (3).
20. [1949] 1 All E. R. 1033; [1949] 2 K. B. 397.
1. [1903] 1 K. B. 81. See also *Mercantile Credit, Co., Ltd.* v. *Garrod*, [1962] 3 All E. R. 1103.
2. Partnership Act 1890, ss. 10, 11.

member of the firm is agent for the rest[3]. The liability for wrongs is "joint and several". A judgment against one partner is therefore not a bar to a subsequent action against the others[4].

The cases decided on this point are numerous and sometimes difficult to distinguish. The following are fair specimens, and will, for present purposes, sufficiently illustrate the rules:

> Two solicitors are partners, and to one of them a client hands money to be invested on a specific security; this partner makes away with the money, and the other is entirely ignorant of the transaction; nevertheless he is liable, for it is within the ordinary scope of a solicitor's business to receive money to invest on specific securities[5]. Had the money been given to invest at discretion the case would have been different, such investments not being part of a solicitor's work[6].

If a partner, being a trustee, improperly employs trust-property in the business of the firm, the other partners are not liable to replace the trust-property: provided that:

1. Any partner will be liable who has notice of the breach of trust; and
2. Trust-money may be followed and recovered from the firm if still in its possession or under its control[7].

VII RIGHTS AND DUTIES OF THE PARTNERS AS BETWEEN THEMSELVES

It has been said already that it is usual for the partnership agreement to be comprised in written Articles of Partnership or a Partnership Agreement. The rights and duties of the partners will then be regulated by the written terms but a number of rights and duties are implied by s. 24 and these are operative subject to any express agreement to the contrary. It is a basic obligation that each partner will observe the utmost fairness and good faith towards his fellow partners.

The mutual rights and duties of the partners, whether contained in an agreement or implied by the Act, may be varied at any time by the consent of the partners and such consent (which must be unanimous) may be inferred from a course of dealing[8].

---

3. *Ibid.*, s. 12.
4. Law Reform (Married Women and Tortfeasors) Act 1935, s. 6.
5. *Blair* v. *Bromley* (1847), 2 Ph. 354.
6. *Harman* v. *Johnson* (1853), 22 L. J. Q. B. 297. See also *Cleather* v. *Twisden* (1885), 28 Ch. D. 340; *Rhodes* v. *Moules*, [1895] 1 Ch. 236 and *Meekins* v. *Henson*, [1962] 1 All E. R. 899; [1964] 1 Q. B. 472.
7. Partnership Act 1890, s. 13.
8. Partnership Act 1890, s. 19.

When the partnership expires by effluxion of time, and the partners continue together, there is an implied arrangement that the partnership shall continue on the old terms so far as applicable, and the same rule applies when surviving partners continue the business after the death of a member of the old firm. Lord WATSON said:

> "When the members of a mercantile firm continue to trade as partners after the expiry of their original contract, without making any new ageement, that contract is held in law to be prolonged or renewed by tacit consent"[9].

Nevertheless, if the partnership is for a fixed term, and is carried over, the new partnership will be at will only, and its continuance on the old terms will be presumed only so far as these are consistent with the incidents of a partnership at will[10].

Amongst the rights of a partner implied by law (so far as they are unmodified by agreement), are:

1. The right to take part in the management of the business[11]. No remuneration can ordinarily be claimed[12], but compensation for extra trouble caused by the wilful inattention of a co-partner to business may be allowed to the partner or partners upon whom the additional burden is thrown[13].

2. To have the business carried on according to agreement. Its nature cannot be changed without the unanimous consent of all the partners; in ordinary matters connected with the business, a majority will bind the others[14].

3. To prevent the admission of a new partner. No person can be introduced as a partner without the consent of all those who, for the time being, are members of the firm[15]. A partner may assign his share of profits, or may mortgage it; this will only enable the other partners to demand a dissolution if the agreement so provides.

Where a fixed term has been agreed on, a partner may retire only with the consent of all the partners, but where it is a partnership "at will", any partner may retire by giving notice to the other partners[16].

A majority of the partners cannot expel any partner unless a power to do so has been conferred by *express* agreement[17].

---

9. *Neilson* v. *Mossend Iron Co.* (1886), 11 App. Cas. 298, decided on the particular words of the articles.
10. Partnership Act 1890, s. 27.
11. *Ibid.*, s. 24 (5).
12. *Ibid.*, s. 24 (6)
13. *Airey* v. *Borham* (1861), 29 Beav. 620.
14. Partnership Act 1890, s. 24 (8).
15. *Ibid.*, s. 24 (7).
16. *Ibid.*, s. 26.
17. Partnership Act 1890, s. 25; and see *In Re A Solicitor's Arbitration*, [1962] 1 All E. R. 772; [1962] 1 W. L. R. 353.

4. To be indemnified by the firm against personal liabilities incurred and payments made by him in the ordinary and proper conduct of the business; or in or about anything necessarily done for the preservation of the business or property of the firm; *e.g.* a partnership is formed to work a mine, and the business cannot be continued until a new shaft is sunk; a partner who pays the cost required is entitled to indemnity[18].

5. To have interest at the rate of five per cent. per annum on any actual payment or advance to the firm made by him beyond the capital he has agreed to subscribe, from the date of such payment or advance[19]. Apart from agreement, express or implied, no partner is entitled to receive interest on his capital; and if there is a mere agreement to pay interest and nothing more, such interest will only be payable out of profits, *i.e.* it will not be treated as an outgoing or loss of the business[20].

6. To have the books kept at the principal place of business of the firm, and to be allowed to examine and copy them whenever he may desire[1]. The right of a partner to examine the books is not personal to himself, and he may employ an agent to whom no reasonable objection can be taken to examine the books on his behalf; but the agent must undertake not to make use of the information so acquired except for the purpose of advising his principal[2].

7. In the absence of any special agreement, the partners are entitled to share equally in the capital and profits of the business, and must contribute to the losses equally[3].

8. To be dealt with by his colleagues with the utmost good faith in all partnership matters. A number of rules exemplify this principle. Thus:

(*a*) Partners are bound to render true accounts and full information of all things affecting the partnership to any partner or his legal representatives[4].

(*b*) Every partner must account to the firm for any benefit he may derive which is obtained by him (without the assent of the others) from any transaction concerning the partnership or from any use by him of the partnership name or business connection[5]. Thus,

---

18. *Ibid.*, s. 24 (2), and *Ex parte Chippendale* (1853), 4 De G. M. & G. 36.
19. *Ibid.*, s. 24 (3).
20. *Ibid.*, s. 24 (4).
1. Partnership Act 1890, s. 24 (9).
2. *Bevan* v. *Webb*, [1901] 2 Ch. 59.
3. Partnership Act 1890, s. 24 (1).
4. Partnership Act 1890, s. 28.
5. *Ibid.*, s. 29.

A, B, C and D are partners in business as sugar refiners, A being also in trade for himself as a sugar merchant, the other partners being cognisant, and not objecting; A, without the knowledge of the firm, sells sugar at a profit to it. *Held:* he must account for and share this profit with the partnership[6].

(c) A partner who carries on a *competing* business without the consent of the others, must account for and pay over to the firm all profits made by him therein[7].

(d) If in the sale by one partner to another of a share in the partnership business, the purchaser knows, and is aware that he knows, more about the partnership accounts than the vendor, he must put the vendor in possession of all material facts and not conceal what he alone knows; and unless such information is furnished the same may be set aside[8].

After dissolution.—When the partnership is put an end to, new rights accrue to its members:

1. A public notification of the dissolution may be demanded by any partner, and, as the practice of the *Gazette* Office is to require the signature of all the partners, any partner may take action to compel a recalcitrant member to sign[9].

2. Each partner has an equitable lien on the property owned by the firm at the date of dissolution, entitling him to have it applied in payment of the firm's debts, and then in payment of what may be due to the partners[10]. If a partner has been induced to enter the partnership by fraud or misrepresentation, and has, on that ground, obtained rescission of the partnership contract, he will be entitled to repayment of the amount given by him for his share, after the partnership liabilities have been satisfied; and to secure payment of that amount he has a lien on the surplus assets[11].

3. In settling the accounts between the partners after a dissolution, *subject to any agreement*, the assets of the firm (including sums contributed by partners to make up deficiencies of capital) must be distributed in the following order:

6. *Bentley* v. *Craven* (1853), 18 Beav. 75; and see *Featherstonehaugh* v. *Fenwick* (1810), 17 Ves. 298.
7. Partnership Act 1890, s. 30.
8. *Law* v. *Law*, [1905] 1 Ch. 140.
9. Partnership Act 1890, s. 37.
10. *Ibid.*, s. 39. The right of a partner to have the goodwill sold when the firm has been dissolved is referred to *post*, p. 170.
11. Partnership Act 1890, s. 41. He is also entitled to stand in the place of creditors for any payment made by him in respect of partnership liabilities, and is entitled to be indemnified by the person guilty of the fraud against all the debts and liabilities of the firm (*ibid.*).

(i) in paying the debts and liabilities of the firm to persons who are not partners;
(ii) in paying partners rateably what is due from the firm to them for advances as distinguished from capital;
(iii) in paying each partner rateably what is due from the firm to him in respect of capital;
(iv) in distributing the ultimate residue among the partners in the proportion in which profits are divisible[12].

Losses (including deficiencies of capital) must be paid first out of profits; next out of capital; if this is exhausted, then individually by the partners, in the same proportions as the profits would have been divided had any existed[12].

Where partners have contributed unequal capitals and have agreed to share profits and losses equally, if the assets are insufficient to repay each partner the whole of his capital and one of the partners is unable to contribute his share of the loss, the solvent partners are not bound to contribute for him. This, in *Garner* v. *Murray*[13],

> G, M and W became partners on the terms that they should contribute the capital in unequal shares and divide the profits equally. On a dissolution, after satisfying all liabilities to creditors and the advances of the partners, the assets were insufficient to make good the capital. A larger sum was due to G than to M. Nothing could be recovered from W. *Held:* that the true principle of division was for each partner to be treated as liable to contribute an equal third share of the deficiency, and then to apply the assets in paying to each partner rateably what was due to him in respect of capital.

4. Any partner may, on dissolution, require that the property, including the goodwill[14], shall be sold, and he may restrain any other partner from doing anything tending directly to decrease the value, *e.g.* using the firm's name, when an attempt is being made to sell the goodwill. And the goodwill may be sold when a partner dies, for the right to it does not vest in the survivors[15].

5. When one partner on entering into a partnership for a fixed term pays a premium, and before the expiration of the term the firm is dissolved otherwise than by the death of a partner, the court may order a return of all or a certain amount of this premium, but not when the dissolution is wholly or chiefly due to the misconduct of the partner who paid the premium, nor when the firm has been dissolved by

---

12. *Ibid.*, s. 44.
13. [1904] 1 Ch. 57.
14. See *post*, pp. 176–178.
15. *Smith* v. *Everett* (1859), 27 Beav. 446.

an agreement containing no provision for a return of any part of the premium[16].

The entire question is in each case in the discretion of the court and such order will be made as, under the circumstances, will work justice. In *Atwood* v. *Maude*[17],

> one partner took another into business with him for a fixed term, asking a premium as compensation for the latter's inexperience. After two years the original partner demanded a dissolution on the ground of the latter's incompetence, whereupon the new partner sued the original partner for a dissolution and a return of the premium, and the court awarded dissolution and a return to the former of such part of the premium as bore the same proportion to the total amount as the unexpired period of the term bore to the total term agreed upon.

From this judgment it appears that the court will ordinarily order the return of the premium, having regard to the terms of the contract, the position of the parties, and their conduct, and that the amount will be calculated on a proportion similar to that taken in the case mentioned.

6. When a member of a firm ceases to be a partner, he is entitled to a settlement in due course and the amount due is deemed to be a debt accruing due at the date of the dissolution or retirement, unless otherwise agreed[18].

If the continuing or surviving partners trade with the capital or assets of the firm without any final settlement of accounts, the outgoing partner or his estate is, in the absence of agreement to the contrary[19], entitled to such share of the profits made since the dissolution as the court may find to be attributable to the use of the outgoing partner's share of the assets, or, at the option of the outgoing partner or his representatives, to interest at the rate of five per cent. per annum on the amount of such share[20]. If profits are claimed they are not to be measured by the amount to which a partner would have been entitled before his retirement or death, but by his proportionate interest in the assets (including goodwill) used in carrying on the business, and subject to a proper allowance to the continuing partner or partners for personal superintendence and management[1].

---

16. Partnership Act 1890, s. 40.
17. (1868), L. R. 3 Ch. 369.
18. Partnership Act 1890, s. 43.
19. It is advisable to provide for such an event in the articles of partnership, and to fix in them the basis upon which an outgoing partner's share or his rights in the goodwill are to be valued.
20. Partnership Act 1890, s. 42.
1. *Manley* v. *Sartori*, [1927] 1 Ch. 157. See also *Pathirana* v. *Pathirana*, [1967] 1 A. C. 233, P. C.

Where a partnership between a British subject and an alien enemy has been dissolved by the outbreak of war, and the business in England is continued by the English partner with the aid of the alien partner's share of the capital, the latter is not deprived of the rights conferred by s. 42, but nothing can be paid to him until after the conclusion of peace[2].

VIII PROPERTY OF THE FIRM

The assets which are to make up the property of the firm should be defined as fully as possible in the articles of partnership or partnership agreement. Unless otherwise agreed, all property and rights and interests in property originally brought into the partnership stock or acquired, whether by purchase or otherwise, on account of the firm, or for the purposes and in the course of the partnership business, is partnership property. It must be held and applied by the partners exclusively for the purpose of the partnership and in accordance with the partnership agreement[3]; and property bought with the money of the firm is deemed, unless a contrary intention appears, to be partnership property[4].

During the continuance of the firm, the members are joint owners of the property, *i.e.* each owns the whole, and the property is not divided up into portions which belong separately to the members. In ordinary cases of joint ownership, when one joint owner dies, his co-owners succeed to his share: but in the joint ownership arising out of partnership this is not so, and the representative of the deceased succeeds to his interest.

If land is conveyed to partners for partnership purposes, the partners hold the legal estate as joint tenants on trust for sale. As between the partners, and as between the heirs of a deceased partner and his personal representatives, it is treated as personalty not realty[5].

Assignment of share.—A partner who assigns his share of the property to another person, either absolutely or by way of mortgage, gives, according to the terms of the assignment, the assignee the right to receive, in whole or in part, the share of profits and (on dissolution) of the property which would have come to that partner; but the assignee cannot during the continuance of the partnership, inspect the firm's books or interfere in the business[6].

---

2. *Hugh Stevenson & Sons* v. *Aktiengesellschaft für Cartonnagen-Industrie,* [1918] A. C. 239.
3. Partnership Act 1890, s. 20 (1).
4. *Ibid.,* s. 21.
5. Partnership Act 1890, s. 22; *Fuller's Contract, Re,* [1933] Ch. 652.
6. Partnership Act 1890, s. 31.

The assignee cannot complain of a *bona fide* agreement subsequent to the assignment to pay salaries to the partners even though this may diminish the profits[7]; he must also accept the account of profits agreed to by the partners, but on a dissolution he is entitled to have an account taken for the purpose of ascertaining the value of the share assigned, irrespective of any agreement between the partners themselves as to the value of such share[8].

IX DISSOLUTION

The rights and duties consequent upon dissolution have already been considered; it now remains to show how, when, and on what grounds it is brought about. It may be caused in any of the following ways:

1. At the will of a partner where no fixed term has been agreed upon[9]. If the partnership was constituted by deed, the partner desiring to terminate the partnership must give notice in writing; in other cases verbal notice will suffice[10]. But a partnership where no fixed term has been agreed upon, or a partnership entered into for an undefined time, may not be a partnership at will, if the partners have made an agreement to the contrary, *e.g.* that the partnership should be terminated "by mutual arrangement only"[11].

2. By effluxion of the time agreed upon as the term, or if entered into for a single adventure or undertaking, by the termination of that adventure or undertaking[12].

3. Transfer of a partner's interest—

(i) By bankruptcy or death, unless otherwise agreed (as it frequently is)[13];

(ii) At the option of the other partners, if any partner suffers his share to be charged by the court for his separate debt on the application of any of his creditors[14].

Under s. 23 of the Act:

A judgment creditor of any partner may obtain from the court an order charging the share of the partner in the partnership property with the payment of the debt, and may obtain the appointment of a receiver of that partner's share of profits and other moneys coming to

---

7. *Re Garwood's Trusts*, [1903] 1 Ch. 236.
8. *Watts* v. *Driscoll*, [1901] 1 Ch. 294.
9. Partnership Act 1890, ss. 26 (1), 32 (c).
10. *Ibid.*, s. 26 (2).
11. *Moss* v. *Elphick*, [1910] 1 K. B. 846.
12. Partnership Act 1890, s. 32 (a), (b).
13. *Ibid.*, s. 33 (1).
14. *Ibid.*, s. 33 (2).

him in respect of the partnership. The other partners may redeem the interest charged, or if a sale is directed, may buy it. These are alternatives to the partners serving notice to dissolve the partnership. A writ of execution cannot issue against any partnership property save on a judgment against the firm; hence the necessity for this procedure.

4. Occurrence of an event making the partnership illegal[15]: *e.g.* war breaking out between the countries in which the different members of the partnership are trading;

5. Fraud, making the original contract voidable;

6. In addition, the court may decree a dissolution of partnership in any of the following cases:

(i) Where it appears necessary or expedient to the court with regard to a partner who is under a mental disability[16];

(ii) Permanent incapacity of a partner to perform his part of the contract[17];

(iii) Misconduct of a partner calculated to prejudice the business, or persistent breach of the agreement, or such other conduct as makes it not reasonably practicable for the other members to continue in partnership with him[18];

(iv) When the business can only be carried on at a loss[19];

(v) Whenever the court thinks it just and equitable to decree dissolution[20].

In the cases of permanent incapacity, misconduct and persistent breach of agreement, a partnership cannot be dissolved on the application of the partner who is in fault, but a partnership may be dissolved on the application of a partner who is under a mental disability, as well as at the instance of the other members.

Administration of partnership estates

The following rules apply to the administration of the estates of bankrupt and insolvent partners. The partnership property is termed the *joint estate*, and the separate properties of the individual partners the *separate estates*.

---

15. Partnership Act 1890, s. 34.
16. Mental Health Act 1959, s. 103 (1) (f).
17. Partnership Act 1890, s. 35 (b).
18. *Ibid.*, s. 35 (c), (d).
19. *Ibid.*, s. 35 (e).
20. *Ibid.*, s. 35 (f).

The general rule is:

> that joint estate is applied in payment of the debts of the partnership, and separate estate in payment of the individual debts of the partner to whom it belongs; if in either case any surplus remains, the surplus of a separate estate will be transferred to the joint estate, if that is deficient; the joint estate surplus being dealt with as part of the respective separate estates in proportion to the right and interest of each partner in the joint estate[1].

Thus:

> A and B are partners; A owes his separate creditors £100, and his separate estate is £75. B owes £150, and has £175; the firm's debts are £500, and assets £450. The separate creditors of A take the £75, those of B take £150 of the £175, the joint creditors taking the remaining £25.

Again:

> if A and B are partners, and A is insolvent, B being solvent, the joint creditors will recover the full amount from B, B being then allowed to prove against A's estate to the amount which he has paid beyond his proportion.

Similar principles hold in the administration of the estate of a deceased partner in the Chancery Division.

Exceptions:—

1. If there is no joint estate and no solvent partner, the joint creditors may prove against the separate estates on an equal footing with the separate creditors[2].

2. If anyone is defrauded by the partners or one of them so that the firm is liable for the fraud, he may prove his debt at his election *either* against the joint estate *or* against the separate estates of the fraudulent partners[3].

3. When a partner has fraudulently, and without the consent of the others, converted partnership property to his own use, the joint estate may prove against that partner's separate estate in competition with the separate creditors, even though it is not shown that the separate estate has benefited by the conversion[4].

As regards the fraudulent conversion, it was said by JESSEL, M.R., in *Lacey* v. *Hill*, that

> "it is not necessary for the joint estate to prove more than . . . that this overdrawing was for private purposes, and without the

---

1. See Bankruptcy Act 1914, s. 33 (6).
2. *Re Budgett, Cooper* v. *Adams*, [1894] 2 Ch. 557.
3. *Re Collie, Ex parte Adamson* (1878), 8 Ch. D. 807; possibly against the estate of an innocent partner (*Re Stratton, Ex parte Salting* (1884), 25 Ch. D. 148).
4. See *Read* v. *Bailey* (1878), 3 App. Cas. 94.

knowledge, consent, privity, or subsequent approbation of the other partners. If that is shown, it is *prima facie* a fraudulent appropriation within the rule"[5].

And such consent or knowledge must have been real, not constructive, for it is the better opinion that the doctrine of constructive notice is not applicable here[6].

4. If a joint creditor petitions against a partner in respect of his joint debt and that partner is adjudged bankrupt, he is allowed as petitioning creditor to prove his joint debt in competition with the separate creditors[7].

5. Where a partner has carried on a distinct and separate trade and has incurred a debt to the firm or become a creditor of the firm, one estate can prove against the other.

Proof by solvent partner against estate of bankrupt co-partner.—Partners may not compete in an administration with the firm's creditors, either against the joint or against any of the separate estates. But if a solvent partner has paid off the joint creditors or if there is no possibility of a surplus in the separate estate of the co-partner so that the firm's creditors could never obtain anything from him, the solvent creditor may prove for a contribution *pari passu* with the separate creditors of his co-partner[8].

Secured creditor.—A creditor of the firm who holds a security for the debt on the separate property of a partner may prove against the joint estate and retain his security against the separate estate, provided he does not receive in the whole more than the full amount of his debt. And a separate creditor of a partner holding a security on the joint property is in a corresponding position. The reason of the above rule is that the surrender of the security would not augment the estate against which proof was being made[9].

X GOODWILL

The nature of goodwill is intimately connected with the law of partnership, and questions concerning it arise so frequently in partnership matters, that it may be very properly discussed in this place.

---

5. (1876), 4 Ch. D. 543.
6. See *Lacey v. Hill* (1876), 4 Ch. D. 543, and Pollock on Partnership (15th ed.), pp. 155 *et seq.*
7. Bankruptcy Act 1914, s. 114.
8. *Head, Re, Ex parte Head*, [1894] 1 Q. B. 638.
9. *Re Turner* (1882), 19 Ch. D. 105.

The term is one which is seldom misunderstood, but it is not easy to give a definition of it. Lord MACNAGHTEN, in *Trego v. Hunt*[10], says: "What 'goodwill' means must depend on the nature and character of the business to which it is attached. Generally speaking, it means much more than what Lord ELDON took it to mean in the particular case actually before him of *Cruttwell v. Lye*[11] where he says: 'The goodwill which has been the subject of sale is nothing more than the probability that the old customers will resort to the old place.' Often it happens that the goodwill is the very sap and life of the business, without which the business would yield little or no fruit. It is the whole advantage, whatever it may be, of the reputation and connection of the firm, which may have been built up by years of honest work or gained by lavish expenditure of money."

In some forms of business, the goodwill is personal[12], *e.g.* made by the skill of the person owning it; whilst in others, the goodwill attaches itself rather to the property than to the owner's person, *e.g.* the goodwill of a well-situated public-house[13]. Some businesses depend so entirely upon personal skill and influence, that goodwill in the ordinary sense can hardly exist, *e.g.* a solicitor's business[14]. A personal goodwill is capable of transfer, and so is the other kind, and this latter attaches itself to the property, and may go with it, *e.g.* to a mortgagee[15].

Where a person assigns the goodwill of a business to another, without expressly binding himself not to compete with the assignee, whether he does so as sole owner of the goodwill or as a partner transferring his interest therein to his co-partner, the legal position may be summed up as follows:

1. The person who acquires the goodwill alone may represent himself as continuing or succeeding to the business of the vendor.

2. But the assignor may nevertheless carry on a similar business in competition with the purchaser, though not under a name which would amount to a representation that he was carrying on the old business.

3. The assignor may publicly advertise his business, but he may not personally or by circular solicit the customers of the

---

10. [1896] A. C., at pp. 23, 24. See also *per* WARRINGTON, J., in *Hill v. Fearis* [1905] 1 Ch., at p. 471.
11. (1810), 17 Ves. 346.
12. *Cooper v. Metropolitan Board of Works* (1884), 25 Ch. D. 472.
13. *Ex parte Punnett* (1881), 16 Ch. D. 226.
14. *Austen v. Boys* (1858), 27 L. J. Ch. 714; *Arundell v. Bell* (1883), 31 W. R. 477; but BAGGALLAY, L.J., thought that something might exist analogous to a goodwill.
15. *Cooper v. Metropolitan Board of Works, supra; cf. Re Bennett,* [1899] 1 Ch. 316.

former firm; although he may deal with customers of the old firm, he must not *solicit* those who do not come to him of their own accord[16].

The rule against the soliciting of old customers does not apply to an involuntary alienation, *e.g.* to the sale of a person's business by his trustee in bankruptcy[17], or by the trustee under a deed of assignment for the benefit of creditors[18]; but it applies to the executor of a deceased partner who sells the goodwill to the surviving partner in pursuance of an obligation imposed by the partnership deed[19].

The way in which the goodwill should be dealt with on the dissolution of a firm has already been mentioned[20].

XI LIMITED PARTNERSHIPS

After January 1st, 1908, it became lawful to form limited partnerships under the Limited Partnerships Act 1907. Such a partnership must not consist of more than ten persons in the case of a banking firm and, as a general rule, must not consist of more than twenty persons in any other type of firm. However, this restriction does not apply to partnerships of solicitors or accountants or members of a recognised stock exchange, and the Board of Trade has power by regulations to exempt other types of partnership from the general rule[1]. They are rare because of the greater advantages of private limited companies.

A limited partnership is not a legal entity distinct from the individuals who compose the firm[2].

It must consist of one or more:

General partners, liable for all the debts and obligations of the firm, and

Limited partners, who shall at the time of entering into partnership contribute a sum as capital, or property valued at a stated amount.

The following points should be noted:

1. A limited partner is not liable for debts beyond the amount so contributed, but he must not during the continuance of the partnership,

---

16. *Trego* v. *Hunt*, [1896] A. C. 7; *Curl Brothers, Ltd.* v. *Webster*, [1904] 1 Ch. 685.
17. *Walker* v. *Mottram* (1882), 19 Ch. D. 355.
18. *Green & Sons, Ltd.* v. *Morris*, [1914] 1 Ch. 562.
19. *Boorne* v. *Wicker*, [1927] All E. R. Rep. 388; [1927] 1 Ch. 667.
20. *Ante*, p. 170.
1. Limited Partnerships Act 1907, s. 4 (2), as amended by Companies Act 1967, s. 121. Regulations have been made exempting from the general rule limited partnerships engaged in surveying, auctioneering, estate agency, valuing, land agency and estate management: Limited Partnership (Unrestricted Size) No 1 Regulations 1971.
2. *Re Barnard*, [1931] All E. R. Rep. 642; [1932] 1 Ch. 269; and see *ante*, p. 154, as to the meaning of the word "firm".

either directly or indirectly, draw out or receive back any part of his contribution, and if he does so he will be liable for the debts of the firm up to the amount so drawn out or received back.

2. A body corporate may be a limited partner[3].

3. Unless a limited partnership is registered with the Registrar of Joint Stock Companies, every limited partner will be liable as a general partner[4].

4. A limited partner must not take any part in the management of the business, and he cannot bind the firm, but he may inspect the books, look into the state and prospects of the business, and advise with the partners thereon. If a limited partner does take part in the management of the business he will be liable as a general partner for debts incurred while he so takes part in the management.

5. Unless the agreement specifies otherwise, a limited partner may only assign his share with the consent of the general partners[5].

6. A partner may be introduced without the consent of the limited partner[6].

7. *Dissolution.*—

(a) The general partners may not dissolve the partnership by reason of a limited partner suffering his share to be charged for his separate debt[7].

(b) A limited partner may not dissolve the partnership by notice[8].

(c) The death or bankruptcy of a limited partner does not dissolve the partnership, and the insanity of a limited partner is only a ground for dissolution if his share cannot be otherwise ascertained and realised[9].

Registration.—On registration particulars must be furnished containing:

1. The firm name;
2. The general nature of the business;
3. The principal place of business;
4. The full name of each partner;
5. The term, if any, for which the partnership is entered into, and date of its commencement;
6. A statement that the partnership is limited, and the description of every limited partner as such;

3. Limited Partnerships Act 1907, s. 4.
4. *Ibid.*, s. 5.
5. *Ibid.*, s. 6 (5) (b).
6. *Ibid.*, s. 6 (5) (d).
7. *Ibid.*, s. 6 (5) (c).
8. *Ibid.*, s. 6 (5) (e).
9. *Ibid.*, s. 6 (2).

7. The sum contributed by each limited partner, and whether paid in cash or how otherwise[10].

Changes in any of the above matters must be registered from time to time[11].

Any arrangement under which a general partner becomes a limited partner, or a limited partner assigns his share to another person, must be advertised in the London Gazette, before it becomes effective[12]. The statements made under the Act are filed by the registrar, and are open to the inspection of any person on payment of a small fee[13].

Subject to certain modifications, limited partnerships may be made bankrupt in the same way as ordinary partnerships, and if the general partners are adjudged bankrupt the assets of the firm vest in the trustee[14].

---

10. Limited Partnerships Act 1907, s. 8.
11. *Ibid.*, s. 9.
12. *Ibid.*, s. 10.
13. *Ibid.*, ss. 13, 16.
14. Bankruptcy Act 1914, s. 127.

PART III

The Principal Types of Mercantile Contracts

CHAPTER 13

Sale of Goods

The law relating to the sale of goods was codified by the Sale of Goods Act 1893 to which Act reference is intended whenever in the course of the chapter the letters S. G. A. are used.

I THE CONTRACT OF SALE

A contract of sale of goods is a

"contract whereby the seller transfers, or agrees to transfer, the property in goods to the buyer for a money consideration, called the price"[1].

The definition draws a distinction between a *sale* and an *agreement for sale*. Where the transfer of property takes place at once, the contract is called a sale, and where the transfer of property is to take place at a future time or subject to some condition that has to be fulfilled, such as payment of the price, the contract is an agreement to sell[2]. An agreement to sell becomes a sale when the time elapses or the conditions are fulfilled subject to which the property in the goods is to be transferred[3].

Goods are defined as including "all chattels personal other than things in action and money . . . The term includes emblements, industrial growing crops, and things attached to or forming part of the land which are agreed to be severed before sale or under the contract of sale"[4]. It follows from the definition that sales of ships are included[5]. A sale of minerals is not included unless they are already detached from the land[6]. "Emblements" and "industrial growing crops" are crops that are not naturally growing but are grown by the industry of men. "Things attached to or forming part of the land" include things that are growing naturally on the land such as timber.

A contract of sale of goods should be distinguished from a *contract*

---

1. S. G. A. 1893, s. 1 (1). A contract of sale may be absolute or conditional (*ibid.*, s. 1 (2)).
2. S. G. A. 1893, s. 1 (3).
3. S. G. A. 1893, s. 1 (4). As to the effect of this, see *post*, pp. 185–189 *et seq.*
4. S. G. A.. 1893, s. 62.
5. *Behnke* v. *Bede Shipping Co.*, [1927] 1 K. B. 649.
6. *Morgan* v. *Russell*, [1909] 1 K. B. 357.

for work and labour. In *Robinson* v. *Graves*[7], the Court of Appeal held that a contract to paint a portrait was a contract for work and labour, not a contract of sale of goods, on the ground that the "substance of the contract" was the skill and experience of the artist and it was only ancillary that there would pass to the customer some materials, namely the paint and canvas. If a contract is one for work and labour, then the terms implied by the Sale of Goods Act, *e.g.* that goods supplied are of good quality and reasonably fit for the purpose for which they are required, do not apply. However, it has been held by the House of Lords that in a contract to do work and to supply materials, two warranties may be implied in respect of the materials supplied, a warranty of their reasonable fitness for the purpose and a warranty of their good quality, in particular against latent defects. Where the materials are chosen by the party for whom the work is done, warranty of their fitness is not implied but, unless excluded by the circumstances (or by the terms of the contract), a warranty of quality will be implied[8].

Mistake and Frustration.—If at the time of the contract for the sale of specific goods, *i.e.* goods identified and agreed on at the time of the contract, the goods have perished without the knowledge of the seller, the contract is void[9]. "Perishing" includes physical destruction and theft, even of part of the goods only if they were sold as an indivisible whole[10].

If there is an agreement to sell specific goods and later, without any fault on the part of the seller or buyer, they perish before the risk of loss passes to the buyer, the agreement is avoided, *i.e.* frustrated[11]. As will be seen, the risk of loss generally passes to the buyer at the same time as ownership[12].

The goods which form the subject of a contract of sale may be either *existing goods* owned or possessed by the seller, or goods to be manufactured or acquired by the seller after the making of the contract of sale. The latter are referred to in the Act as *future goods*[13].

Where by contract of sale the seller purports to effect a present

---

7. [1935] All E. R. Rep. 935; [1935] 1 K. B. 579.
8. *Young and Marten, Ltd.* v. *McManus Childs, Ltd.,* [1968] 2 All E. R. 1169; *Gloucestershire County Council* v. *Richardson,* [1968] 2 All E. R. 1181.
9. S. G. A. 1893, s. 6.
10. *Barrow, Land and Ballard, Ltd.* v. *Phillip Phillips & Co., Ltd.,* [1929] 1 K. B. 574.
11. S. G. A. 1893, s. 7.
12. *Post*, p. 185.
13. S. G. A. 1893, s. 5 (1). There may be a contract for the sale of goods the acquisition of which by the seller depends upon a contingency which may or may not happen (*ibid.*, s. 5 (2)).

sale of future goods the contract operates as an agreement to sell the goods[14].

The price must consist of money[15] or else the contract is one of exchange and not of sale. If the amount is fixed in the contract, this, of course, is the price payable; sometimes the price is left to be fixed in a manner stated in the contract, or it may be determined by the ordinary course of dealing between the parties.

Under all other circumstances a reasonable price is presumed to have been intended[16]. A reasonable price is not necessarily the market price; what is reasonable depends on the circumstances of each particular case[17]. If the price is to be fixed by the valuation of a third party, and that third party cannot, or does not value, the agreement is avoided; except that—

1. So far as goods have already been delivered to and appropriated by the buyer, he must pay a fair price for them; and
2. If the third party is prevented from making the valuation by the act of a party to the contract of sale, that party may be sued for damages.

II FORM OF CONTRACT

A contract for the sale of goods may be in any form; whatever the price, it may be made by word of mouth or in writing, partly in writing and partly by word of mouth, or merely implied from the conduct of the parties[18]. By statute some sale contracts must be in writing, *e.g.* those credit sale and conditional sale agreements to which the Hire-Purchase Act 1965 applies[19].

III TRANSFER OF PROPERTY FROM SELLER TO BUYER

It is often necessary to determine at what exact point of time the property (or ownership) in goods passes to the purchaser, and more especially as, in the absence of agreement to the contrary, and where neither party is in default, the risk of loss as a rule, lies on the owner: *res perit domino*[20]. The question is also material where a seller, who has received money from the buyer, becomes bankrupt with goods

---

14. *Ibid.*, s. 5 (3). See also *post*, p. 187, for the rule that determines when the property in future goods normally passes to the buyer.
15. *Ibid.*, 1893, s. 1 (1). So long as part of the consideration is money, the transaction is one of sale of goods: *Aldridge* v. *Johnson* (1857), 7 E. & B. 885.
16. *Ibid.*, s. 8.
17. *Ibid.*, s. 9.
18. *Ibid.*, s. 3. As to the repeal of s. 4, see *ante*, p. 8.
19. *Post*, p. 233.
20. S. G. A. 1893, s. 20.

in his possession which could have been delivered in conformity with the contract of sale. The Act makes a distinction between *specific* goods and *unascertained* goods. Specific goods are defined as goods identified and agreed upon at the time the contract of sale is made[1]. Unascertained goods are not defined in the Act but examples will be given below.

Sale of specific goods

The cardinal question when the goods are specified or ascertained is, what is the intention of the parties? If an answer to this can be obtained, the time when the property passes is fixed by that answer, for the intention of the parties governs the matter[2]; and where that intention does not otherwise appear, the following are rules for ascertaining it:

Rule 1—"Where there is an unconditional contract for the sale of specific goods in a deliverable state[3], the property in the goods passes to the buyer when the contract is made, and it is immaterial whether the time of payment or time of delivery, or both, be postponed"[4].

A buyer is not necessarily entitled to possession of the goods because the property in them has passed, the general rule being that the seller is entitled to retain possession until the buyer has paid the price.

Rule 2—"Where there is a contract for the sale of specific goods and the seller is bound to do something to the goods, for the purpose of putting them in a deliverable state, the property does not pass until such thing be done, and the buyer has notice thereof"[5].

For instance, if the seller is to repair or alter the goods, the property passes only when the repairs or alterations are done and the buyer has notice of that fact.

Rule 3—"Where there is a contract for the sale of specific goods in a deliverable state, but the seller is bound to weigh, measure, test, or do some other act or thing with reference to the goods for the purpose of ascertaining the price, the property does not pass until such act or thing be done, and the buyer has notice thereof"[6].

This rule does not apply if the "weighing, measuring, or testing" is to be done by the buyer[7].

Rule 4—"When goods are delivered to the buyer on approval or 'on

---

1. *Ibid.*, s. 62.
2. *Ibid.*, s. 17 (1). See for example, *Re Anchor Line (Henderson Bros.), Ltd.*, [1937] 1 Ch. 1.
3. *I.e.* in a state in which the buyer is bound to accept (*ibid.*, s. 62 (4)).
4. *Ibid.*, s. 18, r. 1.
5. S. G. A. 1893, s. 18, r. 2.
6. *Ibid.*, s. 18, r. 3.
7. *Nanka Bruce* v. *Commonwealth Trust, Ltd.*, [1926] A. C. 77.

sale or return' or other similar terms the property therein passes to
the buyer:—

   (a) When he signifies his approval or acceptance to the seller or
does any other act adopting the transaction.

   (b) If he does not signify his approval or acceptance to the seller
but retains the goods without giving notice of rejection, then,
if a time has been fixed for the return of the goods, on the
expiration of such time, and, if no time has been fixed, on
the expiration of a reasonable time. What is a reasonable
time is a question of fact"[8].

If the buyer pledges the goods, he does an "act adopting the
transaction"[9], but the property will not pass if there is an express
term in the contract that the property will not pass until the goods are
paid for, because all the rules are subject to contrary intention shown
in the contract[10].

In *Poole* v. *Smith's Car Sales (Balham), Ltd.*[11],

   A car was left by the plaintiff with the defendant dealers on
"sale or return" terms in August 1960. After several requests,
the car was returned in November 1960 in a damaged state owing
to unauthorised use by the defendants' servants. *Held:* as the car
had not been returned within a reasonable time, the property in
the car had passed to defendants under s. 18, r. 4. The defendants
were therefore liable for the price agreed.

Sale of Unascertained goods

The contract is here merely an executory agreement, and until the
goods are ascertained[12], *i.e.* identified after the contract as being in
accordance with the agreement, the property does not pass. Such
cases will include those which were described in *Gillett* v. *Hill* as:

   "a bargain for a certain quantity, *ex* a greater quantity"[13];

e.g. sale of so many tons of hay out of a certain year's produce and a
sale of goods of a certain kind, *e.g.*, a new Ford Capri 1973. Rule 5
of s. 18 shows that generally the property in unascertained goods will
not pass until goods of the description agreed are *appropriated* to the
contract.

Rule 5—"(1) Where there is a contract for the sale of unascertained
or future goods by description, and goods of that description and in a
deliverable state are unconditionally appropriated to the contract,

---

8. S. G. A. 1893, s. 18, r. 4.
9. *Kirkham* v. *Attenborough*, [1897] 1 Q. B. 201.
10. *Weiner* v. *Gill*, [1905] 2 K. B. 172; [1906] 2 K. B. 574.
11. [1962] 2 All E. R. 482; [1962] 1 W. L. R. 744.
12. S.G.A. 1893, s. 16.
13. (1834), 2 C. & M. 530.

either by the seller with the assent of the buyer, or by the buyer with the assent of the seller, the property in the goods thereupon passes to the buyer. Such assent may be express or implied, and may be given either before or after the appropriation is made.

(2) Where, in pursuance of the contract, the seller delivers the goods to the buyer or to a carrier or other bailee or custodian (whether named by the buyer or not) for the purpose of transmission to the buyer, and does not reserve the right of disposal, he is deemed to have unconditionally appropriated the goods to the contract"[14].

If the seller sends notice of appropriation to the buyer and the latter does not reply promptly, it must be inferred that he assents to the appropriation and the property in the goods will be deemed to pass on the expiration of a reasonable time after receipt of the notice[15].

It follows from Rule 5 that if the thing sold is in course of manufacture the *prima facie* rule is that the property in it does not pass to the buyer before completion. But the parties may expressly or impliedly agree by the contract itself or during the course of the construction of the chattel that the property in the partly finished article shall pass to the purchaser, and such an agreement is generally presumed where payments are to be made in respect of particular stages of manufacture coupled with the fact that the buyer has agreed to accept the corpus so far as completed, *e.g.* by inspecting and approving it. This kind of question has arisen most frequently in connection with ship-building contracts. Materials provided by the manufacturer ready to be incorporated into the fabric of the subject-matter of the sale cannot be regarded as "sold" unless they have been fixed or in a reasonable sense made part of the corpus, or unless there is evidence of a separate agreement that the property in the unfinished materials should pass[16].

Right of disposal reserved

If when selling specific goods or when appropriating goods to a contract for the sale of unascertained goods, the seller reserves the right of disposal to the goods, *i.e.* retains a *jus disponendi*, until some condition is satisfied, generally that the price be paid, the property will not pass until that condition is fulfilled[17].

Where goods are shipped, and by the bill of lading the goods are deliverable to the order of the seller, the seller is *prima facie* deemed

---

14. S. G. A. 1893, s. 18, r. 5. See *e.g. Wardar's (Import and Export) Co., Ltd.* v. *W. Norwood & Sons, Ltd.,* [1968] 2 All E. R. 602; [1968] 2 Q. B. 663, C.A.
15. *Pignataro* v. *Gilroy,* [1919] 1 K. B. 459.
16. *Re Blythe Shipbuilding and Dry Docks Co., Ltd.,* [1926] Ch. 494; *McDougall* v. *Aeromarine of Emsworth, Ltd.,* [1958] 3 All E. R. 431.
17. *Ibid.,* s. 19.

to reserve the right of disposal[18]. But this presumption will be rebutted if on the facts it appears to have been the intention of the parties that the property in the cargo should pass to the buyer on shipment; *e.g.* where the sellers have only taken the bills of lading in their own name to preserve their lien.

If a purchaser receives the bill of lading together with a bill of exchange for acceptance, this is evidence of intention on the part of the vendor not to part with the goods till acceptance of the bill[19]; but upon acceptance of the bill or payment of the price, the property will vest in the buyer, the seller's conditional appropriation of the goods having thereby become unconditional[20].

IV TRANSFER OF TITLE

Capacity to buy and sell is governed by the general law of contract subject to a specified requirement in the Act for minors and persons lacking capacity through mental incapacity or drunkenness to pay for necessaries[21].

As a general rule, only the owner is capable of passing a good title in goods to a buyer: *nemo dat quod non habet*. There are however a number of exceptions to this rule.

In *Bishopsgate Motor Finance Corpn., Ltd.* v. *Transport Brakes, Ltd.*[1], DENNING, L.J., said:

"In the development of our law, two principles have striven for mastery. The first is the protection of property. No one can give a better title than he himself possesses. The second is the protection of commercial transactions. The person who takes in good faith and for value without notice should get a good title. The first principle has held sway for a long time, but it has been modified by common law itself and by statute so as to meet the needs of our times."

General exceptions

1. *Agency.*—If the seller of goods sells them under the authority of or with the consent of the owner, the buyer obtains a good title. Moreover, a buyer obtains a good title if the owner of goods is precluded by his conduct from denying the seller's authority to sell[2]. But merely permitting someone else to have possession of goods does not estop the owner from denying that person's authority to sell.

---

18. *Ibid.*, s. 19 (2); and see *Wait* v. *Baker* (1848), 2 Exch. 1; *Turner* v. *Trustees of the Liverpool Docks* (1851), 6 Exch. 543.
19. *The Parchim*, [1918] A. C. 157.
20. S. G. A., s. 19 (3).
21. S. G. A., s. 2. See *ante*, p. 59.
1. [1949] 1 K. B. 322; [1949] 1 All E. R. 37, at p. 46.
2. S. G. A. 1893, s. 21 (1).

In *Central Newbury Car Auctions, Ltd.* v. *Unity Finance, Ltd.*[3]:

> X agreed with Y that X would sell a car to a finance company which would let it on hire-purchase to Y. Before the arrangements were completed X handed the vehicle and its registration book to Y. The finance company refused to complete but meanwhile Y, who was a rogue, sold the car to Z. *Held:* Z got no title, for Y had no title and X's conduct in handing over the vehicle did not estop him from disputing Y's authority.

2. *Sale under special common law or statutory powers of sale.*—Thus a sale by a pledgee of an unredeemed pledge[4] and the sale of a guest's goods by an innkeeper whose bill is unpaid[5] give the purchaser a good title as against the pledgor or guest respectively.

A court has wide powers under the Rules of the Supreme Court to order a sale of goods.

Special exceptions

1. *Sale in market overt.*—When goods are sold in "market overt" to a *bona fide* purchaser, without notice of the seller's defect or want of title, and according to the usage of the market, the sale is binding on the true owner, though he neither sold them nor authorised their sale[6].

Goods are sold in "market overt" if they are sold in a recognised market established by grant or prescription or under statutory powers. The sale need not be effected by a trader if sales by private treaty habitually take place in the market[7]. But by custom sales by a trader in a shop in the City of London made in the ordinary course of his business on any day except Sunday are treated as being made in market overt[8].

Until the Theft Act 1968 it was the rule that if goods were stolen, and the offender prosecuted to conviction, the property in the goods so stolen revested in the original owner, notwithstanding any intermediate dealing with them, whether by sale in market overt or otherwise[9].

2. *Sale under a voidable title.*—Where the seller of goods has a

---

3. [1956] 3 All E. R. 905; [1957] 1 Q. B. 371.
4. See *post*, p. 398.
5. Innkeepers Act 1878.
6. S. G. A. 1893, s. 22 (1). Horses were excluded by s. 22 (2), but this provision was repealed by the Criminal Law Act 1967, Sched. III.
7. *Bishopsgate Motor Finance Corpn., Ltd.* v. *Transport Brakes, Ltd., ante,* p. 189.
8. *Hargreave* v. *Spink,* [1892] 1 Q. B. 25.
9. S. G. A. 1893, s. 24 (1), repealed by the Theft Act 1968, Sched. III. The Theft Act 1968, s. 28, enables a court on conviction of an offender to order restitution of the goods to the owner but s. 31 (2) provides that the conviction of an offender does not affect title so that, for example, on a sale in market overt, the purchaser will be the "owner".

voidable title, *e.g.* because he has obtained the goods by fraud, but his title has not been avoided at the time of the sale, the buyer acquires a good title to the goods, provided he buys them in good faith and without notice of the seller's defect of title[10].

3. *Sale by mercantile agent.*—This exception is dealt with in the Chapter on "AGENCY"[11].

4. *Sale by the possessors of goods or documents of title to them.*—Where a person having sold goods "continues or is in possession" of the goods or the documents of title[12] thereto, delivery or transfer of the goods or documents of title by such vendor or his mercantile agent[13], under any sale, pledge, or other disposition thereof, has the same effect as if such vendor or other person were expressly authorised by the owner of the goods to make the same, provided that the person to whom the sale or disposition has been made acts *bona fide* and without notice of the previous sale[14]. The Court of Appeal held in *Worcester Works Finance, Ltd.* v. *Cooden Engineering Co., Ltd.*[15] that "continues . . . in possession" means continuity of physical possession and it is irrelevant whether the seller remains in possession as a bailee or a trespasser or whether the buyer has consented or not to the seller remaining in possession.

Where a person having bought or agreed to buy goods, obtains, *with the consent of the seller*, possession of the goods or the documents of title to the goods, the delivery or transfer by that person, or by a mercantile agent acting for him, of the goods or documents of title, under any sale, pledge, or other disposition thereof, to any person receiving the same in good faith and without notice of any lien or other right of the original seller in respect of the goods, has the same effect as if the person making the delivery or transfer were a mercantile agent in possession of the goods or documents of title with the consent of the owner[16]—*i.e.* his disposition of the goods or documents of title

---

10. S. G. A. 1893, s. 23.
11. See *ante*, p. 119.
12. "Document of title" has the same meaning as in the Factors Act 1889 (S. G. A. 1893, s. 62). As to what the expression includes, see *ante*, p. 135. The registration book of a motor car is not a document of title.
13. For the meaning of this, see *ante*, p. 135.
14. S. G. A. 1893, s. 25 (1). A similar provision is to be found in the Factors Act 1889, s. 8.
15. [1971] 3 All E. R. 708; [1972] 1 Q. B. 182, C. A., following *Pacific Motor Auctions Proprietary, Ltd.* v. *Motor Credits (Hire Finance), Ltd.*, [1965] 2 All E. R. 105; [1965] A. C. 887, P. C.
16. S. G. A. 1893, s. 26 (2); and see Factors Act 1889, s. 9. The fact that the consent of the seller was obtained by deception does not exclude the section. See *Pearson* v. *Rose and Young, Ltd.*, [1950] 2 All E. R. 1027; [1951] 1 K. B. 275; *Du Jardin* v. *Beadman Brothers, Ltd.*, [1952] 2 All E. R. 160; [1952] 2 Q. B. 712; *Newtons of Wembley, Ltd.* v. *Williams*, [1964] 3 All E. R. 532; [1965] 1 Q. B. 560

will, in general, give a good title to the innocent sub-purchaser or pledgee, though in fact he has no right to sell or pledge the goods[17].

So in *Cahn* v. *Pockett's Bristol, etc. Co., Limited*[18],

the seller of goods forwarded to the buyer a bill of lading indorsed in blank, together with a draft for the price for acceptance. The buyer did not accept the draft, but transferred the bill of lading to the plaintiffs, who took it in good faith and for value. The seller stopped the goods *in transitu*. The Court of Appeal *held* that the plaintiffs had acquired a good title to the goods, as, although it was not intended that any property should pass to the original buyers until acceptance of the draft, they had nevertheless obtained possession of the documents of title with the consent of the seller.

A person who takes goods on hire-purchase is not a person who has "agreed to buy" goods within the meaning of this section. In consequence, subject to the provisions of the Hire-Purchase Act 1964 giving protection to the purchasers of motor vehicles (see *post*, pp. 192–193) and to the possibility of the hirer of goods selling them in market overt (see *ante*, p. 190), the general rule is that a hirer in possession of goods under a hire-purchase agreement is not able to give a good title to a purchaser even if the purchaser takes in good faith[19].

A person has "agreed to buy" within the meaning of the section although the contract of sale was conditional[20], but the section has no application to certain "conditional sale" agreements under which the total purchase is payable by instalments, and the property is to remain in the seller until such conditions as to payment of instalments or otherwise, as may be specified in the agreement, are fulfilled[1]. Conditional sale agreements to which the section does apply are those made by or on behalf of a body corporate as the buyer of the goods, or those where the total purchase price exceeds £2,000.

5. *Protection of purchasers of vehicles.*—If a motor vehicle has been let under a hire-purchase agreement or has been agreed to be sold under a conditional sale agreement and, before the property has passed to the hirer or buyer, he disposes of the vehicle to a "private purchaser" who takes the vehicle in good faith and without notice of the hire-purchase agreement or conditional sale agreement, the disposition has effect as if the title of the owner or seller had been vested in the hirer

17. Factors Act 1889, s. 2.
18. [1899] 1 Q. B. 643; 4 Com. Cas. 168.
19. *Helby* v. *Matthews*, [1895] A. C. 471.
20. *Marten* v. *Whale*, [1917] 2 K. B. 480, C. A.
1. Hire-Purchase Act 1965, s. 54.

or buyer immediately before the disposition[2]. Further, where the disposition is to "a trade or finance purchaser", *i.e.* a dealer in motor vehicles or a finance company, then if the person who is the first private purchaser of the vehicle after that disposition is a purchaser in good faith and without notice of the hire-purchase or conditional sale agreement, the disposition to the first private purchaser has effect as if the title of the owner or seller had been vested in the hirer or buyer immediately before he disposed of it to the original purchaser. A private purchaser of a vehicle which is still subject to a hire-purchase agreement is protected if he honestly believes that, although the vehicle was once subject to such an agreement, the instalments have been paid off[3].

6. *Sale after delivery of writ of execution.*—Where a writ of execution has been delivered to the sheriff to be executed, the sheriff has a legal right to seize them to sell and thus satisfy the judgment debt. But while the writ remains unexecuted, the debtor is able to pass a good title to the goods to anyone who purchases them in good faith for valuable consideration without notice of the writ[4].

V CONDITIONS AND WARRANTIES

Definitions

There is more in a contract for the sale of goods than simply payment of the price and delivery of the goods. For instance:

A may buy a second-hand motor car and then find that the seller had no title to it; or that it is a 1965 model when it was said to be a 1970 model; or that it is so defective that it is only fit for the scrap-heap.

A's rights in these events may be covered expressly in the contract, but more probably nothing will have been said about them. In order

---

2. Hire-Purchase Act 1964, s. 27. A "conditional sale agreement" means an agreement in which the total purchase price is payable by instalments, and the property is to remain in the seller until such conditions as to payment of instalments or otherwise, as may be specified in the agreement, are fulfilled: *ibid.*, s. 21 (5). A "private purchaser" means someone buying the vehicle or taking it on hire-purchase who does not carry on the business of purchasing vehicles for resale or of providing finance by purchasing vehicles in order to dispose of them under hire-purchase or conditional sale agreements: *ibid.*, s. 29 (1) and (2).
3. *Barker* v. *Bell*, [1971] 2 All E. R. 867; [1971] 1 W. L. R. 983, C. A.
4. S. G. A. 1893, s. 26, amended by the Administration of Justice Act 1965, s. 22. Once the writ is executed, *e.g.* by the sheriff seizing the debtor's goods, the debtor cannot pass title to the goods even though he is left temporarily in possession of them: *Lloyds and Scottish Finance Ltd.* v. *Modern Cars and Caravans (Kingston), Ltd.*, [1964] 2 All E. R. 732; [1966] 1 Q. B. 764.

to give business efficacy to the contract, it is necessary therefore for the law to imply certain terms[5].

These terms may be such that they go to the root of the contract so that failure to comply gives the buyer a right to treat the contract as repudiated. Such terms are known as *"conditions"*. Or they may be less important terms, collateral to the main purpose of the contract in which case a breach will give rise to a right to damages only. Such terms are known as *"warranties"*.

The Sale of Goods Act does not include a definition of a condition. But a warranty is defined as

> an agreement with reference to goods which are the subject of a contract of sale, but collateral to the main purpose of such contract, the breach of which gives rise to a claim for damages, but not to a right to reject the goods and treat the contract as repudiated[6].

Express conditions and warranties

A statement about the goods made by the seller at the time of sale may amount merely to a representation[7] or it may be a promise which becomes a term of the contract. Which it is, is a matter which depends on the intention of the parties to be gathered from their words and behaviour[8].

> "When the seller states a fact which is or should be within his own knowledge and of which the buyer is ignorant, intending that the buyer should act on it and he does so it is easy to infer a warranty . . . But, if the seller, when he states a fact, makes it clear that he has no knowledge of his own but has got his information elsewhere and is merely passing it on, it is not so easy to imply a warranty"[9].

If the statement does become a term of the contract, then whether it is a condition or a warranty depends in each case on the construction of the contract[10]. The intention of the parties must be ascertained, and it may well be that the same phrase in two different contracts may in one case amount to a condition and in the other merely to a warranty. A stipulation may be a condition, though the parties have in the contract termed it a warranty[11].

---

5. As to implying terms generally, see *ante*, p. 114.
6. S. G. A. 1893, s. 62.
7. For the remedies for fraudulent and innocent misrepresentation, see *ante*, pp. 37–40.
8. *Heilbut, Symons & Co.* v. *Buckleton*, [1913] A. C. 30; *Oscar Chess, Ltd.* v. *Williams*, [1957] 1 All E. R. 325, C. A.
9. *Per* DENNING, L.J., in *Oscar Chess, Ltd.* v. *Williams*, [1957] 1 All E. R. 325, C. A.
10. S. G. A. 1893, s. 11 (1) (b).
11. *Ibid.*, s. 11 (1) (b); *Wallis Son and Wells* v. *Pratt and Haynes*, [1911] A. C. 394.

A stipulation as to time *of payment* is not of the essence of the contract, *i.e.* is not a condition unless a different intention appears from the terms of the contract[12]. Other stipulations as to time in mercantile contracts are usually construed as conditions[13]. In particular, a stipulation as to time of delivery is generally construed as a condition, so that if the seller fails to deliver on time, the buyer may treat the contract as repudiated[14].

A buyer may waive a condition or elect to treat the breach of it as a breach of warranty and in certain circumstances he can only treat the breach as a breach of warranty[15].

Implied conditions and warranties

Conditions and warranties may be implied where the circumstances require it. Thus:

> If an export licence is required, the person whose duty it is to get it may either warrant that he will get it—that is an absolute warranty; or he may warrant that he will use all due diligence in getting it. When nothing is said in the contract it is almost invariably the latter class of warranty that is implied, but each case must be decided according to its own circumstances[16].

The Sale of Goods Act has codified the conditions and warranties usually implied in a contract of sale. These are exceptions to the rule that the buyer must make express stipulations or take his chance: *caveat emptor*. They may be negatived by express agreement[17], or they may be impliedly waived. But an express condition or warranty does not negative a condition or warranty implied by the Act unless inconsistent with it[18]. So also custom may negative a condition or warranty usually implied[17]. On the other hand, custom may annex an implied warranty or condition[19].

The courts construe very narrowly agreements purporting to exclude the statutory conditions and warranties. Thus an agreement excluding warranties does not exclude conditions[20]. An agreement excluding implied warranties does not exclude express ones[1], and the

---

12. S. G. A. 1893, s. 10. But as to delivery and payment being concurrent conditions, see *post*, p. 202.
13. *Bowes* v. *Shand* (1877), 2 App. Cas. 455, 463.
14. See *ante*, p. 84.
15. See *post*, pp. 206, 207.
16. *Per* DEVLIN, J., in *Peter Cassidy Seed Co.* v. *Osuustukkukauppa*, [1957] 1 All E. R. 484.
17. S. G. A. 1893, s. 55.
18. *Ibid.*, s. 14 (4).
19. *Ibid.*, s. 14 (3).
20. *Wallis, Son and Wells* v. *Pratt and Haynes*, [1911] A. C. 394.
1. *Andrews Bros. (Bournemouth), Ltd.* v. *Singer & Co., Ltd.*, [1933] All E. R. Rep. 479; [1934] 1 K. B. 17.

courts will normally construe an exemption clause as not having been intended to cover a fundamental breach of contract[2]. So if there is a sale by description a stipulation that "no allowance will be made for errors of description" will not assist the seller if he supplies an article essentially different from the one contracted for[3].

The conditions and warranties implied under the Sale of Goods Act 1893 are:

1. *Condition and warranties of title.*—Unless the circumstances of the contract show a different intention there is:

   (i) *an implied condition on the part of the seller that, in the case of a sale, he has a right to sell the goods, and that in the case of an agreement to sell he will have a right to sell them at the time when the property is to pass*[4].

This condition is broken by the sale of goods with marks or labels which infringe a registered trade mark[5].

A breach of this condition entitles the buyer to recover the price as upon a total failure of consideration. The fact that the buyer has used the goods before being deprived of them by the true owner makes no difference, because a buyer of goods pays the price in order to enjoy the ownership of them, not just their use[6].

   (ii) *An implied warranty that the buyer shall have and enjoy quiet possession of the goods*[7].

   (iii) *An implied warranty that the goods shall be free from any charge or encumbrance in favour of any third party not declared or known to the buyer before or at the time when the contract is made*[8].

2. *On sale of goods by description.*—There is:

An implied condition that the goods shall correspond to the description, and if the sale was also by sample, a condition that the bulk shall correspond to such description, as well as corresponding with the sample[9].

It may in some cases be difficult to decide whether a sale is a sale by description, but in cases where the purchaser has not seen the goods

---

2. *Suisse Atlantique Société d'Armement Maritime S.A.* v. *N.V. Rotterdamsche Kolen Centrale*, [1966] 2 All E. R. 61; [1967] 1 A. C. 361. See also *Harbutt's Plasticine, Ltd.* v. *Wayne Tank and Pump Co., Ltd.*, [1970] see E. R. 225; [1970] 1 Q. B. 447, C. A. and p. 17 *ante*.
3. *Pinnock Brothers* v. *Lewis and Peat, Ltd.*, [1923] 1 K. B. 690, and see *ante*, p. 16.
4. S. G. A. 1893, s. 12 (1).
5. *Niblett* v. *Confectioners' Materials Co.*, [1921] 3 K. B. 386.
6. *Rowland* v. *Divall*, [1923] 2 K. B. 500.
7. S. G. A. 1893, s. 12 (2).
8. *Ibid.*, s. 12 (3).
9. S. G. A. 1893, s. 13.

and buys them relying on the description alone, whether the goods be specific or unascertained, there is a contract for the sale of goods by description"[10].

There is a sale by description if goods are ordered from a catalogue; or if they are ordered over the counter by a trade name[11].

Even where the buyer does see the goods it may still be a sale by description.

In *Beale* v. *Taylor*[12],

> The seller of a car advertised it as a "Herald Convertible, white, 1961 . . ." The buyer saw the car before agreeing to buy it and later discovered that while the rear half of the car was part of a 1961 Herald Convertible, the front half was part of an earlier model. *Held:* buyer entitled to damages for breach of the condition implied by s. 13 of the Sale of Goods Act.

The goods must correspond in all respects with the description

> "every item in a description which constitutes a substantial ingredient in the identity of the thing sold is a condition"[13].

If goods are bought by description *from a seller who deals in goods of that description*[14] (whether he be a manufacturer or not), there is:

An implied condition that the goods shall be of merchantable quality; provided that if the buyer has examined the goods, there shall be no implied condition as regards defects which such examination ought to have revealed[15].

Goods are of "merchantable quality" if they are

> "in such an actual state that a buyer fully acquainted with the facts and therefore knowing what hidden defects exist and not being limited to their apparent condition would buy them without abatement of the price obtainable for such goods if in reasonable sound order and condition and without special terms"[16].

---

10. *Varley* v. *Whipp*, [1900] 1 Q. B. 513.
11. *Morelli* v. *Fitch*, [1928] All E. R. Rep. 610; [1928] 2 K. B. 636.
12. [1967] 3 All E. R. 253.
13. Per SCOTT, L.J., in *Couchman* v. *Hill*, [1947] K. B. 554, 559; [1947] 1 All E. R. 103.
14. It seems to be sufficient that the seller has previously dealt in goods of the *kind* now being sold though he has not previously sold goods of precisely the description now being sold: *Ashington Piggeries, Ltd.* v. *Christopher Hill, Ltd.*, [1971] 1 All E. R. 847; [1972] A. C. 441, H. L. by a three to two majority.
15. S. G. A. 1893, s. 14 (2). See *Wren* v. *Holt*, [1903] 1 K. B. 610.
16. Per DIXON, J., in *Australian Knitting Mills* v. *Grant* (1933), 50 C. L. R. 387, 418, approved by Lords GUEST, PEARCE and WILBERFORCE in *Henry Kendall & Sons* v. *William Lillico & Sons, Ltd.*, [1968] 2 All E. R. 444, H. L.

Goods may be regarded as of "merchantable quality" although they happen not to be saleable in the place where the seller knew the buyer intended to resell them[17] and the fact that the goods are saleable only at a slightly reduced price does not make them unmerchantable[18]. The buyer is not bound to incur any expense in order to make the goods merchantable[19].

In *Wilson* v. *Rickett, Cockerell & Co., Ltd.*[20]:

> A ton of coalite was sold to the plaintiff. The consignment included a piece of coal in which explosive was embedded. *Held:* the consignment considered as a whole was "unmerchantable" having defects unfitting it for its only proper use—burning.

3. *Goods wanted for a particular purpose.—Where the buyer expressly or by implication makes known to the seller the particular purpose for which goods are required, so as to show he relies on the seller's skill or judgment, and the goods are of a description which it is in the course of the seller's business to supply, there is implied a condition that they are reasonably fit for the intended purpose*[1].

The particular purpose for which the goods are required may be made known to the seller by the recognised description of the article, if that description points to one particular purpose only.

> The plaintiff asked for a hot-water bottle and was supplied with one which burst. *Held:* the plaintiff had sufficiently made known the use for which he required it[2].

The implied condition extends to latent defects, *e.g.* where milk contains disease germs, the existence of which can only be discovered by prolonged examination[3]. It applies to goods "supplied under a contract of sale, *e.g.* bottles containing mineral water, although by the terms of the contract no property in the bottles passes to the buyer[4].

Reliance on the seller's skill or judgment need not be total or exclusive; but it must be substantial and effective. A contract to

---

17. *Sumner, Permain & Co.* v. *Webb & Co.*, [1922] 1 K. B. 55, at p. 63, *per* SCRUTTON, L.J.
18. *B. S. Brown & Son, Ltd.* v. *Craiks, Ltd.*, [1970] 1 All E. R. 823; [1970] 1 W. L. R. 752, H. L. Thus the phrase "without abatement of the price" in the test of "merchantable quality" approved by three Law Lords in *Henry Kendall & Sons* v. *William Lillico & Sons, Ltd.* should perhaps be read as "without substantial abatement of the price".
19. *Jackson* v. *Rotax Motor, etc. Co.*, [1910] 2 K. B. 937.
20. [1954] 1 All E. R. 868; [1954] 1 Q. B. 598, C. A.
1. S. G. A. 1893, s. 14 (1).
2. *Preist* v. *Last*, [1903] 2 K. B. 148. See also *Godley* v. *Perry*, [1960] 1 All E. R. 36.
3. *Frost* v. *Aylesbury Dairy Co.*, [1905] 1 K. B. 608; C. & T., p. 185.
4. *Geddling* v. *Marsh*, [1920] 1 K. B. 668.

manufacture an article in accordance with a plan and specification may still leave some matters to the skill or judgment of the manufacturer in respect of which he must comply with the implied condition of fitness[5]. Thus, in *Ashington Piggeries, Ltd.* v. *Christopher Hill, Ltd.*,[6]

> The owners of mink companies asked a company of feeding stuff compounders to compound a mink food in accordance with a formula supplied by the mink companies. The feeding stuff compounders agreed to do this and when the compound supplied resulted in serious loss of mink because an ingredient was toxic to mink, they were *held* liable under s. 14 (1). Reliance on their skill and judgment was only partial because the buyer provided the formula for the compound but they relied on the sellers to see that the ingredients were of suitable quality.

Reliance on the seller's skill and judgment will usually arise by implication from the circumstances, and if the particular purpose for which the buyer requires the goods are either obvious (*e.g.* a car is obviously required for driving on the roads) or the buyer's special purpose is made known to the seller, then in the absence of anything to the contrary, reliance on the seller's skill and judgment is implied[7].

Where a retailer sells goods obtained from a manufacturer, which owing to some latent defect cause injury to the ultimate buyer or consumer, the latter can recover damages from the retailer in contract and in certain circumstances from the manufacturer in tort[8].

The manufacturer's liability is based on actionable negligence, the existence or non-existence of which is immaterial to the contractual liability of the retailer.

> A manufacture of products which he sells in such a form as to show that he intends them to reach the ultimate consumer in the form in which they left him with no reasonable possibility of intermediate examination, and with the knowledge that the absence of reasonable care in the preparation or putting up of the products will result in an injury to the consumer's life or property, owes a duty to the consumer to take that reasonable care[9].

5. *Cammell Laird & Co.* v. *Manganese Bronze, etc. Co.*, [1934] All E. R. Rep. 1; [1934] A. C. 402.
6. [1971] 1 All E. R. 847; [1972] A. C. 441, H. L.
7. *Henry Kendall & Sons* v. *William Lillico & Sons, Ltd.*, [1968] 1 All E. R. 444, H. L.; *Teheran-Europe Corporation* v. *S. T. Belton, Ltd.*, [1968] 2 All E. R. 886; [1968] 2 Q. B. 545, C. A.; *Vacwell Engineering Co., Ltd.* v. *B. D. H. Chemicals Ltd.*, [1969] 3 All E. R. 1681; *Ashington Piggeries, Ltd.* v. *Christopher Hill Ltd.*, [1971] 1 All E. R. 847, 861, *per* Lord GUEST.
8. *Grant* v. *Australian Knitting Mills*, [1935] All E. R. Rep. 209; [1936] A. C. 85.
9. *Donoghue* v. *Stevenson*, [1932] A. C. 562, *per* Lord ATKIN, at p. 599. The tortious liability of a manufacturer may be excluded by the terms of a "Guarantee" issued by him if the buyer accepts its terms, *e.g.*, signing it and returning it to the manufacturer.

The principle only applies where the defect is hidden and unknown to the retailer or consumer.

There is no implied condition as to quality or fitness on the sale of a specified article under its patent or trade name[10].

However, the fact that an article is described by its patent or trade name will not exclude a condition that it is fit for a particular purpose if reliance is still placed on the seller's skill or judgment[11]. In any event the goods must be merchantable. A "trade name" must be acquired by user, and the question whether it has or has not been so acquired is one of fact.

4. *Sale by sample.*—There is an implied condition[12]:—

I. *That the bulk shall correspond with the sample in quality*; the correspondence must be complete. It is not sufficient that with a small amount of labour and expense the bulk could be made to correspond with the sample[13].

2. *That the buyer shall have a reasonable opportunity of comparing the bulk with the sample before acceptance*[14]; and

3. *That the goods shall be free from any defect rendering them un-merchantable, which would not be apparent on reasonable examination of the sample.*

Sale by sample does not of necessity take place whenever a sample is shown; sale by sample takes place when there is a term in the contract, express or implied, to that effect[15]; the whole of the circumstances must be looked to.

Lord MACNAGHTEN, in *Drummond* v. *Van Ingen*, laid it down that:

"The office of the sample is to present to the eye the real meaning and intention of the parties with regard to the subject-matter of the contract which, owing to the imperfection of language, it may be difficult or impossible to express in words. The sample speaks for itself. But it cannot be treated as saying more than such a sample would tell a merchant of the class to which the buyer belongs, using due care and diligence, and appealing to it in the ordinary way and with the knowledge possessed by merchants of that class at the time. No doubt the sample might be made to say a great deal more. Pulled to pieces and examined by unusual tests which curiosity or suspicion might suggest, it would doubtless

---

10. S. G. A. 1893, s. 14 (1), Proviso.
11. *Baldry* v. *Marshall*, [1925] 1 K. B. 260.
12. *Ibid.*, s. 15 (2).
13. *Ruben (E. & S.), Ltd.* v. *Faire Brothers & Co., Ltd.*, [1949] 1 All E. R. 215; [1949] 1 K. B. 254.
14. Place of delivery is, *prima facie*, the place of inspection (*Perkins* v. *Bell*, [1893] 1 Q. B. 193).
15. S. G. A. 1893, s. 15 (1).

reveal every secret of its construction. But that is not the way in which business is done in this country"[16].

It should be noted that when anyone redeems trading stamps for goods, certain *warranties* are implied by the Trading Stamps Act 1964, s. 4:

(a) that the promoter of the trading stamp scheme has a right to give the goods in exchange,

(b) that the person obtaining the goods shall have and enjoy quiet possession of them,

(c) that the goods shall be free from any charge or encumbrance in favour of any third party, not declared or known to the person obtaining the goods,

(d) that the goods shall be of merchantable quality except that if the person obtaining the goods has examined the goods before or at the time of redemption, there shall be no implied warranty as regards defects which the examination ought to have revealed.

This provision is subject to the terms on which redemption is made, so far as these terms expressly exclude or modify these implied warranties.

VI RIGHTS OF THE BUYER

The rights of each party correspond to the duties of the other; it suffices, therefore, to deal with the rights of each. The buyer's rights fall under two heads:

1. He is entitled to delivery, and
2. He is entitled to have any conditions and warranties observed.

Delivery

Delivery is defined in s. 62 of the Act as the

"voluntary transfer of possession from one person to another".

The vendor must deliver the goods in accordance with the terms of the contract of sale[17]. The expenses of and incidental to putting the goods into a deliverable state must be borne by the seller unless otherwise agreed[18].

Delivery does not necessarily involve placing the buyer in actual possession; it may be *constructive,* as by handing to the buyer the

---

16. (1887), 12 App. Cas., at p. 297. See also *Heilbutt* v. *Hickson* (1872), L. R. 7 C. P. 438.
17. S. G. A. 1893, s. 27.
18. *Ibid.,* s. 29 (5).

key of the warehouse in which bulky goods are stored. Again, the seller may agree to retain physical possession of the goods, but on terms which change his possession from that of owner to that of bailee. The transfer of a document of title, *e.g.* a bill of lading, is a symbolic delivery of the goods[19]. If the goods are in the possession of a third person, there is no delivery by the seller to the buyer, unless and until such third person acknowledges to the buyer that he holds the goods on his behalf; but this rule is not to affect the operation of the issue or transfer of any document of title to goods[20].

The vendor must, in the absence of special agreement, deliver the goods upon payment or tender of the price; for subject to agreement to the contrary, *delivery of the goods and payment of the price are concurrent conditions*[1]. If credit is allowed he must deliver at once; but in the latter case, if the buyer becomes insolvent before he gets actual possession, the vendor may retain the goods[2], and as to future deliveries, MELLISH, L.J., said:

> "The seller, notwithstanding he may have agreed to allow credit for the goods, is not bound to deliver any more goods under the contract, until the price of the goods not yet delivered is tendered to him"[3].

Though the vendor is bound to deliver, he cannot, in the absence of agreement to do so, be compelled to carry or send the goods to the buyer. *The place of delivery is, apart from any express or implied agreement, the seller's place of business, if he has one; if not, his residence;* though if the goods sold are specific goods which to the knowedge of the parties when the contract is made are in some other place, then delivery should be made at the place where the goods are located at the time of sale[4].

Where the seller is bound to send the goods to the buyer, and no time is fixed by contract, he must deliver within a reasonable time[5]. Demand or tender of delivery must be made at a reasonable hour; what is a reasonable hour is a question of fact[6].

Delivery to a carrier.—If the seller is authorised or required to send goods to the buyer delivery to a carrier is prima facie delivery to the buyer[7],

---

19. See *Dublin City Distillery Co.* v. *Doherty*, [1914] A. C. 823, where the authorities on constructive delivery are reviewed by Lord ATKINSON.
20. S. G. A. 1893, s. 29 (3).
1. *Ibid.*, s. 28.
2. *Bloxam* v. *Sanders* (1825), 4 B. & C., at p. 948; and see *post*, "Lien" and "Stoppage *in Transitu*," pp. 210-214.
3. *Ex parte Chalmers* (1873), 8 Ch. 291.
4. S. G. A. 1893, s. 29 (1).
5. *Ibid.*, s. 29 (2).
6. *Ibid.*, s. 29 (4).
7. *Ibid.*, s. 32 (1).

but if the seller agrees to deliver at a fixed place, the carrier who takes the goods there is agent for the seller, and there is no delivery till their arrival[8]. The seller must, unless otherwise authorised by the buyer, make a reasonable contract with the carrier having regard to the nature of the goods and the circumstances of the case—should the seller fail to do this and the goods are lost or damaged, the buyer may decline to accept and pay for them, or hold the seller responsible in damages[9].

Where the seller is required to deliver goods at the buyer's premises, he discharges his obligations if he delivers them there without negligence to a person apparently having authority to receive them[10].

Where goods are delivered at a distant place, deterioration necessarily incident to the course of transit will fall on the buyer, though the seller agrees to deliver at his own risk[11], but loss caused by failure on the part of the seller to see that perishable goods are fit to go on the journey must be made good by the seller[12].

When goods are sent by sea, the seller must give such notice to the buyer as may enable him to effect any usual insurance of them during their sea transit, otherwise the goods shall be deemed to be at the risk of the seller[13]. This applies to a sale under an f.o.b. contract, although delivery is complete when the goods are put on board[14].

Delivery of wrong quantity.—When delivery is made it must be of the exact quantity. *If too little is delivered* the buyer may return the whole or keep the goods and pay for them at the contract rate[15].

If too much is delivered the buyer may retain the goods included in the contract and reject the rest, or reject the whole. Alternatively, he may accept the whole delivery. In this case there is virtually a new contract, and he must pay for the whole of the goods at the contract rate[16].

If the contract goods are sent with other goods of a different description

---

8. *Dunlop* v. *Lambert* (1838), 6 Cl. & F. 600, 621. Similarly in c.i.f. contracts (see *post*, p. 215) delivery of the goods is deemed to take place not when the goods are given to the carrier but when the documents relating to them are handed to the buyer.
9. S. G. A. 1893, s. 32 (2); *Thomas Young & Son, Ltd.* v. *Hobson & Partners* (1949), 65 T. L. R. 365.
10. *Galbraith and Grant* v. *Block*, [1922] 2 K. B. 155.
11. S. G. A. 1893, s. 33.
12. *Beer* v. *Walker* (1877), 46 L. J. K. B. 677; *Mash and Murrell, Ltd.* v. *Joseph I. Emanuel, Ltd.*, [1961] 1 All E. R. 485; [1961] 1 W. L. R. 862 (reversed on the facts, [1962] 1 All E. R. 77 *n.*; [1962] 1 W. L. R. 16 *n.*); *Cordova Land Co., Ltd.* v. *Victor Bros.*, [1966] 1 W. L. R. 793.
13. S. G. A. 1893, s. 32 (3).
14. *Wimble, Sons & Co.* v. *Rosenberg & Sons*, [1913] 3 K. B. 743.
15. S. G. A. 1893, s. 30 (1).
16. *Ibid.*, s. 30 (2).

the buyer can keep the contract goods or reject the whole. He cannot keep the other goods except by agreement[17].

Frequently the contract, in naming the quantities, includes some such expression as "say about", "more or less", etc., and the effect of this is to allow in favour of the seller a reasonable variation between the contract quantity and the amount delivered. And the usage of the trade or the course of dealing between the parties may import such terms into the contract[18]. Each case stands by itself, but the following are fair examples. In *McConnel* v. *Murphy*[19],

> the contract was for "all the spars manufactured by X, say about 600, averaging sixteen inches"; 496 were tendered of the specified kind and measurement, and the tender was held good.

In *Morris* v. *Levison*[20],

> the contract was for "a full and complete cargo, say 1,100 tons"; the vessel would take 1,210 tons, and only 1,080 were provided; it was decided that, under the circumstances, this would not suffice.

On the other hand, in *Miller* v. *Borner*[1],

> where the undertaking was to load a "cargo of ore, say about 2,800 tons," the charterer satisfied the contract by loading 2,840 tons, although the capacity of the ship was greater; the absence of the words "full and complete" leading to an opposite result.

But words of quantity may be merely words of estimate and not of contract. Thus,

> on the sale of the "remainder of a cargo (more or less about) 5,400 quarters wheat," the buyers were held bound to accept 5,574 quarters, on the ground that there was a sale of the whole remainder, whatever the quantity might be; the sellers' collateral estimate not affecting the meaning of the governing word "remainder"[2].

In the absence of agreement to the contrary a buyer cannot be compelled to take delivery by instalments[3].

---

17. *Ibid.*, s. 30 (3); *Moore & Co.* v. *Landauer & Co.*, [1921] 2 K. B. 519.
18. S. G. A. 1893, s. 30 (4); *Margaronis Navigation Agency, Ltd.* v. *Henry W. Peabody & Co. of London, Ltd.*, [1964] 3 All E. R. 333; [1965] 2 Q. B. 430.
19. (1874) L. R. 5 P. C. 203.
20. (1876), 1 C. P. D. 155.
1. [1900] 1 Q. B. 691; 5 Com. Cas. 175.
2. *Re Harrison and Micks Lambert*, [1917] 1 K. B. 755. See also *Tebbitts Bros.* v. *Smith* (1917), 33 T. L. R. 508, C. A.
3. S. G. A. 1893, s. 31 (1).

Rights upon Breach of the Contract[4]

Remedy for non-delivery.—Where the seller wrongfully neglects or refuses to deliver the goods to the buyer, the buyer's remedy is an action for damages, and the damages will be the estimated loss directly and naturally resulting, in the ordinary course of events, from the seller's breach of contract[5]. Where there is an available market for the goods in question the buyer is *prima facie* entitled to recover the difference between the contract price and the market price at the time when they ought to have been delivered, or, if no time was fixed, at the time of the refusal to deliver[6]. Any sub-contracts made by the buyer are generally ignored. In *Williams Brothers v. Agius*[7],

> the seller failed to deliver coal, the contract price of which was 16s. 3d. per ton. The buyer had made a contract to resell the coal at 19s. a ton. At the date of the seller's refusal to deliver the market price for such coal was 23s. 6d. per ton. *Held:* buyer entitled to 7s. 3d. per ton as damages the sum necessary to enable him to buy coal on the market and comply with his resale obligations.

Where there is no available market for the goods, the buyer's damage will, as stated, depend on the loss directly and naturally resulting from the breach but if special circumstances are known to the seller, *e.g.*, that non-delivery will mean loss to the buyer of a sub-contract, such special damages may also be claimed[8]. In *Victoria Laundry (Windsor), Ltd. v. Newman Industries, Ltd., Coulson & Co., Ltd. (Third Parties)*[9],

> the defendants delayed delivery of a boiler to the plaintiffs, who required it for the extension of their business. The plaintiffs had in view (*inter alia*) the prospects of certain profitable dyeing contracts of which the defendants had no notice. It was held that, although the defendants could not be held liable for the loss of these particular contracts, they could reasonably have foreseen that some loss of business would result and the plaintiffs were entitled to some general, and perhaps speculative, sum for loss of business reasonably to be expected.

---

4. See the remarks on "BREACH OF CONTRACT," *ante*, p. 84 *et seq.*, which are, in the main, applicable to the present subject.
5. S. G. A. 1893, s. 51 (1), (2).
6. *Ibid.*, s. 51 (3). Where the seller has committed an anticipatory breach of a contract to deliver goods within a reasonable time, the relevant market price is that prevailing at the time when delivery ought to have been made, subject to a duty to mitigate on the part of the buyer (if he accepted the seller's repudiation) by buying at once if the market is rising assuming there is a reasonable opportunity to do so: *Garnac Grain Co. v. H. M. F. Faure and Fairclough and Bunge Corporation*, [1967] 2 All E. R. 353, H. L.
7. *Williams Brothers v. E. T. Agius*, [1914] A. C. 510.
8. S. G. A. 1893, s. 54; *Patrick v. Russo-Grain Export Co.*, [1927] 2 K. B. 535.
9. [1949] 2 K. B. 529.

If the seller fails to deliver in accordance with contract goods which he knew were required to carry out a sub-contract, and the buyer becomes thereby unable to carry out the same, the latter is entitled to recover from the seller not only loss of profit on the resale but also the costs, etc., of reasonably defending an action against him by the sub-purchaser[10].

If the agreement was to deliver by stated instalments, to be separately paid for, and the seller makes defective deliveries in respect of one or more instalments, it is in each case a question depending on the terms of the contract, whether the buyer is entitled to repudiate the contract, or has merely a right to damages[11]. The main tests to be considered are (i) the quantitative ratio which the breach bears to the contract as a whole, and (ii) the degree of probability that such a breach will be repeated. But a single breach may be so serious as to involve repudiation of the contract[12].

Specific performance.—Where chattels are unique or of peculiar importance, the court, on the buyer's application, may order specific performance of a contract to deliver them; the judgment to this effect may be unconditional, or upon such terms and conditions as to damages, payment of the price and otherwise, as to the court may seem just[13]. Accordingly, the court may order specific performance of a contract for the sale of a ship which is of peculiar or practically unique value to the purchaser[14]. In any case, however, the goods must be "specific", *i.e.* identified and agreed upon at the time the contract is made[15] or "ascertained", *i.e.* identified in accordance with the agreement after the contract has been made[16].

Breach of condition.—Unless the buyer waives the condition, the breach of it entitles him to repudiate the contract, or he may, at his option, treat it as a breach of warranty, and claim damages only[17].

If the buyer waives a condition to deliver goods within a stipulated

---

10. *Agius* v. *Great Western Colliery Co.*, [1899] 1 Q. B. 413; *Hammond* v. *Bussey* (1888), 20 Q. B. D. 79.
11. S. G. A. 1893, s. 31 (2). And see *ante*, pp. 88–89.
12. *Maple Flock Co.* v. *Universal Furniture, etc., Ltd.*, [1933] All E. R. Rep. 15; [1934] 1 K. B. 148.
13. S. G. A. 1893, s. 52.
14. *Behnke* v. *Bede Shipping Co.*, [1927] All E. R. Rep. 689; [1927] 1 K. B. 649. Contrast *Cohen* v. *Roche*, [1927] 1 K. B. 169, where Hepplewhite chairs were held not to have sufficient value as antiques to justify an order for specific delivery.
15. S. G. A. 1893, s. 62 (1).
16. *Re Wait*, [1927] 1 Ch. 606, *per* ATKIN, L.J.
17. S. G. A. 1893, s. 11 (1).

time, he cannot afterwards abruptly cancel the contract without first giving notice to the seller fixing a reasonable time for delivery[18].

Unless there be a term of the contract, express or implied, to the contrary, if the contract is not severable and the buyer has accepted[19] the goods or part of them, the buyer is bound to treat the breach of condition as a breach of warranty[20].

Where a buyer rejects goods for breach of condition after he has paid the price, he is not entitled to retain possession of the goods until the money paid has been returned[1].

Breach of warranty.—The buyer may not on account of this repudiate the contract, but he may:

    1. Set up the breach of warranty in diminution or extinction of the price, and

    2. He may bring an action against the seller, and claim damages for the breach[2].

The measure of damages for breach of warranty is the estimated loss directly and naturally resulting in the ordinary course of events from the breach of warranty[3]. In *Bostock & Co.* v. *Nicholson & Sons*[4],

> the plaintiffs claimed damages against the defendants for breach of warranty in not supplying sulphuric acid commercially free from arsenic. The acid, which contained arsenic in large quantities, was used by the plaintiffs in the manufacture of brewing sugar, which the plaintiffs sold to brewers. The defendants did not know the purpose for which the acid was bought. In consequence of the poisonous nature of the sugar, the plaintiffs became liable to pay damages to the brewers and the goodwill of their business was entirely destroyed. The plaintiffs recovered as damages, under sub-s. (2) of s. 53,
>
>   (i) the price paid for the impure acid;
>   (ii) the value of the goods spoilt by being mixed with it.
>
> The other heads of damage were held not to fall within the measure laid down by the sub-section.

In the case of breach of warranty of quality, *prima facie* the measure of damages is the difference between the value of the goods at the time of delivery to the buyer, and the value they would have had if

---

18. *Hartley* v. *Hymans*, [1920] 3 K. B. 475; *Rickards (Charles), Ltd.* v. *Oppenheim*, [1950] 1 All E. R. 420; [1950] 1 K. B. 616.
19. As to what is "acceptance", see *post*, p. 208.
20. S. G. A. 1893, s. 11 (1) (c), as amended by the Misrepresentation Act 1967, s. 4 (1).
1. *J. L. Lyons & Co.* v. *May and Baker*, [1923] 1 K. B. 685.
2. S. G. A. 1893, s. 53 (1).
3. *Ibid.*, s. 53 (2).
4. [1904] 1 K. B. 725.

they had answered the warranty[5]. Larger damages will be claimable if, *e.g.* the defects cause personal injury or damage to property.

If the seller commits a breach by late delivery then *prima facie* the buyer is entitled to the difference between the market price at the time the goods ought to have been delivered and the (lower) market price of the goods when they are actually delivered plus any damage, *e.g.* for loss of use naturally arising or reasonably contemplated by the parties. Where, however, the buyer has made a resale contract at a price higher than the market price at the time of actual delivery the damages may be reduced to the difference between the market price at the time the goods ought to have been delivered and the resale price[6].

VII RIGHTS OF THE SELLER

The seller is entitled to be paid, and unless otherwise agreed, delivery of the goods and payment of the price are concurrent conditions[7]. The seller is also entitled to have the goods accepted subject to the right of the buyer to examine the goods, if he has not previously done so[8].

Acceptance

By s. 34 S. G. A., where goods are delivered to a buyer which he has not previously examined he is not deemed to have accepted them until he has had a reasonable opportunity of examining them. There is acceptance by the buyer either:

1. When he intimates to the seller that he accepts them, or
2. Except where s. 34 provides otherwise, when after delivery of the goods to him, he does any act in relation to them which is inconsistent with the ownership of the seller, or
3. Except where s. 34 provides otherwise, when after the lapse of a reasonable time, he retains the goods without intimating to the seller that he has rejected them[9].

Once a buyer has "accepted" the goods, he is bound to treat any breach of condition as a breach of warranty. If the buyer, having had an opportunity of examining the goods, despatches all or part of them to a sub-buyer that is an act which is inconsistent with the ownership of the seller. If the buyer, however, has not had an opportunity to examine them, despatch of all or part of them to a sub-buyer is not *acceptance* of the goods because this part of s. 35 is made subject to s. 34.

---

5. S. G. A. 1893, s. 53 (3).
6. *Wertheim* v. *Chicoutimi Pulp Co., Ltd.*, [1911] A. C. 301.
7. S. G. A. 1893, s. 28.
8. *Ante*, pp. 198–200.
9. S. G. A. 1893, s. 35, as amended by the Misrepresentation Act 1967, s. 4 (2).

Under ordinary circumstances a seller cannot compel the buyer to return rejected goods; he is entitled only to notice of the rejection[10]. If the contract is broken by the buyer, the seller acquires other rights— viz., the right to bring an action against the buyer, and, in some cases, rights against the goods.

A. Actions against the Buyer

Where the property in the goods has passed to the buyer[11] the seller may,

1. If the buyer makes default in payment, bring an action for the price[12]; or
2. If the buyer neglects or refuses to accept, he may bring an action for damages for not accepting the goods[13].

Where the property in the goods has not passed to the buyer, the action which usually lies is one for not accepting[13].

To this latter statement there is an exception—viz., that where the price is payable on a day certain, irrespective of delivery, and the buyer wrongfully neglects or refuses to pay the price, the seller may maintain an action for the price, although the property in the goods has not passed, and the goods have not been appropriated to the contract[14].

The damages for non-acceptance will be such as directly and naturally result in the ordinary course of events from the breach.

Where there is an available market for the goods in question, the measure of damage is prima facie to be ascertained by the difference between the contract price and the market or current price at the time or times when the goods ought to have been accepted[15].

Where there is no available market, *e.g.* where goods are made to a special specification of the buyer, the measure of damages will be the loss of profit expected by the seller[16].

Similarly, if supply of the kind of goods being sold exceeds demand, there is no "available market" and, should a buyer break his contract, the seller is entitled to his loss of profit on the sale[17]. It is otherwise if

10. *Ibid.*, s. 36.
11. *Ante*, pp. 185–189.
12. S. G. A. 1893, s. 49 (1).
13. *Ibid.*, s. 50 (1).
14. *Ibid.*, s. 49 (2).
15. *Ibid.*, s. 50.
16. *Vic Mill, Ltd., Re*, [1913] 1 Ch. 465. *Cf. Interoffice Telephones, Ltd.* v. *Robert Freeman Co., Ltd.*, [1957] 3 All E. R. 479; [1958] 1 Q. B. 190.
17. *W. L. Thompson* v. *Robinson (Gunmakers), Ltd.*, [1955] 1 All E. R. 154; [1955] Ch. 177.

demand exceeds supply because the seller makes just as many deals as he would have done if the buyer did not break his contract—nominal damages only are then awarded[18].

When the seller is ready to deliver the goods, and requests the buyer to take delivery, and the buyer does not within a reasonable time after such request take the goods, he is liable to the seller for any loss occasioned by his neglect or refusal to take delivery, and also for a reasonable charge for the care and custody of the goods[19].

Where the contract is to deliver by stated instalments, refusal to accept or to pay for one or more instalments may entitle the seller to treat the contract as at an end, and sue as for a total breach, or it may give a right to sue only for damages arising from the particular default; the right of the seller in this respect depends upon the terms of the contract in each case[1]. Thus:

> failure to make punctual payment for an instalment delivery may not amount to a repudiation by the buyer, entitling the seller to refuse to make further deliveries[2].

B. Remedies against the Goods
The rights of an "unpaid seller" against the goods are—

1. Lien;
2. Stoppage *in transitu.*
3. Resale.

An *"unpaid" seller* is, for the purposes of the present part of the subject, one to whom the whole price has not been paid or tendered, or who has been conditionally paid by means of a negotiable instrument, which has been subsequently dishonoured[3].

"Seller" includes any person in the position of a seller—*e.g.* agent for the seller to whom the bill of lading has been indorsed[4].

1. Lien
This is the seller's right to hold goods of which he has possession, but not ownership, when the price has not been paid[5]. If the property in the goods has not passed to the buyer, the unpaid seller has a right of withholding delivery, similar to and co-extensive with lien[6].

---

18. *Charter v. Sullivan*, [1957] 1 All E. R. 809; [1957] 2 Q. B. 117, C.A.
19. S. G. A. 1893, s. 37.
1. *Ibid.*, s. 31 (2).
2. *Payzu v. Saunders*, [1919] 2 K. B. 581.
3. S. G. A. 1893, s. 38 (1).
4. *Ibid.*, s. 38 (2).
5. *Ibid.*, s. 39 (1). And see *post*, p. 412.
6. S. G. A. 1893, s. 39 (2).

The unpaid seller may retain possession of the goods until he is paid or tendered the price in the following cases[7]—viz.,

   (i) where the goods have been sold without any stipulation as to credit;

   (ii) where the goods have been sold on credit, but the term of credit has expired;

   (iii) where the buyer becomes insolvent—*i.e.* when he has ceased to pay his debts in the ordinary course of business, or cannot pay his debts as they become due[8].

And if the goods have been part delivered, the unpaid seller may exercise his right of lien on the remainder, unless such part delivery has been made under such circumstances as to show an agreement to waive the lien[9]. It has been decided that if the seller breaks his contract to deliver whilst the buyer is solvent, that even then he will be entitled to retain the goods if the buyer subsequently becomes insolvent[10].

Lien is lost if:

   (i) the seller delivers the goods to a carrier or other bailee for the purpose of transmission to the buyer without reserving the right of disposal; or

   (ii) if the buyer or his agent lawfully obtains possession of the goods; or

   (iii) if the seller waives his lien[11].

2. Stoppage in transitu

This differs from *lien* chiefly in two points:

   (i) it can be exercised only when the buyer is insolvent; and

   (ii) only when the goods have left the possession of the seller.

It is the right conferred on the unpaid seller who has parted with goods to stop them, on insolvency of the buyer, before they have reached the buyer's actual or constructive possession, and to resume possession of the goods and retain them until payment or tender of the price[12].

The general result of the stoppage is to restore the right of possession to the vendor; to place him, in fact, in a position similar to that which he had lost by parting with possession of the goods. The sale is not thereby rescinded[13].

---

7. *Ibid.*, s.41.   8. *Ibid.*, s. 62.
9. *Ibid.*, s. 42. However, if in a severable contract, one instalment is delivered and not paid for, the seller has no lien over another instalment which is paid for.
10. See *Valpy* v. *Oakeley* (1851), 16 Q. B. 941.
11. S. G. A. 1893, s. 43.   12. S. G. A. 1893, s. 44.
13. *Ibid.*, s. 48 (1).

The right can be exercised only against an insolvent buyer, the insolvency being a matter to be determined on the facts[14]. The vendor may take time by the forelock, and stop the goods before actual insolvency; but if, at the termination of the voyage, or at the date when delivery is due, the buyer proves solvent, the vendor must deliver, and may further be liable for expenses[15].

It is only during transit that this right of stoppage exists; it is therefore important to define when the transitus begins and when it ends. It is provided by the Act that goods shall be deemed to be *in transitu* from the time when they are delivered to a carrier or other bailee for the purpose of transmission to the buyer, until the buyer, or his agent in that behalf, takes delivery of them from such carrier or other bailee[16].

Duration of transit.—In every case an inquiry must be made into the particular facts, as the question is really one of the intention of the parties[17]; *e.g.*—

 (i) Goods delivered to a carrier *qua* carrier—transit continues.

 (ii) Goods delivered to a carrier *qua* warehouseman for the buyer—transit ends. But not until the carrier acknowledges to the buyer or his agent that he holds for him[18].

 (iii) Goods delivered to the buyer's servant—transit ends.

 (iv) Goods delivered to the master of the buyer's ship—transit ends. If the goods are delivered to a ship chartered by the buyer, it is a question depending on the facts of each particular case whether they are in the possession of the master as a carrier, or as agent for the buyer[19].

 (v) When the buyer takes possession of the goods away from the carrier[1], even against the carrier's will, and though the destination is not reached, transit ends.

 (vi) When the carrier or bailee wrongfully refuses to deliver the goods to the buyer or his agent in that behalf—transit ends[2].

 (vii) If the buyer or his agent in that behalf takes possession of part of the goods, the circumstances being such as to show an intention on the part of the vendor to retain the rest, the right

---

14. "Insolvency" is defined, *ante*, p. 211.
15. *The Constantia* (1807), 6 Rob. Ad. R. 321.
16. S. G. A. 1893, s. 45 (1).
17. See remarks of JESSEL, M.R., in *Merchant Banking Co.* v. *Phoenix Bessemer Steel Co.* (1877), 5 Ch. D. 205, 219; and of MATHEW, J., in *Bethell* v. *Clark* (1887), 19 Q. B. D. 558.
18. S. G. A. 1893, s. 45 (3).
19. S. G. A. 1893. s. 45 (5).
1. *Ibid.*, s. 45 (2). *London and North Western Rail. Co.* v. *Bartlett* (1862), 7 H. & N. 400, 31 L. J. Exch. 92.
2. S. G. A. 1893, s. 45 (6).

to stop *in transitu* as to these remains; if such as to show an agreement to give up possession of the rest, the right to stop has gone[3].

How effected.—There is no particular form of procedure required in the exercise of the right. Simple notice to the carrier is enough, but it must be given to the person actually in possession (*e.g.* the ship's master), or if to an employer of such person (*e.g.* shipowner), then in time to allow, with the exercise of reasonable diligence, the person in charge to be communicated with[4], and it has been questioned whether or no there is any duty in the shipowner to communicate with the master[5].

Rights and duties of carrier.—Where goods have been stopped *in transitu*, the carrier must re-deliver the goods to, or according to the directions of, the seller[4] and on the other hand the seller comes under an obligation to take possession of the goods and to pay the freight and all attendant charges thereon[6].

But although as between the unpaid seller and the carrier, the latter is entitled to be paid the charges due in respect of the carriage of the particular goods, the carrier is not entitled to assert any general lien which he may have acquired as against the consignee in priority to the seller's right to stop *in transitu*[7].

Rights of third parties.—The vendor's right is superior even to that of a judgment creditor who has attached the goods[8]. Neither the right of lien nor the right to stop *in transitu* is defeated by any sale or other disposition of the goods which the buyer may have made without the seller's consent[9]. But if a document of title to goods, *e.g.* a bill of lading, has been lawfully transferred to any person as buyer or owner of the goods, and that person transfers the document to one who takes it in good faith and for valuable consideration, then if such transfer was by way of sale the right of lien and stoppage *in transitu* is defeated[10]. The same effect is produced whether the transfer is made by the buyer or by a mercantile agent, "entrusted with the bill of lading."

A *bona fide* transfer by way of pledge of the document of title will

---

3. *Ibid.*, s. 45 (7).
4. S. G. A. 1893, s. 46.
5. *Ex parte Falk* (1880), 14 Ch. D. 446; 7 App. Cas. 573, 585.
6. *Booth S.S. Co., Ltd.* v. *Cargo Fleet Iron Co.*, [1916] 2 K. B. 570, C. A.
7. *United States Steel Products Co.* v. *Great Western Rail. Co.*, [1916] 1 A.C. 189.
8. *Smith* v. *Goss* (1807), 1 Camp. 282.
9. S. G. A. 1893, s. 47; *Lickbarrow* v. *Mason* (1793), 1 Sm. L. C. (13th ed.) 703; see also *D. F. Mount, Ltd.* v. *Jay and Jay (Provisions) Co., Ltd.*, [1959] 3 All E. R. 307; [1960] 1 Q. B. 159.
10. *Cahn* v. *Pockett's Bristol, etc. Co., Ltd.*, *ante*, p. 192.

defeat the right to a certain extent; the unpaid seller's right is subject to that of the *bona fide* transferee for value[11].

3. Resale

As the contract of sale is not usually rescinded by the exercise of the right of lien or of stoppage *in transitu*, it follows that, as a rule, re-sale is not allowable. But if, notwithstanding this, the unpaid seller re-sells, although this is generally a breach of contract, the new buyer acquires a good title as against the original and defaulting buyer[12]. In certain cases the unpaid vendor is entitled to re-sell, viz.,

1. Where the right was expressly reserved in the contract of sale[13];
2. Where the goods are perishable[14]; or
3. Where the unpaid seller gives notice to the buyer of his intention to re-sell, and the buyer does not, within a reasonable time, pay or tender the price[14].

In these cases the seller may re-sell and claim damages from the buyer for any loss occasioned by the buyer's breach of contract. The exercise by the unpaid seller of a right of resale under these provisions rescinds the original contract so that any profit made by the unpaid seller on resale is his to keep[15].

VIII RIGHTS UNDER CERTAIN KINDS OF CONTRACT

Where contracts of sale involve the shipment of goods from one country to another, certain obligations of the contract are generally indicated by the initials or words "f.o.b."; "c.i.f."; or "ex ship". Such descriptions of the contract carry with them legal effects founded on the custom of merchants adopted into the law by the decisions of the courts.

F.O.B. contracts.—These initials mean "free on board". Thus, a clause in the contract might run, "Sold to A. B. 200 bags of rice f.o.b. Antwerp". Under such a contract the seller must put the goods on board at Antwerp at his own expense for the account of the buyer; and when on board, whether the goods are specific or unascertained, they are at the risk of the buyer, who is considered to be the shipper[16]. The buyer must name a ship or authorise the seller to select one, and

---

11. S. G. A. 1893, s. 47; *Lickbarrow* v. *Mason, supra.*
12. S. G. A. 1893, s. 48 (2).
13. *Ibid.,* s. 48 (4).
14. *Ibid.,* s. 48 (3).
15. *R. V. Ward, Ltd.* v. *Bignall,* [1967] 2 All E. R. 449; [1967] 1 Q. B. 534, C. A.
16. *Cowasjee* v. *Thompson* (1845), 5 Moo. P. C. C. 165; *Brown* v. *Hare* (1858), 3 H. & N. 484; (1859) 4 H. & N. 622; *Inglis* v. *Stock* (1885) 10 App. Cas. 263.

it is the seller's duty to give the buyer sufficient notice to enable him to protect himself by insurance against loss during the sea transit[17]. Property in the goods will normally pass to the buyer as soon as they are put on board but not if loaded together with other goods of the same description.

C.I.F. contracts.—The initials c.i.f. stand for the words, cost, insurance, freight. Thus, if a merchant agrees to sell goods "at £2 per ton c.i.f. Manchester Docks", that sum will include the price of the goods, the premium for insuring them and the freight payable for carrying them to their named destination, Manchester.

The obligations undertaken by the seller under a c.i.f. contract, in the absence of provision to the contrary, were summarised by Lord ATKINSON[18] as follows:

The seller must—

1. Make out an invoice of the goods sold;
2. Ship at the port of shipment goods of the description contained in the contract;
3. Procure a contract of affreightment under which the goods will be delivered at the destination contemplated by the contract;
4. Arrange for an insurance upon the terms current in the trade which will be available for the benefit of the buyer;
5. With all reasonable despatch send forward and tender to the buyer these shipping documents, namely, the invoice, bill of lading and policy of insurance, delivery of which to the buyer is symbolical of delivery of the goods purchased, entitling the seller to payment of their price.

Property in the goods normally passes when the documents are handed over to the buyers and payment is made.

A c.i.f. contract usually provides for payment of "cash against documents" and the fact that the goods have not arrived at the time when the documents are tendered does not excuse the buyer from making immediate payment; but this does not prejudice the buyer's right to reject the goods and recover the money paid by him if on arrival the goods are found not to be in conformity with the contract[19].

So, a vendor under an ordinary c.i.f. contract who has shipped appropriate goods can effectively tender proper documents to the buyer and require payment, although the seller knows at the time that

---

17. S. G. A. 1893, s. 32 (3); see *ante*, pp. 203.
18. *Johnson* v. *Taylor Brothers & Co.*, [1920] A. C., at pp. 155, 156.
19. *E. Clemens Horst Co.* v. *Biddell Brothers*, [1912] A. C. 18.

the goods have been lost at sea. This is because the risk passes to the buyer as soon as the goods are put on board[20]. The seller's obligation to insure must be strictly complied with. If he does not effect an insurance the buyer is not bound to accept and pay for the goods, although they arrive safely at their destination[1]. If under a c.i.f. contract the bill of lading has been falsely dated so as to make it appear that the goods were shipped in accordance with the contract, and the buyer is thereby induced to accept the documents, he can, on subsequently discovering the fact, recover the difference between the market price and the contract price of the goods as damages for breach of the seller's implied obligation to deliver a correct bill of lading[2].

In practice the buyer frequently agrees to accept documents other than those required under a strict c.i.f. contract, *e.g.* a certificate of insurance instead of a policy or a delivery order instead of a bill of lading. Such deviations must be expressly provided for in the contract and it must be made clear whether or not the seller is to be entitled to sue for the price on tender of the substituted documents[3].

Sales "ex ship".—Lord SUMNER in delivering the judgment of the Privy Council described the characteristics of these contracts in the following words:

> In the case of a sale "ex ship" the seller has to cause delivery to be made to the buyer from a ship which has arrived at the port of delivery and has reached a place therein, which is usual for delivery of goods of the kind in question. The seller has therefore to pay the freight, or otherwise to release the shipowner's lien and to furnish the buyer with an effectual direction to the ship to deliver. Till this is done the buyer is not bound to pay for the goods. Till this is done he may have an insurable interest in profits, but none that can correctly be described as an interest "upon goods," nor any interest which the seller, as seller, is bound to insure for him. If the seller insures, he does so for his own purposes and of his own motion. The mere documents do not take the place of the goods under such a contract[4].

Letters of credit.—In contracts where it is the buyer's duty to pay cash against documents, it is commonly made a condition that the buyer shall open a credit in the seller's favour. This means that the

---

20. *C. Groom, Ltd.* v. *Barber,* [1914-15] All E. R. Rep. 194; [1915] 1 K. B. 316.
1. *Orient Co.* v. *Brekke and Howlid,* [1913] 1 K. B. 531.
2. *Finlay & Co.* v. *N. V. Kwik, etc. Maatschappij,* [1928] All E. R. Rep. 110; [1929] 1 K. B. 400; *Kwei Tek Chao* v. *British Traders and Shippers, Ltd.,* [1954] 1 All E. R. 779.
3. See *Comptoir D'Achat et de Vente du Boerenbond Belge S/A* v. *Luis de Ridder Limitado, The Julia,* [1949] A. C. 293; [1949] 1 All E. R. 269.
4. *Yangtsze Insurance Association* v. *Lukmanjee,* [1918] A. C., at p. 589.

buyer must instruct his own bank (the "issuing bank") to open a credit in the seller's favour at a bank (the "correspondent bank") in the seller's country. The issuing bank then instructs the correspondent bank to pay the seller (or accept a bill of exchange drawn by the seller) when he hands over the shipping documents. If the buyer's obligation is to provide a "confirmed credit", then the seller is entitled to obtain the correspondent bank's undertaking of liability under the credit (in addition to the liability assumed by the issuing bank) before shipment. In every case the buyer must provide the credit a reasonable time before the first day of shipment[5], and if shipment is to take place between two dates the credit must remain open for the whole of that period[6] even if the choice of the exact date is left to the buyer[7]. The banker for his part will be entitled to indemnity from the buyer but only if he complies exactly with his intructions, or if deviation from them is subsequently ratified expressly or by conduct[8]. The banker may refuse to pay the seller if the documents tendered do not on the face of them clearly correspond to what he has been instructed to accept[9].

> But if "clean" bills of lading are presented, the bank is not concerned to see that conditions on the back of them have been complied with[10].

The object of a confirmed credit is to provide an assurance in advance that the seller will be paid and to enable him to discount bills at the best rate. The credit is sometimes made transferable and the seller may be relying on it to obtain the goods themselves. If that fact is known to the buyer and he fails to provide the credit, the measure of damages will be the loss of the profit which would have been made[11]. A confirmed letter of credit constitutes a contract between the correspondent bank and the seller and the buyer cannot cancel it even if he claims that the seller is in breach of the contract of sale[12].

---

5. *Sinason-Teicher Inter-American Grain Corporation* v. *Oilcakes and Oilseeds Trading Co., Ltd.*, [1954] 3 All E. R. 468.
6. *Pavia & Co., S. P. A.* v. *Thurmann-Nielsen*, [1952] 1 All E. R. 492; [1952] 2 Q. B. 84.
7. *Ian Stach, Ltd.* v. *Baker Bosley, Ltd.*, [1958] 1 All E. R. 542; [1958] 2 Q. B. 130.
8. *Bank Melli Iran* v. *Barclays Bank (Dominion, Colonial and Overseas)*, [1951] 2 T. L. R. 1057.
9. *Rayner & Co., Ltd.* v. *Hambro's Bank, Ltd.*, [1942] 2 All E. R. 694; [1943] 1 K. B. 37.
10. *British Imex Industries, Ltd.* v. *Midland Bank, Ltd.*, [1958] 1 All E. R. 264; [1958] 1 Q. B. 542.
11. *Trans Trust S. P. R. L.* v. *Danubian Trading Co., Ltd.*, [1952] 1 All E. R. 970; [1952] 2 Q. B. 297.
12. *Hamzeh Malas & Sons* v. *British Imex Industries, Ltd.*, [1958] 1 All E. R. 262; [1958] 2 Q. B. 127.

IX SALES BY AUCTION

When goods are sold by auction each lot is *prima facie* deemed to be the subject of a separate contract of sale. Anyone who makes a bid is in law making an offer to buy and there is acceptance if the auctioneer knocks down the goods to the last bidder. Thus, the sale is complete when the hammer falls, or as otherwise customary, and after that time the bid may not be retracted. The seller or his agent may bid, but only if an express notification to that effect is given; a contravention of this rule makes the sale fraudulent. The seller may notify that he has placed a reserve price on the goods[13].

By the Auctions (Bidding Agreements) Act 1927 sellers are to some extent protected from loss resulting from agreements designed to stifle competition and bring about a sale of goods at a lower price than might otherwise have been obtained.

By this Act a dealer[14] who gives or offers any gift or consideration to another person as a reward for abstaining or having abstained from bidding at an auction, or any person who accepts or attempts to obtain such reward is guilty of a punishable offence, but this does not prevent a dealer previously to the auction from entering into an agreement in writing with other persons to purchase goods *bona fide* on a joint account, if before the purchase the dealer deposits a copy of the agreement with the auctioneer[15].

If goods have been sold at an auction to a person who is a party to a prohibited bidding agreement (assuming one of the parties to that agreement is a dealer), the seller may avoid the contract and, if the goods are not returned to him, he may recover compensation from *any* party to the prohibited agreement[16].

---

13. S. G. A. 1893, s. 58. As to auctioneers, see *ante*, pp. 148.
14. *I.e.*, a person who in the normal course of his business attends sales by auction for the purpose of purchasing goods with a view to reselling them. Auctions (Bidding Agreements) Act 1927, s. 1 (2).
15. Auctions (Bidding Agreements) Act 1927, s. 1 (1).
16. Auctions (Bidding Agreements) Act 1969, s. 3.

CHAPTER 14

Hire-Purchase

I INTRODUCTION

A hire-purchase agreement is an agreement by an owner of goods to hire them out to a "hirer" and to give the hirer an option to purchase them conditional on his completing the necessary payments for the goods and complying with the terms of the agreement. Normally, the hirer obtains immediate possession of the goods when the contract is made and the hirer thereupon pays a deposit or initial payment which is usually a certain percentage of the cash price, *i.e.*, the price at which the goods could be purchased outright. If the hirer pays the balance of the cash price together with the hire-purchase charges, by instalments as specified in the agreement, ownership of the goods passes to the hirer. Since the hirer is merely given an "option" to buy the goods, he is not in the position of someone who has "agreed to buy" the goods, so that if before he has exercised his option to purchase he sells the goods, he cannot pass a good title to the purchaser under s. 25 (2) of the Sale of Goods Act 1893[1]. Further, the provisions of the Sale of Goods Act which imply certain terms in contracts of sale of goods have no application to contracts of hire-purchase.

Frequently, when a customer wishes to take goods from a dealer on hire-purchase, the dealer himself is not in a position to provide credit, and a common form of hire-purchase transaction is that the dealer sells the goods to a finance company and the finance company, now the owner of the goods, makes the hire-purchase agreement with the customer. The rights and obligations of the hire-purchase agreement exist betwen the customer and the finance company and the dealer is not a party to that agreement.

II COMMON LAW: OBLIGATIONS OF THE OWNER

Where the hire-purchase price does not exceed £2,000, the agreement is subject to certain terms implied by the Hire-Purchase Act 1965,

---

1. *Helby* v. *Matthews*, [1895] A. C. 471. However, he may pass a good title under such other exceptions to the rule of *nemo dat quod non habet* as sale in market overt, or a disposition of a motor vehicle to a private purchaser under the provision of ss. 27-29, Hire-Purchase Act 1964. See *ante*, p. 192.

unless the agreement is made by or on behalf of a body corporate as the hirer of the goods to which the agreement relates[2]. With regard to all agreements made by or on behalf of a body corporate as the hirer and to all agreements where the hire-purchase price does exceed £2,000, the obligations of the parties are governed by common law. Moreover, the provisions of the Hire-Purchase Act are not exclusive, and such common law principles as the law relating to fundamental breach and the measure of damages payable on a breach by the hirer are applicable to agreements governed by the Acts. The common law obligations of the owner are as follows:

1. *To deliver the goods to the hirer.*—Breach of this duty entitles the hirer to repudiate the agreement[3]. Unless the goods are of a special or unique kind, the hirer's only other remedy for breach is damages, not specific performance.

2. *Implied condition as to title.*—In every hire-purchase contract, there is an implied condition that the bailor is the true owner of the goods at the time of their delivery to the hirer[4]. For breach of this term, the hirer may recover any payments (by way of deposit or instalments) that he has made on the ground of total failure of consideration[5].

3. *Implied warranty of quiet enjoyment.*

4. *Implied condition that the goods will correspond to their description[6].*

5. *Implied condition that the owner will keep the goods in repair till delivery[7].*

6. *Implied term that the goods are fit for their purpose.*—In a number of cases concerning simple hire transactions, it has been held that there is an implied condition that the goods are as fit for their purpose as care and skill can make them except where the defect is apparent or where the hirer places no reliance on the owner's skill or judgment[8]. PARKER, L.J., in *Karsales (Harrow), Ltd.* v. *Wallis* put the duty on a stricter basis for hire-purchase transactions[9]:

---

2. Hire-Purchase Act 1965, s. 4.
3. In the case of a motor vehicle, failure to supply the log book means that the hire-purchase contract does not come into operation: *Bentworth Finance, Ltd.* v. *Lubert*, [1967] 2 All E. R. 810; [1968] 1 Q. B. 680, C. A.
4. *Mercantile Union Guarantee Corporation, Ltd.* v. *Wheatley*, [1937] 4 All E. R. 713; [1938] 1 K. B. 490.
5. *Warman* v. *Southern Counties Car Finance Corporation, Ltd.*, [1949] 1 All E. R. 711; [1949] 2 K. B. 576.
6. *Karsales (Harrow), Ltd.* v. *Wallis*, [1956] 2 All E. R. 866; [1956] 1 W. L. R. 936, C. A.; *Astley Industrial Trust, Ltd.* v. *Grimley*, [1963] 2 All E. R. 33; [1963] 1 W. L. R. 584, C. A.
7. *Karsales (Harrow), Ltd.* v. *Wallis*, [1956] 2 All E. R. 866, at p. 868; [1956] 1 W. L. R. 936, *per* DENNING, L.J.
8. *Hyman* v. *Nye* (1881), 6 Q. B. D. 685; *Reed* v. *Dean*, [1949] 1 K. B. 188.
9. [1956] 2 All E. R. 866, at p. 870; [1956] 1 W. L. R. 936, at p. 943.

"I think it is the duty of a hire-purchase finance company, which is letting out a chattel on hire-purchase to ascertain that the chattel is reasonably fit for the purpose for which it is expressly hired."

But whether the obligation is a strict one and whether it applies irrespective of whether or not reliance on the owner's skill or judgment is shown is uncertain[10].

At Common Law, the implied obligations of the owner can be excluded or modified by the express terms of the hire-purchase agreement. However, if the goods delivered are not those contracted for—if there has been, that is to say, a fundamental breach the court will normally construe any exemption clause as not intended to apply in this situation[11]. In *Karsales (Harrow), Ltd.* v. *Wallis*[12],

> The defendant inspected a second-hand Buick car which was in excellent condition and he agreed to take it on hire-purchase. The contract contained a clause to the effect that there was no condition that the vehicle was roadworthy or as to its fitness for any purpose. When the car was delivered, it was found to be in a deplorable condition, having been substantially altered since it was inspected. *Held:* the exemption clause was not effective as there had been a fundamental breach of contract.

As to whether the defects in the goods delivered are serious enough to amount to a fundamental breach of contract, it depends on whether there is "such a congeries of defects as to destroy the workable character" of the goods[13].

III COMMON LAW: OBLIGATIONS OF THE DEALER

Where the dealer sells the goods to a finance company and the latter then lets them out on hire-purchase to the customer, the dealer is not generally privy to the contract of hire-purchase. However, a collateral contract may be implied between the dealer and the customer, based on the dealer undertaking to cause the finance company to enter into a hire-purchase contract with the customer in return for the customer promising to enter into a hire-purchase agreement with the finance company. If, therefore, the dealer has made any express

---

10. *Astley Industrial Trust, Ltd.* v. *Grimley*, [1963] 2 All E. R. 33; [1963] 1 W. C. R. 584, C. A.
11. *Suisse Atlantiqué Société d'Armement Maritime S.A.* v. *N.V. Rotterdamsche Kolen Centrale*, [1966] 2 All E. R. 61; [1967] 1 A. C. 361.
12. [1956] 2 All E. R. 866; [1956] 1 W. L. R. 936, C. A., followed in *Yeoman Credit, Ltd.* v. *Apps*, [1961] 2 All E. R. 281; [1962] 2 Q. B. 508, C. A.; and in *Charterhouse Credit Co., Ltd.* v. *Tolly*, [1963] 2 All E. R. 432; [1963] 2. Q. B. 683, C. A.
13. *Per* Lord DUNEDIN in *Pollock and Co.* v. *Macrae*, 1922, S. C. (H. L.) 192, at p. 200.

warranty to the customer about the goods and this warranty is broken, the dealer may be held liable in damages for breach of contract. Thus, in *Andrews* v. *Hopkinson*[14]:

> The dealer told the customer who was contemplating taking a second-hand car on hire-purchase: "It's a good little bus; I would stake my life on it; you will have no trouble with it." The car was sold to a finance company with whom the customer made a hire-purchase agreement. A week after delivery, the customer was injured while driving the car owing to a failure in the steering mechanism. The terms of the hire-purchase agreement deprived the customer of a remedy against the hire-purchase finance company. *Held:* the dealer was liable in damages for breach of his express warranty which formed part of a collateral contract between the dealer and the customer.

An alternative ground for awarding damages against the dealer in *Andrews* v. *Hopkinson*[14] was that since a dealer in second-hand goods owes a duty of care to ensure that they are not in such a state that personal injuries or damage to property might be caused, he was liable in negligence.

The House of Lords in *Branwhite* v. *Worcester Works Finance Co.*[15] held by a majority that the dealer is not normally the agent in law of the finance company in relation to a hire-purchase transaction. However, the House held unanimously that if the hirer pays a deposit to the dealer and the finance company when paying the purchase price for the goods to the dealer is credited with the amount of that deposit, the finance company is treated as having received it. It follows that if the hire-purchase agreement is void, *e.g.* because the parties were not *ad idem* owing to the dealer having fraudulently inserted figures in the proposal form contrary to those agreed by the hirer, the hirer is entitled to recover the amount of the deposit from the finance company as money had and received on a consideration that has wholly failed.

IV COMMON LAW: OBLIGATIONS OF THE HIRER

1. *To take delivery of the goods.*—If a hirer declines to take the goods, he is liable in damages, but the owner has no right to wait and sue for the instalments as they would have become due had the hirer taken delivery[16].

2. *To take care of the goods.*—The hirer is liable in damages if the agreement is determined and the goods are in a damaged state

---

14. [1956] 3 All E. R. 422; [1957] 1 Q. B. 229, followed in *Yeoman Credit, Ltd.* v. *Odgers*, [1962] 1 All E. R. 789; [1962] 1 W. L. R. 215, C. A.
15. [1968] 3 All E. R. 104.
16. *National Cash Register Co., Ltd.* v. *Stanley*, [1921] 3 K. B. 292.

unless he can prove that he has taken reasonable care of them. In assessing damages in respect of such article,

> "there ought to be evidence as to what its general condition and value were at the inception of the contract and, similarly, evidence as to what its general condition and value were at the termination of the contract"[17].

The hirer is not liable for fair wear and tear.

3. *Liability for loss or damage irrespective of negligence.*—An action in conversion lies against a hirer if he deals with the goods in a manner inconsistent with the owner's title, such as disposing of them or wrongfully withholding possession from the owner after the agreement has been terminated. If the hirer deals with the goods in a way clearly not authorised by the owner, he is strictly liable for any damage to the goods occurring thereafter.

4. *To pay instalment charges.*—The essence of hire-purchase is that the hirer is not bound to *buy* the goods and must be given some option to terminate the agreement and return the goods. If he exercises that option, he must pay all instalments due at that time, together with any further sum which the agreement requires under a "minimum payment" clause should be paid on that event[18].

Damages for default.—Should the hirer default in making his payments as required in the agreement, he is liable for all arrears, and the owner is invariably entitled under the agreement to terminate the agreement and to resume possession of the goods. The hirer is also liable in damages for loss consequent on his breach. The measure of damages depends on whether, by words or conduct, the hirer has repudiated the agreement or not. If he has repudiated the agreement, *e.g.*, by writing a letter to the effect that he cannot go on with the agreement, and this repudiation has been accepted by the owner[19], the measure of damages is the difference between the hire-purchase price (less any "option money") and the sum of the sale price reasonably obtained

---

17. Per DAVIES, L.J., in *Brady v. St. Margaret's Trust,* [1963] 2 All E. R. 275; [1963] 2 Q. B. 494, C. A.
18. *Associated Distributors, Ltd. v. Hall,* [1938] 1 All E. R. 511; [1938] 2 K. B. 83, C. A. Lords DENNING and DEVLIN *obiter* said that case was wrongly decided: *Bridge v. Campbell Discount Co., Ltd.,* [1962] 1 All E. R. 385; [1962] A. C. 600, H. L. In *United Dominions Trust (Commercial), Ltd. v. Ennis,* [1967] 2 All E. R. 345, 348; [1968] 1 Q. B. 54, C. A., Lord DENNING said that a hirer is not to be taken to exercise the option to terminate unless he does so consciously, knowing of the consequences, and avowedly in exercise of the option.
19. The hirer's repudiation of the agreement is not "accepted" by the owner if the owner seeks to enforce a minimum payment clause in the agreement: *United Dominions Trust (Commercial), Ltd. v. Ennis,* [1967] 2 All E. R. 345; [1968] 1 Q. B. 54, C. A.

and any payments paid by or due from the hirer to date[20]. A discount is made to take account of the fact that the owner obtains accelerated receipt of his capital outlay[21]. If, however, the hirer has not repudiated the agreement but is merely in arrears with one or more instalments, or the owner has not accepted the hirer's repudiation but exercises a contractual right to terminate the agreement, the owner may only claim against the hirer the amount of instalments in arrears, damages for any failure on the part of the hirer to take reasonable care of the goods, and the cost of repossessing them[1].

Where the agreement itself provides by a "minimum payment" clause that, on default by the hirer, if the owner exercises his contractual right to end the agreement, the hirer must pay not only the arrears due but some further fixed sum, the court will only allow such sum to be claimed if it represents a genuine pre-estimate of the loss likely to follow from the hirer's default. Otherwise the sum will be irrecoverable as a "penalty" and the owner will be confined to a claim for damages assessed by the court on the principles already discussed[2].

5. *To make certain payments in the event of bankruptcy, levy of execution, etc.*—The agreement may provide that if any distress or execution is levied against the hirer or a receiving order is made against him, the owner may terminate the agreement and retake possession of the goods. Such a term is enforceable and the court has no power to grant equitable relief to the hirer in such a case[3]. Should the agreement also provide that, on such event, the hirer must make certain further payments after the owner repossesses the goods, such sum may be recoverable[4].

V THE HIRE-PURCHASE ACT 1965

Scope of the Act

The Hire-Purchase Act 1965 applies to all hire-purchase agreements where the hire-purchase price does not exceed £2,000, but the Act has no application where the agreement is made by or on behalf of a body

---

20. *Yeoman Credit, Ltd.* v. *Waragowski*, [1961] 3 All E. R. 145; [1961] 1 W. L. R. 1124, C. A.
21. *Overstone, Ltd.* v. *Shipway*, [1962] 1 All E. R. 52; [1962] 1 W. L. R. 117.
1. *Financings, Ltd.* v. *Baldock*, [1963] 1 All E. R. 443; [1963] 2 Q. B. 104, C. A.; *Brady* v. *St. Margaret's Trust*, [1963] 2 All E. R. 275; [1963] 2 Q. B. 494, C. A.
2. *Bridge* v. *Campbell Discount Co., Ltd.*, [1962] 1 All E. R. 385; [1962] A. C. 600, H. L.; *Anglo-Auto Finance Co., Ltd.* v. *James*, [1963] 3 All E. R. 566; [1963] 1 W. L. R. 1042, C. A.
3. *Kelly* v. *Lombard Banking Co., Ltd.*, [1958] 3 All E. R. 713; [1959] 1 W. L. R. 41, C. A.
4. *Re Apex Supply Co., Ltd.*, [1941] 3 All E. R. 473; [1942] Ch. 108, doubted by SOMERVELL, L.J., in *Cooden Engineering Co., Ltd.* v. *Stanford*, [1952] 2 All E. R. 915, at p. 921; [1953] 1 Q. B. 86, at p. 98.

corporate as the hirer of the goods to which the agreement relates[5]. A hire-purchase agreement is defined as

> "an agreement for the bailment of goods under which the bailee may buy the goods or under which the property in the goods will or may pass to the bailee";
>
> "where by virtue of two or more agreements, none of which by itself constitutes a hire-purchase agreement, there is a bailment of goods and either the bailee may buy the goods, or the property therein will or may pass to the bailee, the agreements shall be treated . . . as a single agreement made at the time when the last of the agreements was made"[6].

The phrase "hire-purchase price" means the total sum payable by the hirer to complete the purchase (*i.e.*, the deposit or sum credited to him as a deposit and instalments), exclusive of any sum payable as a penalty or as compensation or as damages for breach of the agreement[7]. If it is agreed in the hire-purchase agreement relating to a motor vehicle that the insurance premium should be paid by the owner and included into the hire-purchase price, the premium is then part of the hire-purchase price[8].

The Hire-Purchase Agreement

Cash price

By s. 6 of the Act, before any hire-purchase agreement is entered into, the owner must state in writing to the prospective hirer, a price at which the goods may be purchased by him for cash, *i.e.*, the cash price. If the hirer has inspected the goods or like goods and tickets or labels were attached to or displayed with the goods clearly stating the cash price, or if the hirer has selected the goods by reference to a catalogue, price list, or advertisement, which has clearly stated the cash price, then s. 6 is deemed to have been complied with.

Written agreement

An owner may not enforce a hire-purchase agreement unless the agreement is signed by the hirer himself and by or on behalf of all other parties to the agreement[9]. The agreement must contain a statement of the hire-purchase price, the cash price of the goods to which the agreement relates, the amount of each of the instalments, the date upon which each instalment is payable, and must contain a

---

5. The 1965 Act consolidated earlier Acts of 1938, 1954 and 1964.
6. Hire-Purchase Act 1965, s. 1.
7. *Ibid.*, s. 58.
8. *Mutual Finance Co., Ltd.* v. *Davidson*, [1963] 1 All E. R. 133; [1963] 1 W. L. R. 134, C. A.
9. Hire-Purchase Act 1965, s. 5.

list of the goods to which the agreement relates sufficient to identify them.   The agreement must also contain a notice in the terms prescribed in the Schedule to the Act, explaining the hirer's statutory right to terminate the agreement and the statutory restrictions on the owner's right of repossession[10].   The Department of Trade has made regulations prescribing the type size, the colour of the paper and lettering used and that a "box" in red print be used for the hirer's signature[11].

Copies

Where the hirer signs the agreement at "appropriate trade premises", *i.e.* premises at which the owner normally carries on business or goods of a similar description are normally offered or exposed for sale in the course of a business carried on at these premises, then if the agreement is signed by or on behalf of all other parties immediately after or immediately before the hirer signs, it is sufficient if a copy is there and then delivered to the hirer.   Otherwise, the hirer must be given a copy of the document he is asked to sign in the form in which it was when presented or sent to him (the "first statutory copy") *and* a copy of the agreement (the "second statutory copy") must be delivered or sent to him within seven days of the making of the agreement[12]. Where the hirer signs elsewhere than at "appropriate trade premises", *e.g.* at his home, he must always be given or sent both a copy of the document in the form he signs it (the "first statutory copy") *and* be sent by post a copy of the agreement (the "second statutory copy") within seven days of the making of the agreement.   Both copies must contain statements of the hirer's right of cancellation, considered below[13].

Effect of non-compliance

If the provisions in ss. 5 to 9 are not complied with, the owner is not entitled to enforce the hire-purchase agreement or any contract of guarantee relating thereto, nor does he have any right to recover the goods from the hirer, nor may any security given by the hirer or guarantor be enforceable against the hirer or guarantor by any holder thereof[14].   However, provided that there is an agreement signed by the hirer and by or on behalf of all other parties to the agreement, if the court is satisfied that a failure to comply with any of the other

---

10. *Ibid.,* s. 7.
11. S. I. 1965, No. 1646.
12. Hire-Purchase Act 1965, s. 8.
13. *Ibid.,* s. 9.
14. The hirer cannot be sued in conversion merely for refusing to give up possession when the owner is in breach of these provisions (Hire-Purchase Act 1965, s. 52).   If he parts with possession to a third party both he and the third party may be liable in conversion (*Eastern Distributors, Ltd.* v. *Goldring,* [1957] 2 All E. R. 525; [1957] 2 Q. B. 600, C. A.).

requirements as to the formation of the agreement has not prejudiced the hirer, the court may dispense with that requirement for the purposes of the action[15].

Hirer's right of cancellation

Where the customer signs a hire-purchase agreement (or a document which would constitute such an agreement if executed by or on behalf of the owner of the goods) at a place other than "appropriate trade premises", he may serve a notice of cancellation of the agreement on the owner or his agent at any time before the end of four days beginning with the day on which he receives the "second statutory copy" of the agreement[16]. "Appropriate trade premises" means premises at which the owner normally carries on a business, or goods of a similar description are normally offered or exposed for sale in the course of a business carried on at those premises. Any contractual provision restricting this right is void. The effect of a notice of cancellation being served is to rescind the agreement, or to constitute a revocation of any offer to enter into such agreement if the agreement has not yet been effected. Notice of cancellation shall be deemed to be served at the time when it is posted, if it is sent by post and addressed to a person specified in the first or second statutory copy of the agreement, or addressed to the owner or the owner's agent. Notice may alternatively be served on the owner or the owner's agent by other means than by post.

Consequences of cancellation.—When the hirer exercises his right of cancellation he is under no obligation to deliver any goods in his possession to which the agreement relates except at his own premises and in pursuance of a written and signed request[17]. In the meantime, he is under an obligation to take reasonable care of them[18]. Any payment made by the hirer in pursuance of the agreement is recoverable by him and he has a lien over the goods in his possession until such sum is recovered[19].

Dealer as agent of owner

Any representations (whether constituting a condition or warranty

---

15. Hire-Purchase Act 1965, s. 10. There is no dispensing power in respect of the requirements in s. 9 that the second statutory copy of an agreement signed otherwise than at appropriate trade premises be sent by post to the hirer (unless it is merely that the seven-day period has not been complied with) and that the statutory copies contain statements of the hirer's right of cancellation.
16. *Ibid.*, s. 11.
17. Hire-Purchase Act 1965, s. 13.
18. The obligation ceases if twenty-one days have elapsed since service of the notice of cancellation unless the hirer has within that time received a written and signed request for delivery and has unreasonably refused or failed to comply with it.
19. *Ibid.*, s. 14. There are provisions in s. 15 concerning the effect of the notice of cancellation where goods have been given in part-exchange.

or not) with respect to the goods to which a hire-purchase agreement relates, made to the hirer by the dealer who conducted the antecedent negotiations, are deemed to have been made by him as agent of the owner[20]. Such dealer is also deemed to be the owner's agent for the receiving of any notice of cancellation or notice of revocation of a customer's offer to enter into a hire-purchase agreement, or any notice given by a hirer, claiming to rescind the agreement, for example for misrepresentation[1]. Any contractual provision excluding or restricting these statutory provisions is void[2].

Implied terms

There is an implied condition on the part of the owner that he shall have the right to sell the goods at the time when the property is to pass, an implied warranty that the hirer shall have and enjoy quiet possession of the goods and an implied warranty that the goods shall be free from any charge or encumbrance in favour of any third party at the time when the property is to pass.[3] These implied terms are implied notwithstanding any agreement to the contrary[4].

There is also an implied condition that the goods shall be of merchantable quality, but no such condition shall be implied if the hirer has examined the goods or a sample thereof, as regards defects which the examination ought to have revealed[5]. Moreover, no such condition shall be implied if the goods are let as second-hand goods, the agreement contains a statement to that effect and a provision that this condition is excluded, and it is proved that such provision was brought to the hirer's notice and its effect made clear to him before the agreement was made[6]. Nor is the condition of merchantable quality implied if the goods are let as being subject to defects specified in the agreement, the agreement contains a provision that the condition is excluded, and it is proved that such provision was brought to the hirer's notice and its effect made clear to him before the agreement was made[7].

If the hirer, expressly or by implication, has made known the particular purpose for which the goods are required, either to the owner (or his servant or agent) or to the dealer (or his servant or agent), there in an implied condition that the goods shall be reasonably fit for that purpose[8]. Such condition may be excluded or modified by a

---

20. *Ibid.*, s. 16. This does not effect the dealer's personal liability at common law for such representations. See *ante*, p. 221.
1. Hire-Purchase Act 1965, ss. 12 (3) and 31.
2. *Ibid.*, s. 29 (3).
3. *Ibid.*, s. 17 (1).   4. *Ibid.*, s. 18 (3).
5. *Ibid.*, s. 17 (2), (3).   6. *Ibid.*, s. 18 (1).
7. *Ibid.*, s. 18 (2).   8. *Ibid.*, s. 17 (4).

provision in the agreement and it then has no application if it is proved that such provision was brought to the hirer's notice and its effect made clear to him before the agreement was made[9].

Where goods are let by reference to a sample, there is an implied condition that the bulk will correspond to the sample in quality and that the hirer will have a reasonable opportunity of comparing the bulk with the sample[10]. Where goods are let by description, there is an implied condition that the goods will correspond with the description, and if the goods are let by reference to a sample as well as by description, the bulk must not only correspond with the sample but also with the description[11]. Any contractual provision excluding or modifying these implied conditions is void[12].

Right of hirer to terminate agreement

At any time before the final payment under the agreement falls due, the hirer may determine the agreement by giving notice in writing to any person entitled or authorised to receive the sum payable under the agreement (frequently, the dealer)[13]. The hirer's liability if he gives such notice, without prejudice to any liability already accrued, is to pay the amount if any by which one-half of the hire-purchase price exceeds the total of the sums paid and the sums due in respect of the hire-purchase price immediately before termination, or such less sum as may be specified in the agreement[14]. However, if the court is satisfied that a sum less than the amount by which one-half of the hire-purchase price exceeds the total of the sums paid and the sums due in respect of the hire-purchase price immediately before termination would be equal to the loss sustained by the owner in consequence of the termination, the court may make an order for the payment of that sum[15]. If the hirer has failed to take reasonable care of the goods, he is liable to pay damages for the failure[16]. Any provision in the agreement excluding or modifying the hirer's statutory right to terminate the agreement is void[17].

Hirer's default

Where the agreement provides that it shall terminate or be terminable, or that the owner shall have the right to recover possession if the

---

9. Hire-Purchase Act 1965, s. 18 (4). *Lowe* v. *Lombank, Ltd.*, [1960] 1 All E. R. 611; [1960] 1 W. L. R. 196.
10. *Ibid.*, s. 19 (1).
11. *Ibid.*, s. 19 (2).
12. *Ibid.*, s. 29 (3) (c).
13. *Ibid.*, s. 27.
14. *Ibid.*, s. 28 (1).
15. *Ibid.*, s. 28 (2).
16. *Ibid.*, s. 28 (3).
17. Hire-Purchase Act 1965, s. 29 (2) (b).

hirer defaults in the payment of one or more instalments, such "specified consequences" will not follow on such default, unless a notice of default is served on the hirer (by post or otherwise), giving him at least seven days in which to make the payments due[18]. The "specified consequences" will only follow if the notice is not complied with.

"Protected Goods."—Part III of the Hire-Purchase Act 1965 contains provisions restricting the owner's right to recover possession of goods when one-third of the hire-purchase price has been paid. By s. 33 the phrase "protected goods" is used to describe goods where for the time being the following conditions are fulfilled:

(a)   that the goods have been let under a hire-purchase agreement;
(b)   that one-third of the hire-purchase price has been paid (whether in pursuance of a judgment or otherwise) or tendered by or on behalf of the hirer or a guarantor; and
(c)   that the hirer has not terminated the hire-purchase agreement or the bailment by virtue of any right vested in him.

The owner may not enforce any right to recover possession of "protected goods" from the hirer otherwise than by court action.

Should the owner contravene this provision, the agreement determines, and the hirer and any guarantor are entitled to recover from the owner any sums paid under the agreement or contract of guarantee or under any security given in respect thereof[19].

The action has to be commenced in the county court of the district where the hirer resides or carries on business or resided or carried on business at the date on which he last made a payment[20]. On the hearing of the action the court may:

(1)   make an order for the specific delivery of all the goods to the owner; or
(2)   make an order for the specific delivery of all the goods to the owner but postpone the operation of the order on condition that the hirer or any guarantor pays the unpaid balance

---

18. *Ibid.*, s. 25. The Court of Appeal held in *Eshun* v. *Moorgate Mercantile Co., Ltd.* that a notice was invalid if it failed to refer to the provision of the agreement under which the notice was given, did not specify the consequences of non-payment of arrears due, and failed to give the date of service of the notice: [1971] 2 All E. R. 402; [1971] 1 W. L. R. 722.
19. *Ibid.*, s. 34 (2). In *Mercantile Credit Co.* v. *Cross*, [1964] 1 All E. R. 603; [1965] 2 Q. B. 205, the Court of Appeal held that the owner does not contravene s. 34 if he serves the hirer with a termination notice telling the hirer to surrender possession of the goods and the hirer acquiesces by doing as he is asked. Nor is s. 34 contravened if the owner retakes possession after the hirer has abandoned the goods: *Bentinck* v. *Cromwell Engineering Co.*, [1971] 1 All E. R. 33; [1971] 1 Q. B. 324, C. A.
20. *Ibid.*, s. 49 (1).

of the hire-purchase price at such times and in such amounts as the court thinks just; or

(3) make an order for the specific delivery of a part of the goods to the owner and for the transfer to the hirer of the owner's title to the remainder of the goods[1].

If the second type of order is made, *i.e.* a "postponed order", the court may revoke the postponement or vary the conditions of the postponement at any time[2].

If at any time the court has made an order for specific delivery of goods to the owner (including a "postponed order") which has not been complied with and the owner has not recovered possession of all such goods, the owner may apply to the same court to revoke the order and instead to make an order for the payment of a sum equal to the balance of the outstanding payments subject to a discount for accelerated receipt[3]. Even if the owner has recovered possession, he may apply to the court for an order requiring the hirer to pay any instalments accrued due before the action for repossession was brought and for any sum payable under a valid minimum payment clause[4].

Requirements as to information

At any time before the final payment has been made under a hire-purchase agreement, the hirer is entitled, by making a request in writing and on the payment of twelve and one half pence, to have the owner supply him with a copy of the agreement together with a statement containing certain particulars relating to the amounts paid, due, and to become payable under the agreement[5]. Failure by the owner to comply with this provision, without reasonable cause, and so long as the default continues, means that the agreement cannot be enforced against the hirer, nor can any contract of guarantee be enforced, nor can the owner enforce any right to recover the goods. No security given by the hirer or by any guarantor is enforceable.

If the agreement requires the hirer to keep the goods comprised in the agreement under his possession or control, the hirer must, on receipt of a request in writing from the owner, inform him where the goods are[6].

Void provisions

Any contractual provision whereby the owner or any person acting

---

1. Hire-Purchase Act 1965, s. 35 (4).
2. *Ibid.*, s. 39.
3. *Ibid.*, s. 42.
4. *Ibid.*, s. 44. Such a clause is void if it subjects the hirer to a liability greater than that specified in s. 28. See *ante*, p. 229.
5. *Ibid.*, s. 21.
6. Hire-Purchase Act 1965, s. 24.

on his behalf may enter premises for the purpose of taking possession of goods let under a hire-purchase agreement or that relieves the owner from any liability for such entry is void[7]. Also void is any provision whereby anyone acting on the owner's behalf in connection with the formation or conclusion of a hire-purchase agreement is deemed to be the agent of the hirer or whereby an owner is relieved from liability for the acts or defaults of anyone acting on his behalf in connection with the formation or conclusion of a hire-purchase agreement[8].

Appropriation of payments

Where a hirer has two or more hire-purchase agreements with the same owner and owes money at a given date on two or more of them, he may specify, when making a payment insufficient to satisfy his total debt, which debt he is paying. If he does not so specify the payment must be appropriated by the owner in the proportion which the sums due at the time under each agreement bear to one another[9].

Death of hirer

If a hire-purchase agreement provides that on the death of the hirer the agreement shall terminate or be terminable, or the owner shall have the right to recover possession, or any sum shall be payable or any right of the hirer shall cease to be exercisable or shall be restricted or postponed, it shall to that extent be void[10]. Detailed statutory provisions restrict the recovery of possession of goods after the hirer's death if one-third of the hire-purchase price has been paid or tendered before or after his death[11].

Guarantees and indemnities

A contract of guarantee relating to a hire-purchase agreement and any security given by such guarantor is not enforceable unless, within seven days of the making of the contract of guarantee or of the hire-purchase agreement, whichever is the later, there is delivered or sent to the guarantor a copy of the hire-purchase agreement and a copy of a note or memorandum of the contract of guarantee[12]. If a court is satisfied that failure to comply with this requirement has not prejudiced the guarantor and that it would be just and equitable to do so, the court may dispense with the requirement. A guarantor is given similar rights to require information to be provided as has the hirer

---

7. *Ibid.*, s. 29 (2) (a).
8. *Ibid.*, s. 29 (2) (d) and (e).
9. *Ibid.*, s. 51.
10. *Ibid.*, s. 30.
11. *Ibid.*, Schedule 3.
12. Hire-Purchase Act 1965, s. 22.

(see *ante*, p. 231). For the purposes of these provisions and of other provisions in the Hire-Purchase Act, any contract made at the request (express or implied) of the hirer to *indemnify* the owner against any loss that he may incur under the hire-purchase agreement, is to be treated in the same way as a contract of guarantee[13].

Conditional sale agreements

By s. 1 (1) of the Hire-Purchase Act 1965, a conditional sale agreement is defined as "an agreement for the sale of goods under which the purchase price or part of it is payable by instalments, and the property in the goods is to remain in the seller (notwithstanding that the buyer is to be in possession of the goods) until such conditions as to the payment of instalments or otherwise as may be specified in the agreement are fulfilled". The provisions of the Hire-Purchase Act are to apply to conditional sale agreements as they do to hire-purchase agreements, provided that the total price does not exceed £2,000 and the agreement is not made by or on behalf of a body corporate as the buyer of the goods to which the agreement relates. The significance of this provision, *inter alia*, is that the buyer of goods under a conditional sale agreement has the benefit of the same statutory implied terms and the same right to terminate the agreement before the final payment is made as the hirer under a hire-purchase agreement. Of course, the provisions of the Acts must, in relation to conditional sale agreements be read subject to modifications of wording, so that, for example, any reference to "hirer" means "buyer" and any reference to "hire-purchase price" means "total purchase price". Sections 12 to 15 of the Sale of Goods Act, which imply certain conditions and warranties in contracts of sale, do not apply to such conditional sale agreements.

The buyer under a conditional sale agreement where the total price is not more than £2,000 and the agreement is not made by or on behalf of a body corporate as the buyer is not deemed to be a person who has "agreed to buy" the goods for the purposes of s. 25 (2) of the Sale of Goods Act[14]. Generally speaking, therefore, if a buyer under such an agreement disposes of the goods to a third party before the property in them has passed to him, he cannot pass a good title to the third party.

Credit-sale Agreements

For the purposes of the Hire-Purchase Act, a credit-sale agreement means "an agreement for the sale of goods under which the purchase

---

13. *Ibid.*, s. 58 (1).
14. Hire-Purchase Act 1965, s. 54. See *ante*, p. 191.

price is payable by five or more instalments not being a conditional sale agreement"[15].

Certain provisions of the Hire-Purchase Act apply to credit-sale agreements, as so defined, provided that the total purchase price does not exceed £2,000 and the agreement is not made by or on behalf of a body corporate as the buyer of the goods to which the agreement relates.

Thus, if the total purchase price exceeds £30, the price at which the goods may be bought for spot cash must be stated in writing before the agreement is signed, and there must be an agreement signed by the buyer and by or on behalf of all other parties to the agreement, with similar requirements as to contents and with regard to the delivery of the first and second statutory copies as is required in the case of hire-purchase agreements, save that "total purchase price" takes the place of "hire-purchase price", "seller" the place of "owner" and "buyer" the place of "hirer". A buyer of goods under a credit-sale agreement in which the total price exceeds £30 has the same right of cancellation as a hirer under a hire-purchase agreement where the agreement (or a document which would constitute such an agreement if executed by or on behalf of the seller of the goods) is signed by the prospective buyer at a place other than appropriate trade premises. Also, where the total price exceeds £30, a guarantor or indemnifier must be sent copies of the credit-sale agreement and a note or memorandum of the contract of guarantee or indemnity within 7 days of the making of the contract of guarantee or indemnity or of the credit-sale agreement (whichever is the later)[16].

Sections 16 and 31 of the Hire-Purchase Act 1965, by which the dealer may be deemed the agent of the owner or seller, apply to credit-sale agreements as they do to hire-purchase agreements. The provisions requiring information to be given on request by the owner or seller to the hirer or buyer or guarantor apply also to credit sales.

VI THE ADVERTISEMENTS (HIRE-PURCHASE) ACT 1967

The Advertisements (Hire-Purchase) Act 1967 (consolidating earlier legislation) requires certain information to be included in any advertisement of goods available for disposal on hire-purchase or credit-sale, if the advertisement contains an indication that a deposit

---

15. *Ibid.*, s. 1 (1). Since a person who has bought goods under a credit-sale agreement is already the owner of them, clearly he is able to pass a good title to them even if he sells them before he has paid all the instalments due on them.

16. Hire-Purchase Act 1965, s. 22.

is payable, or that no deposit is payable, or of the amount of one or more of the instalments. The information required consists of:

(*a*) the total number of instalments payable;

(*b*) the length of the period in respect of which each instalment is payable; and

(*c*) if any instalments are payable before delivery of the goods, the number of instalments so payable.

The Act applies irrespective of whether the hire-purchase price or total purchase price exceeds £2,000 and "credit sale" is so defined as to *include* conditional sales.

Where the amount of the deposit or of any instalment is given in the advertisement or a sum is stated as the hire-purchase price or total purchase price, the advertisement must also state the cash price of the goods, the amount of each instalment, either a statement that there is no deposit or a statement of the amount of the deposit expressed as a sum of money or as a fraction or percentage of a stated sum, and the hire-purchase price or total purchase price of the goods.

If the advertisement contains a fraction represented as the rate of interest to be borne by the hirer or buyer the advertisement must contain not only the details already referred to but also the instalments must be expressed as instalments of equal amounts, the fraction must be expressed as a specified amount per cent. per annum and the amount so specified must be not less than the amount calculated in accordance with a prescribed formula[17].

---

17. The formula is set out in the Advertisements (Hire-Purchase) Act 1967, Sched. 1, Part III.

CHAPTER 15

Bills of Exchange and other Negotiable Instruments

I INTRODUCTION

A negotiable instrument was defined by the late Judge WILLIS, as

"one the property in which is acquired by any one who takes it *bona fide*, and for value, notwithstanding any defect of title in the person from whom he took it; from which it follows that an instrument cannot be negotiable unless it is such and in such a state that the true owner could transfer the contract or engagement contained therein by simple delivery of the instrument"[1].

This definition involves the following characteristics of a negotiable instrument:

1. Property in it passes from hand to hand by mere delivery;
2. The holder in due course, *i.e.* someone who acquires it *bona fide* and for value, is not prejudiced by defects of title of his transferor or of previous holders;
3. He can sue in his own name;
4. He is not affected by certain defences which might be available against previous holders, *e.g.* fraud to which he is no party[2].

This may be illustrated by examples:

A owes B £500; he gives a written recognition of the debt—say the shortened form of acknowledgment known as an I. O. U. The debt evidenced by this I. O. U. can be *assigned* by B to C and such assignment will be effective under s. 136 of the Law of Property Act 1925 or in equity if certain conditions are satisfied[3] but any defence good against B, *e.g.* no consideration, will be good against C. However, if A gives B a bill of exchange payable to bearer for £500, then B can *negotiate* the bill to C simply by delivery of the bill and if C is a holder in due course, he is not liable to be defeated by any defence personal to B, *e.g.* fraud by B in obtaining the bill from A.

The character of negotiability does not attach itself to every

---

1. Willis on Negotiable Securities (5th ed.), pp. 5, 6.
2. See *per* BOWEN, L.J., in *Simmons* v. *London Joint Stock Bank*, [1891] Ch., at p. 294.
3. See *ante*, p. 70.

1882 Act was mainly declaratory and made but few alterations in the law[17].

How a bill is used

The simplest way to understand a bill of exchange is to consider the position where A owes money to B, *e.g.* for goods sold to him, and requests C to pay his debt for him, C being, perhaps, an agent or financier whom A has put, or has agreed to put, in funds. A then draws a bill requiring C to pay the money to B or to B's order. A is the "drawer", B is the "payee" and C is the "drawee". C is not automatically bound to pay B: he may "accept" the bill by signing his name across the face of it (in which case he is referred to as the "acceptor") or he may refuse to accept it or he may give a "qualified acceptance". It may be necessary for B to "present" the bill to C in order to see whether C will accept it, *e.g.* if the money is not payable until C has had notice of the bill, in other words if it is payable so many days "after sight". Meanwhile B may have transferred his rights under the bill, *i.e.* negotiated the bill, and it may have passed through several hands. In order to back the bill with their credit other persons may have "indorsed" it. The right of the holder of the bill to sue on it may be affected by the question whether he or a predecessor has given value for it and whether he was aware of any defects in the title to the bill of the person from whom he received it.

In due course the bill will normally be "presented for payment" to the acceptor. If he fails to meet it, or has refused to accept it, the bill is said to be "dishonoured". It may be necessary or advisable to obtain formal evidence of dishonour and in this case the bill is "protested". The holder will then have rights against the other parties who have signed the bill. In certain cases he may be able to sue the drawer and indorsers without first presenting the bill for payment to the acceptor, for presentment is excused in some circumstances where it would serve no useful purpose or is not practicable.

A bill may be used in various ways. Thus, in order to make the buyer primarily liable on the bill, the seller might draw the bill payable to his own order. The buyer would then accept it and a third party might indorse it as guarantor.

Definition of a bill

Section 3 (1) of the Bills of Exchange Act 1882 gives the following definition of a bill of exchange:

---

17. Lord BLACKBURN, in *McLean* v. *Clydesdale Banking Co.* (1884), 9 App. Cas. 105, 106; Lord HERSCHELL, in *Bank of England* v. *Vagliano Brothers*, [1891] A. C., at p. 145.

"A bill of exchange is an unconditional order in writing, addressed by one person to another, signed by the person giving it, requiring the person to whom it is addressed to pay on demand, or at a fixed or determinable future time, a sum certain in money to or to the order of a specified person, or to bearer."

From this it will be seen that what is required is:

1. A written instrument to which there are three parties.
2. The instrument must be an order to pay money, and
3. The order to pay must be unconditional[18].

Thus, it may not order any act to be done, in addition to the payment of money[19]; nor must it order payment out of a particular fund, for this would not be unconditional[20]; but it may specify a fund out of which the payer may reimburse himself, or may specify a particular account to be debited with the amount[20]. The definition of a bill of exchange includes cheques[1], and in *Bavins* v. *London and South Western Bank*[2],

> a document in the form of an ordinary cheque ordering a banker to pay a sum of money *"provided the receipt form at foot hereof is duly signed, stamped and dated,"* was held not to be unconditional, and therefore not a cheque within the meaning of the Act.

Some usual forms of bills are as follows:

(I)

£100.   *London, January 1st, 1973.*

Two months after date pay C. D., or order, the sum of one hundred pounds sterling for value received.

To Mr. E. F.   A. B.
London.

(II)

£50.   *Bristol, March 5th, 1973.*

On demand pay C. D. the sum of fifty pounds sterling for value received.

To E. F.   R. S.
York.

Accepted, E. F.

---

18. As to conditional acceptances and indorsements, see *post*, p. 248–249.
19. Bills of Exchange Act 1882, s. 3 (2).
20. *Ibid.*, s. 3 (3).
1. *Post*, p. 271.
2. [1900] 1 Q. B. 270; 5 Com. Cas. 1. *cf. Nathan* v. *Ogdens, Ltd.* (1905), 94 L. T. 126, where the document contained the words: "the receipt at the back must be signed." It was held that these words were addressed to the payee, not the drawee, the order on the drawee was therefore unconditional, and the document a valid bill of exchange.

£70.

Accepted payable at the Westminster Bank Ltd., Lothbury only.

(III)

Newcastle, March 1st, 1973.

... to ...X. Y. sixty days after sight seventy pounds sterling.

To A. B. C.

F. G.

£100.

Accepted payable Coutt's Bank.

ARTHUR JAMES.

(IV)

Newcastle, October 3rd, 1973.

Pay James Brown or bearer on November 1st, 1973, the sum of one hundred pounds for value received.

To Mr. ARTHUR JAMES.

F. ROBERTS.

£150.

Accepted payable Child's Bank.

HENRY BROWN.

(V)

London, June 1st, 1973.

Ten days after date pay to my order the sum of one hundred and fifty pounds for value received.

To HENRY BROWN.

JOHN SMITH.

The three parties are styled respectively in the case of Form I, the drawer A B, the payee C D, and the drawee (who, if he accepts, becomes acceptor) E F, but the bill is good if it is drawn payable to the drawer (see Form V above) or to the drawee[3]. If the drawer and drawee are the same person as in a banker's draft, the holder may at his option treat the instrument as a promissory note, thereby excusing himself from the duties of a holder of a bill of exchange[4].

Drawee.—The drawee must be named or indicated with reasonable certainty, and if the bill is not payable to bearer, the same will apply to the payee[5]. There may be several joint drawees, but alternative or successive drawees are not allowed[6]; a drawee or referee, in case of need, may be named who, after dishonour and protest for non-acceptance, may accept or pay the bill with the holder's assent[7].

Payee.—The payee is the bearer if the bill is expressed to be payable

---

3. Bills of Exchange Act 1882, s. 5 (1).
4. *Ibid.*, s. 5 (2). So also if the drawee is a fictitious person or without legal capacity.
5. *Ibid.*, ss. 6 (1) and 7 (1). It is permitted to add the drawer's name after the acceptor's death (*Carter* v. *White* (1884), 25 Ch. D. 666).
6. *Ibid.*, s. 6 (2).
7. *Ibid.*, ss. 15, 67.

to bearer, or if the only or last indorsement is an indorsement in blank; it is payable to order if it is so expressed, or if it is expressed to be payable to a particular person, and does not contain words prohibiting transfer[8]. An instrument payable to "cash" is not a bill of exchange as it is not payable either to a specified person or to bearer[9]. By s. 7 (3), "where the payee is a fictitious or non-existing person, the bill may be treated as payable to bearer". As is shown more fully later, when the holder of a bill payable to a specified person (an order bill) claims payment on it, his claim will normally fail if one of the indorsements on which his title rests is forged or unauthorised[10]. However, any indorsements on a bearer bill are superfluous since a bearer bill is negotiable simply by delivery. In *Clutton* v. *Attenborough & Son*[11],

> A clerk employed by the appellants falsely represented to them that work had been done on their account by one George Brett and persuaded them to draw cheques in Brett's favour. No one of that name was known to the appellants or had in fact done any work for them. The clerk indorsed the cheques in the name of "George Brett" and negotiated them to the respondents who gave value for them in good faith. The House of Lords *held* that as the payee on the cheques was fictitious they could be treated as payable to bearer and the respondents' title did not depend on any forged indorsement as bearer cheques are negotiable without indorsement. The respondents had a good title to the cheques.

Contrast *Vinden* v. *Hughes*[12]. In that case,

> the plaintiff's clerk filled up cheques payable to the order of certain customers with the names of the customers and sums of money which were not in fact owing to them. The clerk obtained the plaintiff's signature as drawer, forged the indorsements and negotiated the cheques to the defendant, who took them in good faith and for value. It was *held* that the payees were not "fictitious", because the drawer believed when signing the cheques that he owed the sums mentioned to the persons whose names appeared on the cheques. In consequence, the drawer was able to recover the amount of the cheques which his bankers had paid to the defendant.

---

8. *Ibid.*, s. 8 (3), (4). The effect of this is dealt with, *post*, p. 249.
9. *Cole* v. *Milsome*, [1951] 1 All E. R. 311; *Orbit Mining and Trading Co.* v. *Westminster Bank, Ltd.*, [1962] 3 All E. R. 565; [1963] 1 Q. B. 794.
10. See *post*, p. 251.
11. [1897] A. C. 90.
12. [1905] 1 K. B. 795.

In an earlier case, *Bank of England* v. *Vagliano Brothers*[13],

> the House of Lords *held* that the payee is "fictitious" within the meaning of s. 7 (3) even though the name is that of an existing person if the name of the payee has been inserted by whoever in fact signed the bill as drawer, by way of pretence, without any intention that the person named as payee should ever receive payment.

Date.—The date should be inserted, but if a bill is issued undated, the omission is not fatal[14], and the holder may insert the true date; if by *bona fide* mistake he inserts the wrong date, and in every case where a wrong date is inserted and the bill comes into the hands of a holder in due course, the bill is payable as if the date inserted had been the true date[15]. An instrument to which the Act applies may be ante-dated, post-dated, or dated on a Sunday[16].

Amount payable.—The sum payable by a bill is "certain"[16], although required to be paid:

1. With interest, or
2. By stated instalments, or
3. By stated instalments with a provision that, on default in payment of any instalments, the whole shall become due, or
4. According to an indicated rate of exchange to be ascertained as directed by the bill[17].

If the words and figures differ, the amount payable is that expressed in words[18].

The words "value received" are usually inserted, but there is no necessity for this, as value is presumed until contradicted[19]. The place where the bill is drawn or payable need not be stated[20].

The bill may be written on paper, or on parchment, or on anything except on a metallic substance, and it may be written in pencil, or in ink, or may be partially or wholly printed. Stamp duty on bills of exchange and promissory notes has been abolished[1].

---

13. [1891] A. C. 107.
14. Bills of Exchange Act 1882, s. 3 (4) (a).
15. *Ibid.*, s. 12. "Holder in due course" is defined, *post*, p. 252.
16. *Ibid.*, s. 13.
17. See definition of a bill of exchange, *ante*, p. 240.
18. Bills of Exchange Act 1882, s. 9.
19. *Ibid.*, s. 3 (4) (b).
20. *Ibid.*, s. 4.
1. Finance Act 1970, s. 32.

III. PARTIES

The Act declares that capacity to incur liability on a bill is co-extensive with capacity to contract[2], as to which see *ante*, Chapter 5. But the following rules are peculiar to the present subject:

1. No person who has not signed as such can be liable as drawer, indorser, or acceptor, except that a trade signature, or signature under an assumed name, is the equivalent of signature in the signer's own name[3].

The signature of the name of a firm is equivalent to the signature by a person so signing of the names of all persons liable as partners of that firm[4].

2. A limited company incorporated for the purposes of trade or otherwise having capacity, may be a party to a bill, and will be bound if the bill is made, accepted, or indorsed in the name of, or by or on behalf or on account of the company by any person acting under its authority[5]. If the signature is by procuration, *e.g.* "per pro", it operates as a notice that the agent has but limited authority to sign, and the principal is only bound if the agent was acting within the actual limits of his authority[6]. But where by the constitution of the company the person signing a bill on its behalf might have been so authorised, any one taking the bill as a holder in due course is entitled to assume that such person had authority in fact unless he is put upon inquiry by some unusual circumstance[7]. The name of the company must appear in legible letters, and the word "limited" or "Ltd." after it; otherwise the officer who causes the signature to be attached is liable to a penalty and, unless the bill is duly paid by the company, he is also personally liable on the bill[8].

3. Where a person signs a bill but adds words tending to show that he signs *qua* agent merely he incurs no personal liability[9]. But

---

2. Bills of Exchange Act 1882, s. 22 (1). A minor cannot bind himself by accepting a bill whether it is in respect of necessaries or not (*Re Soltykoff* [1891] 1 Q. B. 413).
3. Bills of Exchange Act 1882, s. 23.
4. *Ibid.*, s. 23.
5. Companies Act 1948, s. 33.
6. Bills of Exchange Act 1882, s. 25.
7. *Dey* v. *Pullinger Engineering Co.*, [1921] 1 K. B. 77.
8. Companies Act 1948, s. 108. However, where the holders of a bill had prepared it with the name of the company as drawee incorrectly stated, they were estopped from enforcing the personal liability under this section of the director of the company who had signed the bill on behalf of the company without ensuring that the company's name was correctly written out: *Durham Fancy Goods, Ltd.* v. *Michael Jackson (Fancy Goods), Ltd.*, [1968] 2 All E. R. 987.
9. Bills of Exchange Act 1882, s. 26 (1).

it does not follow because a man signs his name with words describing himself as agent, manager, etc., that he will be relieved from liability; the point to be determined is whether the words used suffice to give notice that the signature was affixed in the capacity of agent, or whether they are words of description. Thus,

> X accepts bills as "X, manager"; he is liable[10]. But if he accepts "For the A Co. Ltd., X, manager," he is not liable[11].

Where it is not clear whether the signature is that of the principal or of the agent by whose hand it is written, the construction most favourable to the validity of the instrument must be adopted[12]. Thus

> a bill was addressed to the F Co., Ltd. It was accepted "A.B.; C.D.; directors, F Co., Ltd.", and also indorsed "F Co. Ltd., A.B.; C.D.; directors." The bill was held to be validly *accepted* by the company, but *indorsed* by the directors personally on the ground that if the company was to be treated as indorsing a bill on which they were already liable as acceptors nothing would be added to its value, and consequently it was most favourable to the validity of the bill to construe the indorsement as the personal indorsement of the directors[13].

4. As to bills signed by one partner or more on behalf of the firm, see under "PARTNERSHIP"[14].

5. Where a bill is drawn or indorsed by a minor, or by a corporation having no capacity to incur liability on the bill, the holder may nevertheless enforce it against any other parties having power to contract[15]; *i.e.* the title to the bill is passed by the minor's signature, but is passed *sans recours* to him.

IV ACCEPTANCE

The liability of the drawee does not arise until he has accepted the bill, and this is done by writing his name across the face of it; sometimes the word "accepted" is added, though this is not necessary. The Act defines acceptance as

> "the signification by the drawee of his assent to the order of the drawer"[16];

and it enacts that

> 1. The signature of the drawee must be written on the bill;

---

10. *Liverpool Bank* v. *Walker* (1859), 4 De G. & J. 24.
11. *Alexander* v. *Sizer* (1869), L. R. 4 Ex. 102.
12. Bills of Exchange Act 1882, s. 26 (2).
13. *Elliott* v. *Bax-Ironside*, [1925] 2 K. B. 301.
14. *Ante*, p. 162.
15. Bills of Exchange Act 1882, s. 22 (2).
16. *Ibid.*, s. 17 (1).

2. The acceptance must not stipulate for performance by any other means than the payment of money[17].

The bill may be accepted though it has not yet been signed by the drawer or is otherwise incomplete, or though already dishonoured, or though overdue[18]; but no signature will be binding and irrevocable against any person until after unconditional delivery of the instrument, in order to give effect thereto. An acceptance becomes irrevocable if the drawee gives notice to or according to the directions of the person entitled to the bill that he has accepted it[19].

Only the person to whom the bill is addressed can accept it, unless he accepts *suprà protest* for the honour of a party liable on the bill[20].

Delivery between immediate parties and any remote party who is not a holder in due course may be shown to have been conditional only; but a valid delivery of the bill by all parties prior to him is conclusively presumed in favour of a holder in due course[1]. A valid delivery is also presumed to have taken place where the bill is no longer in the possession of a party who has signed it as drawer, acceptor, or indorser, but this presumption may be rebutted[2].

Presentment for Acceptance

It is always advisable to present the bill for acceptance, for if it is refused, the parties, other than the drawee, become immediately liable, though the bill has not yet matured[3]; and it is sometimes necessary, *e.g.* where a bill is payable after sight, presentment is necessary to fix the maturity of the instrument; and when it is payable at a place other than the place of residence or business of the drawee, or when it is expressly stipulated that presentment shall be made, it must be presented for acceptance before it can be presented for for payment[4].

The holder must present a bill payable after sight for acceptance, or negotiate it, within a reasonable time; what is a reasonable time depending upon usage and the facts of the particular case[5]. Thus, in *Fry* v. *Hill,*

on Friday a person received at Windsor a bill on London, and the bill being payable after sight it had to be presented for

---

17. Bills of Exchange Act 1882, s. 17 (2).
18. *Ibid.*, s. 18.
19. *Ibid.*, s. 21 (1).
20. *Jackson* v. *Hudson* (1810), 2 Camp. 447; *post*, p. 247.
1. Bills of Exchange Act 1882, s. 21 (2).
2. *Ibid.*, s. 21 (3).
3. *Ibid.*, s. 43 (2).
4. *Ibid.*, s. 39: unless the holder has not time to present for acceptance before presenting for payment (*ibid.*, s. 39 (4)).
5. Bills of Exchange Act 1882, s. 40 (3).

acceptance; the holder presented it on Tuesday, and the jury, considering the fact that there was no post on Saturday, thought the time reasonable[6].

The effect of failing to comply with this requirement as to a bill payable after sight is to discharge the drawer and all prior indorsers[7].

The following rules as to presentment for acceptance are given in s. 41 of the Act:

"(a) The presentment must be made by or on behalf of the holder to the drawee or to some person authorised to accept or refuse acceptance on his behalf at a reasonable hour on a business day and before the bill is overdue:

"(b) Where a bill is addressed to two or more drawees, who are not partners, presentment must be made to them all, unless one has authority to accept for all, then presentment may be made to him only:

"(c) Where the drawee is dead, presentment may be made to his personal representative:

"(d) Where the drawee is bankrupt, presentment may be made to him or to his trustee:

"(e) Where authorised by agreement or usage, a presentment through the post office is sufficient."

Presentment, though otherwise necessary, is excused in the following cases, and the holder may treat the bill as though acceptance had been refused, *i.e.* may (in fact, must if he desires to hold his remedies against the drawer and the indorsers)[8] treat the bill as dishonoured for non-acceptance:

"(a) Where the drawee is dead or bankrupt, or is a fictitious person or a person not having capacity to contract by bill:

"(b) Where, after the exercise of reasonable diligence, such presentment cannot be effected:

"(c) Where, although the presentment has been irregular, acceptance has been refused on some other ground"[9].

"The fact that the holder has reason to believe that the bill, on presentment, will be dishonoured does not excuse presentment"[10].

Acceptance for honour suprà protest

If the drawee does not accept upon presentment, it is the duty of the holder at once to treat the bill as dishonoured[11], and he may,

---

6. (1817), 7 Taunt. 398; and see *Shute* v. *Robins* (1828), 1 Moo. & M. 133; 3 C. & P. 80.
7. Bills of Exchange Act 1882, s. 40 (2).
8. See *ibid.*, s. 43 (1) (b).
9. Bills of Exchange Act 1882, s. 41 (2).
10. *Ibid.*, s. 41 (3).
11. *Ibid.*, s. 48.

if he thinks fit, note and protest[12] the bill for non-acceptance. In that case, if the bill is not overdue, and if the holder consents, any person not being a party already liable on the bill may accept it for the whole or part of the sum drawn[13], and such person is styled an *acceptor for honour suprà protest*. He must sign the bill, and indicate thereon that his acceptance is for honour, and it is presumed to be an acceptance for the honour of the drawer, unless it states some other party for whose honour it has been made. Usually the acceptance for honour is attested by a notarial "act of honour" recording the process, but this may not be necessary.

The holder of a bill dishonoured by non-acceptance, who has an offer of an acceptance for honour should first cause the bill to be protested, and then to be accepted *suprà protest*. At maturity he should again present it to the drawee for payment, in case in the meantime he has been put in funds by the drawer for that purpose. If payment is refused the bill should be protested a second time for non-payment, and then presented for payment to the acceptor for honour[14].

Qualified acceptances

The following are qualified acceptances:

1. Conditional, *i.e.* which make the bill payable on a condition therein stated;
2. Partial, *i.e.* which limit the agreement to pay to a named portion of the amount for which the bill is drawn;
3. Qualified as to time;
4. Acceptance by some, but not all, of the drawees;
5. Local qualification, *e.g.* "accepted payable at the Westminster Bank, Ltd., Lothbury only" (as in Form III, *ante*, p. 241). But an acceptance to pay at a particular place is unqualified, and payment may be demanded anywhere, unless it states that the payment is to be made at a particular place only, and not elsewhere[15]. An acceptance will not be treated as qualified unless the words used clearly make it so[16].

The holder is not bound to take a qualified acceptance, and if the drawee refuses any other, the bill may be treated as dishonoured by

---

12. See *post*, p. 263 and see *ibid.*, ss. 51, 93.
13. *Ibid.*, s. 65. This may be done if the acceptor is insolvent or bankrupt, and the bill is protested for better security (*ibid.*, s. 51 (5)).
14. Bills of Exchange Act 1882, s. 67; *Williams* v. *Germaine* (1828), 7 B. & B. 477.
15. Bills of Exchange Act 1882, s. 19.
16. *Decroix* v. *Meyer*, *per* BOWEN, L.J. (1890), 25 Q. B. D., at p. 349; affirmed, [1891] A. C. 520.

non-acceptance[17]; and except in the case of a partial acceptance of which due notice has been given, if the holder without the express or implied authority or subsequent assent of the drawer or any indorser, takes a qualified acceptance, he will release those who have not authorised it or assented to it[18].

V NEGOTIATION AND INDORSEMENT

Negotiation

A bill may contain words prohibiting transfer or indicating an intention that it should not be transferable, and if it contains such words, although valid between the parties, it is not negotiable; but the intention to prohibit negotiation must be clearly expressed[19]. The words "not negotiable" written across an ordinary bill prohibit transfer, although in the case of cheques which are crossed "not negotiable", the words have a special and restricted meaning which does not prohibit transfer altogether[20].

The characteristics of negotiability have already been pointed out, and it now remains only to show in what manner the instrument is put in circulation. The Act says that a bill is negotiated when it is so transferred as to make the transferee the holder of the bill[1]. In the case of bills payable to bearer, this is done by mere delivery[2]. In the case of those payable to order, indorsement, in addition to delivery, is required[3]; and transfer, though for value, without indorsement gives only such rights as the transferor had in the bill, with a right to require indorsement[4]. Thus,

> if A has a bill payable to bearer, and he gives it in due course to B, B holds it with all A's rights of suit on it, and without A's defects of title; if it be payable to order, B may require A to indorse it, but until this is done he holds it subject to any defence which could be raised against A; such indorsement operates as a negotiation, but will not cure any defect of the transferor's title of which the indorsee had notice before the indorsement was obtained[5].

---

17. Bills of Exchange Act 1882, s. 44 (1).
18. *Ibid.*, s. 44 (2), (3).
19. *Ibid.*, s. 8 (1); *National Bank* v. *Silke*, [1891] 1 Q. B. 435.
20. *Hibernian Bank, Ltd.* v. *Gysin and Hanson*, [1939] 1 All E. R. 166; [1939] 1 K. B. 483. The bill in this case was made payable to the order of a particular person only. As to cheques, see *post*, p. 273.
1. Bills of Exchange Act 1882, s. 31 (1).
2. *Ibid.*, s. 31 (2).
3. *Ibid.*, s. 31 (3).
4. *Ibid.*, s. 31 (4).
5. *Whistler* v. *Forster* (1863), 14 C. B. N. S., at pp. 257, 258.

Indorsements

An indorsement must be written on the bill, and signed by the indorser (in general, the signature alone is placed on the back, or, if there be not sufficient room on the bill, then on an annexed paper styled an "allonge", and this is sufficient)[6]; if his name is misspelt, he may sign according to the misspelling, and then add his correct name[7]. Indeed, the indorsement should always correspond with the drawing. Thus, a cheque payable to A B per X, must be indorsed "A B per X"; and not simply "X". X must show that he indorses as agent for A B[8].

A partial indorsement, *i.e.*, a purported transfer of part only of the amount, is useless as a negotiation[9]; so would be the signature of one of several parties (not being partners) to whose joint order the bill is payable, unless such party is authorised by the others to act in this matter for them[10].

An indorsement may be made in blank or special:

1. *In blank,* when the signature of the indorser is written without any direction as to whom or to whose order the bill is to be payable; the bill is then payable to bearer.
2. *Special,* when the indorsement specifies the indorsee[11].

Thus:

if A indorses a bill "Pay to B & Co. or order," this operates as a special indorsement, and if B & Co. desire to negotiate the bill they must themselves indorse it; this they may do either in blank or specially.

It is always at the option of a holder to convert a blank into a special indorsement: he does so by writing above the indorser's signature a direction to pay the bill to, or to the order of himself or of some other person[12].

Indorsements are sometimes:

Conditional, e.g. "Pay D on his obtaining a degree"[13]. A particular form of conditional indorsement is the *restrictive indorsement.*

A *restrictive indorsement* may be a mere authority to deal with the bill as directed, or it may be an indorsement prohibiting further negotiation; *e.g.*

---

6. Bills of Exchange Act 1882, s. 32 (1).
7. *Ibid.,* s. 32 (4).
8. *Slingsby* v. *District Bank, Ltd.,* [1931] 2 K. B. 588; affirmed, [1931] All E. R. Rep. 143; [1932] 1 K. B. 544.
9. Bills of Exchange Act 1882, s. 32 (2).
10. *Ibid.,* s. 32 (3).
11. *Ibid.,* s. 34.
12. *Ibid.,* s. 34 (4).
13. The acceptor may pay the indorsee on maturity though the condition has not yet been fulfilled (*ibid.,* s. 33).

"Pay D only",
"Pay D or order for collection",
"Pay to A B or order for my use".

Such an indorsement gives the indorsee the right to receive payment of the bill and to sue any party that his indorser could have sued, but he cannot transfer his rights as indorsee unless it expressly authorises him to do so. If the restrictive indorsement authorises further transfer, all subsequent indorsees take the bill with the same rights and subject to the same liabilities as the first indorsee under the restrictive indorsement[14].

Forged and unauthorised indorsements

A forged or unauthorised indorsement is wholly inoperative and anyone taking the bill after such an indorsement has no title to it, or right to sue it, even though he may have no knowledge that the indorsement is forged or unauthorised[15]. The only proviso to this statutory rule is if the party against whom it is sought to retain or enforce payment of the bill is precluded (*i.e.* estopped) from setting up the forgery or want of authority[16]. An unauthorised signature may be ratified unless it amounts to a forged signature which would be the case if put on for a fraudulent purpose.

Although anyone taking the bill after a forged or unauthorised signature has no right to sue on the bill, he will have a claim against anyone who indorsed the bill after the forged or unauthorised signature. This is because an indorser is precluded from denying to his immediate or a subsequent indorsee that the bill was at the time of his indorsement a valid and subsisting bill and that he then had a good title thereto[17].

Transferor by delivery

A holder who negotiates a bill payable to bearer by delivery without indorsement is styled a transferor by delivery; he incurs no liability on the instrument. However, such transferor by delivery does warrant to his immediate transferee being a holder for value:

1. That the bill is what it purports to be;
2. That he has a right to transfer it;
3. That at the time of the transfer he is not aware of any fact which renders it valueless[18].

---

14. Bills of Exchange Act 1882, s. 35 (3).
15. *Ibid.*, s. 24.
16. *Ibid.*, s. 24, *Greenwood* v. *Martins Bank, Ltd.*, [1933] A. C. 51; *post*, p. 271.
17. *Ibid.*, s. 55 (2).
18. *Ibid.*, s. 58.

VI RIGHTS AND LIABILITIES

Rights of the holder

The holder is defined as the payee or indorsee of a bill or note who is in possession of it, or the bearer[19]. Holders fall into one of two divisions, viz.:

1. Those who are holders in due course, and
2. Those who are not.

1. A *holder in due course* is one who has taken a bill,
   (i) complete and regular on the face of it[20];
   (ii) before it was overdue, and without notice that it had been previously dishonoured, if such was the fact;
   (iii) in good faith and for value; and
   (iv) without notice of any defect in the title of the person who negotiated it.

All four are requisite[1].

The rights of the holder in due course are to sue in his own name any or all of the parties to the bill, and to do so free of any defence depending upon any defect of title or any mere personal defence available to prior parties amongst themselves[2].

The original payee of a bill cannot be a holder in due course; the bill is not negotiated to him[3].

2. A holder who has not obtained the bill in due course may sue on it in his own name if he is simply a holder for value but he is liable to be defeated by some defect of title in his predecessors or by defences of a personal nature available against them, other than set-off[4]. He may, however, indorse it to a holder in due course, in which case the latter obtains a good and complete title; he may also receive payment in due course, and may give the payer a valid discharge for the bill[5]. Section 29 (3) enacts:

"A holder (whether for value or not), who derives his title to a bill through a holder in due course, and who is not himself a party to any fraud or illegality affecting it, has all the rights of that holder in due course as regards the acceptor and all parties to the bill prior to that holder"[6].

---

19. *Ibid.*, s. 2.
20. The face includes the back (*Arab Bank, Ltd.* v. *Ross*, [1952] 1 All E. R. 709 at p. 715; [1952] 2 Q. B. 216, at p. 226). An indorsement is irregular if it raises any doubt whether it is the indorsement of the named payee (*ibid.*).
1. *Ibid.*, s. 29. As to what constitutes a defective title, see below. A forger's title is not defective—he has no title at all. See *ante*, p. 251.
2. Bills of Exchange Act 1882, s. 38.
3. *R. E. Jones* v. *Waring and Gillow*, [1926] A. C. 670.
4. Bills of Exchange Act 1882, s. 38; *Ex parte Swan* (1868), L. R. 6 Eq. 344.
5. *Ibid.*, s. 38 (3).   6. *Ibid.*, s. 29 (3).

From the above it is clear that a holder cannot be "in due course", unless he is ignorant of any fraud or illegality in connection with the bill on the part of the person who negotiated the bill to him, *and* unless he has given value for it.

The defects of title specially mentioned in the Act, which afford an answer to an action on the bill by any party with notice of the defects are—

1. Fraud,
2. Duress [force and fear],
3. Other unlawful means,
4. Illegal consideration, and
5. Negotiation in breach of faith, or under circumstances amounting to a fraud[7].

Though actual notice of these defects is, of course, sufficient to invalidate the title of a person claiming to be a holder, notice will be imputed to him if it can be shown that he received information which cast upon him the duty of making further inquiries, and that he abstained from doing so because they might injure his title. However,

> "It is not enough to show that there was carelessness, negligence or foolishness in not suspecting that the bill was wrong, when there were circumstances that might have led a man to suspect that. All these are matters which tend to show that there was dishonesty in not doing it, but they do not, in themselves, make a defence to an action upon a bill of exchange"[8].

Negligence will not affect the title of the holder if his conduct is, in fact, honest[8].

"*Valuable consideration*" in connection with bills of exchange means any consideration necessary to support a simple contract[9] or an antecedent debt or liability[10]; and where value has at any time been given for a bill, the holder for the time being is deemed to be a holder for value, as regards the acceptor, and all parties who became such prior to the time when value was given[11]. And as the law does not

7. Bills of Exchange Act 1882, s. 29 (2). These are not exhaustive; "force and fear" is a technical term of Scottish law, inserted because the Act applies to Scotland.
8. Bills of Exchange Act 1882, s. 90; *Jones* v. *Gordon* (1877), 2 App. Cas., at p. 628, *per* Lord BLACKBURN; *Miller* v. *Race* (1791), 1 Sm. L. C. (13th ed.), 524.
9. See as to the common law, *ante*, p. 000.
10. Bills of Exchange Act 1882, s. 27. See *ante*, p. 24. If a cheque is paid into a bank on the footing that the amount may be at once drawn on, the bank is a holder for value (*Ex parte Richdale* (1882), 19 Ch. D. 409).
11. *Ibid.*, s. 27. It is not necessary that the holder should have given value *to* someone not a party to the bill: *Diamond* v. *Graham*, [1968] 2 All E. R. 909; [1968] 1 W. L. R. 1061, C. A.

inquire into the adequacy of a consideration, taking a bill at a considerable undervalue is not of itself sufficient to affect a holder's title, though in the circumstances of any particular case it may be evidence that he was not acting honestly[12].

Where the holder of a bill has a lien on it, he is deemed to be a holder for value to the extent of the lien[13]. Thus, if the payee of a cheque for £100 asks his bank to collect payment for him and he has a £75 overdraft at the bank, the bank has a lien on the cheque for £75. The bank will be holders for value to the full amount of a cheque if that is less than the payee's overdraft[14].

"*Accommodation party.*"—Sometimes a bill is signed by a person as drawer, acceptor, or indorser without consideration for the purpose of lending his name to some other person. The person so signing is an "accommodation party" to the bill, and is in substance a surety for the person accommodated; but a holder for value may sue the accommodation party, although he knew him to be such when he took the bill[15].

Presumption in favour of holder.—It often becomes important to decide on whom lies the burden of proof of showing *bona fides* and the giving of value. The ordinary rule is this:

> when it is shown that the acceptance, issue, or negotiation of the bill is affected with fraud, duress, or illegality, the holder (unless he is the person to whom the bill was originally delivered[16] must prove that after the alleged fraud, etc., value has in good faith been given for the instrument[17]. But until such defect is shown a holder is deemed to be a holder in due course[18].

Overdue bills.—It has already been said that to constitute a "holder in due course", he must have acquired the bill before it was overdue, for a bill which is negotiated after that date is taken subject to any defect of title affecting it at maturity, and henceforth none can give a better title than they themselves have[19]. A bill payable on demand is overdue when it appears on the face of it to have been in circulation for an unreasonable time[20]; the maturity of other bills depends upon

12. *Jones* v. *Gordon* (1877), 2 App. Cas. 616.
13. Bills of Exchange Act 1882, s. 27 (3).
14. *Barclays Bank* v. *Astley Industrial Trust*, [1970] 1 All E. R. 719; [1970]
    2 Q. B. 527.
15. Bills of Exchange Act 1882, s. 28.
16. *Talbot* v. *Von Boris*, [1911] 1 K. B. 854.
17. Bills of Exchange Act 1882, s. 30 (2); and see *Hall* v. *Featherstone* (1858),
    3 H. & N. 284; *Tatam* v. *Haslar* (1889), 23 Q. B. D. 345.
18. Bills of Exchange Act 1882, s. 30.
19. *Ibid.*, s. 36 (2).
20. *Ibid.*, s. 36 (3). This is not so with promissory notes. See *post*, p. 279.

their date and wording[21]. Payment before maturity will not discharge the bill, and if it is put in circulation afterwards such payment will be no answer to a holder in due course[22]. Where a bill, which is not overdue, has been dishonoured by non-acceptance, any person who takes it with notice of the dishonour takes it subject to any defects of title attaching to it at the time of dishonour[1].

Lost bill.—If the bill is lost before it is overdue, the drawer may be compelled to give another bill of the same tenor, at the request of the person who was the holder; the latter giving security against the claims of any person who may become possessed of the lost instrument[2].

Negotiation back to holder.—A case of some peculiarity arises when the bill is negotiated back to a holder, who has previously signed it as a drawer or indorser, *e.g.*

> A draws a bill in favour of C; C indorses it to D, D to E, and E to A. In this case A cannot enforce the bill against any intervening party, for they themselves have an exactly corresponding right against him (see next paragraph). He is said to be precluded from suing on the ground of "circuity of action"; but he may reissue the bill[3].

However, if, owing to the circumstances, the holder would not have been liable to the particular indorser whom he is suing, then his own previous signature is no answer in the action. For instance:

> A bought goods of B, and C was to be surety for the price; B drew bills on A, indorsed them to C, who reindorsed them to B, and it was decided that as in this case there was a state of facts negativing the intention of reserving in C a right of action against B, "circuity of action" would not avail as a defence in an action by B against C[4].

Rights of parties other than the holder

Each of the indorsers of the bill is liable to the holder, and to any subsequent indorser who pays the bill at maturity. Correlatively each party who has put his name to the bill may claim against any who previously have signed it, whether by way of acceptance, drawing, or indorsement; *e.g.* the drawer may fall back on the acceptor for compensation; the first indorser has his remedy against the acceptor

---

21. See *post*, pp. 266.
22. *Burbridge* v. *Manners* (1812), 3 Camp. 193.
1. Bills of Exchange Act 1882, s. 36 (5).
2. Bills of Exchange Act 1882, s. 69. And the court may in any proceeding upon a bill (even against some other party than the drawer) order that the loss of it shall not be set up, provided an indemnity be given against the claims of any other person upon the instrument (*ibid.*, s. 70).
3. *Ibid.*, s. 37.
4. *Wilkinson & Co.* v. *Unwin* (1881), 7 Q. B. D. 636.

and the drawer, and so forth. Any party but the acceptor may sign the bill *sans recours, i.e.* may put his name on the bill, expressly and on the instrument itself disclaiming any personal liability, and any party taking after this is bound by the disclaimer[5].

It will be seen from the above that a bill with several names attached is a form of contract of suretyship[6]; the acceptor being the principal debtor, the other parties being sureties with regard to him, but generally not in regard to each other[7]; they have no right of contribution *inter se*. The indorser who pays a holder is entitled, as a surety who pays the creditor would be, to any securities held by the holder in respect of the bill[8]. So if the holder agrees to give time to the acceptor after maturity, the indorsers who do not assent are discharged[9]. If the bill has been accepted for the accommodation of the drawer, the acceptor is liable to the holder, but he has a right of indemnity against the drawer, and the rights of a surety in connection therewith[10].

Liabilities

Liability of the acceptor.—The drawee is not obliged to accept the bill, and in the event of refusal is under no liability on it[11]. If he does accept, he engages to pay according to the tenor of his acceptance[12] and this is so whether or not he has received consideration. By accepting he is precluded from denying to a holder in due course:

1. The existence of the drawer,
2. The genuineness of his signature,
3. His capacity, and
4. His authority to draw,

and if the bill is payable to the drawer's order:

5. His then capacity to indorse.

Further, if the bill is payable to the order of a third person, he admits:

1. The existence of the payee, and
2. His then capacity to indorse.

But these admissions do not include the genuineness of validity of the indorsements[13].

---

5. Bills of Exchange Act 1882, s. 16.
6. See *Jones* v. *Broadhurst* (1850), 9 C. B. 173.
7. *Macdonald* v. *Whitfield* (1883), 8 App. Cas. 733, 744.
8. *Duncan, Fox & Co.* v. *North and South Wales Bank* (1881), 6 App. Cas. 1.
9. *Tindal* v. *Brown* (1786), 1 T. R. 167. See under "Suretyship," *post*, pp. 376–388.
10. *Bechervaise* v. *Lewis* (1872), L. R. 7 C. P., at p. 377.
11. Bills of Exchange Act 1882, s. 53 (1).
12. *Ibid.*, s. 54 (1).
13. Bills of Exchange Act 1882, s. 54 (2).

If he has given his acceptance for honour, "*suprà protest*", the liability is not absolute, but accrues only if the drawee does not pay, and then only when the bill has been duly presented for payment and dishonoured, and has been again protested (the protest on non-acceptance of itself insufficient), and of these facts he is entitled to notice[14]. His liability, when it attaches, is to the holder and to all parties subsequent to the party for whose honour the bill was accepted[15].

Liability of the drawer.—He must pay the bill if it is dishonoured by non-acceptance or by non-payment on the part of the drawee if due notice of dishonour is given[16]. He may not deny to a holder in due course the existence of the payee, and his then capacity to indorse[17].

Liability of the indorser.—He engages, if the bill is duly presented and dishonoured, to compensate the holder or any subsequent indorser, provided he has the requisite notice of dishonour[18]. He must be taken to admit to a holder in due course the genuineness of the signatures of the drawer and of the previous indorsers; and he may not deny to a subsequent indorsee the validity of the bill, and that he had a good title to it at the time of indorsement[19].

A person who signs a bill otherwise than as drawer or acceptor thereby incurs the liability of an indorser to a holder in due course[20]. Suppose that A sells goods to B Co. Ltd., and it is arranged that A will draw a bill of exchange on B Co. Ltd. in favour of A, that B Co. Ltd. will accept it and, because A does not consider that the liability of the company itself is sufficient security, that one of the directors of the company should also sign the bill in his personal capacity. If the bill is drawn and signed by the various parties as arranged, the director's personal indorsement of the bill will render him liable to a holder in due course under s. 56. The director is said to be a quasi-indorser of the bill and to have "backed" it.

As has been stated above, each indorser may be called on to pay, by way of indemnity, the whole amount (unless he protected himself against this by the form of his indorsement) paid on the bill by a subsequent indorser, and the liabilities of indorsers *inter se* will ordinarily be determined according to this rule. But any special circumstances may be considered, in order to ascertain the true relations of the parties. Thus:

---

14. *Ibid.*, s. 66 (1).
15. *Ibid.*, s. 66 (2).
16. *Ibid.*, s. 55 (1).
17. *Ibid.*, s. 55 (1).
18. *Ibid.*, s. 55 (2).
19. Bills of Exchange Act 1882, s. 55 (2).
20. *Ibid.*, s. 56.

when A, B, and C, directors of a company, mutually agreed with each other to become sureties to a bank for a certain debt of the company, and in pursuance of that agreement indorsed three promissory notes of the company, it was decided that the first of the three indorsers need not indemnify the others, but that each was liable in a proportionate amount[1].

The rule is that indorsements are presumed to have been made in the order in which they appear on the bill; but this presumption may be displaced by evidence[2].

Inchoate Bills

A signature on blank stamped paper, *e.g.* what is commonly known as a blank cheque, may be delivered by the signer for the purpose of being converted into a bill, and such delivery operates as a *prima facie* authority to fill it up as a complete bill for any amount the stamp will cover.   Such an instrument after completion cannot be enforced against any person who became a party to it before completion, unless it was filled up within a reasonable time, and strictly in accordance with the authority given; except where after completion it is negotiated to a holder in due course[3].   Thus, if A signs a cheque form as drawer but does not complete the cheque and delivers it to someone to fill up for, say, the purchase price of a television set, *prima facie* A is not liable on the cheque unless it is filled up within a reasonable time and according to A's instructions.   But, if after it has been completed the cheque comes into the hands of a holder in due course who has no knowledge that it has been filled up contrary to instructions A is liable on it to such holder in due course for the amount now on the cheque.

The original holder of a bill cannot be a holder in due course[4], but he may be able to rely on the doctrine of estoppel: Thus, in *Lloyds Bank Ltd.* v. *Cooke*[5],

where the defendant signed his name on a blank stamped piece of paper and handed it to a customer of the plaintiffs with authority to fill it up as a promissory note for a certain sum payable to the plaintiffs and deliver it to the plaintiffs as security for an advance to be made by them, and the customer fraudulently filled in a larger amount and obtained that amount from the plaintiffs, who did not know of the fraud, it was held that the defendant was estopped from denying the validity of the note as between himself

---

1. *Macdonald* v. *Whitfield* (1883), 8 App. Cas. 733, 734.
2. Bills of Exchange Act 1882, s. 32 (5).
3. Bills of Exchange Act 1882, s. 20.
4. *R. E. Jones* v. *Waring and Gillow*, [1926] A. C. 670, *ante*, p. 245.
5. [1907] 1 K. B. 794; *cf. Wilson and Meeson* v. *Pickering*, [1946] 1 All E. R. 394; [1946] K. B. 422.

and the plaintiffs. The plaintiffs could not have relied on s. 20, Bills of Exchange Act, because the note had not been negotiated to them—they were the original payees.

In *Smith* v. *Prosser,*

> where the defendant signed blank forms of promissory notes and handed them to an agent for safe custody, it was held that the defendant was not liable to a *bona fide* indorsee for value to whom the agent had fraudulently negotiated them: for having handed the notes to his agent as custodian only, he was not estopped from denying their validity[6].

VII PRESENTMENT FOR PAYMENT AND NOTICE OF DISHONOUR

Presentment for payment

Presentment for payment is necessary (except in the cases mentioned below), and without it there is no right to enforce payment against the drawer and indorsers of the bill[7], but if the bill be accepted generally no presentment is required to render the acceptor liable[8].

The time of presentment is determined as follows:

> if the bill is payable on demand it must (to affect the drawer) be presented within a reasonable time after its issue, and (to affect an indorser) within a reasonable time after its indorsement; if payable otherwise, then it must be presented on the day on which the bill falls due[9].

The place of presentment is determined by the terms of the acceptance. If accepted payable at a particular place, presentment must be made at the place named; if the acceptor's address is on the bill, this (if no other place is specified) will demonstrate the proper place; if no place is specified and no address given, it should be presented to the acceptor at his place of business if known, and if not, at his ordinary residence; otherwise it may be presented to the acceptor at his last-known place of business or residence, or to himself wherever he may be found[10]. In *Yeoman Credit, Ltd.* v. *Gregory*[11], a bill, accepted payable at the N.P. Bank, fell due for payment on December 9, 1959. The bill was not presented there until December 10. *Held:* the defendant indorser was discharged from liability.

The presentment must be made by the holder or by some person

---

6. [1907] 2 K. B. 735.
7. Bills of Exchange Act 1882, s. 45.
8. *Ibid.*, s. 52 (1).
9. *Ibid.*, s. 45. The acceptor cannot always demand the exact carrying out of this dury. See s. 52 (2).
10. Bills of Exchange Act 1882, s. 45.
11. [1963] 1 All E. R. 245; [1963] 1 W. L. R. 343.

authorised to receive payment on his behalf at a reasonable hour on a business day. It must be made to the person designated by the bill as payer or to some person authorised by him to pay or to refuse payment, if such can be found. If there are several designated payers and no place of payment is specified, then to all of them, unless they are partners. If the drawee or acceptor is dead, presentment must be made, if possible, to his personal representative. Agreement or usage may authorise presentment through the post office[10].

Delay in making presentment is excused by circumstances beyond the control of the holder and not imputable to his default, misconduct or negligence. Presentment will be dispensed with:

   (i) where after the exercise of reasonable diligence it cannot be effected;
  (ii) where the drawee is a fictitious person[12];
 (iii) as regards the drawer, where the drawee or acceptor is not bound, as between himself and the drawer, to accept or pay the bill, and the drawer has no reason to believe that the bill would be paid if presented[13];
  (iv) as regards an indorser, where the bill was accepted or made for the accommodation of that indorser, and he has no reason to expect that the bill would be paid if presented;
   (v) if it is waived, expressly or by implication[14].

The holder must, on presentment, exhibit the bill to the person from whom payment is demanded[15].

Notice of dishonour

When a bill has been dishonoured either by non-acceptance or by non-payment, there is, in the former case, an immediate right of recourse against the drawer and indorsers, and in the latter against the acceptor, the drawer, and the successive indorsers; but these have, in general, a right to notice of dishonour, and those who receive no notice when such is requisite are freed from liability. The acceptor is not entitled to notice of dishonour[16].

The notice must be given within a reasonable time after dishonour, and, in the absence of special circumstances, these rules apply:

Time.—The following points should be noted:

   1. Where the parties who are to give and receive notice respectively, reside in the same place, it should be sent in such time as

---

12. See *ante*, p. 242.
13. *E.g.* if as between them it is an accommodation bill.
14. Bills of Exchange Act 1882, s. 46.
15. Bills of Exchange Act 1882, s. 52 (4).
16. *Ibid.*, s. 52 (3).

to reach the person to whom it is sent on the day after dishonour;

2. Where they live in different places it should be sent on the day after dishonour, or if there be no post at a convenient hour on that day, then by the next post thereafter[17].

Notice of dishonour *posted before* the bill is dishonoured can be effective[18]. If the bill when dishonoured is in the hands of an agent, he has a similar time allowed him wherein to communicate with his principal, and then the principal in turn has a similar allowance; the agent may, however, give notice direct to the parties interested[19]; and each person who receives notice has a similar time after receipt of notice wherein to communicate with prior parties[20].

Delay in giving notice of dishonour is excused if it is caused by circumstances beyond the control of the party giving notice, and is not imputable to his negligence[21].

To and by whom to be given.

1. It should be given by the holder, or by an indorser who is himself liable on the bill, or by an agent acting on behalf of either[1];

2. It must be given to the person entitled to it, or to his agent in that behalf[2]; or (if the drawer or indorser entitled to notice is dead, and the holder knows it) to his personal representative, if there be one, and he can be found with reasonable diligence[3]; or (if he is bankrupt) either to the party himself or to his trustee in bankruptcy[4].

Where there are two or more drawers or indorsers, not being partners, notice must be given to each, unless one of them has authority to receive notice for the others[5]. When a bill drawn or indorsed by partners is dishonoured after the dissolution of the firm, notice to one partner is sufficient[6].

No form of notice.—No particular form is required; writing or oral communication, or partly one and partly the other, will suffice, provided

17. *Ibid.*, s. 49 (12). When the letter is duly addressed and posted, subsequent miscarriage will not affect the party's rights (*ibid.*, s. 49 (15)).
18. *Eaglehill, Ltd.* v. *J. Needham, Builders, Ltd.*, [1972] 3 All E. R. 895; [1972] 3 W. L. R. 789, H. L.
19. *Ibid.*, s. 49 (13).
20. *Ibid.*, s. 49 (14).
21. *Ibid.*, s. 50 (1).
1. Bills of Exchange Act 1882, s. 49 (1), (2).
2. *Ibid.*, s. 49 (8).
3. *Ibid.*, s. 49 (9).
4. *Ibid.*, s. 49 (10).
5. *Ibid.*, s. 49 (11).
6. *Goldgarb* v. *Bartlett and Kremer*, [1920] 1 K. B. 639.

that the identity of the bill and its dishonour by non-acceptance or non-payment is sufficiently indicated; so also will return of the dishonoured bill to the drawer or indorser[7]. When given by the holder it enures for the benefit of all subsequent holders, and of all prior indorsers who have a right against the party to whom it has been given; and notice given by an indorser enures for the benefit of the holder and all indorsers subsequent to the party who has received notice[8].

Notice is required in the generality of cases, and that this should be so is clearly equitable. A man may have indorsed a bill, value £100, due on September 3rd; if he hears nothing about it, by, say, September 12th, his remedies against parties liable to him might become less valuable or be lost by his being unable to enforce them promptly. If afterwards he is asked to pay, great hardship might be inflicted upon him: hence the necessity for notice of dishonour. But in the following cases either this would not apply, or else a greater hardship would be inflicted on the holder by requiring him to give notice.

Thus, an omission to give notice of dishonour will not operate as a discharge:

1. Where the bill is dishonoured by non-acceptance, and notice of dishonour is not given, the rights of a holder in due course subsequent to the omission will not be prejudiced, and
2. Where due notice of dishonour is given on non-acceptance, and no acceptance is in the meantime given, notice of subsequent dishonour by non-payment is unnecessary[9].

Excuses for non-notice.—Notice of dishonour is dispensed with in the following cases[10]:

1. Where reasonable diligence is used, but notice is impossible, or does not reach the person sought to be charged;
2. Where notice is waived by the party entitled to it;
3. As regards *the drawer* when—
    (i) drawer and drawee are the same person;
    (ii) where the drawee is a fictitious person or a person having no capacity to contract;
    (iii) where the drawer is the person to whom the bill is presented for payment;

---

7. Bills of Exchange Act 1882, s. 49 (5)–(7).
8. *Ibid.*, s. 49 (3), (4).
9. Bills of Exchange Act 1882, s. 48.
10. *Ibid.*, s. 50 (2).

(iv) where the drawee or acceptor is as between himself and the drawer under no obligation to accept or pay the bill[11];

(v) where the drawer has countermanded payment;

4. As regards the *indorser*—

(i) where the bill was accepted or made for his accommodation;

(ii) where the indorser is the person to whom the bill is presented for payment;

(iii) where the drawee is a fictitious person or person not having capacity to contract, to the knowledge of the indorser at the time of indorsement. The meaning of "fictitious" has been examined already[12].

Noting and Protesting

In the case of an inland bill, protest, though sometimes useful, is optional, save where acceptance or payment for honour is desired[13]. But in the case of a foreign bill[14], appearing on the face of it to be such, the drawer and indorsers are discharged if, in the event of non-acceptance, the bill is not protested; and protest is necessary also, if a foreign bill which was not dishonoured by non-acceptance is dishonoured by non-payment[15]. Protest may be excused under circumstances similar to those mentioned above in the case of notice of dishonour[16].

Form of protest.—Protest of a foreign bill after it has been dishonoured (or more accurately, noting and protesting such a bill) involves handing the bill to a notary public who again formally presents the bill for acceptance or payment. Upon redishonour, the notary makes a memorandum on the bill of his initials, his charges, the date and a reference to his register where the details are entered and he attaches a slip to the bill giving the "answer he receives". That is the "noting" and the "protest", strictly so called, is the formal document recording the fact of dishonour. A protest must:

1. Contain a copy of the bill;

2. Be signed by the notary making it;

3. Must specify the person at whose request the bill is protested;

4. The place and date of protest;

---

11. For instance, where a banker has no funds to meet a cheque, or the bill was accepted for the accommodation of the drawer.
12. *Ante,* p. 242.
13. Bills of Exchange Act 1882, s. 51 (1).
14. *Post,* p. 270.
15. Bills of Exchange Act 1882, s. 51 (2).
16. *Ibid.,* s. 51 (9).

5. The cause or reason for protesting the bill;
6. The demand made and the answer given, if any, or the fact that the drawee or acceptor cannot be found[17].

If the services of a notary cannot be obtained, any householder or substantial resident of the place may, in the presence of two witnesses, give a certificate, signed by them, attesting the dishonour of the bill, and the certificate will in all respects operate as a formal protest[18].

Time for protest.—The bill should be protested on the day of dishonour, but if noted on that day, or not later than the next succeeding business day[19], it may be protested afterwards as of that day[20], delay is excused if caused by circumstances beyond the control of the holder, not imputable to his default, misconduct, or negligence[1].

Place of protest.—A bill must be protested at the place where it is dishonoured, save that:

1. When a bill is presented through and returned dishonoured through the post, it may be protested at the place to which it is returned, and
2. If the bill is drawn payable at some place of business or residence other than that of the drawee, and is dishonoured by non-acceptance, it must be protested at the place where it is expressed to be payable[2].

Measure of damages on a dishonoured bill

This differs in the case of a bill dishonoured in the British Isles and one dishonoured abroad. The measure of damages on a bill dishonoured at home is:

1. The amount of the bill; added to
2. Interest from the date of maturity, or if the bill is payable on demand, of presentment for payment; added to
3. The expenses of noting, and of any necessary protest[3].

On a bill dishonoured abroad the measure is[4] the amount of the re-exchange with interest till the time of payment[5], *i.e.*

---

17. Bills of Exchange Act 1882, s. 51 (7). If the bill is lost or destroyed or is wrongfully detained from the person entitled to hold it, protest may be made on a copy or written particulars thereof (*ibid.*, s. 51 (8)).
18. *Ibid.*, s. 94. A special form is given in the Schedule to the Act.
19. *Ibid.*, s. 51 (4); Bills of Exchange (Time of Noting) Act 1917, s. 1.
20. Bills of Exchange Act 1882, s. 93. "Noting" is the minute made by the notary on which the formal notarial certificate—the protest—is based.
1. *Ibid.*, s. 51 (9).
2. *Ibid.*, s. 51 (6).
3. *Ibid.*, s. 57 (1). See *ante*, p. 263.
4. The holder has no option to sue for the damages provided for the case of a dishonour at home (*Re Commercial Bank of South Australia* (1887), 36 Ch. D. 522).
5. Bills of Exchange Act 1882, s. 57 (2).

"the sum for which a sight bill (drawn at the time and place of dishonour at the *then rate of exchange* on the place where the drawer or indorser sought to be charged resides) must be drawn in order to realise at the place of dishonour the amount of the dishonoured bill and the expenses consequent on its dishonour"[6].

It has been decided that notwithstanding the above, if a bill drawn abroad is dishonoured at home and the drawer is by foreign law under a liability to the holder to pay re-exchange, he may, if the bill is duly protested, recover such re-exchange from the acceptor[7].

If justice requires it, the interest may be withheld whether the bill be an inland or a foreign bill[8].

VIII DISCHARGE OF THE BILL

The grounds of discharge are these:

1. Payment in due course,
2. Waiver,
3. Cancellation,
4. Merger,
5. Alteration.

In addition certain parties may be discharged by want of notice of dishonour or by omission to duly present the bill.

1. Payment in due course

In order to operate as a discharge, this must be made by the proper person and in due course. Payment by or on behalf of the acceptor at or after maturity will always operate as a discharge if made *bona fide* to the holder without notice of any defect there may be in his title[9]. An accommodation bill is discharged if paid by the party accommodated[10] but with other bills payment by the drawer or an indorser does not discharge the bill but merely discharges subsequent indorsers from liability[11]. Where a bill payable to the order of a third party is paid by the drawer, the drawer may enforce payment against the acceptor but not reissue the bill. On the other hand, where a bill payable to the drawer's order is paid by the drawer, or where any bill is paid by an indorser, the party paying may strike out his own and subsequent indorsements and again negotiate the bill[11].

---

6. See Chalmers on Bills of Exchange (13th ed.), p. 192.
7. *Re Gillespie, Ex parte Robarts* (1887), 18 Q. B. D. 286.
8. Bills of Exchange Act 1882, s. 57 (3).
9. Bills of Exchange Act 1882, s. 59.
10. *Ibid.*, s. 59 (3).
11. *Ibid.*, s. 59 (2).

To whom.—Payment must be made to the party entitled[12], and it is on this account that the payee must be in the first instance a person named or indicated with reasonable certainty, though a bill may be made payable to several payees jointly, or alternatively to one of them, or to the holder of an office for the time being[13], and it may be made payable to bearer. If a fictitious[14] or non-existing person is named as payee the bill may be treated as payable to bearer[15].

Amount payable.—The amount paid must be the correct amount, which, therefore, must be a sum certain[16]. If interest has been agreed, then the amount payable is the amount due plus interest and such interest runs from the date of the bill, or (if it be undated) from date of issue, unless the bill otherwise provides[17]; a partial acceptance makes the acceptor liable only to the amount for which he has accepted. When the drawer pays off a certain part of the amount, is the acceptor freed *pro tanto* or can he be sued for the whole, the holder being then liable to the drawer for the excess recovered? In an action by a holder against the acceptor, payment by the drawer or an indorser of any part is no answer[18], unless the bill is an accommodation bill, given for the accommodation of the drawer[19].

When.—The bill is payable at maturity. It is payable on demand, if it is so expressed, or if no time for payment is named, or if it is stated to be payable at sight or on presentation; also if it is accepted or indorsed when overdue, it is, as regards such acceptor or indorser, deemed to be payable on demand[20]. If it is payable at a fixed period after date or sight or on or after a fixed period after any specified event which is certain to happen, the date is determined according to the tenor[1].

A bill on demand is payable on the day of demand, but in other cases the bill is due and payable on the last day of the time of payment as

---

12. But see *post,* p. 274, as to payment by a banker of a demand draft bearing a forged indorsement.
13. Bills of Exchange Act 1882, s. 7.
14. See *Bank of England* v. *Vagliano Bros., ante,* p. 243.
15. Bills of Exchange Act 1882, s. 7 (3). See *ante* p. 242.
16. *Ante,* p. 243.
17. Bills of Exchange Act 1882, s. 9 (3).
18. *Ibid.,* s. 59 (2).
19. *Lazarus* v. *Cowie,* [1842] 3 Q. B. 459; *Cook* v. *Lister* (1863), 32 L. J. C. P. 121 (*ibid.,* s. 59 (3)).
20. Bills of Exchange Act 1882, s. 10.
1. *Ibid.,* s. 11. It must be observed, however, that an instrument drawn payable on a contingency cannot be a valid bill of exchange. In *Williamson* v. *Rider,* [1962] 2 All E. R. 268; [1963] 1 Q. B. 89, it was held that an instrument drawn payable "on or before December 31, 1956" created an uncertainty and a contingency in the time of payment; and see s. 12, as regards filling up the date when the instrument has been issued undated, *ante,* p. 243.

fixed by the bill[2], or if that is a non-business day[3], on the succeeding business day.

The whole day is available for payment, *i.e.* in general the whole of the business hours of the day[4]. Payment may be made before it is due, but it will not then operate as a discharge except between the parties to the payment, and will be no answer to a holder in due course[5].

When a bill is paid the holder may be compelled to deliver it up to the party paying it[6].

Payment for honour

If a bill is not paid at maturity it becomes dishonoured by non-payment, and the holder immediately acquires his consequent rights against the parties. If it has been protested for non-payment, any person may intervene and pay it for the honour of any party liable thereon or for whose account the bill is drawn[7]; the intervention is then called "payment for honour", and the payer steps into the place of the holder, to the extent of his rights against the defaulter and those who were liable to him; parties subsequent to the party for whose honour the bill is paid are discharged[8]; this "payment for honour *suprà protest*" must be attested by a notarial act of honour, which may be appended to the protest[9].

2. Renunciation

When the holder of a bill *at* or *after* maturity absolutely and unconditionally renounces his rights against the acceptor, the bill is discharged. The renunciation must be in writing unless the bill is delivered up to the acceptor[10]. If *in like manner* a holder renounces his rights against a particular indorser of the bill *before*, *at* or *after* maturity, that indorser will be discharged. If a holder renounces his rights against a party before maturity and then negotiates the bill to a holder in due course who is ignorant of the renunciation, the holder in due course is not affected by the renunciation[11]. At common law

---

2. *Ibid.*, s. 14 as amended by the Banking and Financial Dealings Act 1971, s. 3.
3. Non-business days mean Saturday, Sunday, Good Friday, Christmas Day, a bank holiday and a day appointed by Royal proclamation as a public fast or thanksgiving day: Bills of Exchange Act 1882 s. 92 as amended by the Banking and Financial Dealings Act 1971, s. 3.
4. *Kennedy* v. *Thomas*, [1894] 2 Q. B. 759.
5. Bills of Exchange Act 1882, s. 59 (2).
6. *Ibid.*, s. 52 (4).
7. Bills of Exchange Act 1882, s. 68 (1).
8. *Ibid.*, s. 68 (5).
9. *Ibid.*, s. 68 (3).
10. *Ibid.*, s. 62 (1).
11. *Ibid.*, s. 62 (2).

accord without satisfaction does not operate to discharge a party from liability, unless a release under seal is given; the law merchant did not adopt this principle and permitted the holder of a bill to discharge the acceptor without consideration; and, subject to the conditions above mentioned, the Act has recognised the peculiar rule of the law merchant.

3. Cancellation[12]

Cancellation discharges the person whose name is cancelled, and also all indorsers who would have a right of recourse against him, unless

(i) the cancellation was not intentional; or

(ii) was made without the holder's consent; or

(iii) was made by mistake; the burden of proving that the cancellation took place under these conditions is on the party seeking to support the bill.

If the bill as a whole is thus cancelled, all parties are discharged.

4. Merger

Under some circumstances this will discharge the bill, *e.g.* when the acceptor becomes holder of the bill in his own right, at or after maturity[13]. The acceptor must, however, receive back the bill with a right good against the world and not subject to that of any other person, so that if it is transferred to him without consideration in fraud of a previous holder in due course, he will still remain liable on it[14].

5. Alteration

Material alteration of the bill or acceptance without the assent of all parties liable, avoids the bill, except as against a party who has made, authorised, or assented to the alteration and except as against subsequent indorsers. If, however, the alteration is not apparent, the holder in due course may sue for the amount of the bill as it stood before alteration[15]. Material alterations are, *inter alia*, alterations of date, amount, time and place of payment, or the addition of a particular place of payment, where the original acceptance was general[16].

So also, the alteration of the place of drawing of a completed bill which converts the instrument from an inland into a foreign bill is material[17]; but such an alteration is not material if made by the

---

12. Bills of Exchange Act 1882, s. 63.
13. *Ibid.*, s. 61.
14. *Nash* v. *De Freville*, [1900] 2 Q. B. 72.
15. See *Scholfield* v. *Earl of Londesborough*, [1896] A. C. 514.
16. Bills of Exchange Act 1882, s. 64. See also *Slingsby* v. *District Bank, post*, p. 264, where an alteration in the name of the payee was held to be material.
17. *Koch* v. *Dicks*, [1932] All E. R. Rep. 476; [1933] 1 K. B. 307.

drawer before the bill is completed[18]. A bill is not avoided by an alteration which is not material. In *Garrard* v. *Lewis*[19],

> defendant signed an acceptance, the amount being left in blank, but the figures in the margin were £14 0s. 6d.; the drawer filled up the bill for £164 0s. 6d., and altered the figures to make them correspond, and it was decided that the marginal figures not being a material part of the bill, the alteration was no defence to an action by a *bona fide* holder[20].

But s. 64 does not apply to alterations resulting from mutilation. Thus, where the note of a bank was accidentally broken into fragments and then pieced together so as to contain all the elements necessary to render it valid and effectual as a negotiable instrument and establish its identity as a note of the bank, but not so as to show the number of the note, the holder was held entitled to recover from the bank the amount for which the note had been issued[1].

IX BILL IN A SET

Bills are frequently drawn in a set[2], *e.g.* two, three, or more parts, and if they are numbered and refer one to the other, the whole of the parts constitute one bill. The drawee should accept one part only, and, if he accepts more than one he will be liable on each part as though it were a separate bill, save where all get into the hands of one holder; he should not pay unless the accepted part is produced to him, for if he does so, and that part is eventually presented by a holder in due course, he must pay again.

If a holder of a set indorses different parts to different persons, he is liable on each part for the full amount, and so will be all subsequent indorsers on the parts they indorse. Subject to the above, payment of one part discharges the set. Where two or more parts of a set are negotiated to different holders in due course, the holder whose title first accrues is as between such holders deemed the true owner of the bill; but this must not prejudicially affect the position of a person who in due course accepts or pays the first part presented to him.

---

18. *Foster* v. *Driscoll*, [1928] All E. R. Rep., at p. 138; [1929] 1 K. B., at p. 494.
19. (1883), 10 Q. B. D. 30.
20. These rules do not apply to Bank of England notes. See *post*, pp. 280–281.
1. *Hong Kong, etc., Banking Corporation* v. *Lo Lee Shi*, [1928] A. C. 181. *Semble*, even a material part of the instrument might be supplied by clear verbal evidence of its destruction (*Hong Kong, etc., Banking Corporation* v. *Lo Lee Shi, supra*).
2. Bills of Exchange Act 1882, s. 71.

X FOREIGN BILLS

An inland bill is one which is or purports on the face of it to be both drawn and payable within the British Isles, or to be drawn within them, upon the same person resident therein. Any other bill is a foreign bill. Unless the contrary appear on the face of it, a bill may be treated by the holder as an inland bill[3].

The form of a foreign bill usually differs from an inland bill, the former being drawn, as a rule, in sets, and at one or more *usances* (*i.e.* the time for payment allowed by custom as between the country of draft and the country of payment). When a foreign bill is dishonoured, protest is necessary save as against the acceptor; in the case of an inland bill it is optional[4].

It is a matter of some difficulty to decide what law governs a foreign bill, whether the law of the place of draft, or of the place of payment. The rules relating to this are to be found in s. 72 of the Bills of Exchange Act 1882; their main result seems to be that the law of the place where the act is done is to be the law governing the validity in form and the interpretation of that act, *e.g.* a bill drawn in England, accepted in France, payable in Holland; here English law governs the drawing, French law the acceptance, Dutch law the payment. Thus, where a foreign bill drawn on an English acceptor payable to the order of a named payee was indorsed in France with the authority of the payee by an agent *in his own name* simpliciter, then, that indorsement being valid by French law, although it would not be recognised by the law of England as a good indorsement of an inland bill, was sufficient to entitle the indorsee to sue the English acceptor[5].

---

3. Bills of Exchange Act 1882, s. 4.
4. *Ibid.*, ss. 51, 52 (3).
5. *Koechlin et Cie* v. *Kestenbaum Bros.*, [1927] 1 K. B. 889.

CHAPTER 16

Cheques, Promissory Notes and Bank Notes

I CHEQUES

The present law relating to cheques is contained in the Bills of Exchange Act 1882 and the Cheques Act 1957. Section 73 of the Bills of Exchange Act defines cheques as bills of exchange drawn on a banker, payable on demand; the definition of a bill of exchange given in the Act applies to cheques, and so generally do all provisions of the Act applicable to bills payable on demand, except as otherwise provided in Part III of the Bills of Exchange Act (ss. 73–81).

Duties of a banker

When a cheque is presented, the banker must pay it if he has funds in his hands belonging to the drawer available for the purpose; otherwise he becomes liable to an action at the suit of the customer for wrongfully dishonouring the cheque. If the customer is not a trader he will only receive nominal damages unless the damage he has suffered is alleged and proved as special damage[1] but if a trader's cheque is wrongfully dishonoured, the customer can recover substantial damages without giving evidence of having sustained any special loss[2].

The other main responsibility that the banker has to his customer is to make payment out of the customer's account only on the customer's signature and only according to the customer's directions. *Prima facie*, therefore, the banker has no right to debit his customer's account for the amount of a cheque on which the customer's signature has been forged[3] and, if the banker pays someone whose title rests on a forged indorsement the banker is not entitled to debit the customer's account. However, there are statutory provisions to be considered shortly which protect a banker in some circumstances. Further, where the banker's error is occasioned by the customer's breach of his duty to

---

1. *Gibbons* v. *Westminster Bank*, [1938] 3 All E. R. 577; [1939] 2 K. B. 882.
2. *Fleming* v. *Bank of New Zealand*, [1900] A. C. 577.
3. Bills of Exchange Act 1882, s. 24. See *ante*, p. 251. But the customer may be estopped by conduct from questioning the banker's payment of the cheque—*e.g.* if he has delayed informing the bank of the forgery after he has become aware of it. *Greenwood* v. *Martins Bank*, [1932] All E. R. Rep. 318; [1933] A. C. 51.

draw his cheques properly the banker is also protected. A customer does owe a duty to take reasonable precautions against forgery and if he carelessly draws a cheque with spaces which can be utilised to alter fraudulently the amount of the cheque and this is in fact done, the customer must bear the loss caused by payment of the cheque as altered[4]. It has, however, been held not to be a breach of duty to leave a blank space after the payee's name on a cheque payable to order[5].

In the case of a company account (or the account of any incorporated or unincorporated body), the bank will be authorised to pay only on a cheque which is signed by specifically authorised persons. Moreover, as the paying bank owes a duty of care to its customer, even where a cheque contains the authorised signatures, if the bank knows or ought to know that the cheque has been drawn for an unauthorised purpose (*e.g.* purchase of the company's own shares), it will be liable to its customer should it pay out on the cheque[6].

Duty of a holder

The holder of a cheque must present it for payment within a reasonable time of its issue[7]. If the drawer is entitled at the time of such presentment as between himself and the banker to have the cheque paid, and if owing to non-presentment within a reasonable time he is damnified (*e.g.* by the insolvency of the banker), he is discharged to the amount of the damage suffered; in such a case, the holder may obtain judgment for the amount against the banker[8].

Revocation of banker's authority

A banker's authority to pay a customer's cheque is revoked:

1. By countermand of payment[9];
2. By notice of the customer's death[9]; and
3. By notice of the presentation of a bankruptcy petition by or against a customer, and in any case, by the making of a receiving order against him[10].

---

4. *London Joint Stock Bank* v. *Macmillan*, [1918] A. C. 777.
5. *Slingsby* v. *District Bank, Ltd.*, [1932] 1 K. B. 544.
6. *Selangor United Rubber Estates, Ltd.* v. *Cradock (No. 3)*, [1968] 2 All E. R. 1073; *Karak Rubber Co., Ltd.,* v. *Burden (No. 2)*, [1972] 1 All E. R. 1210; [1972] 1 W. L. R. 602.
7. Bills of Exchange Act 1882, s. 74 (2).
8. Bills of Exchange Act 1882, s. 74 (1), (3).
9. *Ibid.*, s. 75. The banker is not bound to act on an unauthenticated telegram (*Curtice* v. *London, City and Midland Bank*, [1908] 1 K. B. 293).
10. Bankruptcy Act 1914, s. 46 and *Re Dalton (a bankrupt)*, *Ex parte Herrington and Carmichael (a firm)* v. *Trustee of Property of Bankrupt*, [1962] 2 All E. R. 499; [1963] Ch. 366. But where payment has been made to a third party in ignorance of a receiving order and before it is gazetted, the trustee must endeavour if practicable to seek to recover the sum from the payee of the cheque: Bankruptcy (Amendment) Act 1926, s. 4.

He may refuse to pay a cheque on an account which is the subject of a garnishee order[11]; and the common form of order will apply to the "client account" kept by a solicitor unless the order is modified so as not to affect such an account[12].

A cheque is not an equitable assignment of the drawer's balance, and accordingly a third party has no right of action against a banker for refusing to honour it[13].

Crossed cheques

A cheque, across the face of which two parallel lines are drawn (between which the words "and Company", or any abbreviation of them, may be placed), is styled a crossed cheque. A cheque crossed generally contains the above only; a cheque crossed specially contains the name of a banker in addition, and then is said to be crossed to that banker[14].

This crossing (which is a material part of the cheque[15]) may be added to an uncrossed cheque by the drawer or the holder, and either may turn a general into a special crossing[16]. A banker may convert:

1. An uncrossed cheque into a crossed one, or
2. A general crossing into a special crossing to himself[16].

He may

3. Re-cross a specially crossed cheque to another banker for collection[17].

In no other case may a specially crossed cheque be crossed to more than one banker, and if it is so crossed, the duty of the banker to whom it is presented is to refuse payment[18].

When a cheque is crossed generally it must be paid to a banker, and if it is crossed specially, to the banker whose name is on it[19]. For safety's sake the words *"not negotiable"* are often added, and although they do not affect the transferability of the cheque, they limit its negotiable character, rendering a transferee liable to have set up against him the defects of title available against a previous holder. In the words of the Act,

> "he shall not have and shall not be capable of giving a better title to the cheque than that which the person from whom he took it had"[20].

---

11. *Rogers* v. *Whiteley*, [1892] A. C. 118.
12. *Plunkett* v. *Barclay's Bank*, [1936] 2 K. B. 107.
13. *Schroeder* v. *Central Bank of London* (1876), 34 L. T. 735.
14. Bills of Exchange Act 1882, s. 76.
15. *Ibid.*, s. 78.   16. *Ibid.*, s. 77.
17. Bills of Exchange Act 1882, s. 77.
18. *Ibid.*, s. 79 (1).   19. *Ibid.*, s. 79 (2).
20. *Ibid.*, s. 81. See *ante*, p. 249, as to the meaning of the words "not negotiable" when written on an ordinary bill of exchange.

Thus, if A draws a bearer cheque crossed "not negotiable" and the cheque is stolen from the bearer, C may take a transfer of that cheque in good faith and for value but he cannot obtain a good title to the cheque.

Frequently the cheque is further crossed "account payee", which, as shown below, seems to put the collecting banker under a greater duty of care than his ordinary duty of care[1].

The paying banker

A banker who pays a cheque drawn on him otherwise than according to the crossing is liable to the true owner[2] for any loss he may sustain by such payment[3]. If the crossing is obliterated, or if the cheque appears not to be crossed, and not to have been added to, or altered otherwise than in accordance with the Act, then if the banker acts in good faith and without negligence, he is not responsible if he treats the cheque as uncrossed[4].

Further statutory protection is provided for the paying banker by s. 60 and s. 80 of the Bills of Exchange Act and by s. 1 of the Cheques Act.

1. *Section 80 of the Bills of Exchange Act.*—If the banker pays in conformity with the crossing in good faith and without negligence, he is placed in the same position as if he had paid the true owner, and if the cheque has reached the payee, the drawer is entitled to the same protection. It follows that if a crossed order cheque is stolen from the payee and the thief forges the payee's indorsement, then so long as the paying bank pays according to the crossing in good faith and without negligence, it is entitled to debit the drawer's account with the amount and the drawer is in no way liable to the payee.

2. *Section 60 of the Bills of Exchange Act.*—This provides wider protection as it applies to uncrossed as well as to crossed cheques and the paying banker is deemed to have paid a cheque in due course despite the existence of a forged indorsement on the cheque provided the paying banker has acted in good faith and "in the ordinary course of business".

3. *Section 1 of the Cheques Act.*—The main purpose of the Cheques Act 1957 was to make it unnecessary for the payee of a cheque or a subsequent indorsee to indorse the cheque before paying it into his own bank account. Indorsement remains necessary to effect the negotiation of an order cheque. By s. 1 of the Act, if a banker in good faith and "in the ordinary course of business" pays a cheque which is

---

1. See *post*, p. 278.
2. As to who is "true owner", see *Bute (Marquess)* v. *Barclays Bank, Ltd.*, [1954], 3 All E. R. 365, at pp. 368, 369; [1955] 1 Q. B. 202 at pp. 211, 212.
3. Bills of Exchange Act 1882, s. 79 (2).   4. *Ibid.*, s. 79 (2).

not indorsed or is irregularly indorsed he is deemed to have paid it in due course. Thus, if an order cheque is stolen from the payee and the thief opens a bank account in the name of the payee, the bank on which the cheque is drawn may pay the amount to the bank at which the thief has opened this account and if it does so it may be able to rely on the protection of this section.

The collecting banker

At common law, if a banker collected a cheque for his customer and that customer had no rightful title to it, he would be liable in conversion to the true owner. However, by statutory provision, where a banker in good faith and without negligence receives payment of a cheque, whether crossed or not, or having credited a customer's account with the amount of a cheque receives payment for himself, he does not incur any liability to the true owner by reason only of having received payment even if the customer has no title or a defective title to the cheque[5]. The banker need not concern himself with the absence of, or irregularity in, indorsement of the cheque[6].

Who is a "customer"?—Lord DUNEDIN in *Taxation Commissioners v. English, Scottish and Australian Bank*, said:

"The word 'customer' signifies a relationship in which duration is not of the essence. A person whose money has been accepted by a bank on the footing that they undertake to honour cheques up to the amount standing to his credit is a customer of the bank in the sense of the statute, irrespective of whether his connection is of short or long standing. The contrast is not between a habitué and a newcomer, but between a person for whom the bank performs a casual service, such as, for instance, cashing a cheque for a person introduced by one of their customers, and a person who has an account of his own at the bank"[7].

The meaning so given to the words "customer" is of importance because it sometimes happens that a person opens an account for the purpose only of clearing cheques to which he has no title, and if this is not coupled with circumstances which ought to put the banker on inquiry, the protection of the section is not lost.

---

5. Cheques Act 1957, s. 4, superseding Bills of Exchange Act 1882, s. 82 (as amended), which only applied to *crossed* cheques. Formerly in the case of an *uncrossed* cheque the bank had to prove that it was a holder for value to avoid liability for conversion of the cheque.
6. Cheques Act 1957, s. 4 (3). It seems clear, however, that a bank collecting for someone other than the payee must ensure that there are indorsements on the back of the cheque linking the payee with the present holder and that they are not irregular. Breach of that duty would amount to negligence.
7. [1920] A. C. 683, at p. 687. See also *Great Western Rail. Co. v. London and County Banking Co.*, [1901] A. C. 414.

276 Part III—Types of Mercantile Contracts

A bank collecting cheques for another banker does so for a "customer"[8].

What is negligence?—Negligence must be considered with reference to an implied duty to use due care to protect the true owner of the cheque; and the onus of proving absence of negligence lies on the banker[9]. Negligence must be connected with a particular cheque, and, coupled with the circumstances antecedent and present, must involve a departure from the standard of care required by the practice of bankers[10]. Examples are as follows:

> Where a cheque drawn payable to the order of or indorsed by a public official is paid into a private account, as the transaction is quite out of the ordinary course of business, the banker cannot safely collect the cheque without inquiry into his customer's title[11].

So, again

> Where an official of a limited company, even though he be the sole director of a one-man company, pays into his private account cheques drawn in favour of the company, the banker must make proper business inquiries into the reason justifying the collection of such cheques for the personal account of a servant or agent of the company[12].

Contrast

> Where W and E were jointly authorised to sign cheques on the plaintiff company's account and W left some blank cheques, signed by himself on the company's behalf, in E's possession. E drew the cheques "Pay Cash or order", added his own signature and the defendant bank collected the amount for E's private account. *Held:* the defendant bank was not negligent because E's signature on the instruments was not legible and it did not know of E's connection with the plaintiff company whose name appeared on them. It made no difference that being drawn "Pay Cash" the instruments were not strictly cheques as s. 4 (2) of the

---

8. *Importers Co.* v. *Westminster Bank*, [1927] All E. R. Rep. 683; [1927] 2 K. B. 297.
9. *Lloyd's Bank* v. *Savory & Co.*, [1932] All E. R. Rep. 106; [1933] A. C. 201; *Midland Bank* v. *Reckitt*, [1932] All E. R. Rep. 90; [1933] A. C. 1.
10. *Bissell* v. *Fox* (1884), 51 L. T. N. S. 663; (1885), 53 L. T. N. S. 193; *Taxation Commissioners* v. *English, Scottish and Australian Bank* (1920), A. C. 683; *Lloyds Bank* v. *Chartered Bank of India, etc.*, [1928] All E. R. Rep. 285; [1929] 1 K. B. 40.
11. *Ross* v. *L. C. & W. Bank*, [1919] 1 K. B. 678.
12. *Underwood (A. L.), Ltd.* v. *Bank of Liverpool*, [1924] 1 K. B. 775. See also *Bute (Marquess)* v. *Barclays Bank, Ltd.*, [1954] 3 All E. R. 365; [1955] 1 Q. B. 202.

Cheques Act gives a collecting bank protection in the case of "Pay Cash" documents, bankers' drafts, etc., as well as cheques[13].

And

> A cheque for £3,000 was signed on behalf of a company in favour of E. K, calling himself E, sought to open an account at a branch of the Midland Bank in the name of E. The bank agreed to do this and obtained a reference from A who knew K as E and had been a valued customer of the bank for six years. The bank collected the cheque for K (known as E) and after a few weeks K withdrew all the money from his account and left the country. *Held:* the bank acted according to the current practice of bankers and, relying on A's reference, was not negligent in failing to ask for identification or inquire as to K's employment[14].

Where cheques are paid in at one branch for the account of a customer at another branch, the branch which first receives and clears the cheques, which are not seen by the crediting branch, ought to inform the latter of the names of the drawers of the cheques: otherwise a dishonest servant or agent might pay into his private account his employer's or principal's cheques without the risk of detection he would run by delivering the cheques to the branch at which his account was kept which is more likely to know the name of his employer[15].

Even if a collecting bank is held not to be protected by s. 4 of the Cheques Act because of negligence, the damages it must pay in conversion to the true owner may be reduced by the contributory negligence of the owner[16].

Notwithstanding s. 25 of the Bills of Exchange Act, where a banker collects a cheque drawn or indorsed *per pro*, he is not negligent merely because he does not inquire into the authority of the drawer or indorser; s. 25 affects rights and liabilities while the bill is current and ceases to operate when the bill has been discharged by payment; s. 4 of the Cheques Act 1957, deals with rights and liabilities after the bill has been so discharged[17].

But where cheques were drawn in the form "R by T his attorney", and paid by T into his own *overdrawn* banking account, his bankers, having notice by the form of the cheques that the money was not T's money, were held to have been negligent by omitting to ask to see T's

---

13. *Orbit Mining and Trading Co., Ltd.* v. *Westminster Bank, Ltd.*, [1962] 3 All E. R. 565; [1963] 1 Q. B. 794.
14. *Marfani & Co., Ltd.* v. *Midland Bank, Ltd.*, [1968] 2 All E. R. 573, C. A.
15. *Lloyds Bank* v. *Savory & Co.*, [1932] All E. R. Rep. 106; [1933] A. C. 201.
16. *Lumsden & Co.* v. *London Trustee Savings Bank*, [1971] 1 Lloyd's Rep. 114.
17. See *ante*, p. 244, and *Morison* v. *L. C. & W. Bank*, [1914] 3 K. B. 356.

power of attorney or to make any inquiry as to T's authority to pay the moneys into his own account[18].

"Account payee" crossing.—If a cheque is marked "account payee" the collecting banker is under a duty to make inquiry to see that it collects for the payee named on the cheque or that its customer has the payee's authority. It does not restrict the negotiability of the cheque, but if the banker does not make such inquiry, it will be liable in conversion if it collects for someone other than its true owner. If such a cheque is being collected for *another banker*, as the collecting bank cannot control the ultimate destination of the money, it is sufficient for it to hand the proceeds to the proper receiving banker and leave it to him to comply with the direction[19].

Collecting banker as holder for value or holder in due course[20].—Value is deemed to have been given by a collecting bank to the customer who asks it to collect payment on a cheque if (i) there is an express or implied agreement to apply the cheque in reduction of an overdraft, or to allow him to draw against it before it is cleared, or (ii) if *in fact*, it gives him cash at once for the cheque or allows it to be drawn against before the proceeds have been cleared, or (iii) if the bank has a lien on the cheque—where the customer is overdrawn the bank has a lien on any cheque paid in up to the amount of the overdraft[21].

By s. 2 of the Cheques Act, a collecting banker, who gives value for or has a lien on an order cheque given to him for collection without any indorsement on it, is a holder for value of the cheque despite the lack of indorsement. Thus, where the payee of an order cheque gives no value for it and therefore could not sue upon it, hands the cheque in to a bank (with or without his indorsement) for collection for his account (or even for someone else's account) the bank is able to enforce payment provided it can show it is a holder for value[22].

If the bank has not only given value but fulfils all the particulars of the definition of a holder in due course, by reason *inter alia* of being in good faith and having no knowledge of any defect in the title of its customer, it has a good defence to any claim in conversion even if it could not, by reason of negligence, claim the protection of s. 4 of the

---

18. *Midland Bank* v. *Reckitt*, [1932] All E. R. Rep. 90; [1033] A. C. 1.
19. *Importers Co.* v. *Westminster Bank*, [1927] All E. R. Rep. 683; [1927] 2 K. B. 297.
20. For the meanings of a holder for value and a holder in due course, see *ante*, p. 252–253.
21. See *Barclays Bank* v. *Astley Industrial Trust*, [1970] 1 All E: R. 719; [1970] 2 Q. B. 527, *ante*, p. 254.
22. *Midland Bank, Ltd.* v. *R. V. Harris, Ltd.*, [1963] 2 All E. R. 685; [1963] 1 W. L. R. 1021; *Westminster Bank, Ltd.* v. *Zang*, [1966] 1 All E. R. 114; [1966] A. C. 182, H. L.

Cheques Act. Of course, the collecting bank cannot claim to be a holder in due course of a cheque if its title rests on a forged indorsement.

Cheque as a receipt

By s. 3 of the Cheques Act, "an unindorsed cheque which appears to have been paid by the banker on whom it is drawn is evidence of receipt by the payee of the sum payable by the cheque".

II PROMISSORY NOTES

A promissory note is defined by the Act to be[1]:

> "an unconditional promise in writing made by one person to another signed by the maker, engaging to pay, on demand or at a fixed or determinable future time, a sum certain in money, to, or to the order of, a specified person or to bearer."

An instrument in the form of a note payable to maker's order is not a note until indorsed by the maker. If on the face of the note it purports to be both made and payable within the British Isles, it is an inland note; any other is a foreign note. The usual form of a promissory note is as follows:

£50.   *York, August 5th,* 1973.

[Three] months after date [or on demand] I promise to pay
A B or order [or bearer] fifty pounds.

A. F. G.

Here A F G is the maker and A B the payee; when A B puts his name on the back he becomes an indorser. The differences between a note and a bill are manifest; a bill has three original parties, a note has but two.

The contract of the maker is to pay the note according to its tenor, and he may not deny to a holder in due course the existence of the payee, and his then capacity to indorse[2]. This liability may be:

1. Joint, or
2. Joint and several,

according to the number of makers—for any number may jointly make a note—and their liability depends upon the tenor of the note. Thus:

1. "I promise to pay", etc., signed by more than one person, is a joint and several promise[3];
2. "We jointly agree", etc., is a joint promise.

---

1. Bills of Exchange Act 1882, s. 83.
2. Bills of Exchange Act 1882, s. 88.
3. *Ibid.*, s. 85.

There is no liability till delivery of the note, for until then the instrument is incomplete[4].

A holder of a demand note is treated as the holder in due course of it although more than a reasonable time has elapsed between its issue and its negotiation to him—it is not deemed to be overdue as a promissory note is treated as a continuing security; in this respect the law relating to bills and to notes differs[5].

Presentment for payment

Where a note is in the body of it made payable at a particular place it must be presented for payment at that place; in any other case presentment for payment is not necessary to make the maker liable; but presentment (within a reasonable time of the indorsement in the case of a demand note and on the third day of grace in the case of time notes) is always necessary to make the indorser liable. Further, presentment must be at the place specified in the body of the note, if any, to make the indorser liable[6]. A note is only made payable "in the body of it" if the stipulation is part of the actual terms of the contract made by the maker of the note; a memorandum indicating a place of payment is not sufficient to render presentation for payment necessary to render the maker liable.

In cases where presentment for payment is necessary, the Limitation Act will not commence to run until that has taken place[7].

Generally

Subject to the necessary modifications, the provisions of the Act as to bills apply to notes, except as above, and except those relating to:

1. Presentment for acceptance;
2. Acceptance;
3. Acceptance *suprà protest*:
4. Bills in a set.

And protest of a foreign note on dishonour is not necessary.

In applying such provisions to notes, the maker of the note corresponds to the acceptor of a bill, and the first indorser of a note corresponds to the drawer of an accepted bill payable to drawer's order[8].

III BANK NOTES

These are promissory notes issued by a banker, payable to bearer on demand. Their properties were considered in the leading case of

---

4. *Ibid.*, s. 84.
5. *Ibid.*, s. 86 (3); *Glasscock* v. *Balls* (1890), 24 Q. B. D. 13.
6. *Ibid.*, s. 87.
7. *Re British Trade Corporation*, [1932] All E. R. Rep. 671; [1932] 2 Ch. 1; and see *ante*, p. 99.
8. Bills of Exchange Act 1882, s. 89 (2).

Miller v. *Race*[9], where Lord MANSFIELD recognised them as negotiable instruments:

> "They are not goods, nor securities, nor documents for debts, nor are so esteemed; but are treated as money, as cash, in the ordinary course and transaction of business, by the general consent of mankind; which gives them the credit and currency of money, to all intents and purposes."

In a later case, DENMAN, J., said that Bank of England notes differ from ordinary promissory notes and notes of other banks in two important characteristics, viz., they are always payable to bearer without indorsement, and they are legal tender for the amounts represented by them. He did not consider that the ordinary rules relating to bills would of necessity relate to bank notes, though they do relate to promissory notes generally. For example, any alteration of a bank note makes it void as against the issuing bank irrespective of whether the alteration is apparent or not.

So also, in *Suffell* v. *Bank of England*[10], JESSELL, M.R., said:

> "A Bank of England note is not an ordinary commercial contract to pay money. It is, in one sense, a promissory note in terms, but no one can describe it as simply a promissory note. It is part of the currency of the country. It has long been made so by Act of Parliament"[11].

---

9. (1791), 1 Sm. L. C. (13th ed.) 524.
10. (1882), 9 Q. B. D. 555.
11. See at p. 563; and see remarks of BRETT, L.J., at p. 567. A Bank of England note is now legal tender for any amount, see *ante*, p. 77.

CHAPTER 17

Insurance

A. Introduction—Liability Insurance—Life Insurance—Fire Insurance

I INTRODUCTION

A contract of insurance is a contract either to indemnify against a loss which may arise upon the happening of some event, or to pay, on the happening of some event, a definite sum of money to the person insured. The instrument containing the contract to insure is called a *policy of insurance*, the person insured is called the *assured* or *insured*, and the persons who insure are called the *insurers* or, in the case of insurance provided by members of Lloyd's, *underwriters*.

There are many forms of this contract, for a man may agree to insure anything, from a pane of glass to his own life: but three forms of considerable importance are:

1. *Life Insurance*,
2. *Fire Insurance, and*
3. *Marine Insurance.*

These will be considered separately.

In *Carter* v. *Boehm*[1] Lord MANSFIELD said:

"Insurance is a contract on speculation";

and this being the case, it is frequently hard to distinguish a contract to insure from an ordinary wager. In *Godsall* v. *Boldero*[2], Lord ELLENBOROUGH said that insurance was in its nature a contract of indemnity, as distinguished from a contract by way of gaming or wagering. This means that it is not an agreement to pay money on the mere happening of a certain event, but to compensate the insured for any damage suffered owing to its occurrence. This statement, though true of marine and fire insurance, does not accurately describe the contract of life insurance; the latter is an engagement to pay a certain sum of money on the death of a person, and when once fixed it is constant and invariable[3].

Another distinction suggested is, that in the case of a wager, there

---

1. (1765), 1 Sm. L. C. (13th ed.) 546, 549.
2. (1807), 2 Sm. L. C. (13th ed.) 238, 245.
3. *Dalby* v. *India and London Life Assurance Co.* (1855), 15 C. B. 365; 2 Sm. L. C. (13th ed.), at p. 248.

is no interest except the interest provided by the stake, whereas in all insurance contracts such an interest must exist, *i.e.* there must be what is styled an *insurable interest.*

Principle of Indemnity

Apart from contracts of life assurance and accident or sickness insurances, all contracts of insurance are contracts of *indemnity, e.g.*

A insures a house against fire for £10,000; in course of time suppose the house to be burnt down; if £5,000 will restore it, that amount, and that amount only, can be obtained.

BRETT, L.J., said:

"The very foundation, in my opinion, of every rule which has been promulgated and acted on by the courts with regard to insurance law is this, viz., that the contract of insurance contained in a marine or fire policy is a contract of indemnity, and of indemnity only, and that this contract means that the assured, in case of a loss against which the policy has been made, shall be fully indemnified, but shall never be more than fully indemnified"[4].

Thus

A agreed to sell a house to B for £3,100, and had insured the premises against fire. Before completion of the contract to sell, the house was burnt, and the insurance company not having been informed of the contract of sale, paid the amount of damage; subsequently the purchase was completed, and the vendor obtained the full value agreed, and it was decided that the amount of the insurance money must be refunded to the company[5].

In giving judgment, BOWEN, L.J., said:

"What is really the interest of the vendors, the assured? Their insurable interest is this—they had insured against fire, and they had then contracted with the purchasers for the sale of the house, and, after the contract, but before completion, the fire occurred. Their interest, therefore, is that at law they are the legal owners, but their beneficial interest is that of vendors, with a lien for the unpaid purchase-money. That was decided in the case of *Collingridge* v. *Royal Exchange Assurance Corporation*[6]; but can they keep the whole, having lost only half? Surely it would be monstrous to say that they could keep the whole, having lost only

---

4. *Castellain* v. *Preston* (1883), 11 Q. B. D. 380, 386.
5. *Castellain* v. *Preston, supra.* But see now s. 47 of the Law of Property Act 1925 (*post*, p. 294), as to the right of a purchaser in such cases to receive the insurance money on completion. This change in the law does not affect the principle illustrated in the text.
6. (1878), 3 Q. B. D. 173.

half. . . . They would be getting a windfall by the fire, their contract
of insurance would not be a contract against loss, it would be
a speculation for gain"[7].

Subrogation

In an indemnity contract, the insurer is entitled to every right of
the assured, or, as BRETT, L.J., says:

> "As between the underwriter, and the assured, the underwriter
> is entitled to the advantage of every right of the assured, whether
> such right consist in contract, fulfilled or unfulfilled, or in remedy
> for tort capable of being insisted on or already insisted on, or in
> any other right, whether by way of condition or otherwise, legal
> or equitable, which can be, or has been, exercised or has accrued,
> and whether such right could or could not be enforced by the
> insurer in the name of the assured by the exercise or acquiring
> of which right or condition the loss against which the assured is
> insured can be, or has been, diminished"[8].

This is called the *doctrine of subrogation*. It entitles the insurer who
pays the insured not only to the value of any benefit received by the
latter by way of compensation for actual loss, but also to the value of
any rights or remedies the insured may have against third parties in
respect of the damage. The doctrine applies not only to fire policies
but to all indemnity policies. Thus—

If A's servant negligently drives A's vehicle and injures B, A's
insurers after paying B can sue A's servant for damages for breach
of the contract of service[9].

If the insured renounces rights to which the insurer would be
subrogated, he is bound to make up the amount to the insurer. The
doctrine does not apply to non-indemnity insurance, *e.g.* life assurance
and personal accident insurance.

Uberrima fides

Contracts of insurance are *uberrimae fidei*, and therefore, the insured
owes a duty to disclose before the contract is made every material fact
of which he knows or ought to know. If a material fact is not so
disclosed, the insurers have the right at any time to avoid the contract.
Lord MANSFIELD said:

---

7. *Castellain* v. *Preston* (1883), 11 Q. B. D., at p. 401.
8. *Castellain* v. *Preston* (1883), 11 Q. B. D., at p. 388.
9. *Lister* v. *Romford Ice and Cold Storage Co., Ltd.*, [1957] 1 All E. R. 125;
   [1957] A. C. 555.

"Good faith forbids either party, by concealing what he privately knows, to draw the other into a bargain from his ignorance of that fact and his believing the contrary"[10];

and in these contracts the rule is strictly enforced, as the facts are generally within the knowledge of the insured alone. Life insurance stands on the same footing. In the case of *London Assurance Co. v. Mansel*[11], JESSEL, M.R., said:

"As regards the general principle, I am not prepared to lay down the law as making any difference in substance between one contract of assurance and another. Whether it is life, or fire, or marine insurance, I take it good faith is required in all cases, and though there may be certain circumstances, from the peculiar nature of marine insurance, which require to be disclosed, and which do not apply to other contracts of insurance, that is rather, in my opinion, an illustration of the application of the principle, than a distinction in principle."

It has now been settled that this principle applies to all contracts of insurance, *e.g.* a policy which covers the risk of a debtor becoming insolvent[12].

Every material fact must be disclosed. A fact is material if it would influence the judgment of a prudent insurer in deciding whether to accept the risk, and if so, at what premium. A material fact need not necessarily relate exclusively to the particular kind of risk. Thus, a fire policy may be avoided for non-disclosure of a previous refusal of motor-car insurance on grounds which affected the moral integrity of the proposer.

The duty to disclose continues up to the conclusion of the contract and covers any material alteration in the character of the risk which may take place between proposal and acceptance[13].

Insurers are also entitled to avoid liability under a policy where the insured, in the course of negotiations or in the proposal form for insurance, has made any fraudulent misstatement or has made an innocent misstatement of a material fact[14]. Moreover, if the policy contains a declaration that the proposal form constitutes the "basis of the contract", the insurers are entitled to avoid liability if any

10. Lord MANSFIELD, in *Carter v. Boehm* (1765), 1 Sm. L. C. (13th ed.), at p. 550.
11. (1879), 11 Ch. D. 363; and see *Lindenau v. Desborough* (1828), 8 B. & C. 586, 592.
12. *Seaton v. Heath*, [1899] 1 Q. B. 782; 4 Com. Cas. 193; reversed on the facts, *sub nom. Seaton v. Burnand*, [1900] A. C. 135; 5 Com. Cas. 198.
13. *Canning v. Farquhar* (1886), 16 Q. B. D. 727; *Looker v. Law Union, etc., Insurance Co.*, [1928] 1 K. B. 554.
14. *London Assurance v. Mansel* (1879), 11 Ch. D. 363.

answer in the proposal form is incorrect, irrespective of whether the insured made the answer fraudulently or innocently and irrespective of whether the answer relates to a material fact. Thus, in *Dawsons, Ltd.* v. *Bonnin*[15],

> the proposal form for the insurance of a lorry against fire required the proposer to state the full address at which the lorry would be garaged, and inadvertently the wrong address was inserted. A claim was made under the policy when the lorry was lost by fire. The House of Lords *held* that as the proposal form was clearly expressed by the terms of the policy to be "the basis of the contract", the answer in the proposal form amounted to a contractual promise as to its accuracy. Since the answer was not accurate the insurers had a right to avoid the policy for breach of warranty. It made no difference that the answer was not material, *i.e.* the premium would have been no different had the correct address been shown, nor that the inaccuracy was inadvertent.

II LIABILITY INSURANCE

One common type of insurance is against the liability which one may incur to third parties. A statutory obligation exists to take out such insurance in relation to the liability that may arise from the negligent driving of a motor vehicle and in respect of an employer's liability for injury to his employees but these are not the only kinds of liability insurance. It is, however, contrary to public policy for a claim to be allowed under a liability policy in respect of a deliberate unlawful act by the insured. In *Gray* v. *Barr*[16],

> B shot and killed G in a struggle. B was acquitted of murder and manslaughter but G's personal representatives sued B under the Fatal Accidents Acts and B sought an indemnity, in respect of such damages as he might be required to pay, under his accident liability policy. *Held:* B was not entitled to claim under the policy.

Where any person is entitled to claim from insurers in respect of liabilities which he may incur to third parties, then—

> if either before or after the events mentioned below any such liability is incurred by the person insured, his rights against the insurer are transferred to and vest in the third party to whom the liability was incurred.

---

15. [1922] All E. R. 88; [1922] A. C. 413.
16. [1971] 2 All E. R. 949; [1971] 2 Q. B. 554, C. A.

Such transfer of rights comes into operation

(i) if the person insured is an individual: when he becomes bankrupt, or makes a composition or arrangement with his creditors;

(ii) if the person insured is a company: when it goes into liquidation[17], or holders of any debentures secured by a floating charge appoint a receiver or manager of the company's business[18].

Thus, suppose a company has an insurance policy that covers its liability in negligence to members of the public up to £5,000 and someone injured by the company's negligence obtains judgment against the company for £8,000. If, before or after judgment, the company has gone into liquidation, the injured party can claim direct against the insurers for the amount of the policy, £5,000[19]. The insurers may rely on any defence which they could have raised against the insured, such as breach of a condition to give prompt notice of a claim[20] but may not claim a set off in respect of premiums due under the policy[21].

The Road Traffic Act 1972.—This Act compels users of motor vehicles to insure against any liability which may be incurred in respect of the death or bodily injury of any persons arising out of the use of the vehicle on the road. Insurers issuing policies to comply with such requirements of the Act must indemnify the persons or classes of persons specified in the policy (*e.g.* persons using the vehicle with the owner's consent) in respect of any liability which the policy purports to cover in the case of those persons or classes of persons[1]. Such persons have a direct right to sue the insurers notwithstanding the common law rule that only parties to a contract can enforce it[2].

Judgments against persons insured against such third-party risks covered by the terms of the policy must be satisfied by the insurer

---

17. This does not include voluntary liquidation merely for the purposes of reconstruction or amalgamation with another company.
18. Third Parties (Rights against Insurers) Act 1930.
19. No such claim could be made by the injured party against the insurers unless the *liability* of the company had been established, either in litigation or by arbitration or by agreement: *Post Office* v. *Norwich Union Fire Insurance Society, Ltd.*, [1968] 1 All E. R. 577; [1967] 2 Q. B. 363, C. A.
20. *Farrell* v. *Federated Employers Insurance Association*, [1970] 3 All E. R. 632; [1970] 1 W. L. R. 1400, C. A.
21. *Murray* v. *Legal and General Assurance Society*, [1969] 3 All E. R. 794; [1970] 2 Q. B. 495.
1. Road Traffic Act 1972, ss. 143, 148 (4). This Act consolidates earlier legislation. Compulsory insurance in respect of liability to third parties other than passengers has existed since 1930. The Motor Vehicles (Passenger Insurance) Act 1971 extended compulsory cover to passengers.
2. *Tattersall* v. *Drysdale*, [1935] All E. R. Rep. 112; [1935] 2 K. B. 174.

direct to the person(s) entitled to the benefit of the judgment but this liability does not attach to the insurer unless before or within 7 days after the commencement of the proceedings in which judgment was given he had notice of the bringing of the proceedings[3].

The rights so conferred on third parties are not effective unless and until the insurer has delivered a "certificate of insurance" to the assured[4].

If the policy is by its terms limited to the user of the vehicle in a particular way (*e.g.* user for private purposes only), then, if an accident happens while the vehicle is not being used in manner permitted by the policy, a third party who is injured cannot recover damages against the insurer. However, certain restrictions contained in a motor vehicle policy are of no effect as regards a person killed or injured, liability to whom is compulsorily insurable under the Road Traffic Act. Such restrictions include restrictions as to the age or physical or mental condition of the driver, the condition of the vehicle and the number of persons carried[5]. Similarly any condition in the policy relieving the insurers of liability, in the event of some specified thing being done or not being done *after* the accident, is of no effect as regards a person killed or injured, liability to whom is compulsorily insurable under the Act[6].

Sometimes a judgment is obtained against a motorist in respect of a liability required by the Road Traffic Act to be covered by a policy of insurance, but the judgment is unsatisfied. This may happen, for example, because no insurance policy was taken out or because the insurers have gone into liquidation. To meet these eventualities, the Motor Insurers' Bureau was set up in 1946 by the motor vehicle insurers who undertake to keep it in funds. By agreement with the Ministry who undertake to keep it in funds. By agreement with the Department of the Environment (the current agreement was made in 1971 and is published by H.M.S.O.) the Bureau will meet any such unsatisfied judgment provided that, where there is no insurance policy notice of proceedings is given to the Bureau before or within 7 days after the commencement of the proceedings. The Bureau will, however, not meet an unsatisfied judgment against a motorist unless it is in respect of a risk which was compulsorily insurable. The Court of Appeal held in *Hardy* v. *Motor Insurers Bureau*[7] that the Bureau was liable to

---

3. Road Traffic Act 1972, s. 149. In certain cases and subject to certain conditions the insurer may be relieved from liability when he has avoided or cancelled, or is entitled to avoid the policy (*ibid.*).
4. Road Traffic Act 1972, s. 147.
5. Road Traffic Act 1972, s. 148.
6. *Ibid.*, s. 206 (2).
7. [1964] 2 All E. R. 742; [1964] 2 Q. B. 745, C. A.

indemnify a man who had been deliberately injured by being dragged along the ground by the driver of an uninsured van. Insurance is compulsory in respect of "any liability" whether arising out of deliberate or negligent action.

Employers Liability (Compulsory Insurance) Act 1969.—This Act compels employers to insure against liability for bodily injury or disease sustained by his employees and arising in the course of their employment.

III LIFE ASSURANCE

Life assurance is

> "a contract by which the insurer, in consideration of a certain premium, either in a gross sum, or by annual payments, undertakes to pay to the person for whose benefit the insurance is made, a certain sum of money or annuity on the death of the person whose life is insured"[8].

To prevent gambling in these transactions, the Life Assurance Act 1774 was passed. This enacts that—

> 1. No insurance shall be made by any person or persons, bodies politic or corporate, on the life or lives of any other person or persons, wherein the person or persons for whose use, benefit, or on whose account such policies shall be made, shall have no interest (which means pecuniary interest) or by way of gaming or wagering; and every insurance made contrary to the true intent and meaning hereof shall be null and void to all intent and purposes[9];
> 2. The name of the person so interested, or for whose benefit the policy is made, shall be inserted in the policy[10];
> 3. In all cases where the insured has such an interest, no greater sum shall be recovered than the value of the interest at the date of the policy[11]. If, in the meantime, his interest ceases, he may yet recover at the death, it being essential that he should have his interest only at the date of the making of the policy[12].

It should further be observed that an assignee of a valid policy need not have an interest[13].

A person who has effected a policy on the life of another in which

---

8. Smith's Mercantile Law (13th ed.), p. 514.
9. Life Assurance Act 1774, s. 1.
10. *Ibid.*, s. 2. These requirements do not apply to an insurance against third-party risks under the Road Traffic Act 1972 (*Boss* v. *Kingston*, [1963] 1 All E. R. 177; [1963] 1 W. L. R. 99).
11. Life Assurance Act 1774, s. 3.
12. *Dalby* v. *India, etc., Co.* (1855), 2 Sm. L. C. (13th ed.) 246.
13. *Ashley* v. *Ashley* (1829), 3 Sim. 149.

he has no insurable interest cannot as a rule repudiate the policy and recover the premiums paid[14]; but he may do so if he was induced by the fraud of the insurers to believe that he was effecting a valid and legal policy, because in such case the parties are not *in pari delicto*[15].

Insurable interest

What is an insurable interest? It is difficult to describe, but the following illustrations will show what has been the opinion of the courts:

1. A creditor may insure the life of his debtor to the extent of his debt[16];
2. A trustee may insure in respect of the interest of which he is a trustee[17];
3. A wife may insure her husband[18];
4. A husband may insure his wife[19]; and
5. A man may insure himself;

but a father has not necessarily an insurable interest in the life of his son[20].

Alien enemies

Where a policy has been effected on the life of a person who subsequently becomes an alien enemy, the policy does not become void and the continued payment and receipt of premiums does not involve unlawful intercourse with an alien enemy, but in the event of the death of the assured the right of his executors to demand payment of the policy moneys is suspended during the war[1].

Suicide

In *Beresford* v. *Royal Insurance Co.*[2], a life policy expressly provided that it would be invalidated if the assured should die by his own hand whether sane or insane within one year from the date of the policy. The assured committed suicide while sane *after* one year had elapsed from the date of the policy. By implication from the express terms of the policy the policy moneys were payable but the House of Lords held that, since committing suicide while sane was a criminal offence, it was contrary to public policy to allow the moneys to be recovered.

---

14. *Harse* v. *Pearl Life Assurance Co.*, [1904] 1 K. B. 558.
15. *Hughes* v. *Liverpool Victoria, etc., Society*, [1916] 2 K. B. 482.
16. *Godsall* v. *Boldero* (1807), 2 Sm. L. C. (13th ed.) 238.
17. *Tidswell* v. *Ankerstein* (1792), Peake, 151.
18. *Reed* v. *Royal Exchange Assurance Co.* (1795), Peake, Add. Ca. 70.
19. *Griffiths* v. *Fleming*, [1909] 1 K. B. 805.
20. *Halford* v. *Kymer* (1830), 10 B. & C. 724.
1. *Seligman* v. *Eagle Insurance Co.*, [1917] 1 Ch. 519.
2. [1938] 2 All E. R. 602; [1938] A. C. 586.

Since the Suicide Act 1961, sane suicide is no longer a criminal offence but on the general principal of insurance law that no claim may be made on a policy when the assured deliberately brings about the event insured against, if similar facts occurred today the policy moneys may still not be recoverable. However an express term providing clearly that the moneys are payable even on a sane suicide would presumably prevail over the general principle.

Married women

By the Married Women's Property Act 1882, s. 11, it is provided that a married woman may effect a policy upon her own life, or upon the life of her husband, for her own benefit. Further, it provides that if a man or a married woman effect a policy[3] upon his or her own life, or on each other's lives, and the policy is expressed to be for the benefit of the other or for the benefit of the children, this shall create a trust[4], which, so long as any object of the trust remains unperformed, shall not form part of the insured's estate, nor be subject to the insured's debts. A policy effected by a husband simpliciter for the benefit of a named wife creates an immediate vested interest, and if the wife pre-deceases her husband the policy will pass to her executors as part of her estate[5]; but the husband is entitled to a lien on the policy moneys for premiums paid by him since his wife's death as being money expended by a trustee to preserve the property of a certain given trust[6]. If it be proved that the policy was effected, and the premiums paid to defraud the creditors of the insured, these will be entitled out of the moneys payable under the policy to a sum equal to the premiums paid.

Assignment of the policy

The Policies of Assurance Act 1867 provided for the legal assignment of a life policy before legal assignments of choses in action generally became possible under the Judicature Act 1873. The assignment must be in writing, either by endorsement on the policy or by a separate instrument, but:

    1. The assignee is liable to be defeated by defences which would have been good against the assignor[7];

---

3. This includes a policy providing for payment of money upon death by accident (*Re Gladitz*, [1937] 3 All E. R. 173).
4. Apart from the statute the person named as beneficiary would have no rights (*Cleaver* v. *Mutual Reserve Fund Life Association*, [1892] 1 Q. B. 147). See *ante*, p. 66.
5. *Cousins* v. *Sun Life Assurance Society*, [1932] All E. R. Rep 404; [1933] 1 Ch. 126.
6. *Re Smith's Estate*, [1937] 3 All E. R. 472; [1937] Ch. 636.
7. Policies of Assurance Act 1867, s. 2.

2. He should give written notice to the insurance company, for in the event of a second or further assignment, the priorities will depend upon the date of this notice; and further, any *bona fide* payment made by the company previous to such notice will be valid in favour of the company[8].

The company must specify on the policy the place of business at which such notices may be given, and upon receiving notice it must upon a written request and payment of a fee not exceeding five shillings acknowledge the receipt of it in writing[9]. An assignment is also effective at law if it complies with the provisions of the Law of Property Act, s. 136[10].

IV FIRE INSURANCE

Fire insurance is a contract, one party to which undertakes to indemnify the other against the consequence of a fire[11] happening within an agreed upon period, in return for the payment of money in a lump sum or by instalments. The insured must have an insurable interest in the premises or goods insured at the time of the loss[12], *i.e.* he must be in such a position that he incurs loss by the burning; thus:

1. A creditor may insure a house over which he has a mortgage[13];
2. A bailee may insure his customer's goods for the full value and, if loss occurs, he may retain so much of the policy moneys as would cover his own interest while being trustee for the owners in respect of the rest[14]. Alternatively a bailee may take out a policy which covers merely his own liability as bailee and it is a matter of construction which type of policy has been taken out.

---

8. *Ibid.*, s. 3.
9. Policies of Assurance Act 1867, ss. 4, 6.
10. See *ante*, p. 71.
11. "Fire" is not confined to fires started accidentally. The policy covers loss through accidentally putting articles into the grate (*Harris* v. *Poland*, [1941] 1 K. B. 462). There is a distinction between fire and an explosion although the latter involves combustion of gas which may have been ignited by a flash (*Boiler Inspection and Insurance Co. of Canada* v. *Sherwin-Williams Company of Canada, Ltd.*, [1951] A. C. 319, P. C., at p. 338).
12. The Life Assurance Act 1774 (see *ante*, p. 289) applies to insurances on buildings but not to insurances of "ships, goods or merchandise." It follows that an insurance on a building is only legal under the Act if the insured has an insurable interest in the building at the time of the contract *and*, by virtue of the principle of indemnity, at the time of the loss.
13. *Westminster Fire Office* v. *Glasgow Provident Investment Society* (1888), 13 App. Cas. 699.
14. *Waters* v. *Monarch Assurance Co.* (1856), 5 E. & B. 870; and *Hepburn* v. *A. Tomlinson (Hauliers), Ltd.*, [1966] 1 All E. R. 418; [1966] A. C. 451, H. L.

But a shareholder of an incorporated company, even though he may hold all the shares, has no insurable interest in the company's property; nor has an unsecured creditor such an interest[15].

A contract of fire insurance made by an agent without authority cannot be ratified by the principal after and with knowledge of the loss by fire of the subject-matter insured[16].

The contract being one of indemnity, only the amount of loss actually suffered can be recovered; this BOWEN, L.J., calls "the infallible rule"[17]. But the parties may agree beforehand the value of the premises or goods insured. And in the absence of fraud the agreement will be binding. Thus in *Elcock* v. *Thomson*[18]:

> Premises were insured in 1940 and it was agreed that £106,850 was the true value and that in the event of loss the property would be assumed to be of such value and would be assessed accordingly. A fire occurred in 1947 and it was found that immediately before the fire the real value of the premises was £18,000 and immediately after the fire it was £12,600.
>
> It was held that estimate was binding on the insurers and, as the real value of the premises had been depreciated by 30 per cent, the insurers were liable to pay 30 per cent of £106,850.

"Subject to average" clause

Where fire causes only partial loss to premises or goods, the general rule is that the insured is entitled to the full cost of repairs, provided that comes within the total amount covered by the policy. However, if the policy contains a "subject to average" clause and the property is under-insured, the insurers are only liable for that proportion of the actual loss which the sum insured bears to the value of the property[19].

Reinstatement

By the Fires Prevention (Metropolis) Act 1774, s. 83, it is provided that any interested person may procure that the insurance money shall be laid out in rebuilding the premises, but a clear and unambiguous request to the insurance company to rebuild should be made. This right is of general and not merely of local application to the Metropolis, and a judgment creditor of the person insured who seeks to attach the insurance moneys cannot deprive a person interested of his right to

---

15. *Macaura* v. *Northern Assurance Co.*, [1925] A. C. 619.
16. *Grover and Grover* v. *Matthews*, [1910] 2 K. B. 401. This rule does not apply to contracts of marine insurance. See *post*, p. 295.
17. *Castellain* v. *Preston* (1883), 11 Q. B. D., at p. 401. See also *ante*, p. 283, where the facts of the case are set out and the application of this principle generally to contracts of insurance is discussed.
18. [1949] 2 All E. R. 381.
19. *Acme Wood Flooring Co., Ltd.* v. *Marten* (1904), 90 L. T. 313.

have the moneys expended in rebuilding[20]. Instead of rebuilding the place themselves, the insurers may permit the parties claiming the money to do so upon sufficient security being given that the money shall be laid out in such rebuilding[1].

Assignment and transferability of policies

The right to receive the proceeds under a fire policy (or any other policy) is assignable, but in the case of a fire policy, being an indemnity policy, the assignee may only claim if the insured still has an insurable interest in the property at the time of loss.

Although the right to receive the proceeds under a fire policy is assignable, the policy cannot itself be transferred so that it attaches to different property or so that there is a different insured person *unless* the insurers consent. If, therefore, A sells property to B, any purported transfer by A to B of his fire policy on the premises can only be effective if the insurers consent. However, if insurance money becomes payable to a vendor in respect of damage to or destruction of property between the date of the contract of sale and the completion of the purchase, the money when received by the vendor must be paid to the purchaser on or after completion, subject to any stipulation to the contrary and any requisite consent of the insurers. The purchaser must pay the proportionate part of the premium from the date of the contract[2].

---

20. *Sinnott* v. *Bowden,* [1912] 2 Ch. 414.
1. See *Westminster Fire Office* v. *Glasgow Provident Investment Society* (1888), 13 App. Cas. 699.
2. Law of Property Act 1925, s. 47. Apart from the section the benefit of the insurance does not run with the property. See *Rayner* v. *Preston* (1881), 18 Ch. D. 1, and *ante,* p. 283.

CHAPTER 18

Insurance

B. Marine Insurance

I INTRODUCTION

The law relating to marine insurance was codified by the Marine Insurance Act 1906. It is unnecessary, therefore, to cite earlier cases as authorities for propositions of law laid down in the Act but some are referred to for purposes of illustration where the scope and meaning of a section in the Act are not at first sight apparent.

Marine insurance is a contract whereby the insurer undertakes to indemnify the assured in the manner and to the extent thereby agreed, against marine losses, that is to say, the losses incident to marine adventure[1]. The person who is indemnified is called the *"assured"*, or the *"insured"*, the other party being styled the *"insurer"* or the *"underwriter"*.

The policy may be so extended as to protect the assured against losses on inland waters or on any land risk which may be incidental to a sea voyage[2].

The contract is generally entered into through the agency of brokers, who are responsible to the underwriters for the premium[3], and the mode of contracting and the various details are largely determined by the custom of the different associations whose members are engaged in this particular kind of transaction.

All persons who have insurable interests may be insured, unless they are alien enemies[4], and any companies or persons not under disability may be insurers.

Amongst subject-matters of marine insurance may be named the ship, the goods connected therewith, the cargo, freight, money lent on bottomry, etc.; but as in other contracts, so in marine insurance, there can be no valid agreements with regard to illegal trading.

Assignment of policy

When a person has insured his interest in any vessel, cargo, or freight,

---

1. Marine Insurance Act 1906, s. 1. See *post*, p. 296, for the statutory definition of a "marine adventure".
2. *Ibid.*, s. 2 (1).
3. See *ante*, p. 146.
4. *Brandon* v. *Nesbitt* (1794), 6 T. R. 23.

he may assign his policy to another, unless the terms of the policy forbid it, and that other may sue in his own name, but is liable to be met by the same defences as would have been valid against the original assured; *e.g.*

that the policy is void through the non-disclosure of material facts by the assignor[5].

The policy may be assigned either before or after loss[6]. An assured who has no interest cannot assign; but this rule does not affect the assignment of a policy after loss[7]. An assignment can be made by indorsement, or in other customary manner[6].

II INSURABLE INTEREST

A person has an insurable interest when he is interested in a marine adventure, and in particular where he stands in any legal or equitable relation to the adventure or to an insurable property[8] at risk therein, in consequence of which he may benefit by the safety or due arrival of insurable property, or may be prejudiced by its loss, damage, or detention, or may incur liability in respect thereof[9].

There is a *marine adventure* where insurable property[8] is exposed to maritime perils, or where the earning of freight, etc., or the security for advances is endangered by the exposure of insurable property to maritime perils, or where any liability is incurred by a person interested in or responsible for insurable property, by reason of maritime perils. *Maritime perils* means the perils consequent on, or incidental to, the navigation of the sea, that is to say, perils of the sea, fire, war perils, pirates, rovers, thieves, captures, seizures, restraints and detainments of princes and peoples, jettison, barratry, and any other perils, either of the like kind or which may be designated by the policy[10].

The assured must be interested in the subject-matter insured at the time of the loss though he need not have more than an expectation of an interest when the insurance is effected and if the goods are insured, "lost or not lost", the policy is valid although the property may already be lost at the time the policy is effected, unless at the time of effecting the insurance, the assured was aware of the loss and the insurer was not[11]. Defeasible and contingent interests are insurable, and so is a partial interest of any nature[12].

---

5. *W. Pickersgill & Sons* v. *London and Provincial, etc., Insurance Co.*, [1912] 3 K. B. 614.
6. Marine Insurance Act 1906, s. 50.
7. *Ibid.*, s. 51.
8. Ship, goods or other movables (*ibid.*, s. 3 (2) (a)).
9. *Ibid.*, s. 5.
10. Marine Insurance Act 1906, s. 3 (2).
11. *Ibid.*, s. 6.   12. *Ibid.*, ss. 7, 8.

The following are examples of persons having an insurable interest:

1. Shipowners and owners of goods—to the extent of the value of their interest[13].
2. A mortgagee—to the extent of the sum due to him[14].
3. A mortgagor—to the full value of the property[14].
4. An insurer—who may reinsure to the extent of his liability[15].
5. A bottomry bondholder—to the extent of the amount payable to him under the bond[16].
6. A person who has advanced money for the ship's necessaries[17].
7. A person advancing freight—if such freight is not repayable in case of loss[18].
8. The master and crew may insure their wages[19].

An assignment of the interest of the assured in the subject-matter insured, does not, in the absence of express or implied agreement, transfer the rights of the assured under the policy[20].

Gambling Policies

Where the assured has no insurable interest and no expectation of acquiring such an interest at the time of the contract, the policy is void. So are policies made:

1. "Interest or no interest", or
2. "Without further proof of interest than the policy itself", or
3. Policies made "without benefit of salvage to the insurer", except in cases where there is no possibility of salvage[1].

A policy containing a P. P. I. clause (policy proof of interest) is rendered void by s. 4 (2)(b), even though the assured had an insurable interest when the policy was signed and issued[2]. A slip attached to a policy containing such a clause, which the assured is expressly permitted to detach and which he does detach, remains none the less part of the policy and makes it void[3].

Gambling on loss by maritime perils is an offence punishable by fine or imprisonment. The prohibition extends to:

---

13. *Ibid.*, s. 14 (3). On a sale "ex ship" the purchaser has no insurable interest "upon goods" until they have been delivered to him (*Yangtsze Insurance Association* v. *Lukmanjee*, [1918] A. C. 585). See *ante*, p. 216.
14. *Ibid.*, s. 14 (1).   15. *Ibid.*, s. 9.
16. *Ibid.*, s. 10. Bottomry is a pledge of the ship or the ship and cargo. See *post*, p. 423.
17. *Moran & Co.* v. *Uzielli*, [1905] 2 K. B. 555.
18. Marine Insurance Act 1906, s. 12.
19. *Ibid.*, s. 11.   20. *Ibid.*, s. 15.
1. Marine Insurance Act 1906, s. 4.
2. *Cheshire & Co.* v. *Vaughan Bros. & Co.*, [1920] 3 K. B. 240; *John Edwards & Co.* v. *Motor Union Assurance Co.*, [1922] 2 K. B. 249.
3. *Re London County Commercial Re-insurance Office*, [1922] 2 Ch. 67.

1. Contracts made by a person without having any *bona fide*
    interest in the safe arrival of the ship or the safety of the
    subject-matter insured, or a *bona fide* expectation of acquiring
    such an interest, and
2. To contracts made by any person in the employment of the
    shipowner (not being a part owner) where the contract is
    made—
    (i) "Interest or no interest", or
    (ii) "Without further proof of interest than the policy
         itself", or
    (iii) "Without benefit of salvage to the insurer", or
    (iv) Subject to any like term.

Any broker through whom and any insurer with whom such a contract has been effected is also guilty of an offence, if he knew
the nature of the contract[4].

III DISCLOSURE AND REPRESENTATIONS

A contract of marine insurance requires the utmost good faith,
and if that be not observed by either party, the other party may avoid
the contract[5].

It is the duty of the person intending to insure to communicate to
the insurer every circumstance known to him or which in the ordinary
course of business he ought to know, which is material to the risk,
that is, every circumstance which would influence the judgment of a
prudent insurer in fixing the premium, or determining whether he
will take the risk[6].

The obligation to disclose extends to communications made to, or
information received by the assured[6]. Thus:

1. He must communicate news tending to show that a vessel is
    overdue,
2. That it is damaged,
3. That it is lost[7],
4. That goods have already been damaged so as to increase the
    risk[8].

But there is no need to communicate circumstances which diminish the
risk or knowledge which the underwriters are likely to know, such as:

1. General trade customs,

---

4. Marine Insurance (Gambling Policies) Act 1909.
5. Marine Insurance Act 1906, s. 17.
6. *Ibid.*, s. 18; and see *Associated Oil Carriers, Ltd.* v. *Union Insurance Society*,
   [1917] 2 K. B. 184.
7. *Gladstone* v. *King* (1813), 1 M. & S. 35.
8. *Greenhill* v. *Federal Insurance Co.*, [1927] 1 K. B. 65. See also s. 18.

2. Speculations as to war,
3. Tempest, etc.,

nor need the intending assured disclose his opinion on matters relating to the adventure[9]; or any circumstance as to which information is waived by the insurer[10].

A principal is deemed also to know, and to be bound by the non-communication of, circumstances within the knowledge, or which in the ordinary course of business ought to be within the knowledge of his agent[11]. LINDLEY, L.J., said:

> "It is a condition of the contract that there is no misrepresentation or concealment, either by the assured or by any one who ought as a matter of business and fair dealing to have stated or disclosed the facts to him, or to the underwriter for him"[12].

But this must not be carried too far. Lord WATSON says[13]:

> "The responsibility of an innocent insured for the non-communication of facts which happen to be within the private knowledge of persons whom he merely employs to obtain an insurance upon a particular risk, ought not to be carried beyond the person who actually makes the contract on his behalf."

Similarly, every material representation made by the assured or his agent during the negotiations for, and before the conclusion of, the contract must be true, or the insurer may avoid the policy. A representation may be of fact, of expectation, or of belief. It is sufficient if a representation of fact be substantially correct, and if a representation of expectation or belief be made in good faith[14].

IV THE POLICY

A marine policy must be signed by or on behalf of the insurer and it must specify the name of the assured or of some person who effects the policy on his behalf. Where the insurer is a corporation, the policy *may* be under seal[15].

The slip

It is customary to draw up a memorandum of the terms, which is initialled by the underwriters before the execution of the formal

---

9. *Carter* v. *Boehm* (1765), 1 Sm. L. C. (13th ed.) 546.
10. Marine Insurance Act 1906, s. 18 (3).
11. *Ibid.*, s. 19.
12. *Blackburn* v. *Vigors* (1886), 17 Q. B. D. 578.
13. *Blackburn* v. *Vigors* (1887), 12 App. Cas. 531, where the point was fully considered; and see *Blackburn* v. *Haslam* (1888), 21 Q. B. D. 144.
14. Marine Insurance Act 1906, s. 20.
15. *Ibid.*, ss. 23, 24.

policy, and the general practice of the commercial community is to recognise this memorandum (called *The Slip*) as though it were the contract; reference may be made to the slip for the purpose of showing when the proposal was accepted, that being the date when the contract is deemed to be concluded[16]. The initialling of the slip creates a contract to enter into a policy[17].

Kinds of Marine Policies

Among the most important divisions is that into—

1. *Valued policies* which specify the agreed value of the subject-matter insured[18].
2. *Unvalued policies*, which do not state the value of the subject-matter of the insurance; hence, after a loss, the amount to be paid by the underwriter remains a matter of assessment, subject to the limit of the sum insured[19].

Policies may also be divided into:

3. *Voyage policies*, which cover the subject-matter "at and from" or from one place to another or others.
4. *Time policies* covering the subject-matter during a specified period[1].
5. *Mixed policies.*—A time policy in which the voyage also is specified, is styled a mixed policy, *e.g.* A to X for six months[2].
6. *Floating policies* which describe the insurance in general terms, and leave the name of the ship or ships and other particulars to be defined by subsequent declaration[3].

As a general rule, the name of the ship must be stated accurately in the policy, but when cargo is insured under a floating policy and the ship in which it is to go is at the time of insuring not yet determined, the name of the ship may be communicated later by indorsement on the policy or in other customary manner. In such cases the insured should declare the shipment and the value of it as soon as he knows of it, and the policy attaches to the goods in the order in which they are shipped. Unless otherwise agreed, where a declaration of value is

---

16. Marine Insurance Act 1906, ss. 21 (as amended by Finance Act 1959, s. 37, Sch. VIII), 89.
17. *Fisher* v. *Liverpool Marine Insurance Co.* (1874), L. R. 9 Q. B. 418. This will not apply to the case of a fire policy (*Thompson* v. *Adams* (1889), 23 Q. B. D. 361).
18. Marine Insurance Act 1906, s. 27. See *post*, p. 305.
19. *Ibid.*, s. 28.
1. Time limits on such policies were removed by Finance Act 1959, ss. 30, 37, Sch. VIII.
2. Marine Insurance Act 1906, s. 25.
3. *Ibid.*, s. 29.

not made until after notice of loss or arrival, the policy must be treated as unvalued.

Form of Marine Policy

The policy may be in print or writing, or partly written and partly printed. The form set out below is known as Lloyd's S. G. policy, and is the form of policy scheduled to the Marine Insurance Act 1906. The notes which follow will, it is hoped, elucidate it. It should be noted that the words or clauses appearing in black type in the following form are those commented upon hereafter.

S. G.

£——

BE IT KNOWN THAT *A and or as Agent* **as well in** *his* **own name** as for and in the name and names of all and every other person or persons to whom the same doth, may, or shall appertain, in part or in all doth make assurance and cause *himself* and them, and every of them, to be insured (1), **lost or not lost** (2) **at and from** (3) *London*. Upon any kind of goods and merchandises, and also upon the body, tackle, apparel, ordnance, munition, artillery, boat, and other furniture, of and in the good ship or vessel called the *Mary*, whereof is master under God, for this present voyage, *John Smith*, or whosoever else shall go for master in the said ship, or by whatsoever other name or names the said ship, or the master thereof, is or shall be named or called; **beginning the adventure upon the said goods** and merchandises from the loading thereof aboard the said ship (3)   upon the said ship, etc.   and so shall continue and endure, during her abode there, upon the said ship, etc.; and further, until the said ship, with all her ordnance, tackle, apparel, etc., and goods and merchandises whatsoever shall be arrived at *Melbourne* upon the said ship, etc., **until she hath moored** at anchor twenty-four hours in good safety (4); and upon the goods and merchandises, **until the same be there discharged** and safely landed (5). And it shall be lawful for the said ship, etc., in this voyage, **to proceed and sail to and touch and stay** (6) at any ports or places whatsoever *on the West Coast of Africa* without prejudice to this insurance. The said ship, etc., goods and merchandises, etc., for so much as concerns the assured, by agreement between the assured and assurers in this policy, are and **shall be valued at** (7).

Touching the adventures and **perils** which we, the assurers, are contented to bear and do take upon us in this voyage: they are **of the seas** (8), men of war, **fire** (9), enemies, **pirates** (10), rovers, **thieves** (11), **jettisons** (12), letters of mart and countermart, surprisals, **takings at sea, arrests, restraints, and detainments of all kings, princes, and people** (13) of what nation, condition, or quality soever, **barratry** (14) **of the master and mariners,** and of **all other perils** (15), losses, and misfortunes, that have or shall come to the hurt, detriment, or damage of the said goods and merchandises and ship, etc., or any part thereof; And **in case of any loss or misfortune** it shall be lawful to the assured, their factors, servants and assigns, to sue, labour, and travel for, in and about the defence, safeguards, and recovery of the said goods and merchandises, and ship, etc., or any part thereof, without prejudice to this insurance; to the charges whereof we, the assurers, will contribute each one according to the rate and quantity of his sum herein assured (16). And it is expressly declared and agreed that no acts of the insurer or insured in recovering, saving or preserving the property insured, shall be considered as a **waiver, or acceptance of abandonment** (16). And it is agreed by us, the insurers, that this writing or policy of assurance shall be of as much force and effect as the surest writing or policy of assurance heretofore made in Lombard Street, or in the Royal Exchange, or elsewhere in London. **And so we, the assurers,** are contented, and do hereby promise and bind ourselves, each one for his own part, our heirs, executors, and goods to the assured, their executors, administrators, and assigns, for the true performance of the premises (17), **confessing ourselves paid** the consideration (18) due unto us for this assurance by the assured, at and after the rate of

IN WITNESS whereof we, the assurers, have subscribed our names and sums assured in *London*.

N.B.—Corn, fish, salt, fruit, flour, and seed are warranted free from average, unless general, or the ship be stranded; sugar, tobacco, hemp, flax, hides, and skins are warranted free from average under five pounds per cent; and all other goods, also the ship and freight, are warranted free from average, under three pounds per cent, unless general, or the ship be stranded (19).

Notes on the above Form of Policy

1. **"As well in his own name".** etc.—The words of the policy are sufficient to protect all persons who possessed an insurable interest at the time of the insurance or acquire one during the risk; and under them a person interested, who did not authorise an insurance to be effected for him, may subsequently, even after the loss, adopt and claim the benefit of the insurance[4].

But it is not enough that the person claiming the benefit of the policy should be within the description of those insured, if the person effecting the policy did not in fact intend to insure on his behalf[5].

---

4. Marine Insurance Act 1906, s. 86.
5. *Boston Fruit Co.* v. *British and Marine Insurance Co.*, [1906] A. C. 336.

2. **"Lost or not lost".**—The words cover the assured, although the subject-matter of the insurance has been partially or entirely lost at the conclusion of the contract of insurance unless the assured was aware of the loss and the insurer was not[6]. They also entitle the underwriter to his premium although the subject-matter has actually arrived safely at the time when the contract was concluded unless at such time the insurer knew of the safe arrival[7].

3. **"At and from". "Beginning the adventure on the said goods",** etc.—These are the words which determine the time from which the insurer is at risk. If the ship is insured "from" a place, the insurer's risk dates from the time when she starts on the voyage insured[8]; if she is insured "at and from", the risk dates from the time when the contract is concluded, if at that time she is in safety at that place; otherwise, the risk commences from the time she arrives in good safety at that place[9]. If freight is insured the risk, under the words "at and from", attaches immediately the ship is in good safety at that place, provided that the freight is chartered freight, otherwise it usually attaches *pro rata* as the cargo is loaded[10].

Whether the ship is insured "at" or "at and from" it is an implied condition that she shall commence the venture within a reasonable time unless the delay was caused by circumstances known to the insurer before the conclusion of the contract, or the insurer has waived the condition[11]. If a place of departure is mentioned, no risk will attach to the underwriter if the ship does not sail from that place[12].

The insurer's risk on goods insured "from the loading thereof" does not attach until they are on board, the risk during transit from shore to the ship is on their owner[13]. To meet this and the case of loss whilst unloading, a clause is often put in the margin of the policy to the following effect:

"including all risk of craft to and from the vessel."

4. and 5. **"Until she hath moored",** etc. **"Until the same be there discharged",** etc.—These words are intended to fix the date of cessation of the insurer's risk. Where the risk on goods continues until they are "safely landed", they must be landed in the customary manner and within a reasonable time after arrival at the port of discharge, and if they are not so landed the risk ceases[14]. So, if it is

---

6. Marine Insurance Act 1906, Sched. I, r. 1.
7. *Ibid.*, s. 84 (3) (b).
8. *Ibid.*, Sched. I, r. 2.
9. *Ibid.*, Sched. I, r. 3 (a), (b).
10. *Ibid.*, Sched. I, r. 3 (c), (d).
11. Marine Insurance Act 1906, s. 42.
12. *Ibid.*, s. 43.
13. *Ibid.*, Sched. I, r. 4.
14. *Ibid.*, Sched. I, r. 5.

customary at the port to land the goods by means of lighters, the risk continues until the goods are safely landed after transport in the lighters[15].

6. "To proceed and sail to and touch and stay", etc.—It is the duty of the assured not to deviate, that is to say, not to go out of the proper course, as agreed or as prescribed by custom, between the termini of the voyage.

Deviation, without lawful excuse, entitles the underwriter to avoid the policy, even though the ship has regained her course before any loss occurs, and the risk was not increased by such deviation[16]. But a mere intention to deviate which is not carried into effect will not discharge the insurer from his liability[17].

Deviation is excused if:

   (i) specially authorised by the policy, or
  (ii) if caused by circumstances beyond the control of the master or his employer, or
 (iii) if reasonably necessary to comply with a warranty; or
 (iv) to ensure the safety of the ship, or
  (v) to save human life; or
 (vi) to obtain medical or surgical aid for any person on board, or
(vii) if caused by barratrous conduct of master or crew, if barratry be a peril insured against[18].

But a deviation for the mere purpose of saving property is not justifiable[19].

The words quoted at the head of this note authorise the subject of insurance to proceed to and stay at certain ports mentioned in the policy, but not even to stay at such ports may the ship deviate from the voyage; she may touch and stay at them in the course of the voyage from the port of departure to the port of destination[20]. Thus, liberty given to a ship insured on a voyage from London to Plymouth to touch at any port in the English Channel will not excuse a call at Penzance, this last-named port being beyond the voyage in question, but it would allow a call at Newhaven in Sussex.

If after the commencement of the risk the destination of the ship is voluntarily changed from that contemplated by the policy there is said to be a change of voyage, and not a mere deviation, and is not

---

15. *Hurry* v. *Royal Exchange Co.* (1801), 2 Bos. & P. 430.
16. Marine Insurance Act 1906, s. 46.
17. *Ibid.*, s. 46 (3).
18. Marine Insurance Act 1906, s. 46. "Barratry" includes every wrongful act wilfully committed by the master or crew to the prejudice of the owner, or as the case may be, the charterer: *ibid.*, Sched. I, r. 11.
19. *Scaramanga* v. *Stamp* (1880), 5 C. P. D. 295. But see the Carriage of Goods by Sea Act 1924, *post*, p. 363.
20. Marine Insurance Act 1906, Sched. I, r. 6.

authorised by the clause now being considered[1]. Where there is a change of voyage, the insurer is discharged from the time when the determination to change is manifested, even though the ship be lost before she has actually changed the course of the voyage for which the insurance was effected[2].

Where the destination is specified and the ship sails for a different destination, the risk does not attach[3].

The voyage must be prosecuted with reasonable diligence, and unjustifiable delay will discharge the insurer[4]. The reason is that—

"the voyage commenced after an unreasonable interval of time would have become a voyage at a different period of the year, at a more advanced age of the ship, and, in short, a different voyage than if it had been prosecuted with proper and ordinary diligence; that is, the risk would have been altered from that which was intended"[5].

Circumstances which excuse deviation will also excuse delay[6].

7. **"Shall be valued at"**, etc.—The value of the subject-matter as stated is accepted for the purposes of assessing compensation when a loss has happened as the true value, and is conclusive between the insurers and the assured except for the purpose of determining whether there has been a constructive total loss[7]; unless there is evidence that the amount fixed was fraudulently stated, or intended by both parties as a mere wager. It has been stated that:

"An exorbitant valuation may be evidence of fraud, but when the valuation is *bona fide*, the valuation agreed upon is binding"[8].

The effect of a valued policy may be illustrated by the case of *Balmoral Company (S.S.) v. Marten*[9].

The defendant in that case insured a ship valued in the policy at £33,000. The ship incurred salvage expenses and a general average loss. In the salvage action the real value of the ship was proved to be £40,000, and in the average statement the rights of the parties were adjusted upon the footing that £40,000 was the contributory value of the ship. The insurers were held liable to make good to the owners only 33-40ths of the salvage and general

---

1. *Ibid.*, s. 45 (1).
2. *Ibid.*, s. 45 (2).
3. *Ibid.*, s. 44.
4. *Ibid.*, s. 48.
5. *Mount v. Larkins* (1832), 8 Bing. 122, *per* TINDAL, C.J.
6. Marine Insurance Act 1906, s. 49. See *ante*, p. 304.
7. *Ibid.*, s. 27.
8. BOVILL, C.J., in *Barker v. Janson* (1868), L. R. 3 C. P. 306. See also *The Main*, [1894] P. 320.
9. [1902] A. C. 511; 7 Com. Cas. 292.

average losses; that is, to pay in the proportion of the insured value to the contributory or salvage value.

8. "Perils . . . of the seas".—The clause in which these words occur defines the various dangers against loss in connection with which the insurers agree to indemnify the assured. The term "perils of the seas" refers only to fortuitous accidents or casualties of the seas, and does not include the ordinary action of the winds and waves[10]. The indemnity is against accidents which may happen, not against events which must happen; nor need the loss be occasioned by extraordinary violence of the winds or waves. If a vessel strikes upon a sunken rock in fair weather and sinks, this is a loss by perils of the sea. And a loss by foundering, owing to a vessel coming into collision with another vessel, even when the collision results from the negligence of that other vessel, falls within the same category[11].

A loss brought about by negligent navigation will be covered, if that which immediately caused the loss was a peril of the sea, even if the negligence is that of the assured himself, so long as it does not amount to wilful misconduct[12]. Damage done by rats to a vessel which prevents her from sailing is not a peril of the sea; but if in consequence of the ravages of rats sea water enters the ship and damages the cargo, there is a loss by a peril of the seas[13]. The burden of proving, on a balance of probabilities, that loss has occurred by perils of the sea lies on the assured[14].

The case of *The Inchmaree*[15] should be noted.

> In that case a vessel was lying at anchor off the shore, about to proceed on her voyage; the boilers were being filled by means of a donkey-engine; owing to a failure on the part of somebody on board to see that a certain valve was open, the valve remained closed, and consequently, in the operation of pumping, water was forced back, split the air chamber, and disabled the pump.

The House of Lords decided that the damage was not caused by

---

10. Marine Insurance Act 1906, Sched. I, r. 7. Under perils of the seas are comprehended winds, waves, lightning, rocks, shoals, collisions, and in general all causes of loss and damage to the property insured, arising from the elements, and inevitable accidents, other than those of capture and detention. See *The Stranna*, [1938] P. 69, where the meaning of the term was fully considered.
11. *The Xantho* (1887), 12 App. Cas. at p. 509, *per* Lord HERSCHELL.
12. *Trinder & Co.* v. *Thames, etc., Marine Insurance Co.*, [1898] 2 Q. B. 114; 3 Com. Cas. 123.
13. *Hamilton* v. *Pandorf* (1887), 12 App. Cas. 518; *cf. E. D. Sassoon* v. *Western Assurance Co.*, [1912] A. C. 561.
14. *Compania Nairera Santi S.A.* v. *Indemnity Marine Insurance Co., Ltd.*, [1960] 2 Lloyd's Rep. 469.
15. *Thames and Mersey Marine Insurance Co.* v. *Hamilton, Fraser & Co.* (1887), 12 App. Cas. 484.

"perils of the seas", nor by any cause similar to "perils of the seas", and that the insurers were not liable on the policy.

In consequence of this decision a special clause—styled *The Inchmarree* clause—is now usually added to the policy. It covers (amongst other things):

   (i) certain losses caused by the negligence of master, mariners, engineers, and pilots, or
   (ii) through explosives, etc., or
   (iii) any latent defect in the machinery or hull.

But the operation of the clause must be confined to the specific causes of loss enumerated, and not extended to matters *ejusdem generis*.

Thus, the clause has been held not to cover damage caused to the hull of a ship by a boiler falling into the hold while it was being lowered by a floating steam crane of which the tackle was defective[16].

9. "Fire".—The peril insured against is not merely unintentional burning; for instance, a fire voluntarily caused in order to avoid capture by an enemy is covered by the policy[17]; or a fire intentionally caused by a person other than the assured[18]. Of course, no claim may be made in respect of a fire deliberately caused by the assured, but once it is shown that the loss has been caused by fire, the plaintiff has made out a *prima facie* case and the onus lies upon the defendant to show on a balance of probabilities that the fire was caused by or connived at by the plaintiff. If the court determines that the loss is equally consistent with arson as it is with an accidental fire, the plaintiff would win on that issue[19]. A policy on goods will not cover any loss caused by a fire resulting from the condition in which they were shipped[20].

10. "Pirates".—The term includes passengers who mutiny and rioters who attack the ship from the shore[1]. But the expression must be construed in its popular sense as meaning persons who plunder indiscriminately for private gain and not persons who seize property for some public political end[2].

---

16. *Stott (Baltic) Steamers, Ltd.* v. *Marten*, [1916] 1 A. C. 304
17. *Gordon* v. *Rimmington* (1807), 1 Camp. 123.
18. *Midland Insurance Co.* v. *Smith* (1881), 6 Q. B. D. 561.
19. *Slattery* v. *Mance*, [1962] 1 All E. R. 525; [1962] 1 Q. B. 676.
20. *Boyd* v. *Dubois* (1811), 3 Camp. 133. It follows that generally it is not necessary for the insured to disclose information relating to their condition. However, the previous history or condition of goods may in certain circumstances be a material fact which ought to be disclosed: *Greenhill* v. *Federal Insurance Co.*, [1927] 1 K. B. 65, disapproving a dictum of Lord ELLENBOROUGH in *Boyd* v. *Dubois*.
 1. Marine Insurance Act 1906, Sched. I, r. 8.
 2. *Republic of Bolivia* v. *Indemnity Mutual Marine Assurance Co.*, [1909] 1 K. B. 785.

11. **"Thieves".**—Clandestine theft, or theft committed by any of the crew or passengers, is not included in the term "thieves" as used in this clause of the policy[3].

12. **"Jettisons".**—This means the throwing overboard of tackle or cargo to lighten the ship *bona fide* and in an emergency. As a rule the insurer is not liable to indemnify the owner of the goods if they were being carried on deck or in deck houses; but custom of the trade or express agreement may throw the loss on the insurer[4].

13. **"Takings at Sea, Arrests, restraints, etc. . . . of kings, princes, and people".**—This includes political or executive acts, such as capture in time of war by an enemy, stoppage of neutral vessels suspected of carrying enemy goods, embargo in time of peace, etc.[5]. A declaration of war by Her Majesty which renders the further prosecution of a voyage to an enemy port unlawful is a restraint of princes, although the assured may voluntarily abandon the adventure[6]. Thus in *Rickards* v. *Forestal Land, Timber and Rail. Co.*[7]

> British subjects shipped goods in German vessels to various ports. The goods were insured by the appellants. Shortly before the outbreak of war the German government ordered all German vessels to put in at a neutral port and, if possible, to return to Germany. The ship tried to get back to Germany but when intercepted was scuttled by her crew. It was held that this was a "restraint of princes" as the order was carried out on behalf of the German government.

But this principle does not apply merely because the captain of the ship voluntarily puts into a neutral port of refuge to avoid the risk of capture, before the peril has actually begun to operate[8]. There must be an actual restraint in existence; a reasonable apprehension that a restraint will be imposed, though justified by the event, does not excuse the abandonment of the voyage[9].

"Takings at sea" covers not only capture and seizure but where, for example, the master on instructions from the owner of the ship,

3. Marine Insurance Act 1906, Sched. I, r. 9.
4. *Milward* v. *Hibbert* (1842), 3 Q. B. 120.
5. Marine Insurance Act 1906, Sched. I, r. 10.
6. *British and Foreign Marine Insurance Co.* v. *Sanday & Co.*, [1916] 1 A. C. 650; and see *post*, p. 308.
7. [1942] A. C. 50; [1941] 3 All E. R. 62. *Cf. Czarnikow, Ltd.* v. *Java Sea and Fire Insurance Co., Ltd.*, [1941] 3 All E. R. 256.
8. *Becker, Gray & Co.* v. *London Assurance Corporation*, [1918] A. C. 101.
9. *Watts, Watts & Co.* v. *Mitsui & Co.*, [1917] A. C. 227; but see *Atlantic Maritime Co., Inc.* v. *Gibbon*, [1953] 2 All E. R. 1086; [1954] 1 Q. B. 105, C. A.

assumes a dominion over the cargo inconsistent with the cargo owner's rights—this is a taking at sea of the cargo[10].

The operation of a muncipal law preventing the delivery of goods at their destination (*e.g.* the landing the cattle suffering from disease) is a "restraint of people"[11].

The property of an alien enemy cannot of course be insured against capture during war with this country; but if such property were insured and seized by the Government of the assured before an actual state of war existed, the subsequent breaking out of war would not invalidate the contract of insurance, although the right to recover would be suspended during the continuance of hostilities[12]. The insurer is not liable under this heading for loss occasioned by riot, or by ordinary judicial process[13].

F. C. & S. Clause.—It is not unusual for insurers to stipulate by a special clause in the policy that they shall not be liable for loss caused by capture or seizure. This clause is known as the F. C. & S. clause (free of capture and seizure), and since the Second World War runs as follows:—

> "Warranted free of capture, seizure, arrest, restraint or detainment, and the consequences thereof and of any attempt thereat; also from the consequences of hostilities and warlike operations, whether there be a declaration of war or not; but this warranty shall not exclude collision, contact with any fixed or floating object (other than a mine or torpedo), stranding, heavy weather or fire unless caused directly (and independently of the nature of the voyage or service which the vessel concerned or, in the case of collision, any other vessel involved therein, is performing) by a hostile act by or against a belligerent power; and for the purpose of this warranty 'power' includes any authority maintaining naval, military or air forces in association with a power.
>
> "Further warranted free from the consequences of civil war, revolution, rebellion, insurrection, or civil strife arising therefrom, or piracy."

It withdraws from the protection of the policy certain risks which would otherwise be covered. For instance,

> where in anticipation of war the Government of the South African Republic seized gold belonging to its own subject, it was held

---

10. *Nishina Trading Co., Ltd.* v. *Chiyoda Fire and Marine Insurance Co.*, [1969] 2 All E. R. 776; [1969] 2 Q. B. 449, C. A.
11. *Miller* v. *Law Accident Insurance Co.*, [1903] 1 K. B. 712.
12. *Janson* v. *Driefontein Consolidated Mines*, [1902] A. C. 484; 7 Com. Cas. 268.
13. Marine Insurance Act 1906, Sched. I, r. 10.

that there was a seizure within the meaning of the warranty and that the insurers were not liable on the policy[14].

But if a loss occurs the assured is not bound to prove that his vessel was *not* lost by the excepted causes, and if nothing more is proved than the loss of the vessel at sea, that loss will fall upon the marine underwriters[15].

When the policy contains a warranty of freedom from capture, the insurer's liability ceases on capture of the vessel. Thus,

in a policy against total loss by perils of the sea, containing the F. C. & S. clause, a neutral ship carrying contraband during the Russo-Japanese war, was captured by the Japanese. While being navigated towards a Court of Prize, the ship was wrecked and became a total loss. She was afterwards condemned in the prize Court. On a claim by the owners under the policy, it was held that when the ship was first seized there was a total loss by a capture, the lawfulness of which was authoritatively determined by a subsequent decision of the Prize Court and that the *captors* and not the *assured* had lost the vessel by shipwreck. Accordingly, the owners failed to recover[16].

14. "Barratry of the master and mariners".—The term "barratry" includes every wrongful act wilfully committed by the master or crew to the prejudice of the owner or charterer[17]. For example, setting fire to or scuttling a ship or employing it for smuggling[18] are barratrous acts.

15. "All other perils".—This means all other perils of a nature similar to those which have already been enumerated in the policy[19]. Thus:

it does not include the scuttling of a ship with the connivance of the owner[20].

16. "In case of any loss or misfortune . . . waiver or acceptance of abandonment".—This is styled the "sue and labour clause". The object is to encourage the insurer and the assured to do work to preserve after an accident the property covered by the policy, and to make the best of a bad state of affairs. Should they do so, the clause

---

14. *Robinson Gold Mining Co.* v. *Alliance Insurance Co.*, [1902] 2. K. B. 489; affirmed, [1904] A. C. 359.
15. *Munro Brice & Co.* v. *War Risks Association*, [1918] 2 K. B. 78.
16. *Andersen* v. *Marten*, [1908] A. C. 334.
17. Marine Insurance Act 1906, Sched. I, r. 11; and see *Earle* v. *Rowcroft* (1806), 8 East. 126.
18. *Cory* v. *Burr* (1883), 8 App. Cas. 393.
19. Marine Insurance Act 1906, Sched. I, r. 12.
20. *Samuel (P.) & Co.* v. *Dumas*, [1924] A. C. 431.

provides that their respective rights shall be in no wise prejudiced by any acts done in pursuance of such object, and that the assured shall be entitled to obtain his expenses consequent on the work from the insurers. But for this clause an assured might abstain from any attempt to safeguard wrecked property for fear that such conduct might be deemed a waiver of his right to abandon; under such a clause it is his duty to take reasonable measures to avert or minimise loss[21]. General average losses and contributions and salvage charges are not recoverable under the clause, nor are expenses incurred to avert loss not covered by the policy[1]. Moreover, if the insurer incurs expenses which, if they had been incurred by the assured, would have been recoverable from the insurer under the clause, the insurer cannot recover them from the assured[2].

17. **"And so we the assurers"**, etc.—This clause requires modification to adapt it to the needs of an underwriting limited liability company. Each insurer who signs, signs on his own behalf only, and agrees to indemnify the assured to an amount not exceeding the sum he places next his name. Where there is a loss recoverable under the policy, each insurer, if there are several, is liable for such proportion of the loss as the amount of his subscription bears to the value or assessed amount of the loss; one insurer is not liable for another's default unless it is expressly so agreed[3].

18. **"Confessing overselves paid"**, etc.—This recital is sometimes varied by stating that the persons negotiating the policy have agreed to pay: in either case, unless otherwise agreed, the broker is directly responsible to the insurer for the premium[4]. The custom making the broker and not the assured liable to the insurer for the premium extends also to a "company's policy", which contains a promise by the assured to pay. Even this does not make the assured directly liable to the insurer, for payment must be made according to the custom, *i.e.* by the broker[5]. In the absence of fraud, an acknowledgment on the policy of the receipt of the premium is conclusive as between the insurer and the assured, but not as between the former and the broker[6].

---

21. Marine Insurance Act 1906, s. 78 (4).
1. *Ibid.*, s. 78 (2), (3).
2. *Crouan* v. *Stanier*, [1904] 1 K. B. 87.
3. *Cf. Tyser* v. *Shipowners' Syndicate (Reassured)*, [1896] 1 Q. B. 135; 1 Com. Cas. 224.
4. Marine Insurance Act 1906, s. 53 (1). See *ante*, p. 146.
5. *Universo Insurance Co. of Milan* v. *Merchants' Marine Insurance Co.*, [1897] 2 Q. B. 93; 2 Com. Cas. 28, 180.
6. Marine Insurance Act 1906, s. 54.

19. "N.B." etc.—This clause is styled the "memorandum"; its object is to prevent the insurers from being liable for loss on certain goods peculiarly liable to damage on a sea voyage, or for certain small losses which must almost necessarily occur, but which might increase the liability of the insurer beyond what he could calculate on.

The meaning of the clause has been much considered, and it is believed that the result of the cases may be summarised thus:

(i) the insurer is not liable to indemnify against a partial loss or damage to the first group of goods (viz., corn, fish, etc.) unless the loss is a general average loss[7], or unless the ship is stranded[8];

(ii) he is not liable to indemnify against a partial loss or damage to the second group (viz., sugar, etc.) unless the damage amounts to five per cent. of the value of the thing damaged.

(iii) he is not bound to indemnify against partial loss or damage to the ship, freight, or any goods other than the above, unless the loss amounts to three per cent. of the value of the thing lost or damaged, or unless it is a general average loss, or unless the ship is stranded.

It should be stated that a general average loss may not be added to a particular average loss to make up the specified percentage[9]; but in a voyage policy successive losses, though from different perils, may be added together for this purpose, and in a time policy successive losses occurring on the same voyage may be added together, but not losses occurring on distinct and separate voyages[10].

The meaning of "stranding" in this memorandum is not always very clear; it means that the ship has by some accident, or (at any rate) out of ordinary course[11], touched the sea bottom or something in immediate contact with it, and has thereby been retarded on her course for an appreciable length of time. The fact that the stranding has taken place renders the insurer liable (save to goods in class 2) for all losses on the goods, though happening before or after the stranding, and not attributable to it[12]; but the goods must be actually on board at the time of the stranding[12].

The words "sunk or burnt" are sometimes added at the end of the

---

7. See *post*, pp. 367–370.
8. The term "average unless general," means a partial loss of the subject-matter insured, other than a general average loss, and does not include "particular charges."
9. Marine Insurance Act 1906, s. 76 (3).
10. *Stewart* v. *Merchants' Marine Insurance Co.* (1886), 16 Q. B. D. 619.
11. *Kingsford* v. *Marshall* (1832), 8 Bing., at p. 463.
12. Marine Insurance Act 1906, Sched. I, r. 14.

memorandum. In such case a ship is not "burnt" within the meaning of the policy, unless the injury by fire is such as to constitute a substantial burning of the ship as a whole[13].

The F. P. A. Clause

Another clause, being an additional limitation of the insurer's liability, is of frequent occurrence; it is styled the F. P. A. (free of particular average) clause, and runs thus:

> "Warranted *free from particular average* unless the vessel or craft be stranded, sunk, or burnt, each craft or lighter being deemed a separate insurance. Underwriters, notwithstanding this warranty, to pay for any damage or loss caused by collision with any other ship or craft, and any special charges for warehouse, rent, re-shipping, or forwarding, for which they would otherwise be liable. Also to pay the insured value of any package or packages which may be totally lost in transhipment. Grounding in the Suez Canal not to be deemed a strand, but underwriters to pay damage or loss which may be proved to have directly resulted therefrom."

Save in the matters specially referred to in this clause, the warranty "free from particular average" prevents the assured from recovering for a loss of part other than a loss incurred by a general average sacrifice; but if the policy covers parcels separtely valued, or when by usage the contract is apportionable, the risk for loss of an apportionable part is on the insurer[14]. This warranty does not exonerate the insurer from salvage charges or from liability under the suing and labouring clause, if expense is incurred to save the subject-matter of insurance from a loss for which the insurers would have been liable[15]. Such expenses are terms "particular charges"[16].

The Running Down Clause

A further clause, which is either printed in the body of the policy, or put in the margin, or otherwise attached to the policy, is the *Running Down Clause*, the object of which is to cover the shipowner from loss in the nature of damages payable by him by way of compensation for collisions between his and other ships caused by the default of those in charge of his ship. The collision need not be directly between

---

13. *The Glenlivet*, [1894] P. 48.
14. Marine Insurance Act 1906, s. 76 (1). See *Fabrique de Produits Chimiques* v. *Large*, [1923] 1 K. B. 203.
15. *Ibid.*, s. 76 (2).
16. *Ibid.*, s. 64 (2).

the insured ship and the vessel entitled to compensation, and where, owing to the negligent navigation of the insured ship, a third vessel is run down by a ship which has been forced into it through being struck by the insured ship, the damages payable to the third vessel will be covered by this clause[17].

V RE-INSURANCE AND DOUBLE INSURANCE

Re-insurance

Re-insurance occurs when one insurer insures the risk he has undertaken with another insurer. An agreement to re-insure is a policy of "sea insurance" which must comply with the statutory requirements affecting an original policy[18].

The law applicable is in the main the same as that which governs an original insurance. The contract of re-insurance is also a contract of indemnity, and if the original insurer enters into a compromise with the original assured, paying less than he was liable for, the re-insurer is entitled to the benefit of that compromise[19]. The re-insurer usually undertakes, with regard to the original policy, "to pay as may be paid thereon". These words do not create any liability unless the re-insured actually became bound to pay under the original policy; it is not sufficient that he has paid in good faith in the belief that he was liable[20].

A re-insurer need not give the notice of abandonment that is usually necessary in the case of constructive total loss[1]. The doctrine of subrogation[2] applies to re-insurance, and the re-insurer is entitled to his proper proportion of any money which has been or could be recovered by enforcing a right that would diminish the loss of the original insurer[3].

Double insurance

A double insurance occurs when the assured effects two or more policies on the same interest and adventure. If the two together cause an over-insurance the excess cannot be recovered, but the assured

---

17. *Fenwick (W. F.) & Co.* v. *Merchants' Marine Insurance Co.*, [1915] 3 K. B. 390.
18. *English Insurance Co.* v. *National Benefit Assurance Co.*, [1928] All E. R. Rep. 441; [1929] A. C. 114; *Genforsikrings Aktieselskabet* v. *Da Costa*, [1911] 1 K. B. 137, and see *ante*, p. 299. Some of the statutory requirements were removed by Finance Act 1959, ss. 30, 37, Sch. VIII.
19. *British Dominions General Insurance Co.* v. *Duder*, [1915] 2 K. B. 394.
20. *Chippendale* v. *Holt* (1895), 1 Com. Cas. 197.
1. Marine Insurance Act 1906. s. 62 (8); and see *post* pp. 316, 317.
2. See *ante*, p. 284, *post*, pp. 321–323.
3. *Assicurezioni Generali de Trieste* v. *Empress Assurance Corporation*, [1907] 2 K. B. 814.

may sue on whichever policy he desires, and may recover the whole sum to which he is entitled by way of indemnity[4].

Where the policy is a valued policy, the assured must give credit as against the valuation for any sum received by him under any other policy without regard to the actual value of the subject-matter insured[5]; and where the policy is unvalued, he must give the like credit as against the full insurable value[6].

As between the insurers each is liable to contribute rateably his proportionate part[7], the assured holding any excess he may have received in trust for such of the insurers as are *inter se* entitled to it[8]. Any insurer who pays more than his proportion of the loss is entitled to contribution from the other insurers in the same way as a surety who has paid more than his proportion of the debt[9].

VI ALTERATION OF A POLICY

In accordance with the general principles of insurance contracts an unauthorised alteration in a policy has the effect of making it void as against all who were not parties to the alteration[10]. A material alteration by consent is usually made by indorsement signed by the parties.

VII LOSSES

Except where otherwise agreed, the insurer is liable for any loss proximately caused by a peril insured against, even though the loss would not have occurred but for the negligence or misconduct of the master or crew. The rule that the loss must be traced to a "proximate cause" has always been rigorously applied in insurance cases[11]. The cause which is truly proximate is that which is proximate in efficiency. That efficiency may have been preserved although other causes may have meantime sprung up which have not yet destroyed it, or truly impaired it, and it may culminate in a result of which it still remains the real efficient cause to which the event can be ascribed[12]. Thus,

---

4. Marine Insurance Act 1906, s. 32 (2) (a).
5. *Ibid.*, s. 32 (2) (b).
6. *Ibid.*, s. 32 (2) (c). For the mode of ascertaining insurable value, see *ibid.*, s. 16.
7. *Ibid.*, s. 80 (1).
8. *Ibid.*, s. 32 (2) (d).
9. Marine Insurance Act 1906, s. 80 (1).
10. *Ante*, p. 268.
11. See *per* Lord SUMNER in *Becker, Gray & Co.* v. *London Assurance Corporation*, [1918] A. C., at pp. 112 *et seq.*
12. *Leyland Shipping Co.* v. *Norwich Union Fire Insurance Co.*, [1918] A. C. 350, *per* Lord SHAW OF DUNFERMLINE, at p. 369.

if a ship insured against all consequences of hostilities runs upon the sunken wreck of a vessel torpedoed by an enemy submarine, the act of hostility is not the proximate cause of the loss; but it would be otherwise if the enemy had deliberately sunk a vessel in a narrow and shallow entrance to a port for the purpose of damaging vessels trying to make the port[13].

But the insurer is not liable for ordinary wear and tear, nor for loss caused by inherent vice of the subject-matter insured, or by rats or vermin[14].

Losses are of two kinds:

Partial, where the subject-matter of the insurance is only partially damaged, or where there is only an obligation to contribute to general average, and

Total, where the subject-matter is wholly destroyed, or has become so damaged that the owner is justified in abandoning it.

Total Losses

These are subdivided into
1. *actual total losses* and
2. *constructive total losses*.

1. Actual total loss

This occurs:

   (i) when the subject-matter is actually destroyed, or irreparably damaged, or

   (ii) where the assured is irretrievably deprived of it[15]; *e.g.* when a ship ceases any longer to be a ship, and becomes a mere bundle of planks; or

   (iii) when goods are so damaged as to have ceased to exist in such condition or form as to answer the denomination under which they were insured; or

   (iv) when lost to the owner by an adverse valid decree of a court of competent jurisdiction in consequence of a peril insured against[16].

But possession restored after action brought does not disentitle the owners to recover as for a total loss[17].

---

13. *William France Fenwick & Co.* v. *North of England, etc., Association*, [1917] 2 K. B. 522.
14. Marine Insurance Act 1906, s. 55. Subject to agreement, salvage charges incurred in preventing a loss by perils insured against, may be recovered as a loss by those perils (*ibid.*, s. 65).
15. *Ibid.*, s. 57 (1).
16. *E.g.* sale by the Court of Admiralty (*Crossman* v. *West* (1888), 13 App. Cas. 160).
17. *Ruys* v. *Royal Exchange Assurance Corporation*, [1897] 2 Q. B. 135; 2 Com. Cas. 201.

Where the ship concerned is missing, her actual total loss may be presumed, if no news be received after the lapse of a reasonable time.

2. Constructive total loss

This occurs:

(i) where the subject-matter insured is reasonably abandoned[18] on account of its actual loss appearing to be unavoidable, or

(ii) because it could not be preserved from actual loss without an expenditure which would exceed its value when the expenditure had been incurred[19].

In particular, there is a constructive total loss:

(i) where a vessel has sunk in deep water and cannot be raised without incurring an expense greater than her value[1], or

(ii) when a ship has been so damaged that the cost of repair would exceed her value when repaired[2].

The insurers cannot by gratuitously intervening and incurring an expense which a prudent uninsured owner would not have done, convert a constructive total loss into a partial one; *e.g.*

by raising a vessel which has been sunk in deep water and abandoned by the assured[3].

Again, there is a constructive total loss where the assured is deprived of his ship or goods by a peril insured against and it is *unlikely* that he can recover them; but if at the date of the commencement of the action on the true facts as then existing the recovery of the vessel or goods is a matter of uncertainty and the assured cannot show that on the balance of probability the ship or goods will not be recovered his claim will fail[4].

When goods are insured at and from a port of loading to a port of destination, there is a loss if the adventure is frustrated by a peril insured against, although the goods themselves may continue in existence uninjured and be under the control of the owner. The subject-matter of the insurance is primarily the physical safety of the merchandise; but it is also an insurance of its safe arrival at the

---

18. "Abandoned" here means simply "given up for lost," not formally surrendered to the underwriters: *Court Line, Ltd.* v. *R., The Lavington Court*, [1945] 2 All E. R. 357.
19. Marine Insurance Act 1906, s. 60 (1).
1. *Ibid.*, s. 60 (2) (i); *Kemp* v. *Halliday* (1866), L. R. 1 Q. B. 520.
2. As to taking general average contributions into account, see s. 60 (2) (ii); *Kemp* v. *Halliday, supra.*
3. *Sailing Ship Blairmore Co.* v. *Macredie*, [1898] A. C. 593; 3 Com. Cas. 241.
4. Marine Insurance Act 1906, s. 60 (2); *Polurrian S.S. Co.* v. *Young*, [1915] 1 K. B. 922; C. & T., p. 268 (capture of neutral ship by belligerent); *Marstrand Fishing Co.* v. *Beer*, [1937] 1 All E. R. 158 (barratrous seizure of ship).

designated port. Accordingly, although in possession of the goods, the owner may in such case, on giving due notice of abandonment, recover for a constructive total loss[5].

Where goods were insured and the policy contained a clause "warranted free of any claim based upon loss of, or frustration of, the insured voyage or adventure" and both the goods and the adventure were lost to the owners as a result of restraint of princes, it was held that the exception did not apply, for it was confined to a case where the goods were not physically lost, but became a constructive total loss by reason of the frustration of the adventure[6]. In other words the "frustration clause" as it is called confines the insurance to the safety of the goods and excludes the right of the insured to claim merely because it has not been possible to convey them to their destination owing to a peril insured against.

Notice of abandonment.—In cases of constructive total loss, notice of abandonment must generally be given; otherwise—unless notice is waived by the insurer—the loss will be considered as partial[7]. A notice of abandonment must indicate the intention of the assured to abandon his insured interest unconditionally[8], *e.g.* an owner cannot abandon part of a ship. The notice must be given with reasonable diligence after the receipt of reliable information, a reasonable time for inquiry being allowed where the information is of doubtful character[9], *i.e.* at the earliest opportunity consistent with making inquiry as to the circumstances; and it must be given by the owner or a properly authorised agent. It need not be in writing[10].

Where notice of abandonment is properly given the assured is not prejudiced by the refusal of the insurer to accept it, but the notice is irrevocable after acceptance, express or implied, and acceptance is a conclusive admission of liability for the loss[11].

When an insurer receives valid notice of abandonment, he is entitled to stand in the place of the assured as to the subject-matter of the policy[12]; hence, the effect of a proper notice of abandonment is to

---

5. *British and Foreign Marine Insurance Co.* v. *Sanday & Co.*, [1916] I A. C. 650.
6. *Rickards* v. *Forestal Land, Timber and Rail. Co.*, [1941] 3 All E. R. 62; [1942] A. C. 50. For the facts, see *ante*, p. 308.
7. Marine Insurance Act 1906, s. 62 (1), (8). Notice of abandonment is also unnecessary where, at the time when the assured receives notice of the loss, the insurer could not possibly benefit if notice were given to him (*ibid.*, s. 62 (7)). See also *Roura and Forgas* v. *Townend*, [1919] I K. B. 189.
8. Marine Insurance Act 1906, s. 62 (2).
9. *Ibid.*, s. 62 (3).
10. Marine Insurance Act 1906, s. 62 (2).
11. *Ibid.*, s. 62 (4)–(6).
12. *Ibid.*, s. 63.

transfer the rights (including the right to any freight earned subsequently to the accident) formerly possessed by the assured to the insurer, and such transfer dates back to the time of the accident[13]. If a ship is carrying the owner's goods, the insurer is entitled to reasonable remuneration for the carriage of the goods subsequent to the casualty causing the loss[14].

If after payment of the loss the vessel arrives safe, she is treated as having been abandoned, and becomes the property of the insurers[15].

Total loss of freight.—Different considerations apply to a total loss of chartered freight. On a claim against underwriters for such a loss it is sufficient for the shipowner to show that before loading or in the course of the contemplated voyage the ship has sustained damage which prevents it from commencing or continuing the voyage, and that a prudent owner, uninsured, would not incur the cost even of such temporary repairs as might be necessary to complete the voyage and earn the freight[16].

Adjustment of Losses

The settlement between the assured and the insurer is styled the adjustment, and is usually settled on behalf of the parties by their brokers. If an insurer settles with the broker, the former is, according to Lloyd's rules, discharged as against the claims of the assured; but at law this rule has not been fully recognised, nor, unless it can be shown that the assured was aware of the custom, is it likely that in future the courts will act on it[17].

On ship

As to the amounts allowed (in the absence of express provision in the policy)—

1. In the case of *partial loss* to the ship, the insurers will have to pay the cost of repairs less customary deductions[18], which means generally that they will pay two-thirds of the expenditure on the repairs, the other third being an arbitrary amount supposed to be equivalent to the gain obtained by the owner by the substitution of new materials and work for old. But

---

13. *Ibid.* See *Barclay* v. *Stirling* (1816), 5 M. & S. 6.
14. Marine Insurance Act 1906, s. 63 (2).
15. *Houstman* v. *Thornton* (1816), Holt, N. P. 242.
16. *Carras* v. *London and Scottish Assurance Corporation,* [1935] All E. R. Rep. 246; [1936] 1 K. B. 291; *Kulukundis* v. *Norwich Union Insurance Society*, [1936] 2 All E. R. 242; [1937] 1 K. B. 1.
17. *Todd* v. *Reid* (1821), 4 B. & Ald. 210; *Bartlett* v. *Pentland* (1830), 10 B. & C. 760; but see *Stewart* v. *Aberdein* (1838), 4 M. & W. 211.
18. Marine Insurance Act 1906, s. 69 (1).

on a first voyage they usually have to pay the whole. If the ship is not repaired, or only partially repaired, the assured is entitled to indemnity for the reasonable depreciation arising from the unrepaired damage; but he cannot recover more than if the ship had been repaired[19].

2. In the case of a *total loss*, if the policy is a valued policy, the amount payable is fixed in the policy. If the policy is unvalued, the amount payable is the full insurable value of the ship at the commencement of the risk[20]; which includes outfit, stores, provisions, money advanced for seamen's wages, together with the cost of insurance[1]. In the case of a steamer, "ship" includes machinery, boilers and coals, etc.[1].

On goods[2]

In the case of

1. A total loss of goods, when the policy is:

   (i) unvalued, the assured may recover the insurable value, *i.e.* the prime cost of the goods, plus expenses of shipping and insurance charges[3];

   (ii) if valued, then the amount agreed.

2. A *partial* loss, subject to any agreement, where part of the goods is totally lost and the policy is valued, the sum recoverable is such proportion of the sum fixed by the policy as the insurable value of the part lost bears to the insurable value of the whole, ascertained as in the case of an unvalued policy[4]. Where part of the goods is lost and the policy is unvalued, the sum recoverable is the insurable value of the part lost[5].

Where all or part of the goods arrive damaged, the assured is entitled to such proportion of the sum fixed (in the case of a valued policy), or of

---

19. *Ibid.*, s. 69 (2), (3).
20. *Ibid.*, s. 68. The sum recoverable is called the measure of indemnity, each insurer being liable for such proportion of the measure of indemnity as the amount of his subscription bears to the value fixed by the policy or to the insurable value (*ibid.*, s. 67).
1. *Ibid.*, s. 16 (1); Sched. I, r. 15.
2. The term "goods" means goods in the nature of merchandise, and does not include personal effects or provisions and stores for use on board. In the absence of any usage to the contrary, deck cargo and living animals must be insured specifically and not under the general denomination of goods (*ibid.*, Sched. I, r. 15).
3. Marine Insurance Act 1906, s. 16 (3).
4. *Ibid.*, s. 71 (1).
5. *Ibid.*, s. 71 (2).

the insurable value (in the case of an unvalued policy), as the difference between the gross sound and damaged values at the place of arrival bears to the gross sound value[6].

General average loss

Unless the policy expressly provides to the contrary, where the assured has incurred a general average[7] expenditure or suffered a general average sacrifice, he may recover from the insurer without enforcing his rights of contribution[8].

Again, if the assured has paid or is liable for any general average contribution, he is, subject to any special terms of the policy and to the limit of the sum insured, entitled to be indemnified to the full amount of his general average contribution or to a proportionate part, depending on whether the subject-matter liable to contribution is or is not insured for its full contributory value[9]. The same rule obtains where the assured is owner of the different interests, although in such a case there could be no contribution in fact[10].

In the absence of express stipulation, the insurer is not liable for any general average loss or contribution, which was not incurred for the purpose of avoiding a peril insured against.

Successive losses

Unless the policy otherwise provides, an insurer is liable for successive losses, even though the total amount may exceed the sum insured; but a partial loss, not made good, followed by a total loss under the same policy, can only be treated as a total loss[11]. The same rule applies where the subsequent total loss is not covered by the policy, because payment for the previous partial loss would involve indemnification for an expenditure which could never be made[12].

VIII SUBROGATION

Where the insurer pays for a total loss either of the whole or in the case of goods of any apportionable part, he becomes entitled to the interest of the assured in the subject-matter insured, and is subrogated to all his rights and remedies therein; and where an insurer pays for

---

6. *Ibid.*, s. 71 (3). As to the meaning of "gross value," see *ibid.*, s. 71 (4).
7. See *post*, pp. 367–370, where the meaning of "general average" is given.
8. Marine Insurance Act 1906, s. 66 (4).
9. *Ibid.*, s. 73. The insurer's liability for salvage charges must be determined on the like principle (*ibid.*). See *ante*, p. 305, as to mode of assessing amount payable under a valued policy for a general average loss.
10. *Ibid.*, s. 66 (7).
11. *Ibid.*, s. 77.
12. *British and Foreign Insurance Co.* v. *Wilson Shipping Co.*, [1921] 1 A. C. 188.

a partial loss, he acquires no title to the subject-matter insured, or such part of it as may remain, but is subrogated to the assured's rights and remedies therein, in so far as the assured has been indemnified by payment[13]. However, in *Yorkshire Insurance Co., Ltd.* v. *Nisbet Shipping Co., Ltd.*[14], it was held that where insurers paid the assured the full value of a ship at the time of the loss and subsequently the assured brought proceedings against the Canadian Government and received an agreed sum which exceeded that paid by the insurers owing to the devaluation of the pound against the dollar, the insurers could not recover under s. 79 anything more than they had paid.

Thus, the insurer is subrogated to the rights of the assured only to the extent to which he has insured, the assured being entitled to benefit to the extent to which he has left himself uninsured. The following case will serve as an illustration:

> The owners of a schooner insured her for £1,000 under a policy stating her value to be £1,350. The schooner was totally lost in a collision with a steamship, and the insurers, having paid the £1,000, sued the steamship owners and recovered £1,000, which was found to be the value of the schooner in the action. *Held:* that the owners of the schooner were entitled to be treated as their own insurers for £350, and, therefore, the £1,000 must be divided between them and the insurers in the proportion of their respective interests, viz., $\frac{350}{1350}$ and $\frac{1000}{1350}$[15].

On the other hand, if the ship is valued in the policy at less than the real value, and a proportion of the loss is recovered by the assured from the owners of another vessel in a collision action in which both ships were held to blame, and such proportion is based on the real or higher value, the underwriters who have paid a *total* loss will be entitled to the whole sum recovered, up to the amount paid by them on the policy[16]. The same principle applies where underwriters are liable for a *partial* loss under a valued policy; they are entitled to

---

13. Marine Insurance Act 1906, s. 79. See further as to subrogation, *ante*, p. 284.
14. [1961] 2 All E. R. 487; [1962] 2 Q. B. 330. But where insurers, having paid out the assured, are given an assignment of the assured's rights against third parties, the insurers are entitled to bring such action in their own name and may recover more than 100 per cent. of their loss: *Compania Colombiana de Seguros* v. *Pacific Steam Navigation Co.*, [1964] 1 All E. R. 216; [1964] 2 W. L. R. 484.
15. *The Commonwealth*, [1907] P. 216; and see s. 81.
16. *Thames and Mersey Marine Insurance Co.* v. *British and Chilian S.S. Co.*, [1915] 2 K. B. 214; affirmed, [1916] 1 K. B. 30, C. A.

deduct the full amount recovered by the assured from third persons in respect of that loss[17].

Where property is insured for its full value and a subsequent and subsidiary "increased value" policy is taken out with other insurers and both policies are paid in full on a total loss occurring, the whole of the salvage, if it does not exceed the amount covered by the primary policy, belongs to the original insurers. It might be different if by the terms of the primary policy the assured had reserved a right to effect a further insurance for increased value[18].

IX RETURN OF THE PREMIUM

In the absence of fraud or illegality on the part of the assured or his agents,

1. Where the consideration for the payment of the premium totally fails the premium becomes returnable to him;
2. Where the consideration partially fails, a proportionate part is returnable, but only if the premium is apportionable and there is a total failure of any apportionable part of the consideration[19].

Thus the premium, or a part of it, is returnable:

1. If the policy is void or is avoided by the insurer from the commencement of the risk[20];
2. If the subject-matter insured, or an apportionable part of it, is never subjected to the risk[1];
3. If the assured had no insurable interest at any time during the currency of the risk unless the policy was a contract of wagering[2].

When the assured:

1. Over-insures on an unvalued policy, a proportionate part of the premium is returnable[3].

---

17. *Goole, etc., Towing Co.* v. *Ocean Marine Insurance Co.*, [1927] All E. R. Rep. 621; [1928] 1 K. B. 589.
18. *Boag* v. *Standard Marine Insurance Co.*, [1937] 1 All E. R. 714; [1937] 2 K. B. 113. See *ante*, p. 315, as to contribution between insurers in cases of double insurance.
19. Marine Insurance Act 1906, s. 84 (1), (2).
20. *Ibid.*, s. 84 (3) (a).
1. Marine Insurance Act 1906, s. 84 (3) (b). But if insured "lost or not lost," the fact that, unknown to the insurer, the ship had in fact arrived in safety at the date of the conclusion of the contract to insure, does not entitle the assured to a return of premium (*ibid.*).
2. *Ibid.*, s. 84 (3) (c).   3. *Ibid.*, s. 84 (3) (e).

2. Over-insures by double insurance a proportionate part of the several premiums is returnable, except when the double insurance is effected knowingly by the assured.

When the policies have been effected at different times, no premium is returnable in respect of any earlier policy which has borne the entire risk, or on which a claim has been paid in respect of the full sum insured[4].

X WARRANTIES

By a warranty the assured undertakes that some particular thing shall or shall not be done, or that some condition shall be fulfilled, or he affirms or negatives the existence of a particular state of facts[5]. Lord MANSFIELD has stated:

"A warranty in a policy of insurance is a condition or contingency, and unless that be performed there is no contract; it is perfectly immaterial for what purpose a warranty is introduced, but being inserted the contract does not exist, unless it is literally complied with"[6].

A warranty, therefore, when once introduced must be exactly complied with, whether it be material to the risk or not, otherwise, subject to any express provision in the policy, the insurer will be discharged from the date of the breach of warranty, though the loss had nothing whatever to do with it[7], and though the breach of warranty arose owing to events beyond the control of the warrantor[8]. A warranty may be:

1. *Express*, or
2. *Implied*.

If express, it must be inserted in or incorporated by reference into the contract[9].

If, owing to a change of circumstances, the warranty no longer applies to the circumstances of the contract, or if it is rendered unlawful by legislation, a non-compliance with it is excused[10]. Where a warranty has been broken, it is of no avail for the assured to remedy the breach and comply with the warranty before loss; but the breach may be waived by the insurer[10].

---

4. *Ibid.*, s. 84 (3) (f).   5. Marine Insurance Act 1906, s. 33.
6. *De Hahn* v. *Hartley* (1786), 1 T. R. 343, 345.
7. Marine Insurance Act 1906, s. 33.
8. *Hore* v. *Whitmore* (1778), 2 Cowp. 784.
9. Marine Insurance Act 1906, ss. 33, 35.
10. *Ibid.*, s. 34.

A representation is a statement made by the assured to the insurer regarding the proposed risk, but it is not an integral part of the contract itself. If made, and if material, it must be substantially complied with[11]. It seems then to differ in effect from a warranty in this, that whereas a misrepresentation if untrue entitles the insurer to avoid the policy only if it is material, a warranty avoids the contract under any circumstances; and further, that whereas substantial compliance is sufficient in the case of a representation, strict compliance is needed for a warranty[12].

The more usual express warranties are—

1. To sail on a given day;
2. That the vessel is safe on a particular day. This is complied with if the vessel is safe at any time on that day, though at the hour when the policy is signed she has been lost[13];
3. To sail with convoy;
4. That the ship is neutral. This implies a condition that she shall be neutral at the commencement of the risk, and that, as far as the assured can control the matter, she will remain neutral during the risk, and will carry the proper papers[14];
5. That the goods are neutral; which implies that they are neutral owned, and, so far as the assured can control the matter, that they will be carried to a neutral destination by a neutral ship[14].

The implied warranties are—

1. In a voyage policy, that at the commencement of the voyage the ship shall be seaworthy for the purpose of the particular adventure[15]. If the policy contemplates a voyage in different stages, involving different or varied risks, it will suffice if, at the commencement of each distinct stage, she is seaworthy in view of the risks to be encountered on the next stage[16]. In a time policy there is no implied warranty of seaworthiness at any stage of the adventure[17]; but where, with the privity of the assured, the ship is sent to sea in an unseaworthy state, the insurer is not liable for any loss attributable to unseaworthiness. This means, however, the particular unseaworthiness of which the

---

11. *De Hahn* v. *Hartley* (1786), 1 T. R. 343, 345.
12. The word "warranty" has not in insurance law the meaning it bears in general contract law.
13. Marine Insurance Act 1906, s. 38.
14. *Ibid.*, s. 36.
15. *Ibid.*, s. 39 (1). A ship is seaworthy if she is reasonably fit to encounter the ordinary perils of the seas in view of the adventure insured (*ibid.*, s. 39 (4)). *Cf.* Carriage of Goods by Sea Act 1924, *post*, p. 359.
16. Marine Insurance Act 1906, s. 39 (3); and see *Greenock Steamship Co.* v. *Maritime Insurance Co.*, [1903] 2 K. B. 657. See also *post*, p. 338.
17. Marine Insurance Act 1906, s. 39 (5).

assured had knowledge, and if a ship is unseaworthy in two respects, to one only of which the assured was privy, he can recover for a loss caused by the other[18].

2. In a voyage policy attaching whilst a ship is in port, an implied warranty that she is reasonably fit, at the commencement of the risk, to encounter the ordinary perils of that port[19].

3. In a voyage policy on goods, there is an implied warranty that at the commencement of the voyage the ship is not only seaworthy as a ship, but also that she is reasonably fit to carry the goods. But in a policy on goods or other movables, there is no implied warranty that the goods or movables are seaworthy[20].

4. That the venture is a lawful one, and will, so far as the assured can control it, be carried out in a lawful manner[1].

There is no implied warranty as to the nationality of a ship, or that her nationality shall not be changed during the risk[2]; but if a ship is expressly warranted neutral there is an implied condition that, so far as the assured can control the matter, she shall be properly documented[3].

---

18. *Thomas* v. *Tyne and Wear S.S. Freight Insurance Association*, [1917] 1 K. B. 938.
19. Marine Insurance Act 1906, s. 39 (2).
20. *Ibid.*, s. 40. See *Daniels* v. *Harris* (1875), L. R. 10 C. P. 1.
1. Marine Insurance Act 1906, s. 41.
2. *Ibid.*, s. 37.
3. *Ibid.*, s. 36 (2).

CHAPTER 19

Carriage of Goods on Land

I INTRODUCTORY

Carriers at common law

The common law recognises two classes of carrier, common carriers and private carriers, the distinction being that the former holds himself out as being ready to carry goods or passengers or both[1] for *anyone* who wishes to engage him, and a private carrier is one whose practice is to pick and choose his customers or who undertakes carriage only as a casual occupation. The importance of this division lies in the fact that a common carrier is under a duty to carry passengers and goods of the class which he professes to carry and cannot refuse custom except on certain well-defined grounds. His liability in respect of passengers depends on negligence, but his liability in respect of goods is that of an "insurer", *i.e.* he is strictly liable for all loss or damage irrespective of negligence subject to express contractual terms excluding or limiting such liability. The position of a private carrier on the other hand is that, subject to the terms of the contract in which he has entered, he is liable in respect of passengers and goods only for such injury, loss or damage as is caused by his negligence though in respect of goods the burden of proof is on the carrier. A person who reserves the right of accepting or rejecting offers of goods for carriage is not a common carrier[2].

Statutory modifications

The position of land carriers has been considerably modified by various statutory provisions, all of which directly or indirectly affect the terms and conditions upon which goods or passengers are carried.

The chief of these are the following:

1. The Carriers Act 1830 limits the liability of the common carrier in respect of loss or damage to certain types of goods[3];
2. Railway companies before the Transport Act 1947 were controlled by a number of statutory provisions the underlying objects of which were to secure that:

---

1. *Clarke* v. *West Ham Corporation*, [1909] 2 K. B. 858.
2. *Belfast Ropework Co., Ltd.* v. *Bushell*, [1918] 1 K. B. 210.
3. *Post*, pp. 332–334.

(*a*) reasonable facilities were provided for the public; and
(*b*) no undue preference was shown to any individual.

3. The Transport Act 1947 created a new public corporation known as the British Transport Commission to which was given a monopoly in rail transport.

4. The Transport Act 1962 divided the functions of the Commission into various Boards of which the British Railways Board is the most important[4]. The Boards are not common carriers.

5. The Carriage of Goods by Road Act 1965 (which came into effect in June 1967) enacts the Geneva Convention for the International Carriage of Goods by Road (1956) which governs all contracts where the place of taking over the goods and the place designated for delivery are situated in two different countries, at least one of which is a party to the Convention. The provisions of the Convention, covering *inter alia* liability for loss, damage and delay are set out in the Schedule to the Act and cannot be contracted out of.

6. The Transport Act 1968 created the National Freight Corporation which has taken over the Freight Liner division of British Rail and the various road haulage companies, already publicly owned, such as British Road Services Ltd; The Corporation is not a common carrier, and has adopted British Rail's General Conditions for the Carriage of Goods[5].

II RIGHTS AND DUTIES AT COMMON LAW

Common Carriers of goods

At common law a common carrier of goods must carry the goods of the class he professes to carry of anybody who delivers them to him, and who offers to pay reasonable hire[6]. He may claim payment in advance, *i.e.* before he carries, but not before he receives the goods[7]. This duty of taking anybody's goods is that which makes him a common carrier, *i.e.* a carrier common to all. He should:

1. Carry the goods by his ordinary route, not of necessity the shortest, but without unnecessary deviation or delay[8];

---

4. The others are the British Transport Docks Board, the British Waterways Board and the London Transport Board (replaced by the London Transport Executive by the Transport (London) Act 1969).
5. See *post*, p. 334.
6. *Garton* v. *Bristol and Exeter Rail. Co.* (1861), 1 B. & S. 112, at p. 162.
7. *Pickfords* v. *Grand Junction Rail. Co.* (1841), 8 M. & W. 372.
8. *Briddon* v. *Great Northern Rail. Co.* (1859), 28 L. J. Ex. 51; *Myers* v. *London and South Western Rail. Co.* (1870), L. R. 5 C. P. 1.

2. Deliver them to the consignee, at the place (if any) designated by the consignor; unless the consignee requires the goods to be delivered at another place, in which case he may deliver them according to the orders of the consignee[9]; and if as between the consignor and the consignee there was a right in the former to change the destination of the goods, the carrier, on receiving due notice, must take the goods to the new destination if it is within the area of his operations[10].

He cannot be compelled to take the goods[11]:

1. If his vehicle is already full;
2. If the goods are such as he cannot, or does not profess to convey;
3. If they are of a nature such as to subject him to extraordinary risk[12].
4. If they are inadequately packed[13].

A consignor who delivers goods of a dangerous character to a common carrier (although the consignor may be ignorant of the danger) impliedly warrants that the goods are fit to be carried with safety. This implied warranty does not arise in cases where the carrier knows of the danger. Thus, in *Bamfield* v. *Goole and Sheffield Transport Co.*[14],

> the defendants, who were forwarding agents, delivered "ferro-silicon" in casks to a common carrier under the description of "general cargo," but did not inform him that it was ferro-silicon, although they were aware of the fact. The ferro-silicon during carriage gave off poisonous gases, which caused the death of the carrier.

The judge found on the evidence that ferro-silicon was liable under certain conditions to be dangerous, that neither the defendants nor the carrier knew this, and that the defendants were not guilty of negligence in not knowing the dangerous character of the goods. The defendants were held liable in damages for causing the death of the carrier.

The carrier has a lien for his charges on the goods carried in respect of which the claim arises, but it is a particular and not a general lien[15].

---

9. *London and North Western Rail. Co.* v. *Bartlett* (1862), 7 H. & N. 400.
10. *Scothorn* v. *South Staffordshire Rail. Co.* (1853), 8 Ex. 341.
11. *Batson* v. *Donovan* (1820), 4 B. & A., at p. 32.
12. *Edwards* v. *Sherratt* (1801), 1 East. 604.
13. *Sutcliffe* v. *Great Western Rail. Co.*, [1910] 1 K. B. 478, at p. 503.
14. [1910] 2 K. B. 94. The warranty also applies to goods delivered to a private carrier (*Great Northern Rail. Co.* v. *L. E. P. Transport and Depository*, [1922] 2 K. B. 742).
15. *Rushforth* v. *Hadfield* (1805), 6 East, 519; (1806), 7 East, 224.

Liability for loss or damage

At common law, the common carrier must make good any loss or damage whether or not it is caused by his negligence, for his agreement is to carry safely and securely, unless the loss or damage is caused by:

1. An act of God[16]. This is some unforeseen accident occasioned by the elementary forces of nature unconnected with the agency of man or other cause, the occurrence of which could not have been reasonably foreseen and the consequence of which could not have been prevented by reasonable precautions[17].

2. The Queen's enemies.

He is, in fact, in the "nature of an insurer" whereas one who carries goods, not being a common carrier, is bound only to carry with due care[18]. The exceptions to the common carrier's liability, whether those mentioned above or whether fixed by contract, do not avail him if the loss or damage to the goods is contributed to by his negligence, or if he does not provide a proper vehicle[19].

He is responsible for the safety of the goods so long as they are in his custody; *i.e.* during transit and (as his duty is usually to deliver as well as to carry) after transit for a reasonable time, varying with circumstances. After the lapse of such time he becomes a mere bailee, and is liable only for negligence, unless otherwise agreed[20].

If the consignee refuses to take the goods, the carrier must do what, in all the circumstances, is reasonable[21], and may recover expenses properly incurred in consequence of the refusal to accept delivery[1]. It will be safer for him to give notice of the refusal to the consignor, though this not be always necessary[2].

A carrier is not liable for damage or loss to goods which has arisen owing:—

1. To an inherent vice in or natural deterioration of the goods delivered to be carried; or

2. To the neglect of the owner, without negligence on the part of the carrier; or

---

16. *Forward v. Pittard* (1785), 1 T. R. 27.
17. *Nugent v. Smith* (1876), 1 C. P. D. 423; C. & T., p. 273.
18. *Coggs v. Bernard* (1703), 1 Sm. L. C. (13th ed.), 175.
19. *The Xantho* (1887), 12 App. Cas., at p. 510; and see *per* BOWEN, L.J., in *Steinman & Co.* v. *Angier Line*, [1891] 1 Q. B., at p. 624.
20. *Per* COCKBURN, C.J., in *Chapman v. Great Western Rail. Co.* (1880), 5 Q. B. D., at pp. 281, 282; *Mitchell v. Lancashire and Yorkshire Rail. Co.* (1875) L. R. 10 Q. B. 256.
21. *Crouch v. Great Western Rail. Co.* (1857), 2 H. & N. 491; 3 H. & N. 183.
1. *Great Northern Rail. Co.* v. *Swaffield* (1874), L. R. 9 Ex. 132.
2. *Hudson v. Baxendale* (1857), 2 H. & N. 575.

3. If the packing is defective, although that fact is known to him at the time when the goods are received[3].

And if from any cause (*e.g.* the nature of the goods) special care is required, the carrier is entitled to be informed of this, otherwise he will not be liable for damage which but for such cause would not have occurred.

In *Baldwin* v. *London, Chatham and Dover Rail. Co.*[4]

rags were sent for transit to the company, and by mistake the company failed to send them in proper time to their destination; the rags were packed wet, and were in consequence spoilt by the delay, but had they been dry, no damage would have been suffered.

The court decided that in the absence of notice of the state of the rags to the carriers, they were not liable for the loss, and that nominal damages would suffice to meet the damage suffered through their default.

Exclusion and limitation of liability of common and private carriers of goods

Even at common law, a common carrier (and of course a private carrier) could agree with his customer that his liability should be excluded or limited. Thus, if the owner of goods received a ticket, on which was a notice limiting the carrier's liability, this would be strong evidence that he agreed to the terms so that the owner was bound by the condition though not actually aware of it if the carrier had taken all reasonable steps to bring it to his notice[5].

Those carriers who are members of the Road Haulage Association normally contract on the basis of the Association's Conditions of Carriage which were last revised in 1967. Clause 2 states that "the carrier is not a common carrier and will accept goods for carriage only on these conditions". Clause 10 provides time limits for claims and by Clause 11 it is provided that there is no liability for loss, misdelivery or damage which has arisen from Act of God, war, seizure under legal process, act or omission of the trader, inherent vice, insufficient packing or labelling, or riots. Otherwise, Clause 12 provides for liability on the carrier subject to a limit of £800 per ton where the loss or damage is in respect of the whole consignment and a

---

3. *Gould* v. *S. E. and C. Rail. Co.*, [1920] 2 K. B. 186. But being aware of the facts the carrier must do what is reasonable to prevent further loss (*Beck* v. *Evans* (1812), 16 East, 244, 247).
4. (1882) 9 Q. B. D. 582.
5. See *per* BLACKBURN, J., in *Peek* v. *North Staffordshire Rail. Co.* (1863), 10 H. L. Cas., at p. 494; and see *ante*, p. 15.

proportion of that sum where loss or damage is in respect of part of a consignment.

A contractual clause excluding or limiting the carrier's liability will normally be construed as not applicable where the carrier has committed a fundamental breach of contract, *e.g.*, subcontracting the carriage of a valuable consignment without the owner's consent[6].

Common carriers of passengers.—A common carrier of passengers must carry any passenger, not being an objectionable person, who offers himself and is willing to pay the fare, provided that there is accommodation[7]. He is not an "insurer" of his passengers but is bound to exercise due care for their safety[8].

Any contract for the conveyance of passengers in a public service vehicle is void in so far as it purports to restrict liability in respect of the death of or personal injury to a passenger while being carried in, entering or alighting from the vehicle[9].

Common carriers to-day.—Most road hauliers reserve the right to accept or reject offers of goods for carriage and are therefore not common carriers, or, as in the case of those contracting on the basis of the Road Haulage Association's Conditions of Carriage, expressly state that they are not common carriers. However, a bus or coach running as part of a regular transport service (and known in law as a public service vehicle) is still a common carrier of any passenger's luggage that it carries.

III THE CARRIERS ACT 1830

Protection of carriers.—By the Carriers Act 1830[10], it is enacted:

1. That no common carrier by land[10] for hire shall be liable for loss or injury to certain articles when the value exceeds £10, unless at time of delivery the value and nature of the property shall have been declared, and an increased charge paid or

---

6. *Garnham, Harris and Elton, Ltd.* v. *Alfred W. Ellis (Transport), Ltd.*, [1967] 2 All E. R. 940; [1967] 1 W. L. R. 940; see also *Suisse Atlantique Société d'Armement Maritime S.A.* v. *N.V. Rotterdamsche Kolen Centrale*, [1966] 2 All E. R. 61; [1967] 1 A. C. 361, and *John Carter (Fine Worsteds)* v. *Hanson Haulage, Ltd.*, [1965] 1 All E. R. 113; [1965] 2 Q. B. 405.
7. *Clarke* v. *West Ham Corporation*, [1909] 2 K. B. 258.
8. *Barkway* v. *South Wales Transport Co.*, [1950] 1 All E. R. 392; [1950] A. C. 185.
9. Road Traffic Act 1960, s. 151. Even a condition to like effect on a free pass may be ineffective: *Gore* v. *Van der Lann*, [1967] 1 All E. R. 360; [1967] 2 Q. B. 31, C. A.
10. This is applicable where the transit is *partly* by sea, if the loss occurs on land (*Le Conteur* v. *London and South Western Rail. Co.* (1866), L. R. 1 Q. B. 54). .

agreed to be paid[11]. Such notice must be express. Amongst the articles mentioned are:

(i) gold, (ii) jewellery, (iii) watches, (iv) negotiable paper, (v) pictures, (vi) china, (vii) furs, and (viii) silks.

The amount is the aggregate value of the parcel. The protection extends to cases where the goods are lost by the gross negligence of the carrier's servants[12].

2. All common carriers may demand on such packages an increased charge, but the amount per scale must be notified in legible characters in some conspicuous part of the office where the parcels are received. Such notice will bind those sending goods, without proof that it was brought to their knowledge[13].

The exemption from the common law liability is given only where this notification and demand have been made[14], or when the declaration of value has not been given. When an extra charge is made, the person making payment is entitled to a receipt[15].

3. Other than as provided for by the Act, no public notice shall be allowed to limit the liability of carriers[16].

4. Special contracts are not affected by the statute if their provisions are inconsistent with the exemption in favour of carriers contained in s. 1 of the Act and that protection is renounced: but the carrier is not deprived of the protection, unless the terms of the special contract are inconsistent with the goods having been received by him as a common carrier[17].

5. A criminal act on the part of a servant of the carrier, or of a sub-contractor carrying for him[18], resulting in damage or loss to the goods, will render the carrier liable notwithstanding any other provision of the Act[19]. To determine who are included under servants, see the section, and *Machu* v.

---

11. Carriers Act 1830, s. 1.
12. *Hinton* v. *Dibbin* (1842), 2 Q. B. 646.
13. Carriers Act 1830, s. 2. A ticket containing conditions is not such a notice; but may form the basis of a special contract (*Walker* v. *York and North Midland Rail. Co.* (1854), 2 E. & B. 750).
14. *Great Northern Rail. Co.* v. *Behrens* (1862), 7 H. & N. 950.
15. Stamping is dispensed with (Carriers Act 1830, s. 3).
16. Carriers Act 1830, s. 4.
17. *Ibid.*, s. 6; *Baxendale* v. *Great Eastern Rail. Co.* (1869), L. R. 4 Q. B. 244.
18. *Machu* v. *London and South Western Rail. Co.* (1848), 2 Ex. 415.
19. Carriers Act 1830, s. 8.

London and South Western Rail. Co.[20], and *Stephens v. London and South Western Rail. Co.*[1].

The carrier's exemption applies only in the case where there is loss[2] or injury to the goods; he is therefore liable as heretofore for damage caused by delay.

Most road hauliers today (as well as British Rail) are not common carriers and, therefore, the significance of the Carriers Act 1830 is now small.

IV RAIL TRANSPORT

The railways were taken into public ownership by the Transport Act 1947, and a public corporation, the British Railways Board, now manages the railways.

The British Railways Board have power to demand such charges as they think fit, and are not subject to any control as regards charges by the Transport Tribunal. The Board are under no duty to provide reasonable facilities to the public for receiving forwarding and delivering goods and are not common carriers of goods or passengers[3]. Because the Board are not common carriers, the Carriers Act 1830 no longer has any application to goods carried on the railways.

Conditions of carriage of goods

The Board enjoy complete freedom to make the use of their services and facilities "subject to such terms and conditions as they think fit"[4]. The Board have issued sets of conditions on the basis of which they are prepared to carry goods. The principal set contains "General Conditions for the Carriage of Goods (other than Goods for which Conditions are specially provided)". Under these conditions, the Board are liable for any loss, or misdelivery of, or damage to, merchandise during transit, unless the Board can prove it has arisen from act of God, war, seizure under legal process, act or omission of the trader, inherent vice, insufficient or improper packing, labelling or addressing, riot or strikes, or the consignee not taking delivery within a reasonable time.

---

20. (1848), 2 Ex. 415.
1. (1887), 18 Q. B. D. 121. As to the amount of evidence required to cause the court to infer that the theft was committed by a servant of the carrier, see *Vaughton v. London and North Western Rail. Co.* (1875), L. R. 9 Ex. 93; *McQuenn v. Great Western Rail. Co.* (1875), L. R. 10 Q. B. 569.
2. This includes a temporary loss (*Millen v. Brasch* (1883), 10 Q. B. D. 142).
3. Transport Act 1962, s. 43 (6).
4. *Ibid.*, s. 43 (3).

However, liability is limited in respect of loss of the whole consignment to £800 per ton, and in respect of a partial loss to such proportion of £800 per ton as the value of the part lost bears to the whole consignment. The Board is not liable where the consignor or consignee is fraudulent.

With regard to goods carried at Owner's Risk (in which case, the charges are lower), the Board's only liability for loss, damage, misdelivery, delay, or detention is where wilful misconduct on the part of the Board or their servants can be proved. However, there is liability without proof of wilful misconduct where there has been a misdelivery of the whole consignment or of a separate package forming part of a consignment.

In the case of damageable goods not properly protected by packing the Board are generally liable only for wilful misconduct. However, the Board are also liable if it can be proved that the damage would still have been suffered even if properly packed.

Written notice of any claim must be made within 3 days of the transit terminating, and the claim itself must be made within 7 days. These times give way to longer periods of 28 days and 42 days where the claim is in respect of non-delivery of the whole consignment or of a separate package forming part of a consignment.

Carriage of passengers

The Board's liability for injury to a passenger depends on proof of negligence. By s. 43 (7) of the Transport Act 1962, the Board may not carry a passenger by rail on terms or conditions which (*a*) purport directly or indirectly to exclude or limit their liability in respect of the death of or bodily injury to any passenger other than a passenger travelling on a free pass, or (*b*) purport directly or indirectly to prescribe the time within which or the manner in which any such liability may be enforced. Any such term or condition is void.

CHAPTER 20

Carriage of Goods by Sea

I INTRODUCTION

A contract for the carriage of goods by sea is also known as a contract of affreightment, the consideration being called "freight". It is found in two forms:—

1. A charter-party, which provides for the hiring of the ship itself;
2. A contract for the conveyance of goods in a general ship, the terms of which are evidenced by a bill of lading. A bill of lading also operates as a receipt for the goods shipped on board and as a document of title to the goods[1].

These two contracts have many incidents in common. Sometimes the charterer (*i.e.* the person who hires the ship from the shipowner) uses the ship as a general ship, carrying goods of third parties under bills of lading. Alternatively, the charterer may find the cargo himself in which case there may well be a bill of lading as well as a charter-party because the charterer may wish to use the bill of lading as a document of title to transfer the cargo while it is still in transit—the charter-party, not the bill of lading, will comprise the contract between the shipowner and the charterer. However, as regards assignees of the bill of lading, the bill of lading contains the terms of the contract of carriage made with the shipowners, and unless the bill of lading refers to and incorporates with itself any or all of the terms of the charter-party in clear terms, the assignee is not affected by the charter-party[2]. If the bill of lading contains a statement,

"freight and all other conditions as per charter-party,"

the terms of the charter-party govern the payment of freight and all other conditions which would have to be performed by the receiver of the goods, so far as these are not in conflict with any express stipulations of the bill of lading; but conditions of the charter-party which are not to be performed by the consignee of the goods are not incorporated, so that a provision in the charter-party that deck cargo

---

1. See further as to bill of lading, *post*, pp. 350 *et seq.* A "general ship" is one used to carry the goods of a number of persons.
2. See *per* ESHER, M.R., and BOWEN, L.J., in *Oriental Steamship Co.* v. *Tylor*, [1893] 2 Q. B., at pp. 521, 526.

is to be carried at merchant's risk will not protect the shipowner against a claim by the assignee of the bill of lading[3].

II CHARTER-PARTIES

"When the agreement is to carry a complete cargo of goods or to furnish a ship for that purpose, the contract of affreightment is almost always contained in a document called a *charter-party*, the *shipowner* letting the ship for the purpose of carrying, or undertaking to carry, the *charterer* hiring the ship for such purpose, or undertaking to provide a full cargo"[4].

The person whose goods are to be taken is called the charterer.

The charter-party may, but need not, be under seal. It may amount to a complete demise of the ship; that it to say, it may put the vessel altogether out of the power and control of the owner, and vest that power and control in the charterer, so that during the hiring the master and crew are servants of the charterer and the shipowner is under no liability with regard to the cargo carried during the demise[5]. However, a charter-party by demise is uncommon[6] and generally the ship remains in the possession of the owner, the charterer acquiring the right only to put his goods on the vessel, and to have them carried[7]. It is a matter of construction whether the charter-party is one by demise or not, but the most common types of charter-party are (i) a *voyage charter-party*, where the ship is chartered for a particular voyage, and (ii) a *time charter-party*, where the ship is chartered for a particular period of time.

It would seem that the charterer's right to the use of the ship can be disregarded by a person who purchases the ship even with notice of the terms of the charter-party. For he is no party to the contract and although in equity certain covenants run with the land, there is no similar doctrine applicable to chattels[8]. Of course, if the owner sold the ship during the currency of a charter-party the owner would be liable to the charterer for breach of contract.

---

3. *Serraino* v. *Campbell*, [1891] 1 Q. B. 283; *Diederichsen* v. *Farquharson*, [1898] 1 Q. B. 150; 3 Com. Cas 87.
4. Scrutton on Charter-parties and Bills of Lading (17th Edn., 1964), p. 1.
5. *Baumwoll, etc.* v. *Furness*, [1893] A. C. 8.
6. *Sea and Land Securities, Ltd.* v. *Dickinson & Co., Ltd.*, [1942] All E. R. 503; [1942] 2 K. B. 65, 69.
7. *Sandeman* v. *Scurr* (1867), L. R. 1 Q. B. 86, 96.
8. *Port Line, Ltd.* v. *Ben Line Steamers, Ltd.*, [1958] 1 All E. R. 787; [1958] 2 Q. B. 146, not following the Privy Council decision in *Lord Strathcona S.S. Co.* v. *Dominion Coal Co.*, [1926] A. C. 108. For the principle that a contract is not binding on third parties, see *ante*, p. 66.

Voyage Charter-parties

An example is given below of the *express* terms commonly found in a voyage charter-party. There are, however, a number of terms that are *implied* by law. In our earlier chapter on "CONSTRUCTION OF CONTRACTS"[9] it was pointed out that the introduction of an implied term into a contract can be justified only when it is not inconsistent with an express term of the contract, and where the implied term is necessary to give business efficacy to the contract. There is a wealth of judicial precedent establishing the following three terms as implied obligations of the shipowners in a voyage charter-party—the first one mentioned is also an implied obligation of the shipowners in a time charter-party:—

   (i) that the ship is seaworthy at the time of sailing from the port of loading;

   (ii) that the voyage will be commenced and carried out without unreasonable delay; and

   (iii) that there shall be no unwarranted deviation from the route.

The charterer is under an implied obligation not to ship goods which involve the risk of unusual danger or delay to the ship. This applies to both voyage and time charters.

Any of these implied obligations can be excluded or varied by an express term in the charter-party provided this is done by clear unambiguous language[10].

Implied obligations of shipowner

   (i) *Seaworthiness.*—In the case of both voyage and time charter-parties, there is implied by law an obligation on the part of the shipowner that the ship is seaworthy and fit to receive cargo at the time of sailing from the port of loading. This means that the ship is fit to encounter the ordinary perils of navigation and that the ship, its furniture, and equipment are fit to carry the cargo[11]. It is not enough that the shipowner does his best to make the ship fit—it must in fact be fit. There is thus an absolute twofold obligation on the shipowner as to seaworthiness at the time of sailing from the port of loading and as to the ship's fitness to receive the particular cargo at the time of loading. If the ship is seaworthy and fit to receive cargo at these times, defects arising subsequently do not amount to breach of this obligation but if the voyage is of necessity divided into stages, *e.g.* to take in coal, the vessel must be made seaworthy at the commencement of each stage.[12]

---

9. *Ante*, p. 111.
10. *Nelson Line (Liverpool), Ltd.* v. *James Nelson & Sons, Ltd.*, [1908] A. C. 16.
11. *Steel* v. *State Line Steamship Co.* (1878), 3 App. Cas. 72; *McFadden* v. *Blue Star Line*, [1905] 1 K. B. 697.
12. *The Vortigern*, [1899] P. 140.

Bad stowage will amount to unseaworthiness only if it endangers the safety of the ship as distinct from merely the safety of the cargo[13].

If the shipowner is in breach of his implied undertaking of seaworthiness, this does not automatically discharge the contract of affreightment. The charterer is entitled, of course, to sue for damages and where he learns of the unseaworthiness before the journey begins he is entitled to repudiate the contract if the ship cannot be rendered seaworthy within a reasonable time[14] but the charterer is not entitled to repudiate for a trifling breach. As DIPLOCK, L.J., said in a leading case[15]:

> "The shipowner's undertaking to deliver a seaworthy ship is neither a 'condition' nor a 'warranty' but one of that large *class* of contractual undertakings one breach of which may have the same effect as that ascribed to a breach of 'condition' under the Sale of Goods Act 1893 and a different breach of which may only have the same effect as that ascribed to a breach of 'warranty' under that Act."

If the ship is unseaworthy at the start of the voyage, the shipowner is liable for damage to cargo which would not have occurred but for the unseaworthiness, even if other causes contribute to the loss[16]. Where, however, unseaworthiness at the start of the voyage does not cause some subsequent damage to cargo, the shipowner's liability will depend on whether the damage is due to an "excepted peril", *i.e.* is covered by a term in the charter-party exempting the shipowner from liability in the circumstances that have occurred[17].

(ii) *Reasonable despatch.*—There is an implied obligation on the shipowner under a voyage charter-party that the voyage will be be commenced and carried out without unreasonable delay[18]. If the breach is so serious that the commercial purpose of the charterer is substantially defeated, he may repudiate the contract but otherwise he is confined to a remedy in damages.

(iii) *No unwarranted deviation.*—The shipowner is under an implied obligation to ensure that there is no unnecessary or unwarranted deviation of the ship from its proper course. The route may be specified in the contract but otherwise the proper course is either the shortest geographical route or the usual route[19].

---

13. *Elder Dempster & Co.* v. *Paterson Zochonis & Co.*, [1924] A. C. 522.
14. *Stanton* v. *Richardson* (1874), L. R. 9 C. P. 390.
15. *Hong Kong Fir Shipping Co., Ltd.* v. *Kawasaki Kisen Kaisha, Ltd.*, [1962] 1 All E. R. 474, 487; [1962] 2 Q. B. 26, 41.
16. *Smith, Hogg & Co., Ltd.* v. *Black Sea and Baltic Insce. Co.*, [1940] 3 All E. R. 405; [1940] A. C. 997; see also *Monarch Steamship Co.* v. *Karlshamns Oljefabriker (A/B)*, [1949] 1 All E. R. 1; [1949] A. C. 196.
17. *The Europa*, [1908] P. 84.
18. *M. Andrew* v. *Adams* (1834), 1 Bing. N. C. 29.
19. *Reardon Smith Lines, Ltd.* v. *Black Sea and Baltic Lines Insurance Co., Ltd., The Indian City*, [1939] 3 All E. R. 444; [1939] A. C. 562.

Voluntary unwarranted deviation renders the contract of affreightment voidable so that, at the charterer's option, a voyage charter-party
is voided as from the beginning of the voyage, no matter when or where
the deviation took place. Moreover, if loss or damage to cargo occurs,
the shipowner cannot rely on the excepted perils clause in the charter-
party even though the loss or damage to cargo was not caused by the
deviation[20]. In *James Morrison & Co.* v. *Shaw, Savill & Co.*[1],

A ship was torpedoed by an enemy submarine during an unwarranted deviation. *Held:* the shipowners could not rely on the
excepted perils clause; nor could they rely on the exceptions
available to common carriers at Common Law that the loss was
caused by the King's enemies unless they could prove that the
loss would have occurred if the ship had been on her proper
course. Clearly the shipowners could not prove this here.

Breach of the obligation also entitles the charterers to claim damages for
any loss resulting.

Deviation is permissible where it is necessary for the safety of the
ship or crew even though this necessity was caused by unseaworthiness
or was due to some culpable act on the part of the ship's master. If,
therefore, the ship is in peril the master is not faced by the alternative
of having to choose between the safety of his ship and crew and the
loss of the contract of affreightment[2]. Furthermore, there is a general
right to deviate in order to save life, *e.g.* the crew of another ship in
distress, but not to save property[3].

The contract may of course contain an express term allowing the ship
to call at ports that are not on the usual route or to make other
deviations not warranted at Common Law.

Implied Obligation of Charterer

In both voyage and time charter-parties, the charterer is under an
implied obligation not to ship goods which involve the risk of unusual
danger or delay to the ship, *e.g.* goods which the charterers know
cannot be discharged at the port of discharge without violating the law
prevailing at that port[4].

---

20. *Joseph Thorley, Ltd.* v. *Orchis Steamship Co., Ltd.*, [1907] 1 K. B. 405.
1. [1916] 2 K. B. 783 (a bill of lading case, but the same principle applies to
   charter-parties).
2. *Kish* v. *Taylor*, [1912] A. C. 604.
3. *Scaramanga* v. *Stamp* (1880), 5 C. P. D. 295. But in bills of lading governed
   by the Carriage of Goods by Sea Act 1924 or by the Carriage of Goods by
   Sea Act 1971, deviation to save property is permissible. See *post*, p. 363.
4. *Mitchell, Cotts & Co.* v. *Steel Brothers & Co., Ltd.*, [1916] 2 K. B. 610.
   Under a time charter-party, the charterer is also under an implied obligation
   to use only good and safe ports.

Form of Charter-party

While a charterparty may be in any form, a shipowner and charterer will normally employ one of the various standard forms originating in agreement between the Chamber of Shipping of the United Kingdom and the Baltic and International Maritime Conference whose membership comprises shipowners, shipbrokers and chartering agents. These standard contracts are known by various code names such as "Gencon", "Nubaltwood", "Austwheat" etc. The following is the "Gencon" form reproduced by kind permission of the Baltic and International Maritime Conference. It is used the world over and considered particularly suitable for cargoes of grain, fertilizers, salt, scrap iron, bricks, cattle and several other types of cargo.

PART A   Place and date:

1. IT IS THIS DAY MUTUALLY AGREED between

                              Owners of the steamer
or motor-vessel

                   of   tons gross/net Register
and carrying about   tons of deadweight cargo, now

and expected ready to load under this Charter about   and
Messrs.   of   as Charterers.

That the said vessel shall proceed to

                 or so near thereto as she may safely get
and lie always afloat, and there load a full and complete cargo (if shipment of deck cargo agreed same to be at Charterers' risk) of

(Charterers to provide all mats and/or wood for dunnage and any separations required, the Owners allowing the use of any dunnage wood on board if required) which the Charterers bind themselves to ship, and being so loaded the vessel shall proceed to

               as ordered on signing Bills of Lading
or so near thereto as she may safely get and lie always afloat and there deliver the cargo on being paid freight—on delivered/intaken quantity—as follows:

2. The freight to be paid in cash without discount on delivery of the cargo at mean rate of exchange ruling on day or days of payment, the receivers of the cargo being bound to pay freight on account during delivery, if required by Captain or Owners.

Cash for vessel's ordinary disbursements at port of loading to be advanced by Charterers if required at highest current rate of exchange, subject to two per cent. to cover insurance and other expenses.

3. Cargo to be brought alongside in such a manner as to enable vessel to take the goods with her own tackle and to load
the full cargo in
running working days. Charterers to procure and pay the necessary men on shore or on board the lighters to do the work there, vessel only heaving the cargo on board.

If the loading takes place by elevator cargo to be put free in vessel's holds, Owners only paying trimming expenses.

Any pieces and/or packages of cargo over two tons weight, shall be loaded, stowed and discharged by Charterers at their risk and expense.

Time to commence at 1 p.m. if notice of readiness to load is given before noon and at 6 a.m. next working day if notice given during office hours after noon.

The notice to be given to the Shippers, Messrs.

Time lost in waiting for berth to count as loading time.

4. Cargo to be received by Merchants at their risk and expense alongside the vessel not beyond the reach of her tackle and to be discharged in
running working days.   Time to commence at 1 p.m. if notice of readiness to discharge is given before noon, and at 6 a.m. next working day if notice given during office hours after noon.

Time lost in waiting for berth to count as discharging time.

5. Ten running days on demurrage at the rate of   per day or pro rata for any part of a day, payable day by day, to be allowed Merchants altogether at ports of loading and discharging.

6. Should the vessel not be ready to load (whether in berth or not) on or before the   Charterers have the option of cancelling this contract, such option to be declared, if demanded, at least 48 hours before vessel's expected arrival at port of loading. Should the vessel be delayed on account of average or otherwise, Charterers to be informed as soon as possible, and if the vessel is delayed for more than 10 days after the day she is stated to be expected ready to load, Charterers have the option of cancelling this contract, unless a cancelling date has been agreed upon.

7. In every case the Owner shall appoint his own Broker or Agent both at the port of loading and the port of discharge.

8.   brokerage on the freight earned is due to

In case of non-execution at least 1/3 of the brokerage on the estimated amount of freight and dead-freight to be paid by the Owners to the Brokers as indemnity for the latter's expenses and work.   In case of more voyages the amount of indemnity to be mutually agreed.

9-15.: as in part B, which constitutes a part of this Charter as though fully set forth herein.

PART B

9. Owners are to be responsible for loss of or damage to the goods or for delay in delivery of the goods only in case the loss, damage or delay has been caused by the improper or negligent stowage of the goods

(unless stowage performed by shippers or their stevedores or servants) or by personal want of due diligence on the part of the Owners or their Manager to make the vessel in all respects seaworthy and secure that she is properly manned, equipped and supplied or by the personal act or default of the Owners or their Manager.

And the Owners are responsible for no loss or damage or delay arising from any other cause whatsoever, even from the neglect or default of the Captain or crew or some other person employed by the Owners on board or ashore for whose acts they would, but for this clause, be responsible, or from unseaworthiness of the vessel on loading or commencement of the voyage or at any time whatsoever.

Damage caused by contact with or leakage, smell or evaporation from other goods or by the inflammable or explosive nature or insufficient package of other goods not to be considered as caused by improper or negligent stowage, even if in fact so caused.

10. The vessel has liberty to call at any port or ports in any order, for any purpose, to sail without pilots, to tow and/or assist vessels in all situations, and also to deviate for the purpose of saving life and/or property.

11. Owners shall have a lien on the cargo for freight, dead-freight, demurrage and damages for detention. Charterers shall remain responsible for dead-freight and demurrage (including damages for detention), incurred at port of loading. Charterers shall also remain responsible for freight and demurrage (including damages for detention) incurred at port of discharge, but only to such extent as the Owners have been unable to obtain payment thereof by exercising the lien on the cargo.

12. The Captain to sign Bills of Lading at such rate of freight as presented without prejudice to this Charterparty, but should the freight by Bills of Lading amount to less than the total chartered freight the difference to be paid to the Captain in cash on signing Bills of Lading.

13. General average to be settled according to York–Antwerp Rules, 1950, Proprietors of cargo to pay the cargo's share in the general expenses even if same have been necessitated through neglect or default of the Owner's servants (see clause 9).

14. Indemnity for non-performance of this Charterparty, proved damages, not exceeding estimated amount of freight.

15. **Strike-Clause, War-Clause and Ice-Clause as below.**

GENERAL STRIKE CLAUSE

Neither Charterers nor Owners shall be responsible for the conse-sequences of any strikes or lock ·outs preventing or delaying the fulfilment of any obligations under this contract.

If there is a strike or lock-out affecting the loading of the cargo, or any part of it, when vessel is ready to proceed from her last port or at any time during the voyage to the port or ports of loading or after her arrival there, Captain or Owners may ask Charterers to declare, that they agree to reckon the laydays as if there were no strike or lock-out. Unless Charterers have given such declaration in writing (by telegram, if necessary) within 24 hours, Owners shall have the option of cancelling this contract. If part cargo has already been loaded, Owners must proceed with same, (freight payable on loaded quantity only) having liberty to complete with other cargo on the way for their own account.

If there is a strike or lock-out affecting the discharge of the cargo on or after vessel's arrival at or off port of discharge and same has not been settled within 48 hours, Receivers shall have the option of keeping vessel waiting until such strike or lock-out is at an end against paying half demurrage after expiration of the time provided for discharging, or of ordering the vessel to a safe port where she can safely discharge without risk of being detained by strike or lock-out. Such orders to be given within 48 hours after Captain or Owners have given notice to Charterers of the strike or lock-out affecting the discharge. On delivery of the cargo at such port, all conditions of this Charter-party and of the Bill of Lading shall apply and vessel shall receive the same freight as if she had discharged at the original port of destination, except that if the distance of the substituted port exceeds 100 nautical miles, the freight on the cargo delivered at the substituted port to be increased in proportion.

GENERAL WAR CLAUSE

If the nation under whose flag the vessel sails should be engaged in war and the safe navigation of the vessel should thereby be endangered either party to have the option of cancelling this contract, and if so cancelled, cargo already shipped shall be discharged either at the port of loading or, if the vessel has commenced the voyage, at the nearest safe place at the risk and expense of the Charterers or Cargo-Owners.

If owing to outbreak of hostilities the goods loaded or to be loaded under this contract or part of them become contraband of war whether absolute or conditional or liable to confiscation or detention according to international law or the proclamation of any of the belligerent powers each party to have the option of cancelling this contract as far as such goods are concerned, and contraband goods already loaded to be then discharged either at the port of loading, or if the voyage has already commenced, at the nearest safe place at the expense of the Cargo-Owners. Owners to have the right to fill up with other goods instead of the contraband.

Should any port where the vessel has to load under this Charter be blockaded the contract to be null and void with regard to the goods to be shipped at such port.

No Bills of Lading to be signed for any blockaded port, and if the port of destination be declared blockaded after Bills of Lading have been signed, Owners shall discharge the cargo either at the port of loading, against payment of the expenses of discharge, if the ship has not sailed thence, or, if sailed at any safe port on the way as ordered by Shippers or if no order is given at the nearest safe place against payment of full freight.

GENERAL ICE CLAUSE

(a) In the event of the loading port being inaccessible by reason of ice when vessel is ready to proceed from her last port or at any time during the voyage or on vessels arrival or in case frost sets in after vessel's arrival, the Captain for fear of being frozen in is at liberty to leave without cargo, and this Charter shall be null and void.

(*b*) If during loading the Captain, for fear of vessel being frozen in, deems it advisable to leave, he has liberty to do so with what cargo he has on board and to proceed to any other port or ports with option of completing cargo for Owner's benefit for any port or ports including port of discharge. Any part cargo thus loaded under this Charter to be forwarded to destination at vessel's expense but against payment of freight, provided that no extra expenses be thereby caused to the Receivers, freight being paid on quantity delivered (in proportion if lumpsum), all other conditions as per Charter.

(*c*) In case of more than one loading port, and if one or more of the ports are closed by ice, the Captain or Owners to be at liberty either to load the part cargo at the open port and fill up elsewhere for their own account as under section *b* or to declare the Charter null and void unless Charterers agree to load full cargo at the open port.

(*d*) This Ice Clause not to apply in the Spring.

(*a*) Should ice (except in the Spring) prevent vessel from reaching port of discharge Receivers shall have the option of keeping vessel waiting until the re-opening of navigation and paying demurrage, or of ordering the vessel to a safe and immediately accessible port where she can safely discharge without risk of detention by ice. Such orders to be given within 48 hours after Captain or Owners have given notice to Charterers of the impossibility of reaching port of destination.

(*b*) If during discharging the Captain for fear of vessel being frozen in deems it advisable to leave, he has liberty to do so with what cargo he has on board and to proceed to the nearest accessible port where she can safely discharge.

(*c*) On delivery of the cargo at such port, all conditions of the Bill of Lading shall apply and vessel shall receive the same freight as if she had discharged at the original port of destination, except that if the distance of the substituted port exceeds 100 nautical miles, the freight on the cargo delivered at the substituted port to be increased in proportion.

Notes on the Form of Charter-party

1. *Now . . .*—This is to indicate the position of the ship at the date of the charter-party. A statement as to where the ship is will generally be construed as a condition precedent, the falsity of which entitles the charterers to rescind[5].

2. *Shall proceed to . . .*—The owner must bring the ship to the agreed place of loading at the port where the voyage is to commence within a reasonable time.

3. *Or so near thereto as she may safely get and lie always afloat.*—If the ship cannot safely reach the place named, the shipowner complies with his obligation by taking the ship as near to that place as is safe.

---

5. *Behn* v. *Burness* (1863), 3 B. & S. 751.

The first part of this phrase entitles the shipowner to demand that the cargo be loaded at some place other than at the named place if she is prevented from getting there by some permanent obstacle, *e.g.* ice or a blockade in wartime, which cannot be overcome by the shipowner within such time as according to all the circumstances of the case may reasonably be allowed[6]. The phrase "always afloat" means that if the ship cannot load without touching ground at the named port, the master is entitled to load at the nearest safe port. If, however, the ship can safely lie at the named port in order to load for a certain time only, the master is bound to load there[7].

4. *A full and complete cargo.*—But for this provision, a shipowner paid at a rate per ton of the cargo might find that owing to waste of space his freight has not come up to what he had contemplated. If the ship is described in the earlier part of the document as—"of 340 tons or thereabouts" and the words—"full and complete cargo" are unqualified, the charterer does not fulfil his obligation by putting on board a cargo of 340 tons, if in fact the ship will take more; he must pay freight not only on the 340 tons shipped but also "dead" freight, *i.e.* damages for failing to provide a full and complete cargo[8]. The charterer is of course not liable for putting less than 340 tons on board if the ship cannot take that quantity.

Sometimes the charter-party runs thus:

"a full and complete cargo, say [about 1,100] tons";

in such a case the charterer is not bound to load the ship up to her actual capacity, but his obligation will be satisfied if he loads to about three per cent. in excess of the 1,100 tons, though the ship's capacity is over 1,200 tons[9]. But the word "cargo" alone, in the absence of anything in the charter-party to qualify it, means the entire load of the vessel, and therefore the omission of the words "full and complete" is often immaterial[10].

On the other hand, subject to the stipulations of the charter-party, it is an implied condition that the shipowner shall not use the ship

---

6. BRETT, L.J., in *Nelson v. Dahl* (1879), 12 Ch. D., at p. 592.
7. *Carlton Steamship Co. v. Castle Mail Packets Co.*, [1898] A. C. 486.
8. *Hunter v. Fry* (1819), 2 B. & Ald. 421; *Morris v. Levison* (1876), 1 C. P. D. 155. However, the *de minimis* rule applies in determining whether "a full and complete cargo" has been loaded: *Margaronis Navigation Agency, Ltd. v. Henry W. Peabody & Co. of London, Ltd.*, [1964] 3 All E. R. 333; [1965] 2 Q. B. 430, C. A.
9. *Morris v. Levison, supra; cf. Miller v. Borner,* [1900] 1 Q. B. 691; 5 Com. Cas. 175, where the charterer contracted only to load a "cargo of ore, say about 2,800 tons," not a "full and complete cargo".
10. *Borrowman v. Drayton* (1877), 2 Ex. D. 15; *Jardine, Matheson & Co. v. Clyde Shipping Co.*, [1910] 1 K. B. 627; *cf. Miller v. Borner,* [1900] 1 Q. B. 691, where on the construction of the particular charter-party the omission of the words "full and complete" was held to be material.

in a manner prejudicial to the charterer, *e.g.* he cannot load bunker coal intended for a future voyage so as to prevent the charterer having full advantage of the ship[11].

Where the charter-party provides for a cargo of "lawful merchandise", the cargo must be such that it not only can be loaded without breach of the law in force at the port of loading, but also can be lawfully discharged at the port of destination[12].

5. *Which the Charterers bind themselves to ship.*—When the charterer has notice that the ship is ready to load, he must bring the cargo alongside the ship and deliver it to the master of the ship[13]. If under the local rules the ship cannot proceed to the dock area until the cargo is ready, the charterer is liable in damages for delay in producing the cargo[14].

In the absence of express stipulation in the charter-party, the charterer is liable for not producing a cargo, even if he is not personally at fault in failing to do so[15]. As a rule the shipowner is responsible for proper storage[16] but the exceptions are numerous[17].

6. *The vessel shall proceed to . . . or so near thereto as she may safely get and lie always afloat and there deliver the cargo.*—The phrases "so near thereto as she may safely get" and "always afloat" have already been explained.

In *Nelson v. Dahl*, BRETT, L.J., stated that:

"The liability of the shipowner as to the commencement of the unloading is to use all reasonable dispatch to bring the ship to the named place where the carrying voyage is to end, unless prevented by excepted perils, and when the ship is there arrived, to have her ready with all reasonable dispatch to discharge in the usual or stipulated manner"[18].

The shipowner is not under an obligation to give notice that he is ready to unload. The consignee or charterer must be ready without any such notice to take the cargo from alongside, and for that purpose provide the proper appliances for taking delivery there[19]; the shipowner should put the cargo over the rail of the ship, and in such a position that the consignee can take it.

---

11. *Darling v. Raeburn*, [1906] 1 K. B. 572; *affirmed*, [1907] 1 K. B. 846.
12. *Leolga Compagnia de Navigacion v. John Glynn & Son, Ltd.*, [1953] 2 All E. R. 327; [1953] 2 Q. B. 375.
13. *Per* SELBORNE, L.C., in *Grant v. Coverdale* (1884), 9 App. Cas., at p. 475.
14. *The Aello*, [1957] 3 All E. R. 626; [1958] 2 Q. B. 385.
15. *Grant v. Coverdale* (1884), 9 App. Cas. 470 is a good example.
16. *Blaikie v. Stembridge* (1859), B. C. B., N. S. 894.
17. *E.g. Canadian Transport Co., Ltd. v. Court Line, Ltd.*, [1940] A. C. 934; [1940] 3 All E. R. 112.
18. (1879), 12 Ch. D., at p. 584.
19. *Dahl v. Nelson Donkin & Co.* (1881), 6 App. Cas., *per* Lord BLACKBURN, at p. 43.

The shipowner must deliver the goods to the consignee or charterer or an agent thereof unless by custom or contract some mode of delivery other than personal delivery is permissible. Normally the goods must be delivered only against production of the bill of lading[20].

Under the Merchant Shipping Act 1894, the master of a ship has certain statutory powers of landing goods in the United Kingdom where the owner of goods imported into the United Kingdom fails to take delivery of them. If such owner fails to land or take deliver of the goods at the time agreed (or if no time is agreed, within seventy-two hours, exclusive of a Sunday or holiday), from the time of the report of the ship (required by the Customs laws) the shipowner may land or unship the goods and place them at certain places according to circumstances. The shipowner may, by giving written notice to the person in whose custody the goods are placed, retain his lien for freight on the same, and then, subject to certain conditions, the person with whom the goods are deposited may, and if required by the shipowner shall, if the lien is not discharged as provided by the Merchant Shipping Act 1894, at the expiration of ninety days from the time when the goods were placed in his custody (or earlier if they are perishable), sell by public auction sufficient of the goods to satisfy the Customs dues, the expenses, and the freight[1].

7. *On being paid freight.*—Freight is dealt with later; see *post*, pp. 365–367.

8. *Running working days and Demurrage.*—Normally, a charter-party specifies the number of "lay days", *i.e.* the number of days allowed for loading and discharging the cargo. Where they are referred to as "running working days" as in clause 3 (for loading) and clause 4 (for discharging), this means days on which work is usually done in the port. Lay days commence when the ship arrives at the place agreed on in the charter-party, and the charterer has notice that she is ready to load (no notice is required that she is ready to discharge). The days run continuously, each day being counted from midnight to midnight and not periods of 24 hours[2].

If a port only is named without, e.g., any particular dock or mooring being specified, the ship is deemed to be an "arrived" ship when she comes within the commercial area of the port even though no berth is available for her[3]. Dispatch money may be payable to the charterers

---

20. *Sze Hai Tong Bank, Ltd.* v. *Rambler Cycle Co.*, [1959] 3 All E. R. 182; [1959] A. C. 576.
1. Merchant Shipping Act 1894, ss. 492-501.
2. *The Katy,* [1895] P. 56.
3. *Leonis Steamship Co., Ltd.* v. *Rank, Ltd.*, [1908] 1 K. B. 499; *The Johanna Oldenorff, E. L. Oldenorff & Co. G. M. B. H.* v. *Tradex Export S. A.*, [1972] 3 All E. R. 420; [1972] 3 W. L. R. 623, C. A.

if the loading or discharging is completed early[4]. However, charterers are entitled to use the whole of the lay time for loading and need not hurry to suit the convenience of the owners[5].

"*Demurrage*" properly signifies the agreed additional payment, generally per day (*i.e.* agreed damages) for delay beyond the "lay days". This is the strict meaning of demurrage and the freighter who agrees to pay demurrage for detention beyond the lay days will have to pay so long as the ship is in such condition that she cannot be handed back to the use of the shipowner, even if the delay is not caused by the freighter's default[6].

The House of Lords has held[7] that the shipowner's claim is confined to the amount of demurrage agreed even though, because of the extent of the charterer's delays, the charterer is guilty of a fundamental breach of contract and the shipowner is therefore entitled to repudiate the contract. The shipowner cannot claim instead unliquidated damages based, *e.g.* on loss of profit through the ship being able to make fewer voyages during the period of the charter.

The word "demurrage" is also used to mean compensation by way of unliquidated damages for undue detention when the agreement has not specially provided for agreed damages[8]. Thus, if no lay days are mentioned, the charterer is liable to pay damages if he detains the ship beyond what, in the actual circumstances, is a reasonable time[9]. But in either case, the charterer is not liable to pay if the delay is due to the default of the owner or of those for whom the owner is responsible or if the contract clearly specifies.

Demurrage in the sense of unliquidated damages is only damages for the detention of the ship. It does not exclude damages under a totally different head[10].

9. *Owners are to be responsible for loss of or damage to the goods . . .*— There is some doubt as to the Common Law liability of a carrier of goods by sea, but invariably the matter is provided for by the terms of the contract. Thus the effect of this clause is to confine the shipowner's liability for loss of or damage to the cargo or for delay in delivery of the goods to cases where such loss, damage or delay is

---

4. See *e.g. Alma Shipping Co., S.A.* v. *V. M. Salgeances e Irmaos, Ltd.*, [1954] 2 All E. R. 92.
5. *Margaronis Navigation Agency* v. *Henry W. Peabody & Co. of London, Ltd.*, [1964] 3 All E. R. 333; [1965] 2 Q. B. 430.
6. ESHER, M.R., in *Budgett* v. *Binnington*, [1891] 1 Q. B. 38.
7. *Suisse Atlantique Société d'Armement Maritime S.A.* v. *Rotterdamsche Kolen Centrale*, [1966] 2 All E. R. 61; [1967] 1 A. C. 361.
8. BOWEN, L.J., in *Clink* v. *Radford*, [1891] 1 Q. B., at p. 630.
9. *Hick* v. *Rodocanachi*, [1891] 2 Q. B. 626; [1893] A. C. 22.
10. *Aktieselskabet Reider* v. *Arcos, Ltd.*, [1926] All E. R. Rep. 140; [1927] 1 K. B. 352, C. A.

caused by improper or negligent stowage where stowage has been by or on behalf of the shipowner, or by personal want of due diligence on the part of the owner or his manager to make the ship seaworthy and to see that she is properly manned, equipped and supplied. The clause makes it clear that the owners are responsible for no loss or damage or delay "arising from any other cause whatsoever". It is thus much broader in exempting the owner from liability than a charter-party which sets out a number of specific excepted perils such as act of God and perils of the sea and leaves the owner liable for any damage not caused by one of the excepted perils mentioned.

10. *The vessel has liberty . . . to deviate for the purpose of saving life and/or property.*—As was said in discussing the implied obligation of the shipowner that there shall be no unwarranted deviation from the route, there is a general right in order to save life but not to save property. The terms of this clause do entitle the ship to deviate to save property.

11. *Receivers shall have the option of keeping the vessel waiting until such strike . . . is at an end against paying half demurrage after expiration of the time provided for discharging.*—Where a strike continued beyond the lay days, but goods were discharged on the strike ending and the ship was delayed through congestion at another port, it has been held that half demurrage only was payable both for the period from the end of the lay days to the end of the strike and for the period from then until the end of discharging at the last port[11].

III BILLS OF LADING

A bill of lading is a document acknowledging the shipment of goods, signed by or on behalf of the carrier[12]. It is, secondly, excellent evidence of the contract for the carriage of goods but is not in itself the contract of carriage and evidence may be given that a contract was made before the bill of lading was signed and that the contract differs in some respect from the provisions of the bill of lading[13]. Its third function is as a document of title and this aspect is considered below[14].

---

11. *The Onisilos, Salamis Shipping (Panama) S. A.* v. *Edm. Van Meerbeck & Co. S. A.*, [1971] 2 All E. R. 497; [1971] 2 Q. B. 500, C. A.
12. *Caldwell* v. *Ball* (1786), 1 T. L. 216. A document acknowledging the receipt of goods "for shipment" was held to be a bill of lading by the Privy Council in "*Marlborough Hill*" *(Ship)* v. *Cowan & Sons*, [1921] 1 A. C. 444, but in the subsequent case of *Diamond Alkali Export Corporation* v. *Fl. Bourgeois*, McCARDIE, J., refused to treat such a document tendered by the sellers under a C.I.F. contract as a good bill of lading.
13. *The Ardennes*, [1950] 2 All E. R. 517; [1951] 1 K. B. 55.
14. See *post*, p. 355.

A bill of lading is generally used even when the ship is chartered. If the charterer finds the cargo himself, the bill of lading is usually, but not always, a mere receipt for the goods given by the master and a document of title but does not contain the contractual terms of the carriage. The form of a bill of lading varies much according to the practice of the parties thereto, but a usual form is as follows[15]:

> "Shipped in good order and condition by   , in and upon the good ship called the 'British Tar,' whereof   , is master for this present voyage, and now in the port of   , and bound for   , with liberty to call at any ports on the way for coaling or other necessary purposes, fifty casks of wine being marked and numbered as per margin, and to be delivered in the like good order and condition at the aforesaid port of   , the act of God, the Queen's enemies, fire, barratry of the master and crew, and all and every other dangers and accidents of the seas, rivers, and navigation of whatever kind or nature soever excepted, unto   or to his assigns, he or they paying freight for the said goods £   per ton, delivered with primage and average accustomed. In witness whereof, the master of the said ship hath affirmed to   bills of lading all of this tenor and date, one of which bills being accomplished, the others to stand void.
> "Dated, etc.
> "Weight, value, and contents unknown."

Many matters already mentioned in connection with charter-parties apply equally to bills of lading. Several of these are mentioned in the notes to the form of charter-party given above[16]. There is, however, this difference: a shipowner, when the contract is contained in a charter-party, may have duties to perform before the time of shipment of the goods; this is not so often the case when the contract is evidenced by a bill of lading only.

Bill of Lading and Mate's Receipt

The bill of lading is signed generally by the master (or by the shipowner's loading broker) though in practice, where the goods are shipped, the acknowledgment first given is a less formal receipt (*"mate's receipt"* —not a document of title), which is afterwards exchanged for a bill of lading. But there is nothing to prevent the giving of a bill of lading without production of the mate's receipt, if the goods are on board,

---

15. As to what the bill of lading must show where the Carriage of Goods by Sea Act 1924 or the Carriage of Goods by Sea Act 1971 applies, see *post*, pp. 358–365.
16. *Ante*, p. 345 *et seq.*

and if there is no interest in them known to the master except that of the shipper[17].

The shipowner is justified in delivering bills of lading to the holder of the mate's receipt if he has no notice of other claims[18]. If the mate's receipts and the bills of lading get into different hands the goods must be delivered to the holder of the bills[19].

Whose agent is the master

The master, when he signs, affixes his signature as agent of the owners of the vessel; except that when a vessel has been chartered, and the charterers put up the vessel as a general ship, then the master may be agent of the charterer and not of the owner, the decision in each case depending upon the facts. If the ship has been demised[20] to the charterer, the master is generally the charterer's agent[21], but the mere fact that the charter-party provides that the master shall be the agent of the charterer does not of itself bind those who deal with the ship without actual notice of this clause[1]. The law on this subject may be stated in the words of COCKBURN, C.J., in *Sandeman* v. *Scurr*[2]:

> "where a party allows another to appear before the world as his agent in any given capacity, he must be liable to any party who contracts with such apparent agent in a matter within the scope of such agency. The master of a vessel has by law authority to sign bills of lading on behalf of his owners. A person shipping goods on board a vessel, unaware that the vessel has been chartered to another, is warranted in assuming that the master is acting by virtue of his ordinary authority, and therefore acting for his owners in signing bills of lading.

In this case

> the charterers put up a vessel as a general ship, and plaintiff put on board wine, and received bills of lading in ordinary form signed by the master, and the owners were held liable for loss by leakage arising from improper stowage, it being questioned whether an action would not lie also against the charterers.

An indorsee of the bill of lading, who takes it *bona fide*, and for value, and without notice of the charter-party, may hold the shipowner to the terms of the bill of lading; but if this indorsee was aware of the

---

17. *Hathesing* v. *Laing* (1874), L. R. 17 Eq. 92.
18. *Evan* v. *Nichol* (1842), 3 M. & G. 614.
19. *Baumwoll, etc.* v. *Furness*, [1893] A. C. 8.
20. See *ante*, p. 337.
21. *Baumwoll, etc.* v. *Furness*, [1893] A. C., at p. 14.
1. *Manchester Trust* v. *Furness*, [1895] 2 Q. B. 539; 1 Com. Cas. 39.
2. (1866), L. R. 2 Q. B. 86, 97.

charter-party when he took the bill, the shipowner will not be bound if the bill of lading was signed without the shipowner's authority[3].

Effect of master's signature

The master has no authority to sign a bill of lading for goods not actually received on board[4], and if he does so, the owners are not liable; but his signature is *prima facie* evidence against the owners that the goods were shipped, and it lies on the owners to rebut this evidence if they allege that the goods never were on board[5]; however, a bill of lading will not be even *prima facie* evidence of quantity, if it contains qualifying words, such as—

"A quantity of 937 tons, weight, etc. unknown"[6].

By express stipulation the bill of lading may be made conclusive evidence against the shipowners of the quantity shipped[7].

As regards the *master's liability*, by section 3 of the Bills of Lading Act 1855,

"every bill of lading in the hands of a consignee or indorsee for valuable consideration, representing goods to have been shipped on board a vessel, shall be *conclusive evidence* of such shipment as against the master or other person signing the same, notwithstanding that such goods or some part thereof may not have been so shipped."

But even the master will not be liable if—

1. The holder of the bill at the time of receiving it is aware that the goods have not been actually shipped; or
2. The misrepresentation in the bill was caused by the fraud of the shipper, the holder, or of some person under whom the holder claims[8].

Neither does the section estop the person signing the bill of lading from showing that goods incorrectly described in the bill of lading by mere marks of identification, having no significance in respect of their quantity, quality, or commercial value, are in fact the goods which were shipped under the bill of lading[9].

---

3. *The Patria* (1872), L. R. 3 Ad. & Ec. 436.
4. *McLean* v. *Fleming* (1872), L. R. 2 H. L. Sc. 128; *Grant* v. *Norway* (1851), 10 C. B. 665.
5. *Smith* v. *Bedouin Steam Navigation Co.*, [1896] A. C. 70.
6. *New Chinese Antimony Co.* v. *Ocean S.S. Co.*, [1917] 2 K. B. 664; *Att.-Gen. Ceylon* v. *Scindia Steam Navigation Co., Ltd.*, [1961] 3 All E. R. 684; [1962] A. C. 60, P. C.
7. *Lishman* v. *Christie* (1887), 19 Q. B. D. 333.
8. Bills of Lading Act 1855, s. 3; and see *Valieri* v. *Boyland* (1866), L. R. 1 C. P. 382.
9. *Parsons* v. *New Zealand Shipping Co.*, [1901] 1 K. B. 548; 6 Com. Cas. 41.

Duty of shipowner

Like the obligations of a shipowner implied in a charter-party, the shipowner impliedly undertakes in a bill of lading that the ship is seaworthy, that she will proceed with reasonable despatch, and that she shall proceed without any unwarranted deviation[10]. The meaning of these obligations was considered in the discussion of Charter-parties[11] and they can likewise be excluded or varied by express terms. The shipowner is not liable for loss or damage to cargo if caused by a cause listed in the excepted perils clause of the bill of lading, *e.g.*:

   (i) "Act of God and the Queen's enemies".

   (ii) "Accidents from machinery", etc.

When the bill states that the goods are shipped

   "in good order and condition."

it is called a *clean* bill of lading. These words refer to the apparent and external condition. They operate as *prima facie* evidence in favour of the shipper and as conclusive evidence in favour of the indorsee of the bill of lading. If the words are untrue, the shipowner will be liable in damages to an indorsee of the bill of lading who suffers loss by acting on the faith of the representation[12]. This statement is not sufficiently qualified by adding the words "condition unknown" so as to convey to a transferee of the bill of lading notice that the goods are or may be in a damaged state[13]. If the master signs a clean bill of lading knowing that the goods shipped are not in good order and condition in return for an indemnity by the shipper, such indemnity is illegal and unenforceable[14].

Duty of shipper

The shipper is under an implied obligation not to ship goods which involve the risk of unusual danger or delay to the ship unless the shipowner is aware or ought to be aware of this fact as a result of notice from the shipper or otherwise.

---

10. For the measure of damages for loss caused by deviation, see *Monarch Steamship Co., Ltd.* v. *Karlshamns Oljefabriker (A/B),* [1949] A. C. 196; *Mehmet Dogan Bey* v. *G. G. Abdeni & Co., Ltd.,* [1951] 2 All E. R. 162; [1951] 2 K. B. 405.

11. *Ante*, p. 338 *et seq.*

12. *Compania Naviera Vasconzada* v. *Churchill,* [1906] 1 K. B. 237; *Brandt* v. *Liverpool, etc. Steam Navigation Co.,* [1924] 1 K. B. 575; see also *Silver* v. *Ocean S.S. Co., post,* p. 361.

13. *The Skarp,* [1935] P. 134. But see *Canada and Dominion Sugar Co., Ltd.* v. *Canadian National Steamship, Ltd.,* [1947] A. C. 46.

14. *Brown, Jenkinson & Co.* v. *Percy Dalton (London), Ltd.,* [1957] 2 All E. R. 844; [1957] 2 Q. B. 621.

Transfer of bill of lading

A bill of lading is not only a document containing the terms of a contract of carriage, it is in addition a document of title; it is the symbol of goods at sea, and remains so until the goods have come to the hands of a person entitled under the bill of lading to the possession of them[15].

The person to whom the bill is made out may transfer his rights under it; if the bill is drawn to order, he does so by indorsing the bill and delivering it to the assignee; and if it is drawn to bearer he may transfer his rights under it by mere delivery. Where the bill is indorsed, it may be indorsed in blank (*i.e.* the mere signature of the transferor on the back of the bill) or be specially indorsed (*i.e.* on indication of the transferee's name together with the transferor's signature). Where a bill of lading is transferred by indorsement and delivery or by delivery, the transferee is entitled to demand possession of the goods as owner or pledgee according to the nature of the transaction[16].

The transfer of a bill of lading drawn to order, though it passed the goods, did not until 1855 transfer the right to sue on the contract or the obligations under the contract. But by the Bills of Lading Act 1855, s. 1, it was provided that—

"every consignee of goods named in a bill of lading, and every indorsee of a bill of lading, to whom the property in the goods therein mentioned shall pass, upon or by reason of such consignment or indorsement, shall have transferred to and vested in him all rights of suit, and be subject to the same liabilities in respect of such goods as if the contract contained in the bill of lading had been made with himself."

It has been decided that the pledge of a bill of lading does not *per se* pass the property within the meaning of this section, so that the pledgee is not liable to pay the freight; but the case is otherwise if the pledgee exercises his right to take possession of the goods[16].

Delivery of goods

The master must deliver the goods to the consignee upon payment of freight; or if the bill has been properly assigned, then he should deliver to the holder of the bill. Sometimes the bill of lading is executed in duplicate or triplicate, and the different parts may get into the hands of different persons; in such case the first transferee for value is entitled to the goods[17].

---

15. *Barber* v. *Meyerstein* (1870), L. R. 4. L. 317.
16. *Sewell* v. *Burdick* (1885), 10 App. Cas. 74. It should be noted that s. 2 of the Bills of Lading Act enables the shipowner alternatively to claim the freight direct from the original shipper even after he has assigned the bill of lading.
17. *Barber* v. *Meyerstein* (1867), L. R. 2 C. P. 38, 661; (1870), L. R. 4 H. L. 317.

But the master who, acting *bona fide* and without notice of conflicting claims, delivers to a holder who presents any of the parts of the bill of lading to him, is not liable if it should prove that that holder is not the first transferee[18]. This is a consequence of the clause found in bills of lading drawn in a set:

"one of these bills of lading accomplished, the other shall stand void."

If the master has notice of conflicting claims, it is his duty to interplead.

If the bill is drawn to a specified person without the addition of the words "or order or assigns" the bill cannot be transferred. Where the bill can be transferred the transferee cannot normally obtain a better title than the transferor as a bill of lading is not a negotiable instrument. However, a bill of lading is often said to be quasi-negotiable because the rights of a *bona fide* transferee for value of a bill of lading can prevail over the lien of an unpaid seller of goods and over his right to stop the goods in the course of transit[19].

IV LIMITATIONS ON LIABILITY OF SEA CARRIERS

The Merchant Shipping Act 1894

The Merchant Shipping Act 1894, as amended, gives protection to the "owner" of a *British ship* and the term "owner" now covers "any charterer and any person interested in or in the possession of the ship and, in particular, any manager or operator of the ship", when certain kinds of damage occur to goods without any actual fault or privity on his part[20].

Where a claim arises from the act or omission of any person in his capacity as master or member of the crew or as servant of the owners, charterer, etc., similar protection is given to employer and employee alike.

No liability at all arises in the following cases unless there is actual fault or privity on the part of the "owner":—

1. When goods or other things on board are lost or damaged by reason of fire on board the ship[21]. Where fire has been caused by unseaworthiness of the ship that does not deprive the

---

18. *Glyn, Mills & Co.* v. *East and West India Docks* (1882), 7 App. Cas. 591.
19. *Ante*, p. 213.
20. Merchant Shipping Act 1894, s. 503; Merchant Shipping (Liability of Shipowners and Others) Act 1958, s. 3. A master who is also owner of a ship is entitled to this protection: *The Annie Hay*, [1968] 1 All E. R. 657.
21. This includes damage done by smoke, or water used in putting out the fire (*The Diamond*, [1906] P. 282).

shipowner of the statutory exception[1] but the onus is upon the shipowner to prove that the loss happened without his fault; if the owner knew or had the means of knowing of the danger, but gave no special instructions and took no proper steps to previous injurious consequences arising, he will not be entitled to protection. A corporate body can be made liable if the negligence was that of its head or brain, or central or governing managment, and the faulty decision falls within the purview of that authority[2]. A shipowner is, however, not liable merely because of the fault or privity of his servants.

2. When gold, silver, diamonds, watches, jewels, or precious stones are lost or damaged by reason of any robbery, embezzlement, making away with or secreting thereof, and when the shipowner or master had not at the time of shipment received a written declaration of their true nature and value[3].

By s. 503[4] *liability is limited* in the cases mentioned below if the misfortune has occurred without his actual fault or privity, *irrespective of whether the ship is British or foreign.*

1. Where any loss of life or personal injury is caused to any person being carried in the ship;
2. Where any damage or loss is caused to any goods, merchandise, or other things on board;
3. Where any loss of life or injury is caused to any person not carried on the ship or any damage is caused to any property not on the ship or any rights are infringed by improper navigation of the ship, or by acts or omission of any person in loading carriage or discharge of its cargo or embarkation carriage or disembarkation of its passengers[5]. Failure of owners to take steps to ensure that the master used radar in a proper manner may constitute "actual fault", disentitling them to limit their liability[6].

---

1. *Dreyfus (Louis) & Co.* v. *Tempus Shipping Co., Ltd.*, [1931] A. C. 726.
2. *Lennard's Carrying Co.* v. *Asiatic Petroleum Co.*, [1915] A. C. 705. As to the shipowner's right to recover a general average contribution, where he is relieved from liability by the section, see *post*, pp. 367–370.
3. Merchant Shipping Act 1894, s. 502. Protection is not now confined to sea-going ships: Merchant Shipping (Liability of Shipowners and Others) Act 1958, s. 8 (1).
4. *Ibid.*, s. 503, as amended by the Merchant Shipping (Liability of Shipowners and Others) Act 1958, s. 2.
5. See *The Bramley Moore*, [1964] 1 All E. R. 105; [1964] P. 200.
6. *The Lady Gwendolen*, [1964] 3 All E. R. 447; [1964] 3 W. L. R. 1062.

It is the duty of the owner to give instructions to the master where an owner knows that owing to the special construction of the vessel particular precautions of an unusual character require to be taken to keep her seaworthy, and the facts are such that a competent and experienced master might not be aware of the danger to be guarded against. An omission by the owners to give such instructions amounts to "actual fault or privity", and they are not entitled to have their liability limited[7].

The limit in respect of loss of life or personal injury (with or without damage to vessels or goods) is an aggregate amount equivalent to 3,100 gold francs for each ton of the ship's tonnage[8], and in respect of damage to vessels or goods (with or without loss of life or personal injury) an aggregate amount not exceeding 1,000 gold francs[9].

If there are claims in respect of loss of life and goods, the claims for loss of life will be entitled to 3,100 gold francs per ton, and the balance of the claims for loss of life and the claims for goods will rank equally against the remaining 1,000 gold francs[10]. The limits of liability apply to the aggregate of such liabilities which are incurred on any distinct occasion[11]. The fault of one part owner does not take away the right of another part owner to limit his liability[12].

The Carriage of Goods by Sea Act 1924

By this Act the responsibilities, liabilities, rights and immunities attaching to carriers under *bills of lading* are governed by the Hague Rules which are set out in the Schedule to the Act, the operation of which is limited to the carriage of goods[13] by sea in ships carrying goods

---

7. *Standard Oil Co. of New York* v. *Claudine Steamers, Ltd.*, [1924] A. C. 100 (turret ship lost through master emptying water ballast tanks).
8. Where the tonnage is less than 300 tons the sum is multiplied by 300. The Department of Trade may specify the equivalent of gold francs and the conversion rate applicable at the date of judgment prevails: *The Abadesa*, [1968] 2 All E. R. 726; [1968] P. 656; *The Mecca*, [1968] 2 All E. R. 731; [1968] P. 665.
9. Merchant Shipping Act 1894, s. 503, as amended by Merchant Shipping (Liability of Shipowners and Others) Act 1958, s. 1, and s. 69 of the Merchant Shipping Act 1906. There are special provisions for calculating the tonnage for this purpose.
10. *The Victoria* (1888), 13 P. D. 125.
11. Merchant Shipping Act 1894, s. 503 (3), as substituted by Merchant Shipping (Liability of Shipowners and Others) Act 1958, s. 8 (2).
12. *The Obey* (1886), L. R. 1 A. & E. 102.
13. "Goods" does not include live animals and cargo which by the contract of carriage is stated as being carried on deck and is so carried (Carriage of Goods by Sea Act 1924, Sched., Art. I (c)); and see *Svenska Traktor Aktiebolaget* v. *Maritime Agencies (Southampton), Ltd.*, [1953] 2 All E. R. 570; [1953] 2 Q. B. 295 (cargo carried in fact on deck but not so stated). If bills of lading are issued in the case of a ship under a charter-party, they must comply with the Rules.

from any port in Great Britain or Northern Ireland to any other port whether in or outside Great Britain or Northern Ireland[14]. The Hague Rules were amended in 1968 and these amendments were given effect to in the Carriage of Goods by Sea Act 1971. Although the 1971 Act is not yet in force, the principal changes made by it are noted below[15].

As Lord HODSON said of the 1924 Act, it was "not passed for the relief of shipowners but to standardise within certain limits the rights of the holder of every bill of lading against the shipowner"[16]. "Carriage of goods" includes the operation of loading. In *Pyrene Co., Ltd. v. Scindia Navigation Co., Ltd.*[17].

A fire tender was dropped and damaged while being lifted from the quay and before it crossed the ship's rail. It had been sold f.o.b. and the property in it had not passed. The contract of affreightment with the shipowners who undertook the loading had been made by the buyers. *Held:* the shipowners could invoke the Rules in an action against them by the sellers, for (1) the operation of carriage by sea had begun; (2) in all the circumstances the sellers as well as the buyers must be taken to be parties to the contract of affreightment.

In cases to which the Rules apply[18]:

1. The undertaking to provide a seaworthy ship is not absolute; but the carrier is bound, before and at the beginning of the voyage, to exercise due diligence to make the ship seaworthy. The phrase "before and at the beginning of the voyage" means that the obligation is a continuing one from at least the beginning of loading until the ship starts on her voyage[19]. Where the voyage is in stages, the carrier must exercise due diligence before and at the beginning of the voyage to have the vessel adequately bunkered for the first part of the voyage and to arrange for adequate bunkers at intermediate ports[20]. He must also use due diligence properly to man, equip and supply the ship and

---

14. Carriage of Goods by Sea Act 1924, s. 1. This Act, where it applies, does not exclude the limitations on liability provided by the Merchant Shipping Act 1894. See Carriage of Goods by Sea Act 1924, s. 6 (2). It should be noted that most contracts for the carriage of goods by sea are governed by the Hague Rules because many other countries have in fact adopted them.
15. *Post*, pp. 364–365.
16. *Riverstone Meat Co.* v. *Lancashire Shipping Co.*, [1961] 1 All E. R. 495, 527; [1961] A. C. 807.
17. [1954] 2 All E. R. 158.
18. Where the Rules are incorporated into a *charter-party*, though designed only for bills of lading, the owner's liability to the charterer is limited as provided by the Rules: *Adamastos Shipping Co., Ltd.* v. *Anglo-Saxon Petroleum Co., Ltd.*, [1958] 1 All E. R. 725; [1959] A. C. 133.
19. *Maxime Footwear Co., Ltd.* v. *Canadian Government Merchant Marine, Ltd.*, [1959] 2 All E. R. 740; [1959] A. C. 589.
20. *The Makedonia*, [1962] 2 All E. R. 614; [1962] P. 190.

to make all parts of the ship in which goods are carried fit and safe for their reception, carriage and preservation[21]. The burden of proving due diligence is on the carrier, but if due diligence has been exercised neither the carrier nor the shipowner is liable for loss or damage arising from unseaworthiness[1]. The diligence required of the carrier to make the ship seaworthy and fit for the carriage of goods is not limited to his personal diligence; his responsibility extends to the acts of his servants and agents. If the ship has been built for him or bought by him and is defective, he is not liable if he has taken all reasonable and proper precautions to satisfy himself that the ship is fit for service[2], but if he has delegated the work of repairing the ship to an independent contractor the carrier is liable for negligence on the part of such contractor[3]. Breach of this statutory obligation disentitles the shipowner from relying on the "excepted perils" set out in the Act and listed in para. 5 below.

2. The carrier must properly and carefully load, handle, stow, carry, keep, care for and discharge the goods carried[4].

The carrier will not be liable if damage to the cargo was caused by negligence in the *management of the ship*, but that expression does not include an act done solely in relation to the cargo, and not directly or indirectly in relation to the management of the ship as such[5]. Thus, a distinction is drawn between want of care of the cargo and want of care of the vessel indirectly affecting the cargo. It follows that the carrier will not be protected if cargo is damaged by want of care in the management of the refrigerating machinery[6].

3. The carrier must, on demand of the shipper, issue a bill of lading showing:

(i) The leading marks necessary for identification of the goods[7] as furnished in writing by the shipper, and clearly stamped or otherwise shown on the goods or on their cases or coverings in such a manner as would ordinarily remain legible until the end of the voyage.

---

21. Carriage of Goods by Sea Act 1924, s. 2; Sched., Art. III, para. 1.
1. *Ibid.*, Sched., Arts. I, IV, para. 1.
2. *W. Angliss & Co.* v. *P. & O. Steam Navigation*, [1927] 2 K. B. 456.
3. *Riverstone Meat Co.* v. *Lancashire Shipping Co.*, [1961] 1 All E. R. 495; [1961] A. C. 807.
4. Carriage of Goods by Sea Act 1924, Sched., Art. III, para. 2.
5. *Ibid.*, Sched., Art. IV, para. 2; *Gosse Millard* v. *Canadian Government Merchant Marine*, [1928] All E. R. Rep. 97; [1929] A. C. 223.
6. *Foreman and Ellams* v. *Federal Steam Navigation Co.*, [1928] 2 K. B. 424.
7. See p. 358, note 13.

(ii) The number of packages or pieces, or the quantity or weight as furnished in writing by the shipper[8].

(iii) The apparent order and condition of the goods.

The carrier is not bound to state any mark number, quantity or weight which he has reasonable ground for suspecting does not accurately represent the goods, or which he has no reasonable means of checking.

The bill of lading must contain an express statement that it is subject to the Hague Rules as applied by the Act (the Paramount Clause), and it is *prima facie* evidence of the receipt of the goods as described therein[9]. As against a transferee of a bill of lading who has taken it on the faith of the statement that the goods were shipped in "apparent good order and condition", the shipowner is estopped from alleging that the goods were not in that condition when shipped[10]. The shipowner is, however, entitled to disclaim liability for any defect which would not have been apparent on reasonable examination at the time of loading.

4. Unless written notice of loss or damage stating the general nature thereof is given to the carrier at the port of discharge before or at the time of the removal of the goods into the custody of the person entitled to them, or if the loss or damage be not apparent, within three days, such removal shall be *prima facie* evidence of the delivery by the carrier of goods as described in the bill of lading. The notice need not be given if the state of the goods has at the time of their receipt been the subject of joint survey or inspection. In any event the carrier and the ship shall be discharged from all liability in respect of loss or damage unless suit is brought within one year after delivery of the goods or the date when the goods should have been delivered[11]. The period has been enlarged to two years under the British Maritime Law Agreement 1950.

---

8. The shipper is deemed to guarantee the accuracy of these particulars, and must indemnify the carrier against loss resulting from inaccuracies (Carriage of Goods by Sea Act 1924, Sched., Art. III, para. 5).
9. Carriage of Goods by Sea Act 1924, s. 2; Sched., Art. III, paras. 3 and 4.
10. *Silver* v. *Ocean S.S. Co.*, [1930] 1 K. B. 416; see *ante*, p. 354, as to effect of a clean bill of lading at common law.
11. Carriage of Goods by Sea Act 1924, Sched., Art. III, para. 6. For the effect of this on a general average claim, see *Goulandris Brothers, Ltd.* v. *B. Goldman & Sons, Ltd.*, [1957] All E. R. 100; [1958] 1 Q. B. 74. The requirement of bringing an action within one year is not satisfied by the same plaintiff bringing an action relating to the same subject-matter against the same defendants in another jurisdiction within the one year: *Compania Colombiana de Seguros* v. *Pacific Steam Navigation Co.*, [1964] 1 All E. R. 216; [1965] 1 Q. B. 101.

5. The exemptions from liability conferred on the carrier by the Act are very extensive. Thus, neither the carrier nor the ship shall be responsible for loss or damage arising or resulting from:

(a) Act, neglect, or default of the master, mariner, pilot or the servants of the carrier in the navigation or in the management of the ship[12].

(b) Fire, unless caused by the actual fault or privity of the carrier.

(c) Perils, dangers and accidents of the sea or other navigable waters.

(d) Act of God.

(e) Act of war.

(f) Act of public enemies.

(g) Arrest or restraint of princes, rulers or people, or seizure under legal process.

(h) Quarantine restrictions.

(i) Act or omission of the shipper or owner of the goods, his agent or representative.

(j) Strikes or lock-outs or stoppage or restraint of labour from whatever cause, whether partial or general.

(k) Riots and civil commotions.

(l) Saving or attempting to save life or property at sea.

(m) Wastage in bulk or weight or any other loss or damage arising from inherent defect, quality, or vice of the goods.

(n) Insufficiency of packing.

(o) Insufficiency or inadequacy of marks.

(p) Latent defects not discoverable by due diligence.

(q) Any other cause arising without the actual fault or privity of the carrier, or without the fault or neglect of the agents or servants of the carrier, but the burden of proof shall be on the person claiming the benefit of this exception to show that neither the actual fault or privity of the carrier nor the fault or neglect of the agents or servants of the carrier contributed to the loss or damage[13].

A recent case where the shipowner was able to rely on para (q) is *Leesh River Tea Co. v. British Indian Steam Navigation Co.*[14]:—

Tea carried under a bill of lading incorporating the Hague Rules was damaged by water getting into the hold through a storm

---

12. As to the meaning of "management of the ship," see *ante*, p. 360.

13. Carriage of Goods by Sea Act 1924, Sched., Art. IV, para. 4. For the relation of this clause to an express clause in the bill of lading, see *G. H. Renton & Co., Ltd.* v. *Palmyra Trading Corporation of Panama*, [1956] 3 All E. R. 957; [1957] A. C. 149.

14. [1966] 3 All E. R. 593; [1967] 2 Q. B. 250.

valve. This occurred because the brass cover of the valve had been stolen by stevedores at an intermediate port which made the ship unseaworthy but the theft could not reasonably have been detected. *Held:* the shipowner was exempt from liability by para. (*q*) as while stealing the cover the stevedores were not the shipowner's servants or agents because it was unconnected with the cargo they were engaged to unload.

The "excepted perils" cannot be relied on if the shipowner is in breach of his obligation to exercise due diligence to make the ship seaworthy and this breach causes the damage.

Where the carrier is not exempted from liability, his liability is nevertheless limited. He is not liable for any loss or damage to goods exceeding £100 per package or unit unless the nature and value of the goods have been declared by the shipper before shipment and inserted in the bill of lading, but a higher maximum may be fixed by agreement. In fact, under the British Maritime Law Association Agreement 1950, known as the Gold Clause Agreement, British shipowners accept liability up to £200 instead of £100. Neither the carrier nor the ship shall be responsible if the nature or value of the goods has been knowingly misstated by the shipper in the bill of lading[15].

6. *Deviation* for the purpose of saving life *or property* is expressly permitted; so also is any "reasonable deviation"[16]. This has been defined by Lord BUCKMASTER as meaning "a deviation which, where every circumstance has been duly weighed, commends itself to the common sense and sound understanding of sensible men[17]. Lord ATKIN in the same case gave as examples where some person on board is a fugitive from justice or the presence of someone on board was urgently needed on a matter of national importance.

Unwarranted deviation disentitles the shipowner from relying on any of the excepted perils listed in para. 5.

7. Inflammable, explosive or dangerous goods shipped without the knowledge of the carrier may be landed, destroyed or rendered innocuous without liability on the part of the carrier and the shipper will be liable for all resulting damages and expenses. Even if such goods were shipped with the carrier's knowledge they may be disposed of in the same manner as they become a danger to the ship or cargo without liability on the part of the carrier, except to general average, if any[18].

8. The carrier may surrender rights and immunities and increase

---

15. Carriage of Goods by Sea Act 1924, Sched., Art. IV, para. 5.
16. *Ibid.*, Sched., Art. IV, para. 4.
17. *Stag Line, Ltd.* v. *Foscolo, Mango & Co.*, [1931] All E. R. Rep. 666; [1932] A. C. at p. 336.
18. *Ibid.*, Sched., Art. IV, para. 6.

his responsibilities, if such surrender or increase is embodied in the bill of lading[19]. But, in general, the extent of the immunity given to a carrier by the Act cannot be increased and *any contractual clause purporting to relieve him of his statutory liability is void.*

The carrier and shipper may make any special conditions with regard to particular goods[20] if no bill of lading is issued, provided the circumstances, terms and conditions under which the carriage is to be performed reasonably justify a special agreement[1].

In the coasting trade[2], if no bill of lading is issued, the carriage of goods of any class may be the subject of special agreement[3].

The Carriage of Goods by Sea Act 1971

This act does not come into operation until an Order in Council is made and this has not been done at the time of writing. The Act is intended to give effect to amendments to the Hague Rules agreed in Brussels in 1968. The new Rules will apply not only where the port of shipment is in Great Britain or Northern Ireland but also where the bill of lading is issued in another Contracting State or the port of shipment is in such State.

It will not be necessary for the bill of lading to specify expressly that it is subject to the Rules. The right of the carrier or ship to limit liability is altered so that, unless the nature and value of the goods shipped are shown in the bill of lading, liability is limited to an amount not exceeding 10,000 gold francs per package or unit or 30 gold francs per kilo of gross weight, whichever is the higher. Where a container is used to consolidate goods, if the number of packages or units are enumerated in the bill of lading this number shall be deemed the number of packages or units. There is no limitation of liability if it is proved that the damage to the goods arose from an act or omission of the carrier done with intent to cause damage or recklessly and with knowledge that damage would result.

A servant or agent of the carrier, but not an independent contractor, shall be entitled to avail himself of the defences and limits of liability which the carrier is entitled to under the Rules. He is not so entitled

---

19. *Ibid.*, Sched., Art. V.
20. These will not include ordinary commercial shipments made in the ordinary course of trade and it has been said that the proviso applies only where the carrier has to perform some service apart from his usual duties as a carrier: Payne and Ivamy's Carriage of Goods by Sea (9th ed., 1972), p. 64.
1. *Ibid.*, Sched., Art. VI.
2. This covers shipment from any port in Great Britain or Northern Ireland to any other port in those places or to a port in the Irish Free State.
3. Carriage of Goods by Sea Act 1924, s. 4.

if it is proved that damage resulted from an act or omission of the servant or agent done with intent to cause damage or recklessly and with knowledge that damage would probably result.

When the bill of lading is transferred to a third party acting in good faith, it will be conclusive evidence as to statements in the bill of lading concerning identification marks, the number of packages, or quantity or weight shown, as well as to statements relating to the apparent order or condition of the goods.

V FREIGHT

Freight is the name given to the reward paid to the shipowner for the carriage of goods. It is not normally payable until the voyage has been completed and the goods delivered, unless non-delivery is caused by the fault of the shipper alone. Even where inability to deliver arises because of one of the excepted perils, the shipowner is not entitled to freight[4]. Nor is freight normally payable if the goods delivered are for business purposes not of the same nature as the goods shipped[5]. Freight is, however, payable where the goods are merely damaged though the charterer would have a cross-claim in respect of the damage[6].

If the shipowner abandons his vessel without any intention to retake possession, even if he does so under stress of weather[7], the cargo owner can treat the contract of affreightment as at an end, and if the cargo is subsequently salved he can take possession of it without paying freight. But where ship and cargo had been abandoned by the master and crew on being attacked by an enemy submarine, and the ship was for a time erroneously believed to have been sunk, but ship and cargo were subsequently salved, the House of Lords *held* there had been no such abandonment of the ship as to entitle the cargo owners to claim possession of the cargo without paying freight[8]. The shipowner is not disentitled to freight on the ground that he has overloaded the ship contrary to Merchant Shipping (Safety and Load Line Conventions) Act 1932[9].

---

4. *Liddard* v. *Lopes* (1809), 10 East, 526. If the vessel is wrecked, the shipowner may tranship the goods to earn freight (*Hunter* v. *Prinsep*, *ibid.*, 378; and see as to lump sum freight, *post*, p. 366).
5. *Asfar & Co.* v. *Blundell*, [1896] 1 Q. B. 123 (dates under water for two days and impregnated with sewage).
6. *Dakin* v. *Oxley* (1864), 15 C. B. N. S. 646.
7. *The Cito* (1881), 7 P. D. 5, C. A.
8. *Bradley* v. *H. Newsum, Sons & Co.*, [1919] A. C. 16.
9. *St. John Shipping Corporation* v. *Joseph Rank, Ltd.*, [1956] 3 All E. R. 683; [1957] 1 Q. B. 267.

"Advance freight"

If payable, is due at the moment of starting, unless otherwise agreed and if the ship is lost there is no right to recover the freight[10]; even if not paid it can be recovered by the shipowner from the charterer upon the loss of the ship[11]. But if any goods are destroyed before the ship sails so as to make it impossible that any freight could be earned on them, advance freight will not be payable on the portion of the cargo destroyed[12]. Each case depends upon its own circumstances, and to these it is necessary to look to determine whether a given payment is intended as freight in advance, or as a loan; and though it be called "freight in advance", it by no means follows as of course that it is such[13].

"Dead freight"

If the charterer fails to load a full cargo according to agreement, he is liable in damages; such damages are styled "dead freight"[14].

Lump sum freight

This is an entire sum to be paid for the hire of the ship for one entire service[15]. If the whole cargo is lost, no freight will be earned, but if a substantial portion is delivered and the residue has been lost by excepted perils, although the ship does not arrive, the whole freight will be recoverable[16].

Freight pro rata

This is the term given to a payment which is sometimes made for carriage of goods when the contract has been performed in part only. If the original contract has not been performed no claim can arise under it, but if there is a *voluntary* acceptance of the goods at a point short of their destination in such circumstances that the shipowner was able and willing to carry the goods to their destination, a new contract will be implied to pay freight for that part of the voyage actually performed.

But where owing to the outbreak of war a ship was compelled to discharge its cargo at an intermediate port because further prosecution

---

10. *De Silvale* v. *Kendall* (1815), 4 M. & S. 37.
11. *Byrne* v. *Schiller* (1871), L. R. 6 Ex. 319; and *per* ESHER, M.R., in *Smith & Co.* v. *Pyman & Co.*, [1891] 1 Q. B., at p. 744.
12. *Weir & Co.* v. *Girvin & Co.*, [1900] 1 Q. B. 45; 5 Com. Cas. 40.
13. *Allison* v. *Bristol Marine Insurance Co.* (1876), 1 App. Cas. 209, 217, 233.
14. *McLean* v. *Fleming* (1872), L. R. 2 H. L. Sc. 128.
15. *Robinson* v. *Knights* (1873), L. R. 8 C. P. 465, *per* KEATING, J.
16. *Thomas* v. *Harrowing S.S. Co.*, [1915] A. C. 58, where cargo was delivered from a ship wrecked outside the port of discharge.

of the voyage was illegal, the shipowners could not recover the freight in whole or in part—no fresh agreement by the cargo owners to pay freight *pro rata* was inferred from the fact of their taking possession of the goods[17].

Shipowner's lien

The shipowner possesses a lien upon the goods which he carries, until he has received payment of freight; it ceases upon delivery of the goods. The lien extends to all the property consigned on the same voyage under the same contract by the person from whom the freight is due so that delivery of a part does not defeat the lien on the remainder.

In many cases it may be inconvenient to retain them on board, and yet if landed the lien upon them would be in danger of being lost; this difficulty is provided for by certain sections of the Merchant Shipping Act 1894[18]. The shipowner has a possessory lien for general average[19] contributions, and also for expenses incurred in protecting the goods[20].

VI AVERAGE

Average is of two kinds:

1. Particular average

This arises whenever any damage is done to the property of an individual by accident or otherwise, which is not suffered for the general benefit, *e.g.*

    (i) loss of an anchor,
    (ii) damage by water to cargo.

These losses remain where they fall, and no extraordinary compensation is granted in respect of them.

2. General average

A general average loss is caused by or directly consequential on a general average act, which occurs where any extraordinary sacrifice or expenditure is voluntarily and reasonably made or incurred in time of peril for the purpose of preserving the property imperilled in the common adventure. The loss must be borne rateably by all interested[1].

Extraordinary expenditure must be connected with an extraordinary

---

17. *St. Enoch Shipping Co.* v. *Phosphate Mining Co.*, [1916] 2 K. B. 624.
18. See *ante*, p. 348.
19. See below.
20. *Hingston* v. *Wendt* (1876), 1 Q. B. D. 367.
1. Marine Insurance Act 1906, s. 66 (1), (2), (3).

occasion, and the expense of hiring a tug to accelerate the voyage in time of war so as to minimise the risk of destruction by enemy submarines is not a general average act, because the risk of being attacked by the Queen's enemies during war is not an extraordinary or abnormal peril[2].

The essentials of a general average sacrifice are:

   (i) that it was incurred to avoid a danger which was real and not just imagined by the master and which was common to all interests[3];

   (ii) that it was necessary to incur some sacrifice[4];

   (iii) that it was voluntary[5];

   (iv) that it was

"a real sacrifice and not a mere destruction or casting off of that which had become already lost and consequently of no value"[6].

   (v) that the ship, cargo, or some portion have actually been preserved[4];

   (vi) the danger must not be one which arises through the default of the person demanding a general average contribution which fault might result in legal liability[7].

Thus—

where coal shipped without any negligence, caught fire owing to its liability to spontaneous combustion, and water was poured into the holds to extinguish the fire, the owners of the coal were held entitled in respect of damage done by water to the coal which was not ignited, to a general average contribution from the ship[8].

Again, if a fire on board gives rise to a general average loss, the fact that the fire was caused by the general unseaworthiness of the ship, but without the actual fault or privity of the shipowner, will not deprive him of his right to a general average contribution from the cargo; because the shipowner is relieved from liability for damage resulting from the fire by s. 502 of the Merchant Shipping Act 1894[9].

2. *Société Nouvelle d'Armement* v. *Spillers and Bakers,* [1917] 1 K. B. 865.
3. *Nesbitt* v. *Lushington* (1792), 4 T. R. 783.
4. *Pirie* v. *Middle Dock Co.* (1881), 44 L. T. 426.
5. *Shepherd* v. *Kottgen* (1877), 2 C. P. D. 585; *cf. Athel Line, Ltd.* v. *Liverpool and London War Risks Insurance Assc., Ltd.,* [1944] K. B. 87; [1944] 1 All E. R. 46; where the master obeyed the orders of the commodore of a convoy.
6. Per WILLIAMS, J., in *Pirie* v. *Middle Dock Co.* (1881), 44 L. T., at p. 430; *Iredale* v. *China Traders' Insurance Co.,* [1899] 2 Q. B. 356; 4 Com. Cas 256.
7. *Strang* v. *Scott* (1889), 14 App. Cas. 601.
8. *Greenshields, Cowie & Co.* v. *Stephens & Sons,* [1908] 1 A. C. 431.
9. *Dreyfus (Louis) & Co.* v. *Tempus Shipping Co.,* [1931] All E. R. Rep. 577; [1931] A. C. 726; and see *ante*, p. 356.

On the other hand—

Thus where the circumstance giving rise to a general average loss is the shipowner's failure to use due diligence to make the ship seaworthy, his claim for general average can be met by a corresponding cross claim in damages which can be set up as a defence[10].

Examples of general average sacrifices

Ordinary cases of loss which amount to a general average loss are:

(i) jettison of cargo[11];

(ii) voluntary stranding to avoid wreck;

(iii) damage to cargo by scuttling the ship to extinguish fire;

(iv) expenses of putting into a port of refuge for the preservation of ship and cargo.

Interests liable to contribute

Whatever comes under the head of general average loss must be shared by those who have been in a position to be benefited by the sacrifice, *e.g.* the owners of the ship and the freight, and

"all merchandise put on board for the benefit of traffic must contribute";

but the wages of the seamen are not affected.

The position of cargo owners who are liable to contribute to general average expenditure is not one of insurers of the shipowners. General average expenditure is incurred on behalf of all concerned. Thus in *Morrison Steamship Co., Ltd. v. Greystoke Castle (Cargo Owners)*[12],

A collision occurred between two ships the *Cheldale* and the *Greystoke Castle*. The *Cheldale* was held to be partly to blame. The *Greystoke Castle* had to put into port and incurred general average expenditure. It was held that owners of cargo in the *Greystoke Castle* had a direct right of action against the owners of the *Cheldale* in respect of their contributions. Had they been merely liable to indemnify the owners of the *Greystoke Castle*, only the latter could have sued.

Where the general average act involves a voluntary injury to the property of third persons, *e.g.* to the pier of a dock, those benefited

---

10. *Goulandris Brothers, Ltd.* v. *B. Goldman & Sons, Ltd.*, [1957] 3 All E. R. 100; [1958] 1 Q. B. 74.
11. If cargo stowed on deck is jettisoned, there is no right of general average contribution from the other interests, unless deck stowage is allowed by express agreement or by custom of the trade or port.
12. [1946] 2 All E. R. 696; [1947] A. C. 265.

must contribute their share of the damages payable, although they may be in the position of joint tortfeasors[13].

Cargo which had been landed to ensure its safety and not for the purpose of lightening the ship, is not liable to contribute in respect of a general average loss subsequently incurred; such cargo was not then at risk, and derived no benefit from the sacrifice[14]. It is the duty of the master to retain the cargo until he has been paid the amount due in respect of it for general average.

The rules relating to the amounts to be made good vary in different countries. In the absence of agreement, adjustment of the amounts to be contributed in respect of general average will take place at and according to the law of the port of discharge, *i.e.* in general, the place to which the vessel is destined, unless the voyage is justifiably terminated at an intermediate port[15]. But a temporary suspension of the voyage at a port of refuge does not justify an average adjustment there[16].

It frequently happens that, in marine insurance policies, the underwriter agrees to be liable for general average "as per foreign statement"; this binds him as to the correctness of the statements of the foreign average stater, and to accept as general average whatever is such according to the law of any foreign place at which the adjustment is properly made[17]. A set of rules intended to be the basis of a uniform practice in all countries was adopted in 1877. The present rules known as the York-Antwerp Rules 1950 are frequently adopted in contracts of affreightment and marine insurance, and provide a complete code governing the law of general average for those who are parties to the contract[18].

---

13. *Austin Friars S.S. Co.* v. *Spillers and Bakers, Ltd.*, [1915] 3 K. B. 586. The common law doctrine that there cannot be contribution between joint tortfeasors was held in this case not to apply to a contribution in general average. This doctrine was abolished by the Law Reform (Married Women and Tortfeasors) Act 1935, s. 6.
14. *Royal Mail Steam Packet Co.* v. *English Bank of Rio Janeiro* (1887), 19 Q. B. D. 362.
15. *Simonds* v. *White* (1824), 2 B. & C. 805.
16. *Hill* v. *Wilson* (1879), 4 C. P. D. 329.
17. *Mavro* v. *Ocean Marine Insurance Co.* (1875), L. R. 10 C. P. 414.
18. *Vlassopoulos* v. *British and Foreign Marine Insurance Co.*, [1929] 1 K. B. 187.

CHAPTER 21

Carriage by Air

A virtual monopoly of civil aviation was given by the Civil Aviation Act 1946 to three corporations, the British Overseas Airways Corporation, the British South American Airways Corporation and the British European Airways Corporation. The first two of these corporations were amalgamated in 1949 and their monopoly was ended in 1960 since when private airline operators have been permitted to run scheduled flights as well as charter flights. By the Civil Aviation Act 1971 two bodies have been established with important functions for the regulation of civil aviation. The Civil Aviation Authority, appointed by the Secretary of State for Trade and Industry, is given the function of securing that British airlines provide adequate air transport services. Any aircraft operator must obtain a licence from the Authority if the aircraft is registered in the United Kingdom or if the flight begins or ends in the United Kingdom. The other body is the British Airways Board, also appointed by the Secretary of State for Trade and Industry, with power to promote the formation of air transport undertakings and to control all activities of B.O.A.C. and B.E.A.

The development of international air transport gave rise to special codes of rules agreed on at international Conventions. The principal Convention, the Warsaw Convention of 1929, laid the foundation of the present law and was given statutory force in this country by the Carriage by Air Act 1932. The Warsaw Convention was amended at The Hague in 1955 and the Carriage by Air Act 1961 enabled the Government to ratify the Hague Protocol which it eventually did in 1967. The purposes of these Conventions was to unify the rules relating to international carriage by air so that the same rules would govern the contractual requirements and the liability of an airline for passengers and goods, irrespective of the nationality of the airline or persons concerned or the route being travelled. However, since each Convention binds only those countries that have acceded to it, the ideal has not entirely been achieved.

The Warsaw Convention as amended by the Hague Protocol applies to all journeys between the countries adhering to both the Convention and the Protocol and the following are the rules governing such journeys. It should, however, be appreciated that many countries that acceded to the Warsaw Convention have not acceded to the Hague Protocol and in respect of, *e.g.*, a journey between Britain and such a country, the unamended Warsaw Convention (set out in Schedule I of the repealed Carriage by Air Act 1932) continues to apply.

The amended Convention (which is set out in the First Schedule to the Carriage by Air Act 1961) applies to "international carriage" as therein defined[1] but power was reserved by s. 10 of the Act to apply it to non-international carriage by air (*i.e.*, carriage between two points within the U.K., or between the U.K. and a country that has not acceded to the Warsaw Convention) and in fact the Convention has been applied with modifications (shown in footnotes hereafter) to non-international carriage by air[2].

The principal provisions of the amended Convention are:—

1. *Passenger Ticket.*—The carrier must deliver to the passenger a passenger ticket containing prescribed particulars. The ticket is *prima facie* evidence of the conditions of the contract of carriage. The absence, irregularity or loss of the ticket does not affect the existence or validity of the contract but, if the carrier accepts a passenger without delivering the ticket, the carrier is not entitled to rely on Article 22 (to be referred to) which entitles the carrier to limit his liability[3].

2. *Baggage Check.*—In respect of the carriage of registered baggage, a baggage check must be delivered (containing prescribed particulars unless combined with or incorporated in a passenger ticket complying with the requirements of Article 3). The baggage check is *prima facie* evidence of the conditions of the contract of carriage. The absence, irregularity or loss of the check does not affect the existence or validity of the contract of carriage but if the carrier accepts baggage without delivering the check, the carrier is not entitled to rely on Article 22 (to be referred to) which entitles the carrier to limit his liability[4].

3. *Air Waybill.*—Every carrier of cargo has a right to require that the consignor make out and hand over to him an "air waybill" (air consignment note) and the consignor has the right to require the carrier to accept this document. Its absence, irregularity or loss does

---

1. "any carriage in which . . . the place of departure and the place of destination . . . are situated either within the territories of two High Contracting Parties or within the territory of a single High Contracting Party if there is an agreed stopping place within the territory of another State, even if that State is not a High Contracting Party": Carriage by Air Act 1961, Sched. I, Art. 1.
2. Carriage by Air Act (Application of Provisions) Order 1967 (S. I. 1967 No. 480).
3. Carriage by Air Act 1961, Sched. I, Art. 3.
4. Carriage by Air Act 1961, Sched. I, Art. 4.

not affect the existence or validity of the contract of carriage[5]. The air waybill must contain certain particulars[6] and, if all the particulars required by the Convention are not given, the carrier is not entitled to limit his liability in accordance with the provisions of Article 22[7].

4. *Consignor's Rights.*—Subject to his liability to carry out all his obligations under the contract of carriage the consignor may dispose of the goods by withdrawing them at the aerodrome of departure or destination, or by stopping them in the course of the journey on any landing, or by calling for them to be delivered at the place of destination or in the course of the journey to a person other than the named consignee, or by requiring them to be returned to the aerodrome of departure. These rights cease when the consignee becomes entitled to delivery[8].

5. *Consignee's Rights.*—Unless the consignor has stopped the goods the consignee is entitled to have them delivered to him on payment of the charges due and on complying with the conditions set out in the air consignment note.

Unless otherwise agreed the carrier must give notice to the consignee as soon as the goods arrive; but if the carrier admits the loss of the goods, or if they have not arrived at the expiration of seven days after the due date the consignee is entitled to put in force against the carrier the rights which flow from the contract of carriage[9].

6. *Liability re death or injury and re loss or damage of goods.*—Subject to certain exemptions, the carrier is liable:

(i) For the death of or personal injury caused to a passenger by any accident which takes place on board the aircraft or in the course of the operations of embarking or disembarking[10]. This liability is limited to 250,000 francs[11] for each passenger but the carrier and the passenger may by special contract agree to a higher limit of liability[12].

---

5. *Ibid.*, Sched. I, Art. 5.   6. *Ibid.*, Art. 8.
7. *Ibid.*, Art. 9; *Corocraft, Ltd.* v. *Pan American Airways Inc.*, [1969] I All E. R. 82; [1969] I Q. B. 616, C. A. Neither a passenger ticket nor baggage check nor air waybill are required in the case of non-international carriage.
8. Carriage by Air Act 1961, Sched. I, Art. 12.
9. *Ibid.*, Art. 13.   10. *Ibid.*, Art. 17.
11. This refers to the French franc consisting of 65½ milligrams of gold of millesimal fineness 900 (*ibid.*, Art. 22).
12. *Ibid.*, Art. 22 (1). For journeys which originate from or terminate in or have an agreed stopping place in the United States, most of the world's airlines have agreed to a limit of 875,000 francs. The same limit applies to all non-international carriage, but for journeys governed by the unamended Warsaw Convention (*e.g.*, between Britain and a country that accedes to the Warsaw Convention but not to the Hague Protocol) the limit is only 125,000 francs Carriage by Air Acts (Application of Provisions) Order 1967 (S. I. 1967 No. 480).

(ii) The carrier is liable for the loss of or damage to any registered baggage or any cargo which occurs during the carriage by air, *i.e.* while the baggage or cargo are in charge of the carrier, whether in an aerodrome or on board an aircraft, but not during any carriage by land, sea or river outside an aerodrome[13]. This liability is limited to 250 francs per kilogram unless the passenger or consignor has at the time of handing over the package to the carrier made a special declaration of value and has paid an additional charge if required. In that case the carrier will be liable to pay a sum not exceeding that declared unless he proves *that this sum is greater than the actual value to the consignor at destination[14]. As regards objects of which the passenger himself takes charge the liability is limited to 5,000 francs per passenger[15].

(iii) The carrier is liable for delay in the carriage by air of passengers, baggage or cargo[16].

Any provision tending to relieve the carrier of liability or fix a lower limit than that which is laid down in the Convention is null and void but this does not involve nullity of the whole contract which remains subject to the provisions of the Convention[17]. The limits of liability specified in Article 22 do not apply if it is proved that the damage resulted from an act or omission of the carrier, his servants or agents, done with intent to cause damage or recklessly and with knowledge that damage would probably result[18]. If an employee of the carrier is sued in respect of the death or injury of a passenger or for loss or damage to goods, he is entitled to the same limitation of liability as the carrier himself[19]. By the Carriage by Air (Supplementary Provisions) Act 1962, where the contract of carriage is entered into with one carrier and another carrier, with authority from the first carrier, performs all or part of the carriage, both may be liable to the passenger or consignor, subject to the same statutory exceptions and limits.

7. *Defences of the Carrier.*—The Carriage by Air Act 1961 exempts the carrier from liability in the following circumstances:

(i) If he can prove that his servants or agents have taken all

---

13. Carriage by Air Act 1961, Sched. I, Art. 18.
14. *Ibid.*, Art. 22 (2).
15. *Ibid.*, Art. 22 (3).
16. *Ibid.*, Art. 19.
17. *Ibid.*, Art. 23.
18. Carriage by Air Act 1961, Art. 25.
19. *Ibid.*, Art. 25a.

necessary measures to avoid the damage or it was impossible for them to take such measures[20].

(ii) If the damage was caused by or contributed to by the negligence of the injured person, the Court may, in accordance with the provisions of its own law, exonerate the carrier wholly or partly from liability[1].

(iii) Where baggage or cargo are damaged, a complaint in writing must be made to the carrier at latest in the case of baggage within seven days and in the case of cargo within fourteen days of the receipt thereof respectively. In the case of delay the complaint must be made at the latest within 21 days. If no complaint has been made in accordance with these provisions, no action will lie against the carrier unless there is fraud on his part[2].

(iv) The right to recover damages is extinguished if an action is not brought within two years from the date on which the aircraft arrived or ought to have arrived at its destination or from the date on which carriage stopped[3].

8. *Jurisdiction.*—Actions for damages must be brought at the option of the plaintiff in the territory of one of the High Contracting Parties, either before the court having jurisdiction:

(i) Where the carrier is ordinarily resident; or

(ii) Has his principal place of business; or

(iii) Has an establishment by which the contract was made; or

(iv) At the place of destination[4].

---

20. Carriage by Air Act 1961, Sched. I, Art. 20. In respect of journeys which originate from or terminate in or have an agreed stopping place in the United States, most of the world's airlines have agreed to waive this defence.

1. *Ibid.,* Art. 21. This in England is subject to the Law Reform (Contributory Negligence) Act 1945 which entitles a Court to apportion the damages.

2. Carriage by Air Act 1961, Art. 26.

3. *Ibid.,* Sched. I, Art. 29.

4. *Ibid.,* Art. 28. These provisions do not apply to non-international carriage.

CHAPTER 22

Suretyship and Guarantees

I NATURE AND FORMATION OF THE CONTRACT

A guarantee or contract of suretyship is an engagement to be collaterally answerable for the debt, default, or miscarriage of another person. A simple example is where, in consideration of B lending C £100, A agrees with B that if C does not repay the loan he (A) will repay it.

The assumption of *Personal* liability is not an essential element of suretyship; one who merely charges his property to secure another's debt is a surety[1]. Such an agreement may be intended:

1. To secure the performance of something immediately connected with a business transaction, or
2. To secure the fidelity of a person about to be appointed to some employment, or
3. It may be to secure one person from loss resulting from the torts of another[2]; or
4. It may relate to numerous other matters.

In the present chapter it is proposed to deal with guarantees relating to business transactions only.

An agreement to answer for the debt, default, or miscarriage of another need not be in any special form; but as the contract is one within the unrepealed provisions of s. 4 of the Statute of Frauds, it is not enforceable by action unless it is evidenced by a written note or memorandum of the agreement signed by the party sought to be made liable under it[3]. The contents of a memorandum sufficient to satisfy the statute have been already stated[4]; it is not necessary that the memorandum of a guarantee should contain any statement of the consideration given to the guarantor in return for the guarantee[5].

This last statement must not be misunderstood. It is not intended to indicate that consideration to the guarantor is unnecessary; as in

---

1. *Re Conley*, [1938] 2 All E. R. 127, where it was held that payment to a bank might amount to a fraudulent preference of a third person who had deposited documents of title to secure the overdraft.
2. See, *e.g. Kirkham* v. *Marter* (1819), 2 B. & Ald. 613.
3. See *ante*, p. 8.
4. *Ante*, pp. 8–9.
5. Mercantile Law Amendment Act 1856, s. 3.

all other contracts, consideration must be given to the promisor, save when the guarantee is under seal. What is meant is that the document signed by the guarantor may comply with the Statute of Frauds, although this consideration is not mentioned or referred to in it. The giving of credit to the principal debtor is normally sufficient consideration for the surety's promise. Consideration must "move from the promisee" but not necessarily "to the promisor"[6].

The main features of a guarantee (as applied to business transactions), are the following:

1. The contract of guarantee involves the existence of another valid contract, one party to which is a party to the contract of guarantee; in fact, there must be two contracts, one party being common to each. That party is the creditor; to him the principal debtor is or is about to be under a liability on the principal contract; and to him the guarantor or surety is to be liable if the principal debtor breaks the principal contract. Thus,

if C is asking B to sell goods to him, and A says to B, "Let C have the goods; if he does not pay you, I will," this is an offer of a guarantee on the part of A. Should he say, "Give C the goods, I will be your paymaster," the result is not of necessity the same; for the words may show an intention on A's part to pay for the goods in any event, and not merely if C fails to pay[7]. A's promise in the latter case is one of "indemnity" and is enforceable even though it may not be evidenced in writing.

In *Coutts & Co.* v. *Browne-Lecky*[8]:

A signed a guarantee in respect of the overdraft of his minor son. *Held:* the loan to the minor being void under the Infants Relief Act 1874 there was no debt which could be guaranteed and the guarantee was void.

Where a charge is provided by a company as security for a loan to finance the purchase of shares in the company and the company's obligations are guaranteed, since the charge is illegal under the Companies Act 1948, the guarantee is void too[9].

2. If a contract is properly construed as a guarantee, the guarantor is under no liability whatsoever once the principal debtor

---

6. *Barrell* v. *Trussell* (1811), 4 Taunt. 117; *Crears* v. *Hunter* (1887), 19 Q. B. D. 341. *Cf. ante*, p. 23.
7. *Birkmyr* v. *Darnell* (1704), 1 Smith L. C. (13th ed.), 331.
8. [1947] K. B. 104; [1946] 2 All E. R. 207. Qy. whether the document might not have been construed as an indemnity and enforced as such as in *Yeoman Credit, Ltd.* v. *Latter*, [1961] 2 All E. R. 294; [1961] 1 W. L. R. 828, C. A.
9. *Heald* v. *O'Connor*, [1971] 2 All E. R. 1105; [1971] 1 W. L. R. 497.

has properly complied with all his obligations[10] or the contract is frustrated.

For this reason, in hire-purchase transactions, it is better from the finance company's point of view if the dealer who introduces a potential hirer agrees to indemnify the company against any loss the company may incur as a result of the hirer's default under the hire-purchase agreement rather than merely signs a contract of guarantee. Then, if the hirer exercises a contractual right to terminate the agreement, which may cause the finance company loss even when the payments the hirer has to make on exercising such right are taken into account, the loss can be recouped from the indemnifier[11].

3. A guarantee contract is not a contract *uberrimae fidei* and, therefore, there is no obligation on the creditor to disclose material facts affecting the credit of the debtor or circumstances connected with the transaction which might make the guarantor's position more hazardous[12]. Thus, where a guarantee is given to secure an advance on a banking account, it is not incumbent on the banker, if he is not asked for information, to tell the surety that the account is already overdrawn[13].

4. It is normally the surety's duty to see to it that the principal debtor pays or performs his other duty. In *Moschi* v. *Lep Air Services, Ltd.*[14], the appellant guaranteed performance by a company he controlled of its agreement to pay off its debts to the respondents by instalments. The company repudiated its agreement. The respondents accepted that repudiation and sued the appellant on his guarantee. *Held*: breach of the debtor's obligations entailed a breach by the guarantor of his own contract and he was liable in damages to the same extent as the debtor—acceptance of the debtor's repudiation

---

10. *Western Credit, Ltd.* v. *Alberry*, [1964] 2 All E. R. 938; [1964] 1 W. L. R. 945, C. A.
11. *Goulston Discount Co., Ltd.* v. *Clark*, [1967] 1 All E. R. 61; [1967] 2 Q. B. 493, C. A.
12. *Wythes* v. *Labouchère* (1859), 3 De G. & J. 593; *National Provincial Bank of England, Ltd.* v. *Lord Glanusk*, [1913] 3 K. B. 335. A fidelity guarantee contract is a contract *uberrimae fidei* so that failure by an employer to disclose to someone who gives a guarantee for the fidelity of a servant that the servant has been previously dishonest will entitle the guarantor to avoid liability; *London General Omnibus Co.* v. *Holloway*, [1912] 2 K. B. 72, C. A.
13. *Hamilton* v. *Watson* (1885), 12 Cl. & F. 109, H. L.; *Cooper* v. *National Provincia¹ Bank, Ltd.*, [1945] 2 All E. R. 642; [1946] K. B. 1.
14. [1972] 2 All E. R. 393; [1972] 2 W. L. R. 1175, H. L.

did not bring the guarantor's obligation to an end but transmuted it into an obligation to pay damages.

Where writing not required

There are contracts for which no writing is required, which approach in characteristics closely to guarantees. The object of the contract must be regarded, and if the payment of another's debt is only involved as an incident of a larger purpose, that fact will not bring it within the Statute of Frauds.

Thus, if A sells goods to B, A generally has a right of lien over the goods, *i.e.* a right to retain possession of them until he is paid for them. Suppose B resells the goods to C and, in order to obtain possession of them, C orally promises A that if B does not pay for them he (C) will do so. C's promise is enforceable because made rather to protect his proprietary interest in the goods than to pay off another's debt[15]. Similarly, a *del credere* agent, an agent for sale who undertakes to pay if the buyer becomes insolvent, is liable on such undertaking even though it is not evidenced in writing[16]. On the other hand, a company shareholder who promises to pay off the company's debt in order to prevent the company's goods being taken in execution, he himself having no legal interest or charge over the goods, is only liable if there is evidence of his promise in writing[17].

II LIABILITY OF THE SURETY

The surety's liability (which arises, as has been stated, only on the principal debtor's default) *is limited to the amount which the surety has undertaken to pay on such default.*

This may be the whole amount due to be paid by the principal debtor, or it may be something smaller beyond which it has been agreed that the surety's liability shall not extend.

If the guarantee is one which the surety has entered into jointly with others, he is still liable to pay the whole amount he has agreed to pay on the debtor's default, unless the wording of the guarantee otherwise provides. His right of contribution against co-sureties may be a partial indemnity, but he cannot, in the absence of agreement binding the creditor, compel the creditor to proceed against the other sureties.

It seems also that although the surety's liability arises only on the principal debtor's default, the surety cannot insist that the creditor

---

15. *Fitzgerald* v. *Dressler* (1860), 7 C. B. N. S. 374.
16. *Sutton & Co.* v. *Grey*, [1894] 1 Q. B. 285, and *ante*, p. 152.
17. *Harburg India Rubber Comb Co.* v. *Martin*, [1902] 1 K. B. 778.

shall sue the debtor before resorting to him, even upon giving an indemnity against the cost and delay of such proceedings. The surety is not bound by any decision as to the liability of the debtor in actions to which he was not a party, and may insist (at his own risk as to costs) that the right of the creditor shall be proved against himself[18].

Continuing Guarantee.—Upon the construction of the contract there is sometimes a question whether or not the guarantee is continuing, *i.e.* whether it is intended to continue until recalled, or whether it is to be confined to a single transaction or debt.

If A guarantees B to the extent of any goods he may purchase from C, not exceeding £150, he may mean to guarantee the money due on all B's purchases provided that they never exceed £150, or he may intend to guarantee B until he has obtained £150 worth of things, and then stop.

Each case must be decided on the language of the document, and the presumed intention of the parties, for no definite rule can be drawn from the decisions.[19]

Thus, in *Allnutt* v. *Ashenden*[20],

the agreement ran:

"I hereby guarantee B's account with A for wines and spirits to the amount of £100";

there was at the time when the guarantee was made an account existing between A and B, though at the time the amount due in connection with it was less than £100. *Held:* a guarantee of the existing account only.

But in *Wood* v. *Priestner*[21],

P was indebted to W for coals supplied on credit, and he desired to buy more; his father gave the following guarantee:

"In consideration of the credit given by W to my son for coal supplied by them to him, I hereby hold myself responsible as a guarantee to them for the sum of £100, and in default of his payment of any accounts due, I bind myself by this note to pay W whatever may be owing to an amount not exceeding £100".

Held: a continuing guarantee.

---

18. *Ex parte Young, Re Kitchin* (1881), 17 Ch. D. 668.
19. *Coles* v. *Pack* (1870), L. R. 5 C. P. 65, 70; *Wood* v. *Priestner* (1867), L. R. 2 Ex. 66, 282.
20. (1843), 5 M. & G. 392.
21. (1867), L. R. 2 Ex. 66, 282.

III. RIGHTS OF THE SURETY

When he pays the debt he has the following rights:

1. Against the principal debtor

To recover, with interest[1], from him all money properly paid when due[2] on account of the guarantee, provided, of course, that the debtor was a consenting party to the suretyship[2].

Whether or not the costs of disputing the claim of the creditor can be recovered from the debtor, depends upon whether the expense of resistance to the claim was reasonably incurred; and it is advisable to inform the principal debtor of intended payment of the creditor's demand; this enables such defence to be set up as the debtor thinks fit, and prevents difficulties which might otherwise arise when the surety demands his indemnity from the principal[3].

The surety is also entitled to enforce against the debtor the rights which the creditor enjoyed in regard to the debt in question[4].

Moreover, a surety has the right *before* payment to compel the principal debtor to relieve him from liability by paying off the debt, if the debt is actually ascertained and due and the surety admits liability. In such a case it is not necessary to prove that the creditor has refused to exercise his right to sue the principal debtor[5].

2. Against the creditor

To be placed in the position of the creditor as to all judgments, securities given by the debtor, and other rights, *e.g.* rights of set off. If he is surety for part of the debt only, his rights to the securities also are but partial[6]. These may be used as against the debtor or co-sureties equally, but so that the latter can only be compelled to pay thereunder the proportionate shares to which they are liable.

---

1. *Petre* v. *Duncombe* (1851), 20 L. J. Q. B. 242.
2. *Exall* v. *Partridge* (1799), 8 T. R., at p. 310. The seizure and sale of the surety's property under execution for the debt will entitle the surety to sue the debtor (*Rodgers* v. *Maw* (1846), 15 M. & W. 444).
3. *Duffield* v. *Scott* (1789), 3 T. R. 374.
4. See below. He may have larger rights than the creditor had. See *Badeley* v. *Consolidated Bank* (1887), 34 Ch. D., at p. 556.
5. *Ascherson* v. *Tredegar Dry Dock, etc., Co.*, [1909] 2 Ch. 401; *Thomas* v. *Notts Incorporated Football Club, Ltd.*, [1972] 1 All E. R. 1176; [1972] Ch. 596; *cf. Morrison* v. *Barking Chemicals Company*, [1919] 2 Ch. 325.
6. *Goodwin* v. *Gray* (1874), 22 W. R. 312. This right of the surety does not take from the creditor the right to surrender his security on the debtor's bankruptcy and prove as provided by the Bankruptcy Act 1914 (*Rainbow* v. *Juggins* (1880), 5 Q. B. D. 138, 422). A guarantor of a hire-purchase agreement does not acquire any interest in the property by payment (*Chatterton* v. *Maclean*, [1951] 1 All E. R. 761).

As regards securities, HALL, V.-C., in *Forbes* v. *Jackson*[7], said:

> "The surety is entitled to have all the securities preserved for him, which were taken at the time of the suretyship, or, as I think it is now settled, subsequently. . . . The principle is that the surety in effect bargains that the securities which the creditor takes shall be for him, if and when he shall be called upon to make any payment, and it is the duty of the creditor to keep the securities intact, not to give them up or to burden them with further advances."

The creditor's priority, if he has any, passes also to the surety who pays the debt, *e.g.* a surety who paid a debt due to the Crown was held entitled to the Crown's priority, so far as was necessary for his indemnity[8].

By the Mercantile Law Amendment Act 1856, s. 5,

> "every person who, being surety for the debt or duty of another, or being liable with another for any debt or duty, shall pay such debt or perform such duty, shall be entitled to have assigned to him, or to a trustee for him, every judgment, specialty, or other security which shall be held by the creditor in respect of such debt or duty, whether such judgment, specialty, or other security shall or shall not be deemed at law to have been satisfied by the payment of the debt or performance of the duty, and such person shall be entitled to stand in the place of the creditor, and to use all the remedies[9], and, if need be, and upon a proper indemnity, to use the name of the creditor, in any action or other proceeding, at law or in equity, in order to obtain from the principal debtor, or any co-surety, co-contractor, or co-debtor, as the case may be, indemnification for the advances made and loss sustained by the person who shall have so paid such debt or performed such duty; and such payment or performance so made by such surety shall not be pleadable in bar of any such action or other proceeding by him: Provided always, that no co-surety, co-contractor, or co-debtor shall be entitled to recover from any other co-surety, co-contractor, or co-debtor, by the means aforesaid, more than the just proportion to which, as between those parties themselves, such last-mentioned person shall be justly liable"[10].

---

7. (1882), 19 Ch. D. 615, 621; *Duncan, Fox & Co.* v. *North and South Wales Bank* (1881), 6 App. Cas. 1.
8. *Re Lord Churchill* (1888), 39 Ch. D. 174.
9. If the surety has not obtained an actual assignment of the judgment, he may still have the advantage of this section (*Re McMyn* (1886), 33 Ch. D. 575).
10. He may sue or prove in bankruptcy for the total amount of the debt, but cannot actually get payment of more than his just proportion (*Re Parker*, [1894] 3 Ch. 400).

3. Against co-sureties

To contribution from them[11]. The right to contribution arises when two or more persons are sureties for the same principal and the same engagement although bound by different instruments, and although they became sureties in ignorance of the existence of another surety. If the principal makes default, all must contribute equally, if each is a surety to an equal amount, otherwise they must contribute in proportion to the amount for which each is a surety[12]. And in counting the number of sureties for this purpose, those unable to pay are not reckoned[13]. Thus,

If A, B, and C are sureties for £1,200, and A pays the whole, he can claim £400 from B and £400 from C, or, according to equitable rules, if C is insolvent, A can claim £600 from B.

But a surety who has paid cannot claim from his co-surety unless he has paid more than his proportion of the debt remaining due at the time of such payment, even though the co-surety has so far paid nothing; *e.g.*

X owes a debt of £150 and this is guaranteed by four joint sureties; the liability of two sureties, A and B, is limited to £50 each and that of the other two sureties, C and D, is limited to £25 each. If £48 is due and payable and A pays the full £48 he is entitled to claim £16 from B and £8 each from C and D. But if A pays no more than £16 he has no claim to contribution from his co-sureties even if they pay nothing[14].

Where there is one debt payable by instalments, a surety cannot call on a co-surety to contribute until he has paid more than his proportion of the entire debt, although he has paid more than his share of the part which has become due[15].

The surety may (it seems) insist upon payment to the creditor of the co-surety's proportion, although he has not yet himself actually paid the creditor[16], especially if judgment has been obtained against him[17].

---

11. *Dering v. Lord Winchelsea* (1787), 2 Wh. & Tu. (9th ed.), p. 488. A surety is entitled to interest on the amount owing to him for contribution (*Hitchman v. Stewart* (1855), 3 Drew. 271).
12. *Ellesmere Brewery Co. v. Cooper*, [1896] 1 Q. B. 75; 1 Com. Cas. 210.
13. *Ex parte Snowdon* (1881), 17 Ch. D. 44; *Davies v. Humphries* (1840), 6 M. & W., at p. 168.
14. *Ellesmere Brewery Co. v. Cooper*, [1896] 1 Q. B., at p. 80; 1 Com. Cas., at p. 212.
15. *Stirling v. Burdett*, [1911] 2 Ch. 418.
16. Per JAMES, L.J., in *Ex parte Snowdon* (1881), 17 Ch. D., at p. 47.
17. *Wolmershausen v. Gullick*, [1893] 2 Ch. 514. For this purpose an admitted claim in an administration action is equivalent to judgment (*ibid.*).

A co-surety is entitled to a share of every counter-security which has been delivered to any of the sureties, and such security must be brought into hotchpot in order that the ultimate burden may be equally divided[18].

IV DISCHARGE OF THE SURETY

The surety will be discharged on any of the grounds which suffice to put an end to contracts in general[19], and also on the following, which are peculiar to guarantees[20]:

1. If the creditor has altered the terms of the contract guaranteed without the assent of the surety.

As COTTON, L.J., said in 1878:

> "The true rule in my opinion is, that if there is any agreement between the principals with reference to the contract guaranteed, the surety ought to be consulted, and that if he has not consented to the alteration, although in cases where it is without inquiry evident that the alteration is unsubstantial, or that it cannot be otherwise than beneficial to the surety, the surety may not be discharged; yet, that if it is not self-evident that the alteration is unsubstantial, or one which cannot be prejudicial to the surety, the court will not, in an action against the surety, go into an inquiry as to the effect of the alteration . . . but will hold that in such a case the surety himself must be the sole judge whether or not he will consent to remain liable . . . and that if he has not so consented he will be discharged[1].

In *Polak* v. *Everett*[2], QUAIN, J., said:

> "The contract of the surety should not be altered without his consent, and the creditor should not undertake to alter the contract, and then say, 'Although the contract has been altered, and I put it out of my power to carry it out by my voluntary act, I now offer you an equivalent.' "

Acceptance by the creditor of the debtor's wrongful repudiation of his obligations is not in any sense a variation of the contract[3].

---

18. *Steel* v. *Dixon* (1881), 17 Ch. D. 825.
19. See *ante*, Chapter VII.
20. The contract of suretyship may, however, contain special clauses excluding the ordinary rights of a surety. See, for example, *Perry* v. *National Provincial Bank of England*, [1910] 1 Ch., at p. 470.
1. *Holme* v. *Brunskill* (1878), 3 Q. B. D. 495, at p. 505, followed in *National Bank of Nigeria, Ltd.* v. *Oba M/S Awolesi*, [1964] 1 W. L. R. 1311.
2. (1876), 1 Q. B. D. 669, at p. 677. See also *In Re Darwen and Pearce*, [1927] 1 Ch. 176.
3. *Moschi* v. *Lep Air Services, Ltd.*, [1972] 2 All E. R. 393 [1972] 2 W. L. R. 1175, H. L.

2. Giving time to the principal debtor will, except in certain cases, release the surety, provided that there is a *binding contract* with the debtor (express or implied, written or verbal) to give time, and not merely a forbearance by the creditor to enforce his rights. Lord ELDON, in *Samuell* v. *Howarth*[4], said:

> "The rule is this, that if a creditor, without the consent of the surety, gives time to the principal debtor, by so doing he discharges the surety; *i.e.* if time is given by virtue of a positive contract between the creditor and principal, not where the creditor is merely inactive. And, in the case put, the surety is held to be discharged for this reason, because the creditor, by so giving time to the principal, has put it out of the power of the surety to consider whether he will have recourse to his remedy against the principal debtor or not, and because he, in fact, cannot have the same remedy against the principal as he would have had under the original contract".

Thus, in *Midland Motor Showrooms* v. *Newman*[5],

> the parties to a hire-purchase agreement made a later agreement by which the hirer was given more time to pay off an instalment then due. *Held:* the guarantor of the hire-purchase agreement was discharged.

To this there is an important exception, since a surety is not released by an agreement to give time to the debtor if the creditor expressly reserves his rights against the surety. The reasons why the reservation by the creditor of his rights against the surety does not release the surety are that—

(i) it rebuts the implication there there was any intention to discharge the surety, and

(ii) the principal debtor, by consenting to this reservation, impliedly agrees that the surety shall have recourse against him; so that in effect the rights of the surety are not impaired, and he may, notwithstanding the agreement, pay the creditor and enforce his rights against the debtor[6].

After the creditor has obtained judgment against both the principal and the surety, a binding agreement to give time to the former does not release the surety; the judgment creates a new liability in respect of which the judgment debtors are in the same position[7].

---

4. (1817), 3 Mer. 272, 278.
5. [1929] 2 K. B. 256, C. A.
6. *Kearsley* v. *Cole* (1847), 16 M. & W. 128, at p. 135.
7. *Re A Debtor*, [1913] 3 K. B. 11.

3. If the creditor gives up any security in respect of the debt or takes a new security from the debtor in lieu of the original security or of such kind as to operate by way of merger of the old security[8].

4. A further ground of discharge is:

(i) the negligence of the creditor in his dealings with the debtor, or

(ii) misuse of securities held by him for the debt resulting in detriment to the surety, so that the surety's remedies are affected.

As regards negligence in dealings, the principle was thus stated by COTTON, L.J.[9]:

"If there is a contract express or implied that the creditor shall acquire or preserve any right against the debtor, and the creditor deprives himself of the right which he has stipulated to acquire, or does anything to release any right which he has, that discharges the surety. . . . A surety is not discharged merely by the negligence of the creditor."

For instance,

A lent money to B and P upon the security of certain goods and fixtures, and by the terms of the deed A was entitled to enter on the happening of certain events. The deed required registration, but the creditor did not register, neither did he enter into possession when he became entitled to do so; consequently, B and P becoming bankrupt, the goods were lost, and the sureties were held discharged only to the extent of the value of the goods[10].

But mere passive acquiescence by the creditor in acts which are contrary to the conditions of a bond will not relieve the sureties[11].

5. The absolute discharge of the principal is the discharge of the surety[12]. But a covenant entered into between debtor and creditor that the latter will not sue the former, with a reservation of rights against the surety, will not release the surety[13]. And an agreement which purports to release the debtor, but which reserves rights against the sureties, will, in general, be construed merely as a covenant not to sue the debtor[14].

When the creditor releases one of two or more sureties who have

---

8. *Boaler* v. *Mayor* (1865), 19 C. B. (N. S.) 76.
9. *Carter* v. *White* (1884), 25 Ch. D., at p. 670.
10. *Wulff and Billing* v. *Jay* (1872), L. B. 7 Q. B. 756.
11. *Mayor of Durham* v. *Fowler* (1889), 22 Q. B. D. 394, where all the cases are considered; and see *Black* v. *Ottoman Bank* (1862), 15 Moo. P. C. 472.
12. *Commercial Bank of Tasmania* v. *Jones*, [1893] A. C., at p. 316; *cf. Perry* v. *National Provincial Bank of England*, [1910] 1 Ch. 464.
13. *Price* v. *Barker* (1855), 4 E. & B. 760.
14. Lord HATHERLEY in *Green* v. *Wynn* (1869), L. R. 4 Ch., at pp. 204, 206.

contracted jointly or jointly and severally, the others are discharged because the creditor has broken his contract with them. But where a surety contracts severally he is discharged when the creditor releases another surety only if he can establish that he is thereby deprived of the equitable remedy of claiming contribution which even a several surety has against another surety[15].

6. Death of a surety will, if the consideration be divisible, revoke a continuing guarantee, and his estate is not liable thereon for advances made subsequently to and with notice of the death[16], but on a joint and several continuing guarantee, the death of one surety does not *per se* release his co-sureties[17]. Nor, if the consideration for the guarantee has been given once for all, will the death of the surety release his estate from future liability under the guarantee[18]; and if any notice is required to revoke a continuing guarantee, mere knowledge of the surety's death is not sufficient to determine the liability[19].

7. If the undertaking to become surety be entered into on the faith that another shall also become a surety, and that other refuses to, or for any other reason does not, join in the guarantee, those who have already executed it are entitled to consider their liability at an end[20]. Similarly, if a number of persons agree to be co-sureties for definite amounts and the creditor permits one surety to sign for a smaller amount without his co-sureties consenting, all the co-sureties (including the one who effected the alteration) are discharged[1].

8. Whether a guarantee may be revoked by the surety depends upon circumstances, but speaking generally, it may be said that if the consideration for the guarantee has been given once for all, the guarantee is irrevocable save by mutual consent[1]; if it be a continuing guarantee and the consideration is divisible, it may, as regards future transactions, be revoked by notice[2].

Whether, in the absence of express stipulation, a guarantee given to secure the fidelity of a servant can be revoked, is open to question; it seems that in such a case the revocation cannot be immediate and probably a notice sufficient to enable the employment to be lawfully determined would at least be required[3].

---

15. *Ward* v. *National Bank of New Zealand* (1883), 8 App. Cas. 755.
16. *Coulthart* v. *Clementson* (1880), 5 Q. B. D. 42.
17. *Beckett* v. *Addyman* (1882), 9 Q. B. D. 783.
18. *Lloyd's* v. *Harper* (1881), 16 Ch. D. 290.
19. *Re Crace*, [1902] 1 Ch. 733.
20. *Ward* v. *National Bank of New Zealand* (1883), 8 App. Cas. 755. *Ellesmere Brewery Co.* v. *Cooper*, [1896] 1 Q. B. 75; 1 Com. Cas. 210.
1. *Lloyd's* v. *Harper* (1881), 16 Ch. D. 290.
2. *Coulthart* v. *Clementson* (1880), 5 Q. B. D. 42.
3. *Re Crace*, [1902] 1 Ch. 733.

9. By the Partnership Act 1890, s. 18, a continuing guarantee given to a firm or to a third person in respect of the transactions of a firm, is, in the absence of agreement to the contrary, revoked as to future transactions by any change in the constitution of the firm.

10. Neither the discharge in bankruptcy of the principal debtor, nor the acceptance of an arrangement by his creditors, will operate to discharge sureties for his debts[4].

Limitation of actions

Time begins to run in favour of the surety when the cause of action is complete. Generally where there is a present debt and an agreement to pay "on demand", a request for payment is not a condition precedent to the right to sue[5], but in the case of a surety, the debt is considered to be collateral, and if his promise is to pay on demand, no right of action accrues against him, until a demand for payment has been made[6].

---

4. Bankruptcy Act 1914, ss. 16 (20), 28 (4).
5. *Norton* v. *Ellam* (1837), 2 M. & W. 461.
6. *Bradford Old Bank* v. *Sutcliffe*, [1918] 2 K. B. 833.

CHAPTER 23

Moneylenders
and Moneylenders' Contracts

Definition

The expression "moneylender" includes every person whose business is that of moneylending, or who advertises or announces himself or holds himself out in any way as carrying out that business[1]. However, the expression "moneylender" does not include:—

(i) a pawnbroker[2]; or

(ii) a friendly society; or

(iii) any person *bona fide* carrying on the business of banking or insurance. A certificate given by the Department of Trade that a person can properly be treated as being a person *bona fide* carrying on the business of banking is conclusive evidence that he is so carrying on that business[3]; or

(iv) any person *bona fide* carrying on any business not having for its primary object the lending of money, in the course of which and for the purposes whereof he lends money[4]; or

(v) any body corporate for the time being exempted from the Moneylenders Acts by order of the Department of Trade.

Licences

Every moneylender, whether carrying on business alone or as a partner in a firm, must take out annually in respect of every address at which he carries on his business as such a moneylender's licence obtainable from the relevant local authority. It will be void if not

---

1. Moneylenders Act 1900, s. 6.
2. Except in connection with special contracts, see *post*, p. 399.
3. Moneylenders Act 1900, s. 6, as amended by the Companies Act 1967, s. 123. The Department of Trade's certificate may be revoked without prejudice to the effect of the certificate as respects any period before the revocation.
4. Moneylenders Act 1900, s. 6. Thus, a loan made for the purposes of the business of an issuing house is not governed by the Moneylenders Acts: *Frank H. Wright (Constructions), Ltd.* v. *Frodoor*, [1967] 1 All E. R. 433; [1967], 1 W. L. R. 506. But it has been held that when a hire-purchase company made loans to dealers that were not linked to any hire-purchase transaction, the loans were governed by the Moneylenders Acts and as the provisions of these Acts had not been complied with the loans were irrecoverable: *Premor, Ltd.* v. *Shaw Brothers*, [1964] 2 All E. R. 583; [1964] 1 W. L. R. 978, C. A.

taken out by a moneylender in his true name and it must show his authorised name and authorised address[5].

No licence will be granted to a moneylender unless he has first obtained a certificate from the magistrates' court having jurisdiction in the district where the business is proposed to be carried on or, in the metropolitan police district, from a metropolitan magistrate. This certificate must show the moneylender's true name and the name under which, and the address at which, he is authorised by the certificate to carry on business; and no certificate shall authorise him to carry on business at more than one address or under more than one name. Consequently a separate certificate must be taken out in respect of each licence.

Penalties may be imposed on a moneylender who has not complied with the requirements of this section but prosecutions are rare. The borrower is entitled to refuse repayment of any loan if the moneylender has not complied with the section as the loan is then illegal.

A moneylender can only be authorised to carry on business under:

(1) his true name; or
(2) the name of a firm in which he is a partner not required to be registered under the Registration of Business Names Act 1916; or
(3) the business name of an individual, or of a firm in which the moneylender is a partner, which had been at the 29th of July, 1927, registered for not less than three years both as moneylender and under the Registration of Business Names Act 1916[6].

The suspension or forfeiture of a moneylender's certificate by the court or his being convicted of an offence under the Betting and Loans (Infants) Act 1892, or the Moneylenders Act 1900, operates to suspend or render void all licences granted to that moneylender[7].

Restrictions on business

A moneylender must not issue any advertisement, circular or business letter which does not show his authorised name, or any document which implies that he carries on a banking business[8]. No person may send or deliver or cause to be sent or delivered any circular or other document to any person without his written request advertising the name, address

---

5. Moneylenders Act 1927, s. 1; Finance Act 1949, s. 15, Sch. II, Pt. II.
6. Moneylenders Act 1927, s. 2.
7. *Ibid.*, s. 3.
8. Moneylenders Act 1927, s. 4. This does not exempt the moneylender, if a company, from complying with s. 201 of the Companies Act 1948, or, if an individual or firm, with s. 18 of the Registration of Business Names Act 1916.

or telephone number of a moneylender or containing an invitation to borrow money from a moneylender or to apply for information and advice as to so doing[9]. But newspaper advertisements and posters exhibited at an authorised address and limited to certain particulars are permitted[10]. No moneylender may employ an agent or canvasser, nor may any person act as such[11].

If a document purports to indicate the terms of interest upon which a moneylender is willing to lend, it must either express the interest in terms of a rate per cent. per annum or show the rate per cent. per annum represented by the interest proposed to be charged as calculated according to Schedule I of the Act of 1927[12].

A moneylending transaction brought about by the contravention of any of the provisions of s. 5 is illegal, unless the moneylender proves that such contravention occurred without his consent or connivance[13]. Where the transaction is illegal repayment of the loan cannot be enforced, and any security given for it must be restored, the borrower being a person whom the Act was designed to protect, and he is therefore entitled to recover, notwithstanding the illegality of the transaction[14].

Form of contract

No moneylender's contract for repayment of money lent to a borrower or his agent or for payment of interest thereon and no security given by the borrower or his agent in respect of such contract is enforceable unless:

(1) a written memorandum of the contract is made and signed personally[15] by the borrower, and

(2) a copy thereof is delivered to the borrower within seven days of the making of the contract.

The memorandum must contain all the terms of the contract, and must show the date when the money was lent, the amount of the principal, and the interest charged expressed in terms of a rate per cent. per annum or the rate per cent. per annum represented by the interest charged as calculated by Schedule I of the 1927 Act[16].

---

9. Moneylenders Act 1927, s. 5 (1).
10. *Ibid.*, s. 5 (2).   11. *Ibid.*, s. 5 (3).
12. *Ibid.*, s. 5 (4).   13. *Ibid.*, s. 5 (6).
14. *Victorian Daylesford Syndicate, Ltd.* v. *Dott*, [1905] 2 Ch. 624; *Bonnard* v. *Dott*, [1906] 1 Ch. 740.
15. If the borrower is a limited company, the memorandum may be signed on behalf of the company by any person acting under its authority and need not be under the seal of the company (*Re British Games, Ltd.*, [1938] 1 All E. R. 230; [1938] Ch. 240).
16. Moneylenders Act 1927, s. 6. The memorandum need not specify mere matters of machinery by which the terms are to be carried into effect: *Re 22 Albion Street, Westminster, Hanyet Securities, Ltd.* v. *Mallett*, [1968] 2 All E. R. 960, C. A.

"Principal" means the amount actually lent to the borrower.
"Interest" does not include any sum lawfully charged in accordance
with the Act for costs, charges, or expenses, but includes any amount
by whatsoever name called, in excess of the principal, paid or payable
to a moneylender in consideration of or otherwise in respect of a loan[17].
The omission or misstatement of a material term of the contract
will render it unenforceable[18]; but if a security is referred to in the
memorandum it may be identified by parol evidence and need not be
set out in full, if it does not impose terms contradicting the contract,
or which are more onerous than those contained in the contract[19].

If a loan is renewed by a substituted or varied agreement, which
includes a promise by the borrower to pay the balance of the money
previously lent to him, a memorandum of the new contract must be
made and a copy sent to the borrower to render the transaction valid[20].
Where a contract is unenforceable against the borrower for non-
compliance with s. 6 of the Moneylenders Act 1927, it is equally
unenforceable against his surety[20].

A memorandum is sufficient which merely contains a request to
allocate a fresh advance to the settlement of an old loan[21]; but it is not
sufficient if the memorandum does not state that payment of an old
loan was a condition of the contract[1] or that a sum was paid out of a
fresh advance to compensate the moneylender for an old loss which
was only provable in the bankruptcy of the borrower[2].

A *bona fide* compromise of a genuine dispute of fact whether or not a
person is a moneylender is binding and enforceable[3].

In *Congresbury Motors Ltd.* v. *Anglo-Belge Finance Co.*[4], moneylenders made a loan to enable a company to pay the purchase price on
certain property and, the purchase money was paid direct by the moneylenders to the vendors. Repayment of the loan was unenforceable
because no note or memorandum had been executed stating the date

---

17. *Ibid.*, s. 15 (1). And see *Dunn Trust* v. *Feetham*, [1935] All E. R. Rep. 280;
    [1936] 1 K. B. 22.
18. *Kent Trust, Ltd.* v. *Cohen*, [1946] 2 All E. R. 273; [1946] K. B. 584.
19. *Reading Trust* v. *Spero*, [1929] All E. R. Rep. 405; [1930] 1 K. B. 492;
    Mitchener v. *Equitable Investment Co.*, [1938] 1 All E. R. 303; [1938]
    2 K. B. 559.
20. *Eldridge and Morris* v. *Taylor*, [1931] All E. R. Rep. 542; [1931] 2 K. B.
    416; *Temperance Loan Fund* v. *Rose*, [1932] All E. R. Rep. 690; [1932]
    2 K. B. 522.
21. *Re Lyle (B. S.), Ltd.* v. *Chappell*, [1931] All E. R. Rep. 446; [1932] 1 K. B.
    691.
1. *Egan* v. *Langham Investments*, [1938] 1 K. B. 667.
2. *Dunn Trust* v. *Feetham*, [1935] All E. R. Rep. 280; [1936] 1 K. B. 22.
3. *Binder* v. *Alachouzos*, [1972] 2 All E. R. 189; [1972] 2 Q. B. 151, C. A.
4. [1970] 3 All E. R. 385; [1971] Ch. 81, C. A.

when the loan was made but the Court of Appeal *held* that the money-lenders were entitled by subrogation to a lien on the property for the money paid to the vendors.

Prohibition of compound interest and certain charges.—It is illegal for a moneylender to charge compound interest, or for the rate or amount of interest to be increased by reason of any default in the payment of sums due under the contract; but he may charge simple interest on sums in respect of which default has been made at a rate not exceeding that payable on the principal apart from default[5].

It is also illegal for a moneylender to make any charge for negotiating or granting a loan, and if he does so the borrower or intending borrower may recover the amount charged as a debt, or set it off against the amount actually lent, which shall be deemed to be reduced accordingly[6].

Information as to the loan.—A moneylender is bound on demand in writing by the borrower and tender of five pence for expenses, to supply information as to the state of the loan and also (if a reasonable sum is tendered for expenses) copies and documents relating thereto. If the moneylender fails without reasonable excuse to comply with such demand within a month he cannot, so long as the default continues, sue for any sum due under the contract and interest ceases to be chargeable in respect of the period of his default[7].

Limitation of actions.—A moneylender's right to take proceedings under a contract either to recover money lent and interest or to enforce a security is barred unless the proceedings are commenced within twelve months from the date on which the cause of action accrued; where payments become due from time to time under the contract, the time of limitation does not commence to run until a cause of action accrues in respect of the last payment. But if during the twelve months, or any subsequent period during which proceedings may be taken, the borrower acknowledges in writing the amount due and gives a written undertaking to pay it, proceedings may be brought within a further period of twelve months from the date of such acknowledgment and undertaking[8].

If a moneylender sues before the whole amount is due under the contract, the court may order any principal outstanding to be paid

---

5. Moneylenders Act 1927, s. 7. In *Spector* v. *Ageda*, [1971] 3 All E. R. 417; [1971] 3 W. L. R. 498, it was *held* that a loan made by a solicitor to enable the borrower to discharge a debt incurred to a moneylender on which compound interest had been charged was itself illegal and irrecoverable. The solicitor knew the moneylender's loan was illegal.
6. *Ibid.*, s. 12.
7. Moneylenders Act 1927, s. 8.
8. *Ibid.*, s. 13 (1), as amended by Limitation Act 1939, s. 34 (4); Sched.

to the moneylender with such interest, if any, as it may allow up to the date of payment[9].

Assignment of moneylender's debt or security

An assignor of a moneylender's debt or security (whether he is the moneylender himself or a previous assignee), must give written notice to the assignee that the debt or security is affected by the Act of 1927. He must also supply the assignee with all information necessary to enable such assignee to supply information and furnish copies of documents to the borrower, if so required pursuant to s. 8. A moneylender or previous assignee who contravenes the above provisions must indemnify the person to whom the debt or security is assigned against any loss caused thereby, and is also guilty of an offence[10].

Any agreement with, or security[11] taken by, a moneylender will be valid in the hands of a *bona fide* assignee or holder for value without notice of any defect due to the operation of the Act, and also in the hands of any person deriving title under him; and the right to take proceedings by such persons to enforce the security will not be barred in the same manner as they would have been if the moneylender or an assignee with notice were suing[11]. Subject to the rights conferred on such assignees and holders, the Act continues to apply to the debt or security notwithstanding assignment; and if the borrower or any person is prejudiced by an assignment he has a direct right to be indemnified by the moneylender against any consequent loss[12].

Re-opening of moneylending transactions

Since the abolition of the usury laws in 1854, moneylenders have been entitled to charge any rate of interest agreed upon. The Moneylenders Act 1900, however, provides that if the interest on a loan is excessive and the whole transaction is harsh and unconscionable or such that a court of equity would give relief, the court may reopen the transaction and give reasonable relief to the borrower[13]. Under the Moneylenders Act 1927, if the interest charged exceeds the rate of 48 per cent. per annum, it will be presumed that the interest is excessive and that the transaction is harsh and unconscionable unless the moneylender proves the contrary[14]. Even the consent of the

---

9. Moneylenders Act 1927, s. 13 (2).
10. Moneylenders Act 1927, s. 16.
11. Post-dated cheques given in repayment of the loan are "securities", *Stirling* v. *John*, [1923] 1 K. B. 557.
12. Moneylenders Act 1927, s. 17.
13. Moneylenders Act 1900, s. 1. The court has no jurisdiction to re-open a transaction which has been made the subject of a judgment in a previous action: *Cohen* v. *Jonesco*, [1916] 1 K. B. 127.
14. Moneylenders Act 1927, s. 10.

borrower to judgment is not of itself sufficient to rebut this presumption; the court must be satisfied by the moneylender that interest exceeding 48 per cent. is not in the circumstances excessive[15]. The presumption was rebutted in one case where loans had been made to a businessman for a highly speculative and very profitable business with interest at 60 and 80 per cent[16].

In the case of loans where the interest charged does not exceed the rate of 48 per cent. whether the rate is excessive is a question of fact. If money is lent on good security, a rate of interest that might not have been regarded as excessive for a loan on personal security may be outrageous and extortionate[17]. Even where the rate of interest charged does not exceed 48 per cent., an excessive rate of interest, having regard to the nature of the risk and other circumstances, may of itself be evidence that the bargain is harsh and unconscionable[18].

---

15. *Mills Conduit Investment, Ltd.* v. *Leslie*, [1931] All E. R. Rep. 442; [1932] 1 K. B. 233.
16. *Reading Trust, Ltd.* v. *Spero*, [1930] 1 K. B. 492.
17. *Kruse* v. *Seeley*, [1924] 1 Ch. 136, *per* EVE, J., at p. 144.
18. *Samuel* v. *Newbold*, [1906] A. C. 461; *Verner-Jeffreys* v. *Pinto*, [1929] 1 Ch. 401.

CHAPTER 24

Bailment, Pledge, Mortgage and Lien

I BAILMENT

Bailment is the delivery of the possession of goods on a condition, express or implied, that they shall be returned to the bailor or dealt with according to his directions as soon as the purpose for which they were bailed is ended. There are many common everyday transactions of bailment—the deposit of goods for safe custody or storage, the leaving of goods for the purposes of cleaning or repair, the hiring out of goods, and the pledge of goods as a security for money lent. Carriage of goods, already dealt with, is yet another example. In practice the relationship between bailor and bailee is usually based on contract but this is not necessarily so. Thus, there is a bailment where the carrier or repairer of goods is acting gratuitously and if the bailee of goods, B, delivers possession of them to a sub-bailee, C, with the owner's consent, there is a bailment relationship between the owner and C and C owes the owner the same duties as B does[1]. In *Gilchrist Watt & Sanderson Property, Ltd.* v. *York Products Property, Ltd.*[2],

> Shipowners carried two cases of clocks belonging to the plaintiffs from Hamburg to Sydney. The two cases were unloaded by the defendants but one of the cases was missing when the plaintiffs were ready to take delivery. *Held:* the defendants owed a duty of care to the plaintiffs although there was no contract between them—the defendants, obligation was the same as that of a bailee whether or not it could with strict accuracy be described as being the obligation of a bailee.

The principal liabilities of a bailee are:

1. to allow the bailor to repossess the goods bailed when proper demand for them is made by the bailor. Failure on the part of the bailee to do this renders him liable to the bailor in conversion or detinue, and he is also liable for any loss or

---

1. *Morris* v. *C. W. Martin & Sons, Ltd.*, [1965] 2 All E. R. 725; [1966] 1 Q. B. 716, C. A.
2. [1970] 3 All E. R. 825; [1970] 1 W. L. R. 1262, P. C.

damage to the goods occurring while the bailee is wrongfully detaining the goods irrespective of negligence[3].

Where the goods bailed are entrusted by the bailee to his servant who steals them the bailee is liable in conversion for their loss to the bailor[2].

2. to take reasonable care of the goods bailed[4]. It was at one time felt that the degree of care required depended on the type of bailment and, in particular, on whether it was a gratuitous bailment or a bailment for reward. However, in the case of *Houghland* v. *R. R. Low (Luxury Coaches), Ltd.*[5], the Court of Appeal held that the standard of care required of a bailee is the same whether the bailment is gratuitous or for reward. ORMEROD, L.J., said:

"The question that we have to consider in a case of this kind, if it is necessary to consider negligence, is whether in the circumstances of this particular case a sufficient standard of care has been observed by the defendants or their servants."

Moreover, the onus of proof is on the bailee. Thus, if the goods bailed are lost or returned to the bailor in a damaged state, the bailee is liable in damages unless he can prove that all reasonable care was taken by himself, by his servants and by any independent contractor to whom he has entrusted the goods[6].

The bailee is liable for any loss or damage, irrespective of negligence, if the loss or damage occurs after the bailee has dealt with the goods in a manner fundamentally inconsistent with the bailment[7].

Distinguished from licence

A bailment involves a handing over of possession. If a barber's shop or café provides hooks on which a customer may leave his coat but no employee of the proprietors of the shop or café take possession of the coat from the customer, there is no bailment and hence, no duty of care on the part of the proprietors. In *Ashby* v. *Tolhurst*[8]:

---

3. *Shaw & Co.* v. *Symmons & Sons, Ltd.*, [1917] 1 K. B. 799.
4. *Coggs* v. *Bernard* (1704), 1 Sm. L. C. (13th ed.), 175.
5. [1962] 2 All E. R. 159; [1962] 1 Q. B. 694.
6. *British Road Services, Ltd.* v. *Arthur V. Crutchley & Co., Ltd.*, [1968] 1 All E. R. 811, C. A. The ordinary negligence liability of a bailee may be excluded by contractual terms, but such terms are ineffective if there has been a fundamental breach of contract, *ante*, p. 16.
7. *Edwards* v. *Newland & Co.*, [1950] 1 All E. R. 1072; [1950] 2 K. B. 534, where the bailee stored goods in a warehouse other than the one in which he contracted to store them, and was held liable for consequent loss irrespective of negligence.
8. [1937] 2 All E. R. 837; [1937] 2 K. B. 242, followed in *Tinsley* v. *Dudley*, [1951] 1 All E. R. 252; [1951] 2 K. B. 18, C. A.

The plaintiff left his car at the defendant's car park after paying the one shilling charge. On the plaintiff's return, he was informed by the attendant that someone had come for the car on his behalf. The plaintiff claimed for the loss of his car. *Held:* the relationship between the owners of the car park and the car owner was that of licensor and licensee, not of bailee and bailor, so that no duty of care arose.

Duty of the bailor

Where goods are hired out for use, there is an implied term in the contract to the effect that the goods are as fit for their purpose as reasonable care and skill can make them[9].

Involuntary bailees

Where someone receives unsolicited goods and he has no reasonable cause to believe they were sent to him with a view to their being acquired for the purposes of a trade or business, he has certain rights under the Unsolicited Goods and Services Act 1971 to treat the goods as an unconditional gift to him. The conditions are that he does not agree to acquire or return them and either that (a) during the six months' period from delivery the sender did not take possession and the recipient did not unreasonably refuse repossession or that (b) not less than 30 days before the end of the six months' period the recipient gave notice to the sender and during the 30 days the sender did not take possession and the recipient did not unreasonably refuse repossession.

II PLEDGE

This is a delivery of goods by a debtor to his creditor, as security for a debt. Its effect is to transfer possession and consequent rights, and therefore the pledgee can bring an action for the return of the goods if they are taken from him; so also can the pledgor. There is also an implied undertaking on the part of the pledgee to return the article when the debt is paid at the stated date, or if no time is stated, then whenever the pledgor pays or makes proper tender, and the pledgor impliedly undertakes that it is his property[10]. A man cannot ordinarily make an effective pledge of property which does not belong to him; but to this there are exceptions[11].

---

9. *Hyman* v. *Nye* (1881), 6 Q. B. D. 685. An express contractual term may exclude this implied term but the exclusion clause may not be effective if there has been a fundamental breach of contract: *Karsales (Harrow), Ltd.* v. *Wallis*, [1956] 2 All E. R. 866; [1956] 1 W. L. R. 936. See *ante*, p. 16.
10. *Cheesman* v. *Exall* (1851), 6 Ex. 344.
11. See *ante*, pp. 135–137.

The pledgee must use ordinary diligence in his care of the pledge, but if, notwithstanding such diligence, it is lost, he incurs no liability. If then the pledge is stolen, the pledgee must show that it was not lost for want of what an ordinarily prudent man would have done to ensure its safety; and if notwithstanding it was taken by robbery, he is not bound to replace it[12]. He must not use goods pledged unless they are such as will not deteriorate by wear and even in such a case he uses them at his peril[12].

He obtains a power of sale when default is made in payment of the debt at the stipulated time; or if no time is stipulated, then after a proper demand for payment has been made, and a reasonable time for performance has been allowed[13]. Any excess obtained by the sale beyond the amount necessary to liquidate the debt and expenses must be returned to the pledgor.

A pledgee usually loses his rights by parting with the possession of his pledge, but he may redeliver it to the pledgor for a limited purpose without losing such rights[14].

Pledges given to pawnbrokers, *i.e.* to persons carrying on the business of taking goods and chattels in pawn[15], are subject to the provisions of the Pawnbrokers Acts 1872 and 1960. Amongst these may be noted—

1. That the Acts do not apply to loans of over £10[16];
2. Pawn-tickets must be given for the pledge[17];
3. Every pledge is to be redeemable within six months and seven days[18];
4. Pledges above two pounds in value, not redeemed, are to be sold by auction, and those of two pounds or under are forfeited at the end of the period of six months and seven days[19];
5. Pledges over two pounds are redeemable till sale[20];
6. Special contracts may be made on loans of above five pounds, subject to the giving of a special pawn-ticket signed by the pawnbroker and a duplicate signed by the borrower[1]. A

---

12. *Coggs* v. *Bernard* (1703), 1 Sm. L. C. (13th ed.) **175**, at p. **185**.
13. *Re Richardson* (1885), 30 Ch. D., at p. 403, *per* FRY, L.J.
14. *North Western Bank* v. *Poynter*, [1895] A. C. 56.
15. Pawnbrokers Act 1872, s. 5.
16. *Ibid.*, s. 10, and Pawnbrokers Act 1960, s. 1.
17. Pawnbrokers Act 1872, s. 14.
18. Pawnbrokers Act 1872, s. 16, and Pawnbrokers Act 1960, s. 2.
19. Pawnbrokers Act 1872, ss. 17, 19, and Pawnbrokers Act 1960, ss. 2, 3.
20. Pawnbrokers Act 1872, s. 18, and Pawnbrokers Act 1960, ss. 2, 3.
1. Pawnbrokers Act 1872, s. 24, and Pawnbrokers Act 1960, s. 1.

transaction effected under such a contract may be re-opened by the court under s. 1 of the Moneylenders Act 1900[2]. There are, in addition, many provisions, the objects of which are to ensure that the right person gets back the pledge upon payment, and to restrain the commission of crimes.

III MORGAGE OF PERSONAL PROPERTY

In this place it is intended to restrict the remarks made on mortgages to such as affect personal property; information as to mortgages on real property should be sought in special works on that subject.

Mortgages of personal property are in most instances within the Bills of Sale Acts. In cases in which these Acts do not apply, as, for instance, where shares are mortgaged, the mortgagee has an implied power to sell the shares on default by the mortgagor in payment of the amount due at the time appointed. If no time for payment has been fixed, the mortgagee must give a reasonable notice to the mortgagor requiring payment on a day certain before he can sell[3]. If the mortgage was by deed, the mortgagee would have the powers conferred by ss. 101 and 103 of the Law of Property Act 1925.

IV BILLS OF SALE

A Bill of Sale is a document which transfers the property in goods either absolutely or by way of security. If the transferor of the goods, *i.e.* the grantor of the bill of sale, retains possession of the goods, the bill is regulated by:

1. The Bills of Sale Act 1878, whose object is to prevent false credit being given to persons in apparent possession of goods which in reality belong to others; and

2. The Bills of Sale Act 1882, whose object is to protect impecunious persons, who, it was believed, were often induced to sign complicated documents of charge which they did not understand.

Accordingly,

1. It will be found that the Act of 1878—which originally applied to all forms of bills of sale—makes void as against creditors and those representing them a secret disposition by bill of sale of chattels of which the grantor retains possession.

---

2. Moneylenders Act 1927, s. 10 (3); ss. 6, 12 and 13 of the Moneylenders Act 1927 do not apply to a pawnbroker's loan, if he complies with the substituted provisions of s. 14 of that Act: and see *ante*, pp. 391–395.
3. *Deverges* v. *Sandeman, Clarke & Co.*, [1902] 1 Ch. 579.

2. On the other hand, the Act of 1882, which applies only to bills of sale given by way of security for money totally invalidates such bills of sale if they are not in the prescribed form, and makes them of no effect even between the parties.

Although, so far as bills of sale by way of security for money are concerned, the Act of 1878 is superseded by the Act of 1882, some of the provisions of the former Act are retained in the latter, and are therefore applicable to both classes of bills of sale, *i.e.* absolute or by way of security.

Wide ranging changes in the law including the repeal of the Bills of Sale Act were proposed in 1971 by the Crowther Committee on Consumers Credit[4].

Definition

For instance, the definition of bill of sale is the same for both Acts. The term "bill of sale" includes not only—

1. Bills of sale strictly so called (*i.e.* assignments of personal chattels giving a title without delivery),

   but also many other documents, viz.:

2. Assignments,
3. Transfers,
4. Declarations of trust without transfer,
5. Inventories of goods with receipt thereto attached or receipts for the purchase moneys of goods, and other assurances of personal chattels,
6. Licences to take possession of chattels as security for any debt, and also any agreement, whether intended or not to be followed by the execution of any other instrument, by which a right in equity to any personal chattels, or to any charge or security thereon, shall be conferred[5].

Also any attornment or agreement, except a mining lease, whereby a power of distress is given, or agreed to be given, by way of security for any debt or advance and whereby any rent is reserved or made payable as a mode of providing for the payment of interest on such debt or advance, is to be deemed a bill of sale so far as distress is concerned. This does not apply to the mortgage of any land which the mortgagee in possession demises to the mortgagor as his tenant at a fair rent[6].

---

4. Cmnd. 4596.
5. Bills of Sale Act 1878, s. 4.
6. *Ibid.*, s. 6; *Ex parte Kennedy* (1888), 21 Q. B. D. 384.

But the term "bill of sale" is not to include:

1. Assignments for the benefit of creditors[7],
2. Marriage settlements[8],
3. Transfers of ships or shares therein,
4. Transfers of goods in the ordinary course of trade[9],
5. Bills of lading, or any documents used in the course of trade or business as proof of the possession or control of or authorising the possessor to transfer or receive goods,
6. Assignments of fixtures, unless separately assigned[10],
7. An agricultural charge on farming stock and other agricultural assets[11].

The Act of 1882 does not apply to debentures issued by an incorporated company which require to be registered under the Companies Act 1948[12]. By the Industrial and Provident Societies Act 1967, a charge granted by a society registered under the Industrial and Provident Societies Act 1965 is outside the Bills of Sale Acts if application is made to register the charge in the Central Office of the Registry of Friendly Societies within the prescribed period.

Verbal contracts are not within the Acts, which strike at documents and not at transactions[13]; nor is any document which is merely ancillary and which does not give the transferee his title; hence, when property and possession pass under a verbal arrangement, a receipt for money payable in connection therewith given subsequently, will not be a bill of sale[14]. A pledge is not within the Acts[15].

When goods have already passed out of the possession of the transferor, documents subsequently executed evidencing the transaction are not bills of sale[16]; for, as COTTON, L.J., said in *Marsden v. Meadows*[17], the documents to be within the Act must be—

---

7. Though expressed to exclude creditors having notice of the deed, who do not come in within a given time (*Hadley v. Beedom*, [1895] 1 Q. B. 646).
8. Including agreements to settle on marriage, even though informal and not under seal (*Wenman v. Lyon*, [1891] 2 Q. B. 192).
9. This will protect a sale of growing crops, which are "goods" (*Stephenson v. Thompson*, [1924] 2 K. B. 240).
10. Bills of Sale Act 1878, s. 4.
11. Agricultural Credits Act 1928, s. 8 (1).
12. Bills of Sale Act 1882, s. 17; *Re Standard Manufacturing Co.*, [1891] 1 Ch. 622.
13. *North Central Wagon Co. v. M. S. & L. Rail. Co.* (1887), 35 Ch. D. 191; *Newlove v. Shrewsbury* (1888), 21 Q. B. D. 41.
14. *Ramsay v. Margrett*, [1894] 2 Q. B. 18.
15. *Waight v. Waight and Walker*, [1952] 2 All E. R. 290; [1952] P. 282.
16. *Charlesworth v. Mills*, [1892] A. C. 231.
17. (1881), 7 Q. B. D. 80; and see *Ex parte Hubbard* (1886), 17 Q. B. D. 690, contrasting it with *Ex parte Parsons* (1886), 16 Q. B. D. 532; *North Central Wagon Co. v. Manchester, Sheffield and Lincolnshire Rail. Co.* (1888), 13 App. Cas. 554.

"documents on which the title of the transferee of the goods depends, either as the actual transfer of the property, or an agreement to transfer, or as a muniment or document of title taken, to use an expression found in some of the cases, at the time as a record of the transaction."

A constructive delivery is sufficient to constitute an actual transfer of possession; *e.g.*

handing over the keys of a locked room containing the chattels, and the transaction will not be rendered void by a written licence to enter and remove them being subsequently given[18].

In considering whether a document, apparently not within this definition, is nevertheless covered by it, the court not only may but must inquire into the *real* nature of the transaction. Thus,

where the real agreement was one to lend money upon the security of goods in which the borrower had an interest, but took the form of a purchase of the goods by the lender, followed by a hire-purchase agreement with the borrower, the court held the latter agreement to be a bill of sale[19].

But RUSSELL, L.J., in *Snook v. London and West Riding Investments, Ltd.*[1] said that a court will only hold such transaction to be intended to mask a loan if it finds that *both* parties to the transaction so intended it.

Personal chattels.—The Acts refer only to bills of sale of *personal chattels*, a term which will include fixtures and growing crops if assigned separately from the land to which they are attached; also trade machinery though attached to the land. But assignments of—

1. Stocks,
2. Shares,
3. Contracts,
4. Other choses in action,

are not assignments of personal chattels, and hence are not affected by these Acts[2].

Bills of sale are of two kinds:

1. *Absolute,* such as pass the property absolutely to the transferee;

---

18. *Wrightson v. McArthur and Hutchisons,* [1921] 2 K. B. 807.
19. *Beckett v. Tower Assets Co.,* [1891] 1 Q. B. 639; *Mellor v. Maas,* [1903] 1 K. B. 226, affirmed in the House of Lords, *sub nom. Maas v. Pepper,* [1905] A. C. 102, *Polsky v. S. and A. Services, Ltd.,* [1951] 1 All E. R. 185; *affd.* 1062 *n,* followed in *North Central Wagon Finance Co.* v. *Brailsford,* [1962] 1 All E. R. 502; [1962] 1 W. L. R. 1288.
1. [1967] 1 All E. R. 518, 530; [1967] 2 Q. B. 786, C. A.
2. Bills of Sale Act 1878, s. 4.

2. *Conditional,* such as pass it subject to a condition revesting it upon the performance of the condition, viz., upon the payment of money.

The Act of 1882 is confined in its operation to conditional bills.

Requisites and formalities

With one exception the provisions for registration are the same for both Acts[3]:

1. The bill must be registered in the Filing Department of the Royal Courts of Justice within seven days after execution.

To the registrar must be presented
   (i) the original bill, with every schedule or inventory annexed to or referred to in it[4];
  (ii) a true copy[5] of such bill and schedules, and of every attestation of the execution of the bill of sale;
 (iii) an affidavit verifying the execution and attestation, stating also the time of execution, and the names, addresses, and occupations of the grantor and of every attesting witness.

The copy and affidavit must be filed within the seven days. It is not necessary for the grantor to specify every occupation in respect of which he is engaged or liable, it is sufficient to state his occupation in a concise way, and one in which he would be recognised by those acquainted with him and his pursuits[6].

2. In the case of an absolute bill, the execution of it by the grantee must be attested by a solicitor and the attestation must state that the solicitor explained the effect of the execution. In the case of a conditional bill, the attestation may be by any credible witness not a party to the bill[7].

3. The bill must contain a statement of the consideration and this must be substantially true; and it will be sufficient if the facts are accurately stated, either as to their legal or as to their mercantile and business effect[8]. It would not be correct to describe money retained by the grantee as "now paid" to the grantor, unless it was retained

---

3. Bills of Sale Act 1878, ss. 8, 10; Bills of Sale Act 1882, ss. 8, 10.
4. A bill of sale contained an assignment of "1,800 books as per catalogue"; and it was decided that the catalogue was not a schedule or inventory which required registration (*Davidson* v. *Carlton Bank*, [1893] 1. Q. B. 82).
5. Or copies of conditional bills of sale if required for transmission to County Court Registrars (Administration of Justice Act 1925, s. 23).
6. *Feast* v. *Robinson* (1894], 63 L. J. Ch. 321. See also *Kemble* v. *Addison,* [1900] 1 Q. B. 430.
7. Bills of Sale Act 1882, s. 10.
8. *Credit Co.* v. *Pott* (1880), 6 Q. B. D. 295.

in respect of a debt actually due[9]. Nor can money advanced contemporaneously with the execution of the deed be properly stated as "now owing". It does not become due until the future date specified in the bill, and should be described as "now paid[10]. On the other hand, money previously paid by the grantee at the request of the grantor to a third person is sufficiently described as "paid to the grantor"[11].

4. If made—

    (i) with a defeasance (*i.e.* any agreement which may enable the bill to be avoided) or

    (ii) subject to any condition or declaration of trust,

the defeasance, condition, or declaration of trust must be set forth on the same paper which contains the bill; and it must be contained in the registered copy[12]. Thus:

> where a promissory note was given at the same time, and for the same consideration as the bill, payable by instalments, and there was a proviso that, if the instalments became in arrear, the whole debt might be claimed at once, it was held that this constituted a defeasance, since by payment of the promissory note the bill of sale would be defeated, and not being contained on the same paper as the bill, the latter was void[13].

It does not matter in whose favour the defeasance or condition operates[14]; if it is of such a nature that some right or liability under the bill of sale is affected, varied or added to[11].

Effect of non-compliance.—If the above requisites are not complied with, the bill of sale, if an absolute bill, is void as regards all goods covered by it in the *apparent possession* of the grantor against the following:

1. Trustee in bankruptcy of the grantor;
2. Assignees for the benefit of his creditors;
3. Those seizing the goods comprised in the bill under executions;
4. All persons on whose behalf the goods have been thus seized[15].

---

9. Bills of Sale Act 1878, s. 8; Bills of Sale Act 1882, s. 8. See *Re Charing Cross Bank* (1881), 16 Ch. D. 35; *Ex parte Rolph* (1882), 19 Ch. D. 98; *Ex parte Firth* (1882), 19 Ch. D. 419; *Richardson* v. *Harris* (1889), 22 Q. B. D. 268; *Parson* v. *Equitable Investment Co.*, [1916] 2 Ch. 527.
10. *Davies* v. *Jenkins*, [1900] 1 Q. B. 133.
11. *Stott* v. *Shaw*, [1928] All E. R. Rep. 549; [1928] 2 K. B. 26.
12. Bills of Sale Act 1878, s. 10 (3).
13. *Counsell* v. *London and Westminster Loan Co.* (1887), 19 Q. B. D. 512. The note would be good (*Monetary Advance Co.* v. *Cater* (1888), 20 Q. B. D. 785. See also *Edwards* v. *Marcus*, [1894] 1 Q. B. 587).
14. *Edwards* v. *Marcus*, *supra*.
15. Bills of Sale Act 1878, s. 8.

To avoid these penalties:

> "there must be something done which plainly takes [the goods] out of the apparent possession of the debtor in the eyes of everybody who sees them"[16].

Where the possession is doubtful, the law attributes it to the person who has the legal title, so that:

> if a husband and wife are living together in premises containing chattels which have been sold or validly given by the husband to the wife, the chattels must be considered as being in the actual possession of the wife and not in the apparent possession of the husband[17].

On the other hand, in *Youngs* v. *Youngs*[18].

> A man sold furniture to his housekeeper. He gave her at the time a receipt with an inventory attached. The furniture was not moved. It was held that possession had not passed to the housekeeper. She used the furniture only as a member of the household and in contrast to the facts of the last-mentioned case there was no "common establishment" between the grantor and grantee.

A conditional bill of sale which is not duly attested or registered or which does not truly set forth the consideration is void in respect of the personal chattels comprised therein even as against the grantor. It is not void as regards the personal covenant to pay the principal and interests[19].

A bill of sale, when registered, takes its priority over others according to the date of registration[20]; no transfer need be registered; at the expiration of every five years re-registration is necessary[1].

Except where otherwise indicated, the above applies to all bills of sale. It is important here to notice a further provision which applies to absolute bills of sale only. If duly registered they are not within the order and disposition clause of the Bankruptcy Act[2]. The exemption does not apply to bills of sale given by way of security[3].

---

16. *Ex parte Jay* (1874), L. R. 9 Ch., at p. 704.
17. *Ramsay* v. *Margrett*, [1894] 2 Q. B. 18; *French* v. *Gething*, [1922] 1 K. B. 236. The principle of *Ramsay* v. *Margrett* was applied to an establishment where a man lived with his mistress in *Koppel* v. *Koppel*, [1966] 2 All E. R. 187.
18. [1940] 1 K. B. 760; [1940] 1 All E. R. 349. See also *Hislop* v. *Hislop*, [1950] W. N. 124, C. A.
19. Bills of Sale Act 1882, s. 8. As to the effect of omitting a defeasance or condition from a conditional bill of sale, see *post*, p. 408.
20. Bills of Sale Act 1878, s. 11.
1. *Ibid.*, s. 10.
2. Bills of Sale Act 1878, s. 20; and see *post*, p. 467.
3. Bills of Sale Act 1882, s. 15.

The Act of 1882

It remains to consider the provisions of the Act of 1882, which applies to conditional bills of sale only. A bill of sale given by way of security for the payment of money must be made in accordance with the form in the schedule to the Act under penalty of avoidance[4]; *i.e.* it must produce the precise legal effect—neither more nor less— of that form, it must preserve all the characteristics of the form, and it must be so framed as not to deceive any reasonable person as to its exact meaning[5]. The form is as follows:

Form of the Bill of Sale

"This indenture made the   day of   between AB of   of the one part and CD of   of the other part WITNESSETH that in consideration of the sum of £   now paid to AB by CD the receipt of which the said A. B. hereby acknowledges [*or whatever else the consideration may be*] he the said AB doth hereby assign unto CD his executors, administrators, and assigns, all and singular the several chattels and things specifically described in the schedule hereto annexed by way of security for the payment of the sum of £ and interest thereon at the rate of   per cent per annum [*or whatever else may be the rate*]. And the said AB doth further agree and declare that he will duly pay to the said CD the principal sum aforesaid, together with the interest then due, by equal   payments of £   on the   day of   [*or whatever else may be the stipulated times or time of payment*]. And the said AB doth also agree with the said CD that he will [*here insert terms as to insurance, payment of rent, or otherwise, which the parties may agree to for the maintenance or defeasance of the security*].

"Provided always, that the chattels hereby assigned shall not be liable to seizure or to be taken possession of by the said CD for any cause other than those specified in s. 7 of the Bills of Sale Act (1878) Amendment Act 1882.

"In witness, etc.

"Signed and sealed by the said AB in the presence of me EF [*add witness's name, address and description*]."

Comments

1. As showing the strictness with which the form must be followed, reference may be had to the following cases in which a divergence was held fatal.

---

4. *Ibid.*, s. 9.
5. *Ex parte Stanford* (1886), 17 Q. B. D. 259; *Thomas v. Kelly* (1888), 13 App. Cas. 506. The fact that the transaction cannot be expressed in a document in the statutory form will be no excuse for diverging from it (*Ex parte Parsons* (1886), 16 Q. B. D. 532).

(i) Omission of the address of the grantee[6]; it will be noticed that the form runs,

A B of   C D of

thereby clearly indicating that the address of both must be given.

(ii) A general assignment in the body of the deed of chattels to be afterwards acquired[7]. These can only be assigned in two cases:

(a) where brought on any place in substitution for such fixtures, plant, and trade machinery as are by definition "personal chattels", and are already described in the schedule to the bill of sale[8];

(b) where assigned for the purpose of maintaining the security—*e.g.*

a covenant to replace such articles (specifically described in the schedule) as may be damaged or worn out, with others of equal value[9].

(iii) The inclusion of anything not a "personal chattel" will not be in accordance with the statutory form[10], but though void as a bill of sale, the deed would in such cases be good as to anything assigned which was not a personal chattel and therefore not within the Acts[11].

(iv) a conveyance of property by the grantor "as beneficial owner", which has the effect of introducing into the statutory form covenants not contained in it[12];

(v) a proviso enabling the grantee to retain the bill of sale after payment of the secured debt[13].

2. Whenever part of the consideration is a present advance, it is essential to the validity of the bill that it should contain an acknowledgment of the receipt of that advance[14].

3. A bill of sale, though on the face of it unobjectionable, is not in accordance with the form if it omits a condition or defeasance which

6. *Altree* v. *Altree*, [1898] 2. Q. B. 267.
7. *Thomas* v. *Kelly* (1888), 13 App. Cas. 506; C. & T., p. 335.
8. Bills of Sale Act 1882, s. 6 (2).
9. *Seed* v. *Bradley*, [1894] 1 Q. B. 319; *Consolidated Credit Corporation* v. *Gosney* (1886), 16 Q. B. D. 24.
10. *Cochrane* v. *Entwistle* (1890), 25 Q. B. D. 116.
11. *Re Burdett* (1888), 20 Q. B. D. 310.
12. *Ex parte Stanford* (1886), 17 Q. B. D. 259. See Law of Property Act 1925, s. 76.
13. *Watson* v. *Strickland* (1887), 19 Q. B. D. 391.
14. *Davies* v. *Jenkins*, [1900] 1 Q. B. 133.

ought to have been inserted in the bill of sale and which, if inserted, would have rendered it void[15].

4. On the other hand, a covenant for unequal repayment is permissible. It is true that the form runs

"by equal payments,"

but a qualification is introduced by the words in brackets—

"[or whatever else may be the stipulated times or time of payment]."

This clearly allows a payment by one instalment, and thereby shows that payment by equal instalments is not the only mode contemplated by the form[16];

5. So also a clause in a bill which provides for payment by equal instalments which include both principal and interest is permitted by the statutory form[17].

6. The form requires the witness's name, address, and description. Description by occupation would be sufficient, but if the witness has no occupation his style must be given[18].

7. The consideration must amount at least to £30[19].

8. It must be noticed that there are three kinds of penalties provided by the Act of 1882.

(i) If the bill:

(a) is not in the prescribed form, or

(b) if the consideration does not amount to £30,

it is absolutely void even as between the parties[20], and the grantee is entitled merely to the return of his money with 5 per cent. interest and without the security of the bill[1].

(ii) If the bill is not duly registered or attested, or if the consideration is not truly stated, the bill is void even as between the parties, but only so far as it gives security over the chattels[2]; an agreement in the bill to pay a given rate of interest would be enforceable.

---

15. *Smith* v. *Whiteman*, [1909] 2 K. B. 437; *Hall* v. *Whiteman*, [1912] 1 K. B. 683.
16. *Re Cleaver* (1887), 18 Q. B. D. 489; and see *Simmons* v. *Woodward*, [1892] A. C. 100.
17. *Linfoot* v. *Pockett*, [1895] 2 Ch. 835; *Rosefield* v. *Provincial Union Bank*, [1910] 2 K. B. 781. *Cf. Goldstrom* v. *Tallerman* (1886), 18 Q. B. D. 1.
18. *Sims* v. *Trollope*, [1897] 1 Q. 3. 24. *Cf.* the provisions of the Bills of Sale Act 1878, s. 10 (2), as to the description of the witness necessary in the affidavit filed on registration. Under that subsection if the witness had no occupation it would not be necessary to give his style (*Ex parte Young, Re Symonds* (1880), 42 L. T. 744).
19. Bills of Sale Act 1882, s. 12.
20. *Ibid.*, ss. 9, 12.
1. *Davies* v. *Rees* (1886), 17 Q. B. D. 408.
2. Bills of Sale Act 1882, s. 8.

(iii) Thirdly, the bill of sale must have a schedule annexed containing an inventory of the personal chattels comprised in the bill, or the bill will be void except against the grantor:

(a) in respect of chattels which are not "specifically described" in the inventory in the schedule[3]; and

(b) in respect of any chattels included in the schedule of which the grantor was not the true owner at the time of executing the bill of sale[4].

9. Even where the provisions of the Acts have been fully complied with, the grantee of a bill of sale in respect of goods in the possession of the grantor in his "trade or business" may still lose his security if the grantor becomes bankrupt. This is because the grantor's trustee in bankruptcy is entitled to take such goods for division among the grantor's creditors[5].

In s. 7 of the Act of 1882 the causes for which the goods covered by a bill of sale given to secure payment of money may be seized are set forth. These are:

1. If the grantor shall make default in payment[6], of the sum or sums of money secured by the bill at the time therein provided for payment, or in the performance of any covenant or agreement contained in the bill of sale, and necessary for maintaining the security;

2. If the grantor shall become a bankrupt or suffer the said goods, or any of them, to be distrained for rent, rates, or taxes;

3. If the grantor shall fraudulently either remove, or suffer the said goods, or any of them, to be removed from the premises;

4. If the grantor shall not, without reasonable excuse, upon demand in writing by the grantee, produce to him his last receipt for rent, rates, and taxes;

---

3. Bills of Sale Act 1882, s. 4. "Specifically described" has been defined to mean described with such particularity as would be used in an ordinary business inventory of the chattels in question (*Witt* v. *Banner* (1888), 20 Q. B. D. 144; *Davidson* v. *Carlton Bank*, [1893] 1 Q. B. 82; and see *Davies* v. *Jenkins*, [1900] 1 Q. B. 133).

4. *Ibid.*, s. 5 (*Thomas* v. *Kelly* (1888), 13 App. Cas. 506). A joint assignment of chattels by husband and wife as "grantor," which belong to one of them alone, is not an assignment by the true owner (*Gordon* v. *S. Goldstein*, [1924] 2 K. B. 779). The grantor of an absolute bill of sale, even if the bill is not registered, is no longer the true owner of the goods (*Tuck* v. *Southern Counties Deposit Bank* (1889), 42 Ch. D. 471). But as a grantor of goods under a conditional bill of sale remains true owner of the equity of redemption of the goods up to seizure, he may give a second bill of sale, subject to the former (*Thomas* v. *Searles*, [1891] 2 Q. B. 408).

5. *Re Ginger, Ex parte London and Universal Bank*, [1897] 2 Q. B. 461. See *post*, p. 467.

6. Though of a single instalment (*Re Wood*, [1894] 1 Q. B. 605).

5. If execution shall have been levied against the goods of the grantor under any judgment at law.

But the grantor may within five days from the seizure or taking possession of any chattels for any of the above-mentioned causes, apply to a judge of the High Court, and the judge may, if he is satisfied that the cause of seizure no longer exists, restrain the removal or sale of the chattels, or may make such other order as may seem just[7]. During the five days the goods may not be removed from the place of seizure[8].

Mention must be made of O. 17, r. 6 of the Rules of the Supreme Court, which deals with interpleader proceedings and provides that:

"where an application for relief under this Order is made by a sheriff who has taken possession of any goods or chattels in execution under any process and a claimant alleges he is entitled, under a bill of sale or otherwise, to the goods or chattels by way of security for debt, the court may order those goods or chattels or any part thereof to be sold and may direct that the proceeds of sale be applied in any manner and on such terms as may be just . . ."

Similar provisions are contained in O. 28, r. 14 of the County Court Rules.

A sale will be ordered under this rule, when there will clearly be a surplus after paying off the bill of sale holder; will not be ordered when there will be clearly no surplus; and will not be ordered where it is doubtful whether there will be a surplus, unless the execution creditor will guarantee the bill of sale holder against loss by the sale[9].

V LIEN

Liens are of various kinds—
(a) possessory,
(b) maritime,
(c) equitable.

(a) Possessory liens

A possessory lien is one which appertains to a person who has possession of goods which belong to another, entitling him to retain them until the debt due to him has been paid. They are of two kinds:

1. *Particular lien.*—This is a right to retain the particular goods in connection with which the debt arose; *e.g.*

(i) a carrier may retain goods given to him for carriage; and

---

7. Bills of Sale Act 1882, s. 7.
8. *Ibid.*, s. 13.
9. *Stern* v. *Tegner*, [1898] 1 Q. B. 37.

(ii) an innkeeper may retain his guest's goods,
until payment of charges due.

A particular lien may arise—
   (i) out of express agreement or
   (ii) by implication;

and the law will give an implied lien over goods which a person is
compelled to receive; *e.g.* to an innkeeper over a guest's goods brought
to the inn[10]. And when the debt has been incurred for labour or skill
exercised upon a particular thing, the creditor has an implied lien
upon that thing for his reward[11]; *e.g.* a shipwright has a lien on a vessel
for the cost of repairs.

2. *General lien.*—This may arise from—
   (ii) custom (long existing, notorious, and reasonable) or
   (ii) contract;

and it is a right of retaining goods not only for the debt incurred in
connection with them, but for the general balance owing by their owner
to the person exercising the right of lien. Amongst trades or professions
which have this lien may be mentioned—
   (i) factors[12],
   (ii) bankers[13],
   (iii) stockbrokers[14],
   (iv) solicitors[15],
   (v) and sometimes insurance brokers[16].

Any right of lien implied from custom can be negatived by contract[17].
A possessory lien (as a rule) gives no right to sale[18], nor in fact any
right, except such as belongs to a possessor merely, as distinguished
from an owner. It is lost by payment and by surrender of possession[19];
taking security may show an intention to abandon the lien[20].

There are several instances where a right of lien can involve a right
of resale. One example is the statutory right of resale to an unpaid
seller of goods. A warehouseman or wharfinger may in certain events

---

10. An innkeeper's lien does not extend to motor cars or other vehicles or
    horses or other animals: Hotel Proprietors Act 1956, s. 2 (2).
11. *Ex parte Ockenden* (1754), 1 Atk. 235.
12. *Cowell v. Simpson* (1810), 16 Ves., at p. 280. *Cf. Rolls Razor, Ltd. v. Cox*,
    [1967] 1 All E. R. 397; [1967] 1 Q. B. 552, C. A. (mere agent to sell in the
    name of his principal *held* to have no lien on his principal's goods).
13. See *ante*, p. 147.
14. *Re London and Globe Finance Corporation*, [1902] 2 Ch. 416.
15. *Ex parte Sterling* (1810), 16 Ves. 258.
16. See *ante*, p. 146.
17. *Rolls Razor, Ltd. v. Cox*, [1967] 1 All E. R. 397; [1967] 1 Q. B. 552, C. A.
18. *White v. Spettigue* (1845), 13 M. & M., at p. 607.
19. *Kruger v. Wilcox* (1755), Amb., at p. 254.
20. *Cowell v. Simpson* (1810), 16 Ves. 275; *Re Taylor, Stileman and Underwood*,
    [1891] 1 Ch. 590.

sell goods placed in his custody[1], and innkeepers may under certain circumstances sell the goods of a guest[2].

By virtue of the Disposal of Uncollected Goods Act 1952, a bailee who has accepted goods in the course of a business for repair or other treatment, *e.g.*, a car repairer, has a statutory right of sale. When the goods so accepted are ready for redelivery but the bailor fails both to pay or tender to the bailee his charges in relation to the goods, and to take delivery of the goods, the bailee may on certain conditions sell the goods. To exercise this statutory right, the bailee must have conspicuously displayed, at all premises used by the bailee for accepting goods of the kind in question, a notice indicating that acceptance is subject to the provisions of the Act and that the Act does give the bailee a right of sale exercisable at least 12 months after the goods are ready for redelivery. Furthermore, the bailee must have given the bailor written notice that the goods are ready for redelivery and after twelve months have expired after such notice, the bailee must thave given fourteen days' notice of his intention to resell. If any amount is recovered in the sale in excess of the charges of the bailee, such excess is recoverable by the bailor.

(b) Maritime liens

A maritime lien is one which attaches to a thing in connection with some liability incurred in relation to a maritime adventure. It does not depend on the possession of the thing, but travels with it into whosoever's hands the thing may come. It is enforced by arrest and sale (unless security be given) through the medium of the Admiralty Court[3].

Amongst maritime liens may be named:

1. The lien of a salvor;
2. The lien of the seamen for their wages;
3. The lien of the master for wages and disbursements;
4. The lien over a colliding ship and freight of one whose property has been damaged by collision with a ship brought about by the default of that ship;
5. The lien of a bottomry bondholder.

The order in which maritime liens are enforceable depends upon their nature and sometimes on equitable grounds which may be applicable to the circumstances of the case. The lien of a later salvor is preferred to that of an earlier salvor, and to a lien for prior damage[4],

---

1. Merchant Shipping Act 1894, s. 497.
2. Innkeepers Act 1878.
3. See *The Bold Buccleugh* (1851), Moo, P. C. 67, 284. The Administration of Justice Act 1970, s. 2, created a separate Admiralty Court in the Queen's Bench Division of the High Court.
4. *The Inna*, [1938] P. 148.

because he has preserved the *res* for the benefit of the earlier liens. So also, bottomry bond liens are payable in inverse order, the last bond taking precedence over former bonds. But this principle does not apply to the liens over a ship which has successively collided with two or more other vessels, nor do the claimants for damage rank in priority according to the dates of the respective collisions; if there is not sufficient to satisfy all the claims, the proceeds of the *res* must be divided rateably between all the claimants[5]. Where the conflict is between different classes of lien, the priorities depend upon varying circumstances and no single general rule can be laid down.

A maritime lien may come into conflict with a possessory lien. Thus, the possessory lien of a shipwright for the cost of repairs is subject to maritime liens which attached to the ship before it was taken into his yard; but the shipwright's possessory lien takes precedence of all maritime liens accruing after the commencement of his possession[6].

The sheriff can only seize a ship under a writ of *fi. fa.* subject to any maritime lien attaching to the ship at the time of seizure[7].

It is doubtful whether a maritime lien is assignable with the debt, but a mere volunteer who pays the debt of a privileged claimant does not thereby acquire his lien[8].

(c) Equitable liens

An equitable lien is nothing but the right to have a specific portion of property allocated to the payment of specific liabilities. The right of a partner on dissolution to have the firm's assets applied in payment of the firm's liabilities is a right of the class styled "equitable liens".

---

5. *The Stream Fisher*, [1926] All E. R. Rep. 513; [1927] P. 73.
6. *The Tergeste*, [1903] P. 26.
7. *The Ile de Ceylon*, [1922] P. 256.
8. *The Petone*, [1917] P. 198.

CHAPTER 25

Shipping

I REGISTRATION OF A BRITISH SHIP

A British ship[1] is one which is owned wholly by those qualified to be owners of a British ship. These are[2]:

1. British subjects.
2. Bodies corporate, established under, and subject to the laws of some part of Her Majesty's Dominions and having their principal place of business in those Dominions.

With certain exceptions, every British ship must be registered or she will not be recognised as a British ship and will not be entitled to the benefits of British ownership or the use of the British flag[3]. Before registration these requisites must be satisfied:

1. The name of the ship[4] must be marked as prescribed on the bows, and her name and the name of her port of registry on the stern;
2. The official number and tonnage must be cut on her main beam, and a scale of feet denoting her draught of water in Roman letters or figures must be painted on the stem and stern post[5].

Before registry, the ship must be surveyed and measured and the *certificate of survey* must be produced, giving the tonnage and build of the vessel, and generally identifying her[6]; also on the occasion of the first registry, *a builder's certificate*, giving particulars as to the build and tonnage of the ship, and of the sale of the vessel to the person desiring to be registered as owner[7].

---

1. "Ship" includes every description of vessel used in navigation not propelled by oars (Merchant Shipping Act 1894, s. 742).
2. Merchant Shipping Act 1894, s. 1, as amended by the British Nationality Act 1948, s. 31, Sched. IV, which ended the preferred position of a natural-born British subject. The administration of this Act is committed to the Department of Trade.
3. Merchant Shipping Act 1894, ss. 2 and 72.
4. The Minister may refuse to register any ship by a name already belonging to a registered British ship or so similar as to be calculated to deceive (Merchant Shipping Act 1906, s. 50). Change of name requires the previous written consent of the Minister (Merchant Shipping Act 1894, s. 47).
5. Merchant Shipping Act 1894, s. 7.
6. *Ibid.*, s. 6.   7. *Ibid.*, s. 10.

The *owner* must then make a *declaration of ownership,* stating:
1. His qualification to hold a British ship;
2. The number of shares he holds in the ship;
3. A denial that, as far as he knows, any unqualified person is entitled to any interest in her;
4. The name of the master;
5. When and where the ship was built[8].

A body corporate makes this declaration through its secretary or other proper officer.

Application for registry should be made by:
1. Those requiring to be registered as owners or some of them, or
2. By their duly authorised agent appointed by individuals in writing, or
3. By a corporation's duly authorised agent appointed under the common seal of the corporation[9];

and the registration is then performed by the chief officer of customs of the port, if it be in the United Kingdom, or by certain specified officers if it be in the colonies[10]. An entry of the particulars contained in the certificate of survey and in the declaration of ownership is made in the *register book*[11], and a *certificate of registry*[12] is given, which must contain the particulars relating to the ship entered in the register book with the name of the owner. The certificate may, if lost, be renewed on following out the procedure prescribed by the Act[13]; and it may not be detained for any lien or other such purpose—it is for use in navigation only[14].

If the ownership changes hands, an indorsement to this effect must be placed on the certificate at the port of registry if the vessel is there; if not, on her first arrival there, or the indorsement may be made at another port if the registrar at the port of registry advises the registrar of the latter port[15]. If a ship is lost, or ceases to be a British ship, the certificate of registry must be given up[16].

Property in a British ship[17]

The property in a British ship is divided into sixty-four shares,

---

8. *Ibid.,* s. 9.
9. *Ibid.,* s. 8.
10. *Ibid.,* s. 4.
11. *Ibid.,* s. 11.
12. *Ibid.,* s. 14.
13. Merchant Shipping Act 1894, s. 18.
14. *Ibid.,* s. 15.
15. *Ibid.,* s. 20.
16. *Ibid.,* s. 21. Section 52 of the Merchant Shipping Act 1906, contains provisions for the protection of mortgagees of ships sold to aliens.
17. Merchant Shipping Act 1894, s. 5.

and no more than sixty-four persons may be registered at the same time as owners of the ship. But any share may be held in joint owner-ship, and the joint owners, not exceeding five in number, may be registered and shall be considered as constituting one person, and any number of persons may have a beneficial title in a single share, the registering owner representing them; a company or corporation may be registered by its corporate name. No person may be registered as owner of a fraction of a share.

II TRANSFERS, TRANSMISSIONS, AND MORTGAGES

1. Sale of ship or shares

A sale will pass a registered ship or any share in her if the professing owner is in a position to give a good title, and if the proper formalities are observed. The method of passing the property is by bill of sale, which must—

    (i) be in the form set forth in the Act of 1894,

    (ii) be executed before and attested by one or more witnesses, and

    (iii) must contain an identifying description, generally the same as is contained in the surveyor's certificate[18].

The transferee must make a declaration (called a *"declaration of transfer"*) stating that he (or his corporation, if he be an officer of a corporation) is in a position to hold a British ship, and that to the best of his knowledge and belief no unqualified person has any interest, legal or beneficial, in the ship, or in any share of her[19]. The bill of sale and the declaration are then produced to the registrar, and the trans-action is recorded in the register book, and a statement of the entry indorsed upon the bill of sale itself[20].

2. Transmission by operation of law

Ownership in a British ship or of shares in her may be transmitted

    (i) by death to the executor or administrator of a deceased owner, or

    (ii) on bankruptcy to the owner's trustee in bankruptcy.

In every case the person to whom the share is transmitted must be one capable of owning a British ship, and he must make and sign a declaration (called a *"declaration of transmission"*) identifying the ship, with the requisite particulars, and stating the mode of transmission, and must produce the proper documentary proof of his right to rep-resent the former owner; whereupon the registrar will make the requisite entries in the register book[1].

---

18. Merchant Shipping Act 1894, s. 24. The Bills of Sale Acts do not apply. See *ante*, p. 402.
19. *Ibid.*, s. 25.
20. *Ibid.*, s. 26.   1. *Ibid.*, s. 27.

If the transmission is to one not qualified to be the holder of a British ship, there is power in the High Court to hold a sale at such person's request if application is made within four weeks of the transmission; the money is paid to such person as the court may direct. The time for making this application may be extended to one year, but if not made within the time limited, the ship or share is subject to forfeiture[2].

3. Mortgages

A registered ship, or any share therein, may be mortgaged in two ways:

    (i) by a direct mortgage with registration;
    (ii) by a mortgage under a mortgage certificate[3].

A direct mortgage must be in the form prescribed, and must, upon the production of the necessary instruments, be recorded by the registrar in the register book[4]. Upon the order in the register book will depend the priority of mortgages *inter se*[5].

It must be noted that the mortgage will not transfer the ownership of the vessel[6], but, subject to the rights of prior mortgagees, it confers a power of sale[7] on non-payment of the debt.

When a mortgage is discharged, the mortgage deed with a receipt for the mortgage money, indorsed, duly signed, and attested, should be produced to the registrar, and an entry recording the matter must be made by him in the register book[8]. Any transfer of the mortgage must also be in a prescribed form and recorded by the registrar[9]. The court has inherent jurisdiction to expunge the entry of an invalid mortgage from the register[10].

Certificates of sale or mortgage.—Difficulties might arise in selling or mortgaging ships which, at the time, are out of the country or colony where the port of registry is situated. To obviate these, the Act in such cases gives power to registrars to give *certificates of sale or mortgage* enabling certain persons to sell or mortgage the ship wherever she may be, but in accordance with the conditions of the certificate. The owner must in applying for the certificate give particulars to the registrar as to:

---

2. *Ibid.*, s. 28.
3. See below.
4. Merchant Shipping Act 1894, s. 31.
5. *Ibid.*, s. 33.
6. *Ibid.*, s. 34.
7. *Ibid.*, s. 35.
8. *Ibid.*, s. 32.
9. *Ibid.*, s. 37.
10. *Brond* v. *Broomhall*, [1906] 1 K. B. 571.

(i) who is to exercise the power;

(ii) the minimum price of sale, if a minimum is to be fixed, or the maximum amount to be raised on the ship, if a maximum is intended to be fixed;

(iii) the place where the power is intended to be exercised or a declaration that it is intended to be exercised anywhere;

(iv) the time within which it is to be exercised.

These particulars are to be entered into the register book[11]. The power is not to be used in the United Kingdom, nor in any British possession, if the port of registry is situated within it[12].

The certificate must give the particulars from the register book which have to be entered therein on the application for the certificate, and must enumerate any registered mortgages or certificates of sale or mortgage affecting the ship[13]. Rules are laid down with respect to certificates of sale amongst which is a rule that no certificate of sale can be granted except for the sale of an entire ship. Certificates of mortgage may be given to allow of the mortgage of a share in a vessel[14].

When a ship is mortgaged in accordance with the powers given in the certificate, the mortgage must be registered by indorsement on the certificate of mortgage by a British consular officer.

In the case of sale, the certificate and the bill of sale must be produced to the registrar of the port where the sale takes place, as also the certificate of original registry; the certificates of sale and registry are then forwarded to the original port of registry, the registration of which closes the original registry, except so far as relates to unsatisfied mortgages or certificates of mortgages entered therein and these will be entered also in the new registry to be opened at the port of transfer.

A certificate not used must be re-delivered to the registrar by whom it was granted[14]. The registered owner may cause the registrar to give notice of revocation to the registrar of the port where the power of sale or mortgage is to be exercised, and after such notice has been recorded the certificate will then be revoked, save in so far as transactions under it have already taken place[15].

Rights of mortgagee.—A mortgagee is entitled to possession if money becomes due under the mortgage, or the mortgagor is doing something to impair the security[16]; and on taking possession he becomes entitled

---

11. Merchant Shipping Act 1894, s. 40.
12. *Ibid.*, s. 41.
13. *Ibid.*, s. 42.
14. *Ibid.*, ss. 43, 44.
15. *Ibid.*, s. 46.
16. *Law Guarantee and Trust Society* v. *Russian Bank*, [1905] 1 K. B. 815; *The Manor*, [1907] P. 339.

to the accruing freight[17], but not to unpaid freight which became due before he took possession[18].

4. Equitable interests

No notice of any trust, express, implied, or constructive, can be entered on the register book, and subject to any limitations appearing on the register book itself, the registered owner of a ship or a share in her has absolute power to dispose of his ship or share; but, subject to this, beneficial interests (including those arising under contracts and other equitable interests) may be enforced by and against owners or mortgagees of ships just as they could against owners of any other personal property[19]. Thus in *Black* v. *Williams*[20],

> the holders of floating debentures given an equitable charge on certain steamships were postponed to persons having a subsequent registered legal mortgage on the same ships, though the latter had notice of the debentures when they took the mortgages; but though the trust for the debenture holders could not be recognised as against the registered mortgagees, it remained valid and enforceable for other purposes.

An unqualified person cannot hold a share in a British ship, even as a beneficial owner[1].

5. Ship's papers

A ship must carry the proper papers, and is bound to show them to (*inter alia*) any:

1. Naval commissioned officer of any of Her Majesty's ships,
2. Officer of the Department of Trade,
3. Chief officer of Customs,
4. Mercantile marine office superintendent,
5. British consular officer, or
6. Registrar-general of seamen or his assistant[2].

Those usually carried are:

1. The certificate of registry;
2. The crew agreement;
3. The charter-party and the bills of lading;
4. The bill of health;
5. Invoices containing the particulars of the cargo;
6. The official log book.

---

17. *Keith* v. *Burrows* (1877), 2 App. Cas. 636.
18. *Shillito* v. *Biggart*, [1903] 1 K. B. 683.
19. Merchant Shipping Act 1894, ss. 56, 57.
20. [1895] 1 Ch. 408.
1. Merchant Shipping Act 1894, ss. 1, 25, 57.
2. *Ibid.*, s. 723.

Regulations may prescribe the particulars to be entered in the log book and the persons by whom such entries are to be made[3].

III POSITION OF OWNERS

The possession of the ship is *prima facie* evidence of ownership[4], so also is the certificate of registry[5]. The owner must appoint a proper master and crew, with a view to the general safety; therefore, a contract to sell a vessel, one condition being the appointment of a particular person as master, was held illegal[6]. His liability at common law and under the Merchant Shipping Acts for the safety of all goods delivered to him to be carried has been mentioned, *ante*, p. 349 *et seq.*

The registered owners are *prima facie* liable to pay for all repairs and necessaries, the term "necessaries" including anchors, cables, coals, and indeed—

> "all that is fit and proper for the service in which the ship is engaged, and that the owner, as a prudent man, would have ordered if present"[7].

But the evidence is *prima facie* only, for ownership does not *per se* carry with it the liability to pay for repairs, etc. If the owner gave the orders himself, or expressly or impliedly authorised another to do it for him, he is liable to pay the cost of the fulfilment of these orders; a master usually has such authority, but not—

> "where the owner can himself personally interfere, as in the home port, or in a port in which he has beforehand appointed an agent who can personally interfere to do the thing required"[8].

Co-owners are not of necessity partners[9], but in many cases are tenants in common, and it depends upon all the circumstances taken together, whether they are the one or the other. If merely tenants in common, each may transfer his share without consulting the others. They are not, in the absence of contract, agents for one another, nor do they bind each other by admissions.

Frequently one owner is appointed by the others, or by some of them, to manage the employment of the ship and to do what is necessary

---

3. Merchant Shipping Act 1970, s. 68.
4. *Robertson v. French* (1803), 4 East, 130.
5. Merchant Shipping Act 1894, s. 695.
6. *Card v. Hope* (1824), 2 B. & C. 661.
7. *The Riga* (1872), L. R. 3 Ad. & Ec. 516.
8. Lord ABINGER, in *Arthur v. Barton* (1840), 6 M. & W., at p. 143; and see *Gunn v. Roberts* (1874), L. R. 9 C. P. 331.
9. The name and address of the person to whom the management is entrusted must be registered (Merchant Shipping Act 1894, s. 59).

in order to make her a profitable speculation[10]; such an owner, termed a *managing owner*[11], can bind such of his co-owners as have given him authority, express or implied, to do so[12], and he has implied authority to do what is necessary in ordinary course to carry out on shore all that concerns the employment of the ship[13], *i.e.*

1. He may make charter-parties;
2. He may not cancel them[14];
3. He may employ a shipbroker and make the consequent payments[15].

If an owner is liable to a creditor for work done to the ship, he may be made to pay the whole, and must rely for contribution on any right he may have against his co-owners.

Control of ship

Disputes may arise between co-owners as to the destination and details of an intended voyage. These are settled in the Admiralty Court (now a separate court in the Queen's Bench Division of the High Court), which has jurisdiction in disputes concerning possession, earnings, etc. If the majority of owners desire to send the vessel on a particular voyage, but this is objected to by the minority, the court will, at the instance of the latter, arrest the vessel till the majority have entered into a bond to an amount equivalent to the value of the shares held by the minority, to return the vessel safe, and to answer judgment in an action[16]. The dissentient who thus gets security for his share has no claim to any freight earned on the voyage in question, nor is he liable for any of the expenses[17].

Part-owners of a ship may be partners but they are not necessarily so, and the mere fact that a person is registered as part-owner of a ship does not give his co-owner authority to pledge his credit for necessary repairs. There must be some evidence of express or implied authority or holding-out[18].

IV POSITION OF THE MASTER

The master.—The master (who must be duly certificated) must start on the voyage in time, and must take care to have a proper crew and

10. *The Huntsman*, [1894] P. 214.
11. If the manager is not a co-owner, he is styled the "*ship's husband*."
12. *Hibbs* v. *Ross* (1866), L. R. 1 Q. B. 534; *Frazer* v. *Cuthbertson* (1880), 6 Q. B. D. 93, at p. 97.
13. *The Huntsman*, [1894] P. 214.
14. *Thomas* v. *Lewis* (1879), 4 Ex. D. 18.
15. *Williamson* v. *Hine*, [1891] 1 Ch. 390.
16. *Re Blanshard* (1822), 2 B. & C., at p. 248.
17. *The Vindobala* (1888), 13 P. D. 42; 14 P. D. 50; *The England* (1887), 12 P. D. 32.
18. *Brodie* v. *Howard* (1855), 17 C. B. 109.

equipment. He should manage the vessel, and navigate her in the agreed-upon manner, employing a pilot, where such is the custom of the port. He must keep an official log, and this, with the ship's papers, he must guard and show to the proper officer when required to do so.

He must take the cargo as quickly as possible, must store it properly, and must sign the bill of lading for all he has taken on board[19]. He should deliver the cargo, on arrival at the destination, to the proper person, subject to his lien for freight[20].

He is, of course, answerable for any fraudulent or illegal conduct of which he is guilty affecting the owner's interest, such conduct being, in his case, styled *barratry*.

He has the same rights as a seaman, including a maritime lien, for the recovery of his wages, and for such disbursements or liabilities as he may properly make or incur on account of the ship[1].

Among his powers are:

1. Hypothecation. The master may, in case of necessity in order to raise money, assign the ship or the ship and cargo by what is known as a *bottomry bond*, the master thereby binding himself to repay the principal and interest of the loan on safe arrival of the ship at the end of her voyage. If the cargo alone is hypothecated, the document is called a *respondentia bond*. Both types of instrument are obsolete[2].

2. Sale, where this course is necessary, and the best course, and communication with the owner in time is impossible;

3. Transhipment, in cases where it is desirable in the interest of his owners;

4. Disciplinary powers over those on board the vessel[3];

5. Jettison, *i.e.* throwing goods overboard to lighten the ship;

6. In the absence of the owners, and if communication is impossible in time, he may bind them by contracts for the supply of necessaries, or may borrow money on their credit to pay for necessaries to be supplied, but not for those already supplied[4].

---

19. See *ante*, pp. 350–356.
20. *Ante*, p. 365.
1. Merchant Shipping Act 1970, s. 18; *The Castlegate* [1893] A. C. 38; *The Orienta*, [1895] P. 49; and cf. *The Ripon City*, [1897] P. 226.
2. Halsbury's Laws of England, 3rd edn., Vol. xxxv, p. 137.
3. He can arrest anyone on board if he has reasonable cause to believe that it is necessary for the preservation of the ship or safety of the passengers: Merchant Shipping Act 1970, s. 79.
4. *Arthur v. Barton* (1840), 6 M. & W. 129.

V SALVAGE

This is a reward allowed to persons who save or assist in saving[5] a ship, apparel and cargo, or what had formed part of these, or freight from shipwreck, capture, or similar jeopardy[6]. The right to salvage may, but does not necessarily, arise out of contract[7]. To support the claim the salvor must show:

1. That the services rendered were voluntary. Accordingly, the services must not be such as would be called for under a pre-existing contract; but if a tug has agreed to tow a vessel and circumstances have arisen which justify the tug in abandoning that contract, she may recover salvage for further services which are outside the scope of the contract of towage[8]. There is no right to recover salvage if the salvor has acted in pursuance of a statutory duty[9].

2. That there was skill and peril, and some enterprise shown in the performance of the work.

3. That the services were beneficial. Actual benefit is not essential where the services are rendered at the request of the vessel in distress. The acceptance of the offer of a particular ship to come to assistance in response to a radio call entitles that ship to a salvage award, although little or no benefit is conferred, if the disabled ship is ultimately saved; but a mere response to an s.o.s. call does not of itself give a right to salvage remuneration[10].

Although "no cure, no pay" is of the essence of salvage, an agreement to pay the salvor some remuneration in the event of failure is enforceable[11].

The owner of a salving ship can recover for services rendered by him to a ship damaged through the fault of a vessel of which the salvor was also the owner. The maxim that "no man can profit by his own wrong" does not apply to such a case[12].

The salvor has a maritime lien, extending to ship, freight, cargo, upon the property salved, the lien ranking first, above all other liens

---

5. For the distinction between salvage and towage, see *The Troilus*, [1951] A. C. 820.
6. *Wells* v. *Owners of Gas Float Whitton*, [1897] A. C., at p. 344.
7. *Five Steel Barges* (1890), 15 P. D. 142; *per* HANNEN, P., at p. 146.
8. See *The Leon Blum*, [1915] P. 90; affd. *The Leon Blum*, [1915] P. 290.
9. *The Gregerso*, [1971] 1 All E. R. 961; [1971] 2 W. L. R. 955.
10. *The Stiklestad*, [1926] P. 205.
11. *Admiralty Commissioners* v. *Valverda*, [1938] A. C. 173, at pp. 187, 197, 202; [1938] 1 All E. R. 162, at pp. 169, 176, 178.
12. *The Beaverford* v. *The Kafiristan*, [1938] A. C. 136; [1937] 3 All E. R. 747.

which have already previously attached to the property. The cargo owners are liable for salvage, and in proportion to its value rateably with the other property salved[13].

The amount payable for salvage is generally assessed by the court, but it is quite competent for the masters of the vessels concerned to enter into an agreement before assistance is rendered fixing the amount to be paid. The master of the salving vessel can bind his owners and crew by such an agreement if it is fair and honest[14]; but the agreement will be set aside if it is inequitable. An agreement to pay an exorbitant sum coupled with the fact that the master of the vessel about to be salved is acting under the stress of circumstances, will be treated as inequitable[15].

The salvage money is apportioned between the owners, master, officers and crew of the salving vessel. Except in the case of a seaman belonging to a ship employed on salvage service, a seaman cannot agree to abandon any right that he may have or obtain in the nature of salvage[16].

Salvors who are guilty of or are privy to the theft of salved property forfeit all claim to salvage; and those who by negligence or lack of supervision fail to prevent or detect such theft are liable to forfeiture or diminution of the award according to the view taken by the Court of their conduct[17]. There is no rule of maritime law that a successful salvor is free from liability for negligence[18].

The Crown is liable in respect of salvage services in assisting any of Her Majesty's ships or aircraft or in saving life therefrom, or in saving cargo belonging to the Crown[19].

The Crown may claim salvage to the same extent as any other salvor[20].

VI POSITION OF THE SEAMAN

Following the Report of a Court of Inquiry into the shipping industry, under the chairmanship of Lord PEARSON[1], the provisions of the

---

13. *The Longford* (1881), 6 P. D. 60. Devaluation of the pound between the date of the termination of the salvage services and the date of the award might not properly be taken into account in fixing the amount of the award: *The Teh Hu,* [1969] 3 All E. R. 1200; [1970] P. 106, C. A.
14. *The Nasmyth* (1885), 10 P. D. 41.
15. *The Medina* (1877), 2 P. D. 5; *The Rialto,* [1891] P. 175; *The Port Caledonia,* [1903] P. 184.
16. Merchant Shipping Act 1894, s. 156.
17. *The Clan Sutherland,* [1918] P. 332; *The Kenora,* [1921] P. 90.
18. *The Tojo Maru,* [1971] 1 All E. R. 1110, H. L.
19. Crown Proceedings Act 1947, s. 8 (1).
20. *Ibid.,* s. 8 (2).
1. Cmnd. 3211 (1967).

Merchant Shipping Acts 1894 to 1967 relating to the conditions of service, discipline and general welfare of merchant seamen have been replaced by the Merchant Shipping Act 1970.

Crew agreements

With certain exceptions, an agreement in writing must be made between each person employed as a seaman in a ship registered in the United Kingdom and the persons employing him and must be signed both by him and by or on behalf of them[2]. The agreements made with the several persons employed in a ship are to be contained in one document—a crew agreement—subject to exceptions approved by the Department of Trade. The Department must approve the provisions and form of a crew agreement and normally the crew agreement must be carried on the ship to which it relates whenever it is at sea. Both the employer and the master of the ship are liable for failure to comply with these provisions. Department of Trade Regulations may provide for notice to be given to a superintendent or proper officer before a crew agreement is made and for requiring copies or extracts of crew agreements to be supplied to members of the crew demanding them[3].

Discharge of seamen

Department of Trade Regulations may prescribe the procedure to be followed in connection with the discharge of seamen from ships registered in the United Kingdom. In particular Regulations may require notice of a discharge to be given to the superintendent or proper officer[4]. Regulations may prescribe that a seaman be not discharged outside the United Kingdom from a ship registered in the United Kingdom without the consent of the proper officer.

Wages

Wages due to a seaman under a crew agreement must normally be paid to him in full when he leaves the ship on being discharged from it[5]. If the amount shown in the account (which must also be delivered to him[6]) exceeds £50, not less than £50 or less than one-quarter of the amount shown must be paid to him at that time and the balance within seven days of that time. If any amount due is not paid when payable the seaman is entitled to wages for a period of 56 days after his discharge

---

2. Merchant Shipping Act 1970, s. 1.
3. *Ibid.*, s. 2.
4. Merchant Shipping Act 1970, s. 3. "Superintendent" means the officer in charge of a port's mercantile marine office. "Proper officer" means a consular officer appointed by H. M. Government.
5. *Ibid.*, s. 7.
6. *Ibid.*, s. 8.

and thereafter all moneys due carry interest at the rate of 20%. The penalties for failure to pay have no application if due to a mistake or a reasonable dispute as to liability.

Regulations may provide for deductions to be made from wages due to a seaman where he has broken his obligations under the crew agreement[7]. Any dispute as to the amount payable may be submitted by the parties to the superintendent or proper officer whose decision is final[8].

A seaman's wages are not subject to attachment and any assignment of such wages before they have accrued is not binding on the seaman[9]. However, a seaman may, by means of an allotment note, allot to any person or persons part of the wages to which he will become entitled[10]. The person named in the allotment note has the right to recover in his own name that part of the seaman's wages allotted to him[11].

If a ship registered in the United Kingdom is wrecked or lost a seaman whose employment in the ship is thereby terminated is entitled to wages for every day on which he is unemployed in the two months following the date of the wreck or loss unless it is proved he did not make reasonable efforts to save the ship and persons and property carried in it[12]. Similarly, where a ship is sold outside the United Kingdom and a seaman's employment is thereby terminated, he is entitled to wages for every day on which he is unemployed in the two months following the date of the sale[13].

A seaman's lien, his remedies for the recovery of his wages, his right to wages in case of the wreck of loss of the ship, and any right he may have or obtain in the nature of salvage are not capable of being renounced by any agreement[14]. This does not affect terms of any agreement made with the seaman belonging to a ship which is to be employed on salvage service, or provide for the remuneration to be paid to them for salvage services rendered by that ship.

If expenses are incurred by Government Departments or a local authority for the benefit of any dependants of a seaman and other expenses provided for by regulations, the persons employing the seaman may be required to retain a proportion of the seaman's net wages[15]. A magistrates' court may make an order for such sum to be paid to the authority concerned.

---

7. Merchant Shipping Act 1970, s. 9.
8. *Ibid*, s. 10.
9. *Ibid.*, s. 11.
10. *Ibid.*, s. 13.
11. *Ibid.*, s. 14.
12. *Ibid.*, s. 15 (1).
13. *Ibid.*, s. 15 (2).
14. *Ibid.*, s. 16.
15. *Ibid.*, s. 17.

Safety, health and welfare

The Act makes provision for regulations to secure safe working conditions and means of access, adequate crew accommodation, provisions, water and medical stores and for the submission of complaints by seamen and for medical treatment[16].

Offences by seamen

Various *criminal* offences specified in the Merchant Shipping Act 1970 include misconduct endangering the ship or persons on board the ship, drunkenness on duty, wilful disobedience to lawful commands, continued or concerted disobedience or neglect of duty and absence without leave at the time of sailing[17].

Regulations may specify any misconduct on board as a *disciplinary* offence and enable the master or other officer to impose fines on seamen committing disciplinary offences[18]. The amount of the fine may not exceed £10. Provision is made for appeal against the imposition of a fine to a superintendent or proper officer[10]. Regulations may provide for the setting up of a ship's disciplinary committee to exercise the powers of the master in dealing with disciplinary offences[20]. The amount of any fine imposed on a seaman for a disciplinary offence may be deducted from his wages or otherwise recovered by the persons employing him and paid by them to a superintendent or proper officer[1].

Civil liability of seamen

A seaman is liable in damages for breach of contract if he is absent from his ship at a time when he is required by his contract of employment to be on board unless he proves his absence was due to an accident or mistake or some other cause beyond his control and that he took all reasonable precautions to avoid being absent[2]. Damages are limited to £10 unless special damages are claimed when the limit is £100.

If a seaman is found in civil proceedings in the United Kingdom to have committed an act of smuggling he is liable to make good any expense that the act has caused to any other person[3].

---

16. Merchant Shipping Act 1970, s. 3. 19–26.
17. *Ibid.*, ss. 27–31.
18. *Ibid.*, s. 34.
19. *Ibid.*, s. 35.
20. *Ibid.*, s. 36.
1. *Ibid.*, s. 38.
2. *Ibid.*, s. 39.
3. *Ibid.*, s. 40.

Relief and repatriation of seamen left behind

Where a seaman in a ship registered in the United Kingdom is left behind in a country outside the United Kingdom or is taken to such a country on being shipwrecked, the persons who last employed him as a seaman must make such provision for his return and for his relief and maintenance until his return as regulations may require[4].

Regulations made in 1972

Several sets of Regulations under the Merchant Shipping Act 1970 were made in the latter part of 1972 as this edition went to press. They cover crew agreements, disciplinary offences, seamen's documents, seamen's allotments, and seamen's wages.

---

4. *Ibid.*, s. 62.

CHAPTER 26

Contracts of Employment

Lord DENNING has pointed out that the master-servant relationship, that is, the relationship that exists between an employer and an employee under a contract of service, is easier to recognise than to define[1]. A chauffeur, for example, is employed under a *contract of service*, but a taxicab driver is not employed under a contract of service with the person who hires him for a journey. The taxicab driver is engaged under a *contract of services*, and is termed an independent contractor, rather than a servant. The usual test cited for determining whether a master-servant relationship exists is to ask if there is a right in the employer to say not only what work is to be done for him but how it is to be done[2]. It is sometimes an artificial test because in many cases of skilled servants, the master cannot in practice control how he does his work, but if the right of control exists, the contract is one of service of employment[3]. In any case, the test is not an exclusive one[4].

If the relationship of master and servant does exist, then not only is the master vicariously liable for any torts committed by the servant while acting in the course of his employment, but certain terms are implied by law in every contract of service which do not necessarily apply to contracts for services. It should also be noted that the Contracts of Employment Act 1972, whose provisions are considered below[5], applies only to persons employed under a contract of service or apprenticeship.

Formation of the contract

The rules as to capacity are the same as for the general law of contract[6]. It follows that if a minor enters into a contract of employment of apprenticeship, it is binding on him if the contract, looked at as a whole, is beneficial to him[7].

---

1. *Stevenson, Jordan and Harrison, Ltd.* v. *MacDonald and Evans*, [1952] 1 T. L. R. 101, at p. 111.
2. *Simmons* v. *Heath Laundry Co.*, [1910] 1 K. B. 543, at p. 550.
3. *Cassidy* v. *Minister of Health*, [1951] 1 All E. R. 574; [1951] 2 K. B. 343.
4. *Amalgamated Engineering Union* v. *Minister of Pensions and National Insurance*, [1963] 1 All E. R. 864; [1963] 1 W. L. R. 441.
5. *Post*, p. 431.
6. *Ante*, p. 56.
7. *Doyle* v. *White City Stadium, Ltd.*, [1934] All E. R. Rep. 252; [1935] 1 K. B. 110.

In general, a contract of service may be in writing or oral and there is no special requirement as to form. However, the Merchant Shipping Act 1970 requires written contracts with each member of the crew[8], and contracts of apprenticeship must be in writing. Furthermore, the Contracts of Employment Act 1972 requires employers (with certain exceptions) to give employees written particulars of the terms of their employment not later than thirteen weeks after the beginning of a period of employment[9]. The statement must identify the parties, specify the date when the employment began, and give the following particulars of the terms of employment as at a specified date not more than one week before the statement is given:

(i) the scale or rate of remuneration, or the method of calculating remuneration,

(ii) the intervals at which remuneration is paid (*e.g.* weekly or monthly),

(iii) any terms and conditions relating to hours of work,

(iv) any terms and conditions relating to holidays and holiday pay, incapacity for work due to sickness or injury (including any provision for sick pay), and pensions and pension schemes, and

(v) the length of notice the employee is obliged to give and entitled to receive to determine the contract.

In addition, the statement must include a note (a) indicating the employee's statutory rights in relation to an agency shop or closed shop agreement and (b) specifying a person to whom the employee can apply for the redress of any grievance relating to his employment.

Where there are no particulars to be entered under any of those heads, that fact must be stated[10]. If the contract is for a fixed term, the date when the contract expires must be stated[11]. Where there is a change in the terms, the employer must, not more than one month after the change, inform the employee of the nature of the change by a written statement, and if he does not leave a copy of the statement with the employee, he must ensure that the employee has reasonable opportunities of reading it or that it is made reasonably accessible to him in some way[12]. Any of the particulars specified may be given by referring the employee to some document which the employee has reasonable opporunities of reading or which is made reasonably accessible to him[13].

---

8. *Ante,* p. 426.
9. Contracts of Employment Act 1972, s. 4.
10. *Ibid.,* s. 4 (2).
11. *Ibid.,* s. 4 (3).
12. *Ibid.,* s. 5.
13. *Ibid.,* s. 6.

Failure on the part of an employer to comply with the Contracts of Employment Act 1972 entitles the employee to require a reference to be made to an Industrial Tribunal. If the Tribunal determines that certain particulars which ought to have been given to the employee have not been given, then "the employer shall be deemed to have given to the employee a statement in which these particulars were included ... as specified in the decision of the tribunal"[14]. The requirements do not apply to any employee who has a written contract of service containing terms affording the same particulars as specified above and a copy of the contract has been given to him, or he has reasonable opportunities of reading such copy or such copy is made reasonably accessible to him in some other way[15]. Nor do the requirements apply to any employee whose hours of work are normally less than twenty-one hours a week[16] or to certain excepted classes of employees, namely registered dock workers, or an employee who is the father, mother, husband, wife, son or daughter of the employer[17].

Termination of contract

Where the contract specifies that it is to endure for a certain fixed period, clearly the contract terminates at the end of such period. If no such fixed period is specified but the terms lay down certain grounds on which the contract may be terminated by the employer, these grounds may be construed as exhaustive, so that if no such ground exists, a dismissal even on reasonable notice would not be valid[18].

The general rule of common law where the contract is for an indefinite term is that the contract may be determined by either party giving reasonable notice to the other. What is "reasonable" depends on the nature of the employment, and the more responsible or specialised the work of the employee the longer will be the notice that must be given[19]. Under the Contracts of Employment Act 1972 certain *minimum* periods of notice are specified, depending on the time served by the employee. Thus, an employee who has been employed for a continuous period of at least thirteen weeks is entitled to a minimum notice of one week if the continuous period is less than two years, two weeks' notice if it is two years or more but less than five years, four weeks' notice if it is five years but less than ten years, six weeks' notice

---

14. Contracts of Employment Act 1972, s. 8.
15. *Ibid.*, s. 6.
16. *Ibid.*, s. 9.   17. *Ibid.*, s. 6.
18. *McClelland* v. *Northern Ireland General Health Services Board*, [1957] 2 All E. R. 129; [1957] 1 W. L. R. 594.
19. *Cf. Savage* v. *British India Steam Navigation Co.* (1930), 46 T. L. R. 294, and *Manubens* v. *Leon*, [1918-19] All E. R. Rep. 792; [1919] 1 K. B. 208.

if it is ten years but less than fifteen years and eight weeks' notice if it is fifteen years or more[20]. The notice required to be given by an employee, who has been continuously employed for thirteen weeks or more, must be not less than one week[1].

Any provision for shorter notice in any contract with a person who has been continuously employed for thirteen weeks or more has effect subject to these statutory provisions, but either party may waive his right to notice on any occasion and may accept a payment in lieu of notice[2]. It should be emphasised, however, that if under the express terms of contract or by virtue of the Common Law, a longer period of notice must be given, such express term or terms implied by Common Law prevails. The Act specifies only *minimum* periods of notice.

A breach of contract only brings about termination if the breach amounts to a repudiation of the contract or a breach of condition and the other party elects to treat the contract as at an end. A contract of employment may be terminated by frustration, for example, by the death or serious illness of either party[3]. It may also be terminated by dissolution of a partnership[4], by bankruptcy of the employer[5], and by the winding up of an employing company[6].

At Common Law, provided a contract of employment for an indefinite term was terminated by the employer giving "reasonable" notice the termination was not a wrongful dismissal and the employee had no remedy. Now, by the Industrial Relations Act 1971, s. 22, if an employee is "unfairly" dismissed he is entitled to claim compensation. In considering whether the dismissal is fair or unfair, the employer must show (a) the reason or reasons for the dismissal and (b) the reason related to the capability or qualifications of the employee or his conduct or was some other substantial reason justifying dismissal[7]. The dismissal is unfair unless the employer acted reasonably. Compensation for unfair dismissal will take into account the employee's duty to mitigate and will not exceed the amount which represents 104 weeks pay or

---

20. Contracts of Employment Act 1972, s. 1.
1. *Ibid.*, s. 1 (2). Due notice by an employee of an intention to take part in a strike is not to be construed as a notice to terminate his contract of employment or as a repudiation of that contract: Industrial Relations Act 1971, s. 47. This rule does not apply if his action is contrary to a term of his contract.
2. *Ibid.*, s. 1 (3).
3. *Poussard* v. *Spiers and Pond* (1876), 1 Q. B. D. 410; *Bettini* v. *Gye* (1876), 1 Q. B. D. 183; *Marshall* v. *Harland & Wolff, Ltd.*, [1972] 2 All E. R. 715; [1972] 1 W. L. R. 899 (illness not such as to frustrate contract).
4. *Phillips* v. *Alhambra Palace Co.*, [1901] 1. K. B. 59.
5. See Bankruptcy Act 1914, s. 34.
6. *Reid* v. *Explosives Co., Ltd.* (1887), 19 Q. B. D. 264.
7. Industrial Relations Act 1971, s. 24.

£4,160 whichever is the less[8]. The unfair dismissal provisions do not apply where less than four employees have been continuously employed, where the employer is the husband or wife or close relative of the employee, to employment as a registered dock worker, or to employment for less than 21 hours weekly[9].

Implied duties of an employee

Subject to any express terms of the contract, the following duties are implied from the master-servant relationship.

1. *To attend the place of work* unless there is reasonable excuse, such as illness.

2. *To obey lawful orders.*—All orders within the scope of the servant's employment must be obeyed unless to do so would imperil the servant's life or limb or would amount to an unlawful act. However, disobedience does not entitle the employer to dismiss unless the servant's conduct evinces a clear intention to flout the essential conditions of the contract[10].

3. *To exercise due care and skill.*—An employee not only undertakes possession of the skill necessary to carry out his job properly but also that he will exercise that skill with reasonable care. In *Lister* v. *Romford Ice and Cold Storage Co., Ltd.*[11],

> A lorry driver employed by the company injured his father, who was a fellow-employee, while backing the lorry. The company was made liable vicariously for the driver's negligence. *Held:* the company was entitled to an indemnity against the driver who was in breach of the duty of care implied in his contract of employment.

4. *To conduct himself properly.*—Insolence, persistent laziness, bad timekeeping, and drunkenness are examples of breach of this duty. Whether such misconduct justifies dismissal is a matter of degree[12] but dishonesty always justifies dismissal[13].

5. *To observe good faith.*—It is a breach of this duty for an employee to take a secret commission[14] or to solicit the employer's customers with a view to transferring their custom to him when he leaves his

---

8. *Ibid.*, s. 116.
9. *Ibid.*, s. 27.
10. *Laws* v. *London Chronicle, Ltd.*, [1959] 2 All E. R. 285; [1959] 1 W. L. R. 698.
11. [1957] 1 All E. R. 125; [1957] A. C. 555.
12. *Clouston & Co., Ltd.*, v. *Corry*, [1904–7] All E. R. Rep. 685; [1906] A. C. 122; *Pepper* v. *Webb*, [1969] 2 All E. R. 216; [1969] 1 W. L. R. 514, C. A.
13. *Cunningham* v. *Fonblanque* (1833), 6 C. & P. 44.
14. *Boston Deep Sea Fishing and Ice Co.* v. *Ansell* (1888), 39 Ch. D. 339.

present employment[15]. Working in his spare-time for a rival employer may also be a breach of the employee's duty of fidelity[16].
In *British Syphon Co., Ltd.* v. *Homewood*[17], ROXBURGH, J., said that

> "in matters concerning the business of his employer, the servant has a duty to be free from any personal reasons for not giving his employer the best possible advice."

As a result, if his duties include giving technical advice, any invention he makes in relation to his master's business must belong to his master. It would be contrary to the servant's duty of fidelity if the employee were permitted to patent the invention.

It is part of the employee's duty of good faith to perform the employment contract in such a way that it does not frustrate the commercial object of the contract and in consequence an employee is in breach if he "works to rule" in a wholly unreasonable way so that the employer's work is disrupted[18].

The implied duty of fidelity survives the termination of the contract in that an ex-employee may be restrained from disclosing his former employer's trade secrets[19] or from using for his own purpose lists of his employer's customers that he has drawn up[20]. But, unless there is an express covenant in restraint of trade, he is free to compete with his former employer, to solicit his former employer's customers, and to advertise that he formerly worked for that employer[1].

Implied duties of the employer

1. *To retain the employee for agreed period.*—While the employer is bound to retain the employee for the period agreed unles the contract permits it to be terminated earlier, there is in general no duty to provide the employee with work. However, exceptionally, there is a duty to provide work in the case of apprentices, and wherever payment

---

15. *Wessex Dairies, Ltd.* v. *Smith*, [1935] All E. R. Rep. 75; [1935] 2 K. B. 80; followed in *Sanders* v. *Parry*, [1967] 2 All E. R. 803; [1967] 1 W. L. R. 753.
16. *Hivac, Ltd.* v. *Park Royal Scientific Instruments, Ltd.*, [1946] 1 All E. R. 350; [1946] Ch. 169.
17. [1956] 2 All E. R. 897; [1956] 1 W. L. R. 1190.
18. *Secretary of State for Employment* v. *Associated Society of Locomotive Engineers and Firemen (No. 2)*, [1972] 2 All E. R. 949; [1972] 2 Q. B. 443, C. A.
19. Unless disclosure is justified in the public interest as where, for example, the employer has engaged in illegal practices: *Initial Services, Ltd.* v. *Putterill*, [1967] 3 All E. R. 145; [1968] 1 Q. B. 396, C. A.
20. *Robb* v. *Green*, [1895] 2 Q. B. 315.
1. For covenants in restraint of trade, see p. 46, *ante*.

is wholly or partly on a commission basis[2]. Similarly, if as with an actor, the opportunity of work is of the essence of the contract, work giving the actor the chance of enhancing his reputation, there is a breach of contract if the work agreed is not provided even though the employer has complied with his obligation to pay the agreed remuneration[3].

2. *To pay agreed remuneration.*—Where an employee is away from work because of illness but the illness is not sufficiently serious to cause frustration of the contract, it is presumed that he is still entitled to be paid his wages. This presumption applies where the written terms are silent and the employer is unable to establish an implied term to the effect that wages are not paid during illness[4].

By the Equal Pay Act 1970, due to come into force on December 29, 1975, women must be given equal treatment as regards terms and conditions of employment with men in the same employment.

3. *To take reasonable care for servant's safety.*—It was held by the House of Lords in *Wilsons and Clyde Coal Co.* v. *English*[5] that an employer owes a personal duty to use due care to provide a competent staff of men, adequate material, a safe system of work and adequate supervision. These are all aspects of the employer's duty to take reasonable care for the servant's safety. Whether or not the duty has been broken is essentially a question of fact, and decisions on fact should not be treated as binding authorities[6]. An employer may be liable for breach even where the employee is working on premises not in the employer's occupation[7], and in determining whether the employer has taken reasonable care, it is relevant that he is aware that a particular employee is susceptible to certain risks[8]. If the employer is in breach and could have foreseen the risk of a certain kind of injury, the employer is liable for all damage directly resulting from the injury, including damage that could not itself be reasonably foreseen[9].

By the Employer's Liability (Defective Equipment) Act 1969, if an employee suffers personal injury because of a defect in equipment provided by his employer and the defect is attributable wholly or partly to the fault of a third party (*e.g.* the manufacturers), the employer

---

2. *Bauman* v. *Hulton Press*, [1952] 2 All E. R. 1121.
3. *Herbert Clayton and Jack Waller, Ltd.* v. *Oliver*, [1930] A. C. 209.
4. *Orman* v. *Saville Sportswear, Ltd.*, [1960] 3 All E. R. 105; [1960] 1 W. L. R. 1055.
5. [1937] 3 All E. R. 628; [1938] A. C. 57.
6. *Qualcast (Wolverhampton), Ltd.* v. *Haynes*, [1959] 2 All E. R. 38; [1959] A. C. 743.
7. *General Cleaning Contractors, Ltd.* v. *Christmas*, [1952] 2 All E. R. 1110; [1953] A. C. 180.
8. *Paris* v. *Stepney Borough Council*, [1951] 1 All E. R. 42; [1951] A. C. 367.
9. *Smith* v. *Leech, Brain Co., Ltd.*, [1961] 3 All E. R. 1159; [1962] 2 Q. B. 405.

is liable. Any agreement purporting to exclude or limit this liability is void.

All employers are required to insure against their liability for damages for personal injuries to their employees by the Employers' Liability (Compulsory Insurance) Act 1969.

One defence that an employer may have when being sued for breach of his implied duty of care is that the servant has voluntarily accepted the particular risk which caused the injury, but it is not enough that the servant knew of the risk. The defence is *volenti non fit injuria*, not *scienti non fit injuria*[10]. Another possible defence is that the injury was caused in fact by the servant's own lack of care for his safety. If this is established, a court has power to apportion damages between them under the Law Reform (Contributory Negligence) Act 1945.

Apart from the Common Law duty of care implied in every contract of employment, the employer may be liable in damages for breach of statutory duties, for example those imposed by the Factories Act 1961.

4. *To make redundancy payments.*—By the Redundancy Payments Act 1965, an employer is bound to make a redundancy payment to any employee who has been continuously employed for one hundred and four weeks or more and is dismissed on the ground of redundancy or is laid off or kept on short-time. The Act does not apply where the employee has attained the age of sixty-five if a man or sixty if a woman, nor where the employee has been properly dismissed for misconduct, nor where the employee has unreasonably refused an offer by his employer to provide suitable employment. The amount of any re- dundancy payment payable is calculated in accordance with the First Schedule to the Act and on payment the employer is entitled to claim a rebate from the Redundancy Fund. Disputes under the Act are determined by the Industrial Tribunals.

Remedies of employer and employee

1. *Employer.*—While an employer may always dismiss an employee instantly if he has been dishonest, in all other cases of breach of duty on the employee's part, it is a matter of degree whether the breach justifies dismissal. Assuming the employer has a right to dismiss his employee, there is no obligation to tell him the grounds, and if the employer is not aware of any good grounds until after the date of the dismissal he still has a good defence to an action for wrongful dismissal if, in fact, good grounds did exist[11].

---

10. *Smith* v. *Baker and Sons*, [1891] A. C. 325.
11. *Boston Deep Sea Fishing and Ice Co., Ltd.* v. *Ansell* (1888), 39 Ch. D. 339.

Where the employee's breach is not sufficiently serious so as to justify dismissal, the employer's only remedy against him is a claim for damages. Specific performance is never awarded of a contract for personal services.

2. *Employee.*—An employee has the right to leave without giving notice only if the employer's breach amounts to a repudiation of the essential conditions of the contract. In these circumstances, the employee is freed from all the obligations of the contract, including any covenants in restraint of trade[12].

Where a servant is working under a statutory scheme of employment he may, in the discretion of the court, obtain a declaratory judgment to the effect that he has been wrongfully dismissed[13]. A declaration will not normally be granted if it is an ordinary contract of employment[14]. However, the rule is not inflexible and in special circumstances a declaration may be granted and even an injunction to prevent wrongful dismissal[15].

The usual remedy for wrongful dismissal is an action for wages accrued due, remuneration for the broken period of employment and damages. The principal measure of damages, where it is a contract for a fixed period, is the amount of wages or salary that would have been paid during the remainder of that period, and if it is a contract terminable by notice, the wages or salary that would have been paid in the period of such notice. However, this amount will be reduced if the employee has failed in his duty to mitigate damages[16]. More significant, in so far as the total loss of wages or salary is not more than £5,000, is that the tax that would have been paid on the earnings must be allowed for in the award of damages. Any sum in excess of £5,000 is taxable in the plaintiff's hands under the Finance Act 1960[17].

Damages for breach of an apprenticeship contract may cover not only pecuniary loss but loss of future training and diminution of future prospects[18].

---

12. *General Billposting Co., Ltd.* v. *Atkinson,* [1908–10] All E. R. Rep. 619; [1909] A. C. 118.
13. *Vine* v. *National Dock Labour Board,* [1956] 3 All E. R. 939; [1957] A. C. 488. And see *Ridge* v. *Baldwin,* [1963] 2 All E. R. 66; [1964] A. C. 40.
14. *Francis* v. *Municipal Councillors of Kuala Lumpur,* [1962] 3 All E. R. 633; [1962] 1 W. L. R. 1411; *Taylor* v. *National Union of Seamen,* [1967] 1 All E.R. 767; [1967] 1 W. L. R. 532. See also *Denmark Productions, Ltd.* v. *Boscobel Productions, Ltd.,* [1968] 3 All E. R. 513, C. A.
15. *Hill* v. *C. A. Parsons & Co. Ltd.,* [1971] 3 All E. R. 1345; [1972] Ch. 305, C. A.
16 *Brace* v. *Calder,* [1895] 2 Q. B. 253.
17. *Parsons* v. *B. N. M. Laboratories, Ltd.,* [1963] 2 All E. R. 658; [1964] 1 Q. B. 95: *Bold* v. *Brough, Nicholson and Hall, Ltd.,* [1963] 3 All E. R. 849; [1964] 1 W. L. R. 201.
18. *Dunk* v. *George Waller & Son,* [1970] 2 All E. R. 630; [1970] 2 Q. B. 163, C. A.

3. *Industrial Relations Act 1971.*—This Act contains detailed provisions about "unfair industrial practices". Where an unfair industrial practice, *e.g.* unfair dismissal, is alleged by an employee, he may seek a remedy from an Industrial Tribunal which is empowered to make a recommendation for re-engagement or to order compensation[19]. An employer who alleges an unfair industrial practice has a right to complain to the National Industrial Relations Court a branch of the Supreme Court created by the Act, or to an Industrial Tribunal depending on the circumstances[20].

The Truck Acts

As a general rule, by virtue of the Truck Acts 1831–1940, all "workmen" must be paid their wages in full in cash. A "workman" means a labourer, servant in husbandry, journeyman, artificer, handicraftsman, miner, or someone otherwise engaged in manual labour not being a domestic or menial servant[1].

Under the provisions of the Truck Acts, any contract to pay a workman wages otherwise than in cash is illegal. Moreover, any contractual provision directing the workman as to how or where to spend his wages is illegal. If payment is made otherwise than in cash the workman can claim the full wages without any set-off for the goods supplied in lieu of wages. It is not contrary to the Truck Acts for an employee to be paid less than the usual rate if, for example, the contract impliedly permits a deduction to be made for bad workmanship in the calculation of wages due[2].

The Acts have been modified to some extent by the Payment of Wages Act 1960. This Act provides that if the workman requests in writing, and the employer agrees, he may have his wages or part of them paid by crediting his bank account with the amount due, or by postal order, money order, or cheque. An arrangement to pay wages by one of these methods may be terminated by either party giving not less than four weeks' written notice and may be terminated at any time by written agreement. A special provision in the Act provides that wages may be paid by postal or money order where the workman is absent from his usual place of employment, either on account of illness or injury or on duty, without any request by the workman or agreement with him, unless the workman notifies his employer in writing that he does not wish his wages to be so paid in such circumstances[3].

---

19. Industrial Relations Act 1971, s. 106.
20. *Ibid.*, s. 101.
1. Employers and Workmen Act 1875.
2. *Sagar* v. *H. Ridehalgh & Son, Ltd.*, [1931] 1 Ch. 310.
3. Payment of Wages Act 1960, s. 4.

Under provisions in the Truck Acts themselves, certain deductions are permitted. For example, if the workman has signed a written agreement, his employer may deduct up to the real value of (i) any medicine or medical treatment, (ii) fuel, (iii) materials, tools or implements used by a workman who is employed in mines, (iv) hay, corn or provender to be consumed by a beast of burden, (v) rent of living accommodation, or (vi) food prepared and consumed on the employer's premises[4]. A fine in respect of some conduct likely to cause damage or loss to the employer may be deducted, provided there is either a written contract signed by the workman or a notice conspicuously displayed, specifying the acts or omission for which fines may be imposed[5]. With the workman's agreement, his employer may deduct the amount of any debt due from the workman to a third party[6], but not the amount of any debt owed by the workman to the employer himself[7].

---

4. Truck Act 1831, s. 23.
5. Truck Act 1896, s. 2.
6. *Hewlett* v. *Allen & Sons*, [1894] A. C. 383.
7. *Williams* v. *North's Navigation Collieries (1889), Ltd.*, [1906] A. C. 136.

PART IV

Bankruptcy

CHAPTER 27

Bankruptcy

I INTRODUCTORY

The earliest bankruptcy statutes date back to the time of Henry VIII, and of Elizabeth and James I. Before 1861 the advantages of bankruptcy belonged only to those who came under the category of traders, but in an Act of that year non-traders were included amongst those who could be made bankrupt. The objects of modern bankruptcy legislation are:

1. To ensure the fair distribution of the property of an insolvent debtor among his creditors.
2. To allow the debtor to relieve himself of the burden of his debts and start afresh.
3. To prevent abuses of the process.

The principal statute governing bankruptcy law today is the Bankruptcy Act 1914.

II WHO MAY BE MADE BANKRUPT

In order that a court may make an adjudication of bankruptcy it is necessary that a "debtor" has committed "an act of bankruptcy." Section 1 of the Act lists a number of acts as "acts of bankruptcy" and these are examined below[1]. A "debtor" is defined[2] to include any person, whether a British subject or not, who at the time when any act of bankruptcy was done or suffered by him:

(*a*) was personally present in England; or

(*b*) ordinarily resided or had a place of business in England; or

(*c*) was carrying on business in England personally or by means of an agent or manager[3]; or

(*d*) was a member of a firm or partnership which carried on business in England.

The position of various special classes of persons is as follows:

1. *Minors.*—A minor can be made a bankrupt in respect of debts legally binding on him, *e.g.* if the debt on which the bankruptcy is founded was incurred for necessaries, or is a judgment debt founded

---

1. *Post*, p. 445.
2. Bankruptcy Act 1914, s. 1 (2).
3. A foreigner who had ceased to trade in England but left debts unpaid in England was treated as still carrying on his business in England (*Theophile* v. *Solicitor-General*, [1950] 1 All E. R. 405; [1950] A. C. 186, H. L.).

on a tort[4], but if there is no debt legally enforceable against him, he cannot be made a bankrupt even on his own petition[5]. When a plea of infancy would have been a defence to an action the court of bankruptcy will give effect to it although judgment has been obtained[6].

2. *Married women.*—Since 1935, a married woman has been subject to bankruptcy law as if she were a *feme sole*[7].

3. *Aliens.*—An alien who commits an act of bankruptcy comes within the definition of a "debtor" and is, therefore, subject to English bankruptcy law if he is either personally present in England at the time of the act of bankruptcy or satisfies any of the other conditions listed above in the meaning given by the Act to a "debtor" and may be made bankrupt on his own petition. However, a *creditor* may only present a petition against a debtor, whether an alien debtor or not, in the more limited circumstances referred to later[8].

4. *Mentally disordered persons.*—Mentally disordered persons cannot commit an act of bankruptcy involving *intent*, *e.g.* fraudulent preference; they can be adjudged bankrupt even without the consent of the Court of Protection where the act of bankruptcy was committed before the debtor came under that court's jurisdiction, but it seems that even if the act of bankruptcy takes place before a receiver of the patient's estate is appointed, the trustee in bankruptcy will not be entitled to the debtor's property to the exclusion of the Court of Protection at any rate if that court asserts its control before the receiving order in bankruptcy[9].

5. *Partnerships.*—A partnership may be made bankrupt[10]. A receiving order against the firm is equivalent to a receiving order against each of the general partners.

6. *Deceased persons.*—A deceased person cannot be made bankrupt on proceedings instituted after his death, but his estate may be administered in bankruptcy[11]. Where a debtor dies after presentation of the petition the proceedings will, unless the court otherwise orders, be continued as if he were alive[12].

7. *Registered companies.*—No corporation or registered company can be made bankrupt[13]. The winding-up of a company under the Companies Act 1948 is the equivalent of bankruptcy in the case of an individual.

---

4. *Re Debtor (No. 564 of 1949)*, [1950] 1 All E. R. 308; [1950] Ch. 282.
5. *Re A. and M.*, [1926] Ch. 274; and *Re Davenport, Ex parte Bankrupt* v. *Eric Street Properties, Ltd.*, [1963] 2 All C. R. 850; [1963] 1 W. L. R. 817, C. A.
6. *Ex parte Kibble* (1875), L. R. 10 Ch. 373.
7. Law Reform (Married Women, etc.) Act 1935, s. 1 (d).
8. *Post*, p. 448.
9. *Re Debtor (No. 1 of 1941)*, [1941] 3 All E. R. 11; [1941] Ch. 487. See *ante*, p, 61.
10. Including limited partnerships; see *ante*, p. 178.
11. See *post*, p. 495.
12. Bankruptcy Act 1914, s. 112.   13. *Ibid.*, s. 126.

III PROCEDURE

To proceed against a person in bankruptcy, it is necessary:

1. That a bankruptcy petition should be presented either by the debtor or by a creditor, and
2. In accordance with this petition, that a receiving order should be made.

This cannot be done unless an act of bankruptcy has been committed by the debtor. There is one exception to this statement:

if a judgment summons is taken out against a debtor, the court may, instead of exercising the jurisdiction to commit, with the creditor's assent, make a receiving order against the debtor; in such case, however, the debtor is deemed to have committed an act of bankruptcy at the time the order is made[14].

The court, however, cannot make a receiving order unless there is evidence of means which would have justified the making of a committal order[15].

Acts of bankruptcy

By section 1 (1) of the Act, a "debtor" commits an act of bankruptcy in each of the following cases:

1. "If in England or elsewhere he makes a conveyance or assignment of his property to a trustee or trustees for the benefit of his creditors generally."

An assignment to one or more particular creditors is not an act of bankruptcy under this head, nor is an assignment of his property by a debtor for the benefit of his trade creditors only: the act of bankruptcy here meant is a conveyance of all or substantially all a debtor's property to a trustee, who is to represent all the creditors[16].

An assignment executed by a foreigner resident abroad but trading in England and intended to operate according to the law of his domicil is not an act of bankruptcy[17].

A creditor who has acquiesced in a deed of assignment or has recognised the title of the trustee thereunder, *e.g.* by trading with him as such, cannot rely on the assignment as an act of bankruptcy, although he may not have assented to the deed so as to be bound thereby[18]. But such a creditor may present a petition founded on an independent act of bankruptcy[19]. Moreover, a creditor whose assent to a deed of

---

14. *Ibid.*, s. 107 (4).
15. *Re A Debtor*, [1905] 1 K. B. 374.
16. *Re Phillips*, [1900] 2 Q. B. 329.
17. *Re Debtors (No. 836 of 1935)*, [1936] 1 All E. R. 875; [1936] Ch. 622.
18. *Ex parte Stray* (1867), L. R. 2 Ch. 374; *Re Brindley*, [1906] 1 K. B. 377.
19. *Re Mills*, [1906] 1 K. B. 389.

assignment has been obtained by fraud or misrepresentation is not precluded from relying upon the execution of the deed as an act of bankruptcy[20]; and a creditor who has assented to a *proposed* deed of assignment may revoke his assent before the execution of the deed, and then rely on any act of bankruptcy connected with the proposed assignment[21].

    2. "If in England or elsewhere he makes a fraudulent conveyance, gift, delivery, or transfer of his property, or of any part thereof."

Section 172 of the Law of Property Act 1925 provides that any conveyance of property made with intent to defraud creditors is voidable at the instance of anyone prejudiced by it though a *bona fide* transferee for value is protected. The Bankruptcy Act provision, quoted here, does not refer to any specific intent but a "fraudulent" conveyance, etc., by the debtor does mean one which is fraudulent as against his creditors or some of them and the Court is entitled to infer fraud in this sense from the circumstances. Thus, if a debtor assigns all his property for the benefit of one or several creditors to the exclusion of others, this is "fraudulent." On the other hand, if he sells or mortgages his property in the ordinary course of business, this is not necessarily "fraudulent." Similarly, if the debtor assigns his property partly in consideration of a past debt and partly as security for a further advance, then if the lender intended to enable the debtor to carry on his business, the assignment is not "fraudulent"; *contra*, if the advance was a mere device for securing payment of or security for an earlier debt[1].

A *bona fide* purchaser for value without notice of the property fraudulently transferred cannot retain it against a trustee in bankruptcy, if the transaction of purchase took place within the period of relation back, *i.e.* three months before presentation of the bankruptcy petition (unless the transaction is protected under s. 45 of the Act[2]).

    3. "If in England or elsewhere he makes any conveyance or transfer of his property or any part thereof, or creates any charge thereon which would under this or any other Act be void as a fraudulent preference if he were adjudged bankrupt"[3].

It should be observed that in both these subsections the fraudulent conveyance is the cause of its being made an act of bankruptcy; a *bona fide* conveyance or gift may be set aside, but it will not ground a petition.

---

20. *Re Tanenberg & Sons* (1889), 6 Morr. 49.
21. *Re Jones Bros.*, [1912] 2 K. B. 234.
 1. *Re Sinclair, Ex parte Chaplin* (1884), 26 Ch. D. 319.
 2. *Re Gunsbourg*, [1920] 2 K. B. 426. See *post*, p. 462. As to protected transactions, see pp. 464–465.
 3. See *post*, pp. 469–470.

4. "If with intent to defeat or delay his creditors he does any of the following things, namely, departs out of England, or being out of England remains out of England, or departs from his dwelling-house, or otherwise absents himself, or begins to keep house."

In this case there is no act of bankruptcy unless there is an intention to defeat or delay creditors; a mere staying at home, or going abroad, though in fact followed by delay in payment, will not be an act of bankruptcy[4]; but, of course, all the circumstances will be looked to, and the court will find the intention from the facts. Leaving a place of business without paying creditors or notifying the change of address is an act of bankruptcy within this sub-section[5].

5. "If execution against him has been levied by seizure of his goods under process in an action in any court, or in any civil proceeding in the High Court, and the goods have been either sold or held by the sheriff for twenty-one days[6]. Provided that, where an interpleader summons has been taken out in regard to the goods seized, the time elapsing between the date at which summons is taken out and the date at which the proceedings on such summons are finally disposed of, settled, or abandoned, shall not be taken into account in calculating such period of twenty-one days."

6. "If he files in the court a declaration of his inability to pay his debts or presents a bankruptcy petition against himself."

7. "If a creditor has obtained a final judgment, or order[7] against him for any amount, and execution thereon not having been stayed[8], has served on him in England, or, by leave of the court, elsewhere, a *bankruptcy notice* under this Act, and he does not, within seven days after service of the notice, in case the service is effected in England, and in case the service is effected elsewhere, then within the time limited in that behalf by the order giving leave to effect the service, either comply with the requirements of

---

4. *Ex parte Brandon* (1884), 25 Ch. D. 500; *Re A Debtor (No. 360 of 1951)*, [1952] 1 All E. R. 519, n., C. A.

5. *Re Worsley*, [1901] 1 Q. B. 309. The section includes a foreigner who leaves business debts in England (*Theophile* v. *Solicitor-General*, [1950] 1 All E. R. 405; [1950] A. C. 186, H. L.).

6. It was held in *Re Dalton (a Bankrupt), Ex parte Harrington and Carmichael (a Firm)* v. *Trustee of Property of Bankrupt*, [1962] 2 All E. R. 499; [1963] Ch. 336, that a sheriff does "hold" goods although, after seizure, the debtor is allowed under a "walking possession" agreement between him and the sheriff to trade in the goods seized provided any goods sold were replaced.

7. This includes any person for the time being entitled to enforce a final judgment or order (Bankruptcy Act 1914, s. 1 (g)).

8. This would include a case where leave to issue execution was necessary and had not been obtained. See *Ex parte Ide* (1886), 17 Q. B. D. 755, and R. S. C., Ord. 81, r. 5.

the notice[9], or satisfy the court that he has a counter-claim set off or cross-demand which equals or exceeds the amount of the judgment debt, or sum ordered to be paid, and which he could not set up in the action in which the judgment was obtained, or the proceedings in which the order was obtained."

A bankruptcy notice in the prescribed form requires the debtor to pay the judgment debt or sum ordered to be paid in accordance with the terms of the judgment or order, or to secure or compound for it to the satisfaction of the creditor or the court[10].

It should be noted that the judgment debt may be of any amount, and that there are but three ways of avoiding committing the act of bankruptcy when a bankruptcy notice has been served, viz.:

   (i) paying;
   (ii) giving satisfactory security;
   (iii) showing a cross-claim equal to or exceeding the judgment debt, which could not have been set up in the action in which judgment was obtained[11].

Bankruptcy notices are strictly construed and any irregularity which might in any way mislead or embarrass the debtor will render the notice void[12].

   8. "If the debtor gives notice[13] to any of his creditors that he has suspended, or that he is about to suspend, payment of his debts."

The petition

This may be presented either by the debtor or by a creditor, or several creditors may join in presenting the petition.

A Creditor's Petition.—The following are the conditions on which a creditor may petition[14]:

---

9. If the debtor gives a promissory note, which is taken, even conditionally, the creditor cannot get a receiving order on the notice (*Ex parte Matthew* (1884), 12 Q. B. D. 506).
10. Bankruptcy Act 1914, s. 2.
11. As to the time limits for setting up payment or a cross-demand, see *In re a Debtor (No. 30 of 1956)*, [1957] Ch. 381, and *In re a Debtor (No. 991 of 1962)*, *Ex parte Debtor* v. *Tousson*, [1963] 1 All E. R. 85; [1963] 1 W. L. R. 51, C. A.
12. *Re a Debtor (No. 21 of 1950)*, [1950] 2 All E. R. 1129; [1951] Ch. 313 (wrong county court named); *Re a Debtor (No. 41 of 1951)*, [1952] 1 All E. R. 107; [1952] Ch. 192 (proceedings in name of liquidator instead of company).
13. This notice need not be in writing; it suffices if the language used be such as to lead any reasonable person to suppose that the debtor intended to suspend payment (*Crook* v. *Morley*, [1891] A. C. 316. See also *Re a Debtor*, [1929] 1 Ch. 362, and *cf. Clough* v. *Samuel*, [1896] A. C. 442.
14. Bankruptcy Act 1914, s. 4.

1. The debt[15] due to him or, if more than one join in the petition, the aggregate amount of the debts, must amount to £50 or more.

2. It must be liquidated and payable immediately or at a certain future time. The debt must be liquidated *before* the act of bankruptcy on which the petition is founded and at the hearing the creditor will have to show that the debt continued to exist at the time of presentation of the petition and at the hearing.

3. The act of bankruptcy on which the petition is grounded must have occurred within three months before the presentation of the petition.

4. The debtor is (*a*) domiciled in England, or (*b*) has ordinarily resided in, or had a dwelling-house or place of business in England, within a year before presentation of the petition, or (*c*) has carried on business in England, personally or by an agent, or is, or has been within the said period a member of a firm which has carried on business by a partner or agent.

   The references to "business" do not apply to anyone who is domiciled, or to a firm having its principal place of business, in Scotland or Northern Ireland.

5. If the creditor is secured, he must in his petition, either state that he is prepared to surrender his security, or give an estimate of its value, and in the latter case there must be a balance of at least £50 owing to him after deducting from his debt the estimated value of it[16].

   If the petition states the wrong figure as the debt owing, but the correct figure would have been sufficient to support the petition, the receiving order will not be rescinded. But if the creditor fails to disclose a security, the order will be rescinded unless there are circumstances to justify leave being given to amend the petition[17].

A Debtor's Petition.—If the petition is that of the debtor, he must allege in it his inability to pay his debt. Presentation of a petition by the debtor is deemed to be an act of bankruptcy without the previous filing by him of any declaration of inability to pay his debt and "the

---

15. Rates are a sufficient debt although only recoverable by distress (*Re McGreavy*, [1950] Ch. 269). Water rates are now recoverable as a civil debt and a magistrates' court judgment for them can ground a bankruptcy petition: see *Re A Debtor (No. 48 of 1952)*, [1953] 1 All E. R. 545; [1953] Ch. 335, C. A.
16. Bankruptcy Act 1914, s. 4 (2). As to the trustee's right to redeem, see *post*, p. 487.
17. *Re Debtor (No. 6 of 1941)*, [1943] Ch. 213; [1943] 1 All E. R. 553.

court shall thereupon make a receiving order"[18]. A debtor's petition cannot be withdrawn without leave of the court.

The place of presentation is:

1. The High Court of Justice, where the debtor:
    (i) has carried on business or has resided in the London bankruptcy district during the greater part of the six months before the presentation of the petition, or
    (ii) for a longer period thereof than in the district of any county court, or
    (iii) when he is not resident in England, or
    (iv) when his residence cannot be ascertained.

2. In any other case in the county court (not comprised in the London bankruptcy district) within whose district the debtor has resided or carried on business during the greater part of the said six months[19].

Preference is to be given to his "business" over his "residential" district[20].

Form of Creditor's Petition[21]

I, CD, of   [*or* we, CD, of   and EF   of   ] hereby petition the Court that a receiving order may be made in respect of the estate of AB   of   and lately residing at   [*or* carrying on business at   ] and say,—

1. That the said AB has for the greater part of six months preceding the presentation of this petition resided [*or* carried on business] at   within the district of this Court [*or, as the case may be, following the terms of s.* 98].

2. That the said AB is justly and truly indebted to me [*or* us] in the aggregate in the sum of £   [*set out amount of debt or debts, and the consideration*].

3. That I [*or* we] do not, nor does any person on my [*or* our] behalf hold any security on the said debtor's estate, or on any part thereof, for the payment of the said sum.

OR

---

18. Bankruptcy Act 1914, s. 6. In *re a Debtor* (*No. 17 of 1966*), [1967] 1 All E. R. 668; [1967] Ch. 590, a judgment of £2,400 damages was required to be paid by weekly instalments of 25s. and the judgment debtor filed a petition for his own bankruptcy. *Held:* an adjudication based on this petition must be annulled as the debtor was able to pay the instalments as they became due though not the whole of the judgment at once.

19. Bankruptcy Act 1914, ss. 98, 99. As to transfers, see *ibid.*, s. 100.

20. Bankruptcy Rules 1952, r. 145 (2).

21. Bankruptcy Rules 1952, r. 143 and 145, Form No. 11.

That I hold security for the payment of [*or* part of] the said sum [but that I will give up such security for the benefit of the creditors of AB in the event of his being adjudged bankrupt] *or* [and I estimate the value of such security at the sum of £].

OR

That I, CD, one of your petitioners, hold security for the payment of *&c.*

That I, EF, another of your petitioners, hold security for the payment of *&c.*

4. That AB within three months before the date of the presentation of this petition has committed the following act [*or* acts] of bankruptcy, namely [*here set out the nature and date or dates of the act or acts of bankruptcy relied on*].

Dated this   day of   19 .

(Signed)   CD
            EF

(Signed by the petitioner in my presence)
Signature of Witness
Address
Description

Proceedings on a creditor's petition

The following points should be noted:

1. A creditor's petition must be verified by an affidavit of the creditor or of some other person on his behalf having knowledge of the facts and served in the prescribed manner[1].

2. The petition will not be heard until after an interval of eight days at least from the date of service.

3. The creditor must be prepared to prove the continued existence of his debt, the service of the petition on the debtor and the act of bankruptcy or, if more than one act of bankruptcy is alleged in the petition, of some one of the alleged acts of bankruptcy[2].

4. If the debtor wishes to oppose the petition he must file a notice specifying the facts which he intends to dispute and send a copy to the petitioning creditor and his solicitor (if known) at least three days before the hearing[3].

5. If there are more than one respondent to the petition, the petition may be dismissed as against one or more without prejudice to the effect of the petition against the other or others of them[4].

---

1. Bankruptcy Act 1914, s. 5 (1).
2. *Ibid.*, s. 5 (2).
3. Bankruptcy Rules 1952, r. 166.
4. Bankruptcy Act 1914, s. 115.

6. If there are several petitions against one debtor, or against joint debtors, these may be consolidated[5].
7. If a creditor who has the conduct of the proceedings does not proceed with due diligence, a new petitioner may be substituted[6].
8. The petition may not be withdrawn without the leave of the court[7].

The receiving order

This may be made at any time after the presentation of the petition, but, in the case of a creditor's petition, not until after the hearing. If, on a creditor's petition, the court is not satisfied with the proof of any of the matters required to be shown (*i.e.* the petitioning creditor's debt, the act of bankruptcy and the service of the petition) or is satisfied by the debtor that he is able to pay his debts or if there is other "sufficient cause," it will dismiss the petition[8]. Examples of sufficient cause are:

1. That the debtor's only asset is a life interest which will be forfeited on bankruptcy[9];
2. That there are no assets *and no reasonable probability of any*[10];
3. That the petition is brought for some collateral end or to extort more than is due[11].

The effect of a receiving order is to constitute the official receiver —an officer appointed by the Department of Trade[12]—receiver of the property of the debtor, and thereafter no creditor has any remedy against the debtor or his property or may commence an action against the debtor without leave of the court. Creditors not subject to this rule are:

1. Secured creditors[13];
2. Creditors whose debts are not provable in bankruptcy[14]; and
3. To a certain extent, the landlord[15].

---

5. *Ibid.*, s. 110.
6. *Ibid.*, s. 111. A receiving order cannot be made when there is no petitioner with a debt before the court: *Re Mann, Ex parte The Debtor*, [1958] 3 All E. R. 660.
7. *Ibid.*, ss. 5 (7) and 6 (2).
8. *Ibid.*, s. 5 (3).
9. *Re Otway, Ex parte Otway*, [1895] 1 Q. B. 812.
10. *Re Betts*, [1897] 1 Q. B. 50.
11. *Re Shaw* (1901), 83 L. R. 754; *Re A Debtor (No. 883 of 1927)*, [1928] Ch. 199; *Re A Judgment Summons (No. 25 of 1952)*, [1953] 1 All E. R. 424; [1953] Ch. 195, C. A.; *Re Majory*, [1955] Ch. 600.
12. *Post*, p. 472.
13. Bankruptcy Act 1914, s. 7.
14. *Post*, pp. 483, 484, and s. 30. See *James* v. *James*, [1963] 2 All E. R. 465; [1963] 3 W. L. R. 331, D. C.
15. *Post*, p. 486.

Even before a receiving order is made, at any time after the petition is presented, the court may, if this is shown to be necessary for the protection of the estate, appoint the official receiver to be interim receiver of the debtor's property[16].

Any proceedings (*e.g.* action, execution) may be stayed by the court when a petition has been presented, though a receiving order has not yet been made[17].

Notice of every receiving order stating the name, address and description of the debtor, the date of the order, the court by which the order is made, and the date of the petition, must be advertised in the *London Gazette* and in a local paper[18].

The court has a general discretion under s. 108 to rescind its orders, and can therefore rescind a receiving order. In exercising this discretion the court is not confined to the grounds on which an order of adjudication can be annulled[19]. Thus, the court may rescind a receiving order not only where it thinks the order was wrongly made or where there has been payment in full (these being the statutory grounds of annulment) but also if it thinks rescission would be for the benefit of creditors and not detrimental to the public. In *re Izod*[20], a receiving order was rescinded when the debtor's father paid the creditors ten shillings in the pound and they withdrew their proofs and released the debtor. But even if the creditors are paid in full and support the debtor's application for rescission of the receiving order, it may be refused if the official receiver considers the debtor's conduct should be subjected to a public examination[21]. If the receiving order is obtained by the presentation of a petition under circumstances which amount to an abuse of the process of the court, it will, of course, be rescinded[1].

Every receiving order must be registered by the official receiver with the chief land registrar if any part of the debtor's property consists of land, but a purchaser is not protected against an unregistered

---

16. Bankruptcy Act 1914, s. 8.
17. *Ibid.*, s. 9.
18. *Ibid.*, s. 11.
19. See *post*, p. 457.
20. [1898] 1 Q. B. 241. This decision was distinguished in *Re a Debtor (No. 12 of 1970) Ex parte Official Receiver* v. *the Debtor*, [1971] 2 All E. R. 1494; [1971] 1 W. L. R. 1212, C. A.
21. *Re Leslie, Ex parte Leslie* (1887), 18 Q. B. D. 619. By s. 12 of the Act a receiving order may be rescinded if a majority of the creditors in number and value are resident in Scotland or Northern Ireland.
1. *Re Betts*, [1901] 2 K. B. 39. In this case the debtor repeatedly presented petitions against himself for the purpose of avoiding the effect of orders for his committal. But in a proper case the debtor may relieve himself from such pressure by seeking the protection of the bankruptcy court: *Re Harry Dunn*, [1949] 2 All E. R. 388; [1949] Ch. 640, C. A.

receiving order unless he acquires a legal estate in good faith for money or money's worth without notice of an available act of bankruptcy[2].

Normal course of proceedings after receiving order

The debtor will attend a *private interview* with the Official Receiver, where he will receive instructions as to preparing his *statement of affairs*. This gives full particulars as to his assets, debts, creditors, securities held by them, etc. It must be verified by affidavit, and made within three or seven days after the receiving order according to whether the petition was presented by himself or by a creditor[3]. If necessary, the official receiver will allow the debtor skilled assistance in the preparation of his statement. If he fails to submit a statement, without reasonable excuse, he may be adjudged bankrupt on the application of the official receiver or of any creditor. He must also attend the *first meeting of creditors* at which he should present any proposals he may have for a composition. The creditors will decide whether a composition is to be accepted. The debtor must also attend a *public examination* which must not be concluded until after the first meeting of creditors has been held. In default of the creditors accepting a composition, an *adjudication order* will be made in due course and a trustee in bankruptcy will be appointed. His property will vest in the trustee who will realise it and distribute it among the creditors in accordance with the Act. At any date after being adjudged bankrupt the debtor may apply for his *discharge*.

Creditors' meetings

The first meeting is generally the most important, and is often the last. On this occasion the chief business consists of the determination whether a proposal for a composition or scheme of arrangement shall be entertained, or whether it is desirable to have the debtor adjudicated bankrupt, and if bankruptcy is resolved upon, the appointment of a trustee and a committee of inspection. This meeting may be adjourned or any particular question may be left to a subsequent meeting. The debtor must attend and submit to such examination and give such information as the meeting may require[4].

The procedure to be observed at these meetings will be found in

---

2. Land Charges Act 1925, ss. 6, 7.
3. Bankruptcy Act 1914, s. 14. By the Bankruptcy Rules 1952, s. 329, the official receiver may require the debtor to furnish him with a trading and profit and loss accounts and a cash and goods account for any period not exceeding two years before the date of the receiving order.
4. Bankruptcy Act 1914, s. 22.

the Bankruptcy Act 1914, s. 13, and Sched. I, and in the Bankruptcy Rules 1952. The following points are important:

1. Notice must be sent to every creditor mentioned in the debtor's statement of affairs as soon as practicable; at least six days notice must be given in the London Gazette and in a local paper.
2. The first meeting must be held not later than fourteen days after the date of the receiving order, unless the court deems it expedient to order otherwise.
3. The official receiver or his nominee shall preside at the first meeting; on subsequent occasions those present may choose their own chairman.
4. Three creditors (if there are as many) will form a quorum, though if there is no quorum the meeting may elect a chairman, admit proofs, and adjourn.
5. All may vote whose proofs are admitted for liquidated debts which are not contingent. The chairman may reject a proof for the purpose of voting, but his decision is subject to revision by the court.
6. A secured creditor may vote after deducting from his proof the value of his security; but the trustee or official receiver may within twenty-eight days of the vote buy him out at the estimated value *plus* twenty per cent. At any time before being bought out he can amend his valuation but then he can be bought out without the twenty per cent. addition[5].
7. A creditor may vote in person or by proxy[6]. A general proxy empowering the holder to act in all matters until the proxy is revoked can be given only to a manager, clerk, or other person in the regular employ of the creditor, and such employment must be stated on the face of the proxy. A creditor may, however, appoint anyone to act as a special proxy with limited power, *e.g.* to vote for or against a specific proposal for a composition.

Public examination[7]

As soon as conveniently after the expiration of time for the submission

---

5. Bankruptcy Act 1914, Sched. I, rr. 10, 12. This must be distinguished from the procedure adopted when the creditor values his security for the purpose of proving for a dividend on the balance. See *post*, p. 487.
6. See as to proxies, *ibid.*, Sched. I, rr. 15-22, and Bankruptcy Rules 1952, rr. 263-266.
7. Bankruptcy Act 1914, s. 15.

by the debtor of his statement of affairs, he must undergo an examination in open court[8] touching his conduct, dealings and property. It is the duty of the official receiver to apply to the court for the appointment of a time and place for the examination, to give notice to the creditors and to the debtor, and to publish it in the London Gazette and in a local paper[9]. The object of the examination is the protection of the public as well as of the interests of the creditors. He must therefore answer questions put to him even if they may incriminate him[10].

The debtor is put upon his oath, and may be examined

1. By the court,
2. The official receiver,
3. The trustee, if appointed before the conclusion of the examination, or
4. By any creditor who has tendered a proof or his representative authorised in writing.

Notes are taken, which must be signed by the debtor after being read over to or by him and may thereafter be used in evidence against him. The court may adjourn the examination if it sees fit, and, if it thinks the debtor is not making a full and true disclosure of his affairs or, without good reason, has failed to attend or comply with any order of the court, may do so *sine die*[11]; this makes it necessary for the debtor, when he desires to have his examination continued, to get a fresh appointment and to bear personally the expense of advertising. Alternatively the registrar may report the matter to the judge who can commit the debtor for contempt of court[12].

If the debtor makes default in attending his public examination, a warrant may be issued for his arrest[13]. The examination must not be concluded till after the first meeting of creditors has been held, but at any subsequent time the court may declare itself satisfied.

Adjudication[14]

The debtor may, at his own request, be adjudged bankrupt at the time of the receiving order or at any time thereafter[15]. Otherwise, any creditor or the official receiver (usually the latter) may apply to

---

8. When the debtor cannot, from incapacity, attend the court, an order may be made dispensing with the examination, or directing that it be held at such place and in such manner as the court thinks expedient (Bankruptcy Act 1914, s. 15 (10)).
9. Bankruptcy Rules 1952, rr. 188 and 189.
10. *Re Paget*, [1927] All E. R. Rep. 465; [1927] 2 Ch. 85.
11. Bankruptcy Rules 1952, r. 192.
12. Bankruptcy Act 1914, s. 102 (4); Bankruptcy Rules 1952, r. 83.
13. Bankruptcy Rules 1952, r. 190.
14. Bankruptcy Act 1914, s. 18.
15. Bankruptcy Rules 1952, r. 217.

the court to adjudge the debtor bankrupt. The court has power to make such adjudication on any of the following grounds:

1. An ordinary[16] resolution of the creditors in favour of adjudication;
2. That no resolution of any kind has been passed;
3. That the creditors have not met;
4. That a scheme has not been approved within fourteen days after the public examination;
5. That the debtor has failed to pay any instalment due under a composition[17];
6. That the debtor has failed without reasonable cause to give a proper account of his affairs[18];
7. That the public examination has been adjourned *sine die*[19].

Notice of the adjudication must be advertised in the London Gazette and in a local paper[20].

Effect.—The effect of adjudication is to vest the bankrupt's property in the trustee whose position is examined below[1]. If an undischarged bankrupt obtains credit to the extent of £10 or more or trades under a different name from that under which he was adjudged bankrupt, without informing his intended creditor that he is an undischarged bankrupt, or without disclosing the name under which he was adjudged bankrupt, he will be liable to imprisonment[2]. An undischarged bankrupt cannot be a director or take part in the management of a company except with the consent of the court[3].

An adjudication may be *annulled*:

1. If the court thinks that the debtor ought not to have been made bankrupt[4]; or
2. If the debts are paid in full or, in the case of disputed debts, secured to the satisfaction of the court[4]; or
3. If a scheme is accepted after adjudication and the court approves the scheme[5].

---

16. An ordinary resolution is one carried by a majority in *value* of the creditors present and voting in person or by proxy (Bankruptcy Act 1914, s. 167).
17. Bankruptcy Act 1914, s. 16 (16).
18. Bankruptcy Act 1914, s. 14 (3); Bankruptcy Rules 1952, r. 219; as to the validity of this Rule, see *Re Fletcher*, [1955] 2 All E. R. 592; [1956] Ch. 28.
19. Bankruptcy Rules 1952, r. 220.
20. Bankruptcy Act 1914, s. 18 (2).
1. See *post*, p. 473.
2. Bankruptcy Act 1914, s. 155. See *R. v. Doubleday*, [1964] 49 Cr. App. Rep. 62, C. C. A.
3. Companies Act 1948, s. 187.
4. Bankruptcy Act 1914, s. 29. "Debts" means proved debts, and if a bankruptcy is annulled, the rights of a creditor, who did not prove, to sue the debtor is revived: *More* v. *More*, [1962] 1 All E. R. 125; [1962] Ch. 424.
5. *Ibid.*, s. 21 (2).

Even where the debts have been paid in full, the court has discretion to refuse an order of annulment. Thus,

> where the bankrupt had been guilty of a falsification of his statement of affairs, and of a substantial concealment of assets, the court refused to annul the adjudication[6]. But, where a minor had been adjudicated bankrupt and there were no debts legally enforceable against him at all, the court did exercise its discretion to annul the order[7].

An unconditional release given to the bankrupt is not equivalent to payment in full[8].

On annulment the property of the bankrupt will be vested in him, or in such other person as the court may appoint[9]. And if on annulment under a composition, which is paid, the court makes no special order, the property of the bankrupt will revest in him[10].

Notice of the order annulling an adjudication must be advertised in the London Gazette and in a local paper.

Discharge of bankrupt[11]

The discharge is the order of the court granting the bankrupt a release[12], and removing from him the status of bankruptcy.

A bankrupt may apply at any time after being adjudged bankrupt for an order of discharge, and the court will appoint some day subsequent to the conclusion of the public examination on which to hear the application. This is heard in open court after fourteen days' notice to the creditors; and the trustee, the creditors, and the official receiver may all oppose. The official receiver's report on the debtor's conduct and affairs, a copy of which must be sent to the bankrupt not less than seven days before the hearing, is read in court and if he intends to dispute any statement contained in it he must give appropriate notice to the official receiver not less than two days before the hearing[13]. The court may put such questions to the debtor and receive such evidence as it thinks fit and, in its discretion, may grant a discharge.

---

6. *Re Taylor*, [1901] 1 Q. B. 744.
7. *Re Davenport, Ex parte Bankrupt* v. *Eric Street Properties, Ltd.*, [1963] 2 All E. R. 850; [1963] 1 W. L. R. 817, C. A.
8. *Re Keet*, [1905] 2 K. B. 666.
9. Bankruptcy Act 1914, ss. 21 (2), 29 (2).
10. *Flower* v. *Lyme Regis Corporation*, [1921] 1 K. B. 488.
11. Bankruptcy Act 1914, s. 26, as amended by s. 1 of the Bankruptcy (Amendment) Act 1926. "Discharge is still quite charily given": Joslin, "Bankruptcy: Anglo-American Contrasts" (1966), 29 Modern Law Review, 149, 150.
12. See *post*, p. 461.
13. Bankruptcy Rules 1952, rr. 229 and r. 230.

The discharge is either:

1. *Unconditional,* which frees the bankrupt at once as from the date of the order.

2. *Conditional,* having the same effect, but subject to conditions as to any future earnings or income or after-acquired property: *e.g.*

    he may be required to set aside for his creditors' benefit so much money each month; or he may be required to consent to judgment being entered against him for a given amount[14].

3. *Suspensive,* which stays the operation of the order till the expiration of a certain time, *e.g.* two years, or until a certain dividend is paid.

4. *Conditional and suspensive.*

Cases where court's discretion is limited.—Where the bankrupt has committed an offence under the Act[15], or any other offence connected with his bankruptcy, or where any of the facts mentioned below are proved, the court cannot grant an unconditional discharge. The discharge must either be:

1. Refused, or

2. Suspended for such period as the court thinks proper (suspension for a nominal period is permissible though in practice this is equivalent to an unconditional discharge), or

3. Suspended until the bankrupt has paid a dividend of 50p. in the £ to the creditors, or

4. Granted, subject to the condition of judgment being entered against the debtor for any part of the unpaid provable debts, such amount to be paid out of future earnings or after-acquired property on such conditions as the court may direct.

In *addition* to one of these four alternatives, the court may include any other conditions which it could impose under the general powers of s. 26, *e.g.* the court may suspend the order for two years *and* then make it conditional on the debtor paying a periodic sum out of future earnings until a particular dividend has been paid[16].

---

14. Execution will not be allowed to issue without the leave of the court (Bankruptcy Act 1914, s. 26 (2) (iv)).

15. *Ibid.*, ss. 154 *et seq.*

16. *Re Tabrisky, Ex parte Board of Trade,* [1947] 2 All E. R. 182; [1947] Ch. 565; *Re Mills, Ex parte Bankrupt* v. *Official Receiver,* [1966] 1 All E. R. 516; [1967] 1 W. L. R. 580.

The facts requiring the court to refuse an immediate unconditional order are as follows:

(i) When the bankrupt's assets are not of a value equal to 50p. in the £ on his unsecured liabilities, unless this has arisen from circumstances for which he cannot justly be held responsible.

(ii) When the bankrupt has omitted to keep such books of account as are usual and proper in the business carried on by him[17], and as sufficiently disclose his business transactions and financial position[18] within the three years immediately preceding his bankruptcy[19].

(iii) When he has continued to trade after knowing himself to be insolvent.

(iv) If he has contracted any debt provable in bankruptcy without having at the time of contracting it any reasonable or probable ground of expectation (proof whereof shall lie of him) of being able to pay it.

(v) If he fails to account satisfactorily for any loss of assets, or deficiency of assets to meet his liabilities.

(vi) If he has brought on or contributed to his bankruptcy by rash and hazardous speculations, or unjustifiable extravagance in living, or by gambling, or by culpable neglect of his business affairs.

(vii) If he has put any of his creditors to unnecessary expense by a frivolous or vexatious defence to any action properly brought against him.

(viii) If he has brought on or contributed to his bankruptcy by incurring unjustifiable expense in bringing any frivolous or vexatious action.

(ix) If he has within three months before the date of the receiving order, when unable to pay his debts as they become due, given an undue preference[20] to any of his creditors.

(x) If within three months before the receiving order, he incurred liabilities with the view of making his assets equal to 50p. in the £ on his unsecured liabilities.

---

17. This is strictly construed and will not apply to speculations outside the business (*Re Mutton* (1887), 18 Q. B. D. 615).
18. And this without the need of long and skilled investigation (*Ex parte Reed and Bowen, Re Reed and Bowen* (1886), 17 Q. B. D. 244).
19. In certain cases where a person has been previously adjudged bankrupt, the failure to keep proper books is an offence. Section 158, as amended by s. 7 of the Bankruptcy (Amendment) Act 1926.
20. Not necessarily a "fraudulent" preference (*Re Bryant*, [1895] 1 Q. B. 420).

(xi) If on any previous occasion he has been adjudged bankrupt, or has made a composition or arrangement with his creditors.

(xii) If he has been guilty of any fraud or fraudulent breach of trust[1].

Certificate of misfortune.—When a person's bankruptcy has been caused by misfortune without any misconduct on his part, the court may grant the discharge with a certificate to that effect, and this frees the bankrupt from certain statutory disqualifications which otherwise prevent him from taking part in a number of public affairs, *e.g.* membership of either House of Parliament, for five years from the date of his discharge[2]. A bankrupt who initiates litigation when he has no prospects of paying the costs if he loses his cases and whose assets are not equal to 50p. in the £ on his unsecured liabilities is not entitled to an immediate discharge from bankruptcy nor to a certificate of misfortune[3].

Effect of discharge.—The effect of discharge is to release the bankrupt (but not his partner, or his surety) from every provable debt, except in the following cases:

1. A debt due on a recognisance or to the Crown[4];
2. Debts incurred for offences against the revenue[4];
3. Debts incurred through fraud, or fraudulent breach of trust;
4. Liabilities under an affiliation order, except to such extent as the court expressly orders[5].

It will not protect him from criminal proceedings.

IV WHAT PROPERTY IS AVAILABLE FOR THE CREDITORS

Subject to a number of exceptions, all property belonging to the debtor vests on adjudication in the trustee and is therefore available for distribution to the creditors. Also available, again subject to exceptions, is all property that may be acquired by or devolve on the bankrupt before his discharge[6]. A fuller examination of the statutory provisions must now be given.

---

1. The making of an ante-nuptial marriage settlement, which is unjustifiable having regard to the state of the settlor's affairs at the time of making it is equivalent to fraud for the purpose of the bankrupt's discharge (Bankruptcy Act 1914, s. 27).
2. Bankruptcy Act 1914, s. 26 (4); Bankruptcy Act 1883, s. 32; Bankruptcy Act 1890, s. 9; Local Government Act 1933, s. 59 (1) (b), and proviso (ii) (b). Should the debtor wish to appeal against refusal of a certificate of misfortune, he must make the official receiver a respondent: *Re Joyce, Ex parte Joyce*, [1955] 2 All E. R. 747; [1955] 1 W. L. R. 800.
3. In *re Wenlock, Times*, May 29, 1968.
4. Unless the Treasury gives its consent in writing.
5. Bankruptcy Act 1914, s. 28.
6. *Ibid.*, s. 38.

1. All property belonging to the bankrupt at the commencement of the bankruptcy

I.e. the date when he committed the act of bankruptcy on which the receiving order was made or, if he is proved to have committed more than one act of bankruptcy, the date of the first of the acts of bankruptcy proved to have been committed within three months of the presentation of the petition. The bankruptcy and the trustee's title are said to *relate back* to such act of bankruptcy[7].

This category of property divisible amongst creditors includes payments to any creditor since that date and the right to bring actions both in contract and in tort. The following limits are suggested[8]:

(i) a right of action arising or a tort resulting immediately in injury to the person, reputation or feelings of the bankrupt, will not pass to the trustee; nor will a right of action for breach of contract similarly resulting (*e.g.* to cure him).

(ii) If the estate is *directly* affected together with the person, the cause of action will be split, and so much of it as relates to the estate will pass to the trustee[9].

(iii) If a bankrupt has been wrongfully dismissed from his employment *after* adjudication, the right to sue for damages remains in him and does not vest in his trustee[10].

The trustee is, under the bankruptcy laws, only statutory assignee of the bankrupt's choses in action, and therefore takes them subject to all equities existing at the date of the commencement of the bankruptcy. Thus, except where the Act expressly allows it, he obtains no better title than the bankrupt had. For example:

if a building contract provides that the building owner may in certain circumstances pay sub-contractors direct, or if the sub-contracts contain an equitable assignment of part of the moneys payable under the main contract, the rights of the trustee of the main contractor are subject to these provisions[11].

Exceptions.—The following property is not available for creditors[12]:

(i) tools of a bankrupt's trade, and the necessary wearing apparel and bedding of himself, his wife and children, to a value, all included, of not more than £20;

---

7. *Ibid.*, s. 37, and see *Re Burrows, Ex parte Official Receiver* v. *Steel*, [1944] Ch. 49 (continuing act of bankruptcy).
8. Williams (18th ed.), pp. 321–322.
9. *Rose* v. *Buckett*, [1901] 2 K. B. 449; *Re Kavanagh, Ex parte The Bankrupt* v. *Jackson (Trustee)*, [1950] 1 All E. R. 39, n. (*prima facie* a lump sum recovered in a compromise will be divided fifty-fifty).
10. *Bailey* v. *Thurston*, [1903] 1 K. B. 137.
11. *Re Tout and Finch, Ltd.*, [1954] 1 All E. R. 127.
12. Bankruptcy Act 1914, s. 38 (1), (2).

(ii) property held on trust for others, if it can be distinguished from the bulk of the bankrupt's property, *i.e.* if it is earmarked[13].

Special Rules must be noted in connection with (a) the rights of execution creditors; (b) protected transactions.

(a) *The rights of execution creditors.*—When execution has issued against the land, goods, or debts of the bankrupt, the execution creditor is not entitled to retain the *benefit of the execution* or attachment unless it is completed by:

(i) the seizure and sale of the goods, or
(ii) seizure or appointment of a receiver over the land, or
(iii) the receipt of the debt[14],

and this before the date of the receiving order and before the execution creditor has notice of any bankruptcy petition or any available act of bankruptcy[15].

In relation to an execution against goods, "the benefit of the execution refers to the charge on the debtor's goods obtained by the execution creditor by the issue of his writ, and does not include any moneys actually received by the creditor in whole or partial satisfaction of his debt, whether under or in consequence of an execution or not. If part of the debt has been discharged by sale or payment, and the execution is still subsisting, a supervening bankruptcy will deprive the creditor of the benefit of the execution in respect of the unpaid balance"[16].

The Act imposes certain duties on a sheriff in relation to goods taken in execution. If previous to sale or completion of the execution by the receipt or recovery of the full amount of the levy, notice is served on the sheriff that a receiving order has been made against the debtor, he must hand over the goods, and any money received in part satisfaction, to the trustee or official receiver on request[17].

Where goods are seized in respect of a judgment exceeding £20, the sheriff must deduct the expenses of execution and retain the balance

---

13. *Re Hallett & Co., Ex parte Blane*, [1894] 2 Q. B. 237.
14. An order for payment out of court is not sufficient (*George* v. *Tompson's Trustee*, [1949] 1 All E. R. 554; [1949] Ch. 322); nor receipt by the creditor's solicitor as stakeholder (*Re Lupkovics*, [1954] 2 All E. R. 125).
15. Bankruptcy Act 1914, s. 40. An execution may be completed by a partial levy followed by a return of *nulla bona* to a subsequent levy (*Re Fairley*, [1922] 2 Ch. 791); or "by the receipt or recovery of the full amount of the levy," s. 41. An execution levied by seizure and sale of the goods of a debtor is not invalid by reason of it being an act of bankruptcy and a person who purchases the goods in good faith under a sale by the sheriff shall acquire a good title to them against the trustee in bankruptcy (s. 40 (3)).
16. *Re Andrew, Ex parte Official Receiver (Trustee) (No. 2)*, [1936] 3 All E. R. 450; [1937] Ch. 122; *Re Love*, [1951] 2 All E. R. 1016; [1952] Ch. 138.
17. Bankruptcy Act 1914, s. 41 (1).

of the proceeds of the sale or of money paid to avoid it[18], for fourteen days; if during that time he is served with notice of a bankruptcy *petition* and a receiving order is made against the debtor thereon or on any other petition of which the sheriff has notice, the sheriff must pay the balance to the official receiver or trustee who is entitled to retain it as against the execution creditor[19].

(b) *Protected transactions.*—Subject to the foregoing provisions of the Act as to the effect of bankruptcy on an execution or attachment, and to the provisions to be examined later with respect to the avoidance of certain settlements, assignments and preferences, any payment by the bankrupt to any of his creditors, any payment or delivery to the bankrupt, and any conveyance by or contract with him for valuable consideration will hold good, provided the transaction takes place before the date of the receiving order, and before any notice to the person dealing with the bankrupt of any "available act of bankruptcy"[20].

A payment made to the bankrupt after the date of the receiving order is not protected, although the person making the payment had no knowledge of the receiving order and could not by any reasonable means have ascertained that it had been made[1]. But the hardship imposed by the above rule on agents and other persons, *e.g.* bankers, in possession of money or property of a bankrupt has to some extent been mitigated. Where such person has paid or transferred the money or property to another person on or after the date of the receiving order without knowledge that it has been made and before it has been gazetted, then, if the transaction is void, the trustee's right to recover from the innocent payer or transferor cannot be enforced except where and so far as the court is satisfied that it is not reasonably practicable to recover from the person to whom the money or property was paid or transferred[2].

A payment of money or delivery of property (*e.g.* on the redemption of securities) to a person who is subsequently adjudged bankrupt is a

---

18. The sale must be public unless the court otherwise orders (Bankruptcy Act 1883, s. 145); this also applies to sales by the registrar of a county court (County Courts Act 1959, s. 132).
19. Bankruptcy Act 1914, s. 41 (2).
20. Bankruptcy Act 1914, s. 45. A past debt may be good consideration for a conveyance by a bankrupt, but if a creditor takes over substantially the whole of a debtor's property in satisfaction for a past debt, knowing that there are other creditors, the transaction will not be protected: *Re Jukes*, [1902] 2 K. B. 58.
1. *Re Wigzell*, [1921] 2 K. B. 835. If, however, a receiving order is made on appeal from the dismissal of a petition and *antedated* to the date when the petition was wrongly dismissed, the "date of the receiving order" for the purposes of s. 45, *ibid.*, is the date on which it was actually made and not the date appearing on the order.
2. Bankruptcy (Amendment) Act 1926, s. 4.

good discharge, although made with notice of an available act of bankruptcy, if made before the actual date of the receiving order in the ordinary course of business or otherwise *bona fide*. Such payment or delivery of property cannot, however, be safely made after notice of the presentation of a bankruptcy petition[3]. This provision enables, *e.g.*, a bank to pay the debtor money it holds on his behalf although the bank know he has committed an act of bankruptcy and thereby may enable the debtor to pay his debts and avert the presentation of a petition[4].

2. **All property acquired by or devolving on the bankrupt before his discharge**

But (*a*) it is important to appreciate that the trustee may only enforce his rights to such property if he intervenes before the bankrupt disposes of it to a *bona fide* transferee for value. All transactions by a bankrupt with anyone dealing with him *bona fide* and for value, in respect of real or personal property, acquired after adjudication are valid against the trustee if completed before the trustee intervenes[5]. It makes no difference that the transferee knows of the bankruptcy.

Ordinary dealings between banker and customer after adjudication are to be deemed transactions for value. But where a banker ascertains that his customer is an undischarged bankrupt he must forthwith inform the trustee or Department of Trade of the existence of the account, and thereafter he must not make any payments out of it except under an order of the court or in accordance with the instructions of the trustee, unless by the expiration of one month from the date of giving the information no instructions have been received from the trustee[6].

(*b*) The trustee has no right to such part of the bankrupt's personal earnings as is necessary for the support of himself and his family[7]. If a bankrupt dies leaving savings out of his personal earnings, the trustee is entitled to the money only subject to the payment of creditors for necessaries supplied since the adjudication and payment to the creditors for funeral expenses after adjudication[8].

---

3. Bankruptcy Act 1914, s. 46. See *Re Dalton (a Bankrupt), Ex parte Herrington and Carmichael (a Firm)* v. *The Trustee*, [1962] 2 All E. R. 499; [1963] Ch. 336.
4. Williams on Bankruptcy (18th ed.), p. 401.
5. Bankruptcy Act 1914, s. 47 (1). The value given need not augment the bankrupt's estate; a settlement on marriage of after-acquired property will be good (*Re Behrend's Trust*, [1911] 1 Ch. 687).
6. Bankruptcy Act 1914, s. 47 (2).
7. *Re Roberts*, [1900] 1 Q. B. 122.
8. *Re Walter*, [1929] 1 Ch. 647.

(*c*) With regard to certain property, the trustee is only entitled to such part of it as may be allotted to him under the provisions of ss. 50 and 51:

    (i) The benefit of a clergyman's stipend does not go to the trustee, but it may be sequestrated[9]. In this event, an amount to be fixed by the bishop must be allowed to the clergyman; and the curate's stipend for services rendered during four months before the date of the receiving order, to an extent not exceeding £50, is payable in priority in full.

    (ii) So much of the salary of an officer[10] or civil servant of the state is obtainable by the trustee in bankruptcy, as the court, with the written consent of the chief officer of the department, may direct, will be paid to the trustee.

    (iii) Where a bankrupt is in receipt of a salary or income, *i.e.* of some income payable at a fixed time, or is entitled to half pay or pension, the court may make an order that such salary or part of it be paid to the trustee[11].

Where a bankrupt wife is in receipt of maintenance under an order of the divorce court, it is salary or income within this section[12].

The expression "income" points to some definite annual payments coming to the bankrupt[13]. Accordingly, it will include sums payable for maintenance to a former wife under an order of the divorce court[14]; but the prospective and contingent earnings of a professional man are not such income, and no part of those earnings can be ordered to be set aside for the benefit of his creditors[15].

3. The capacity to exercise all powers in respect of property which the bankrupt might have exercised for his own benefit

Except the right of nominating to a vacant ecclesiastical benefice[16].

---

9. Bankruptcy Act 1914, s. 50.
10. *Ibid.*, s. 51 (1). An order under this section may be continued on discharge (*Re Gardner, Ex parte Official Receiver* v. *Gardner*, [1942] Ch. 50; [1941] 3 All E. R. 289).
11. Bankruptcy Act 1914, s. 51 (2). See *Re Cohen*, [1961] 1 All E. R. 646; [1961] Ch. 246, it was held that income from the life interest of a bankrupt under his father's will did not come within the word "income." An order under s. 51 (2) was not necessary as the income vested automatically in the trustee in bankruptcy along with the bankrupt's other assets. And see *Re Duckett*, [1964] 1 All E. R. 19; [1964] Ch. 398.
12. *Re Tennant's Application*, [1956] 2 All E. R. 753.
13. See, further, as to the meaning of salary or income (*Re Shine*, [1892] 1 Q. B. 522; *Re Hutton, Ex parte Benwell* (1884), 14 Q. B. D. 301; *Re Landau*, [1934] Ch. 549).
14. *Re Landau, supra.*
15. *Re Hutton, Ex parte Benwell, supra.*
16. Bankruptcy Act 1914, s. 38 (2) (b).

4. **All goods being, at the commencement of the bankruptcy, in the possession, order, or disposition of the bankrupt, in his trade or business, by the consent and permission of the true owner, under such circumstances that he is the reputed owner thereof**

Choses in action, other than debts due or growing due to the bankrupt in the course of his trade or business, are not "goods" within this section[17].

The reputation of ownership may be excluded by a well-known custom, *e.g.*

> hotel furniture is not in the reputed ownership of the bankrupt, since it is well known that such furniture is frequently hired[18].

Where goods are taken by the trustee under this clause, the true owner is entitled to prove for their value[19].

5. Property comprised in certain settlements

(*a*) *Voluntary settlements made before commencement of bankruptcy*[20].—
If a voluntary settlement is not fraudulent and more than ten years have elapsed from the making of it, it is unimpeachable.

If less than ten years but more than two have elapsed, the settlement is voidable[1] by the trustee, unless those claiming under it show:

(i) that the settlor was solvent at the making of the settlement without the aid of the property comprised in it; and

(ii) that the interest of the settlor passed to the trustee of the settlement on the execution thereof.

If it was executed within two years of the commencement of the bankruptcy it is void as against the creditors.

Thus,

> less than two months before the commencement of his bankruptcy, a man paid part of the price of a house which his wife contracted for in her own name and mortgaged in her sole name to raise the rest of the price. The conveyance was also in her sole name.

---

17. Bankruptcy Act 1914, s. 38 (2) (c), which is usually referred to as the "reputed ownership" clause. As to bills of sale, see *ante*, p. 406.
18. *Re Parker*, [1885] 14 Q. B. D. 636.
19. *Re Button*, [1907] 2 K. B. 180.
20. Bankruptcy Act 1914, s. 42 (1). The word "settlement" includes a conveyance of property, and, indeed, any disposition, verbal or not, which is in the nature of a settlement (*Re Vansittart*, [1893] 1 Q. B. 181). This section does not apply to the administration of the estate of deceased insolvents (*Re Gould* (1887), 19 Q. B. D. 92).
1. *Re Brall*, [1893] 2 Q. B. 381; approved *Re Carter and Kenderdine's Contract*, [1897] 1 Ch. 776. As to the deferred right to prove, see p. 489.

Held: the conveyance to the wife was void as against the man's trustee in bankruptcy under s. 42[2].

A gift of personal property—*e.g.* jewellery—will be a settlement within this section, if although there is no restriction on the donee's power of alienation, yet the intention was that the donee should use or retain the property for an indefinite time[3]; but a gift of money which is not intended to be retained, but to be employed in a business, not itself settled, cannot be avoided as a "settlement," if the money has been so employed or spent[4].

The following settlements are excepted from the operation of s. 42 (1); viz.:

(i) a settlement made before and in consideration of marriage;
(ii) a settlement made in favour of a *bona fide* purchaser or incumbrancer for value; or
(iii) a post-nuptial settlement on a wife or children of property which has accrued to the settlor in right of his wife. This includes property to which a husband becomes entitled on the death of his wife intestate, so that a settlement, within two years of his bankruptcy, of such property on a child of the marriage is valid[5].

(*b*) *Contracts for future settlements.*—A covenant made in consideration of the settlor's marriage for the benefit of his spouse or children for the future payment of money or settlement of property in which at the date of the marriage the settlor had no interest is void against the trustee if the settlor is adjudged bankrupt, unless the covenant has been executed before the commencement of bankruptcy. Further, transfers under any covenant to make future payments or a settlement will be void unless

(i) made more than two years before the bankruptcy, or
(ii) at a time when the settlor was able to pay his debts without the aid of the money paid or property transferred, or
(iii) the payment or transfer was made in pursuance of a covenant to pay or transfer money or property expected to come from a person named in the covenant was made within three months after it comes into the possession of the settlor[6].

(*c*) *Assignments of book debts.*—A general assignment of book debts by a person engaged in trade or business is void against the trustee as

---

2. *Re a Debtor, Ex parte Official Receiver, Trustee of the Property of the Debtor* v. *Morrison,* [1965] 3 All E. R. 453; [1965] 1 W. L. R. 1498.
3. *Re Tankard,* [1899] 2 Q. B. 57.
4. *Re Plummer,* [1900] 2 Q. B. 790.
5. *Re Bower Williams,* [1927] All E. R. Rep. 275; [1927] 1 Ch. 441.
6. Bankruptcy Act 1914, s. 42 (2), (3).

to any debts not paid at the commencement of the bankruptcy, unless it has been registered as if it were a bill of sale. This provision does not apply to debts due from specific debtors or growing due under specific contracts, or to book debts included in a transfer of a business made *bona fide* and for value, or to debts included in any assignment for the benefit of creditors generally[7].

6. Property used to give a fraudulent preference to any creditor

If a person unable to pay his debts when they become due within *six* months[8] before the presentation of a bankruptcy petition upon which he is adjudged bankrupt, with a *view to prefer* a creditor, or any surety for the debt due to such creditor[9], transfers property to that creditor, pays the debt, or allows his property to be taken for the debt, he has made a fraudulent preference, which is void against the trustee in bankruptcy, to whom the creditor must return the property or money. Preference must be the "dominant" intention[10] and "with a view to prefer" means with the intention of preferring though the intention can be inferred from the circumstances[11].

The word "preference" implies an act of free will, and therefore any facts showing that the advantage given to the creditor was not voluntary will be entitled to great weight. Thus,

(i) pressure by the creditor, especially where it involves a threat of legal proceedings, has been held to negative a fraudulent preference[12].

(ii) A mistaken apprehension that legal proceedings would be taken negatives a fraudulent preference[13].

(iii) So also if the debtor's object was to shield himself against the possibility of criminal proceedings for breach of trust[14].

(iv) And even a desire upon the debtor's part to repair a wrong that he has committed (*e.g.* a breach of trust), though the breach was at the time only known to himself, has been treated as warranting the conclusion that there was no view to prefer[15].

---

7. *Ibid.*, s. 43.
8. Bankruptcy Act 1914, s. 44 (1), amended by the Companies Act 1947, s. 115 (3).
9. A person who merely deposits documents to secure another's debt without assuming any liability to pay the debt is a "surety" within the meaning of the section (*Re Conley*, [1938] 2 All E. R. 127).
10. *Peat* v. *Gresham Trust, Ltd.*, [1934] All E. R. Rep. 82; [1934] A. C. 252.
11. *Pe Eric Holmes (Property)*, [1965] 2 All E. R. 333; [1965] Ch. 1052.
12. *Ex parte Taylor* (1886), 18 Q. B. D. 295; C. & T., p. 357.
13. *Thompson* v. *Freeman* (1786), 1 T. R. 155.
14. *Sharp* v. *Jackson*, [1899] A. C. 415.
15. *Re Lake*, [1901] 1 Q. B. 710.

An example of the facts from which the intent to prefer may be inferred is *Re Kushler (M.), Ltd.*[16],

A director had guaranteed the overdraft of a private company. He was advised that it was insolvent. From then on payments were made to the bank till the overdraft was cleared off. No substantial trade creditor had been paid during that period. The bank had not been pressing, though a creditor had. The fact that the overdraft was guaranteed by the director was concealed at a meeting of creditors. It was held that the intention to prefer the director was proved.

The rights of a third person who for value and *bona fide* has obtained the bankrupt's property from such creditor, are not affected.

Fraudulent Transfer of Property.—By s. 172 of the Law of Property Act 1925, already referred to, a transfer of property made with intent to defraud creditors to the knowledge of all parties concerned in the transaction can be set aside at the instance of anyone thereby prejudiced.

V CONTROL OVER THE PROPERTY AND PERSON OF THE DEBTOR

After a receiving order has been made the court may, on the application of the official receiver or the trustee, order any of the following to come before it and be examined on oath concerning the debtor, his dealings, or property:

1. The debtor[17],
2. His wife,
3. Any person known or suspected to have in his possession property of the debtor, or supposed to be indebted to him; or
4. Any person deemed capable of giving information respecting the debtor, his dealings or property[18].

These persons may be required to produce any relevant documents in their custody or power. If any person on examination admits that he is indebted to the debtor or in possession of property belonging to him, an immediate order may be made for payment of the debt or delivery up of the property.

The debtor must give such inventory of his property, such lists of his creditors and debtors, and generally do all such acts in relation to

---

16. [1943] Ch. 248; [1943] 2 All E. R. 22. And see *Re Cutts*, [1956] 2 All E. R. 537.
17. A bankrupt may be examined even after his discharge has become effective (*Re Coulson*, [1934] 1 Ch. 45); *In re a Debtor (No. 12 of 1958), Re Ex parte Trustee of Property of the Debtor v. Clegg*, [1968] 2 All E. R. 425.
18. Bankruptcy Act 1914, s. 25.

his property and the distribution of the proceeds as may reasonably be required by the official receiver or trustee[19].

The Debtors Act of 1869 abolished imprisonment for debt, except in certain cases[20]; but under the law of bankruptcy the court may order arrest of the debtor and seizure of his books and papers, if a bankruptcy notice has been issued[1], or if a petition has been filed, and if there is reason to believe that the debtor has absconded or is about to abscond, with the view:

1. Of avoiding payment, or
2. Of avoiding service of or appearance to any petition, or
3. Of avoiding examination as to his affairs, or
4. Of otherwise avoiding, embarrassing, or delaying bankruptcy proceedings against him[2].

He may also be arrested:

5. If, after presentation of a bankruptcy petition, there is probable ground for believing that he intends to remove, conceal, or destroy his papers or property[3]; or
6. If after service of a bankruptcy petition he removes any goods above the value of £5, without the leave of the trustee or of the official receiver[4]; or
7. If he fails without due cause to attend any examination ordered by the court[5].

VI OFFICERS

The administration of the estates of bankrupts is now under the control of the court and Department of Trade, and subject to such control there are several classes of officers; *e.g.*

1. Official receivers.
2. Special managers.
3. Trustees.

---

19. *Ibid.*, s. 22.
20. See the Debtors Act 1869, ss. 4, 5; County Courts Act 1959, s. 144 and Administration of Justice Act 1970, s. 11.
1. The notice must be served before or at the time of the arrest (Bankruptcy Act 1914, s. 23).
2. *Ibid.*, s. 23 (1) (a).
3. *Ibid.*, s. 23 (1) (b).
4. *Ibid.*, s. 23 (1) (c).
5. Bankruptcy Act 1914, s. 23 (1) (d).

I. The Official Receiver

Appointment.—He is an official appointed by the Department of Trade but is also an officer of the court to which he is attached[6]. On the making of the receiving order it becomes his duty to receive the bankrupt's property until the appointment of a trustee. It is not usual to nominate a separate receiver for each estate, the practice being to appoint a receiver, who acts in all bankruptcies within a given district. The Department of Trade may at any time appoint a deputy or a temporary receiver, and it has power to remove any person whom it has appointed[7].

His duties are

1. With regard to the debtor's conduct, to report thereon, stating whether anything has occurred which should guide the court as to making an order on the debtor's application for discharge. He should take part in the public examination[8];
2. As regards the property, he must see that the proper statement of affairs is made;
3. He must act as trustee[9] during any vacancy in the office of trustee;
4. He must summon and preside at the first meeting of creditors, and must issue forms of proxy;
5. He may appoint a special manager, and may remove him;
6. He must advertise the receiving order, the date of the creditors' first meeting and of the debtor's public examination;
7. He must report to the creditors on any proposal made by the debtor to liquidate his affairs.

His powers as receiver are such as are possessed by a receiver and manager appointed by the High Court[10].

II. Special Manager[11]

A special manager is a person whose duty it is to manage the business until a trustee is appointed. The appointment is made by the official receiver if he is satisfied that the nature of the bankrupt's business requires it and if asked to do so by any creditor. Such manager must

---

6. The official receiver has been described as being in fact "a somewhat impersonal entity . . . an emanation of a department rather than a specific individual" (*per* EVERSHED, M.R., in *Re a Debtor (No. 416 of 1940)*, [1950] Ch. 423, at p. 428, C. A.). He is entitled to no privileges beyond those of an ordinary trustee: *ibid.*
7. Bankruptcy Act 1914, ss. 70, 71.   8. *Ibid.*, s. 73.
9. And as such can sell the property (*Ex parte Turquand* (1886), 11 App. Cas. 286).
10. Bankruptcy Act 1914, s. 74 (2).
11. *Ibid.*, s. 10; Bankruptcy Rules 1952, rr. 319, 353, 354.

give security to the satisfaction of the Department of Trade, and he may receive remuneration at such rate as the creditors by ordinary resolution may fix, or in default of this as the Department of Trade may determine. His powers are such as are entrusted to him by the official receiver to whom he accounts. He may be removed if the official receiver considers his services unnecessary and he must be removed if the creditors pass a special resolution.

III. The Trustee

Appointment.—He may be appointed:
1. By the creditors by ordinary resolution[12] at any of their meetings[13], after the debtor has been adjudged bankrupt, or the creditors have resolved that he be so;
2. By the committee of inspection[14] after the debtor has been adjudged bankrupt, and the creditors decide to leave the choice to that body;
3. By the Department of Trade, if the creditors do not appoint within four weeks of the adjudication, or within seven days of the failure of negotiations relating to a composition, or within three weeks of a vacancy. But the trustee chosen by the Department ceases to hold office if the creditors subsequently take a trustee of their own choosing[15].

The official receiver must not be trustee except in the following cases[16]:
1. Where there is a vacancy in the trusteeship, then he acts until a new trustee is appointed[17];
2. Where the value of the estate is not likely to exceed £300[18];
3. Where the estate is that of a deceased insolvent[19].

Certificate of appointment.—The appointment of a trustee is not complete until the Department of Trade has given a certificate of appointment, and this is not obtained until the trustee has given security for the due performance of his duties[20]. The security must be given to some person appointed by the Department of Trade, which fixes the amount and nature of such security, and may from time to time increase or diminish the amount[1].

---

12. *I.e.* a majority in value of those present, and voting either in person or by proxy.
13. Bankruptcy Act 1914, s. 19 (1).
14. *Post*, pp. 475–476, and s. 19 (1).
15 Bankruptcy Act 1914, ss. 19 (6), (7), 78.
16. *Ibid.*, s. 19 (5).
17. *Ibid.*, ss. 53 (1), 74 (1) (g), 78.
18. *Ibid.*, s. 129 (1).
19. *Ibid.*, s.130 (4).
20. *Ibid.*, s. 19 (2), (4).
1. Bankruptcy Rules 1952, r. 355.

When that has been given, the certificate of appointment will, unless there is ground for objecting to the trustee, be granted, and the appointment takes effect as from that date[2]; the certificate is conclusive evidence of the appointment[3]. The Department may refuse the certificate if:

1. The trustee was not elected *bona fide*;
2. If he is unfit to act, *e.g.* if he has been previously removed from the office of trustee of a bankrupt's property for misconduct;
3. If his connection with the bankrupt or his estate, or any creditor, makes it difficult for him to be impartial[4].

If the certificate is refused the Department must, on the demand of a majority in value of creditors, signify the fact and the grounds thereof to the High Court and the validity of the refusal may be then tried[5].

The appointment must be advertised in the *London Gazette* and in a local paper; the cost is payable by the trustee, but he may recoup himself out of the estate[6].

Any number of trustees may be appointed[7], but it is usual to select one person only, who may be a creditor or not, as may seem best.

Determination of the appointment

The trustee will cease to be such in the following cases:

1. If he resigns. He should call a meeting of the creditors, and give seven days' notice of the meeting to the official receiver[8]. The meeting has power to accept or refuse the resignation.
2. If he is removed. This may be at the instance of the creditors; to obtain the removal, a meeting, of which seven days' notice should be given, must, at the request of one-sixth in value of the creditors, be specially called by a member of the committee of inspection, or by the official receiver (on a deposit of costs), and an ordinary resolution for removal must be carried[9].

   The Department of Trade also has power to remove a trustee if of opinion

   (i) that he is guilty of misconduct or fails to perform his duties, or
   (ii) that the trusteeship is being needlessly protracted without probable advantage to creditors, or

---

2. Bankruptcy Act 1914, s. 19 (4). 3. *Ibid.*, s. 143.
4. Bankruptcy Act 1914, s. 19 (1), (2). 5. *Ibid.*, s. 19 (3).
6. Bankruptcy Rules 1952, r. 331. 7. Bankruptcy Act 1914, s. 77.
8. Bankruptcy Rules 1952, r. 340.
9. Bankruptcy Act 1914, s. 95 (1); Bankruptcy Rules 1952, r. 345.

(iii) that by reason of mental disorder, continued sickness, or absence he is incapable of performing his duties, or

(iv) that through his connection with or relation to the bankrupt, the bankrupt's estate or a particular creditor, it might be difficult for him to act impartially

or where in any other matter he has been removed from office, but if the creditors by ordinary resolution disapprove of his removal, he or they may appeal to the High Court[10].

3. If a receiving order in bankruptcy has been made against him[11].

4. If he has been released by the Department of Trade[12]. When the estate has been fully realised, or on resignation, or removal, a trustee may, if he wishes, apply for his *release*. This is granted by the Department after a proper investigation has been made into his accounts, and after due notice has been given to the debtor and creditors. Its effect is to free the trustee with regard to all matters done during his trusteeship in his official capacity; but it is revocable on proof of fraud or of material concealment[13]. Appeal against refusal of release lies to the High Court.

The committee of inspection

It will be convenient here to state the nature and functions of this body.

It is a committee, consisting of from three to five persons, appointed by the creditors at the first or a subsequent meeting from amongst the creditors qualified to vote or persons who hold general proxies or powers of attorney from such creditors, or to whom a creditor intends to give a general proxy or power of attorney[14]; but no creditor or holder of a general proxy or power of attorney can act as a member of the committee until the creditor has proved his debt and the proof has been admitted.

A member of the committee is in a fiduciary position, and like any other trustee, he must not purchase any part of the estate or derive

---

10. Bankruptcy Act 1914, s. 95 (2).
11. *Ibid.*, s. 94.
12. *Ibid.*, s. 93 (5). The Board of Trade may also remove the trustee for failure to keep up his security (Bankruptcy Rules 1952, r. 338).
13. Bankruptcy Act 1914, s. 93; Bankruptcy Rules 1952, rr. 341–345.
14. These persons cannot *act* until they hold the proxy or power of attorney (Bankruptcy Act 1914, s. 20 (2) (b)).

any profit from any transaction arising out of the bankruptcy, except by leave of the court[15].

The Committee's duty is to supervise the trustee, and to superintend the general administration of the estate. For certain acts the trustee requires its approval[16]. It audits his books[17]. It may act by a majority of the members present at a meeting, and a majority of its members forms a quorum.

A member ceases to be such:

1. When he resigns by delivery of written notice to the trustee;
2. If he becomes bankrupt or compounds with his creditors;
3. If he is removed by ordinary resolution of the creditors carried at a meeting, seven days' notice of intention to hold which has been given;
4. If he is absent from five consecutive meetings[18].

It is not necessary that a committee should be appointed, and if there is none, the trustee may obtain sanction from the Department of Trade for the exercise of the powers in respect of which he is required to get the permission of the committee[18].

Duties of a trustee

From the date of the adjudication and until the appointment of a trustee, and during any vacancy in the trusteeship, the official receiver is trustee for the purposes of the Act. The trustee when appointed takes the property and when there are resignations and new appointments it passes from trustee to trustee. No conveyance is necessary; the certificate of appointment is sufficient evidence of ownership[19]. In general terms, the trustee's duty is:

1. To realise the estate to the best advantage, and to distribute it as quickly as possible;
2. To have regard to the resolutions of the creditors, and to the orders of the Department of Trade; and
3. To make no profit in any way except what may be specially allowed him as remuneration.

With regard to the bankrupt's property:

1. The trustee must not directly or indirectly purchase the estate, nor may he make a profit out of it.

---

15. Bankruptcy Rules 1952, rr. 349, 350 (2); *Re Bulmer, Ex parte Greaves,* [1937] 1 All E. R. 323; [1937] Ch. 499.
16. See p. 479, *post.*
17. See p. 481, *post.*
18. Bankruptcy Act 1914, s. 20 (10).
19. *Ibid.,* s. 53.

2. The trustee must collect debts and take possession of the estate, real and personal.

3. He may transfer choses in action, stock, shares in ships, and shares and property of the like nature to the same extent as the bankrupt might have done[20].

Disclaimer of onerous property[1]

This is the formal notification by the trustee of his refusal to accept the ownership of onerous property. With regard to any property consisting of land burdened with onerous covenants, unprofitable contracts, shares or stock in companies, or of any other property unsaleable or saleable only with difficulty owing to its burdens, the trustee may disclaim the property; but

1. The disclaimer must be in writing and signed by the trustee. It need not be made by deed[2].

2. It must take place within twelve months after the first appointment of a trustee; or, if he has no knowledge of the property within a month of his appointment, then within twelve months of his acquiring the knowledge[3].

3. If the property consists of leaseholds he must obtain leave of the court, unless the property has not been sublet or mortgaged; and either:

   (i) its value is under £20 per annum; or
   (ii) the estate is being administered summarily; or
   (iii) the lessor does not bring the matter before the court within seven days of being served with notice of the trustee's intention to disclaim.

   If the property has been sublet or mortgaged he must apply to the court for leave to disclaim, unless notice having been served on the lessor, mortgagee, or sub-lessee, none of them within fourteen days requires the matter to be brought before the court[4].

A person interested may make written application to the trustee, requiring him to decide whether he will disclaim or not, and in the event of no disclaimer within twenty-eight days the right is gone, and

---

20. Bankruptcy Act 1914, s. 48.
1. *Ibid.*, s. 54.
2. Law of Property Act 1925, s. 52 (1), (2) (b).
3. Bankruptcy Act 1914, s. 54 (1). The Official Receiver acting as trustee during a vacancy has an independent right to disclaim even if the trustee's time has expired: s. 54 (7). The court can extend the time of a trustee but not of the official receiver (*Re A Debtor (No. 416 of 1940)*, [1950] 1 All E. R. 1085; [1950] Ch. 423, C. A.).
4. Bankruptcy Act 1914, s. 54 (3) and Bankruptcy Rules 1952, r. 278.

the trustee may in consequence become personally liable in respect of the property[5].

Effect.—The effect of the disclaimer is to release the bankrupt and the estate from any liability in respect of the property from the date of the disclaimer, and to discharge the trustee from personal liability, notwithstanding previous acts of ownership[6]; but it will not release a trustee from personal liability to pay rates incurred by his voluntary occupation of the premises disclaimed[7].

A trustee is bound specifically to perform a contract for the sale of real estate for valuable consideration to the same extent as the bankrupt could have been compelled to carry it out[8]. He cannot disclaim the contract so as to defeat the equitable interest vested in the purchaser under the contract[9].

Persons injured by disclaimer.—If they have an interest in the property, they may apply to the court, and get an order vesting it in themselves. If the person is an underlessee or a mortgagee by demise of a lease, the order will make the person taking it subject to the bankrupt's liabilities in connection with the property, or if in the particular case the court thinks fit, subject to the liabilities of an assignee of the bankrupt's interest therein. If the underlessee or mortgagee declines to take a vesting order upon the terms offered by the court, he will be excluded from all interest in the property[10]. In any case, a loss caused by disclaimer is a provable debt[11].

Rescission of contracts.—Any person who is, against the trustee, entitled to the benefit or subject to the burden of a contract made with the bankrupt, may apply to the court for its rescission and the court may rescind such contract on such terms as it thinks equitable. Damages may be awarded to either party and the creditor may prove for these against the estate[12].

Powers of the trustee

On his own responsibility the trustee may do the following:

1. Sell all or any of the bankrupt's property by public or private sale, and may transfer the portions sold to the purchaser[13];

---

5. Bankruptcy Act 1914, s. 54 (4).   6. *Ibid.*, s. 54 (2).
7. *Re Lister*, [1926] Ch. 149.
8. *Ex parte Holthausen* (1874), L. R. 9. Ch. 722.
9. *Re Bastable*, [1901] 2 K. B. 518.
10. Bankruptcy Act 1914, s. 54 (6); and see *Re Carter and Ellis*, [1905] 1 K. B. 735.
11. *Ibid.*, s. 54 (8).   12. *Ibid.*, s. 54 (5).
13. A sole trustee in bankruptcy, being a "trust corporation" in relation to the bankrupt's property, can convey the legal estate in land so as to override certain "equitable interests." Law of Property Act 1925, s. 2; Law of Property (Amendment) Act 1926, s. 3 (1), and Schedule amending s. 2 of the principal Act; Trustee Act 1925, s. 14 (2).

and the trustee is not personally liable for selling goods which are on the debtor's premises, or in his possession, if he does so without negligence and without notice that the goods belong to a third person[14];

2. Give receipts which effectually discharge the person paying;
3. Prove for and draw dividends to which the bankrupt is entitled;
4. Exercise any power given him by the Act, and execute instruments necessary for carrying it out;
5. Deal with property of which the bankrupt is tenant-in-tail, just as could the bankrupt himself[15].

With the permission of the committee of inspection (or if none, the Department of Trade[16]), he may exercise more extended powers; viz. he may:

1. Carry on the business, so far as is necessary for the beneficial winding up of the estate;
2. Bring or defend actions relating to the property;
3. Employ a solicitor or agent to do any particular act;
4. Agree to accept a future payment for property sold, subject to such security as the committee think fit;
5. Mortgage or pledge the property to raise money for the payment of debts;
6. Compromise claims, whether by or against the bankrupt, and refer disputes to arbitration;
7. Divide in its existing form amongst creditors such property as from its nature is not readily or advantageously capable of sale.

In no case must the permission be general; it is requisite for each particular act desired to be done[17].

8. Appoint the bankrupt to carry on his trade for the benefit of his creditors[18];
9. Make an allowance to the bankrupt out of his property for the support of himself and his family or in consideration of services if engaged in winding-up his estate, but any such allowance may be reduced by the court[19].

In every case the wishes of the general body of creditors must be regarded, when such wish is properly and regularly expressed[20]. It

---

14. Bankruptcy Act 1914, s. 61.
15. Bankruptcy Act 1914, s. 55.
16. *Ibid.*, s. 20 (10).
17. *Ibid.*, s. 56.
18. *Ibid.*, s. 57.
19. *Ibid.*, s. 58.
20. *Ibid.*, s. 79 (1).

must be remembered that the assistance of the court may always be invoked against a trustee who is exceeding his powers, or who is exercising them improperly.

Appeal against acts of trustee

If the bankrupt or any of the creditors or any other person is aggrieved by any act or decision of the trustee he may apply to the court which may make such order as it thinks just[1]. The bankrupt himself can only apply to the court if he can show that there will or might be a surplus. Nor can he in the absence of fraud interfere in the day to day administration of the estate or question the exercise by the trustee in good faith of his discretion. Thus if a trustee in good faith decides to admit a disputed claim by a creditor, the bankrupt has no right to object[2].

Trustee's obligation to account

1. *List of creditors.*—If required by any creditor to do so, the trustee must furnish a list of creditors showing the amount of the debt of each creditor[3].

2. *Statement of accounts.*—If required by one-sixth of the creditors, the trustee must furnish a statement of accounts up to the date of such notice[4].

3. *Books to be kept.*—The trustee must keep the following books[5]:

   (*a*) A record book. This will contain an account of all proceedings and information necessary to furnish an accurate record of his administration, *e.g.* resolutions of creditors[6].

   (*b*) A cash book. This must contain the receipts and payments as made from day to day, except those falling under the next head[7].

   (*c*) A trading account book where the trustee is carrying on the debtor's business; it must contain an account of receipts and payments, of which the total weekly amount must be incorporated in the cash book; once in each month it should be verified by affidavit, and be certified by the committee of inspection, or by some member thereof deputed to do it by the committee[8].

---

1. *Ibid.*, s. 80.
2. *Re A Debtor, Ex parte The Debtor* v. *Dodwell (Trustee)*, [1949] 1 All E. R. 510; [1949] Ch. 236.
3. Bankruptcy Act 1914, s. 84.
4. *Ibid.*, s. 85.
5. *Ibid.*, s. 86.
6. Bankruptcy Rules 1952, r. 362.
7. *Ibid.*, r. 363.
8. Bankruptcy Rules 1952, r. 364.

4. *Submission to audit.*—The accounts are audited by two separate bodies, by the committee of inspection, and by the Department of Trade. The committee must see all books and vouchers at least once in every three months, but it may require them at any time; at the close of each audit, it must enter and sign a dated certificate in the Cash Book[9].

The Department of Trade inspects and audits the accounts every six months from the date of the receiving order until the debtor's release, and to enable this to be done, the trustee must send in the vouchers, the certificates of the committee, and a duplicate of the cash book; the audited copy is returned to the Registrar of the court and filed[10]. If the trustee has received nothing and made no payments since the last audit, he must send to the Department of Trade an affidavit to that effect[11].

When the trustee sends his first account, he must further enclose a copy of the debtor's statement of affairs, marking the amounts realised in red, and explaining the non-realisation of the remaining assets. When property is sold through an auctioneer or other agent, the gross amount obtained must be entered, the expenses being allowed on the other side[12].

5. *Annual statement.*—At least once a year the trustee must submit a statement to the Department of Trade showing the proceedings in the bankruptcy up to the date of statement[13].

6. *Receipt and payment of money.*—The trustee must not pay any sums received by him as trustee into his private banking account[14], and if he retains for more than ten days a sum exceeding £50 without the authority of the Department of Trade, he makes himself liable to severe penalties[15]. It should be paid into the Bankruptcy Estates Account kept by the Department of Trade at the Bank of England and a receipt from the Department of Trade should be obtained by the trustee[16]. Any balance in the Bankruptcy Estates Account which the Department considers is not required for the purposes of bankrupts' estates is transferred, under the Insolvency Services (Accounting and Investments) Act 1970, to the Insolvency Services Investments Account and dealt with according to the provisions of this Act.

In some cases money may be left at a local bank. Thus, when a

---

9. *Ibid.*, rr. 367, 368; Form 187.
10. Bankruptcy Act 1914, s. 92; Bankruptcy Rules 1952, rr. 369, 370.
11. *Ibid.*, r. 369.
12. Rr. 369 (2), 372.
13. Bankruptcy Act 1914, s. 87.
14. *Ibid.*, s. 88.
15. *Ibid.*, s. 89 (5).
16. *Ibid.*, s. 89 (2).

debtor has an account at any bank, it is usually kept open for seven days after the first meeting of creditors; and the general funds of the estate may be paid into and out of a local bank, if the trustee, on the application of the committee of inspection, gets permission from the Department of Trade; or where there is no committee, if the Department of Trade for special reasons authorises the trustee to keep a local banking account. All moneys received should be at once paid into this account; all payments out must be made by cheques to order, every cheque must be marked with the name of the estate, and signed by the trustee, by one member of the committee, and, if thought desirable, by one other person specially appointed[17].

Trustee's remuneration

This is settled by the creditors, or by the committee of inspection, if the creditors so resolve. In three cases the Department of Trade will fix the amount, viz.:

1. When a fourth in value or number of the creditors dissent from the amount fixed by the others,
2. When the bankrupt satisfies the Department that the remuneration given is unreasonably large[18], or
3. When the trustee was appointed by the Department of Trade.

The payment must take the form of a percentage partly on the amount realised by the trustee, partly on the amount distributed in dividend[19]. The resolution should state what expenses the remuneration is to cover; if the trustee receives no remuneration, reasonable expenses may be allowed, to be fixed by the creditors, with the sanction of the Department of Trade[20].

The trustee must not under any circumstances make an arrangement to accept remuneration from the bankrupt, or any solicitor, or other person employed about the bankruptcy, nor may he make any arrangement for sharing his remuneration with such persons[1]. An agreement with creditors under which the latter are to receive part of the trustee's remuneration in augmentation of their dividends is a fraud upon the bankruptcy laws and illegal[2].

---

17. *Ibid.*, s. 89, and Bankruptcy Rules 1952, r. 346. See *Re Walker* (deceased), [1972] 1 All E. R. 1096; [1972] 2 W. L. R. 1015: Department of Trade *held* entitled to refuse to authorise a local bank account although such account would have enabled interest to be earned on the £36,000 balance.
18. Bankruptcy Act 1914, s. 82 (1), (2).
19. Bankruptcy Act 1914, s. 82 (1); Bankruptcy Rules 1952, r. 335.
20. Bankruptcy Act 1914, s. 82 (4).
1. *Ibid.*, s. 82 (5).
2. *Farmer's Mart, Ltd.* v. *Milne*, [1915] A, C, 106.

VII DISTRIBUTION OF THE PROPERTY

Generally speaking, a trustee's duty under this head is to pay various costs and charges and then to distribute what is left among the creditors who prove their debts. As will be seen, some creditors are preferred over others, and before any creditor can be paid he must *prove* his debt as soon as possible after the making of the receiving order by sending particulars of the debt and an affidavit verifying the particulars to the trustee. The form of proof and the duties of the trustee when he receives it are examined below.

Costs and charges[3]

These are payable in a certain order, each being entitled to payment in full in the order in which they are listed. Amongst the more ordinary expenses, grouped as they are entitled to payment, are:

1. Actual expense of the official receiver incurred in protecting the assets of the debtor, or incurred by him or by his authority in carrying on the business, including the costs of shorthand notes taken at the instance of the official receiver;
2. Certain fees, percentages and charges payable under the Scale of Fees;
3. The petitioning creditor's deposit;
4. The remuneration of the special manager (if any);
5. .The taxed costs of the petitioner;
6. Subsistence allowance made to the debtor by the official receiver[4];
7. Trustee's disbursements;
8. Allowance to the debtor by the trustee[5];
9. Trustee's remuneration;
10. Necessary out-of-pocket expenses of the committee of inspection subject to the approval of the Department of Trade.

Provable debts

A creditor may prove for all debts and liabilities, present or future, certain or contingent, to which the debtor is subject at the date of the receiving order, or to which he may become subject before his discharge by reason of any obligation incurred before the date of the receiving order[6]. Thus, in *Hardy* v. *Fothergill*[7]:

---

3. Bankruptcy Rules 1952, rr. 115, 116.
4. Bankruptcy Rules 1952, r. 313, giving the official receiver this power is supplementary to the power conferred on the trustee by the Bankruptcy Act 1914, s. 58.
5. Bankruptcy Act 1914, s. 58.
6. *Ibid.*, s. 30 (3).
7. (1888), 13 App. Cas. 351.

Held that the future contingent liability of the assignee of a lease on a covenant to indemnify the lessee is provable unless the lessee obtains a court order that it is a liability incapable of estimation.

A contingent claim must be estimated by the trustee (subject to appeal to the court). If no estimate is possible, the court may on application declare the debt not provable[8].

The following debts are not provable[9]:

1. Demands in the nature of unliquidated damages not arising from a contract, promise, or breach of trust—claims for damages in tort are therefore excluded;
2. Debts contracted by the debtor after knowledge by the creditor of an available act of bankruptcy;
3. Debts contracted after the receiving order;
4. Debts the value of which cannot fairly be estimated. Arrears under a maintenance order have been held to be in this category as the court has a discretion whether or not to enforce them[10].

Preferential debts

The following debts are given priority in bankruptcy[11]:

(i) Parochial and local rates and purchase tax due within the year preceding the date of the receiving order and assessed taxes, land tax and income tax assessed up to April 5th preceding the same date, but not exceeding the amount due for one year. Sums due within the year preceding the relevant date from a bankrupt employer who has deducted P.A.Y.E. but not paid these sums to the Inland Revenue are also preferred[12].

(ii) Wages or salary of any clerk or servant[13], workman or labourer not exceeding £200[14], for services rendered during four months before the receiving order.

---

8. Bankruptcy Act 1914, s. 30 (4), (5), (6).
9. *Ibid.*, s. 30 (1), (2), (6).
10. *James* v. *James*, [1963] 2 All E. R. 465. In consequence, the wife may take proceedings before the magistrates to compel payment without leave of the bankruptcy court.
11. Bankruptcy Act 1914, s. 33.
12. Finance Act 1952, s. 30 (2).
13. The managing director of a company is not a "clerk or servant" within the meaning of this section (*Re Newspaper Proprietary Syndicate, Ltd.,* [1900] 2 Ch. 349).
14. The limit of £200 does not apply to a labourer in husbandry who has contracted for payment in a lump sum at the end of the year of hiring. Persons who have lent money to pay salaries or wages do not stand in the shoes of those who would otherwise have been preferred creditors (Williams on Bankruptcy, 18th ed, p. 228). This contrasts with the priority given to such persons in the winding up of a company by s. 319 (4) of the Companies Act 1948.

(iii) "Accrued holiday remuneration," *i.e.* sums which would have been paid in the normal course to a clerk, servant, workman or labourer had his employment continued until he became entitled to a holiday[15].

(iv) National insurance and pensions contributions payable by statute during the twelve months before the date of the receiving order.

These preferential debts rank equally between themselves and must be paid in full unless the bankrupt's property is insufficient to meet them, in which case they abate in equal proportions between themselves[16]. No composition or scheme will be approved by the court which does not provide for payment in priority of all these preferential debts[17].

The Crown is bound by the provisions of section 33, and has no claim to priority of payment except in respect of the debts mentioned therein[18].

Deceased persons.—The section also applies in the case of a deceased person dying insolvent, the date of his death being substituted for the date of the receiving order[19], but the priority over all other debts given by s. 130 (6) to the payment of funeral and testamentary expenses is not affected.

Apprentices.—An apprentice or articled clerk, who has paid a fee to the master, may, on the latter's bankruptcy, obtain a return of money, varying in amount, according to the time which has elapsed since he entered the service at the trustee's discretion (subject to appeal to the court); or the trustee may, with the apprentice's consent, transfer the indenture of apprenticeship or articles of agreement to some other person[20].

Friendly Societies.—A registered society has by the Friendly Societies Act 1896, s. 35, a preferential right as regards any claims for money or property *virtute officii* in the hands of any of its officers, if such officer becomes bankrupt. The right remains, although the moneys cannot be traced and are no longer in the officer's possession[1], and although he ceased to be such officer before his bankruptcy[2]. Such a

15. Companies Act 1947, ss. 91 and 115.
16. Bankruptcy Act 1914, s. 33 (2).
17. *Ibid.*, s. 16 (19).
18. *Ibid.*, s. 151 *and see Food Controller* v. *Cork*, [1923] A. C. 647.
19. *Ibid.*, s. 33 (5).
20. *Ibid.*, s. 34. Alternatively, a solicitor's articled clerk may apply to the High Court to discharge his articles or to order them to be transferred to another solicitor upon such terms and in such manner as the court may think fit (Solicitors Act 1957, s. 45).
1. *Re Miller*, [1893] 1 Q. B. 327.
2. *Re Eilbeck*, [1910] 1 K. B. 136.

debt must be paid in priority to all the other debts of the bankrupt, including those enumerated in s. 33 of the Bankruptcy Act 1914, as amended by subsequent Acts.

Savings banks.—Depositors in savings banks are secured against loss by the acts or misconduct of any officer employed by a similar preferential right in the event of such officer becoming bankrupt[3].

Other debts

With the exception of the above and of certain deferred debts hereinafter referred to (*post*, pp. 488–490), all debts proved in the bankruptcy are paid *pari passu*[4].

The landlord

The landlord is in a peculiar position as regards his rent. He has no priority over other creditors, unless he has distrained. The position then is as follows:

1. If he distrains within three months before the receiving order, he must pay the preferential creditors out of the proceeds of the distress; if he suffers loss thereby, he acquires the same rights of priority as the persons so paid[5].
2. If he distrains after the commencement of the bankruptcy, he can do so only for six months' rent accrued prior to the adjudication, and distress is not available for rent payable in respect of any period subsequent to the date when the distress was levied; where the landlord does not recover the full rent due to him by distress, he may prove for the balance as an ordinary creditor[6].
3. If the trustee remains in possession without disclaiming, the landlord may distrain for rent accrued due after adjudication in the ordinary way[7].

Secured creditors

A secured creditor is a person holding a mortgage, charge or lien on the property of the debtor, as security for a debt due to him from the debtor. The expression therefore does not include a creditor who is secured by the guarantee, or by a mortgage charge or lien on the

---

3. Trustee Savings Bank Act 1954, s. 61.
4. *Ibid.*, s. 33 (7). If there is a surplus after paying the debts, interest from the date of the receiving order at the rate of £4 per centum per annum is payable on all debts proved (*ibid.*, s. 33 (8)). *Cf. post*, p. 489.
5. Bankruptcy Act 1914, s. 33 (4).
6. *Ibid.*, s. 35 (1).
7. *Ex parte Hale* (1875), 1 Ch. D. 285.

property, of a third person. The test is would the security if given up augment the estate against which proof is made; if not the creditor can prove for the whole debt without deducting the value of his security[8]. He may rely on his security and not prove. If he proves he has three courses open to him[9], viz., he may:

1. Surrender his security and prove for his entire debt;
2. He may realise it, and prove for any deficit after deducting the net amount realised;
3. He may state the particulars in his proof, assess its value, and prove for a dividend on the deficit; but in this case the trustee may redeem the security at the assessed value[10].

Where a security has been valued and the trustee does not redeem, the creditor may require him in writing to elect whether he will do so or not, and the trustee must then, if he wishes to redeem, do so within six months. If the trustee is dissatisfied with the valuation, he may demand a sale of the security, on such terms as he and the creditor may agree or the court may fix; the creditor may, with leave of the court, amend if he can prove that he made a *bona fide* mistake or that the security has altered in value since he put in his proof. Where the secured creditor is also the petitioning creditor, the trustee is not entitled to redeem the security at the value placed upon it in the petition; at the same time, the petitioning creditor is bound by the valuation of his security given in his petition[11].

If it is found at any time that a creditor has omitted to state in his proof that he is secured, the security must be surrendered to the trustee for the general benefit of the creditors, unless the court is satisfied that the omission arose from inadvertence, in which case the court may allow the proof to be amended upon such terms as it considers just[12].

Where the debtor's goods have been pledged as security, the official receiver or trustee may serve written notice of his intention to inspect the goods, and after such notice the pledgee must not realise his security until he has given the trustee a reasonable opportunity to inspect and redeem the goods[13].

---

8. *Ex parte West Riding Union Banking Co.* (1881), 19 Ch. D. 105, 112. Proof allowed against joint estate of firm without valuing security upon separate estate of partner. See also *Re Rushton, Ex parte National Westminster Bank, Ltd.*, v. *Official Receiver*, [1971] 2 All E. R. 937; [1972] Ch. 197.
9. Bankruptcy Act 1914, Sched. II, rr. 10–18.
10. Compare the trustee's power of redeeming when the creditor claims to vote at a meeting, *ante*, p. 455.
11. *Re Vautin*, [1899] 2 Q. B. 549.
12. Bankruptcy (Amendment) Act 1926, s. 11.
13. Bankruptcy Act 1914, s. 59.

Mutual dealings

It may happen that the bankrupt, X, not only owes·money to a particular creditor, Y, but is also owed money by Y. In such a case when the trustee makes a claim against Y, Y is permitted to set-off against the claim the money X owes him. The rule is that if there have been mutual debts, mutual credits, or mutual dealings between the bankrupt and the creditor an account must be taken between them and a balance struck, and that balance only shall be claimed or paid; but the creditor cannot claim the benefit of any set-off where he had notice of an available act of bankruptcy at the time he gave credit to the debtor[14]. The line of set-off must be drawn at the date of the receiving order, unless the creditor's right of set-off has been stopped at an earlier date by notice of an act of bankruptcy[14]. In *re Daintry*[15],

> the bankrupt owed a creditor £86 and, before the receiving order, the bankrupt sold his business to the creditor under an agreement whereby the price comprised a portion of the profits to be earned for three years after the sale. After three years it was found that by reason of this agreement £300 was owing to the bankrupt. *Held:* the creditor was allowed to set off the £86 owed to him against the £300.

However, the debts must be due between the same parties and in the same right, so that a joint debt owing by a partnership cannot be set off against a separate debt owing to one of the parties[16].

The operation of the statutory provision on mutual dealings cannot be excluded by agreement[17].

Deferred debts

To the general rule that all debts other than preferential debts are payable *pari passu*[18], there are six exceptions, being cases where the claimant is postponed to the rights of other creditors:

    1. If there is a claim by a person other than a moneylender for agreed interest exceeding five per cent. per annum, the claim is deferred so far as it relates to interest in excess of five per cent. per annum. Accounts settled within three years before the receiving order may be re-opened if forming substantially one transaction with the debt proved and sums received by the creditor appropriated to principal and

---

14. *Ibid.*, s. 31. As to unliquidated claims, see *Jack* v. *Kipping* (1882), 9 Q. B. D. 113.
15. [1900] 1 Q. B. 546.
16. *Re Pennington and Owen*, [1925] Ch. 825.
17. *National Westminster Bank Ltd.* v. *Halesowen Presswork and Assemblies, Ltd.*, [1972] 1 All E. R. 641; [1972] A. C. 785, H. L.
18. *Ante*, p. 486.

interest in the proportion that the principal bears to the sum payable as interest at the agreed rate, and if a security is realised or its value assessed after the receiving order the amount realised or value assessed must be appropriated in like manner[19];

2. In the case of moneylenders, interest must be calculated at five per cent. per annum until all the debts proved have been paid in full. The moneylender is debarred from presenting a petition and voting at meetings, compositions and schemes in respect of that portion of his debt which represents interest in excess of five per cent. per annum[20]. The moneylender may, however, serve a bankruptcy notice on the borrower founded on a judgment which includes interest at a rate exceeding five per cent. per annum[1]; and if a petition is presented his refusal to accept a tender of principal and five per cent. interest is not a sufficient cause for dismissing the petition[2].

3. Where one partner of a firm is adjudged bankrupt, the claim of a creditor to whom the bankrupt is indebted jointly with the other partners, or any of them, is postponed to the claims of the separate creditors[3].

4. Certain debts within s. 3 of the Partnership Act 1890, *e.g.* loans at a rate of interest varying with profits are deferred. See *ante*, p. 157.

5. Proof for money lent by a wife to a husband, or by a husband to a wife, for use in his or her trade or business is postponed[4].

6. The trustees of a settlement which has been avoided have a deferred right to claim a dividend[5].

Questions sometimes arise as to the priority of these deferred claims among themselves and as to their rights to be satisfied in priority to the statutory four per cent. interest allowed to ordinary creditors[6]. The wording of the various sections differs. In the Moneylenders Act, for example, the

---

19. Bankruptcy Act 1914, s. 66. In a scheme of arrangement the application of this section may be excluded (*Re Nepean*, [1903] 1 K. B. 794).
20. Moneylenders Act 1927, s. 9 (1).
1. *Re A Debtor* (247 of 1930), [1930] 2 Ch. 239.
2. *Re A Debtor (No. 231 of 1936)*, [1936] 3 All E. R. 641; [1937] Ch. 181.
3. Bankruptcy Act 1914, s. 63. *Ante*, pp. 174–176.
4. *Ibid.*, s. 36. Even if a judgment has been obtained (*Re Lupkovics*, [1954] 2 All E. R. 125). But if any money is lent to a partnership of which the spouse is a member the right of proof is not affected (*Re Tuff* (1887), 19 Q. B. D. 88).
5. *Ibid.*, s. 42; *ante*, p. 467.
6. *Ante*, p. 486.

wording is "after all the debts proved in the estate have been paid in full." On the other hand, in the Bankruptcy Act 1914, s. 42, the words used are "until all claims of other creditors have been satisfied." It has been held that the claim of a moneylender is a debt which takes priority to the statutory interest while the claim of the trustees of a settlement which has been set aside is not a "debt" and is postponed to the statutory interest[7].

Apart from these statutory provisions, it has been held that a person who authorises the use of his money as part of the capital of a business, so that it is exposed to the hazards of the business and the danger of being lost, is not in fact a creditor at all and cannot compete with the creditors of the business[8].

Form of proof

A proof should be made as soon as may be[9] after the making of the receiving order, and should be sent to the trustee (or official receiver), verified by affidavit; all particulars must be given, and vouchers necessary to substantiate the claim should be specified, and may be called for by the trustee[10].

A moneylender's proof must contain verified details of the sums lent, the sums repaid and of the balance remaining unpaid in respect of (i) interest and (ii) principal, showing what interest would be included in such balance if it were calculated at five per cent. per annum[11].

When the proof is sent in, the trustee must, within twenty-eight days[12],

1. Admit it,
2. Reject it, or
3. Require further evidence,

and if he rejects a proof, he must send written notice of his decision, with the grounds thereof, to the creditor[13]. The court has power to review the decision, and may expunge or reduce a proof admitted by

---

7. *Re Debtor* (*No. 707 of 1939*), *Ex parte Official Receiver* v. *United Auto and Finance Corporation*, [1947] 1 All E. R. 417; [1947] Ch. 313. The position of the other deferred claims has not been determined.
8. *Re Beale* (1876), 4 Ch. D. 246; *Re Meade*, [1951] Ch. 774.
9. To enable a creditor to vote at a meeting, he must send his proof within the time specified in the notice convening the meeting, not later than mid-day preceding the date of the meeting (Bankruptcy Rules 1952, r. 252).
10. Bankruptcy Act 1914, Sched. II, rr. 1–4.
11. Moneylenders Act 1927, s. 9 (2).
12. Bankruptcy Rules 1952, r. 260.
13. Bankruptcy Act 1914, Sched. II, r. 23.
14. *Ibid.*, Sched. II, rr. 24–26.

the trustee, even on the application of the trustee himself[14]. The trustee cannot recover payments made to a creditor whose proof is subsequently expunged or overpayments made to a creditor whose proof is subsequently reduced, but in the latter case the creditor cannot receive any further dividend on the reduced proof without giving credit for overpayments[15]. Where the trustee has given notice of intention to declare a dividend he must, within fourteen days of a specified date, admit or reject every proof not already admitted or rejected, and send written notice thereof to the creditor, who in case of rejection has seven days in which to give notice of appeal[16].

Interest
Interest on overdue debts (although not agreed for) may in certain cases be included in the proof[17].

Dividends[18]
These are payable to all who have proved, the amount depending upon what remains of the estate after payment of the expenses and the preferential debts. There may be one or more dividends, according as may be found convenient, and the time for declaration, though fixed by the rules, may be varied to suit the circumstances[19]. Due notice must be given to the creditors and to the Department of Trade, and the intention to distribute must be announced in the Gazette.

Any surplus after payment of the creditors in full with interest and the costs of the bankruptcy belongs to the debtor[20].

VIII COMPOSITIONS AND ARRANGEMENTS

Compositions
A debtor may obtain his release by the acceptance of a composition or the adoption of a scheme of arrangement; *e.g.* the creditors may agree to take 50p. in the £ payable by instalments and guaranteed by satisfactory persons. This may take place even after adjudication in bankruptcy[1]; but as a rule it precedes this, and is consented to at a

---

15. *Re Searle, Hoare & Co.*, [1924] 2 Ch. 325. But it is submitted that the creditor might be ordered to refund dividends if his proof was fraudulent.
16. Bankruptcy Rules 1952, rr. 259, 267.
17. Bankruptcy Act 1914, Sched. II, r. 21.
18. See Bankruptcy Rules 1952, rr. 267–273.
19. *Ibid.*, rr. 269, 270.
20. Bankruptcy Act 1914, s. 69.
1. Bankruptcy Act 1914, s. 21.

specially called meeting, which may be the first meeting. The procedure is as follows[2]:

1. The debtor must submit to the official receiver his proposal in writing signed by him[3] as soon as may be after the receiving order[4];

2. The official receiver must then call a meeting of creditors, accompanying his notice with a copy of the debtor's proposal and report on the scheme;

3. The meeting must be held before the conclusion of the public examination;

4. If accepted at this by a majority in number and three-fourths in value of those who have proved, the sanction of the court must then be obtained to the scheme, but not till after the public examination is concluded[5].

Approval of the court.—The court cannot approve the scheme if (i) it is of the opinion that the terms of the proposal are not reasonable, or (ii) it is of the opinion that they are not calculated to benefit the general body of creditors, or (iii) the scheme does not provide for the payment in priority of the preferential debts[6].

Further, if any of the facts disentitling a bankrupt to an immediate discharge are proved[7], the court's power to approve the arrangement is gone, unless the scheme provides reasonable security for a dividend of at least 25p. in the £ on all the unsecured debts provable against the debtor's estate; *i.e.* provable at the time when the scheme comes up for approval. If any creditors have released their debts, those debts can be disregarded[8]. As a general rule, the releases must be absolute and the circumstances under which they were obtained must be fully disclosed[9]; but there may be cases in which a conditional withdrawal will suffice[10]. The court will not refuse to approve a scheme on the ground of the debtor's misconduct unless it is of such a character as to make it against public policy to sanction the scheme[11]. A scheme may

---

2. *Ibid.*, s. 16.
3. No one can sign this proposal on behalf of the debtor (*Re Blucher (Prince)*, [1930] All E. R. Rep. 562; [1931] 2 Ch. 70).
4. Usually within four days after the specified time for lodging the statement of affairs.
5. The desire of the creditors is not of itself sufficient to induce the court to approve the scheme (*Ex parte Reed and Bowen, Re Read and Bowen* (1886), 17 Q. B. D. 244).
6. Bankruptcy Act 1914, s. 16. See *ante*, pp. 484–486.
7. See *ante*, pp. 459–460.
8. *Re E. A. B.*, [1902] 1 K. B. 457.
9. *Re Pilling*, [1903] 2 K. B. 50.
10. *Re Flew*, [1905] 1 K. B. 278.
11. *Re E. A. B.*, *supra*.

be approved if it seems beneficial to the creditiors and there is a reasonable possibility of the statutory 25p. in the £ being paid within a short period[12].

Effect of scheme when approved.—If the approval of the court is given the receiving order is discharged, and the adjudication, if made, is annulled, and the bankrupt's property reverts to himself or goes to such person as is nominated in the scheme; the debtor thereafter being released from all liabilities from which a discharge would have released him, subject, however, to the terms of the scheme. The scheme is binding on *all creditors* so far as it relates to debts due to them and provable in the bankruptcy.

The trustee under a scheme is, so far as possible, in the same position as the trustee in bankruptcy; but he must adhere to the terms of the arrangement.

Powers are reserved to the court to annul an arrangement if it fails to be workable, or if the debtor does not carry out his part of it.

Deeds of arrangement

Creditors may make arrangements with the debtor outside the provisions of the Bankruptcy Acts and thereby avoid bankruptcy, but in such cases the rules of bankruptcy do not apply, and the debtor is released from the claims only of those who assent to the scheme. The arrangement is a contract and subject to the general law relating thereto. Any secret preference given or bargained for by any creditor entitles the others to recede from the arrangement.

Such arrangements will usually come within the Deeds of Arrangement Act 1914 and if they fall within the definition of a "deed of arrangement" they must comply with that Act in order to be valid. The Act defines a deed of arrangement as any instrument, whether under seal or not, made for the benefit of creditors generally or made by an insolvent debtor for the benefit of any three or more creditors. It may be:

    1. An assignment of property;

    2. A deed or agreement for a composition;

and in cases where the creditors obtain control over the debtor's property,

    3. A letter of licence;

    4. An agreement for the carrying on or winding up of the debtor's business[13].

---

12. *Re Murray, a Debtor*, [1969] 1 All E. R. 441; [1969] 1 W. L. R. 246.
13. Deeds of Arrangement Act 1914, s. 1.

A deed of any of these classes will be void unless it is registered at the Department of Trade[14] within seven days after first execution and is properly stamped[15].

A deed for the benefit of creditors generally is also void unless assented to by a majority in number and value of the creditors before or within twenty-one days of registration. Within twenty-eight days of registration a statutory declaration must be filed confirming that the assents have been obtained[16]. Within a further seven days the trustee must give security unless a majority in number and value of the creditors dispense with it. In default the court may declare the deed void or appoint a new trustee[17].

A conveyance or assignment for the benefit of creditors generally, is an act of bankruptcy available for three months to a creditor who has not assented to or recognised the deed[18], but if such creditor has been served by the trustee under the deed with a notice of the execution of the deed, the time is cut back to one month[19]. The trustee should not act under the deed for three months after its execution unless all creditors have assented to it because, if the debtor becomes bankrupt the doctrine of relation back will apply and the trustee under the deed would have to account for all dealings with the debtor's property[20].

Should the deed be void, it follows that the trustee under it must account for dealings with the debtor's property even if a bankruptcy petition is presented *after* the lapse of three months from the deed. But, where a deed of arrangement is void by reason that the requisite majority of creditors has not assented to it, or in the case of a deed for the benefit of three or more creditors, by reason that the debtor was insolvent at the time of the execution of the deed and that the deed was not registered as required by the Act, but is not void for any other reason, and a receiving order is made against the debtor upon a petition presented *after* the lapse of three months from the execution of the deed, the trustee under the deed is not liable to account for dealings

---

14. Administration of Justice Act 1925, s. 22 (1). If the deed affects land, it must also be registered at the Land Charges Registry or it is void against a purchaser of the land: Land Charges Act 1925, s. 13.
15. Deeds of Arrangement Act 1914, s. 2. A deed executed abroad must be registered within seven days after the time when it would reach England if posted within one week.
16. Deeds of Arrangement Act 1914, s. 3. The time can be extended by the court.
17. *Ibid.*, s. 11.
18. See *ante*, p. 445.
19. Deeds of Arrangement Act 1914, s. 24.
20. However the trustee under the deed is allowed expenses incurred in complying with the Act and may be allowed by the trustee in bankruptcy remuneration for work that has benefited the estate. *Ibid.*, s. 21; *Re Geen*, [1917] 1 K. B. 183.

with the debtor's property if he proves he did not know and had no reason to suspect the deed was void[1].

A trustee under a deed of arrangement must account yearly to the Department of Trade and every six months to all assenting creditors. A majority in number and value of creditors can demand an audit during the administration or within twelve months of the date of final accounts[2].

IX BANKRUPTCY OF PARTNERSHIPS AND PARTNERS

As a whole the rules governing the administration of the estate of an individual apply to that of a firm, but in some respects there are variations. In ordinary cases a receiving order may be made against a firm[3], but it operates as an order against each individual member, and the court will order discovery to be made of the names of the partners.

When a receiving order is made against a firm, the debtors must submit a joint statement of their partnership affairs and each partner must submit a statement of his separate affairs[4]. The adjudication is made as against the individuals by name and not against the firm[5].

The first meeting is attended by the joint creditors and by the creditors of each separate partner's estate; the trustee appointed by the joint creditors[6] is trustee of the separate estates of the partners, but each separate set of creditors is entitled to its own committee of inspection. The trustee's remuneration is fixed by each estate separately.

Administration of the joint and separate estates is dealt with, *ante*, pp. 174–176.

X ADMINISTRATION OF ESTATE OF DECEASED INSOLVENT

The legal representative of a deceased debtor or any creditor whose debt would have been sufficient to support a bankruptcy petition if the debtor had been alive may petition to have the estate administered in the local court of bankruptcy; or if an administration on the equity side is in progress, the court may transfer it to bankruptcy.

---

1. Deeds of Arrangement Act 1914, s. 19. If the trustee acts when he knows the deed is void, he is liable to a penalty of £5 a day: *ibid.*, s. 12.
2. *Ibid.*, ss. 13–15.
3. Bankruptcy Act 1914, s. 119; Bankruptcy Rules 1952, r. 285. If a judgment is obtained against a firm without personally serving a partner, a bankruptcy notice cannot be served on that partner without first obtaining leave (*Re Ide, Ex parte Ide* (1886), 17 Q. B. D. 755; R. S. C. Ord. 81, r. 5).
4. Bankruptcy Rules 1952, r. 287.
5. *Ibid.*, r. 288.
6. *Ibid.*, rr. 291, 294.

The creditor who desires an administration order must verify his petition by affidavit, and must show that there is no reasonable probability of the estate being sufficient for the payment of the debts owing by the deceased. An order cannot be made until a personal representative is appointed[7]. Notice to the legal personal representative of the presentation of a petition is, in the event of an order being made, equivalent to notice of an act of bankruptcy. The executor's right of retainer is not affected[8].

The official receiver becomes trustee, unless the creditors by ordinary resolution appoint a trustee (and committee of inspection also, if so desired), and he must pay funeral and testamentary expenses in priority to every other debt; he is entitled to have detailed information as to the assets and liabilities given him by the executor or administrator, and may ask of them every information he requires[9].

Unliquidated damages in tort are provable[10].

XI SMALL BANKRUPTCIES

If the estate is not likely to exceed £300, and a receiving order is made, the court can order a "*summary administration,*" in which case the estate is administered by the official receiver as trustee, and without a committee of inspection, but by special resolution the creditors may select a trustee and have the estate administered in the ordinary way[11].

When a judgment has been obtained in a county court and the debtor is unable to pay, and his debts amount to not more than £300, the county court may, without putting the estate into bankruptcy, make an order for their payment by instalments or otherwise, and either in full or to such an extent as appears practicable and subject to any conditions as to future earnings or income as the court may think just[12].

---

7. *Re A Debtor (No. 1035 of 1938)*, [1939] 2 All E. R. 56; [1939[Ch. 594.
8. *Re Rhoades*, [1899] 2 Q. B. 347.
9. Bankruptcy Act 1914, s. 130; Bankruptcy Rules 1952, r. 304.
10. Law Reform (Miscellaneous Provisions) Act 1934, s. 1 (6). As to the position regarding voluntary settlements and the rights of execution creditors, see Williams on Bankruptcy (18th edn.), 541–542.
11. The procedure is regulated by s. 129. Bankruptcy Rules 1952, r. 298. There are no local advertisements unless ordered; if no satisfactory proposals for a compromise are lodged the debtor can be adjudicated forthwith; creditors whose debts do not exceed £2 get notice only of the first meeting; the estate should be distributed if possible in a single dividend within six months; costs are on a reduced scale.
12. County Courts Act 1959, ss. 148–156, as amended by the Administration of Justice Act 1965, ss. 20 and 21. An application to the county court for an administration order is an act of bankruptcy.

PART V

Arbitrations

CHAPTER 28

Arbitrations

I INTRODUCTORY

The settlement of disputes by arbitration is governed largely by the Arbitration Act 1950 and references to sections throughout the present chapter are to the sections of that Act.

There are three ways in which arbitration may arise:

1. *By order of the court.*—Under the Rules of the Supreme Court the jurisdiction or powers of the High Court can be exercised in certain circumstances by official referees or special referees or by masters, registrars, district registrars or other officers of the court. In certain circumstances, the rules authorise the whole of a case or any particular issue to be ordered to be *tried* by the referee or other officer. Moreover, any question before a court may be referred *for inquiry and report*[1]. The type of case chiefly envisaged is where prolonged examination of documents or scientific or local examination is required or where matters of account are involved.

2. *By certain statutes* the parties are given an option to refer disputes, and in some cases the reference is made compulsory. The Arbitration Act, with the exception of certain sections, applies to statutory arbitrations except in so far as it is inconsistent with the special Act[2].

3. *By consent out of court.*—Parties[3] may agree to submit either present or future disputes to arbitration and the arbitrator may or may not be named in the agreement. Such an agreement is known as an *arbitration agreement* or *submission*. The agreement may be by word of mouth but the Arbitration Act only applies to written agreements, for an arbitration agreement is defined as:

"a *written* agreement to submit present or future differences to arbitration whether an arbitrator is named therein or not"[4].

---

1. Administration of Justice Act 1956, s. 15 (1). By the Courts Act 1971, s. 25, existing official referees became Circuit judges. In future no person will be appointed to the office of official referee but particular Circuit judges will be required to discharge "official referees' business".
2. Section 31.
3. A minor is bound by an arbitration clause if the contract as a whole is for his benefit (*Slade* v. *Metrodent*, [1953] 2 Q. B. 112).
4. Section 32.

II ARBITRATION AGREEMENTS

Arbitrations and actions

Commercial arbitrations, which are usually the result of agreement out of court, are particularly useful where the issues involve expert knowledge of a particular trade and the arbitrator is chosen for his experience in that trade. But where the main issues are questions of commercial law these are frequently handled most speedily and economically by the High Court which has a special procedure for dealing with commercial causes in the Commercial Court[5].

Effect of arbitration agreement upon action

An arbitration agreement will not necessarily bar legal proceedings; but if a party commences an action the court may, on the application of the other party, stay the action if the applicant has not delivered any pleadings or taken any step in the action (except entering an appearance), there is no sufficient reason why the dispute should not be referred to arbitration, and the applicant is ready and willing to do all things necessary to the proper conduct of the arbitration[6]. The court has thus a discretion to grant or refuse a stay and in particular in cases where the court has power to give relief on the ground that the arbitrator is not impartial or that the dispute involves a question of fraud, it may refuse to stay the action[7].

Generally speaking, the court will give effect to an arbitration agreement unless the person opposing a stay of action can prove there is good reason for allowing the action to continue.

Thus,

> where the agreement provided that a foreign court should try disputes but both parties were strangers to the foreign court and many of the witnesses were in this country the court refused a stay[8].

If the court has refused to stay an action, or if no application to stay it has been made, the court has sole jurisdiction to decide the

---

5. See *Peter Cassidy Seed Co., Ltd.* v. *Osuustukkukauppa I.L.*, [1957] 1 All E. R. 484; *J. H. Vantol, Ltd.* v. *Fairclough Dodd and Jones, Ltd.*, [1956] 3 All E. R. 921; *British Imex Industries, Ltd.* v. *Midland Bank, Ltd.*, [1958] 1 All E. R. 264; [1958] 1 Q. B. 542 (judgment eleven days after writ). The Commercial Court is part of the Queen's Bench Division of the High Court—it has been in existence since 1895 but only put on a statutory basis by the Administration of Justice Act 1970, s. 3.
6. Section 4.
7. Section 24 (3).
8. *The Fehmarn*, [1958] 1 All E. R. 333. See also *Olver* v. *Hillier*, [1959] 2 All E. R. 220 (dissolution of partnership—no stay); and *Taunton-Collins* v. *Cromie*, [1964] 2 All E. R. 332; [1964] 1 W. L. R. 633, C. A. (no stay because one party to action not a party to arbitration agreement and multiplicity of proceedings undesirable).

dispute, and it will not tolerate arbitration proceedings with respect to that dispute while the action is pending[9].

Scott v. *Avery clause.*—Any agreement whereby the jurisdiction of the courts to determine matters of law is completely ousted, *e.g.* an arbitrator is given the final power to determine a question of law, is illegal. The court's statutory power under s. 21 to compel an arbitrator to submit a point of law for determination by the courts cannot be ousted[10]. On the other hand, it is lawful for parties to stipulate that no right of action shall accrue, until the amount of the debt or damages has been ascertained by arbitration—the reference to arbitration will be a condition precedent to the right to sue, and the non-observance thereof will afford a defence to the action[11]. This is known as a *Scott* v. *Avery* clause. Despite the clause, where the court orders that the arbitration agreement shall cease to have effect (*e.g.* under s. 25), it may further order that a provision in the agreement making an award a condition precedent to the right to sue shall also cease to have effect[12]. It is also lawful for parties to agree that a claim shall be deemed to be waived and absolutely barred if an arbitrator is not appointed within a certain time. If such a condition is not complied with, the claim cannot be enforced either by action or arbitration[13]. But the court may extend the time if undue hardship would otherwise be caused[14].

In *Ford* v. *Clarksons Holidays Ltd.*[15],

> By an arbitration clause in a "package" holiday contract, it was agreed that the decision of a mutually agreed independent arbitrator should be "accepted by all parties as final". When the plaintiff began an action and the defendants applied to stay the proceedings, the plaintiff contended the clause purported to oust the court's jurisdiction and that a stay should be refused because arbitration

---

9. *Doleman & Sons* v. *Ossett Corporation*, [1912] 3 K. B. 257, C. A.
10. *Czernikow* v. *Roth, Schmidt & Co.*, [1922] 2 K. B. 478.
11. *Scott* v. *Avery* (1856), 5 H. L. C. 811.
12. Section 25 (4). For the practice, see *Kruger Townswear, Ltd.* v. *Northern Assurance Co., Ltd.*, [1953] 2 All E. R. 727 n.
13. *Atlantic Shipping, etc. Co.* v. *Louis Dreyfus & Co.*, [1922] 2 A. C. 250. *Cf. Ford & Co.* v. *Compagnie Furness (France)*, [1922] 2 K. B. 797; *Pinnock Bros.* v. *Lewis and Peat*, [1923] 1 K. B. 690; *Smeaton Hanscomb & Co., Ltd.* v. *Sassoon I. Setty, Son & Co. (No. 1)*, [1953] 2 All E. R. 1471.
14. Section 27. See, *e.g.*, *Liberian Shipping Corporation* v. *A. King & Sons, Ltd.*, [1967] 1 All E. R. 934, 938; [1967] 2 Q. B. 86, C. A., where Lord DENNING, M.R., said that "undue" hardship simply means excessive hardship, *i.e.* greater hardship than the circumstances warrant: "Even though a claimant has been at fault himself, it is an undue hardship on him if the consequences are out of proportion to the fault." The clause on its true construction may only bar the right to arbitration and not the substantive right.
15. [1971] 3 All E. R. 454; [1971] 1 W. L. R. 1412, C. A.

proceedings would be more expensive. *Held:* the clause did not purport to oust the court's jurisdiction and the allegation of expense, even if true, was not a proper reason for refusing a stay.

Construction of arbitration agreement

What is the subject matter of the arbitration agreement is a matter of construction in each case. Words referring to disputes arising "under" or "in respect of" a contract are widely construed and include disputes as to whether the contract has been repudiated or frustrated[16].

If, however, a party denies the existence or the validity of the contract *in toto, e.g.* on the ground that it is illegal, he will be precluded from setting up the arbitration clause as a defence to an action[17]; but this does not apply where a party admits the existence of a binding contract, although he denies liability under it[18].

It is often important to decide whether an agreement to refer a question to a third party is an arbitration agreement or not. If the intention is that the third party is to decide the question by a quasi-judicial process, the agreement is an arbitration agreement. But if the third party is to use his own knowledge and skill, *e.g.* to make a valuation of property which is being transferred, there is no arbitration. The Arbitration Act does not apply to a valuation. The parties are contractually bound by the decision of the valuer although it can be set aside if fraudulently made or if on its face it is made on a wrong basis[19]. An arbitrator, owing to his quasi-judicial functions, cannot normally be sued by the parties[20]. A valuer is similarly protected if he is acting as a quasi-arbitrator between two parties even though not technically an arbitrator[1].

Alteration

A submission may be altered by agreement between the parties, but the arbitrator has no power to alter its terms. The court can amend so as to give effect to the real intention of the parties, but not so as to introduce new matter.

The time for making an award even when fixed by the agreement can be enlarged by order of the court, whether it has expired or not[2].

---

16. *Heyman* v. *Darwins, Ltd.*, [1942] 1 All E. R. 337; [1942] A. C. 356, H. L.; *Government of Gibraltar* v. *Kenney*, [1956] 3 All E. R. 22; [1956] 2 Q. B. 410; *The Tradesman*, [1961] 3 All E. R. 661; [1962] 1 W. L. R. 61.
17. *Jureidini* v. *National British, etc., Insurance Co.*, [1915] A. C. 499.
18. *Woodall* v. *Pearl Assurance Co.*, [1919] 1 K. B. 593, C. A.
19. *Dean* v. *Prince*, [1953] 2 All E. R. 636; [1953] Ch. 590, reversed on the facts, [1954] 1 All E. R. 749; [1954] Ch. 409.
20. *Chambers* v. *Goldthorpe*, [1901] 1 Q. B. 624.
 1. *Finnegan* v. *Allan*, [1943] 1 All E. R. 493; [1943] 1 K. B. 425, C. A.
 2. Section 13 (2).

Revocation

The authority of an arbitrator or umpire appointed by virtue of an arbitration agreement (unless a contrary intention is expressed) is irrevocable except by leave of the court[3]. Such leave will be given only in exceptional circumstances such as misconduct on the part of the arbitrator and the like[4]. But in certain circumstances the court will either remove or give leave to revoke the authority of a particular arbitrator and may order that the arbitration agreement shall cease to have effect. An arbitrator can be removed by the court if he has misconducted himself or the proceedings[5], or if he fails to use reasonable dispatch in entering on or proceeding with the reference[6]. The court will give leave to revoke the authority of an arbitrator for good cause— *e.g.* if he is not or may not be impartial. This is so even if the applicant knew of this when he entered into the agreement provided that the dispute had not already arisen[7].

Where the court has given leave to revoke the authority of an arbitrator it may appoint a person to act as sole arbitrator in place of the person or persons removed, or order that the agreement shall cease to have effect with respect to the dispute referred[8].

Similarly, where under an agreement to refer future disputes, a dispute arises which involves a charge of fraud against any party, the court may order that the agreement shall cease to have effect[9].

Assignment and transmission

An arbitration clause can be enforced by or against an assignee if the contract as a whole is assignable[10]. If the moneys receivable under a contract are assigned, an award cannot be made in favour of the assignor[11]. In such a case it may be necessary for the assignor and assignee to be joined as parties.

An arbitration agreement is not discharged by the death of any party thereto, but in such an event it will be enforceable by or against the personal representative of the deceased[12].

If a contract to which a bankrupt is a party contains an arbitration clause, that clause will be enforceable by or against the trustee in

---

3. Section 1.
4. *City Centre Properties (I. T. C. Pensions), Ltd.* v. *Tersons, Ltd.,* [1969] 2 All E. R. 1121; [1969] 1 W. L. R. 772, C. A.
5. Section 23 (1).   6. Section 13 (3).
7. Section 24 (1).   8. Section 25 (2).
9. Section 24 (2).
10. *Shayler* v. *Woolf,* [1946] 2 All E. R. 54; [1946] Ch. 320, C. A.
11. *Cottage Club Estates* v. *Woodhouse Estates Co. (Amersham),* [1927] All E. R. Rep. 397; [1928] 2 K. B. 463.
12. Section 2. The authority of an arbitrator is not revoked by the death of his appointor (*ibid.*).

bankruptcy if he adopts the contract[13]. In other cases, if a bankrupt was before the commencement of the bankruptcy party to an arbitration agreement which applies to some matter requiring to be determined for the purpose of the bankruptcy, the court having jurisdiction in the bankruptcy may, on the application of any other party or the trustee with the consent of the committee of inspection, order the matter to be determined in accordance with the agreement, if it is of opinion that it ought to be so determined[14].

Illegality

A submission may be unenforceable as a contractual obligation. Thus a submission which is an integral part of a betting contract is void under the Gaming Act 1845[15].

III ARBITRATORS AND UMPIRES

The arbitrator

Any person may be appointed arbitrator, and an interest in the subject-matter known to both parties at the time of appointment is no objection[16].

The agreement may name the arbitrator or arbitrators or provide how they are to be appointed, *e.g.* by the President of the Law Society or even by lot. Unless a contrary intention is expressed in the agreement, it is deemed to include a provision that the reference be to a single arbitrator[17].

If the reference is to a single arbitrator and the parties do not concur in appointing one, or if after appointment the arbitrator refuses to act or is incapable of acting, or dies, and the parties do not supply the vacancy, any party may serve the others with notice to concur in appointing an arbitrator, and if no appointment is made within seven clear days after service of such notice, the court may appoint[18].

If the reference is to two arbitrators, and one party fails to appoint his arbitrator, either originally or by way of substitution, the other party having appointed his arbitrator may serve a notice requiring his opponent to make the appointment. If such notice is not complied with within seven clear days, the party serving it may appoint his

---

13. Section 3 (1).   14. Section 3 (2).
15. *Joe Lee, Ltd.* v. *Dalmeny*, [1927] 1 Ch. 300.
16. *Johnston* v. *Cheape* (1817), 5 Dow. 247. But see *ante*, p. 503.
17. Section 6.
18. Section 10. If the application is made by an alien resident out of the jurisdiction, the court may require him to give security for the costs of the arbitration as a condition of making the appointment (*Re Bjornstad and The Ouse Shipping Co.*, [1924] 2 K. B. 673).

arbitrator to act as sole arbitrator in the reference, but the court may set aside any appointment so made[19].

Where arbitrators have been removed or their authority revoked by leave of the court, the court may appoint a person or persons to act in the place of the person or persons removed[20].

The umpire

If the reference is to two arbitrators, they must immediately appoint an umpire[21]. If they fail to do so, or if the umpire refuses to act is incapable, or dies, and the arbitrators do not supply the vacancy, the court may appoint in like manner as in the case of a sole arbitrator[22]. The duties of the umpire commence when he is called upon to act, not when he is appointed. He is called on to act when the arbitrators deliver to the parties or to him a notice in writing that they cannot agree[1]. The court may order him to enter on the reference at any time[2].

If the submission provides that each party shall appoint an arbitrator, and that the appointed arbitrators shall appoint a third, the agreement will have effect as if it provided for the appointment of an umpire; but if the agreement provides for the appointment of three arbitrators otherwise than as above, the award of any two of them will be binding[3].

Invalid appointment

If an arbitration agreement specifies the qualifications of an arbitrator or umpire, any award made by someone purporting to act as arbitrator or umpire who does not possess such qualifications is void and the defect in appointment is not cured by subsequent appearance of the parties before him[4].

Duties of umpire

The umpire enters on the reference in lieu of the arbitrators, who, in a commercial arbitration, may give evidence before the umpire—they are not disqualified from so doing by the mere fact that they have acted in the matter in a judicial capacity[5].

---

19. Section 7. 'Appointment' is not complete until the nominated arbitrator is told of his appointment and he consents to it: *Tradex Export S. A.* v. *Volkswagenwerk A. G.*, [1970] 1 All E. R. 420; [1970] 1 Q. B. 537, C. A.
20. Section 25 (1), (2).   21. Section 8 (1).
22. Section 10   1. Section 8 (2).
2. Section 8 (3).   3. Section 9.
4. *Rahcassi Shipping Co. S.A.* v. *Blue Star Line, Ltd.*, [1967] 3 All E. R. 301; [1967] 3 W. L. R. 1382.
5. *Bourgeois* v. *Weddell & Co.*, [1924] 1 K. B. 539; *Wessenen's Koniklijke Fabrieken N.V.* v. *Isaac Modiano Brother & Sons, Ltd.*, [1960] 3 All E. R. 617; [1960] 1 W. L. R. 1243.

The umpire must decide the whole matter between the parties, and not particular points upon which the arbitrators cannot agree. He has the same powers and is bound by the same rules as the arbitrators.

A judge as arbitrator

Under the Administration Act 1970, s. 4, a judge of the Commercial Court may accept appointment as sole arbitrator or umpire if in all the circumstances he thinks fit. Fees payable are to be taken by the High Court.

IV CONDUCT OF THE PROCEEDINGS

Once the arbitrator or arbitrators have been appointed, the first step is usually to take an appointment for directions as to preliminary steps such as pleadings, or discovery of documents. The arbitration agreement may provide that the reference is to be governed by the rules of a particular trade association. But where a custom is alleged to have grown up in a particular association which conflicts with the ordinary rules of procedure it will only be incorporated in the arbitration agreement if it is consistent with the tenor of the agreement as a whole. There can be no prescriptive right to commit an irregularity[6].

Unless a contrary intention appears, the parties and persons claiming through them are bound subject to any legal objection to produce all documents in their possession or power which may be required and to do all other things which the arbitrator or umpire may require[7]. This entitles him to order pleadings[8], disclosure of documents or interrogatories on oath[9]. But he cannot order security for costs[10]. In addition the court may make orders in respect of the following matters: (1) security for costs; (2) discovery of documents; (3) giving evidence on affidavit; (4) examination of witness before an examiner or on commission abroad; (5) the preservation, interim custody or sale of any goods; (6) the detention, preservation or inspection of any property, the taking of samples or trying of experiments; (7) interim injunctions or the appointment of a receiver[11].

---

6. *London Export Corporation, Ltd.* v. *Jubilee Coffee Roasting Co., Ltd.*, [1958] 2 All E. R. 411.
7. Section 12 (1).
8. *Re Crighton and Law Car and General Insurance Corporation*, [1910] 2 K. B. 738.
9. *Kursell* v. *Timber Operators and Contractors, Ltd.*, [1923] 2 K. B. 202.
10. *Re Unione Stearinerie Lanza and Wiener*, [1917] 2 K. B. 558.
11. Section 12 (6) (h).

The hearing

The arbitrator has, with regard to the parties to the submission, some of the powers of a judge, and the proceedings resemble those of an action[12]. The arbitrator may, at his discretion, exclude persons, other than the parties, who are going to be examined before him during the time that any of the other witnesses are giving evidence. A lay arbitrator is generally allowed to have a legal adviser to sit with him or assist him during the hearing.

An arbitrator may, generally speaking, take skilled advice, but it is not advisable that he should do so without the consent of the parties. Where an arbitrator is authorised to appoint an accountant, "if not objected to by the parties," he may not appoint one without communicating with the parties[13]. An arbitrator skilled in a particular trade may use his own knowledge and experience, *e.g.* in determining the quality of goods sold and the amount of damages without hearing evidence[14].

The arbitrator will fix the time and place of the hearing and notify the parties. If one party fails to attend the arbitrator can proceed in his absence, but he should first give distinct notice of his intention to do so[15].

If a question arises whether the arbitrator has jurisdiction or not, it is his duty to consider the point, although if he wrongly decides that he has jurisdiction, that will not make his award good[16].

Evidence

The arbitrator or umpire is bound to observe the rules of evidence no less than judges[17]. The arbitrator must hear both sides, and take evidence in the presence of both parties. Any practice to the contrary is absolutely wrong and is a ground for setting aside any award[18]. In the absence of agreement to the contrary, the parties are deemed to have agreed to submit to examination on oath or affirmation and that witnesses shall similarly be examined if the arbitrator thinks fit. The arbitrator has power to administer the oaths or take the affirmations[19].

He should receive all the evidence tendered, taking notes of everything material, but if he rejects evidence under a mistake as to its value

---

12. *Re Enoch and Zaretzky*, [1910] 1 K. B. 327.
13. *Re Tidswell* (1864), 33 Beav. 213.
14. *Mediterranean and Eastern Export Co., Ltd.* v. *Fortress Fabrics (Manchester), Ltd.*, [1948] 2 All E. R. 186.
15. *Gladwin* v. *Chilcote* (1841) 9 Dowl. 550.
16. *Christopher Brown, Ltd.* v. *Genossenschaft Oesterreichischer Waldbesitzer*, [1953] 2 All E. R. 1039.
17. *Re Enoch and Zaretzky*, [1910] 1 K. B. 327.
18. *Ramsden & Co.* v. *Jacobs*, [1922] 1 K. B. 640, *per* BRAY, J. See *post*, p. 512.
19. Section 12 (1), (2), (3).

it is not sufficient ground for setting aside the award; similarly, if he receives evidence upon matters not coming within the scope of the reference, his award will not on that ground alone be set aside[20].

He has no right to call a witness without the consent of the parties[1].

The attendance of a witness to give evidence or to produce documents can be enforced by a writ of subpœna issued by the High Court[2]. In the case of a prisoner a writ of *habeas corpus ad testificandum* must be issued[3]. Any witness giving false evidence is guilty of perjury[4].

Special case

An arbitrator or umpire may, and must if so directed by the court, state:

(a) any question of law arising in the course of the reference; or

(b) an award or any part of an award,

in the form of a special case for the decision of the court[5].

In stating an award in the form of a special case, the arbitrator should state the facts on which the award is based and pose the questions of law which the court is to settle. As Lord PEARSON has said:

"The procedure by special case is a valuable safeguard, because without it there might grow up a system of arbitrators' law independent of, and divergent from, the law administered by the courts; and also, if different arbitrators took different views as to the meaning of a clause in a standard contract, there would be no means of obtaining an authoritative decision. On the other hand, the procedure should be kept within its proper limits, confined to questions of law, and should not be extended so as to encroach on the general finality of the arbitrator's decision as provided by s. 16 of the Arbitration Act 1950"[6].

The court may direct a special case to be stated with respect to an interim award or on a question of law arising in the course of the reference although the proceedings under the reference are still pending[7]. If the arbitrator refuses to state a case asked for on reasonable grounds, and makes his award summarily so as to preclude an

---

20. *Falkingham* v. *Victorian Railway Commissioners*, [1900] A. C. 452.
1. *Re Enoch and Zaretzky.*
2. Section 12 (4).
3. Section 12 (5).
4. Perjury Act 1911, s. 1.
5. Section 21 (1). No appeal lies from a decision of the court under para. (a) of this subsection without the leave of the court or the Court of Appeal (s. 21 (3)).
6. *Tersons, Ltd.* v. *Stevenage Development Corporation, Ltd.*, [1963] 3 All E. R. 863, 872; [1965] 1 Q. B. 37, 55.
7. Section 27 (2).

application to the court, that is misconduct, and the award may be sent back with an order to state a case[8], or set aside[9].

It is the duty of the parties to see that all the relevant facts are found, but the court will not construe a special case too rigidly[10] and may draw inferences of fact[11].

These provisions do not apply to references for trial by order of the court[12]. Appeals from an official or special referee are governed by the Rules of the Supreme Court[13].

An agreement not to require an arbitrator to state a special case is contrary to public policy and invalid because it ousts the special statutory jurisdiction of the courts to compel arbitrators to submit a point of law for determination by the courts[14].

Where the arbitrator states his award in the form of a special case, he is *functus officio*, and the court pronounces judgment upon the facts found by him. It is, however, competent for an arbitrator to state his award in the form of a special case with a limited time for setting it down for hearing and with an alternative final award which is to become operative if the case is not set down within the time limited[15].

V THE AWARD

Time for award

In the absence of a provision to the contrary in the arbitration agreement an arbitrator or umpire has power to make his award at any time[16] except where the reward has been remitted for reconsideration[17]. If a time is fixed by the Act or the agreement the court has power to extend it[18].

Form and requisites

The arbitrator should decide all matters submitted to him under the submission, but he should not go beyond them; if he transgresses in either respect the award is void.

8. *Re Palmer & Co. and Hosken*, [1898] 1 Q. B. 131.
9. *Re Fischel & Co. and Mann and Cook*, [1919] 2 K. B. 431.
10. *Anglo-Saxon Petroleum Co., Ltd.* v. *Adamastos Shipping Co., Ltd.*, [1957] 2 All E. R. 311, at p. 314; [1957] 2 Q. B. 233, at p. 264, C. A. For decision in the House of Lords, see *ante*, p. 359.
11. *Universal Cargo Carriers Corporation* v. *Citati (No. 2)*, [1958] 2 All E. R. 563; [1958] 2 Q. B. 254, C. A.
12. See *ante*, p. 499.
13. See Administration of Justice Act 1956, s. 15 (2).
14. *Czarnikow* v. *Roth, Schmidt & Co.*, [1922] 2 K. B. 478.
15. *Re Olympia Oil and Cake Co., and MacAndrew Moreland & Co.*, [1918] 2 K. B. 771.
16. Section 13 (1). But a dilatory arbitrator may be removed: see p. 503, *ante*,
17. See *post*, p. 511.
18. Section 13 (2).

Unless the agreement specifies otherwise, as soon as the arbitrator has executed the award, he should give notice to the parties that it is ready to be delivered.

The arbitrator may correct in an award any clerical mistake or error arising from any accidental slip or omission[19]. But if he puts down what he intended to put down, although the legal effect may be doubtful, he cannot alter his award for the purpose of expounding his meaning[20].

All awards (unless they otherwise direct) carry interest at the same rate as a judgment debt[1]. An arbitrator is not empowered to fix whatever rate of interest he chooses so that, unless he directs that the award will carry no interest, it will carry interest at the same rate as a judgment debt[2].

Subject to anything in the agreement the arbitrators or umpire have the same power as the court to order specific performance of any contract other than a contract relating to land or any interest in land[3].

The chief requisites of an award are three in number, viz.:

1. *The award must be certain* in meaning, so that the parties to the reference can understand how they are affected by it; but the court will assist the parties to interpret it, if possible, and make any alterations necessary to make the meaning clear. If its meaning cannot be interpreted, the award is bad.

2. *The award must be final;* this does not prevent the arbitrator from making an interim award[4] in a proper case unless the agreement precludes it; but any award should deal with the whole of the subject-matter to which it relates and which ought to be determined[5].

3. *The award must be possible and reasonable, e.g.* an award that a party should deliver up a deed not in his custody or under his control would be void.

If the award is bad in part it is not necessarily void; if the good can be separated from the bad, the latter alone is void, as where an arbitrator had awarded on some matters not within the submission; but if the two parts are not separable the whole award is void.

---

19. Section 17.
20. *Sutherland & Co.* v. *Hannevig Bros.*, [1921] 1 K. B. 336.
1. Section 20.
2. *Timber Shipping Co. S. A.* v. *London & Overseas Freighters, Ltd.*, [1971] 2 All E. R. 599; [1972] A. C. 1, H. L. The current rate of interest is $7\frac{1}{2}\%$: Judgment Debts (Rate of Interest) Order 1971 (S. I. 1971 No. 491). See p. 83 *ante*.
3. Section 15.
4. Section 14.
5. *Samuel* v. *Cooper* (1835), 2 Ad. & E. 752.

Costs

The costs of the reference and award are in the discretion of the arbitrators or umpire[6]. The discretion must be exercised judicially[7] but the arbitrator need not state his reasons[8]. Any costs awarded are taxable in the High Court[9].

Any provision in an arbitration agreement that a party shall bear his own costs, or any part thereof, is void; unless the provision is part of an agreement to submit to arbitration a dispute which has arisen *before* the making of such agreement[10].

If the arbitrator omits to deal with the costs of the reference any party may within fourteen days[11] apply to the arbitrator for an order directing by and to whom the costs shall be paid, and after hearing any party who may desire to be heard, the arbitrator must amend his award by adding thereto directions as to costs which he thinks proper[12].

Referring back the award

The award is final and binding on the parties and persons claiming through them[13]. But the court may remit matters referred to the reconsideration of the arbitrators or umpire[14]; they must make their award within three months after the date of the order for remission[15]. The following grounds for remission have been held to be adequate:

1. Any defect sufficient to empower the court to set it aside[16].
2. Omission through inadvertence, *e.g.* where a case is stated but the relevant facts have not been found[17].
3. Formal defects.
4. Mistake admitted by the arbitrator.
5. Where new and material evidence has been discovered.

It seems, however, that the court's discretion to refer back an award is not limited exclusively to the above grounds[18].

---

6. Section 18 (1).
7. *L. E. Cattan, Ltd.* v. *A. Michaelides & Co.*, [1958] 2 All E. R. 125; *Heaven and Kestarton, Ltd.* v. *Sven Widaeus A/B.*, [1958] 1 All E. R. 420; *Ceylon Government* v. *Chandris*, [1963] 2 All E. R. 1; [1953] 2 Q. B. 327.
8. *Perry* v. *Stopher*, [1959] 1 All E. R. 713.
9. Section 18 (2).
10. Section 18 (3).
11. The court or a judge may extend the time.
12. Section 18 (4).
13. Section 16.
14. Section 22 (1).
15. Section 22 (2).
16. See *post*, p. 512.
17. *Universal Cargo Carriers Corporation* v. *Citati*, [1957] 3 All E. R. 234, C. A.
18. *Margulies Brothers, Ltd.* v. *Dafnis Thomaides & Co. (U.K.), Ltd.*, [1958] 1 All E. R. 777.

The right to call in question the decision of an official or special referee is governed by the Rules of the Supreme Court[19].

Setting aside the award

Among the grounds upon which an award may be set aside are the following:

1. Where the arbitrator or umpire has misconducted himself or the proceedings, or the award has been improperly procured[20].

   Irregularity in the conduct of the proceedings, although the arbitrator may not have acted from any corrupt or improper motive, is misconduct. Thus, an award will not stand if the arbitrator:

   (i) hears one party and refuses to hear the other;
   (ii) holds private communication with one party on the subject-matter of the reference;
   (iii) examines witnesses on one side in the absence of the other party, unless justifiably proceeding *ex parte*; or
   (iv) examines witnesses in the absence of both parties;
   (v) refuses to state a case for the opinion of the court on a substantial point of law[1].

2. If the award is uncertain or not final.

   In a reference by consent the court will not set aside the award for mistake, unless it is bad on the face of it in point of law, or such error in law appears upon some document accompanying and forming part of the award[2].

3. If the award is based on an illegal contract[3].

The court will not grant an application to set aside the award unless convinced of its necessity, but will rather remit the award if the error can be corrected without the expense of starting afresh[4].

---

19. Section 16; Administration of Justice Act 1956, s. 15 (2).
20. Section 23 (2).
1. *Re Fischel & Co. and Mann and Cook*, [1919] 2 K. B. 431.
2. *Giacomo Costa Fu Andrea* v. *British Italian Trading Co., Ltd.*, [1962] 2 All E. R. 53; [1963] 1 Q. B. 201. A reference in the award to the pleadings is not sufficient to incorporate them into the award and they may not be looked at when an error on the face of the award is alleged: *Belsfield Court Construction Co., Ltd.*, v. *Pywell*, [1970] 1 All E. R. 453; [1970] 2 Q. B. 47.
3. *David Taylor & Son, Ltd.* v. *Barnett Trading Co.*, [1953] 1 All E. R. 843, C. A.
4. *Kiril Mischeff, Ltd.* v. *Constant, Smith & Co.*, [1950] 1 All E R. 890; [1950] 2 K. B. 616.

Pending an application to set aside an award the court may order any money payable under it to be brought into court or secured[5].

Enforcing an award

1. An award may, by leave of the court, be enforced in the same manner as a judgment, and where such leave is given judgment may be entered in terms of the award[6]:

2. By action on the award. (This is the only remedy where the submission is not in writing.)

3. By attachment.

The court may also grant specific performance of an award.

Certain foreign awards may be enforced by action, or in the same manner as a judgment[7]. Such awards include those made between subjects of Powers who have made reciprocal arrangements with this country and are parties to a Convention on the Execution of Arbitral Awards, which was signed on behalf of His Majesty at Geneva on September 26, 1927[8]. But a foreign award is not enforceable unless it is valid and final in the country in which it was made; it must also be in respect of a matter which may lawfully be referred to arbitration under the law of England, and its enforcement must not be contrary to the public policy or the law of England[9].

Lien on award for remuneration

An arbitrator or umpire has a lien on the award and submission, and may retain them until his charges are paid. He can also recover any agreed or reasonable remuneration by action; for the appointment of a person as arbitrator in a mercantile dispute raises an implied promise by the parties to the submission to pay for his services. Thus, the unsuccessful party to an arbitration must pay the remuneration of an arbitrator appointed by the other side, if so ordered by the umpire under his award, and the arbitrator can sue for the amount in question[10].

If an arbitrator or umpire refuses to deliver his award except on payment of the fees demanded by him, the court may order him to do so on payment into court by the party applying of the fees demanded. Those fees will then be taxed, and the sum found reasonable on taxation will be paid out of court to the arbitrator or umpire and any balance

---

5. Section 23 (3).
6. Section 26.
7. Section 36.
8. Section 35.
9. Section 37.
10. *Crampton and Holt* v. *Ridley & Co.* (1887), 20 Q. B. D. 48; *Brown* v. *Llandovery Terra Cotta Co.* (1909), 25 T. L. R. 625.

will be returned to the applicant. But no such taxation will be ordered where the fees demanded have been fixed by a written agreement between the applicant and the arbitrator or umpire[11].

Limitation

The Limitation Act applies to arbitration proceedings, and its operation is not affected by a term in the agreement that an award shall be a condition precedent to the right to sue. An arbitration is deemed to commence when one party serves the other with notice to appoint an arbitrator or to submit the dispute to the named arbitrator. Where the court sets an award aside or, after the commencement of the arbitration, orders that the agreement shall cease to have effect, it may order that the period between the commencement of the arbitration and the date of the order shall be excluded in computing the time for the commencement of proceedings with respect to the dispute referred[12].

---

11. Section 19.
12. Limitation Act 1939, s. 27.

PART VI

Protection of Commerce

CHAPTER 29

Monopolies and Restrictive Trade Practices

I THE COMMON LAW

The attitude of the common law to monopolies and restrictive trade practices has varied from time to time. Attempts by the Crown since the time of Edward III to claim the right to grant monopolies were challenged by the Courts[1] and the Statute of Monopolies[2] confined the Crown's prerogative of granting monopolies to letters patent in favour of inventors.

Contracts tending to create a monopoly by eliminating competition, restricting output and regulating prices and wages have in certain cases been held to be in illegal restraint of trade and void, particularly where they purported to be unrestricted in point of time and did not reserve a right to the parties to withdraw[3]. But the growing reluctance of the courts to declare contracts void on grounds of public policy[4] had the effect that few agreements were upset on this ground. In *A.-G. of Australia* v. *Adelaide Steamship Company*[5], Lord PARKER said:

"It is clear that the onus of showing that any contract is calculated to produce a monopoly or enhance prices to an unreasonable extent will be on the party alleging it, and that if once the Court is satisfied that the restraint is reasonable as between the parties the onus will be no light one."

It was thus held that a price-maintenance agreement between producers was not necessarily in unreasonable restraint of trade[6] and a similar agreement between manufacturers and a retailer could be enforced either directly by action[7] or by the use of "stop-lists" and other forms

---

1. *Case of Monopolies* (1602), 11 Co. Rep. 84b.
2. (1624), 21 Jac. 1, c. 3. See *post*, p. 536.
3. *Hilton* v. *Eckersley* (1856), 6 E. & B. 47; *Evans* v. *Heathcote*, [1918] 1 K. B. 418; *Kores Manufacturing Co., Ltd.* v. *Kolok Manufacturing Co., Ltd.*, [1958] 2 All E. R. 65. As to restraint of trade, see *ante*, pp. 46–49.
4. See *ante*, pp. 46–49.
5. [1913] A. C. 781, 796. See also *North Western Salt Co.* v. *Electrolytic Alkali Co.*, [1916] A. C. 461.
6. *English Hop Growers, Ltd.* v. *Dering*, [1928] 2 K. B. 174.
7. *Palmolive Company of England, Ltd.* v. *Freedman*, [1928] Ch. 264.

of coercion[8]. On the other hand a manufacturer could not enforce resale price conditions by action against anyone with whom he had not directly contracted[9].

II THE MONOPOLIES COMMISSION

Appointment of Commission

The Monopolies and Restrictive Practices (Inquiry and Control) Act 1948, the first of a series of "anti-trust laws," established the Monopolies and Restrictive Practices Commission, now known simply as the Monopolies Commission[10], consisting of not less than four and not more than twenty-five members[11]. The Department of Trade appoints one of the members Chairman[12]. The general duty of the Commission is to investigate and report upon matters referred to it by the Department of Trade under the Act and to give information and assistance to the Department in matters relating to the existence of conditions of monopoly[13]. The 1948 Act applied only to monopoly in the supply of goods but by the Monopolies and Mergers Act 1965, the Commission's jurisdiction was extended to cover the supply of services and proposed mergers of companies that may lead to monopoly.

Reference by Department of Trade

Where it appears to the Department of Trade that it is or may be the fact that conditions of monopoly prevail as respects:

(a) the supply of goods of any description; or
(b) the supply of services; or
(c) the export of goods of any description from the United Kingdom either generally or to any particular market,

the Department may, if they think fit, refer the matter to the Commission for investigation and report[14]. But the Commission has no power to deal with cases where the conditions of monopoly are alleged to arise from an agreement registrable under the Restrictive Trade Practices Act 1956[15].

Conditions of monopoly

The conditions to which the Act applies are deemed to prevail:

---

8. *Thorne* v. *Motor Trade Association*, [1937] A. C. 797. *Cf. Mogul Steamship Co., Ltd.* v. *McGregor Gow & Co.*, [1892] A. C. 25.
9. *Dunlop Pneumatic Tyre Co., Ltd.* v. *Selfridge & Co., Ltd.*, [1915] A. C. 847. See *ante*, p. 66.
10. Monopolies and Mergers Act 1965, s. 1.
11. *Ibid.*, Sched. I.   12. *Ibid.*, Sched. I.
13. Monopolies and Restrictive Practices (Inquiry and Control) Act 1948, s. 2.
14. Monopolies and Restrictive Practices (Inquiry and Control) Act 1948, s. 2; Monopolies and Mergers Act 1965, s. 2.
15. Restrictive Trade Practices Act 1956, s. 29.

(a) in relation to the supply of goods, if *either* at least one-third of all the goods of that description which are supplied in the United Kingdom or any substantial part thereof are supplied by or to any one person (or by or to two or more persons if they are interconnected bodies corporate or so conduct their affairs whether by agreement or not as to prevent or restrict competition[16]), *or* any agreements or arrangements (whether legally enforceable or not) have the result that goods of that description are not supplied at all in the United Kingdom or any substantial part thereof[17];

(b) in relation to the supply of services of any description, if *either* the supply of services of that description in the United Kingdom or any substantial part thereof is, to the extent of at least one-third, by or for any one person (or by or for any two or more persons being interconnected bodies corporate or so conduct their affairs whether by agreement or not so as to prevent or restrict competition[18]), *or* any agreements or arrangements (whether legally enforceable or not) are in operation the result of which is that in the United Kingdom or any substantial part thereof services of that description are not supplied at all[19];

(c) in relation to exports, if:

(i) at least one-third of the goods of the description in question which are produced in the United Kingdom are produced by one person or group of interconnected companies; or

(ii) arrangements[20] affecting at least one-third of the goods of that description which are produced in the United Kingdom prevent or restrict export from the United Kingdom or prevent or restrict competition in relation to such export; or

(iii) arrangements[20] affecting at least one-third of the goods of that description which are produced in the United Kingdom prevent or restrict supply of goods of that description (whether from the United Kingdom or not) to a particular market or prevent or restrict competition in relation thereto[1].

---

16. Arrangements as to employment of workers are to be left out of account.
17. 1948 Act, s. 3.
18. Arrangements as to employment of workers are to be left out of account.
19. Monopolies and Mergers Act 1965, s. 2 (3).
20. Arrangements as to employment of workers are to be left out of account.
1. 1948 Act, s. 5, amended by the Restrictive Trade Practices Act 1956, s. 29 (2).

In deciding whether one-third of all goods or services of a certain description is supplied or produced by a monopoly group the Department and the Commission are to apply such criterion (value, cost, price, etc.) as they think fit[2].

Scope of references

The Commission may be required simply to investigate and report on the facts, viz. whether conditions of monopoly do in fact prevail, and if so in what manner and to what extent, and what is done by the parties concerned as a result of, or for the purpose of preserving those conditions. It may also be asked to report further whether the conditions or any of the things done operate or may be expected to operate against the public interest[3]. The reference may confine the investigation to specified practices of the parties, or to specified parts of the United Kingdom[4]. References may be varied[5].

In addition the Commission may be required to submit a report (i) on the general effect on the public interest either of practices of a specified class commonly adopted to preserve monopoly conditions or of any specified practices which may prevent or restrict competition, or (ii) on the desirability of action to remedy mischiefs which result from monopoly conditions or conditions preventing or restricting competition[6].

In deciding what is in the public interest all relevant matters are to be taken into account, particularly the need for efficient and economical production; for progressive efficiency in industry and the encouragement of new enterprise; for the fullest and best distribution of men, materials and industrial capacity; and for the development of technical improvements, the expansion of existing markets and the opening up of new ones[7].

Proceedings and Reports of Commission

The Commission can require the attendance of witnesses and administer oaths. It can determine its own procedure and decide who may be heard and who may cross-examine witnesses[8]. After completing its investigations it submits its Report which must deal with

---

2. 1948 Act, s. 20 (3), as amended by the 1965 Act, s. 11 (5) and Sched. III.
   The Department decides in making the reference what goods or services can be treated as goods or services of a separate description: *ibid.*, s. 20 (4).
3. 1948 Act, s. 6 (1).
4. *Ibid.*, s. 6 (2), (3).
5. *Ibid.*, s. 6 (4), (5), as amended by Restrictive Trade Practices Act 1956, s. 29 (3).
6. Monopolies and Mergers Act 1965, s. 5.
7. 1948 Act, s. 14.
8. *Ibid.*, s. 8.

the questions referred to it and give reasons and a survey of the general position to facilitate a proper understanding of the matter. Where the reference is not confined to fact-finding it must consider whether any and if so what action is needed to remedy any mischief which it finds[9]. In the case of an equality of votes the Chairman has a casting vote[10]. A dissenting member can require a statement of his dissent and the reason for it to be included in the report[11]. The Department of Trade may, and except in the case of a fact-finding reference must, lay the report before each House of Parliament unless it is contrary to the public interest to do so. References to secret processes or to the existence of minerals may be omitted to protect legitimate business interests if the omission does not substantially affect the sense of the report[12]. Reports or parts of reports relating exclusively to the export of goods need not be published unless the report finds that conditions of monopoly do exist and that these or things done as a result of them or to preserve them operate against the public interest[13].

Action on reports

Before any action can be taken there must have been a reference not limited to investigation and report on the facts; the report must have been laid before Parliament, with or without omissions; and it must contain a finding that conditions of monopoly exist and that they or things done as a result of them or to preserve them operate or may be expected to operate against the public interest[14]. When these conditions are satisfied, power is given to the Department of Trade to make orders declaring it to be unlawful to make certain agreements (unless it is one to which the Restrictive Trade Practices Act 1956 applies) or requiring any party to determine an existing agreement. The order may also prohibit the withholding of, or threats to withhold supplies or services, or the attaching of conditions to the supply of goods or services[15].

The Department may also (i) declare it to be unlawful to discriminate between any persons in the prices to be charged or to give preferences in other ways; (ii) require the publication of price lists; (iii) regulate the prices charged where the Board considers that prices operate

---

9. *Ibid.*, s. 7 (1), (2).
10. Monopolies and Mergers Act 1965, Sched. I, Part III.
11. 1948 Act, s. 7 (3).
12. *Ibid.*, s. 9.
13. Restrictive Trade Practices Act 1956, s. 31 (2).
14. 1948 Act, s. 10 and 1965 Act, s. 3.
15. 1965 Act, s. 3 (3). For example, the Restriction on Agreements (Estate Agents) Order 1970 (S. I. 1970 No. 1696) renders unlawful agreements between estate agents relating to charges for the supply of their services in connection with the disposal of unfurnished dwellings.

against the public interest; (iv) prohibit the acquisition of another person's trade or business; (v) require the division of any trade or business[16].

Contraventions of such an order do not give rise to criminal proceedings, but the Crown can bring civil proceedings for an injunction or for any other appropriate relief. And the absence of criminal liability is not to limit the right of private persons to bring civil proceedings in respect of any contravention or apprehended contravention[17].

The Department of Trade can ask the Commission to investigate and report whether any recommendation made by the Commission in their report or by a competent authority and conveyed to the parties concerned has been compiled with[18].

These powers are without prejudice to any other powers exercisable by any Government department or other authority[19].

Mergers

The Monopolies and Mergers Act 1965 contains provisions for the Department of Trade to refer proposed mergers of companies to the Monopolies Commission and special provision is made for proposed newspaper mergers.

If as a result of the merger of two or more enterprises, *either* (i) monopoly conditions (as defined above) will prevail or will be strengthened, *or* (ii) the value of the assets taken over will exceed £5 millions, the Department of Trade may refer the matter to the Commission for investigation and report[1]. If the Commission find that the merger will operate against the public interest, the Commission must consider what action ought to be taken and may include recommendations as to such action in their report[2]. The Commission's report must be made within such period not exceeding six months as may be specified by the Department of Trade or within such further time not exceeding three months, as the Department of Trade may allow[3]. If the Commission reports that a proposed merger operates against the public interest, the Department of Trade may order *inter alia* that it is unlawful to carry out the merger and, in order to prevent action being taken which might prejudice the making of such an order,

---

16. 1965 Act, s. 3 (4), (5), (6).
17. 1948 Act, s. 11 (1), (2).
18. 1948 Act, s. 12.
19. *Ibid.*, s. 13.
1. Monopolies and Mergers Act 1965, s. 6.
2. *Ibid.*, s. 6 (2).
3. Monopolies and Mergers Act 1965, s. 6 (b).

the Department of Trade may require that the merger be held up pending the Commission's report[4].

Newspaper Mergers.—The transfer of a newspaper or of newspaper assets to a newspaper proprietor whose newspapers have an average circulation per day of publication amounting, with that of the newspaper concerned, to 500,000 or more copies, is unlawful and void unless the Department of Trade consents[5]. The Department of Trade must refer such a proposed transfer to the Commission (within one month of application for consent to transfer) except where it is satisfied that the newspaper concerned has an average circulation of less than 25,000 copies per day of publication or is satisfied that the newspaper is not economic as a going concern and *either* (i) that it is not to continue as a separate newspaper *or* (ii) that if it is, that the case is one of urgency.

Where a reference is made to the Commission, the Commission must report (within three months or within such further time not exceeding three months as the Department of Trade may allow) whether or not the transfer may operate against the public interest "having regard (amongst other things) to the need for accurate presentation of news and free expression of opinion"[6]. For the purposes of a reference to the Commission of a proposed newspaper merger, the Department of Trade may appoint three to five additional members to the Commission from a special panel maintained by the Department[7].

III RESTRICTIVE TRADE PRACTICES

The Restrictive Trade Practices Act 1956

This Act provided for the appointment of a Registrar of Restrictive Trading Agreements and the setting up of a Restrictive Practices Court. Certain agreements are made registrable and the Restrictive Practices Court can inquire into registered agreements and decide whether restrictions contained in them are contrary to the public interest. If it so finds, the agreement is void as regards those restrictions and the Court can make certain consequential orders.

The Registrar and the Court

The Registrar is appointed by the Crown and holds office during Her Majesty's pleasure. He is charged with the duty of compiling and maintaining a register of agreements made registrable by the Act and of taking proceedings before the Court in respect of registered agreements[8].

---

4. *Ibid.*, s. 6 (10), s. 6 (11).
5. Monopolies and Mergers Act 1965, s. 8.
6. *Ibid.*, s. 8 (3).   7. *Ibid.*, Sched. I.
8. Restrictive Trade Practices Act 1956, s. 1.

The Registrar determines where the Register is to be kept and its form. There must be a special section for information, publication of which would be contrary to the public interest and information as to secret processes. The rest of the register is open to inspection by the public who may obtain certified copies[9].

The Court consists of five judges and not more than ten other members. The judges are three judges of the High Court nominated by the Lord Chancellor, one of the Court of Session, nominated by Lord President of the Court, and one of the Supreme Court of Northern Ireland nominated by the Lord Chief Justice of Northern Ireland. The nominated judges must give priority to the work of the Court which is a superior court of record. In the case of temporary absence or inability to act, other judges may be nominated[10]. The other members are appointed by the Crown on the nomination of the Lord Chancellor being persons with knowledge of or experience in industry, commerce or public affairs. Their appointment is for not less than three years and is renewable. They may resign at any time or may be removed by the Lord Chancellor for inability or misbehaviour or on the ground of any employment or interest incompatible with their functions[11].

The number of members of the court, whether judges or other members, may be increased[12].

The Court may sit anywhere in the United Kingdom, but its central office is in London[13]. It may sit as a single court or in divisions and either in private or in open court. For a hearing there must be a presiding judge and at least two other members[14]. The opinion of the judge or judges sitting as members prevails on a point of law; otherwise decisions are by a majority of all members, the presiding judge having a casting vote. The judgment is delivered by the presiding judge[15]. The Lord Chancellor can make rules of procedure covering in particular the persons to be made respondents[16], the place where the Court is to sit and the evidence which may be required or admitted. The rules

---

9. *Ibid.*, s. 11.
10. Restrictive Trade Practices Act 1956, ss. 2, 3.
11. *Ibid.*, s. 4.
12. *Ibid.*, s. 5.
13. *Ibid.*, Sched., paras. 1, 2. The address is Chancery House, Chancery Lane, W.C.2.
14. *Ibid.*, Sched., paras. 3, 4.
15. *Ibid.*, Sched., paras. 5, 6.
16. Every person who has the right of audience at the trial of an action in the High Court or in the Court of Session has the like right at the hearing of an application to the Court whether sitting in England, Wales or Scotland: Restrictive Trade Practices Act 1956, Sched., para. 11.

can provide *inter alia* for preliminary statements, discovery of documents, consolidation of applications, the summary decision of issues where similar issues have already been decided in other cases and costs in the event of unreasonable conduct[17]. The Court proceeds as far as possible on documentary evidence, the proofs of witnesses and memoranda being exchanged and submitted to the Court before the hearing[18].

The decision of the Court on questions of fact is final but an appeal by way of case stated lies to the Court of Appeal on questions of law[19].

Registration of agreements

Subject to exceptions later referred to, all agreements[20] are registrable if (1) they are made between two or more persons carrying on business in the United Kingdom[1] in the production or supply of goods or in the application to goods of any process of manufacture; and (2) restrictions[2] are accepted by two or more parties in respect of:

(a) the prices to be charged, quoted or paid for goods supplied, offered or acquired, or for the application of any process of manufacture to goods;

(b) the terms or conditions on or subject to which goods are to be supplied or acquired or any such process is to be applied to goods;

(c) the quantities or descriptions of goods to be produced, supplied or acquired;

(d) the process of manufacture to be applied to any goods, or the quantities or descriptions of goods to which any such process is to be applied; or

---

17. *Ibid.*, s. 23.
18. *Re Chemist's Federation Agreement* (1958), L. R. 1 R. P. 43.
19. Restrictive Trade Practices Act 1956, Sched., paras. 7, 8. There is a further right of appeal to the House of Lords.
20. This includes arrangements not intended to be enforceable: *ibid.*, s. 6 (3). And see *Re British Basic Slag, Ltd.'s Agreements*, [1963] 2 All E. R. 807, C. A., where DIPLOCK, L.J., followed the words of CROSS, J.: ". . . all that is required to constitute an arrangement is that the parties to it shall have communicated with one another in some way and that as a result of the communication each has intentionally aroused in the other an expectation that he will act in a certain way."
1. The addition of other parties does not affect the position. Where a trade association is a party, the agreement is treated as if it were made between or restrictions accepted by all the members: *ibid.*, s. 6 (6), (8). If specific recommendations are made by a trade association to its members, the agreement for the constitution of the association is deemed to include a term that members will comply with them: s. 6 (7). See *National Federation of Retail Newsagents Booksellers and Stationers v. Registrar of Restrictive Trading Agreements*, [1972] 2 All E. R. 1269, H. L.
2. An agreement which confers privileges only on those complying with conditions is equivalent to acceptance of restrictions: *ibid.*, s. 6 (4), (5).

(*e*) the persons or classes of person to, for, or from whom, or the areas or places in or from which, goods are to be supplied or acquired, or any such process applied[3].

By the Restrictive Practices Act 1968, the Department of Trade may apply the registration provisions of the 1956 Act to any class of "information agreement"[4]. An "information agreement" is an agreement for the furnishing of information on prices charged, terms of supply, costs, quantities or descriptions of goods, processes of manufacture, or persons or places supplied.

Excepted matters

In determining whether agreements are registrable certain restrictions are to be disregarded under section 7 and certain agreements are exempted from registration under section 8. The most important exceptions and exemptions are:

(1) in agreements for the supply of goods or for the application of any process of manufacture, terms relating exclusively to the goods supplied or processed are to be disregarded. But this does not apply where two or more suppliers or processors or two or more customers accept restrictions, unless this is done in pursuance of a registered agreement or is exempt from registration[5];

(2) an agreement for the supply of goods between two persons neither of whom is a trade association is exempt from registration if no other person is a party and the only restrictions accepted are restrictions accepted—

(*a*) by the party supplying the goods, in respect of the supply of goods of the same description to other persons; or

(*b*) by the party acquiring the goods, in respect of the sale or acquisition for sale of other goods of the same description[6].

In *Re Austins Motor Co., Ltd.'s Agreement*[7], it was held that where a manufacturer enters into a series of identical bipartite agreements with each distributor and dealer, these are exempt from registration unless there is evidence of an agreement or "gentlemen's agreement" that the distributors and dealers will all be treated alike.

---

3. Restrictive Trade Practices Act 1956, s. 6 (1).
4. Restrictive Trade Practices Act 1968, s. 5. An Order of 1969 (S. I. 1969 No. 1842) did apply the 1956 Act to certain information agreements.
5. Restrictive Trade Practices Act 1956, s. 7 (2).
6. *Ibid.*, s. 8 (3).
7. [1957] 3 All E. R. 62; [1958] Ch. 61.

Other excepted restrictions and exempted agreements include terms as to complying with British Standards or as to conditions of employment, agreements made under certain statutes or relating to patents, designs and the use of trade marks, agreements for exchange of information as to processes and agreements relating exclusively to exports or trade outside the United Kingdom[8].

By the Restrictive Trade Practices Act 1968, the Department of Trade may make an order exempting from registration certain agreements of importance to the national economy and any of a number of Ministers may make an order exempting from registration agreements designed to prevent or restrict price increases or to secure reductions in prices[9].

It seems that the Acts have no application to agreements conferring rights or interests on the Crown which might be affected by registration[10].

Registration procedure

The particulars to be furnished are the names and addresses of the parties and the whole of the terms of the agreement, but regulations may provide for excluding certain matters of detail[11]. An agreement which has become registrable remains so notwithstanding subsequent variation or determination and particulars of the variation or determination must be furnished to the Registrar[12].

Where the agreement in question is in writing the original or a true copy must be furnished, otherwise a memorandum must be produced[13]. The time within which registration must be effected is normally before the date on which any relevant restriction accepted under the agreement takes effect and in any case within three months of the agreement[14].

The Restrictive Practices Court has power to order the register to be rectified by the variation or removal of particulars and may also declare whether an agreement is registrable or not[15].

---

8. Restrictive Trade Practices Act 1956, ss. 7, 8.
9. Restrictive Trade Practices Act 1968, ss. 1 and 2.
10. *Re Automatic Telephone and Electric Co., Ltd.'s Application*, [1963] 2 All E. R. 302; [1963] 1 W. L. R. 463, C. A.
11. Restrictive Trade Practices Act 1956, ss. 10, as amended by the Restrictive Trade Practices Act 1968, Sched. III.
12. *Ibid.*, s. 10 (2).
13. *Ibid.*, s. 10 (4).
14. Restrictive Trade Practices Act 1968, s. 6.
15. 1956 Act, s. 13, as amended by the Restrictive Trade Practices Act 1968, s. 13.

Enforcement of registration

The Registrar may give notice to persons or trade associations who he has ground to suppose are or may be parties to a registrable agreement requiring them to say whether they are parties and if so to register particulars[16]. After giving such notice he may apply to the Restrictive Practices Court for an order that the person (or an officer of the body corporate) attend and be examined on oath[17]. There are penalties for failure to comply with a notice and for furnishing false particulars knowingly or recklessly or wilfully altering, suppressing or destroying documents[18]. If particulars of a registrable agreement are not duly furnished, the agreement is void in respect of all relevant restrictions accepted thereunder, and it is unlawful for any party to the agreement carrying on business in the United Kingdom to enforce it in respect of such restrictions. The Restrictive Practices Court, on application by the Registrar, may make an order restraining a party from enforcing the agreement in respect of any relevant restrictions[19].

Investigation by Restrictive Practices Court

The function of the Court is to declare whether or not any of the restrictions which make an agreement registrable are contrary to the public interest[20]. Application is made by the Registrar. A party against whom an Order has been made by the High Court can also apply after two years[1]. Where the restrictions are found to be contrary to public policy they are void and the Court may grant an injunction restraining the parties from giving effect to or enforcing or purporting to enforce the agreement in respect of those restrictions or from making any other agreement to the like effect[2]. The Court may discharge any previous declaration or order and make a new one. Applications to discharge can only be brought by leave which will not be given unless the Court is satisfied of *prima facie* evidence of a change of circumstances[3]. The House of Lords in *Associated News-*

---

16. 1956 Act, s. 14.
17. *Ibid.*, s. 15, as amended by the Restrictive Trade Practices Act 1968, s. 13.
18. Restrictive Trade Practices Act 1956, ss. 16, 17.
19. Restrictive Trade Practices Act 1968, s. 7.
20. 1956 Act, s. 20 (1).
1. *Ibid.*, s. 20 (2).
2. *Ibid.*, s. 20 (3). By the European Communities Act 1972, s. 10, the Court may decline or postpone the exercise of its powers having regard to the operation of Article 85 of the Treaty of Rome or exemptions granted under that Article. Generally, s. 10 makes it clear that all the requirements of the 1956 Act continue to apply irrespective of the operation of Article 85 which prohibits practices affecting trade between E.E.C. countries which distort competition within the E.E.C.
3. Restrictive Trade Practices Act 1956, s. 22.

papers v. *Registrar of Restrictive Trading Agreements*[4], held that all agreements entered on the register, whether subsisting or determined, are referable to and justiciable by the Restrictive Practices Court. But, by the Restrictive Trade Practices Act 1968, if a registered agreement has been determined in respect of all relevant restrictions before proceedings have been taken, the Registrar at his discretion may decline to take such proceedings. Moreover, on the representation of the Registrar, the Department of Trade may discharge the Registrar from taking proceedings where the relevant restrictions accepted under a registered agreement are "not of such significance as to call for investigation" by the Restrictive Practices Court[5].

Public interest

There is a presumption that any restriction is contrary to the public interest[6]. To rebut it the Court must be satisfied of one or more of the following circumstances:

(*a*) that it is reasonably necessary to protect the public against injury;

(*b*) that the removal of the restriction would deny to the public as purchasers, consumers or users of goods, other substantial benefits;

(*c*) that it is reasonably necessary to counteract restrictive action by any one person not a party to the agreement;

(*d*) that it is reasonably necessary to enable the parties to negotiate fair terms with a monopolistic supplier or customer;

(*e*) that its removal would be likely to have a serious and persistently adverse effect on the general level of unemployment in an area;

(*f*) that export business might be substantially affected;

(*g*) that the restriction is reasonably required to maintain another restriction which is found not to be contrary to public policy;

(*h*) that the restriction does not restrict or discourage competition to any material degree and is not likely to do so[7].

The Court must first of all be satisfied that the restriction can be brought within one or more of these subsections. Then it must also be satisfied that the restriction is not unreasonable, having regard to

---

4. [1964] 1 All E. R. 55; [1964] 1 W. L. R. 31, H. L.
5. Restrictive Trade Practices Act 1968, s. 9.
6. Restrictive Trade Practices Act 1956, s. 21.
7. This paragraph was added by the Restrictive Trade Practices Act 1968, s. 10.

the balance between those circumstances and any detriment to the public which may result from the operation of the restrictions.

1. *Protection of public against injury.*—The first ground on which a restrictive agreement may be justified was considered in *Re Chemists' Federation Agreement (No. 2)*[8].

> The objects of the Federation were that proprietary medicines should be sold to the public only through registered pharmacists. The main arguments in support of this policy were that without the restriction some retail chemists might be driven out of business and that some injury to the public might result from sale by other retailers. It was *held* that the protection which the restriction was supposed to afford was not reasonably necessary and that the removal of the restriction would not deprive the public of substantial benefit or enjoyment. Accordingly the restrictions were declared contrary to public policy.

Delivering the judgment of the Court, DEVLIN, J., said this as to what was "reasonably necessary":

> "We have to ask ourselves whether a reasonable and prudent man who is concerned to protect the public against injury would enforce this restriction if he could. He would not do so unless he was satisfied, first, that the restriction afforded an adequate protection and, secondly, that the risk of injury was sufficiently great to warrant it . . . We find that the protection which the existence of this restriction is supposed to afford is not reasonably necessary because the risk of injury is too slight to justify so wide a restriction and because, if the risk were greater than we think it is, the restriction affords no real protection against it."

2. *Denial to the public of substantial benefits.*—This ground has been the one most frequently relied on in the thirty or so cases that have been contested before the Restrictive Practices Court. For example, in *Associated Newspapers, Ltd.* v. *Registrar of Restrictive Trading Agreements*[9].

> Restrictions were imposed on new entrants into the newsagency trade. It was said that if the restrictions were discontinued, the influx of new entrants would cause existing newsagents to lose profits and to restrict delivery services. The argument was rejected as a "gloomy prophesy" and the agreement declared void.

---

8. (1958), L. R. 1 R. P. 75. See also *Re Motor Vehicle Distribution Scheme Agreement*, [1961] 1 All E. R. 161; [1961] 1 W. L. R. 92; and *Re Tyre Trade Register Agreement*, [1963] 1 All E. R. 890; [1963] 1 W. L. R. 367.
9. [1961] 3 All E. R. 428; [1961] 1 W. L. R. 1149.

A successful attempt to rely on the same ground was made in *Re Net Book Agreement*, 1957[10].

Publishers agreed not to permit the retailing of "net books" below their published prices. The court accepted that if the agreement was abolished, resale price maintenance in such books would cease, and the public would suffer because it would lead to fewer stockholding booksellers, higher overall prices, and fewer new titles. The agreement was upheld.

In few price-fixing agreements has the court been convinced by the argument that termination would lead to substantial deterioration in quality or to a curtailment of research and development[11]. But while the court has several times stated as a general view that a free market is preferable to price stabilization, a price-fixing agreement was upheld in *Re Black Bolt and Nut Association's Agreement*[12].

The association's members manufactured 90 per cent. of the black bolts and nuts, carriage bolts and nuts and railway fastenings used in the U.K., in some 3,000 standard sizes. The association recommended prices at which members would sell their products, subject to certain discounts and rebates. The court upheld the restrictions, mainly because the prices recommended were reasonable as compared with those charged by foreign competitors and also because purchasers were saved the expense of "going shopping," *i.e.* enquiring of several manufacturers to find out the lowest price.

3. *To counteract restrictive action by others.*—This paragraph has not yet been pleaded.

4. *To negotiate fair terms with a monopoly.*—This has been pleaded in two cases where the preponderant purchaser was the Central Electricity Generating Board—*Re Water-tube Boilermakers' Association's Agreement*[13] and *Re Associated Transformer Manufacturers' Agreement*[14]. In neither case were the restrictions as to minimum tenders held to be justified. In the latter case, the court said that in

---

10. [1962] 3 All E. R. 751; [1962] 1 W. L. R. 1347.
11. But see *Re Permanent Magnet Association's Agreement*, [1962] 2 All E. R. 775; [1962] 1 W. L. R. 781, where the court held that the provisions in the association's rules for establishing a minimum tender price were essential for the continuation of joint research, which had already shown beneficial results. See also *Re Distant Water Vessels Development Scheme*, [1966] 3 All E. R. 897; [1967] 1 W. L. R. 203.
12. [1960] 3 All E. R. 122; [1960] 1 W. L. R. 884; followed in *Re Cement Makers' Federation Agreement*, [1961] All E. R. 75; [1961] 1 W. L. R. 581; and *Re Standard Metal Window Group's Agreement*, [1962] 3 All E. R. 210; [1962] 1 W. L. R. 1020.
13. [1959] 3 All E. R. 257; [1959] 1 W. L. R. 1118.
14. [1961] 2 All E. R. 233; [1961] 1 W. L. R. 660.

order to justify restrictions on this ground, it must be shown that without them they would be unable to obtain terms comparable with those paid or charged by other buyers or sellers who had not got preponderant bargaining power. In a later case, *Re National Sulphuric Acid Association's Agreement*[15], U.K. manufacturers formed a joint buying organization, agreeing not to buy sulphur otherwise than through this body. The members relied for a large part of their supplies of sulphur on one American supplier who had in the past forced up the price of sulphur. The restrictions accepted by the association's members were held by the court to be justified.

5. *Avoidance of unemployment.*—This was relied on in *Re Yarn Spinners' Agreement*[16].

> The members of the Yarn Spinners' Association agreed not to sell yarn at prices lower than those fixed in the agreement. The court accepted that the effect of ending the scheme would be to raise the level of unemployment by five per cent. or more. However, there were countervailing detriments to the public in the maintenance of a higher price for yarn, high prices were a handicap in the export trade and they encouraged an excess of capacity. Although the agreement was justified under s. 21 (1) (e), this was outweighed by detriment to the public of higher prices; and the agreement was held to be void.

6. *The protection of exports.*—This ground has been relied on in several cases but was only successfully relied on in *Re Water-tube Boilermakers' Association's Agreement*[17].

7. *Restrictions necessary for the maintenance of other proper restrictions.*—If parties have justified a price-fixing agreement under, say, para. (b), this para. may enable them to justify reasonable uniform conditions of sale[18].

8. *Restrictions not discouraging competition to a material degree.*—This was a new ground introduced by the Restrictive Trade Practices Act 1968[19].

IV RESALE PRICE MAINTENANCE

Collective enforcement prohibited

It is unlawful for two or more[20] suppliers to make any agreement or arrangement to withold supplies from dealers who do not observe

---

15. [1963] 3 All E. R. 73; [1963] 1 W. L. R. 848.
16. [1959] 1 All E. R. 299; [1959] 1 W. L. R. 154.
17. [1959] 3 All E. R. 257; [1959] 1 W. L. R. 1118.
18. *Re Black Bolt and Nut Association's Agreement*, [1960] 3 All E. R. 122; [1960] 1 W. L. R. 884.
19. Section 7.
20. Interconnected bodies corporate or partners count as one: Restrictive Trade Practices Act 1956, s. 26 (2).

resale[21] price conditions[1]; or to offer them supplies only on less favourable terms than those applicable to other dealers; or to deal only with wholesalers who undertake to operate such restrictions. Similarly it is unlawful for dealers to agree to withhold orders from or discriminate against suppliers who do not enforce resale price maintenance. An agreement for the exaction of penalties is likewise unlawful[2]. These provisions do not affect an agreement between seller and buyer to which no third person is a party where the undertakings are confined as regards the buyer to the goods sold and as regards the seller to goods of the same description[3]. The sanction for this section is not criminal proceedings but a civil action. The Crown can sue for an injunction or other appropriate relief[4].

Individual enforcement

Subject to the Resale Prices Act 1964, where goods are sold by a supplier subject to a resale price condition, the condition can be enforced by the supplier against any person not party to the sale who has notice of the condition as if he had been party thereto[5]. This right does not apply against a person who did not buy the goods for resale in the course of business or against one who derives title from such a person. Nor does it apply to sales pursuant to an order of a court or by way of execution or distress. Nor does this provision permit the enforcement of restrictions which have been declared by the Restrictive Practices Court to be contrary to public policy[6]. An injunction granted under the section can extend to any goods of the supplier concerned and not merely goods of the same description[7].

Resale Prices Act 1964

This Act imposed restrictions on contractual and other means of maintaining minimum resale prices. Subject to a claim for exemption and powers given to the Restrictive Practices Court by the Act, any

---

21. Selling includes letting on hire-purchase: *ibid.*, s. 26 (3).
1. This includes conditions as to discount and allowances in part exchange: Restrictive Trade Practices Act 1956, s. 26 (1).
2. *Ibid.*, s. 24 (1), (2). A recommendation by one dealer or supplier to others is as unlawful as if there were an agreement: s. 24 (4). An association is in the same position as an individual for this purpose: s. 24 (5).
3. *Ibid.*, s. 24 (3).
4. *Ibid.*, s. 24 (6), (7). Trade Unions can be sued: s. 24 (8).
5. *Ibid.*, s. 25 (1). If the dealer has "notice" of the existence of the restriction, it is not necessary that he should know all its terms: *Goodyear Tyre and Rubber Co. (Great Britain), Ltd.* v. *Lancashire Batteries, Ltd.*, [1958] 3 All E. R. 7.
6. Restrictive Trade Practices Act 1956, s. 25 (2), (3).
7. *Ibid.*, s. 25 (4).

term of a contract for the sale of goods by a supplier to a dealer, or relating to such a sale, is void so far as it provides for the establishment of minimum prices to be charged on the resale of goods in the U.K.[8]. This prohibition applies to patented goods as it applies to other goods. Moreover, subject to the exemption provisions of the Act, it is made unlawful for supplies to be withheld from a dealer or for there to be discrimination against a dealer on the ground that he has sold or is likely to sell such goods below their recommended resale price[9]. Withholding goods is, however, permitted if the dealer has been using such goods as "loss leaders"[10]. Breach of the Act gives rise not to criminal proceedings, but to civil proceedings at the instance either of a dealer or of the Crown[11].

A supplier may claim exemption from the Act by registration with the Registrar of Restrictive Trading Agreements, and the Court may grant exemption on one or other of the grounds specified in the Act. There are five gateways through one or other of which the class of goods must pass for the Court to be able to grant exemption. An exemption order may be made if it appears to the Court that in default of a system of maintained minimum resale prices applicable to the goods:

(a) the quality of goods available for sale, or the varieties of the goods so available, would be substantially reduced to the detriment of the public as consumers or users of those goods; or

(b) the number of establishments in which the goods are sold by retail would be substantially reduced to the detriment of the public as such consumers or users; or

(c) the prices at which the goods are sold by retail would in general and in the long run be increased to the detriment of the public as such consumers or users; or

(d) the goods would be sold by retail under conditions likely to cause danger to health in consequence of their misuse by the public as such consumers or users; or

(e) any necessary services actually provided in connection with or after the sale of the goods by retail would cease to be so provided or would be substantially reduced to the detriment of the public as such consumers or users;

and in any case that the resulting detriment to the public as consumers or users of the goods in question would outweigh any detriment to

---

8. Resale Prices Act 1964, s. 1.
9. Resale Prices Act 1964, s. 2.
10. *Ibid.*, s. 3.
11. *Ibid.*, s. 4.

them as such consumers or users (whether by the restriction of competition or otherwise) resulting from the maintenance of minimum resale prices in respect of the goods. The onus of proof is on the supplier claiming exemption[12].

In *re Chocolate and Sugar Confectionery Reference*[13] the manufacturers' application for exemption from the general ban on resale price maintenance was dismissed on the ground that the evidence did not show there was likely to be a substantial shift of trade to supermarkets and self-service grocers with a consequent closure of a large number of small confectionery shops. However, the Restrictive Practices Court has declared that ethical and proprietary drugs are exempted goods under the Resale Prices Act 1964[14]. The Court considered that removal of r.p.m. would cause a substantial reduction in the services provided by pharmaceutical wholesalers and a reduction in the number of chemists' shops. The Registrar did not oppose an exemption order in favour of books.

Unless and until the Court refuses to grant exemption in respect of a class of goods for which exemption has been claimed, a contractual term as to resale price is valid and s. 25 of the 1956 Act enabling a supplier to enforce such a price against a retailer with whom he is not in privity of contract, but who has notice of the existence of such a price, remains operative[15].

---

12. Resale Prices Act 1964, s. 5.
13. [1967] All E. R. 261; [1967] 1 W. L. R. 1175.
14. *Re Medicaments Reference (No. 2)*, [1971] 1 All E. R. 12; [1970] 1 W. L. R. 1339.
15. *E.M.I. Records, Ltd.* v. *Morris*, [1965] 2 All E. R. 781; [1965] 1 W. L. R. 989.

CHAPTER 30

Patents and Designs

I INTRODUCTION

There is a common law right inherent in the Crown to grant to a subject the monopoly of a trade or manufacture. This right was restricted by the Statute of Monopolies 1623–4[1] but the prerogative of the Crown to grant letters patent for the sole working of new trades or manufactures to the true inventor for a period of fourteen years or under[2] was preserved by s. 6 of that Act which enacted as follows:

> "Provided also that any declaration before mentioned shall not extend to any letters-patent and grants of privilege for the term of fourteen years or under, hereafter to be made, for the sole working or making of any manner of new manufactures within this realm, to the true and first inventor and inventors of such manufactures, which others at the time of making such letters-patent and grants shall not use, so as also they be not contrary to the law nor mischievous to the state, by raising prices of commodities at home, or hurt of trade, or generally inconvenient; the said fourteen years to be accounted from the date of the first letters-patent or grants of such privilege hereafter to be made; but that the same shall be of such force as they should be if this Act had never been made, and of none other."

This section of the Statute of Monopolies which forms the basis of all modern grants of letters-patent has sustained no alteration in principle during the intervening three hundred years. The various statutory provisions dealing with the machinery of patent practice have been consolidated in two enactments, the Patents Act 1949 and the Registered Designs Act 1949. A departmental committee (the Best Committee) was set up in 1967 to inquire into the working of the patents system and patents law "in the light of the increasing need for international collaboration in patent matters and, in particular, of the U.K. Government's intention to ratify the recent Council of Europe Convention on patent law." The Report of the Committee was published in 1970[3].

---

1. 21 Jac. I, c. 3.
2. Now sixteen years or more; see *post*, p. 539.
3. Cmnd. 4407.

II PATENTS

Letters patent may be applied for by:

1. Any person claiming to be the true and first inventor[4]; or
2. The assignee of the inventor; or
3. The personal representative of the inventor or of his assignee.

Particular rules govern a "convention application," *i.e.* one where the applicant has already applied for protection in a country with which this country has entered into a treaty or convention and which has been declared by Order in Council to be a "convention country"[5].

Patent agents

Patent agents, *i.e.* persons who carry on the business of acting as agent for others for the purpose of applying for patents, must be registered and are liable to be struck off the register by the Department of Trade for professional misconduct. No person can be recognised by the Comptroller General of Patents as a patent agent unless he either resides or has a place of business in the United Kingdom or Isle of Man[6].

Procedure[7]

The applicant for letters-patent must, in the first instance, send to the Comptroller General of Patents at the Patent Office his application in the prescribed form[8]. The applicant must name the inventor and if he himself is an assignee he must declare that he believes the person named to be the true inventor and file the consent of the inventor to the application. He must also produce either a complete specification or a provisional specification of his invention[9]. If a provisional specification is produced, a complete specification must be filed within twelve months of filing the application or it is deemed to be abandoned[10]. The claim with certain exceptions obtains a priority date

---

4. Patents Act 1949, s. 1. Disputes between employer and employee may be determined summarily by the comptroller (Patents Act 1949, s. 56). See *Sterling Engineering Co.* v. *Patchett*, [1955] 1 All E. R. 369; [1955] A. C. 534, and *British Syphon Co.* v. *Homewood*, [1956] 2 All E. R. 897, as to the rights of employer and employee.
5. Patents Act 1949, ss. 1 (1), 68 (1). If the inventor applies, an assignee can claim to be substituted as the applicant (*ibid.*, s. 17).
6. *Ibid.*, ss. 88, 89.
7. Procedure is governed by the Patent Rules 1968, S.I. 1968 No. 1389.
8. *Ibid.*, s. 2. The Patent Office is a branch of the Department of Trade.
9. *Ibid.*, ss. 3, 4.
10. *Ibid.*, s. 3 (2). The time may extend to fifteen months if a prescribed fee is paid.

as from the date of the first application[11]. The specification is referred
to an *examiner* for its first examination; he reports to the *comptroller*[12].

The examiner has to investigate whether the invention has previously
been published in any specification or otherwise or whether any prior
claim has been made[13]. If the invention cannot be used without
infringing another patent the applicant may be ordered to insert a
reference to that patent in the complete specification[14].

The applicant is given a limited time to put his application in order
for acceptance and failure to comply with the time limits, taking into
account such extensions as are permitted, may be fatal[15].

The application may be refused if it appears to the comptroller
that it is frivolous, or that its use would be illegal or if it claims as an
invention a food or medicine produced by mixing known ingredients[16].
There is a right of appeal from the decision of the comptroller to the
Appeal Tribunal[17].

The effect of the acceptance of a complete specification is to give
the applicant the like privileges and rights as if the patent had been
sealed on the date of acceptance, but he is not entitled to institute any
proceeding for infringement until the patent has been sealed[18].

Grant opposed

After acceptance the grant of letters-patent may be opposed at any
time within three months from the date of publication of a complete
specification by any person giving notice at the Patent Office on any of
the following grounds:

    1. That the applicant has obtained the invention from the
       opponent;

---

11. Patents Act 1949, s. 5.
12. *Ibid.*, s. 6.
13. *Ibid.*, ss. 7, 8.
14. *Ibid.*, s. 9. See *R. v. Patents Appeal Tribunal, Ex parte J. R. Geigy, S.A.*,
    [1963] 1 All E. R. 850; [1963] 2 Q. B. 728.
15. *Ibid.*, s. 12, as amended by Patents Act 1957, ss. 1, 2.
16. Patents Act 1949, s. 10. It is also the practice of the patent office to refuse
    a grant in respect of processes for the treatment of human beings. How-
    ever, a method of contraception is not such a process: *Re Schering Aktien-*
    gesellschaft's Application. [1971] 3 All E. R. 177; [1971] 1 W. L. R. 1715,
    P. A. T.
17. *I.e.* to one or more judges of the High Court nominated by the Lord
    Chancellor (Patents Act 1949, s. 85, as amended by the Administration of
    Justice Act 1969, s. 24). The proceeding is not a proceeding in the High
    Court and excess of jurisdiction can be the subject of certiorari: *Baldwin*
    and Francis v. *Patents Appeal Tribunal*, [1959] 2 All E. R. 433; *R. v.*
    Patents Appeal Tribunal Ex parte Swift, [1962] 1 All E. R. 610; [1962]
    2 Q. B. 647.
18. *Ibid.*, s. 13.

2. That the invention has been published before the priority date of the claim in a specification, deposited in the United Kingdom and dated within fifty years before such date; or has been made available to the public in any document (other than a United Kingdom specification) published in the United Kingdom before such date;

3. That the invention has been claimed in a complete specification for a United Kingdom patent, which though not *published* at the priority date of the applicant's claim was *deposited* pursuant to an application for a patent which has an earlier priority date;

4. That the invention was used in the United Kingdom before the priority date of the claim;

5. That the invention is obvious and clearly does not involve any inventive step;

6. That the subject of the claim is not an "invention" within the meaning of the Act;

7. That the complete specification in question is insufficient;

8. That, in the case of a convention application, the application was not made within twelve months from the date of the first application in the convention country[19].

Apart from opposition, the comptroller may refuse to grant the patent if it comes to his notice that the invention has already been published[20]. And if the invention is one of importance for defence matters, the application may not proceed further than the acceptance of the complete specification until the appropriate Ministry has consented[1].

Sealing

Patents when granted to applicants are sealed "as soon as may be," but the request must be made within four months from the date of publication of the complete specification except in those cases where the comptroller has allowed an extension of time, or where the sealing has been delayed by an appeal or by the death of an applicant[2]. The patent is granted for sixteen years[3], but the term may be extended on the application of the patentee or an exclusive licensee for a further term of five, or in exceptional cases ten years on the grounds that the

---

19. Patents Act 1949, s. 14. See *R* v. *Patents Appeal Tribunal, Ex parte Beecham Group, Ltd.* (1972), *Times*, November 30.
20. *Ibid.*, s. 15.
1. *Ibid.*, s. 18.
2. *Ibid.*, s. 19. The application may be restored if the failure to make the request was unintentional (*ibid.*, s. 28).
3. *Ibid.*, s. 22.

patentee has not been adequately remunerated or has suffered loss by reason of war with a foreign state. The application is made by petition not more than twelve or less than six months before expiration of the patent[4].

Date of patent

A patent is dated as of the date of filing of the complete specification, but no proceedings in respect of an infringement committed before the acceptance of the complete specification may be taken[5].

Restoration of lapsed patents

Where a patent has become void owing to default in payment of any prescribed fee within the prescribed time, the patentee may apply to the comptroller for an order restoring the patent. If it appears that the omission was unintentional and that the application was made without undue delay, the comptroller must advertise the application so as to entitle any person within a limited time to give notice of opposition; and after such time has expired the comptroller will hear the case and either restore the patent or dismiss the application. Every order restoring a patent must contain a provision for the protection of persons who may have availed themselves of the subject-matter of the patent after it had ceased to have effect[6].

Improvements

After a patent has been applied for or granted the patentee may apply for a patent for an improvement in his invention as a patent of addition which lasts for as long as the original patent; but if the original patent is revoked, then the patent of addition, if the court or comptroller so orders, becomes an independent patent for a period which must not exceed the unexpired term of the original patent[7]. A patentee is also allowed, under certain circumstances and within certain limits, to make amendments of his patent[8].

Licences of right

At any time after the sealing of a patent the patentee may request the comptroller to indorse the patent "licences of right," and thereupon any person is, so long as such indorsement remains upon the patent,

---

4. Patents Act 1949, ss. 23–25. See *R* v. *Comptroller-General of Patents, Ex parte Farmacy Supplies*, [1971] 2 All E. R. 419, D. C. The time may be extended by the court.
5. *Ibid.*, s. 22 (1).
6. *Ibid.*, s. 27.
7. *Ibid.*, s. 26.
8. *Ibid.*, ss. 29–31.

entitled as of right to a licence under the patent upon such terms as, in default of agreement, may be settled by the comptroller[9].

Compulsory endorsement.—Any person interested may at any time after the expiration of three years from the date of sealing a patent apply to the comptroller alleging that there has been an abuse of the monopoly rights thereunder and asking for relief. Patents are granted not only to encourage invention but to secure that new inventions shall, as far as possible, be worked on a commercial scale in the United Kingdom without undue delay[10]. The monopoly rights under a patent are abused therefore if:

1. The patentee, without sufficient reason, is not working his patent on a commercial scale to the fullest extent reasonably practicable; or
2. The demand for the article in the United Kingdom is not being met to an adequate extent and on reasonable terms; or
3. The working of the invention on a commercial scale is being hindered by the importation from abroad of the patented article by the patentee; or
4. The patentee is prejudicing the export trade or home industry by his refusal to grant a licence or by insistence upon unreasonable terms.

The comptroller may, subject to an appeal to the court:

1. Order the patent to be indorsed "licences of right."
2. Order the grant of a licence to the applicant on such terms as he may think expedient. The licence may be an exclusive one. Existing licences may be revoked or new licences granted in their places[11].

If after two years the grant of a compulsory licence proves ineffective, the comptroller may revoke the patent[12]. Proceedings may be referred to an arbitrator if the parties consent or a prolonged examination of documents or a scientific or local investigation is required[13].

Revocation of patent[14]

Revocation of patent may be obtained on various grounds on petition

---

9. Patents Act 1949, s. 35.
10. *Ibid.*, s. 37. *Re Brownie Wireless Co.'s Application* (1929), 46 R. P. C. 457.
11. Patents Act 1949, ss. 37–39. The Crown may make the application (*ibid.*, s. 40). If the patent relates to food or medicine a compulsory licence must be granted even though the three years have not expired unless there are good reasons for refusing it (*ibid.*, s. 41); and see *Parke Davis & Co.* v. *Comptroller-General*, [1954] 1 All E. R. 671, H. L.
12. *Ibid.*, s. 42.
13. Patents Act 1949, s. 44 (3).
14. *Ibid.*, s. 32.

to the court. Among other grounds a petition for revocation may also be presented:

1. By a Government department on the ground that the patentee has failed to comply with a request to use the invention upon reasonable terms for the services of the Crown or any person authorised by it; or

2. By any interested person alleging—

    (i) that the patent was obtained in contravention of his rights;

    (ii) that the patent was obtained by a person not entitled to apply for it, or on a false suggestion or representation;

    (iii) that the invention is not new, or is obvious or not useful or that its intended use is contrary to law.

A defendant in an action for infringement, if entitled to present a petition for revocation may, instead, apply by way of counterclaim in the action for the revocation of the patent[15].

Power of comptroller to revoke[16]

Any person who would have been entitled to oppose the grant of a patent may within twelve months from the date of sealing the patent apply to the comptroller for an order revoking the patent on any of the grounds on which the grant might have been opposed.

Subject to an appeal to the court, the comptroller, after hearing the parties, may revoke the patent if the circumstances are such that he would have been justified in refusing to grant the patent if the proceedings had been proceedings in an opposition to the grant.

Or he may order the specification to be amended by disclaimer, correction or explanation.

Surrender of patent

The patentee may at any time, by giving notice to the comptroller, offer to surrender his patent, and the comptroller may, if he thinks fit, accept the offer and make an order revoking the patent[17].

Restrictions on patentees

Patentees are forbidden to impose certain restrictive conditions on the purchasers of patented articles or on licensees[18]; but otherwise a

---

15. *Ibid.*, s. 61.
16. *Ibid.*, s. 33.
17. Patents Act 1949, s. 34.
18. *Ibid.*, s. 57. See *Tool Metal Manufacturing Co., Ltd.* v. *Tungsten Electric Co., Ltd.*, [1955] 2 All E. R. 657.

patentee may impose restrictive conditions on the sale of a patented article so as to bind all persons acquiring it with notice of the restrictions[19].

Threats of action

A person threatened with an action of infringement may institute proceedings himself for a declaration that the threats are unjustifiable and for an injunction and damages, if he has sustained any[20]. A letter from a solicitor to the effect that he has been instructed by his clients to institute proceedings for infringement of a patent has been held to constitute a threat[1]. If the threats were justified the defendant may counterclaim for infringement of the patent to which the threats relate[2].

Register of grantees

A register is kept at the Patent Office of grantees of patents, their mortgagees, and licensees, of equitable assignments and options, and of notices as to amendments and payment of fees. But no notice will be inserted of any trust, express, implied or constructive. A person becoming entitled by assignment, transmission, or other operation of law to a patent may apply to the comptroller to register his title. The court has power to rectify the register[3].

Crown rights

Any Government department has the right to use patents for the services of the Crown. Similarly, a Government department may authorise any person to "make, use, or exercise" any patented invention for the services of the Crown[4]. The House of Lords held in *Pfizer Corporation* v. *Minister of Health*[5] that the administration of medicines by hospitals to patients under the National Health Service was part of the service rendered on behalf of the Minister in the discharge of his statutory duty and such use of medicines was a use for the services of the Crown. Hence, the Minister could properly authorise importers of a patented drug to supply it to hospitals in Britain.

---

19. *National Phonograph Co. of Australia* v. *Menck*, [1911] A. C. 336. The general ban on resale price maintenance imposed by the Resale Prices Act 1964 (*ante*, p. 533) does not affect the validity of any term of a licence granted by a patentee as to the price at which goods produced by the licence may be sold by him: s. 1 (2) of the Resale Prices Act 1964.
20. Patents Act 1949, ss. 65–66.
1. *H. V. E. (Electric), Ltd.* v. *Cufflin Holdings, Ltd.*, [1964] 1 All E. R. 674; [1964] 1 W. L. R. 378, C. A.
2. Patents Act 1949, s. 65.
3. *Ibid.*, ss. 73–75.
4. *Ibid.*, s. 46.
5. [1965] 1 All E. R. 450; [1965] A. C. 512.

If, before the priority date of the application, the invention has been recorded or tried by a Government department, but not in consequence of communication by the patentee, no royalty is payable. Otherwise payment must be made as agreed between the patentee and the Government department and approved by the Treasury or as decided by a tribunal. The holder of an exclusive licence has a right to a share of the payments[6].

It is a criminal offence, punishable on summary conviction by a fine not exceeding £5, falsely to represent that an article is patented[7].

III REGISTERED DESIGNS

Design means:

"features of shape, configuration, pattern, or ornament applied to any article by any industrial process or means, being features which in the finished article appeal to and are judged solely by the eye, but does not include a method or principle of construction, or features of shape or configuration which are dictated solely by the function which the article . . . has to perform"[8].

Before a design can be registered, it must be new or original[9]. The effect of registration is to give the proprietor copyright in the registered design for five years from the date of registration. The proprietor is entitled to two extensions of five years each[10]. Damages cannot be awarded against innocent infringers[11]. To protect the proprietor the registered number of the design must be marked on the article[11]. A claim for a compulsory licence may be made at any time[12]. Government departments have rights similar to those relating to patents[13]. Applications made in convention countries give priority similar to that accorded to applications for patents[14].

---

6. Patents Act 1949, ss. 46–49, as amended by the Defence Contracts Act 1958.
7. *Ibid.*, s. 91 (1).
8. Registered Designs Act 1949, s. 1 (3).
9. *Ibid.*, s. 1 (2).
10. *Ibid.*, ss. 7, 8.
11. *Ibid.*, s. 9.
12. Registered Designs Act 1949, s. 10.
13. *Ibid.*, s. 12, Sched. I.
14. *Ibid.*, ss. 13–16.

CHAPTER 31

Trade Marks, Passing-off and Trade Libel

I INTRODUCTION

At common law there is a right of action against any person for "passing off" goods as those of another person; the usual method of "passing off" is to adopt or to imitate the "mark" which that other person generally applies to his goods for the purpose of identifying them. Trade marks have been protected by legislation which is now embodied in the Trade Marks Act 1938 and the general effect of the Act is that if a trade mark is *registered*, unauthorised use of the mark is conclusive evidence that the tort of "passing-off" has been committed. This does not affect the common law with regard to other forms of passing-off and, therefore, the owner of an unregistered trade mark may still suceed in a claim for damages in a passing-off action[1].

II TRADE MARKS

A trade mark means "a mark used or proposed to be used in relation to goods for the purpose of indicating, or so as to indicate, a connection in the course of trade between the goods and some person having the right either as proprietor or as registered user to use the mark, whether with or without any indication of the identity of that person"[2]. This definition does not apply to a "certification trade mark" (referred to below) which means a mark registered or deemed to be registered under s. 37.

A trade mark which is equally apt to describe the goods of other firms does not fulfil the definition and will not be registered[3]. Thus in *Re Wheatcroft Bros.' Trade Marks*[4]

the respondents had registered eleven variety names in respect of roses. The name was intended to be used not only for instances of the variety raised by the respondents but for all instances of the variety. *Held:* the register must be rectified by removal of the marks.

1. Trade Marks Act 1938, s. 2.
2. *Ibid.*, s. 68.
3. *Yorkshire Copper Works, Ltd.* v. *Registrar of Trade Marks,* [1954] 1 All E. R. 570, H. L.
4. [1954] 1 All E. R. 110; [1954] Ch. 210.

Registration

The main object of the Act is to fix the proprietorship of a trade mark; the registration of a person under the Act as proprietor of a trade mark gives him the exclusive right to the use of the trade mark upon or in connection with the goods for which it is registered and consequently if another person adopts this mark or an imitation of it, upon the same or analogous goods, the registered proprietor has a right of action for infringement, and in an action of "passing off" (the two actions are usually combined) the adoption of a registered trade mark is conclusive evidence against the defendant. The underlying idea is that goods of different qualities but of apparent similarity should be clearly distinguished from one another in the interest both of the manufacturer and of the purchasing public. It differs thus from "design" in that the trade mark is intended to indicate the origin of the merchandise whereas the design is primarily an artistic feature in the goods themselves.

The register of trade marks is kept at the Patent Office under the control of the Comptroller-General of Patents, Designs and Trade Marks (referred to in the Act as the Registrar) and is divided into two parts: Part A and Part B[5].

Class A.—A trade mark (other than a certification trade mark) can only be registered in respect of particular goods or classes of goods[6], and to be registrable in class A must contain or consist of at least one of the following essential particulars:

1. The name of a company, individual or firm represented in a special or particular manner;
2. The signature of the applicant for registration or some predecessor in his business;
3. An invented word or invented words;
4. A word or words having no direct reference to the character or quality of the goods, and not being according to its ordinary signification a geographical name or a surname[7];
5. Any other distinctive mark; but a name, signature, or word other than such as fall within (1), (2), (3) or (4) is not registrable except upon evidence of its distinctiveness[8].

Provision is made for allowing colours to be considered distinctive marks[9].

---

5. Trade Marks Act 1938, s. 1.
6. *Ibid.*, s. 3. Thus it cannot be registered in respect of a repairing process (*Aristoc, Ltd.* v. *Rysta, Ltd.*, [1945] 1 All E. R. 34; [1945] A. C. 68).
7. An application to register "Tastee Freez" as a trade mark for ice cream was refused as it was directly descriptive of the character and quality of the goods: *Re Tastee Freez International's Application*, [1960] R. P. C. 255.
8. Trade Marks Act 1938, s. 9 (1) (e).   9. *Ibid.*, s. 16.

Registration in Part A gives the proprietor an exclusive right to use the trade mark[10].

Class B.—A trade mark may be registered in Part B where it is capable, in relation to the goods in respect of which it is registered, of distinguishing goods with which the proprietor of the trade mark is or may be connected in the course of trade from goods in the case of which no such connection subsists, either generally or, where the trade mark is registered or proposed to be registered subject to limitations, in relation to use within the extent of the registration[11].

The protection afforded by registration in class B is not so complete as that given by class A; and in any action for infringement, no relief of any kind will be granted if the infringer proves to the satisfaction of the court that the user complained of is not likely to deceive, or cause confusion, or to be taken as indicating a connection in the course of trade between the goods and some person entitled as proprietor or as registered user to use the mark[12].

Prohibited marks.—A trade mark which is likely to deceive or cause confusion, whether by reason of similarity to another mark or otherwise, or which is contrary to law or morality, cannot be registered; nor can any scandalous design[13].

Registered users.—A person who is not the proprietor of a trade mark may, on the joint application of himself and the proprietor, be registered as a registered user thereof in relation to goods with which he is connected in the course of trade[14].

Disclaimers.—If a trade mark (*a*) contains any part not separately registered by the proprietor as a trade mark; or (*b*) contains matter common to the trade or otherwise of a non-distinctive character, the Registrar or the Department of Trade or the Court, in deciding whether the trade mark shall be entered or remain on the register may require as a condition of its being on the register that the proprietor disclaim any right to the exclusive use of any part of the trade mark or to the exclusive use of any such matter or that the proprietor shall make any such other disclaimer as is considered necessary[15].

Associated trade marks.—The same proprietor may have what are called associated trade marks, viz., identical or similar marks for certain classes of goods[16]; he may also split up a mark, using its com-

---

10. *Ibid.*, s. 4.
11. *Ibid.*, s. 10 (1).
12. *Ibid.*, s. 5.
13. *Ibid.*, s. 11. See *Bass, Ratcliff and Gretton, Ltd.* v. *Nicholson & Sons, Ltd.*, [1932] A. C. 130, H. L.; *Re Smith Hayden & Co., Ltd.* (1945), 63 R. P. C. 97; *Re Stredóceska Fruta Narodni Podnik's' Application*, [1968] 2 All E. R. 913. [1969] 1 W. L. R. 36.
14. Trade Marks Act 1938, s. 28.
15. Trade Marks Act 1938, s. 14.
16. *Ibid.*, s. 23 (2).

ponent parts as separate trade marks, or have a series of marks for a number of similar goods[17].

Certification trade marks.—Where goods are certified by any person in respect of origin, material, mode of manufacture, quality or other characteristics, to distinguish them from other goods, a certification trade mark may be registered with the consent of the Department of Trade[18]. Accordingly, associations which examine or test particular kinds of goods and certify the result of their examination by marking the goods may register their marks as trade marks. Lloyds' Register (L. R.) on shipbuilding materials is an example of this. The privileges of the Cutlers' Company in relation to Sheffield goods are incorporated into the Act[19]; their register forms part of the general register; a similar arrangement is made for Manchester cotton goods, the marks of which are registered at "The Manchester Branch"[20].

Defensive marks.—Where a well-known trade mark, consisting of an invented word or words, is registered in respect of any goods, a defensive trade mark may be registered (notwithstanding that it is not used or proposed to be used) to prevent its user in relation to other goods, if such user is likely to be taken as indicating a connection in the course of trade between those other goods and the person entitled to use the mark in relation to the first-mentioned goods[1].

Procedure on registration

Any person claiming to be the proprietor of a trade mark who is desirous of registering the same must apply in writing to the registrar. There is a right of appeal from the decision of the registrar either to the Department of Trade or to the court at the option of the applicant[2]. After the application has been accepted, it is advertised by the registrar. Any person may within one month from the date of the advertisement give notice to the registrar of opposition to the registration of the mark stating the grounds of opposition. Thus, he may object that it resembles an existing trade mark or is not sufficiently distinctive[3]. The matter is decided by the registrar subject to appeal to the court[3].

When the time for opposition has expired the trade mark is registered by the registrar as of the date of the application for registration, and a certificate is issued to the applicant[4]. The duration of registration of

---

17. *Ibid.*, s. 21.
18. *Ibid.*, s. 37; Sched. I.
19. *Ibid.*, s. 38.
20. *Ibid.*, s. 39.
1. *Ibid.*, s. 27; and see *Re Eastex Manufacturing Co., Ltd.'s Application*, [1947] 2 All E. R. 55, for the principles to be applied.
2. Trade Marks Act 1938, s. 17.
3. *Ibid.*, s. 18.
4. *Ibid.*, s. 19.

a trade mark is seven years but the registration may be renewed from time to time on payment of the prescribed fees[5].

If the proprietor does not use his trade mark for five years, unless such non-user is due to special circumstances in the trade, any one who is aggrieved may apply to the court to have it removed from the register[6].

Assignment

Subject to certain exceptions, registered trade marks (and some unregistered trade marks) are assignable and transmissible either in connection with the goodwill of a business or not, and in respect of all or some of the goods in respect of which it was registered[7]. The effect of transfer of a mark without the goodwill of a business will be that thenceforth the mark will be applied to goods of a different origin and perhaps made by a different process[8]. For this reason the registrar has power to direct advertisements and it may be that if as a result the trade mark would be deceptive, the assignment would not be valid[9]. The assignee of a trade mark is entitled to be registered as the proprietor[10]. A registered user cannot assign or transmit his right to use a trade mark[11].

Rectification

The register may be rectified by the registrar or by the court, either at the request of the proprietor or on the application of a person aggrieved[12]. In *Berlei (U.K.)* v. *Bali Brassiere Co.*[13]:

> the House of Lords agreed that a trade mark should be removed from the Register on the ground that it was likely to deceive or cause confusion and it was not necessary for the aggrieved persons to prove they had a reasonable chance of success in a passing-off action.

---

5. *Ibid.*, s. 20.
6. *Ibid.*, s. 26. As to special circumstances, see *Aktiebolaget Manus* v. *R. J. Pulwood and Bland, Ltd.*, [1949] 1 All E. R. 205; [1949] Ch. 208, C. A.
7. Trade Marks Act 1938, s. 22.
8. See *R. J. Reuter & Co., Ltd.* v. *Mulhens*, [1953] 2 All E. R. 1160, C. A. (No. 4711 eau-de-Cologne).
9. *Ibid.*, at p. 1176. The use of the trade mark may also amount to a false trade description under the Trade Descriptions Act 1968. See *post*, p. 552.
10. Trade Marks Act 1938, s. 25.
11. Trade Marks Act 1938, s. 28 (12).
12. *Ibid.*, ss. 32–34.
13. [1969] 2 All E. R. 812; [1969] 1 W. L. R. 1306, H. L. But the House of Lords *held* in *General Electric Co.* v. *General Electric Co., Ltd.*, [1972] 2 All E. R. 507, [1972] 1 W. L. R. 729, H. L., that a trade mark liable to cause confusion will not be expunged from the Register unless the likelihood of confusion existed before the original registration or arose subsequently as a result of blameworthy conduct by the registered proprietor.

A fine not exceeding £5 may be imposed on a person for falsely representing a trade mark as registered[14] and any one authorised to use the Royal Arms in connection with his trade may take proceedings against a person in a similar trade using them without authority[15].

III TRADE NAMES AND PASSING-OFF

A person who uses a name or mark, even one which is not a registered trade mark, has at common law the right to prevent others from knowingly using the same or a similar name or mark in such a way as to deceive the public into thinking that the business carried on by those persons or the goods sold by them are his[16]. In general a man may trade under his own name unless he has a fraudulent purpose or the name has become identified with a well-known business. Certainly, he must not use abbreviations likely to deceive:

> Thus it was held that not only could the makers of the well-known "Wrights Coal Tar Soap" prevent Mr. W. F. Wright from selling toilet preparations under styles such as "Wrights Baby Powder" but an injunction would also be granted restraining him from *carrying on business* under any name of which "Wright" or "Wrights" formed part without clearly distinguishing his business from that of the plaintiffs[17].

Similarly a word in common use may become so much connected in the public's mind with goods of a particular trader as to entitle that trader to protection. The burden is on the trader claiming protection to show that a descriptive term has acquired a secondary meaning so as to mean his goods and not merely goods of a class. In *Bollinger* v. *Costa Brava Wine Co.*[18]:

> Injunctions were granted preventing the defendant company from passing off Spanish wine as wine made in the Champagne district and from selling such wine under any name or description, including the word "champagne". The word "champagne", though not associated with one producer only, was associated with a wine produced in the Champagne district of France.

The burden is less if the word in question is one which he

---

14. *Ibid.*, s. 60.
15. *Ibid.*, s. 61; Patents Act 1949, s. 92, also imposes penalties.
16. *Reddaway* v. *Banham*, [1896] A. C. 199. An injunction will be granted without proof of fraud.
17. *Wright, Layman and Umney, Ltd.* v. *Wright* (1949), 66 R. P. C. 149, C. A. Cf. *Baume & Co.* v. *A. H. Moore*, [1958] 2 All E. R. 113; [1958] Ch. 907.
18. [1961] 1 All E. R. 561; [1961] 1 W. L. R. 277. Followed in *John Walker & Sons* v. *Henry Ost & Co. Ltd.*, [1970] 2 All E. R. 106; [1970] 1 W. L. R. 917.

has invented[19]. But even an invented word may lose its distinctive character[20].

Another method of "passing-off" is by imitation of a distinctive get-up which a trader has used for his goods. The question is whether a purchaser looking fairly at the goods without concealment of the marks would be likely to be deceived[1].

IV TRADE LIBEL

Akin to passing-off are cases where one trader (orally or in writing) injures another by disparaging his property without using words defamatory of the trader himself. This is known as the tort of trade libel or injurious falsehood. Such statements are actionable if the plaintiff can prove:

1. that the statements are false and made to some person other than the plaintiff;
2. that they were published with malice; and
3. that they were calculated to produce and did produce actual damage[2]. But it is not necessary to prove actual damage if the words are calculated to cause pecuniary damage and either are published in writing or other permanent form[3], or are calculated to damage the plaintiff in a trade or business carried on by him at the time of the publication[4].

Similarly a false statement that a trader has ceased to carry on business is actionable if it is published maliciously and causes damage[5].

In *Wilts United Dairies, Ltd.* v. *Thomas Robinson Son and Co., Ltd.*[6],

The defendants sold tinned milk manufactured by the plaintiffs, knowing that it was old and would have deteriorated. It was *held* that by so doing they were falsely representing that it was suitable for resale and the plaintiffs were entitled to damages.

---

19. *Cellular Clothing Co.* v. *Maxton and Murray*, [1899] A. C. 326, 343.
20. *Havana Cigar and Tobacco Factories, Ltd.* v. *Oddenino*, [1924] 1 Ch. 179.
1. *Payton & Co.* v. *Snelling, Lampard & Co.*, [1901] A. C. 308.
2. *Ratcliffe* v. *Evans*, [1892] 2 Q. B. 524.
3. *E.g.* broadcasting (Defamation Act 1952, ss. 1, 3 (2)).
4. Defamation Act 1952, s. 3 (1).
5. *Joyce* v. *Motor Surveys, Ltd.*, [1948] Ch. 252.
6. [1958] R. P. C. 94.

CHAPTER 32

Trade Descriptions

The Trade Descriptions Act 1968 replaced and extended earlier legislation imposing criminal sanctions on the use of false or misleading descriptions in relation to goods. The Molony Committee on Consumer Protection, reporting in 1962 that the Merchandise Marks Acts 1887–1953 were obscure in meaning and in sore need of clarification and consolidation, had recommended a new Statute[1].

Prohibition of false trade descriptions

It is an offence for anyone, in the course of a trade or business, to apply a false trade description to goods or to supply or offer to supply any goods to which a false trade description is applied[2]. A "false" trade description is defined to mean a trade description that is "false to a material degree" or, though not false, is "misleading," that is, likely to be taken for such an indication of, say, the composition of goods, as would be false to a material degree[3]. The definition of "trade description" is not simply any statement of fact relating to the goods which is capable of inducing someone to buy them. The Act lists a number of characteristics, e.g. quantity or size, composition, fitness for purpose, testing by any person, place of manufacture, person by whom manufactured, and previous ownership, and only a misstatement as to any of the various characteristics of goods listed is a contravention of the Act[4].

Both written and oral misstatements are covered by the Act[5].

Advertisements.—If a trade description is used in relation to any class of goods in an advertisement, the trade description is taken as referring to all goods of the class, whether or not in existence at the time the advertisement is published[6]. In determining the class of goods to which the trade description used in an advertisement relates, the court is to pay regard not only to the form and content of the advertisement, but also to the time, place, manner and frequency of its

---

1. Cmnd. 1781.
2. Trade Descriptions Act 1968, s. 1. A person exposing goods for supply or having goods in his possession for supply is deemed to offer to supply them: s. 6.
3. *Ibid.*, s. 3.
4. Trade Descriptions Act 1968, s. 2.
5. *Ibid.*, s. 4 (2).
6. *Ibid.*, s. 5.

publication and all other matters making it likely or unlikely that a person to whom the goods are supplied would think of the goods as belonging to the class in relation to which the trade description is used in the advertisement[7].

Definition and marking orders.—The Department of Trade has power by order to assign definite meanings to expressions used in relation to goods and where such meaning is assigned to an expression it shall be deemed to have that meaning when used in a trade description or in such other circumstances as may be specified in the order[8].

The Department of Trade also has power to require by order that goods be marked with or accompanied by any information (*e.g.* as to origin or contents), or instruction relating to the goods and to regulate or prohibit the supply of goods with respect to which the requirements are not complied with[9]. Similarly, an order may be made that an advertisement contain or refer to any information relating to the goods[10].

False indications as to price.—If any supplier of goods gives a false indication that the price at which they are being offered is equal to or less than either a price recommended by the manufacturer or the price at which the goods (or goods of the same description) were previously offered to him, he is guilty of an offence[11]. An indication that goods were previously offered at a higher price or at a particular price is treated as indicating that they were so offered within the previous six months for a continuous period of not less than twenty-eight days[12].

False statements as to services

The law relating to false statements as to services, accommodation or facilities, as distinct from goods, is less stringent as it is an offence only if a person makes a statement as to services etc., in the course of any trade or business, "which he knows to be false" or "recklessly"[13]. The Department of Trade is empowered to make an order assigning a

---

7. *Ibid.,* s. 5 (3). An "advertisement" includes a catalogue, a circular and a price list: s. 39 (1).
8. Trade Descriptions Act 1968, s. 7.
9. *Ibid.,* s. 8. Imported hen eggs must be marked with their country of origin by the Trade Descriptions (Origin Markings) (Eggs) Order 1972 (S. I. No. 1041).
10. *Ibid.,* s. 9.
11. *Ibid.,* s. 11.
12. *Ibid.,* s. 11 (3). The prosecution has the burden of proving that during the whole of the six months' period preceding the offer there was no offer at a higher price which continued for 28 days: *House of Holland* v. *London Borough of Brent,* [1971] 2 All E. R. 296; [1971] 2 Q. B. 304.
13. *Ibid.,* s. 14. See *M.F.I. Warehouses, Ltd.* v. *Nattrass* (1972), *Times,* December 22.

definite meaning to any expression used with respect to services, accommodation or facilities[14].

Imported goods

The Act prohibits the importation into the United Kingdom of any goods bearing a false indication of origin[15] and restricts the importation of goods bearing or infringing a trade mark[16].

Defences

Where anyone is charged with an offence under this Act, it is a defence to prove

(i) that the offence was due to a mistake or to reliance on information supplied to him or to the act or default of another person, an accident or some other cause beyond his control; *and*

(ii) that he took all reasonable precautions and exercised all due diligence to avoid the commission of such an offence by himself or any person under his control[17].

The House of Lords held in *Tesco Supermarkets* v. *Nattrass*[18] that a company will have a good defence under these provisions if it set up an efficient system to prevent the commission of offences and the offence is committed because of the default of one of its employees, *e.g.* a store manager. His was the default of "another person".

With regard to advertisements, it is a defence for the person charged to prove that he is a person whose business it is to publish or arrange for the publication of advertisements and he received the advertisement for publication in the ordinary course of business and did not know and had no reason to suspect that its publication would amount to an offence under the Act[19].

The fact that a trade description is a trade mark or part thereof does not prevent it being a false trade description when applied to any goods, but there is a defence if the trade mark is registered under the Trade Marks Act 1938[20].

Enforcement

A duty to enforce the Act is placed on every local weights and measures authority[1], and such authority has power to make test pur-

---

14. *Ibid.*, s. 15.
15. *Ibid.*, s. 16.
16. *Ibid.*, s. 17.
17. Trade Descriptions Act 1968, s. 24.
18. [1971] 2 All E. R. 127; [1972] A. C. 153, H. L.
19. *Ibid.*, s. 25.
20. *Ibid.*, s. 34.
1. *Ibid.*, s. 26.

chases[2], and to enter premises and inspect and seize goods and documents[3].

A contract for the supply of goods is not void or unenforceable by reason only of a contravention of the Act[4]. Further, the Act provides no civil remedy for the consumer of goods or services which have been supplied on the basis of a trade description contravening the Act—he is left to his ordinary civil remedies under the Sale of Goods Act 1893 and the Misrepresentation Act 1967[5].

By the Trade Descriptions Act 1972, if a U.K. name or mark is applied to goods manufactured outside the U.K., the name or mark must be accompanied by an indication of the country where they were manufactured.

---

2. *Ibid.*, s. 27.
3. *Ibid.*, s. 28.
4. *Ibid.*, s. 35.
5. See *supra*, pp. 33, 193.

CHAPTER 33

Copyright

I INTRODUCTION

Copyright Act 1956

Copyright in new works is governed mainly by the Copyright Act 1956 which made substantial changes in the law. As regards works existing before the Act it may also be necessary to refer to earlier legislation, particularly the Copyright Act 1911.

Nature of copyright

Copyright is primarily "the right to multiply copies" and, as a corollary, the right to prevent unauthorised persons from doing so[1]. But it means in fact much more for there are many ways in which one man may use the original work of another for his own advantage. Thus,

> A book may be dramatised; a drama may be performed in public; the performance of a musical work may be broadcast or recorded; the record in turn may be played in public; an architect's plans may be used to build a house; or a cartoon character may be reproduced as a toy.

Copyright is given in respect of literary, dramatic, musical and artistic works. A "literary work" need not have any literary merit. A compilation is sufficient if it involves skill and painstaking labour[2].

Protection is given not only to the author of original works but to the producers of sound recordings, cinematograph films, broadcasts, etc.

Definition

The scheme of the Act is to define precisely what acts constitute infringement of copyright in different cases and copyright in relation to a work is defined as

---

1. *Walter* v. *Lane*, [1900] A. C. 539.
2. See *e.g. Football League, Ltd.* v. *Littlewoods Pools, Ltd.*, [1959] 2 All E. R. 546 (league fixtures used for football pools), and *Ladbroke (Football), Ltd.* v. *William Hill (Football), Ltd.*, [1964] 1 All E. R. 465; [1964] 1 W. L. R. 273, H. L. (fixed odds betting coupons arranged in a certain general form).

"the exclusive right, by virtue and subject to the provisions of this Act, to do, and to authorise other persons to do, certain acts in relation to that work in the United Kingdom or in any other country to which the relevant provision of this Act extends"[3].

Various sections of the Act enumerate "the acts restricted by the copyright" in a work of the description dealt with in the section.

Infringement thus consists of doing or authorising another to do any of the restricted acts without the licence of the owner[4].

Qualified persons

Copyright is given to individuals who are British subjects, British protected persons, citizens of the Republic of Ireland and to persons domiciled or resident in the United Kingdom or in other countries to which the relevant provision extends. It is also given to corporate bodies incorporated under the laws of any part of the United Kingdom or of another country to which the relevant provision extends[5]. Thus copyright generally does not depend upon where the work originated but upon the status of the person claiming it. Provision was made in the Act to extend it by Order in Council to the Isle of Man, the Channel Islands, colonies and dependencies and for applying it to countries which by a Convention agree to afford similar treatment to works protected in this country[6]. Copyright may also be extended to works of international organisations such as the United Nations Organisation[7].

Ownership of copyright

Prima facie (*i.e.* subject to agreement otherwise), the author of literary, dramatic, musical and artistic works is entitled to the copyright. But where the work is made in the course of the author's employment under a contract of service or apprenticeship the employer is the person entitled. There are, however, two special rules:

(*a*) where the author is employed by a newspaper, magazine or periodical the proprietor is only entitled to copyright so far as it relates to publication in newspapers, etc.; in all other respects the author has the copyright;

---

3. Copyright Act 1956, s. 1 (1); this definition is applied to copyright in sound recordings, etc., by s. 1 (4). "Relevant provision" means the subsection conferring copyright: s. 1 (3).
4. *Ibid.*, s. 1 (2).
5. *Ibid.*, s. 1 (5).
6. *Ibid.*, ss. 31, 32, 35. Thus, Copyright (International Convention) Orders apply the Act to countries that are members of the Berne Copyright Union or parties to the Universal Copyright Convention.
7. Copyright Act 1956, s. 33, and Orders made thereunder.

(*b*) where a photograph, a portrait, or an engraving is commissioned for money or money's worth the person
commissioning it is entitled to the copyright[8].

Anonymous works and works of joint authorship are subject to
special rules[9]. Copyright is also given to the publisher of every published edition of any one or more literary, dramatic or musical work
to prevent imitation of his typography[10].

II ORIGINAL WORKS

Literary, dramatic and musical works

Copyright is given in respect of every original literary, dramatic or
musical work which is *unpublished* if the author was a qualified person
at the time when it was made or for a substantial part of the time while
it was being made[11]. If the work is *published*, copyright subsists in it
or continues to subsist if, but only if:

(i) it was first published in the United Kingdom or a country to
which the section extends; or
(ii) the author was a "qualified person" when the work was first
published; or
(iii) the author had died before that time, but was a qualified person
immediately before his death[12].

Publication.—A work is published if reproductions have been issued
to the public. Performance is not publication nor is the issue of records,
the exhibition of an artistic work, construction of a work of architecture
or the issue of photographs or engravings of a work of architecture or
of a sculpture. Except in so far as it may constitute an infringement of
copyright, a publication which is merely colourable and not intended
to satisfy the reasonable requirements of the public is to be disregarded[13]. No account is to be taken of any unauthorised publication[14].

Duration.—Copyright continues to subsist in a work for fifty years
after the calendar year in which the author died. But if, before the
death of the author, the work has not been published, performed in
public, offered for sale in the form of records or broadcast, the period
does not begin till the end of the calendar year when first one of these
things is done to the work or an adaption of it[15].

---

8. *Ibid.*, s. 4.
9. *Ibid.*, s. 11, Scheds. II, III.
10. *Ibid.*, s. 15. This copyright lasts for only twenty-five years.
11. *Ibid.*, s. 2 (1).   12. *Ibid.*, s. 2 (2).
13. Copyright Act 1956, s. 49 (2). "Reproduction" is defined in s. 48 (1).
14. *Ibid.*, s. 49 (3).   15. *Ibid.*, s. 2 (3), (4).

Acts restricted.—The acts[16] restricted by the copyright in a literary, dramatic or musical work are—

    (*a*) reproducing the work in any material form;
    (*b*) publishing the work;
    (*c*) performing the work in public;
    (*d*) broadcasting the work;
    (*e*) causing the work to be transmitted to subscribers to a diffusion service;
    (*f*) making an adaptation of the work[17];
    (*g*) doing in relation to an adaptation any of the acts specified in (*a*) to (*e*) above[18].

Importation, sale and other dealings with offending articles also constitute infringements[19].

Artistic works[20]

These include paintings, sculptures, drawings, engravings and photographs, irrespective of artistic quality; works of architecture including models for buildings; and other works of artistic craftsmanship. Copyright subsists in published and unpublished works in similar circumstances to those affecting literary, dramatic and musical works. The duration is again fifty years from the end of the year of the author's death, but

    (*a*) in the case of an *engraving* not published before the death time runs from first publication;
    (*b*) in the case of a *photograph* time runs in any case from first publication.

The acts restricted are:

    (*a*) reproducing the work in any material form[1];

---

16. *Ibid.*, s. 2 (5). Acts in relation to a substantial part of a work are included: *ibid.*, s. 49 (1). As to what is "substantial," see *Hawkes & Son (London), Ltd.* v. *Paramount Film Service, Ltd.*, [1934] Ch. 593.
17. "Adaptation" means turning a non-dramatic work into a dramatic one or *vice versa*, translating a work or producing it in picture strips, or arranging or transcribing a musical work: Copyright Act 1956, s. 2 (6). Arranging or transcribing presupposes a conscious and deliberate process. Reproduction, however, by subconscious copying may be an infringement if the composer of the work was in fact familiar with the original work and there was some causal connection between the two works: *Francis, Day and Hunter, Ltd.* v. *Bron*, [1963] 2 All E. R. 16; [1963] Ch. 587.
18. *Ibid.*, s. 2 (5).   19. *Ibid.*, s. 5.
20. Copyright Act 1956, s. 3.
1. *Ibid.*, s. 3 (5). *E.g. King Features Syndicate (Incorporated)* v. *O. & M., Kleeman Ltd.*, [1941] 2 All E. R. 403 (dolls reproducing cartoon figure); *Dorling* v. *Honnor Marine, Ltd.*, [1964] 1 All E. R. 241; [1964] 2 W. L. R. 195, C. A. (boats and kits of boat parts designed from plans comprising the artistic work); *Merchant Adventurers* v. *M. Grew & Co.*, [1971] 2 All E. R. 657; [1972] Ch. 242 (three-dimensional reproductions of drawings of electric light fittings).

(b) publishing the work;

(c) including the work in a television broadcast;

(d) causing a television programme which includes the work to be transmitted to subscribers on a rediffusion service.

Exempted dealings

Fair dealing with a literary, dramatic or musical work is permitted if it is for research or private study, or for purposes of criticism or review or for the purpose of reporting current events in a newspaper or periodical, accompanied by a suitable acknowledgment, or by means of broadcasting or in a film[2]. Reproduction for the purposes of a judicial proceeding (or a report thereof) is no infringement[3]. Recitation by one person in public of a literary or dramatic work accompanied by a suitable acknowledgment is not an infringement[4]. Nor is inclusion of a short passage in a collection for use in schools, provided certain conditions are fulfilled[5]. Where by virtue of an assignment or licence there is a right to broadcast a literary, dramatic or musical work, a reproduction in the form of a record or film may be made for the purpose of that broadcast. Such reproductions must be destroyed within twenty-eight days of their first use for broadcasting[6].

Somewhat similar exemptions apply in relation to artistic works[7]. Painting, drawing, making an engraving of or photographing a sculpture, etc., which is permanently situated in a public place is no infringement, and works of architecture can be similarly treated[8]. An artistic work may be included in a film or television broadcast if it is only by way of background[9]. The author of an artistic work (who may not own the copyright) may reproduce parts of his earlier work as long as he does not repeat or imitate the main design[10]. Reconstruction of a building is not an infringement of copyright[11].

Special exemptions cover copying by certain libraries[12]. Where records of a musical work have been made or imported for retail sale any manufacturer can make records for retail sale or for supply to a

---

2. Copyright Act 1956, s. 6 (1)–(13). The defence of "fair dealing" is not confined to criticising a plaintiff's literary work but also covers criticism of the philosophy underlying the plaintiff's work: *Hubbard* v. *Vosper*, [1972] 1 All E. R. 1023; [1972] 2 Q. B. 84, C. A.

3. *Ibid.*, s. 6 (4).

4. *Ibid.*, s. 6 (5).

5. *Ibid.*, s. 6 (6).

6. *Ibid.*, s. 6 (7). These are known as "ephemeral recordings."

7. *Ibid.*, s. 9.   8. *Ibid.*, s. 9 (3), (4).

9. *Ibid.*, s. 9 (5).   10. *Ibid.*, s. 9 (9).

11. *Ibid.*, s. 9 (10). As to the separate copyright in plans and buildings, see *Meikle* v. *Maufe*, [1941] 3 All E. R. 144.

12. *Ibid.*, s. 7; Copyright (Libraries) Regulations 1957, S.I. 1957 No. 868.

retailer on giving notice and paying a royalty fixed under the Act[13]. Double protection under this Act and the Registered Designs Act 1949 is avoided[14]. Use of copyright material by teachers or in examination papers is protected[15].

There is no royal prerogative to print or authorise others to print any material the printing of which would be a breach of copyright. In *Oxford University and Cambridge University* v. *Eyre and Spottiswoode, Ltd.*[16]:

> Defendants, as Queen's printers, published the "New English Bible: Gospel according to John," which was admittedly a copy of the same gospel in the "New English Bible," published earlier by the plaintiffs. Defendants claimed the right to publish by virtue of a patent from the Crown which under the prerogative had the exclusive right to publish certain books including the Bible. *Held:* the prerogative right to grant exclusive rights to publish certain books was not a right to expropriate private copyright. The defendants had no right to publish "New English Bible: Gospel according to John."

III SOUND RECORDINGS, FILMS AND BROADCASTS

Copyright

Copyright is given in respect of sound recordings, films and broadcasts[17]. In relation to *records* the acts restricted are making a record embodying the recording, causing the recording to be heard in public or broadcasting the recording[18]. But causing it to be heard in public in a residential hotel or holiday camp (unless a special charge is made for admission to the part where the recording is to be heard) or in certain non-profit making clubs (unless a charge is made and the proceeds are not applied to the purpose of the club) is no infringement[19]. As regards films[20], the acts restricted are making a copy of the film, causing it to be seen or heard in public, broadcasting it or causing it

---

13. *Ibid.*, s. 8. See *Chappell & Co., Ltd.* v. *Nestlé & Co., Ltd.*, [1959] 2 All E. R. 701; Copyright Royalty System (Records) Regulations 1957, S.I. 1957 No. 866.
14. *Ibid.*, s. 10, as amended by the Design Copyright Act 1968.
15. *Ibid.*, s. 41.
16. [1963] 3 All E. R. 289; [1963] 3 W. L. R. 645.
17. Copyright Act 1956, ss. 12–14.
18. *Ibid.*, s. 12 (5). Copyright is lost if records have been issued to the public without a label on the records or their containers indicating the year of first publication: s. 12 (6).
19. *Ibid.*, s. 12 (7); *Phonographic Performance, Ltd.* v. *Pontin's Ltd.*, [1967] 2 All E. R. 736; [1968] Ch. 290 (holiday camp).
20. Film includes the sound-track: *ibid.*, s. 13 (9).

to be transmitted to subscribers to a diffusion service[1]. The copyright belongs to the "maker," that is the person by whom the arrangements necessary for the making of the film are undertaken[2]. As regards *television and sound broadcasts* copyright subsists where they are made by the British Broadcasting Corporation or the Independent Broadcasting Authority from a place in the United Kingdom or in any other country to which this provision extends. The copyright belongs to the Authority concerned[3]. The acts restricted are, as regards visual images, making, otherwise than for private purposes[4], a film or copy of a film[5]; as regards sounds making a recording of them otherwise than for private purposes; causing them to be seen or heard in public by a paying audience[6]; or broadcasting them[7].

The period of copyright in these cases is fifty years from the end of the calendar year when the recording or film is first published or the broadcast first made[8]. When the copyright in a film has expired, to show it in public is not an infringement of the copyright in the work on which it was based[9].

Use of films and broadcasts for purposes of judicial proceedings is protected[10].

IV ENFORCEMENT OF COPYRIGHT

Civil remedies

The owner of copyright may sue for damages and for an injunction to restrain infringement. As an alternative to damages he may claim an account of profits[11]. Further, he may treat infringing copies or plates used to make them as if they were his own property and claim

---

1. Copyright Act 1956, s. 13 (5).
2. *Ibid.*, s. 13 (4), (10).
3. *Ibid.*, s. 14 (1), (2). It can be extended to any new authority: s. 34.
4. A "still" is not an infringement, but any sequence of images sufficient to be seen as a moving picture is: s. 14 (6).
5. See s. 14 (7).
6. For the definition of "paying audience," see Copyright Act 1956, s. 14 (8).
7. *Ibid.*, s. 14 (4).
8. *Ibid.*, ss. 12 (3), 13 (3), 14 (2). As regards news films and other registrable films under Part II of the Films Act 1960, the fifty years run from the year of registration: s. 13 (3) (a). It is no infringement to show news films more than fifty years after the year when the principal events depicted occurred: s. 13 (8). Repetition of a broadcast does not increase the length of a copyright: s. 14 (3).
9. *Ibid.*, s. 13 (7).
10. *Ibid.*, ss. 13 (6), 14 (9).
11. Copyright Act 1956, s. 17 (1).

delivery up of those in the defendant's possession and damages for those which have been sold[12]. However, he cannot claim damages for infringement or conversion against an innocent infringer, that is, one who was not aware and had no reasonable grounds for suspecting that copyright subsisted in the work, or had reasonable grounds for believing that the copies or plates in question were not infringing copies used or to be used for making infringing copies[13].

Exemplary damages may be awarded if the circumstances warrant them[14]. An injunction will not be granted for infringement of copyright in respect of the construction of a building after construction has been begun either so as to prevent its completion or to have it demolished[15]. The Commissioners of Customs and Excise may be required to prohibit the import of infringing copies[16].

False attribution of ownership of a copyright work or passing off an altered artistic work as an unaltered one gives rise to an action for damages[17].

Evidence

Certain presumptions are made in copyright actions. Copyright is presumed to subsist in the work and the plaintiff is presumed to be the owner if he so claims unless these matters are put in issue by the defence[18]. Where a work bears the name of an author, the person named is presumed to be the author and owner of the copyright[19]. If no author is named but the publisher is, he is presumed to be the owner[20]. Where the author is dead the burden is put on the defence to show that the work is not original and to disprove any allegation as to first publication[1]. Similar presumptions apply in relation to anonymous or pseudonymous works[2]. And it is for the defence to

---

12. *Ibid.*, s. 18 (1).
13. *Ibid.*, ss. 17 (2), 18 (2). The onus of establishing this defence is a heavy one: see, *e.g.*, *John Lane, The Bodley Head, Ltd.* v. *Associated Newspapers, Ltd.*, [1936] 1 K. B. 715.
14. *Ibid.*, s. 17 (3). See, for example, *Williams* v. *Settle*, [1960] 2 All E. R. 806; [1960] 1 W. L. R. 1072, C. A.
15. Copyright Act 1956, s. 17 (4).
16. *Ibid.*, s. 22.
17. *Ibid.*, s. 43. Such right of action is not limited to professional authors: *Moore* v. *News of the World*, [1972] 1 All E. R. 915; [1972] 1 Q. B. 441, C. A.
18. *Ibid.*, s. 20 (1).
19. *Ibid.*, s. 20 (2). And see s. 20 (3) as to joint authors.
20. *Ibid.*, s. 20 (4); *Warwick Film Productions, Ltd.* v. *Eisinger*, [1967] 3 All E. R. 367; [1967] 3 W. L. R. 1599.
1. *Ibid.*, s. 20 (5).
2. *Ibid.*, s. 20 (6).

disprove certain statements on labels borne by records at the time of issue[3].

Criminal offences

Deliberate infringements of copyright are also offences punishable by a court of summary jurisdiction[4]. And it is an offence knowingly to make records, films or broadcasts of the performance of a dramatic or musical work unless written consent has been given by or on behalf of the performers[5].

V ASSIGNMENTS AND LICENCES

Dealings with copyright

Copyright may be assigned, bequeathed[6] or transmitted by operation of law. Assignments may be limited so as to apply to only some of the acts restricted by the copyright or they may be limited as regards the country or countries in relation to which the owner has exclusive rights or so as to apply to part only of the period of copyright. These limitations may be combined. Any assignment must be in writing signed by or on behalf of the assignor[7]. Where a work has not yet been produced, future copyright can be assigned and it will automatically vest in the assignee when produced[8].

Apart from assignments, licences may be granted and they are binding on successors in title except purchasers in good faith for valuable consideration without notice (actual or constructive) of the licence[9]. The grantee of an *exclusive* licence (which has to be granted in writing) can bring proceedings for infringement in his own name as if he were an assignee. The licensee may make substantial alterations in the work unless the licence expressly or by implication restricts that right[10].

Bankruptcy

By s. 60 of the Bankruptcy Act 1914, where copyright is vested in a bankrupt and he is liable to pay royalties to the author of the work the trustee in bankruptcy cannot sell or authorise the sale of any

---

3. *Ibid.*, s. 20 (7).   4. Copyright Act 1956, s. 21.
5. Dramatic and Musical Performers Protection Act 1958.
6. A bequest of the manuscript of an unpublished work carries the copyright unless a contrary intention is shown: Copyright Act 1956, s. 38.
7. Copyright Act 1956, s. 36 (1)–(3).
8. *Ibid.*, s. 37.
9. *Ibid.*, s. 36 (4).
10. *Frisby* v. *British Broadcasting Corporation*, [1967] 2 All E. R. 106; [1967] Ch. 932.

copies of the work except on the terms of paying to the author the same royalties as would have been payable by the bankrupt; nor can the trustee, without the consent of the author or the court, assign the copyright, except upon terms which will secure to the author payments by way of royalty at a rate not less than that which the bankrupt was liable to pay[11].

Performing right tribunal

To assist composers and publishers of musical works and makers of records to collect royalties from dance halls and other places of entertainment, societies have been formed which negotiate with the proprietors, collect royalties and distribute them according to their rules. The most important perhaps is the Performing Right Society.

To determine disputes between these licensing bodies and persons requiring licences or organisations representing them, the Act establishes the Performing Right Tribunal[12]. It can deal with licence schemes referred to it or with applications by persons requiring a licence either in accordance with a licence scheme or in a case not covered by a licence scheme[13]. If a licence scheme is in operation an individual may complain of the refusal or failure of the licensing body to grant him a licence under the scheme. If no scheme is in operation he may apply if he can show that licence has been unreasonably refused or if the terms offered were unreasonable. The tribunal may declare him to be entitled to a licence on proper terms[14]. Acts authorised by an order made on reference of a scheme or on the application of an individual are not infringements of copyright if all the conditions are compiled with[15]. The Copyright (Amendment) Act 1971 provides for reference back and review by the Tribunal of any proceeding under s. 27 of the Copyright Act 1965.

---

11. This section is not applicable in company liquidations: *Re Health Promotion, Ltd.*, [1931] All E. R. Rep. 59; [1932] 1 Ch. 65.
12. Copyright Act 1956, s. 23.
13. *Ibid.*, s. 24 (1). For the procedure, see ss. 25, 26: Performing Right Tribunal Rules 1957, S.I. 1957 No. 924. Questions of law can be referred to the High Court: s. 30.
14. *Ibid.*, s. 27.
15. *Ibid.*, s. 29.

Index

GOODS. *See* CARRIAGE BY AIR,
    CARRIAGE OF GOODS ON LAND,
    CARRIAGE OF GOODS BY SEA
GUARANTEES. *See* SURETYSHIP
    AND GUARANTEES

H

HAGUE RULES
    carriage of goods by sea, 358, 364
HIRE-PURCHASE
    Act of 1965, 224
    advertisements, 234
    agreement—
        cash price, 225
        copies, 226
        default by hirer, 229
        definition, 225
        hirer's right of cancellation, 227
        implied terms, 228
        non-compliance with provisions,
            effect of, 226
        price, meaning, 225
        termination, right of hirer, 229
        void provisions, 231
        written, 225
    cancellation, hirer's right of, 227
    common law position, 219, 221, 222
    conditional sale agreements, 233
    credit-sale agreements, 233
    dealer—
        as owner's agent, 227
        obligations of, 221
    default, damages for, 223
    generally, 219
    guarantees and indemnities, 232
    hirer—
        death of, 232
        obligations of, 222
    implied terms and conditions, 220,
        228
    information, requirements as to, 231
    loss or damage to goods, 223
    "minimum payment" clause, 224
    owner, obligations of, 219
    payments, appropriation of, 232
    postponed order, 230
    protected goods, 230
    title, implied condition as to, 220
HYPOTHECATION
    power of master of ship, 423

I

INDEMNITY
    principle of, 283
INDUSTRIAL RELATIONS
    contracts of employment, 433
    unfair industrial practices, 69, 439

INDUSTRIAL TRIBUNAL
    contracts of employment, 431
INFANT. *See* MINOR
INJUNCTION
    breach of contract, remedy for, 93
INSURANCE. *See also* FIRE IN-
        SURANCE, LIFE INSURANCE,
        MARINE INSURANCE
    contract, as, 282
    employers, liability of, 289
    good faith, 284
    indemnity, principle of, 283
    liability, 286
    Motor Insurers' Bureau, 288
    Road Traffic Act, 1960, 287
    subrogation, 284
    third party risks, 286
    uberrima fides, 284
    unlawful acts, claims in respect of,
        286
INSURANCE BROKER
    agent, as, 146

J

JETTISON
    meaning, 308
    power of master of ship, 423

L

LAY DAYS
    meaning, 348
LEASES
    doctrine of frustration, 98
LEEMAN'S ACT
    sale of shares, 54
LEX FORI
    enforcement of remedy, 107
LIBEL
    trade, 551
LIEN
    bill of exchange, 254
    equitable, 414
    maritime, 413
    possessory, 411
    sale of goods, 210
    shipowner's, 367
LIFE ASSURANCE
    alien enemies, 290
    insurable interest, 290
    married women, 291
    meaning, 289
    policy assignment, 291
    suicide, 290
LIMITATION OF ACTIONS
    acknowledgements, 102
    arbitration proceedings, 514
    concealed fraud or mistake, 100
    moneylenders, 393
    part payment, 103
    parties under disability, 100